Service
Operations
Management

Improving Service Delivery

PEARSON
Education

We work with leading authors to develop the
strongest educational materials in management
studies, bringing cutting-edge thinking and
best learning practice to a global market.

Under a range of well-known imprints, including
Financial Times Prentice Hall, we craft high quality
print and electronic publications which help
readers to understand and apply their content,
whether studying or at work.

To find out more about the complete range of our
publishing please visit us on the World Wide Web at:
www.pearsoned.co.uk

Robert Johnston
and Graham Clark

Service
Operations
Management

Improving Service Delivery

second edition

FT Prentice Hall
FINANCIAL TIMES

An imprint of Pearson Education
Harlow, England • London • New York • Boston • San Francisco • Toronto • Sydney • Singapore • Hong Kong
Tokyo • Seoul • Taipei • New Delhi • Cape Town • Madrid • Mexico City • Amsterdam • Munich • Paris • Milan

Pearson Education Limited

Edinburgh Gate
Harlow
Essex CM20 2JE
England

and Associated Companies around the world

Visit us on the World Wide Web at:
www.pearsoned.co.uk

First published 2001
Second edition published 2005

ISBN-10: 0 273 68367 5
ISBN-13: 978 0 273 68367 4

British Library Cataloguing-in-Publication Data
A catalogue record for this book can be obtained from the British Library.

Library of Congress Cataloging-in-Publication Data
Johnston, Robert.
   Service operations management / Robert Johnston, Graham Clark.-- 2nd ed.
      p. cm.
   Includes bibliographical references and index.
   ISBN 0-273-68367-5
   1.   Service industries--Management. I. Clark, Graham. II. Title.
   HD9980.5.J647 2005
   658--dc222   2004063108

10 9 8 7 6 5 4 3
10 09 08 07 06

Typeset in 9.5/12.5pt Stone Serif by 30.
Printed by Ashford Colour Press Ltd., Gosport

The publisher's policy is to use paper manufactured from sustainable forests.

34601∕

Contents

Customer Requirement and expectation

part one Introduction   1

part three Service delivery 169

Supporting resources

Visit **www.pearsoned.co.uk/johnston** to find
valuable online resources

For instructors

- Complete downloadable Instructor's Manual
- PowerPoint slides that can be downloaded and used as OHTs

For more information please contact your local Pearson Education
sales representative or visit **www.pearsoned.co.uk/johnston**

Preface

The focus of this book

This book is about the management of operations in service organisations. Our objective is to help students and managers understand how service performance can be improved by studying service delivery and associated management issues. Service delivery is the focus of this book, yet we recognise that success depends not only on the obvious territory of operations in managing processes and resources, but also in understanding how operations managers must be involved in aspects of the organisation's strategy, the service concept, organisational culture, and the way employees are motivated and managed. How well a service is delivered reflects the ability of the organisation to pull all these strands together, providing a service which meets the demands of its various stakeholders, providing appropriate and achievable service to customers whilst meeting required financial targets.

The book also focuses on the service sector. This sector encompasses many types of organisations: public sector, voluntary, mass transport services, professional services, business-to-business services, retailers, internet services, tourism and hospitality, for example. We do not focus on any particular type of service but seek to cover the many decisions operations managers in all these organisations face.

We also refer to many aspects of 'business performance', not simply 'profit'. Although many organisations are motivated by profit, most operations are also assessed on their costs, revenues and adherence to budgets, customer loyalty and technological leadership, for example. We have sought to provide examples and illustrations from many different organisations and many countries to reflect the diversity of service organisations.

Who should read this book?

This book is intended as a textbook for those who want to build on knowledge of the basic principles of operations management. It will also serve as a handbook for operations managers in service organisations as they seek to develop and implement operations strategies. Specifically it is intended for:

● *Undergraduates* on business studies or joint studies degrees or those specialising in hospitality, tourism or the public sector, for example, who wish to enhance their understanding of service operations management.

● *MBA students* who are managing service organisations and want to stretch their understanding of the area and assess and improve their operations.

● *Executives* who want to focus on certain aspects of service delivery, such as design, capacity, recovery, performance measurement or service strategy development, for example, in order to challenge and change their own organisations.

Distinctive features

- *Operations focused*. This text has a clear operations focus and is concerned with managing operations. It explores operational issues, problems and decisions. It exposes undergraduates to the problems faced by service operations managers and helps practising managers deal with those issues.

- *Frameworks and tools*. Each chapter provides tools, frameworks and techniques that will help students not only analyse existing operations but also understand better how they can deal with the issues that operations managers face. The frameworks, approaches and techniques will vary from topic to topic and will include, for example:
  - a list of key points to bear in mind when making decisions in a particular area
  - a diagram or chart showing the relationship between two variables or sets of variables to help position an operation or help identify the nature of the relationships
  - a list of questions, checks or tests that can be applied to a situation
  - ways of quantifying or assessing qualitative variables
  - the key stages in undertaking a particular activity.

- *Real world illustrations*. Operations management is an applied subject so each chapter includes a number of short illustrations from around the world that show how organisations have either identified or dealt with the particular issues being discussed.

- *Underpinned by theory*. Appropriate theoretical underpinning and developments are included and we have tried to explain them in an unobtrusive and accessible way. References and suggestions for further reading are provided for anyone wishing to undertake more work in a particular area.

- *Managing people*. A key task for operations managers is managing people and so this book contains a significant 'managing people' element. This includes not only employees but also customers, as well as managing and changing the culture of the organisation as a whole.

- *E-service*. Information technology, e-service and virtual operations are integrated into the book and their operational implications explored in detail.

- *State of the art*. The book contains some of the most recent ideas and information, covering in particular world-class service, performance management, service concept, service recovery, guarantees, satisfaction and service processes.

- *Summaries*. Each chapter concludes with a bullet-point checklist summarising the key points in terms of the chapter's objectives.

- *Questions for managers*. At the end of each chapter there are some questions aimed at practising managers, which they can ask of their/an operation. We hope that these questions will encourage you to apply the material in the chapter to real situations and allow you to understand better, challenge and improve your service operations.

- *Discussion questions and further readings*. We have also provided some general discussion questions, aimed at undergraduates, to help them both assess and apply the material to a variety of situations. There are also some suggestions for further reading.

- *Case exercises*. Each chapter, with the exception of the final chapter, concludes with a case exercise suitable for class discussion. The cases are short but focused on the topic and are a rich source of material for debate and development.

- *Instructor's manual*. An instructor's manual is available to lecturers adopting this textbook. It can be downloaded from www.pearsoned.co.uk/johnston and includes OHP masters of the figures in the book, which are also available on disk. It provides additional detailed questions to go with the cases and bullet-point answers to the questions.

Acknowledgements

Many people have helped us in the writing of this book. Academic colleagues from around the world have provided encouragement and/or contributions, including important ideas and material, useful feedback, illustrations and case studies. We would like to express our gratitude to all of them, especially Colin Armistead, Bournemouth University; Len Berry, Texas A&M University; Guenther Botschen, Aston Business School; David Bowen, The American Graduate School of International Management; Stan Brignall, Aston Business School; Stephen Brown, Arizona State University; Dick Chase, University of Southern California; Moira Clark, Cranfield School of Management; Simon Croom, Warwick Business School; David Crowther, Aston Business School; David Collier, Ohio State University; Carole Driver, Plymouth Business School; Bo Edvardsson, Karlstad University; Lin Fitzgerald, Loughborough University; Jim Fitzsimmons, University of Texas at Austin; Kim James, Cranfield School of Management; John Haywood-Farmer, University of Western Ontario; Jim Heskett, Harvard University; Sheryl Kimes, Cornell University; Bob Lillis, Cranfield School of Management; Loizos Heracleous, Templeton College, Oxford; David Lyth, Western Michigan University; Steve Macaulay, Cranfield School of Management; John Mackness, Lancaster University; Jan Mattsson, Roskilde University; Bruce Millett, University of Southern Queensland; Andy Neely, Cranfield School of Management; Alistair Nicholson, London Business School; Elaine Palmer, University of Auckland; Parsu Parasuraman, University of Miami; Adrian Payne, Cranfield School of Management; Zoe Radnor, Warwick Business School; Aleda Roth, University of North Carolina; Roland Rust, University of Maryland; Michael Shulver, Warwick Business School; Rhian Silvestro, Warwick Business School; Nigel Slack, Warwick Business School; Bernd Stauss, Ingolstadt Katholische Universität Eichstätt; Mike Sweeney, Cranfield School of Management; David Tansik, University of Arizona; Bridgette Sullivan-Taylor, Warwick Business School; Andrea Vinelli, University of Padova; Chris Voss, London Business School; Paul Walley, Warwick Business School; and Jochen Wirtz, National University of Singapore.

Practising managers from around the world have also been kind enough to provide some rich material about their activities and organisations, either past or present. Our grateful thanks go to Simon Arbuthnot, Lexus; Bob Atkinson, Queensland Police Service; Peter Barnard, Sharnbrook Upper School; Alan Betts, Bedford Falls Learning; Mark Bradley, Customer Service Network; Colin Brown, Anglian Water; Bev Burgess, ITSMA Europe; Roger Clark, independent consultant; Ian Cobbold, 2GC; Stuart Cross, Boots the Chemist; Mike Day, Pegasus; J.J. De Gorter, NHS Direct; Keith Edwards, Anglian Water; Paul Flanagan, The Home Office; Nicholas Georgiades, TLC Ltd; Goh Ban Eng, Singapore Airlines; David Good, Central Samui

Hotel, Thailand; Sean Guilliam, Lombard Direct; Bernard Harrison, Singapore Zoological Gardens; Bob Heapy, New Islington and Hackney Housing Association; Doug Henderson, DHA; Matthew Higgins, First Direct; Alan Hughes, First Direct; John Hughes, Customer Service Network; Tony Hughes, Mitchells & Butlers; Ted Johns, Institute of Customer Service; Lam Seet Mui, Singapore Airlines; Gavin Lawrie, 2GC; Karen Liaw, Singapore Airlines; Lawrence Lim, Singapore General Hospital; Marilyn Merriam; Jean Neumann, the Tavistock Institute of Human Relations; Jan Nowell, Oxfam; Vincent O'Farrell, adabra.com; Nigel Paget, RAC Motoring Services; David Parsons, Institute of Customer Service; Carla Priestley, Customer Service Network; Bruce Rance, Customer Service Network; Kirit Shah, the GP Group, Bangkok; Soo Redshaw, independent consultant; Sara Sheppard, ITSMA Europe; Sim Kay Wee, Singapore Airlines; Roy Staughton, Shape International; Derek Talbot, Northamptonshire Police; Michael Tay, the Institute of Forensic Science and Forensic Medicine, Singapore; Catrin Weston, BUPA; Yap Kim Wah, Singapore Airlines; Laurie Young, independent consultant; and Chris Zane, Zane's Cycles.

We are particularly grateful to the book's reviewers (both first edition and second edition) whose considerable efforts and expertise provided us with comments, ideas and suggestions, all of which have had a significant influence on the text. The reviewers included Par Ahlstrom, Chalmers University of Technology; Thomas Christiansen, Technical University of Denmark; Lesley Kimber, Southampton Business School; Geoffrey Plumb, Staffordshire University; Graham K. Rand, University of Lancaster; Frank Rowbotham, De Monfort University; Michael Shulver, Warwick Business School; Rhian Silvestro, Warwick Business School; Martin Spring, UMIST; Remko Van Hoek, Erasmus and Cranfield Universities; and Jan de Vries, the University of Groningen.

Our colleagues at Cranfield and Warwick have helped us greatly by not only providing ideas and encouragement but also creating the stimulating environment in which we work. We are particularly grateful to our secretaries, Lyn Selby and Mary Walton, whose efforts have kept us focused on the task and as organised as is possible.

We have greatly benefited from the guidance, encouragement and support of Amanda Thompson and the highly polished and professional team at FT Prentice Hall.

It is appropriate also for us to thank all our students, both past and present. They have, over many years, been a source of great stimulation and development. Each one of them has had an influence on this book.

Finally we would like to thank our long-suffering wives, Marilyn and Shirley, and our children; Simon, Jon, Mike and Chris, Kathryn and Sam, for allowing us to dedicate a significant amount of our time to this project. They have been our major source of encouragement; without their support, and also their direct involvement in the book, we would never have completed this task.

Graham Clark and Robert Johnston

Publisher's acknowledgements

We are grateful to the following for permission to reproduce copyright material:

Figures 2.4 and 2.5 from Fitzsimmons, J. & Fitzsimmons, M. (eds), *New Service Development*, pp. 71–91, copyright © 2000 by Sage Publications, Inc. Reprinted by permission of Sage Publications, Inc.; Figure 2.11 from 'Achieving focus in service organisations' in *Services Industries Journal*, vol. 16, no. 1, Taylor & Francis (Johnston, R. 1996); Figure 4.8 from 'Using service incidents to identify quality improvement points' in *International Journal of Contemporary Hospitality Management*, vol. 6, no. 1/2, Emerald Group Publishing Limited (Lockwood, A. 1994); Figure 4.10 from 'The determinants of service quality: satisfiers and dissatisfiers' in *International Journal of Service Industry Management*, vol. 6, no. 5, Emerald Group Publishing Limited (Johnston, R. 1995); Figures 4.12–4.19 from 'The zone of tolerance: exploring the relationship between service transactions and satisfaction with the overall service' in *International Journal of Service Industry Management*, vol. 6, no. 2, Emerald Group Publishing Limited (Johnston, R. 1995); Figure 5.4 from 'How much has really changed between U.S. automakers and their suppliers?' in *Sloan Management Review*, Summer, Massachusetts Institute of Technology (Helper, S. 1991); Figure 5.5 from *Customer Service and Support*, Pearson Education Limited (Armistead, C.G. & Clark, G.R. 1992); Figure 6.13 from 'Service transaction analysis: assessing and improving the customer's experience' in *Managing Service Quality*, vol. 9, no. 2, Emerald Group Publishing Limited (Johnston, R. 1999); Table 9.2 from *Trusting the Internet: Developing an e-service strategy*, Institute of Customer Service (Voss, C. 2000); Figure 10.3 reprinted by permission of *Harvard Business Review*, from 'The Balanced Scorecard – measures that drive performance' by R. S. Kaplan & D.P. Norton, January–February 1992; Figure 11.2 EFQM Excellence Model Copyright © 1999–2003 EFQM; Figure 11.8 from *Service in Britain: A study of service management and performance in UK organisations*, London Business School (Voss, C.A. & Johnston, R. 1995); Figures 11.9, 11.10 and 11.11 from *Achieving world-class service*, London Business School (Voss, C., Blackmon, K., Chase, R., Rose, B. & Roth, A. 1997); Figure 13.6 from *Operations Management*, 4th edition, Pearson Education Limited (Slack, N., Chambers, S. & Johnston, R. 2004); Figure 14.1 from *Organizational Culture and Leadership*, Schein, E.H., Copyright © 1985 John Wiley & Sons, Inc. This material is used by permission of John Wiley & Sons Inc.; Figure 14.3 from 'Moving up: how to handle transitions to senior levels, successfully', Cranfield School of Management (Parker, C. & Lewis, R. 1980).

Box 2.5 from 'Exploiting the service concept for service design and development' by G. Clark, R. Johnston & M. Shulver published in J. Fitzsimmons & M. Fitzsimmons, *New Service Development: Creating Memorable Experiences* (2000), copyright © 2000 by Sage Publications, Inc. Reprinted by permission of Sage Publications, Inc.

Every effort has been made by the publisher to obtain permission from the appropriate source to reproduce material which appears in this book. In some instances we have been unable to trace the owners of copyright material, and we would appreciate any information that would enable us to do so.

About the authors

Robert Johnston is Professor of Operations Management at Warwick Business School. He has a management degree from the University of Aston and a Ph.D. from the University of Warwick. Before moving to academia he held several line management and senior management posts in a number of service organisations in both the public and private sectors. He continues to maintain close and active links with many large and small organisations around the world through his research, management training and consultancy activities. His research interests include service excellence, performance measurement and strategy, and he has written numerous texts, papers and case studies. He has served as Associate Dean at Warwick Business School and as Academic Director of the Warwick MBA Programme and the Diploma in Service Leadership. He was the founding editor of the *International Journal of Service Industry Management* and he also serves on the editorial boards of the *Journal of Operations Management, Journal of Service Research, Cornell Hotel and Restaurant Administration Quarterly, International Journal of Internet and Enterprise Management, International Journal of Tourism and Hospitality Research* and *Managing Service Quality*.

Graham Clark is Senior Lecturer In Operations Management at Cranfield University. He has a degree in mechanical engineering and a master's degree in management from Imperial College, London. He has considerable experience in managing operations. Since moving to Cranfield in 1986, he has focused on research and teaching in service management and he is involved in a wide range of consultancy assignments. He has written a book on customer support for manufacturing companies, and a second book, *Inspired Customer Service*, was co-written with David Clutterbuck and Colin Armistead. His research interests include the management of call centre people and processes, the leadership of change in the implementation of service strategies, and service performance improvement. He has held the appointment of Director of Quality for the School of Management, followed by three years as Director of the Executive MBA Programme. He holds a number of counselling qualifications and is also involved in personal development programmes for the Cranfield MBA.

part one

Introduction

chapter one

Introduction to service operations management

Chapter objectives:

- to explain what we mean by service operations management

- to define 'service'

- to describe some of the key challenges faced by service operations managers

- to identify different types of services and service processes

- to discuss how to judge the success of a service operation

- to explain the structure of the book.

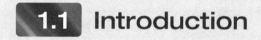 **1.1** **Introduction**

We come into contact with service operations every single day. We are customers or users of a wide range of commercial and public services, such as childcare services, hospitals, shops, schools, holiday firms, police services, restaurants, television and the internet. Indeed, many of us are responsible for delivering service not only as part of our jobs, in organisations such as those above, but also as part of daily life for our friends and families: providing cooking and cleaning services, 'taxi' services, organising holidays and providing emotional support services.

Service operations management is concerned with delivering service to the customers or users of the service. It involves understanding the needs of our customers, managing the processes that deliver the services, ensuring our objectives are met, while also paying attention to the continual improvement of our services. As such, operations management is a central organisational function and one that is critical to organisational success.

It is important to note at the start of this book that service operations covers a far broader field than simply those services that are provided by businesses for consumers. The principles we describe apply to all operations that deploy resources in order to deliver some form of service. These services will include:

- business-to-consumer services (e.g. financial services, retail, leisure)
- business-to-business services (e.g. consultants, office equipment provision and support, communications)
- internal services (e.g. personnel, information technology (IT) services)
- public services (e.g. police, education, health services)
- not-for-profit services (e.g. charities, faith organisations, aid organisations).

In this book we give a detailed coverage of service operations issues and we provide many tools and frameworks that managers can use to understand, assess and improve the performance of their operations. While the development of operations management as a discipline has its roots in production management (for a discussion of this see Johnston 1994 and 1999), this text concentrates on the service operations issues, though many of the concepts are equally relevant to manufacturing organisations. Indeed, all manufacturing companies provide services, such as customer support through the provision of aftersales service and customer training, or internal service functions such as human resources (HR) or IT, or business-to-business services with organisations in their supply chain.

In this introductory chapter we will introduce some definitions and share what we think are the significant problems and challenges facing many service operations managers.

1.2 What is service operations management?

We need to be clear about what we mean by service and service operations management. We will start with service operations management.

1.2.1 Service operations management

Service operations management is the term that is used to cover the activities, decisions and responsibilities of operations managers in service organisations. These managers are often called operations managers but many other titles are used, such as managing partners in consultancy firms, nursing managers in hospitals, head-teachers in schools, fleet managers in transport companies, call centre managers, customer service managers, restaurant managers ...

All these people have a number of things in common:

- They are responsible for the service operation – the configuration of resources and processes that create and deliver service to the customer (see Figure 1.1).
- They are responsible for some of the organisation's resources (we refer to these as inputs – see Figure 1.1), including materials, equipment, staff, technology and facilities. These resources often account for a very large proportion of an organisation's total assets, so service operations managers are responsible for much of an organisation's cost base.
- They are responsible for some or all of the organisation's customers (sometimes referred to as clients, patients or students, for example) and/or the things belonging to their customers, such as their parcels or orders.
- They are responsible for 'processing' their customers or their parcels or orders. (The service process is the set of activities within an operation, or across several operations, that deploy or use those inputs to deliver goods and services to customers.) For the managing partner in a consultancy firm this might involve overseeing meetings with clients, data gathering, analysis and report writing. For the nursing manager it might involve overseeing patient admissions, tests, treatment and discharge.
- They are also responsible for the goods and services delivered to their customers. The nursing manager delivers (discharges) recovering patients together with their prescriptions for medicines and outpatient appointments. The managing partner delivers the final report and the solution to a problem to the client. Thus service operations managers are responsible for generating most, if not all, of an organisation's revenue/income.

1.2.2 Service

Service means many different things in many different contexts. When we talk to managers it is clear that the word service conjures up many different images. For some it is synonymous with complaints or customer care, for others it is the equiv-

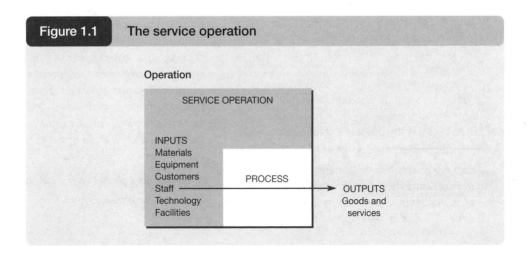

Figure 1.1   **The service operation**

alent of the logistics function, or internal services such as accounting or personnel. For others it means the 10,000 mile check-up to their car. Haywood-Farmer and Nollet (1991, p. 11) neatly summarised this problem:

> *Despite more than 25 years of study, scholars in the field of services management do not agree on what a service is. Indeed, instead of coming closer to a definition they seem to be less certain . . . the problem is trying in a few words to describe 75 per cent of the economic activity of developed nations. Is it any wonder that there are exceptions for all definitions?*

Let us use the example of a hospital to provide some clarity.

A hospital is a very complex service organisation. A hospital employs large numbers of staff, from cleaners and porters to highly skilled surgeons. It will care for hundreds of patients each day, through many different specialists departments, each providing a wide range of treatments. Managing this service operation is extremely challenging. The complexity is in part due to the volumes of patients and the wide range of treatments available, but also due to the fact that, like many service organisations, hospitals comprise many different service operations that must be co-ordinated and linked together in order to deliver healthcare to their customers. For the hospital, these include reception services, diagnostics, pharmacy, theatres (where operations *on* people are carried out), restaurants, physiotherapy, security and so forth. In addition, there are the internal services such as information systems support and finance. Box 1.1 about Singapore General Hospital contains a description from the chief executive officer who explains what is meant by service and how he tries to achieve it.

Singapore General Hospital — Box 1.1

The Singapore General Hospital (SGH) is the country's largest acute tertiary care hospital. It has a total of 1,612 beds and 22 clinical departments providing a comprehensive range of medical services. The hospital employs around 5,500 staff, from clinical and research directors to hospital attendants. SGH is structured as a private limited company for flexibility of operations, but is a not-for-profit organisation owned by the Government of Singapore.

The hospital's mission is to provide excellence in healthcare through cost-effective methods for the benefit of the patient, community and staff. Lawrence Lim is the hospital's chief executive officer and he explains how it delivers its mission:

The hospital has three 'pillars' supporting our mission statement. Service, that is taking care of our patients, is our number-one priority. The second pillar is teaching and nurturing the

next generations of care-givers, doctors, nurses, physiotherapists, etc., and the third area is undertaking clinical research to expand our knowledge and skills in medical science.

In terms of service we aim to offer our patients 'best outcome, best experience'. We want to provide the best outcome by providing the best clinical care. I know people do not wish to come to a hospital, but if they have to, we want to provide them with the best experience possible. This idea was derived and drawn up by the doctors and administrators together and provides a common purpose, mindset and language that permeate the whole hospital. There are four key principles underlying this:

- *assure best outcomes (i.e. clinical quality)*
- *create seamless service (i.e. operational quality)*

- build relationships
- delight with personalised care (i.e. service quality).

We have a quality council comprising doctors and administrators that come together to chart the strategies and programmes for quality in the hospital. They discuss clinical quality, which has to do with getting doctors, nurses, physiotherapists, etc. to produce the best outcome for the patient. We also talk about operational quality, that is how we move a patient around and how we organise our services around the patient. These activities mainly concern operational processes, which we try to 'engineer' in order to create a seamless service for the patient. We are also concerned with service quality, which is about the individual; building a relationship with the patients and showing that we care. From the patients'

perspective all these three types of quality, i.e. clinical, operational and service, are intertwined, but we need to ensure that our staff are focused on all of them too.

We have worked with all the different people in the hospital to try to get everybody to think how they can improve the service. We get them to think about communication skills, even grooming, dress and body language. We are a government hospital and people's concept of a government hospital in the past is that it is bureaucratic, officious and slow to respond. I always tell my staff, let's surprise the patient!

Questions

1 How has Lawrence Lim focused his staff on providing 'best outcome, best experience'?

2 From whom do you think he encountered most resistance, and why?

From the customers' perspective, service is the combination of the customers' experience and their perception of the outcome of the service. The experience at a theme park, for example, includes the experience of the rides and the restaurants, and the outcomes will include the food and drink, the emotions of enjoyment and their view of value for money at the end of the day. It is important to note that customers also have to make an input to the service. These customer inputs include their time and effort plus the financial cost (i.e. the price they pay for the service) (see Figure 1.2). A customer can only receive the 'theme park service' (and have a good day out) if they give up some time, go to the theme park, pay to get in and make the effort to use the rides and enjoy themselves.

Figure 1.2   Service = experience + outcome

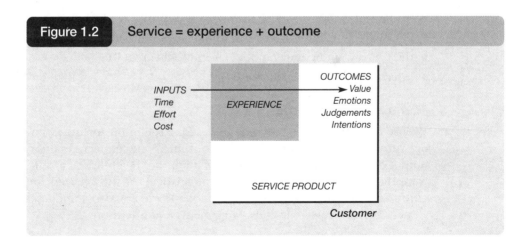

Let us provide some more detail. These two elements, service experience and service outcome, form what is often referred to as the service product or service package (see Figure 1.2). The primary reason customers are paying for, or using, an organisation's services is to receive this service product. Examples of service products might include:

- car insurance
- consultancy advice
- a restaurant meal
- computer maintenance
- healthcare.

Within each of these products there are two key ingredients: the outcomes of the service and the service experience. Although we describe these two aspects separately below, it should be noted that there may be considerable overlap between outcome and experience. It is also important to realise that a customer's evaluation of one component may influence their perception of the other. A service experience that exceeds customer expectations may give rise to a better evaluation of service outcome than might otherwise have been expected.

The service experience

The service experience is the customer's direct experience of the service process and concerns the way the customer is dealt with by the service provider. It contains aspects of how customer-facing staff interact with customers and also the customer's experience of the organisation and its facilities.

It should be noted that the customer's experience of the organisation as a whole will probably start before this point, as expectations are shaped by sales and marketing activities and by word-of-mouth advertising from existing customers.

Aspects of the service experience include:

- the extent of personalisation of the process
- the responsiveness of the service organisation
- the flexibility of customer-facing staff
- customer intimacy
- the ease of access to service personnel or information systems
- the extent to which the customer feels valued by the organisation
- the courtesy and competence of customer-facing staff
- interactions with other customers.

The service outcome

We use the term service outcome to describe the result for the customer of service delivery. The key and most obvious output is the 'expected' and often tangible output of the service. Examples of this might be the ability of a recipient of a software training course to construct a spreadsheet, or for a patient in a hospital to enjoy full mobility after a hip operation. There are also some less tangible outcomes, such as value, emotions, judgements and intentions.

Value (see also Chapter 2) is the customer's assessment of the benefits of the service weighed against all the costs involved. The benefits will include the experience (the pleasantness of the experience and also psychological factors such as a feeling of well-being or being recognised, in a restaurant for example) and the outcomes (such as the quality and quantity of food, feelings of satisfaction and happiness, pleasure resulting from a social occasion) weighed against not only the financial cost that was paid directly or sometimes indirectly by the customer but also the time and effort that was involved for the customer in acquiring and receiving the service.

Emotions are strong mental or instinctive feelings, such as pleasure or frustration, delight or disgust. These may be concerned with the tangible output and/or the way the customer was treated (the experience) (see Box 1.2). For example, a patient may feel annoyed and upset that a hospital operation was not a success, or even if the operation was a success the patient may feel displeasure about the way they were treated by the staff.

Judgements are opinions that form as a result of customers' feelings about their experience and output (including perceived value). These judgements will include views about fairness (or equity), satisfaction (see Chapter 4) or loyalty (see Chapter 3), for example.

Those judgements, good, bad or indifferent, will result in intentions, such as the intention to repurchase or not, the intention to tell friends and relatives how bad the service was or the intention to complain or not. These intentions may or may not result in action.

FinanceCo — Box 1.2

John Smith put down the phone. He had spent the last 45 minutes speaking to various people in the customer service department of FinanceCo Ltd. The problem had started several months earlier when John had taken out a subscription to a gardening magazine charged to his FinanceCo platinum credit card. FinanceCo had offered a 10 per cent discount for the first three months' subscription if customers signed up for at least six months. The amount would be added to customers' credit card accounts each month.

The first magazine arrived promptly, the second was a week late, and the third failed to arrive. John Smith decided to cancel his subscription and rang FinanceCo to do this. A helpful-sounding customer service agent (CSA) agreed that he had received poor service and agreed to end the subscription and refund the last month's payment.

John was more than content with this, feeling that his complaint had been dealt with. The next month's statement, however, did not show the refund and, worse still, a further month's subscription had been put on to his account.

As he had been rather busy, John did not have chance to query this entry until another month had gone by, with a further subscription added, plus interest on subscriptions unpaid. Further calls to the customer service department meant conversations with CSAs who were friendly, made promises, but seemed unable to keep them.

Eventually, after yet another conversation with a sympathetic CSA who seemed unable to resolve the issue, John demanded to talk to the customer services manager. After a lengthy phone call (which John paid for), the matter was finally resolved.

1.2.3 Service and service operations

We have defined service as the combination of outcomes and experiences delivered to and received by a customer. Customers therefore judge the quality of the service on the experience as well as the outcome. Students on a business administration programme or executives on a training course are buying both the experiences – the time in the lecture room, the process of learning and the interaction with other people – as well as the outcomes, which will include increased effectiveness at work, better prospects in the job market, a qualification and their feelings about the way in which they were treated. The role of service operations managers is to manage and integrate both aspects, though long-term success in terms of financial performance, customer satisfaction and competitive advantage, where appropriate, may come from either or both, dependent on the nature of the service and the competitive environment

One of the most important, intriguing and challenging aspects of managing service operations (certainly when compared to manufacturing operations) is that many (though not all) service operations 'process' customers. These are sometimes referred to as customer processing operations (Morris and Johnston 1988). The theme park cannot physically give you the rides unless you turn up, the doctor cannot give you an injection unless you are physically in the same place. This means that the customer's experience is an intrinsic part of the operation's process (see Figure 1.3). As a result, the customer sees much of the process and, in many cases, plays a key role or part in the process itself.

Figure 1.3	Managing service and service operations

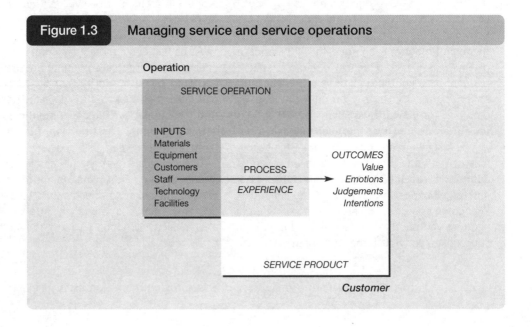

It is important to note that customers may not see and/or experience the whole of the process; they will only be involved in the 'front office' (the overlapping section in Figure 1.3). The 'back office' contains tasks that are carried out usually unseen by the customers, such as cooking the food in some restaurants, or baggage handling at an airport.

This overlap of the process and the customer's experience, together with the intangibility of many services, makes the job of a service operations manager particularly challenging, exciting and, at times, frustrating.

1.3 The challenges facing service operations managers

Managing service operations is something we all do: either unpaid, such as running homes and families, arranging holidays for friends and family, working for faith organisations and charities; or paid, such as managing childcare facilities (see Box 1.3), working in hospitals, hotels, banks, schools or design companies, for example. While each operation has its own particular demands, there are a number of key challenges faced by most if not all service operations and service operations managers:

- managing multiple customers
- understanding the service concept
- managing the outcome and experience
- managing the customer
- managing in real-time
- co-ordinating different parts of the organisation
- understanding the relationship between operations decisions and business/ organisational success
- knowing, implementing and influencing strategy
- continually improving the operation
- encouraging innovation
- managing short-term and long-term issues simultaneously.

In the following sections we have noted the chapters where we explain how service operations managers can deal with these challenges.

1.3.1 Managing multiple customers

Many service organisations do not serve a homogeneous group of customers; they often serve, in different ways, different types of customers. The nursery's customers (see Box 1.3) include both the child for whom it is providing an education and social experience, and also the parents for whom it is providing a 'parental substitute' service. There are other customers, sometimes termed stakeholders, such as education authorities and health and safety officials, for whom the nursery provides informa-

Cybernurseries

Box 1.3

In 1991 a group of Cambridge University students from the School of Computer Science set up the first website camera (web cam). They focused it on the faculty coffee machine so that members of staff could see on their desk computer a 'live' picture, updated every few minutes, of the machine. This allowed them to check that the coffee jug was not empty before they went to use the machine. A higher-profile use of web cams was made in 1996 when Jennifer Ringley, a web-page designer from Washington, DC, trained a camera on her life and broadcast 24 hours a day from her flat.

Because web cams are relatively cheap and easy to set up, with basic systems only requiring a PC with a camera, a video capture card and a connection to the internet, they are now found in a wide variety of situations. Now there are over 10,000 web cams worldwide relaying images every few seconds 24 hours a day. Anyone connected to the internet can now see some breathtaking and bizarre sights, including the conditions at 3,880 metres on Mount Everest, the view of the top of the ski run at Lake Tahoe, sights in the African Bush, views from the Palazzo Senatorio in Rome, weddings at Las Vegas' Little White Chapel, even the contents of a Swedish family's fridge!

One recent innovation has been the arrival of web cams in nurseries so that anxious parents can use their computer at work or home to 'look in' on their children. Security is tight, with pictures being encrypted and passwords required for access. The pictures parents receive are single frames, updated every minute, but the quality is good enough for parents to check if their child is relaxed, happy and well cared for – and to remind them what life is about!

While parents and grandparents are revelling in this innovation, others are queuing up to condemn it. Some psychologists are concerned that it becomes an on-screen substitute for involvement in a child's upbringing that simply assuages the guilt of working mothers. Other people worry about it fuelling the current paranoia about child safety. However, at a time when childcare is needing an injection of trust and with more and more working parents, cybernurseries could soon be commonplace.

Questions

1 What are the advantages and disadvantages of having web cams in nurseries?

2 How do you think the nursery's service has changed as a result of the web cam?

This illustration is based on material in 'Big mother is watching you', *London Evening Standard*, Friday 5 November 1999, pp. 10–11, and 'Around the world in 10,000 web cams', *Daily Mail*, Tuesday 15 February 2000, p. 53.

tion and related services, as well as internal customers – the staff – whose welfare and training needs, for example, need to be considered. Understanding who are the various customers (Chapter 3), understanding their needs and expectations (Chapter 4), developing relationships with them (Chapter 3) and managing the various customers (Chapter 7) are key tasks for service operations managers.

1.3.2 Understanding the service concept

There may be differing views about what an organisation is 'selling' and/or the customer is 'buying'. Some parents may see the nursery as simply a babysitting service; others may see it as a critical educational experience for their offspring. Articulating and communicating the service concept (Chapter 2) is critical for clarifying the organisation's product to all its customers, and for ensuring that it can be delivered (Chapters 6–9) and that it is delivered to specification (Chapter 10).

1.3.3   Managing the outcome and the experience

One of the challenges for the service operations manager is that, for many services, there is no clear boundary between experience and the outcome. Customers in a restaurant are buying both the meal and the way that they are served. The education and the educational experience, likewise the childcare and the childcare experience, are inseparable. This is rather different from most manufacturing operations where the production of the product may be separated from how it is delivered to customers. A critical challenge for service operations is managing both outcomes and experiences simultaneously (Chapters 6–9).

The intangible nature of the experience provides particular problems for both specification and indeed control. Some call centres, for example, use scripts to ensure conformance and clarity, but such scripts lose out on flexibility, development of rapport and maybe also opportunities for cross-selling (see Chapter 7). This requires a clarity about the experience the organisation is selling (Chapter 2), supported by appropriate performance measurement (Chapter 10).

Some service organisations try to manage the intangible parts of the service by attempting to make them more tangible. At the nursery the intangible experience for the child has now been captured as a television product, visible and available to the parent (Chapter 2).

1.3.4   Managing the customer

Many service managers face a challenge not shared by their manufacturing counterparts, which is the presence of the customer inside the operation, often as an essential part of the service production process. In a restaurant customers are not just walking away with a meal inside them (the tangible output); they have also received a service in which they too have played a part. Their mood, attitude and actions may well have an impact not only upon their own experience but also upon that of other diners and the general atmosphere of the restaurant. This means that service operations managers, unlike many of their manufacturing counterparts, have also to manage, so far as this is possible, the customer during the service process. This requires careful design of the processes that handle back office activities but especially those that handle the customer. The service design must manage the customer through the process with an awareness of the impact on the customer's experience and other customers' experiences. A good design will also take account of how delivery processes impact on the employees' feelings, as their attitudes will have a significant bearing on service performance (Chapters 6–9). A key task for the nursery workers is managing the children in their care and recognising that tears or tantrums can easily affect the other children in the group.

The presence of the customer also renders the operation visible to the customer, so the service environment, sometimes referred to as the 'servicescape', needs to be designed to create the right atmosphere for the service (Chapter 6). In the nursery, the facilities and activities are visible not only to the child but also to the parents when dropping off and picking up the child and during the day as they 'drop in' via the web. As such, the servicescape is an important part of the service for customers and employees alike.

1.3.5　Managing in real-time

Many services happen in real-time – they cannot be delayed or put off. A passenger wanting to purchase a ticket for immediate travel may not be willing to return if the agent is busy. Streams of aircraft coming into land cannot easily be put on hold while equipment is serviced or controllers take a break. Children screaming for attention or in danger from hurting themselves in the nursery likewise cannot be ignored. Furthermore, during a service encounter it is not possible to undo what is done or said – things said in the heat of the moment or promises made that cannot be kept. Unlike in manufacturing organisations where it is possible to scrap defective products and remake them, in service there is no 'undo' or 'rewind' button. Smacking a child in the nursery is inexcusable and will not go unnoticed with web cam 'spies' in the room. Managing resources (Chapter 8), managing staff and employees (Chapter 7) and creating an appropriate culture (Chapter 14) are key tasks in managing real-time services.

1.3.6　Co-ordinating different parts of the organisation

The management of service operations is extremely demanding, requiring an integration of marketing, resource management, people management and so on (Chapter 15). The service operations manager is responsible for co-coordinating the various parts of the organisation in the delivery of the service product; this includes not only understanding the needs of customers (Chapter 4) but also overseeing the logistics of the supply chain to ensure that all materials and equipment are in the right place at the right time (Chapter 5). A nursery without staff and the right materials will not only provide a poor experience for the child but could be potentially dangerous. At the same time as delivering service, the service operations manager has to ensure that the operation is viable (Chapter 11) and supports the strategic intent of the organisation (Chapter 13).

1.3.7　Understanding the relationship between operations decisions and business/organisational success

Making the right decisions that lead to business or organisational success is a major challenge for many service operations managers. Business success may mean satisfying and retaining customers, attracting new customers, entering new markets, making profit, reducing costs or meeting budget targets. The problem is in knowing the effect of pulling operations levers (making operations decisions) on business performance (Chapters 10 and 11) and in knowing which improvements are appropriate (Chapter 12). Nursery managers using web cams believe that their introduction provides a highly valued service for their parents, giving them an edge in the market and maybe even allowing them to charge more for their services.

1.3.8 Knowing, implementing and influencing strategy

Operations, besides being the 'doing' part of the business, are also responsible for the implementation of strategy (Chapter 13). It is the nursery operation and its staff that deliver childcare, not its marketers or financial managers, though in a small organisation like the nursery these roles may be undertaken by the same people. It is therefore critical for service operations managers to understand their role not only in implementing strategy but also in contributing to it. Service operations managers can have a significant effect in developing and sustaining a strategy (Chapter 13) by knowing what they can, or could, deliver (Chapters 6–9) and by driving change through the organisation (Chapter 12).

The other strategic challenge for service operations managers is to provide the platform for competitive advantage. Rather than creating a service proposition and matching the operation to this, it may be that there is a competence in operations that can be turned to strategic advantage. The web cam might provide a nursery with a competitive advantage that may be difficult for less technologically advanced nurseries to provide.

1.3.9 Continually improving the operation

A challenge faced by all service operations managers is how continually to improve and develop their processes and products (Chapter 12), ensure that the outcomes are real improvements (Chapters 10 and 11) and that there is a culture that is supportive of service and change (Chapter 14). An important management challenge in this area is in managing the increased complexity resulting from change (Chapter 15). In many cases this includes improving efficiency as well as quality.

1.3.10 Encouraging innovation

Improving the operation is about taking what exists and developing it. Innovation, on the other hand, looks for what is not there, i.e. what is new. Innovation therefore usually requires an element of risk; financial risk because innovations require time and money, and often personal risk as the 'champion' for change puts their reputation on the line. Introducing the web cam to the nursery was an innovation that required some expense and no doubt attracted some detractors. Whether it is a success only time will tell. A critical role for service operations managers is to be alert to, and seek out, new ideas but also to have the will, and support, to assess them carefully and follow through if appropriate (Chapters 7–14).

1.3.11 Managing short-term and long-term issues simultaneously

A significant component of the excitement of operations management is its immediacy. By this we mean the constant challenge of dealing with the needs of a stream of customers, and making operational decisions to ensure the delivery of an appropriate quality of service at an appropriate cost. The danger of this immediacy is that it can lead to a short-term focus. Many service operations managers focus their time and effort on managing the day-to-day operations for the following reasons:

- The pressure on the organisation to perform in the short term leaves little time for medium-term operational improvement activities or longer-term strategic planning. For example, it is difficult for call centre managers to put time into solving underlying problems when they are involved in recruiting emergency staff to try to deal with a flood of calls.

- The contrast between the tangible, rational nature of many short-term operational decisions and the intangible, more intuitive processes required for strategic thinking may mean that the individual manager's style may contain a bias towards the tactical implementation of strategy rather than its formulation. The call centre manager may get a 'buzz' out of 'firefighting' the current problem and may be less inclined to put time into the more routine and less exciting task of data collection, analysis, report writing and high-level debate and discussion to try to resolve underlying and longer term issues.

As a result, the development and strategic aspects of operations management are frequently neglected and so a disproportionate amount of time is spent on managing the day-to-day operations. Operations managers must pay attention to both strategy and the detail of process and resource management to create and sustain a successful organisation (Chapters 6–9, 12 and 13).

1.4 Different types of services

Just as managing service operations involves the general set of challenges set out above, each part of the service sector has its own particular set of problems. Managing a for-profit consultancy with a small number of high-value clients poses rather different problems to managing an aid agency in a disaster-struck, heavily populated region of a developing country.

Each sector of the service economy (such as financial services, tourism, leisure, charities, government, hospitals, business-to-business services) has its own set of specific challenges, although of course much of the general theory and practice described in this book applies to all operations. This section describes some of the differences between the various types of services and outlines some of the particular challenges faced by each sector. In reading this section, it is necessary to be aware that each of these services will also have issues relating to aspects such as:

- The volume of transactions in a given time period. The hypermarket has very different operation challenges from the local grocery store, not least in simply managing the flow of hundreds of customers in the store.

- The mode of service delivery. The retail sector provides a good example of this diversity, with face-to-face service in traditional stores, remote service through mail order or telephone shopping, and, more recently, internet-based services.

Here we explore some of the key differences in service provision between five broad sectors of the service economy (see Table 1.1):

- business-to-business (B2B) services
- business-to-consumer (B2C) services
- internal services
- public services (sometimes referred to as G2C – government-to-consumer)
- not-for-profit services.

It is important to note that we use the term 'customer' as an all-embracing term that covers users, consumers and beneficiaries, for example.

Table 1.1 Types of service

	Business-to-business (B2B) services	Business-to-consumer (B2C) services	Internal services	Public services (G2C)	Not-for-profit services
Description	Services provided for businesses	Services provided for individuals	Services provided by internal functions within organisations	Services provided by central or local government	Services provided by non-government organisations (NGOs) or charities
Examples	Maintenance Consultancy Training Catering	Shops Hotels Banks Food	Finance Purchasing IT Personnel	Prisons Hospitals Schools Leisure	Hospices Counselling Faith organisations Aid agencies
Customers and purchasers	Frequently purchased by professionals, who are not necessarily the end users	Usually purchased by the individual consumer	Users have little or no choice of provider; frequently funded by central budget	Users may have little day-to-day choice; funded through taxation with the allocation of resources influenced by political processes	Beneficiaries are self-selecting or chosen recipients; funded through individual and organisational giving
Challenges	Providing high-quality services to business customers who frequently have high purchasing power	Providing consistent service to a wide variety of customers	Demonstrating value for money against possible external alternatives	Balancing the various political pressures and providing acceptable public services	Dealing with differences between volunteers, donors and beneficiaries Dealing with emotional and sometimes overwhelming needs

1.4.1 Business-to-business (B2B) services

B2B services are provided by businesses for other businesses or organisations. IBM Global Services, for example (see Box 1.4), provides a range of services to its business customers, including computer installation and maintenance and a range of management consulting services. Other B2B services include outsourced catering services, buildings' maintenance or leasing and supporting equipment, financial services and market research. Some of the challenges for B2B services include:

- Dealing with multiple contacts in the organisation. Consultants may have to work with a wide range of employees in their client organisations and so maintain relationships at different levels in the organisation (Chapter 5).

- Working with a complex set of relationships. The users or recipients of a service will frequently not be the purchasers, and this purchasing group may in turn be different from those who commission or specify the service standards (Chapter 3).

- B2B relationships may last for a long time. The challenge here is for the relationship not to become too 'cosy', with the customer or supplier being taken for granted (Chapter 5).

IBM Global Services   Box 1.4

IBM is widely regarded as a successful service company providing its business customers with solutions to their problems. In 2003 IBM had a turnover of over $89 billion and a gross profit of $33 billion. While sales of hardware and software accounted for just over 50 per cent of revenue, the remainder, and around 30 per cent of the gross profit, was generated by IBM Global Services (IGS), a rapidly expanding part of the business. IGS has a wide portfolio of services with, for example, computer installation and maintenance services at one end of the spectrum, and its wide-ranging business consulting services at the other.

Brian Sellwood, the general manager of IBM Global Services, responsible for delivery, operations and applications management services across Europe, Africa and the Middle East, describes the importance of services:

In today's computing industry it is very difficult to differentiate one supplier from another in terms of their hardware and software. The product itself is no longer, or very rarely, a differentiator. It's what you can offer the customer around that product, and that's invariably service, services such as project management, application implementation, fixing a fault with a machine, how you manage and perform that service. It's about what you do with that product, how you manage that relationship, how you treat the customer, how you respond to their problems and the solutions you can offer your customers to make their businesses stronger and better.

This approach is considerably different to just ten years before when IBM was renowned as a product-based company specialising in developing and selling computer hardware and software. It was also making a loss. IBM set about creating an organisation that was focused on its customers and not on the company's products. Brian Sellwood explained:

We were not into services; we were a hardware/software product company. The first step was to start understanding what the customer wanted; what they wanted to buy and how they wanted to see it packaged. Having undertaken some market analysis we decided to start very simply with what we had, and package it better, rather than build a whole new set of new services. Over time we realised that what we had was not quite what the customers wanted to buy; they wanted value-add. That meant we had to change and redefine our portfolio. We had to listen to what our customers were asking for and at the same time observe what the competition were doing and try to see where there were gaps in their portfolios and opportunities for us. And this has been a continuous process ever since. This continual refinement of what we are offering to the customer has played a key role in stimulating our growth over the last ten years.

In the early stages we found that customers were looking for help but had not always been able to express that need because there was not always someone willing to listen. In fact there was no shortage of opportunities for us to go and advise customers on how to make better use of their installed equipment. We found customers wanted almost anything and our challenge was to respond appropriately. No two customers were the same and so the challenge was to be able to offer the customers solutions to their specific problems rather than saying we have this solution and that will fit your business. From that beginning we were able, slowly, to add more services, eventually developing a business consulting capability where we could advise on how to use and manage applications more effectively, *how to install and help customers install applications, and advise customers on process engineering, supply chain development and business transformation.*

Questions

1 What does service mean to IBM?

2 What do you think were the main problems in transforming a product-based organisation into a service-based organisation?

3 What do you think are the key challenges that the organisation faces today?

1.4.2   Business-to-consumer (B2C) services

B2C services are those that individuals purchase for themselves or on behalf of another individual. They range through leisure services such as hotels, restaurants and sports provision, retail services such as shops and supermarkets, financial services such as banks and insurance providers, through to professional services such as lawyers and accountants. The challenges faced by most B2C services include:

- The organisation may deal with many different customers each day. Each have their own special needs and expectations of service delivery and, to make matters more difficult, these may change for the same individual from day to day (Chapters 3 and 4).

- Because the operation serves so many customers, it faces a major challenge in keeping the experience fresh for the next new customer. It may be the first and only time the customer experiences this service, although the customer may be just one out of hundreds that an individual member of staff sees in a day (Chapters 6 and 7).

- Many B2C service operations have the added complication of the need for consistency across many points of contact with customers, frequently spread nationally if not globally (Chapter 6).

1.4.3   Internal services

There are many services in large organisations that do not deal with the external customer, such as personnel, finance, purchasing and IT support. These service functions provide support services to the 'value-adding' parts of the organisation. A considerable number of people are often employed by organisations to provide these services. The particular challenges faced by these service operations include:

- Demonstrating that the internal service provides at least as good 'value for money' as an external alternative. This is a challenge faced by many IT departments, for example, whose users often feel that they could obtain cheaper equipment more rapidly from the local computer store or via the internet (Chapter 2).

- Adapting the service to the business need. If the service provision is effectively a commodity, it can be outsourced (Chapter 5). Internal service providers must demonstrate their ability to tailor their offerings to the changing business needs in a way that external providers cannot (Chapter 13).

- Gaining acceptance from their internal customers. Centrally funded services are frequently viewed with suspicion by local operating units and may not receive the co-operation required to carry out their tasks effectively (Chapter 14).

1.4.4 Public services (G2C)

These services are provided by central or local government for the community at large. Funding comes through the various forms of business and individual taxation, which is then largely allocated by policies set by government. Examples include police, prisons, hospitals and education. Specific challenges for public sector services include:

- The provision of 'best-value' services. Public services are under continual scrutiny. As a result, aspects of service operations that might be taken for granted by their private sector colleagues must be carefully justified in these organisations (Chapters 10 and 11).

- Rationing supply of service. Public sector organisations cannot use the pricing mechanism to regulate demand. With essential services, this can be a very sensitive issue. The health service must make policy decisions as to how much resource can be devoted to heart operations, to maternity services, and so on. Expenditure on intensive care units and accident and emergency provision are particularly sensitive since lives are at stake, but inevitably there will be times when demand outstrips supply (Chapter 8).

- Multiple stakeholders. Public services suffer from having many 'customers'. With B2C services it is reasonably clear who the customers are, and if this group is satisfied, generally speaking the organisation should be successful. This is not the case with the public sector, where the recipients of the service, as individuals, have little power to influence. Politicians and service managers themselves may have far more power to decide current priorities (Chapter 3).

- A confused service concept. The service concept provides direction for the organisation (we devote Chapter 2 to the discussion of the role of the service concept). Some public services are provided for the good of society at large and are not necessarily greatly loved by those who have to deal with them. Prisons, police services and tax collectors may fall into this category.

1.4.5 Not-for-profit services

Charities of various types form the majority of these services. Most engage in a mixture of fund raising, providing information about the cause or issue that concerns them, and in some form of social action. An organisation such as Oxfam must gather funds for famine relief and then organise to supply and distribute aid as required. Challenges for these services include:

- Managing a workforce of volunteers who, though highly motivated, may not follow the organisation's procedures (Chapter 7).
- Managing the allocation of resources to ensure that maximum funds flow to the beneficiaries of the organisation, while developing effective processes and people (Chapters 6–9).
- Dealing with differences between the activities that might influence and impress donors, but which might conflict with the requirements of their 'customers' (Chapter 2).
- Working in a highly emotional area, sometimes being overwhelmed by demand for service (Chapters 6–8).

1.4.6 Different services within a sector

Just as each particular sector has its own set of challenges, there can be significant differences between service operations within sectors. This may relate to the way the organisation has chosen to compete or which customer segments are to be served. Table 1.2 outlines some key differences between two B2C organisations operating in the same sector: a 'low-cost' airline and a 'full-service' airline.

One of the challenges for service operations managers is to match the style of operations, decisions about processes, people and networks to the overall strategy of the organisation (Chapter 13). To do this, the operations manager must have a clear understanding of how the operations function contributes to the overall success of the organisation. We will discuss this question in more detail in section 1.6.

Table 1.2 Comparing airline operations

	Low-cost airline	Full-service airline
Business model	High volume, low cost	Global network, profit made on business travel
Network	Short haul, with no connections to other carriers	Long haul, with connections to global partner airlines
Cabin service	Basic, no food, no frills	Range from economy to first class
Locations	Secondary, low-cost airports	Primary airports to allow interconnections
Volume	Multiple flights per route each day	Range from three flights per day to one flight per week for less popular destinations
Booking system	Direct through own website, and/or own call centre	Usually through intermediaries (travel agents)

1.4.7   A merging of distinctions

Over the last few years the distinctions between different types of organisations that we have outlined above are starting to disappear: 'Old borderlines are evaporating, old categories are merging. The divisions between commercial, public-sector and non-profit organizations are becoming blurred. All organizations now act on the same stage, and need to justify their place on that stage' (Jones 2001, p. 38). Some non-commercial organisations, public sector organisations and charities, for example, emulate the private sector; they have chief executives, strategic plans, marketing departments and customers. Public organisations, although they do not have competitors, recognise that their customers judge their service against for-profit organisations. Charities and government bodies have money-making arms. The British Council, for example, which promotes British culture around the world, also runs for-profit language schools. Universities, charities and faith organisations talk openly about market share.

On the other hand, some commercial organisations commit themselves to adhere to the principles of corporate social responsibility (CSR). Some appoint board members to check that company decisions support human rights, environmental goals and conservation projects, for example, to demonstrate that the organisation stands for something beyond the usual commercial goals. Sir Richard Branson, who heads up the Virgin group of companies, supports a wide range of non-commercial activities, including supporting AIDS work and wildlife and habitat conservation in Africa. Finding himself in a position of power and influence after working hard to establish a profitable set of companies, he is keen to fulfil his lifelong ambition of 'trying to change the world'. He explains: 'I'd always thought that Virgin should be more than just a money-making machine, and that, as Virgin has the wealth of a small nation, we should use that wealth to tackle social issues ... Companies do have a responsibility to tackle them' (Branson 2003, p. 529).

1.5   Different types of service processes

From an operations perspective we tend to be less concerned with the type of organisation or the sector in which we are working and more concerned with the type of process we are managing.

Different processes provide us with different benefits and also different challenges. Extremely flexible processes may be excellent for responding to a wide range of special customer requirements but may be quite costly to maintain. On the other hand, processes suited to delivering high-volume low-cost services are usually not very flexible. A simple example drawn from the hotel industry illustrates the differences:

- A five-star hotel prides itself on providing a wide range of services for its guests. Staff at the reception desk are prepared to spend time dealing with each customer's request and endeavour to answer every question. As a result, each transaction is quite lengthy and the hotel employs extra staff to ensure that the highest levels of service are achieved at all times for guests, who are paying premium prices.

- A budget hotel provides basic, reasonably comfortable accommodation for travellers normally staying for one or two nights. In this case, reception processes are designed to carry out only the basic check-in and payment activities as quickly as possible. Guests are not encouraged to request extra services and the number of receptionists are maintained at the minimum level to keep costs low.

Operational process design is influenced by two key parameters: the volume of transactions to be performed per period per unit, and the variety of tasks to be carried out by a given set of people and processes (we will discuss these in more detail in Chapter 6.)

The budget hotel reception process is close to the 'commodity' position (low process variety/high volume) in Figure 1.4. Processes here are clearly defined, leaving little room for individual customisation. Many consumer services employ these types of processes, having benefits of consistency as well as economy. Other examples include many call centre processes and retail activities. We have termed these commodity processes because there is little differentiation between services. They, however, have the benefit of delivering a clear service offer. A customer knows exactly what to expect when purchasing a Big Mac from McDonald's.

At the other end of the spectrum, we find 'capability' processes. Processes here have much less definition, with each task potentially significantly different from its predecessor. The reception activity in the five-star hotel is probably closer to this position rather than the commodity position of the budget hotel. The service offer is likely to be far less defined than the Big Mac and the 'have-a-nice-day' service that goes with it. In fact, many customers will be buying the ability of the service organisation to work with them to clarify the need or problem to be solved and then to develop a customised solution. Some professional service providers, such as

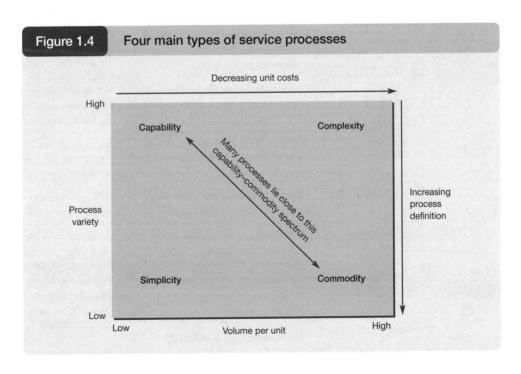

Figure 1.4 **Four main types of service processes**

consultants, will work in this way, although larger, global professional service firms often adopt a relatively standardised way of working, implementing pre-packaged solutions, which places them closer to the bottom right corner of Figure 1.4.

Table 1.3 summarises some of the key differences between capability and commodity processes.

We have provided examples at each end of the capability–commodity spectrum from similar sectors to demonstrate that not all services within a broad sector will employ the same processes. In Chapter 6 we will return to the challenge faced by many services, which is that they must operate in more than one position on this volume–variety matrix.

There are two 'off-diagonal' positions also identified in Figure 1.4:

- **Simplicity (low variety/low volume)**. These include small operations such as microbreweries, and small and specialist consultancies. Some larger organisations may also develop 'simple' operations as start-up services, which then may grow in terms of volume or variety or both (we refer to this as an incubator in Chapter 6).

- **Complexity (high variety/high volume)**. At first sight, this position might seem to be the ideal, providing maximum flexibility for as many customers as possible. In reality, however, providing flexibility for large numbers of customers is invariably expensive, achieved by employing large numbers of highly skilled people and/or high-tech equipment.

Table 1.3 Capability versus commodity processes

	Capability	*Commodity*
Examples	Luxury hotel Management guru Corporate lawyer Builder of architect-designed luxury homes Aviation insurance broker	Budget hotel chain Software package training provider House conveyancer Garden shed erector Motor insurance provider
Process style	Flexible processes allowing for wide range of outcomes and approaches	Relatively rigid processes focused on narrow range of outcomes and proscribed approaches
Service offer	Ability to diagnose customer needs and to develop a customised solution	Ability to provide an economical and consistent service to meet the needs of many customers
What do they do well?	Flexible, innovative and responsive to individual customer needs	Low cost, with consistent quality and often rapid response
Major challenges	Co-ordinating the response of individual employees Maintaining differentiated competencies to justify premium prices Managing productivity Making best use of highly skilled and knowledgeable individuals	Delivering consistently across multi-sites and many providers Employee morale and ownership of process and customer Managing innovation Managing large numbers of staff and customers

One of the challenges for service operations managers is to ensure that the type of process is appropriate to deliver the service concept (Chapter 2). As service concepts change and evolve, existing processes may become less appropriate for the task in hand. Effective managers will recognise this issue and proactively develop new process designs to meet the future requirements.

1.6 Judging the success of a service operation

We hope that it is becoming clear that service operations managers have an important and responsible role:

- They are responsible for a large proportion of the organisation's assets.
- They are responsible for delivering service to the organisation's customers.
- They have a significant impact on the success of an organisation.

The success of service operations managers is not simply about performing a good technical task, such as educating a student, delivering a project on time, or providing a safari holiday. Success is also about making a wider contribution to the success of the organisation, in particular:

- providing customer value
- delivering brand values
- making a financial contribution to the organisation
- delivering an organisational contribution.

Ideally, of course, we would like to see all four types of contribution throughout the organisation's operations, but this is unlikely. What is important is that the service operations manager is clear about the specific role each part plays at the present, and also how this contribution might change in the future.

1.6.1 Customer value

Customer value has a range of components. Customers may recognise value:

- when they receive something that they cannot do for themselves, such as generating electricity or carrying out surgery
- when they receive a service that they do not have the time or inclination to perform for themselves; for example, ironing shirts, shopping or arranging holidays
- when there is a reduction in perceived risk; risk might be perceived at a high level, such as the value of a business transformation consultancy, or at a low level, such as knowing that a train is likely to arrive on time
- through a psychological or emotional advantage of dealing with a particular service provider; for example, a woman may value the service of a doctor's practice because a female doctor is available
- from the status that they feel results from dealing with some service providers; for example, being able to tell their friends that they dine at the most prestigious restaurants or holiday in exotic locations.

A problem for service managers is that the customer's idea of what represents value for money may well vary from customer to customer and shift through time, and even from day to day. At the most basic level, the economising customers will think of value as getting more for their money. Other customers may be prepared to pay more in order to receive a higher service specification. Still others will value the psychological value in being able to say that they are able to afford to be customers of high-status services (even though the specification may be no better than a lower priced service). The service operations manager must be aware of the full range of influences on the customers' assessment of value. A key element in this understanding is the relationship between the service brand values as communicated to the customer and the potential mismatch in terms of customer experience.

1.6.2 Brand values

As indicated in the previous section, service organisations are paying close attention to the link between service delivery and desired brand values (see for example Box 1.5 on Lexus). Pringle and Gordon (2001) outline three imperatives for what they term the 'brand promise':

- to create the brand
- to convey the brand
- to keep the brand.

They argue that brand promises must be kept at four levels:

- The rational level: the need to demonstrate and deliver desired customer experiences and outcomes.
- The emotional level: the need to develop psychological benefits.
- The political level: the need to manage ethical and environmental issues.
- The spiritual level: the need to relate to people's 'higher order' needs.

Service operations must therefore consider how to build processes to deliver the brand values. A major UK electrical retailer developed the brand promise 'Currys, no worries'. An aspect central to this initiative was the organisation's home delivery service, recognising that customers often experience significant hassle in arranging for their new freezer or washing machine to be delivered at a convenient time.

Service operations managers therefore need to pay attention to the following:

- The extent to which the various attributes of customer value are reflected in the brand values of the service.
- The extent to which these brand values are reflected in the design of the service delivery system.
- The difference between the price the customer is willing to pay and the cost of the service operation.
- The extent to which these customer values are understood by the service providers.

Lexus

Box 1.5

Lexus is a division of Toyota Motor Sales, USA, and provides a range of distinctive luxury cars. The company's vision is to deliver the finest automotive experience. Lexus is proud of, and rigorously protects, its brand. It also works hard to reflect the brand in the design of its sales and aftersales service. One way it does this is by defining what it refers to as the 'Customer Journey'. This defines the look and feel of the Lexus Centre for the prospective purchaser.

Simon Arbuthnot, the national marketing manager for Lexus (GB) Ltd, explains:

We purposefully do not call them Dealers, but Centres to give them a retailer feel. These Centres put the customer at the heart of the business, and are planned around the customer's pathway when they visit us. The Lexus Customer Journey incorporates key elements of the brand and maps out the customer's logical progress through the showroom, from prospect to advocate. It also shows how the staff and the environment can be used to deliver consistently high service at every stage.

Some of the key elements of the Customer Journey in the showroom include:

- The entry statement, which defines the Lexus heritage through a historical story board and the brand through emotive visual images.
- The customer is allowed to browse the products at leisure – no sales people are based in the showroom.
- The customer lounge area is informal and relaxed and customers are free to read newspapers, enjoy a cup of coffee or watch TV. This area is modelled on a first-class airline lounge.

The selection areas allow the customer an element of privacy when discussing their car purchase; however, many customers complete the negotiation in the lounge.

Simon adds:

We use a similar approach in aftersales too. The design of all the Customer Journeys is based on three key principles: intelligence, integrity and exclusivity. Intelligence is about serving our customers as easily and effectively as possible while making best use of the space and other resources available. Integrity is being clear and open with our customers and making life easier for staff through the design of the Centres freeing them up to where they add most value, selling and serving. Exclusivity is about providing a warm, confident, exclusive and welcoming environment.

We detail the Lexus Centre standards in a 96-page document and enforce them through the Centre Agreements (our contract with the distributors). If a Centre fails to maintain the qualitative standards (such as cleanliness and appropriate use of the brand and advertising) or quantitative standards (such as the size of showroom, number of parking bays) then they are liable to suffer certain sanctions, up to and including loss of retail margin and ultimately the termination of their Centre Agreement.

This approach seems to work and is much appreciated by the dealers. The 2004 Dealer Attitude Survey in the UK, conducted by the National Franchised Dealers Association (NFDA), showed that Lexus's relationship with its UK network of dealers is stronger, more effective and more rewarding than that of any other manufacturer. It shows Lexus outperforming all other brands and achieving a maximum satisfaction rating in a number of key areas.

Karl Schlicht, Lexus director, added: 'This survey emphatically demonstrates how our determination to make Lexus the best extends to all areas of its business. It is by building such an effective and sustainable relationship with our Centres that we can continue to deliver the very highest standards of service to our customers.'

Questions

1 What are the brand values of Lexus?

2 How does the Customer Journey support those brand values?

This illustration is based on discussions with Simon Arbuthnot and on material from the Lexus websites: www.lexus.co.uk and www.lexus.com

1.6.3 Financial contribution

The process of service delivery should generate revenue for the organisation, either directly from consumers or indirectly from government, sponsors or donors. If the service concept is well thought through, the service operation matches the brand promise and the business model is sound, B2B and B2C services should also generate a surplus (or profit) for the organisation. The amount of this surplus will depend on the difference between the price the customers are willing to pay, based on their perception of value, and the cost of service production.

Service operations managers have a central role in both generating revenue and in managing the costs of production:

- Revenue is linked, directly or indirectly, to customer perceived value, which is influenced by perceptions of the service experience and outcome, both of which have to be designed and delivered by operations.
- The cost of service production is directly managed by service operations, and service operations managers have a key role in the efficient use of resources.

In both these aspects, service operations managers can make a significant contribution to the success of the organisation by being able to provide better customer perceived value and/or by being efficient (or more efficient than their direct competitors).

1.6.4 Organisational contribution

Creating customer value, creating brand value and delivering a financial contribution are three important organisational contributions that service operations managers make. They may also provide some broader organisational contributions, such as:

- enabling the organisation to achieve its goals/objectives/mission
- enabling the functioning of the organisation through the provision of internal services
- supporting the organisation's current strategic intent
- helping shape and develop the organisation's future intent
- developing skills and competencies that will support the development of the organisation.

1.6.5 Economic contribution

A final and important contribution, at a macro level, is the contribution that services, in general, make towards a nation's economy. Service activities are a vital and significant part of most developing and developed economies. In most developed countries services account for in excess of 70 per cent of gross domestic product (GDP), and for over 50 per cent of GDP in developing economies. They also provide employment for a significant number of people. The challenges facing service operations managers throughout the whole range of service organisations – such as financial institutions, government bodies, retailers, wholesalers and personal service providers – need to be taken seriously and managed well to support economic success and development.

We can see that from the standpoint of economic value alone we should pay attention to the service sector, and to service operations in particular as this is where the service, and therefore wealth and value, are created. Services also have an important economic role in non-service organisations. Many manufacturing companies have significant revenue-earning service activities, such as customer support, and also many service activities internal to the organisation, such as payroll, catering, information and IT services etc. Indeed it has been estimated that around 75 per cent of non-service organisations' activities may be directly or indirectly associated with the provision of services (Quinn and Gagnon 1986).

Service companies provide employment for the vast majority of the working population in most developed and developing countries. Some service organisations are indeed people-intensive in the sense of utilising large numbers of relatively low-skilled employees to deliver service. However, many service sectors, such as financial services, have begun to implement large information technology projects to reduce headcount and increase productivity. In many economies the service sector is the only area where new jobs are being created, notably in tourism and leisure.

Finally, we cannot ignore the vast numbers of people employed in the public and voluntary sectors. Managing services, such as education, health, fire, police, social services, famine relief organisations, faith organisations and charities, requires as much expertise as their private-sector counterparts. For example, governments increasingly are subcontracting to the voluntary sector many services that were previously provided directly by the state. In so doing, governments are applying commercial approaches to supplier assessment, and there is therefore a growing pressure on the voluntary sector to apply improvement methodologies (Chapter 12). Although there may not always be as clear a definition of customers and customer satisfaction, there is no doubt that there is ever-increasing pressure to provide higher levels of 'value for money' with the same or reducing resources.

1.7 The structure of the book

Figure 1.5 shows the structure of the book. We have organised its contents around the service concept (covered in Chapter 2), with the five key tasks being covered in the remaining four parts of the book – two of the tasks (customer and supplier relationships) have been combined into one part because they are both part of the supply chain.

Part 1 – Introduction

The second part of this introductory section provides a discussion of the service concept. The service concept provides cohesion and context for these five core operational tasks. Chapter 2 describes the overarching role of the service concept and will explain:

- the nature and power of the service concept
- how the service concept provides organisational alignment

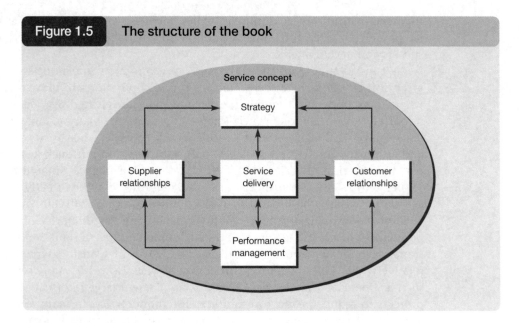

Figure 1.5 The structure of the book

- How the service concept can be used as a strategic tool
- The role of the concept in creating focus.

Part 2 – Customer and supplier relationships

Operations management plays an important part in developing and maintaining relationships with both suppliers and customers. Most operations must pay attention to the management of a wide range of supplier and customer relationships. While Chapter 4 focuses on customer satisfaction and service quality, the themes of quality management and quality improvement are interwoven throughout the whole text. The reason for this is that we believe that quality should be an intrinsic part of service delivery, clearly defined and managed, rather than a separate aspect. In the same way, resource productivity must also be managed as part of service delivery.

Key aspects of managing customer and supplier relationships include:

- managing different types of customers
- developing an understanding of the range of customer relationships, and the issues in developing and maintaining such relationships
- building customer satisfaction by understanding expectations and managing perceptions
- understanding supply chains and supply chain management
- understanding the use and management of intermediaries
- identifying the main types of supply partnerships and how they can be managed effectively.

Part 3 – Service delivery

The prime focus of this book is that of service delivery. The ultimate test of service operations management is at the point of delivery to the customer. In a sense, it may be relatively easy to provide a service that will satisfy (or delight) customers, but very much harder to do this within budget or at a profit. The key aspects of this task include the following:

- managing service processes
- managing people – both staff and customers
- resource allocation and utilisation
- managing networks, technology and information.

Part 4 – Performance management

Performance management covers the measurement of service operations perform-ance, the development of performance measurement systems and structures, and the task of driving changes in performance. Issues covered include:

- assessing the purposes and types of performance measures
- developing interlinkages between the various types of measures
- benchmarking, target-setting and links with improvement and rewards
- understanding the cause–effect relationships between operational decisions and business performance
- using service recovery and service guarantees to drive improvement.

Part 5 – Managing strategic change

This part of the book deals with the process and content of developing service strat-egy. The success of a strategy is clearly influenced both positively and negatively by organisational culture. Equally, operations managers have the opportunity to influ-ence the culture of their organisations, in particular by changing the nature of processes, the organisation structure, and by altering the performance measure-ment and reward systems. This part also shows the complexity faced by service operations managers: that is, the interrelationships between all the tasks that create a complexity that is at the same time both fascinating and frustrating. Issues cov-ered include:

- developing service as a competitive weapon
- identifying operational priorities
- developing and sustaining a service strategy
- understanding organisational culture and how to influence it
- the types of culture and the implications for service delivery systems
- managing change and the pitfalls to avoid
- the nature of complexity and the operational consequences of complexity.

1.8 Summary

What is service operations management?

- Service operations management is the term that is used to cover the activities, decisions and responsibilities of operations managers in service organisations.
- Service operations managers are responsible for delivering service to the organisation's customers.
- Service is the combination of outcomes and experiences delivered to and received by a customer.
- The service experience is the customer's direct experience of the service process and concerns the way the customer is dealt with by the service provider.
- The service outcome includes tangible outputs, plus value, emotions, judgements and intentions.

The challenges facing service operations managers

- The challenges faced by service operations managers include:
  - managing multiple customers
  - understanding the service concept
  - managing the outcome and experience
  - managing the customer
  - managing in real-time
  - co-ordinating different parts of the organisation
  - understanding the relationship between operations decisions and business/ organisational success
  - knowing, implementing and influencing strategy
  - continually improving the operation
  - encouraging innovation
  - managing short-term and long-term issues simultaneously.

Understanding different service operations

- Different types of service organisations face particular challenges.
- There are five broad sectors of the service economy: business-to-business services, business-to-consumer services, internal services, public services and not-for-profit services.
- The key challenges are:
  - B2B – providing high-quality services to business customers who frequently have high purchasing power
  - B2C – providing consistent service to a wide variety of customers
  - internal services – demonstrating value for money against possible external alternatives

- public services (G2C) – balancing the various political pressures and providing acceptable public services
    - not-for-profit services – dealing with differences between volunteers, donors and beneficiaries.
- There are four main types of service processes: capability, commodity, simplicity and complexity. A key challenge for service operations managers is to ensure that the type of process is appropriate to deliver the service concept.

Judging the success of a service operation

- Service operations managers:
    - are responsible for a large proportion of the organisation's assets
    - are responsible for delivering service to the organisations customers
    - have a significant impact on the success of an organisation.
- Success involves performing a good technical task and also:
    - providing customer value
    - delivering brand values
    - making a financial contribution to the organisation
    - delivering an organisational contribution.
- At a macro level services are a critical part of most economies, accounting for a significant proportion of GDP and employment.

1.9 Discussion questions

1 Describe the service experience and outcomes for a fast-food restaurant, a doctor's surgery and an internet-based fashion clothing retailer. Compare and contrast the services of these three organisations.

2 What are the similarities and differences in terms of the challenges faced by a large house-and-contents insurance firm compared to a small commercial insurance broker providing insurance for stately homes?

3 Select a service organisation and identify the key back office and front office tasks. What activities have most impact on outcome and experience? Could any task move from one area to the other and what would be the implications?

1.10 Questions for managers

1 Describe your service in terms of experience and outcomes from both a customer and organisation perspective. Assess the mismatches between these perspectives.

2 With internet access the customer may have greater access through a website to people who previously might have worked in back office functions. On the other hand, customers no longer see the people with whom they are dealing. What are the implications of this for your organisation?

3 What are the key challenges your service operation faces? Are these views shared by your colleagues?

4 How is the success of your operation assessed? Is this approach appropriate?

1.11   Further reading

Davis M. M. and Heineke J., *Managing Services: Using Technology to Create Value*, McGraw-Hill, Boston, Mass., 2003.

Johnston R., 'Service operations management: return to roots', *International Journal of Operations and Production Management*, vol. 19, no. 2, 1999, pp. 104–24.

Jones R., *The Big Idea*, HarperCollinsBusiness, London, 2001.

Lovelock, C.H. and Wirtz J., *Services Marketing: People Technology and Strategy*, 5th edition, Pearson/Prentice Hall, New Jersey, 2003.

Shaw C. and Ivens J., *Building Great Customer Experiences*, Palgrave, Basingstoke, 2002.

Slack N., Chambers S. and Johnston R., *Operations Management*, 4th edition, FT Prentice Hall, Harlow, 2004.

1.12   References

Branson R., *Losing My Virginity: The Autobiography*, Virgin Books, London, 2003.

Haywood-Farmer J. and Nollet J., *Services Plus: Effective service management*, Morin, Boucherville, Quebec, 1991.

Johnston R., 'Operations: from factory to service management', *International Journal of Service Industry Management*, vol. 5, no. 1, 1994, pp. 49–63.

Johnston R., 'Service operations management: return to roots', *International Journal of Operations and Production Management*, vol. 19, no. 2, 1999, pp. 104–24.

Jones R., *The Big Idea*, HarperCollinsBusiness, London, 2001

Morris B. and Johnston R., 'Dealing with inherent variability: the difference between manufacturing and service', *International Journal of Operations and Production Management*, vol. 7, no. 4, 1988.

Pringle H. and Gordon W., *Brand Manners*, Wiley, Chichester, 2001.

Quinn J.B. and Gagnon C.E., 'Will services follow manufacturing into decline? *Harvard Business Review*, vol. 64, no. 6, November–December 1986, pp. 95–103.

Sky Airways   Case Exercise

Robert Johnston and Bridgette Sullivan-Taylor, Warwick Business School

Sky Airways is a major European airline with routes predominantly in Europe but offering daily flights to New York, Johannesburg, Mumbai and St Petersburg. At the last meeting of the board of directors the airline's owner and chief executive,

Bernie Williamson, expressed concern at the growing number of complaints his airline was receiving. His analysis of the increasing trend revealed a strong link between number of complaints and minutes' delay. This did not surprise him. What did surprise him was the large number of underlying complaints that were, in the main (around 72 per cent), about the on-board catering.

Given his desire to increase RPK (revenue passenger kilometre), which had declined by 5 per cent over the past three years, he was keen to hear ideas from his team as to how they could deal with the problem. This was an opportunity seized upon by Angela Carter-Smith, Sky's recently appointed marketing director. She suggested that the airline should consider moving away from pre-packed and reheated meals in tourist class to the business-class style of service, whereby food is pre-cooked but heated, assembled and served in front of the customers. She explained: 'Many international airlines are attempting to enhance their competitive edge by differentiating their in-flight service offering across their global network'. The food costs, she suggested, would be little different but simply require more time by cabin attendants, which they have on the longer flights. If this proved to be successful on the long hauls, it could then be considered on the short hauls. When Bernie reminded her that they needed to provide an upgraded service for the premium-fare passengers, she added that the answer here was to provide 'culturally sensitive' meals: flying to and from Mumbai, the food should be Indian, while to Johannesburg it should have a distinct African flavour. All eyes then turned to Peter Greenwood, the operations director, who had his head in his hands and was groaning. He promised to 'look into it' and report back at the next meeting.

The next day Peter made time to talk about the rising trend in complaints to Christina Towers, the catering subcontract manager, Justin Maude, a senior cabin attendant, and David Goh, senior gate manager.

Christina Towers explained:

The problem we have, like all other catering companies, is consistency. Although we can specify menus, portions and costs there are inevitably wide variations in quantity and quality loaded at various airports around the world. We have the biggest problems at the furthest destinations. You also put us under pressure to maintain costs, so we only try to load the precise number of meals required in order to reduce wastage and space required. It is not easy making pre-flight predictions about both numbers and choices, and you cannot expect it to be right 100 per cent of the time without substantially increasing the number of meals loaded over and above passenger predictions. It is not cost effective and it is weight prohibitive to load two of every meal option, even for a business-class passenger who would expect, more than anyone else, to receive their first choice. I think we would get fewer complaints if we reduced choice of menus.

Justin Maude added:

You would not believe the difficulties we face in providing something as simple as meals to passengers. We frequently have to explain to passengers, in all the cabins, why they can't have their first choice of meal. This creates a great deal of stress for the crew. There is just no room for more meals on board; the galleys are really tight for space. The biggest problem we have is over passengers who order special meals for religious, dietary or health reasons. I reckon one in five is not loaded on to the aircraft. Sometimes we have passengers on board who ask whether the food contains nuts and we have no idea. We can only offer them water and bread rolls to be safe. I think we should ensure the caterers let us know the contents of every meal and always provide extra vegetarian and kosher meals because passengers don't always remember to pre-book them. Another problem is caused by the last-minute passengers whom you want us to take to fill seats, so we often have to ask for more meals shortly before take-off. I know this causes problems but, unlike a restaurant, during flight there is nowhere to find additional supplies. I think it would help if we could have meals that needed less preparation time and take less space, so we can load more meals in anticipation of an increase in passengers and also load additional special meals, just in case.

David Goh then added his views:

The main problem I have is ten minutes before take-off when we find that the incorrect quantity, quality and meal type are loaded and the crew request extra meals. We often end up delaying a plane and missing a slot while the caterers rush over half a dozen extra meals. We should let the plane go. I am sure not everyone actually wants a meal. They only eat because they are bored. I think we should stop providing meals altogether, certainly on the short hauls. Tourist-class passengers often eat at the airport anyway and we already provide food for business class in the executive lounges.

Peter had not dared raise the idea of changing the methods of service in tourist class and increasing the range and type of meals to business-class passengers. His thoughts turned to how he could explain to the board the difference between what might be desirable and what is deliverable and appropriate.

Questions

1 What problems does Peter Greenwood face?

2 If you were Peter Greenwood, what would you say to the board?

chapter two

The service concept

Chapter objectives:

- to define the service concept

- to demonstrate the power of the service concept as a strategic tool

- to use the notion of focus to define four types of service concept

- to examine how unfocused organisations can gain the benefits of focus.

2.1 Introduction

In Chapter 1 Lawrence Lim from Singapore General Hospital said, 'People's concept of a government hospital in the past is that it is bureaucratic, officious and slow to respond'. This is what he thinks some of his customers believe the service will be like; a view he hopes to dispel.

The service concept is a critical element in knowing and defining what the organisation is selling or providing and the customer buying or using. The service concept (and its development) is a core task in managing service operations. It can be used as a central tool in the design, delivery and improvement of services, yet its potential is often underutilised.

Surprisingly little has been written about the service concept, yet it is critical and central to service organisations. This chapter will explain the service concept and show how this powerful yet simple idea can help integrate the various functions of a service organisation. We will also explain, using an example, how by concentrating on the service concept an organisation can develop strategic advantage.

Service concepts focused on a market segment and/or providing a limited range of services offer advantages for both the consumer and the operation, yet many services are unfocused, doing 'everything for everyone'. We will explain how such organisations can gain some of the benefits of focus.

2.2 The service concept

When asked his secret of success, Ingvar Kamprad, the founder of the IKEA chain of furniture stores, replied, 'We are a concept company'. He went on to share his vision and explain the concept: 'Our vision is to contribute to a better everyday life for the majority of people. We do this by offering a wide range of home furnishing items of good design and function, at prices so low that the majority of people can afford to buy them.' This concept has captured the imaginations of both IKEA's employees and customers. People buy IKEA products because they are well made, stylish and inexpensive. They also buy into the idea of self-selection, self-service, self-delivery and self-build.

As products and services are becoming more and more similar and as it becomes easier for organisations to copy others' products and services, organisations may choose to compete through something that transcends their service offering – the service concept.

Over ten years ago, First Direct implemented a new concept in banking. At a time when banks were (unwelcoming) places with lavish banking halls, long queues and a 'you-should-be-grateful' style of service, First Direct created a bank to suit the customer. It is open 24 hours a day and staffed not by traditional bank clerks but by people who are interested in helping people. First Direct is a bank with personality. Its staff are witty and warm, straightforward, informed and informing, and certainly not ordinary. Peter Simpson was one of the originators of the bank and he is First Direct's commercial director:

> We had to find a way to differentiate ourselves from all other banks. Customer satisfaction with banks in general was low and customers felt the banks were all as bad as each other. The existing notion was that a bank required the customer's physical presence. We decided upon the radical idea of a purely telephone operation. Telephone was the obvious channel because just about everybody had a telephone in their house or access to a telephone at work. We went live at midnight on Saturday 1 October 1989. Making a Sunday as our first day of trading made it clear that we were very different and out to provide the customer with a service that they had never experienced before. We took around about 200 calls on the first night and since that day we have never closed.

The service concept is something very important to service organisations, but is often misunderstood and/or underutilised. It is something that is more emotional than a business model, deeper than a brand, more complex than a good idea and more solid than a vision. It is also something that can unite employees and customers and create a business advantage. In section 2.3 we explain in more detail what we mean by a service concept and in section 2.4 we demonstrate how it can be used as a strategic tool.

2.2.1 Customers buy concepts

It is important to recognise that when buying (or using) services customers tend not to be simply buying the elements of a service but something much greater and usually more intangible. Looked at simply, in terms of its elements, a hotel provides a bed, bathroom and food. Looked at as a concept it can provide anything from a low-cost, comfortable night's sleep, through a relaxing and pampered stay, to a truly unique and unforgettable experience (see Box 2.1).

At an elemental level a university provides lectures, food, accommodation and books, but what its customers are looking to acquire is something much greater – an 'educational experience'. Likewise, we go to Disney for a 'magical experience' or a restaurant for a 'great evening out' or to a firm of consultants for 'peace of mind'. These are examples of the essence of a service concept, but the service concept, to be a useful and even a strategic tool, needs to contain more detail than these central themes or 'organising ideas'.

The Icehotel · Box 2.1

Jukkas AB is a company offering a wide range of activities, such as white-water rafting, fishing, reindeer and dog-sledding tours, cross-country skiing, snowmobile safaris and guided tours. It is based in Jukkasjärvi, a small village in Swedish Lapland, which lies 200 kilometres north of the Arctic Circle by the River Torne.

The problem was that visitors were few and far between in the long, dark winter months when the temperature drops to −40 °C. Manager, Yngve Bergqvist, now president of Icehotel, saw this as an opportunity. In the winter of 1989 he invited a group of Japanese ice artists to come to Jukkasjärvi to carve sculptures from the crystal clear ice that forms from the pure waters of the River Torne. He then built a 60-square-metre cylinder-shaped igloo, made out of clear ice blocks, to protect the sculptures. Visitors flocked to see the exhibits in his 'ice gallery'. One day when his hotel was full he was pressed by a good friend to find accommodation for ten colleagues. Yngve could only offer them space in his 'ice gallery' with sleeping bags on reindeer

skins. In the morning the guests enthused about the 'warm and intense experience'. The Icehotel was born.

In winter the Icehotel covers approximately 5,000 square metres and is built out of 30,000 tonnes of snow and 4,000 tonnes of ice. The hotel has a reception, around 40 rooms and 25 suites. It has its own Iceart exhibition, Icebar and Icechurch. Since the hotel melts every spring the number of rooms, as well as the exhibits, varies from year to year!

The temperature in the bedrooms is a relatively warm −5 °C. Guests sleep on a bed of warm insulating reindeer hides in an ultra-warm sleeping bag. In the morning they can enjoy an early morning sauna followed by breakfast. Toilets are located in a small heated building adjacent to the Icehotel. In the evening the guests drink in the Icebar from Iceglasses sculpted from the pure ice of the River Torne. During the day guests eat in the restaurant 100 metres away and take part in the adventure activities such as dog sledding and snowmobile safaris.

Each year a new Icehotel is constructed by around 30 local artists and builders before the arrival of the first guests in mid-December. Snow cannon are used to blast snow on to a frame of arched steel sections, and ice pillars are added for extra support. The walls are made from huge, clear blocks of ice, weighing almost 2 tonnes, cut from the frozen river with special saws and moved by front-loading tractors. Work on the interior starts in early December, when sculptors cut and work the ice to create windows, doors, pillars, beds, lamps and ice sculptures. Guest ice artists are invited each year to design the ice décor in some of the rooms.

When April comes the roof of the Icehotel begins to drip. The hotel is closed and it slowly melts back into the river whence it came.

Questions

1 What are the similarities and differences between an 'ordinary hotel' and the Icehotel?

2 What is the Icehotel's service concept?

This illustration is based on material on the Icehotel website, www.icehotel.com, and discussions with managers.

2.3 The service concept defined

A service concept is a shared understanding of the nature of the service provided and received, which should encapsulate information about:

- *The organising idea*. The essence of the service bought, or used, by the customer.
- *The service experience*. The customer's direct experience of the service process, which concerns the way the service provider deals with the customer.
- *The service outcome*. The result for the customer of the service.
- *The service operation*. The way in which the service will be delivered.
- *The value of the service*. The benefit that customers perceive to be inherent in the service weighed against the cost of that service.

A service concept should provide sufficient detail to make it clear what the organisation is selling/providing and what the customer is buying/receiving. Thus the service concept represents the nature of the service offering, which guides operations staff and managers to know what to deliver and how to deliver it and helps marketing know what to offer to the marketplace (see Figure 2.1).

The service concept needs to be aligned to the organisation's 'organising idea'. For example, a store selling paint, tools and other items for home improvements may be organised around 'providing the cheapest hardware in town' or 'enabling the customer to carry out high-quality home improvements'. The first idea would require an operation focused on 'no frills', efficiency and economy, whereas the second idea might require investment in skilled sales staff to provide guidance for customers as to how best to carry out their do-it-yourself (DIY) projects.

The detailed service concept may be based upon an explicit statement made by the organisation or it may be inferred from marketing information – either direct marketing by the organisation or indirect marketing through experience and word-of-mouth. In Figure 2.1 we provide an example of a service concept and some of its key elements for a theme park in the UK.

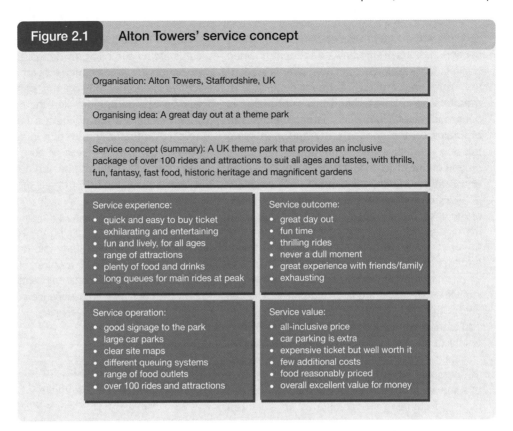

Figure 2.1   Alton Towers' service concept

Organisation: Alton Towers, Staffordshire, UK

Organising idea: A great day out at a theme park

Service concept (summary): A UK theme park that provides an inclusive package of over 100 rides and attractions to suit all ages and tastes, with thrills, fun, fantasy, fast food, historic heritage and magnificent gardens

Service experience:
- quick and easy to buy ticket
- exhilarating and entertaining
- fun and lively, for all ages
- range of attractions
- plenty of food and drinks
- long queues for main rides at peak

Service outcome:
- great day out
- fun time
- thrilling rides
- never a dull moment
- great experience with friends/family
- exhausting

Service operation:
- good signage to the park
- large car parks
- clear site maps
- different queuing systems
- range of food outlets
- over 100 rides and attractions

Service value:
- all-inclusive price
- car parking is extra
- expensive ticket but well worth it
- few additional costs
- food reasonably priced
- overall excellent value for money

The concept may be at an organisational level and describe the nature of service provided by the organisation as a whole, or at an individual service level, thus describing a particular service within a portfolio (see Box 2.2).

The service concept is a mechanism that links operations and marketing, so it is important that it is well defined and agreed so that marketing and operations can be aligned (see section 2.4.1). Yet it is surprising how few organisations have clearly defined service concepts – therefore it is little wonder that customers' expectations are sometimes not met, staff feel frustrated and there is tension between operations and marketing managers. Regular review of the service concept will help prevent the service operation slipping into what may be termed the 'provider mentality': thinking that the customer will love us because we know that what we provide is good!

Trafficmaster   Box 2.2

Trafficmaster utilises sophisticated technology to provide vehicle tracking and route-planning services to vehicle fleet operators and to individual drivers. For a relatively small fee, a monitoring unit can be installed in a vehicle that allows Trafficmaster to use global positioning systems (GPS) technology to track its position in real-time. A regular subscription fee provides access to a range of services, including traffic updates, route-planning services and stolen vehicle tracking systems.

Trafficmaster has in excess of 7,500 sensors positioned around the major routes of the UK, covering some 13,000 kilometres of roads. These sensors monitor traffic flows and identify when traffic is moving slower than normal or is stationary. The likely impact on travelling time can therefore be calculated and this information is passed to the unit in the car, alerting the driver to problems on the chosen route and identifying possible alternatives for the journey.

One of the latest products is SmartNav, which represents a significant change in the service provided to Traffic*master*'s customers. The comprehensive package provides the driver with travel directions at each point and alerts the driver to possible delays en route. The major addition is that drivers can press a button installed in the car, which connects them to the Traffic*master* call centre in Bedfordshire. The call centre agents are termed personal assistants and can draw on a database of over 90,000 points of interest, including banks, restaurants, and tourist attractions. The driver can interrogate the personal assistant to modify the route, and this service may be extended to offer the possibility of making reservations at selected restaurants or hotels en route. This 'concierge' service represents a significant departure from Traffic*master*'s basic services.

Another product, Trackstar, alerts the police if a car is stolen and can provide real-time tracking information to enable early recovery of the vehicle. The customer buying the basic product, Trackstar Standard, must alert the national control centre before the police are informed. For Trackstar protector, the system is automatically activated if the car is moved without the unit first being disarmed. Trackstar has an additional feature that enables the driver to call the emergency services in the event of a breakdown or accident.

Traffic*master* has grown rapidly in a very short space of time, based largely on the success of its technology. In 2003, with the rapid growth in calls to its national control centre, Traffic*master* recruited its first professional call centre manager – to provide much needed experience in dealing with customers as opposed to technical expertise.

Questions

1 Desribe the service concept for each of the Traffic*master* products outlined above. What are the significant differences between them?

2 What guidance can you give to the new manager of Traffic*master*'s national control centre as a result of clarifying the service concepts?

2.3.1 Service value

In Chapter 1 we provided information about the main elements of service and the service concept: experience, outcome, operation and value. It is appropriate here to provide a little more detail about value.

An important element of the marketing mix is price. Price is the value placed on the service. This could be its monetary value, the financial price, or its comparative value if the service is bartered. The price of a service may be referred to in many different ways: the price of money is called interest; the price of poor motoring may be, in financial terms, a fine; while the price for use of equipment is rent.

The cost of a service to a customer is a combination of the financial price together with the cost, or inconvenience, of making the purchase – sometimes called the sacrifice (Zeithaml and Bitner 1996). For example, the cost of buying the weekly groceries involves not only the monetary value of the goods but also the cost of going to the shops to make their purchase – this is not only the bus or train fare but also the sacrifice of effort and time involved, which could have been put to other uses. The cost of poor driving is not only the fine, but also loss of a no-claims bonus, higher insurance premiums and possibly injury or even death, with the mental 'cost' that follows.

To understand value, these costs to the consumer have to be weighed against the benefits consumers perceive in the service. This may not only be the outcome and the experience but also psychological factors, such as a feeling of well-being or being recognised in a restaurant. Value does therefore not necessarily mean low price. Value is the customer's assessment of the benefits of the service weighed against all the costs involved.

A key role of marketers is to try to assess these issues to understand what customers value in order to help the organisation make pricing decisions. Operations management, on the other hand, is the art of creating and delivering value. The task for operations is to find the balance between maximising the value for customers and minimising the cost to the organisation; that is, striking a profitable or in-budget balance between:

- maximising the benefits to the consumer
- minimising the financial and sacrificial costs to the customer
- minimising the cost to the organisation.

The service concept is therefore a key tool that can communicate the set of benefits (outcome, experience, operation, together with the psychological benefits) to the customer in order to demonstrate the potential value of the service.

An operation delivers and creates value by playing a part in the supply chain (Chapter 5): adding value to the supply chain to create its services and value to its customers. Some organisations go further – indeed the more successful organisations do not just *add* value, they *reinvent* it (Normann and Ramirez 1993). Many services have been reinvented over the last few years. For example, internet banking has challenged and radically changed the value delivered by banks and received by their customers. From a customer's point of view, new approaches to banking, such as those pioneered by First Direct, have provided 'a new kind of value. In particular, it eliminated traditional constraints of time and space' (Normann and Ramirez 1993). Now customers can manage their accounts and withdraw cash at any time of day or night, almost anywhere. Telephone and internet banking have not only reinvented value for customers but also changed the nature of value creation by the operation. Managers are now concerned with the design and maintenance of customer-interaction technology (websites, plastic cards and computer networks to support the machines), and in dealing with the inevitable disadvantages of automation, such as trying to maintain a relationship with customers they rarely see.

It is important to emphasise that the ultimate judge of value is the customer. More important still is that the real test is perceived value – whether the customers feel that they are receiving value, based on criteria that are their own, and frequently intangible and intuitive. Here again, the service concept is central to understanding customer requirements: facilitating marketing in presenting the service offer in the most effective manner, and focusing the operation's performance measures on those areas that have most impact on the customers' perceptions.

Understanding and delivering perceived value is central to creating competitive advantage, and we will return to this theme in Chapter 13.

2.3.2 The service concept – a shared view

Because the service concept is a *shared* understanding of the nature of the service, it may not be the same as an organisation's business proposition. The business proposition defines the way in which the organisation would like to have its services perceived by all its stakeholders – customers, employees, shareholders and lenders. This view, however, may not be shared by customers, who may perceive the nature of the service in a different way (see Figure 2.2).

In theory, and in the minds of some managers, these two views are the same; in reality this is often not the case. Customers do not always know what an organisation is trying to provide, or they see it in their own, sometimes irrational, idiosyncratic way. Likewise, organisations do not always understand how their customers view their services. For example, the managers and staff of a conference centre catering for business clients (large and small organisations undertaking training) may see its concept as the provision of excellent conference facilities supported by four-star catering and accommodation. What a (business) customer (the training manager, for example) is buying is a convenient location to undertake company training with minimum hassle with good quality food and accommodation. While these two perspectives may overlap considerably, there may be many important points of misalignment. For example, the conference centre manager may insist on all guests sitting down for a silver-service dinner each evening, whereas training managers may wish to make the most of each evening and have a less formal and quicker, but still high-quality, meal. This important misalignment (see section 2.4.1) may have a considerable impact on the customers' experience, outcome and perception of value.

What is sometimes referred to as the 'marketing concept' (see, for example, Dibb *et al.* 1997) attempts to reconcile these views. The marketing concept is a management philosophy that encourages organisations to understand and then satisfy customers' needs and fulfil the objectives of the organisation (see Figure 2.3).

The service concept should be a shared understanding of what the organisation provides and what the customer receives. In Chapters 3 and 4 we look in more detail at the needs of customers and in Chapter 7 we take a more organisational perspective.

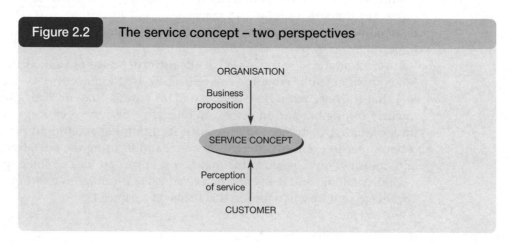

Figure 2.2	The service concept – two perspectives

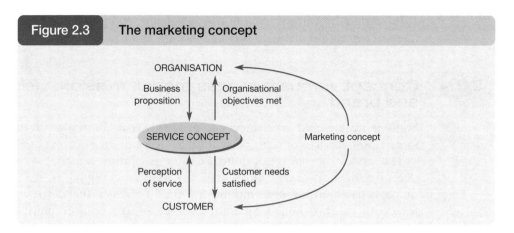

Figure 2.3   The marketing concept

2.3.3   The 'DNA' of the service concept

The service concept is often defined (in operations texts) in terms of the service product – all the different constituent parts that form the service, the outcome and the experience, including the servicescape. This has also been referred to as the 'customer benefit package' (Collier 1994): the things that provide benefit and indeed value for the customer. This approach, defining the nature of the service in terms of its constituent parts, has also appeared in the marketing literature. Lovelock and Wright (1999), for example, use the '8Ps' of marketing, which encompass the elements of the service product – Product, Process, Place, Physical evidence, People, Productivity and quality – plus additional marketing elements: Price and Promotion (the '8Ps' are based on the '7Ps' by Booms and Bitner 1981, which were developed in turn from the '4Ps' by McCarthy 1960).

Deconstructing a service in this way is helpful in that it allows us to identify the various elements of a concept, check them against customers' needs (see Chapter 4), design and deliver those elements (Chapters 6–9) and measure our performance against them (Chapter 10). However, this 'bits and pieces' approach belies the complexity of many services and also ignores the fact that customers' perception of service is integrative. For example, a day out at Disney's Magic Kingdom is more likely to be defined by its designers and its visitors as a 'magical experience' rather than six rides and a burger in a clean park (Clark *et al.* 2000).

The *Concise Oxford Dictionary* (1996) defines a concept as a 'mental picture of a group or class of objects formed by combining all their aspects'. A service concept is thus more than the 'DNA' of a service – the elements of the service product; it is the mental picture that is held by customers, employees and shareholders about the service provided by the organisation. It is 'service in the mind' (Clark *et al.* 2000).

The terminology 'service in the mind' has been adapted from thinking about the psychoanalysis of organisations. The phrase 'organisation in the mind' has been used to express the idea that employees may have very different mental pictures and assumptions about the real purpose of their organisation (Armstrong 1991) – which may be rather different from the version designed for public consumption! When we apply this thinking to service organisations, there is the added dimension of the customer, who may have assumptions or 'service in the mind' that are radically different from either what is intended or what is experienced.

In section 2.4 we will explore the use of the service concept in creating 'alignment of perception' between the organisation and its customers.

2.3.4 Concept versus business model, mission, vision, idea and brand

Many terms are used in business and academia that are similar to, though not the same as, the service concept. We will try to clear up some of this confusion.

The service concept is not quite the same as a business model. A business model describes how an organisation achieves its financial goal. A 'no-frills' airline's model is based on low cost: minimising airport charges, fuel costs, employee costs, food costs etc., providing very limited service, using a point-to-point operation and appealing to large volumes of cost-conscious passengers. This certainly helps describe the value part of the service concept and some of the operations too, but it misses out on the more emotional level – the customer experience.

Neither is the service concept necessarily the same as an organisation's vision or mission. An organisation's vision is usually concerned with where the organisation hopes to be at some time in the future. The service concept is concerned with the present: what the organisation does now and what its customers think it does today. Indeed, the service concept is more likely to be tied to the past based on past marketing or previous experiences, or what people have communicated about past experiences.

The service concept is not usually the same as a mission statement. Organisations' mission statements cover many notions from 'vision statements' to 'company philosophy' (Campbell and Yeung 1990). Like vision statements, mission statements may be concerned with the future rather than today's reality. On the other hand, if they define the organisation's philosophy it is possible that they tend to be more concerned with organisational values rather than the detail of the service that is delivered.

The service concept is much more than an idea. An idea is an initial notion of a service. A service concept is a more complete picture, which includes some details about what the service will be like, the outcomes and the experience. Its value lies in bringing together the various elements of the service – the operational elements, marketing emphasis and customer requirements – to produce a meaningful overarching service definition in sufficient detail to provide a working service specification.

The service concept is more closely related to the notion of brand (see Box 2.3). However, brand has many meanings, including: brand name – the term, design symbol or any other feature that identifies a service (or a product) (Dibb *et al*. 1997); presented brand – how the organisation presents itself and its promise through its marketing efforts; external brand – how the organisation is presented through word-of-mouth communication and the media, for example; and brand meaning – the customers' perception of the organisation and its services (Lovelock and Wirtz 2003). While these four perspectives may be different, a service concept is a shared view and usually articulated in much more detail (sufficient for both marketers to know what they are selling and operations to know what they have to deliver and how it has to be delivered). Thus the service concept is usually more detailed and concrete than a brand or service promise.

RAC Motoring Services

Box 2.3

Founded as the Royal Automobile Club in 1897, RAC Motoring Services is now part of Lex Service plc and provides a range of motoring services to individual members, businesses and car manufacturers. With over 6 million members and one of the world's most advanced computer systems the RAC is committed to providing roadside assistance, repair and vehicle recovery. Its range of products and services also includes travel information, vehicle inspection, route planning and driver training through its subsidiary, BSM. In 2001 RAC was ranked as the number-one Roadside Assistance Provider in Customer Satisfaction by J.D. Power and Associates. This was the second time it had achieved this accolade in the four-year history of the study.

Nigel Paget, the RAC's operations director, explained the reasons for its success:

We deliver an excellent service. Our focus has always been on consistency of delivery and treating the customer as an individual. We try to provide an empathetic, understanding and reassuring service. We try to understand the person's situation. If your car window jams in an open position it may not be an emergency for some people, but if it is pouring with rain or you are about to go on holiday, it needs sorting straight away. We try to respond to the situation at the time.

Our vision is to be the first choice provider of individual motoring solutions to the consumer and to businesses. Our distinction is not just our range of services but our personality. These are the attributes of our organisation, our brand values. They are about how we behave towards our customers and towards each other, day in and day out. RAC's brand values are concerned with being practical, willing, honest, individual, responsible and flexible ... Demonstrating these brand values really sets us apart from our competitors. Some of these values are functional, others are more concerned with the emotional side. In essence, they are about the way we do things around here. For example, we try to select people on their personality.

It's not easy in a business like ours to make it personal for our customers but we do try to do this – it's about empathy and understanding.

For example when someone rings in we don't ask them for their name or car details straight-away, we ask how can we help them. When they tell us their car has broken down and there is steam coming out of it, we will empathise; our colleagues use phrases like 'Oh that sounds awful – don't worry I am sure we can do something about that for you'. While they are saying this they are putting the details into the computer ready to pass on to a patrol. We want it to feel personal and to show that we really care. If a customer is ringing on a mobile we will offer to call them back. We might then say 'And so that I can help you further can I take your registration number please?' We don't give our name first either. We exchange names later because our research tells us people forget the name if they hear it initially.

We let the customer set the agenda. We may find, for example, that the customer has got a problem that does not need a patrol. There is a big difference between putting in a litre of diesel into a petrol vehicle and putting in 10 litres into an already empty tank. If it is the former we can tell them that the vehicle is perfectly drivable and they will believe us – they trust us. Or it may be something they want to sort out for themselves so we put them on to one of our technical engineers who can then advise them. This is obviously of benefit to us. It avoids the cost and time of sending a patrol out and if we can avoid this 2 or 3 per cent of the time then it's a benefit straight on the bottom line. However, the critical thing is the customer benefit. It is customer satisfaction that drives our decisions.

Questions

1 Construct the RAC's service concept encapsulating the experience, outcome, operation and value.

2 How does this differ from its vision, service/brand personality and brand values?

This illustration is an extract of a case commissioned by the Institute of Customer Service as part of a study into service excellence. The author gratefully acknowledges the sponsorship provided by Britannic Assurance, FirstGroup, Lloyds TSB, RAC Motoring Services and Vodafone.

2.3.5 Creating the reality – the role of service operations managers

The role of service operations managers is to understand the organisation's business model and to construct the service concept based upon the organisation's vision, mission, service ideas, brand and brand values, and then acquire and manage the resources to deliver that concept to the organisation's customers.

The service concept acts as a 'service specification' and is also the starting point for the development of an operations strategy. A clear statement of what the customer is buying provides the focus for operational performance criteria and the identification of the key operational decision areas. This is even more important when the operation has to deliver multiple service concepts. Clarification of the differences between concepts will allow the service operations manager to make process design decisions about combining or separating service delivery and will allow clearer communication as to how performance criteria might differ between concepts.

2.4 The service concept as a strategic tool

Besides helping us define and understand the nature of the service we experience or deliver and the value it provides, the service concept can – and we believe should – be used as a strategic tool (see also Van Looey *et al.* 2003). It can be used to:

- create organisational alignment
- assess the implications of design changes
- drive strategic advantage.

2.4.1 Using the service concept to create organisational alignment

We believe there is an opportunity for many service organisations to take control of their service concept and make it explicit. This is the first step in gaining alignment. If you ask a group of individuals, customers and staff, to define the service concept of a particular organisation you will invariably find a range of views. For example, operations managers may be concerned about managing the process, staffing problems and operational costs. Customers may be concerned about the experience, price and value. Marketing may be concerned about brand development, new opportunities and revenue generation. Accounting may be concerned about cash flow and budget projections. Human resource managers may be concerned about staff skills and competencies, attitudes and recruitment. These valid, but none the less differing, perspectives and priorities often result in functional myopia, leading to actions that are functionally appropriate but internally, and externally, inconsistent. Organisations need to eradicate such inconsistency. They must take responsibility for making the nature of their service explicit by ensuring a clear and appropriate marketing message to both employees and customers. Only in this way will they help ensure appropriate, and consistent, service delivery.

We would argue that the service concept can act as an alignment tool that links together different organisational functions with a common purpose and 'standard' against which their actions can be checked. 'In this respect the service concept acts as a lens and filter through which internal functions may see each other's roles and contributions to the service delivered to the customer' (Clark *et al.* 2000). The articulation and agreement of a service concept is a means not only of identifying the nature of the business but also of providing it with a sense of purpose and common direction. It also provides a means of assessing the contributions and interrelationships among the various functional groups.

We would therefore suggest that in order to share, communicate and evaluate a concept, it needs to be written down, discussed and indeed agreed. This allows a check to be made internally to reach agreement about what is being provided and why. It also provides explicit signals to customers, existing and potential, about what the service will be like and the benefits they should expect. Even when written down, the service concept does not have an objective reality in the same way that a manufactured product has; however, it is a means by which organisations can gain internal and external alignment – by ensuring that all constituencies have the same or at least similar 'service in the mind' (Clark *et al.* 2000).

2.4.2 Using the service concept to assess the implications of design changes

The service concept can be used as a driver for long-term service development. By defining the concept, service designers can compare it to alternatives, proposed or already provided by other service suppliers, to help operations managers identify the implications of change. Whether the changes are deliberate changes to the concept or an evolutionary approach with modifications to process or procedures, changes to service concepts have implications for all parts of the organisation. 'There is substantial evidence to suggest that significant changes to service concepts expose the weaknesses in the organisation, its ability to co-ordinate all the various constituencies and its capacity to communicate effectively both internally and externally' (Clark *et al.* 2000).

Such a 'concept audit' can be achieved by using a simple profiling tool. Box 2.4 describes a change of concept in the Natural History Museum in London, which is then profiled in Figure 2.4.

The Earth Galleries at the Natural History Museum, London
Box 2.4

Michael Shulver, Warwick Business School

In 1985 the Geological Museum merged with its neighbour, the Natural History Museum, in Cromwell Road, London. The merger was cemented in 1988 by the construction of new gallery space linking the two sites.

From the mid-1930s to the early 1990s the Geological Museum consisted largely of taxonomic displays of rocks, gems and minerals and was a place for quiet study of 'rocks in boxes' by specialist geologists. This contrasted sharply with the noisy, lively and enthusiastic atmosphere of its neighbour. In the 1970s the Natural History

Museum had begun a programme of exhibition renewal, using advanced and innovative methods of display to interest and entertain visitors, to support its mission 'to maintain and develop its collections and use them to promote the discovery, understanding, responsible use and enjoyment of the natural world'. The resultant Life Galleries are very popular and have won awards for excellence in design. In 1985 the Geological Museum adopted the Natural History Museum's mission and a new name, the Earth Galleries, together with a duty to communicate the natural world to the general public in a way that it could understand.

Putting that mission into operation was not going to be easy. A survey of museum-goers found that they were less than enthusiastic about geology as a subject. It was perceived as dry, dull and had little to do with everyday life – in short, it was just about rocks. The perception was that the only reason you would visit something called the Geological Museum was because you had to pass an exam in geology.

The museum took up this challenge, as Dr Giles Clarke, Head of Department of Exhibitions and Education, explains:

Surely volcanoes are interesting, fascinating things, and earthquakes are really significant, fascinating and important. Gems are beautiful, especially in jewellery, and fossils, they are interesting too. So, there is a whole range of topics there that don't immediately come to mind when people say geology, but nevertheless are perceived as being fascinating. What we can then do is take the breadth of the subject that we want to display and talk about in the galleries, and to shuffle it around so that the high-profile ones come early, and so they will be an attraction to visitors to come in to the subject, and we can use those as a leader to collect people and move them around the exhibitions.

Value, hitherto defined as access to a superlative reference collection of gems and minerals, was now to be reflected more in the degree to which the museum educated, enthused and entertained the public in the earth sciences. The target consumer was now a 15-year-old intellect who would already have had significant exposure to television and film of volcanoes, earthquakes, mining and so on. If the museum was to 'promote the discovery, understanding, responsible use and enjoyment of the natural world' to this consumer group, then it could not rely on the collection alone. Such consumers would need to be helped by staging devices that moved them from the world they knew into the unfamiliar world of geology and inspire engagement with the subject. The exhibits would also have to educate consumers gradually, and gently guide them through the museum's narrative.

The museum would also have to cater for groups, in particular children, who would be more inclined to sample 'chunks' of galleries rather than the whole, so the galleries had to be structured to accommodate short attention spans. Mini-exhibits or galleries, each with a complete story, were created, but the logic of the story was integrated with the overall museum theme. Some displays became interactive, encouraging visitors to experiment with geological processes through hands-on engagement with both hard and soft exhibits, such as minerals, molten surfaces and water, for example. To support the social and family groups in which the public visited the museum, facilities such as restaurants, shops and restrooms had to be developed to be at least as good as those at a theme park.

When the museum completed its work in 1998, geologists still had access to a world-class reference collection, although in very different surroundings. However, the material was now used to enthuse and educate a much wider audience about the secrets of the earth.

Questions

1 How would you describe the concept of the Geological Museum and of the new Earth Galleries?

2 What do you think were the key problems faced by the designers in creating the new concept?

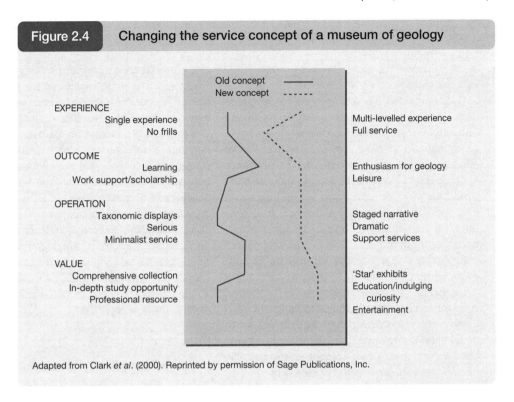

Figure 2.4   Changing the service concept of a museum of geology

Old concept ————
New concept - - - - -

EXPERIENCE
Single experience
No frills

OUTCOME
Learning
Work support/scholarship

OPERATION
Taxonomic displays
Serious
Minimalist service

VALUE
Comprehensive collection
In-depth study opportunity
Professional resource

Multi-levelled experience
Full service

Enthusiasm for geology
Leisure

Staged narrative
Dramatic
Support services

'Star' exhibits
Education/indulging
curiosity
Entertainment

Adapted from Clark *et al.* (2000). Reprinted by permission of Sage Publications, Inc.

A key point here is that of alignment. It is rare that a change to experience, outcome, operation or value can be made in isolation. Changes in one element will have consequences in others. Sometimes these represent opportunity, sometimes the potential for conflict. The use of the service concept and a profiling tool allows the people involved in the design or redesign of a service to understand what is required and to assess and therefore manage the implications of change.

Capability mapping

One enhancement of the profiling tool is the identification not only of the old concept and the new requirement, as in Figure 2.4, but also the capability map of the existing service (see Figure 2.5), i.e. its current potential. This capability envelope can be used by organisations that perhaps do not have a specific new or revised service in mind but can use capability mapping to explore what opportunities there might be for using operational potential.

Box 2.5 explains how one organisation used the capability envelope to identify the areas where the company needed to develop new capabilities.

2.4.3 Using the service concept to drive strategic advantage

Thinking about the service concept not only helps managers understand their business but also challenges them to view their business in ways that can make it stand apart from other organisations. Lord Marshall, chairman of British Airways, made the point:

TECLAN Translation Agency

Box 2.5

Michael Shulver, Warwick Business School

TECLAN provided a one-stop shop for language translation. The company used 35 in-house translators for most European languages, Japanese and Chinese. Translation to and from other languages was subcontracted to a network of some 3,000 translators. Though the company would handle just about any translation work, over time it had developed a distinctive competence in translating technical documentation, particularly computer software. The majority of software translation was the 'localisation' of software written in English – the conversion of hypertextual help-files. However, TECLAN often encountered help-files that lacked sufficient flexibility, and in localising they had to resort to developing completely new help-file structures. Thus it developed a new competence in help-file authoring and rudimentary programming.

By themselves these new competencies were not particularly distinctive, but coupled with the company's translation capability they provided the potential for a highly competitive resource-set.

TECLAN's service concept profile is mapped in Figure 2.5. The profile shows where the company started from and the shaded portion represents the new operations potential that TECLAN developed. The dotted line indicates an idealised service concept for a new service that exploits the newly developed potential. This also highlights the gaps between current capability and that required for the new service. The main areas requiring attention and development were in quality performance and the company's ability to manage relationships with its new class of customers. Although translators had developed the ability to manage relationships with clients' own technicians, TECLAN's account managers lacked the technical knowledge to market and sell the new capabilities.

Questions

1 Summarise TECLAN's current service concept.

2 How does this compare to where it is trying to go and what do you think will be the operational problems in making this change?

This illustration is taken from Clark *et al.* (2000).

Figure 2.5   Capability mapping at TECLAN

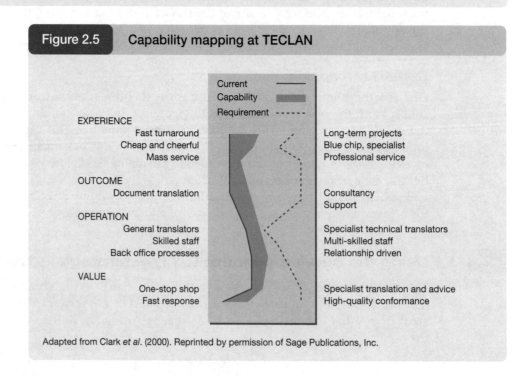

Adapted from Clark *et al.* (2000). Reprinted by permission of Sage Publications, Inc.

There are different ways to think about how to compete in a ... service business such as ours. One is to think that the business is merely performing a function – in our case, transporting people from A to B, on time and at the lowest possible price. That's the commodity mind-set, thinking of an airline as the bus of the skies. Another way to compete is to go beyond the function and compete on the basis of providing an experience. In our case, we want to make the process of flying from A to B as effortless and pleasant as possible. Anyone can fly airplanes but few organisations can excel in serving people. Because it's a competence that's hard to build, it's also hard for our competitors to match. (Prokesch 1995)

By thinking carefully about the market, the different customer segments and the needs of the customers in those segments, together with a dispassionate understanding of the core competencies of the operation, managers may be able to develop totally new and innovative concepts that have great appeal to customers and give the organisation a significant competitive edge (see Figure 2.6).

Box 2.6 describes the development of a new concept at Singapore Zoo, which could be difficult for other organisations to follow. This development springs from the current operational competencies together with a realisation why the Zoo did not attract foreign visitors – a very large and lucrative market.

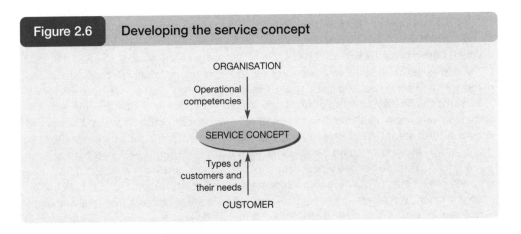

Figure 2.6 Developing the service concept

Singapore Zoological Gardens — Box 2.6

Singapore Zoo is no stranger to innovation. Some years ago the zoo started offering customers the chance to have breakfast or tea with an orang-utan called Ah Meng. Since then she and her companions have played host to some 50,000 guests a year. So well known is the zoo for its innovation that a spoof article in *The Straits Times* on 1 April 1998 offered a new 30-minute low-impact aerobic work-out with Ah Meng before breakfast. Bernard Harrison, the zoo's chief executive, said he was amazed by the flood of interest in the 'new service', the authenticity of which most people did not seem to doubt!

Singapore Zoological Gardens is a public limited company owned by the Government of Singapore and has been in existence since 1983. Its aim is to be a world-class leisure attraction striving to provide excellent exhibits of animals displayed in their natural environment for the purposes of recreation, education and conservation.

The zoo is situated on a 28-hectare site about 30 minutes to the north of the city of Singapore. It houses a collection of 2,800 animals, representing 216 species. It uses an 'open zoo' concept: the animals are kept in spacious, landscaped enclosures, separated from the visitors using psychological restraint techniques based on the animals' natural instincts for defining a territory as their own, or by a natural fear of some elements such as water. The water moats, for example, are concealed with vegetation or dropped below the line of vision. The more dangerous animals, such as leopards and jaguars, are housed in beautifully landscaped glass-fronted enclosures. Oppressive cages, which typify 'old' zoos, are absent. Stimulation is provided by trying to recreate the natural stresses of the wild and bring out the animals' natural instincts and reflexes. For example, instead of throwing neatly chopped chunks of meat to the big cats, the keepers hang a large hunk of meat up high, forcing them to leap for it and grasp it with their claws, much as they would when hunting in the wild.

Despite having a successful world-class zoo, Harrison and his colleagues know that it had limited appeal, in that the majority of the zoo's visitors were local residents. For the large numbers of tourists on short stop-overs, visiting a zoo, which they could easily do at home, was a low priority. The zoo needed a new concept.

After four years of planning and three years of construction, Singapore Zoo's Night Safari was opened in May 1994. The Night Safari is the world's first night-time wildlife park. It occupies a 40-hectare site adjacent to the day zoo, with its own entrance and facilities, from which guests can explore the wildlife in the natural tropical jungle. Over 1,000 nocturnal animals of 100 species can be seen in large naturalistic habitats. Given that most animals are nocturnal, a night safari offers visitors the best chance to see them.

The Night Safari is nothing like an ordinary zoo, but a real safari experience. Quiet electric trams provide guided safaris for visitors around a 3.2 kilometre trail, which takes about 45 minutes to complete, although there are stop-off points. The ride provides the zoo's staff with a chance to edu-cate and inform, and its guests time to relax and enjoy the ride. The same 'open' concept as the day zoo is used, to tremendous effect. Indeed, under the cover of darkness, the moats can be very effectively camouflaged using netting and shade. Other less dangerous animals, such as deer, roam freely in large areas bounded by cattle grids. Occasionally the tram has to stop and wait for an animal to move out of its way. During the ride the landscape changes to provide appropriate settings for its animals, from the rocky outcrops of the Himalayan foothills, to the grassy plains of equatorial Africa, and ending with the forests of South-East Asia. Information boards at intervals provide facts about the animals nearby. Indeed the impression of free-roaming wild animals is so realistic that one visitor was overheard asking his partner how come all the animals were in the right places – could they read?

Three walking trails are well marked and provide opportunities to see all the animals at close range. The dark jungle paths create an eerie atmosphere, and guests come face-to-face with many animals. Because it is dark, the glass-fronted cages that house the big cats are not noticeable – nor are the visitors to the cats because of the lighting differences, so they carry on as normal with their night-time activities.

Lighting is provided by a combination of mercury and incandescent lights, mounted on tall poles to provide a soft bluish moonlight, which neither detracts from the ambience nor disturbs the animals. Only certain areas are 'moonlit', since the dark background adds to the atmosphere and lighting the foreground would spoil the effect of the appearance of freedom. Flash photography is forbidden to ensure the animals are not disturbed.

All the facilities are consistent with the safari theme. The walkways from the car parks to the tram station are constructed from wooden boards with wooden handrails. The central 'rooms' have high ceilings, wooden beams and ceiling fans but no walls, and so are open to the dark jungle. Around the restaurant and shops, and the bongo burger bar with food aimed at the younger visitors, there is no piped music, just the quiet chattering of the wildlife. Even the toilets have a safari feel: they are open to the sky with sinks set in stone outcrops surrounded by jungle.

fying their key characteristics and drawing their profiles using the profiling tool (Figure 2.4).

Questions

2 Why do you think that other zoos will find it difficult to copy this concept?

1 Compare and contrast the service concepts of the Night Safari and a traditional zoo by identi-

This illustration is based on visits to Singapore Zoo, and discussions with staff and material from the zoo's website: www.zoo.com.sg

2.5 Focused and unfocused service operations

In this section we explore four types of service concept and how, together with the important notion of focus, we can understand the issues faced by service organisations and also how some of them can achieve greater efficiencies.

2.5.1 Focused service operations

Providing a narrow range of services is the most efficient way of designing and delivering services. This can be a narrow range for a tightly defined market segment (see Figure 2.7), such as structural testing services for construction industries, or English language courses for working mothers. Or alternatively it can be a narrow range of services for a broad market segment – a 'one size fits all' service (see Figure 2.8). For example, MasterCard and Visa credit cards are held by a whole range of people from low income to high income, low users to high users, personal users and corporate users. Yet their operations are limited essentially to delivering credit facilities through the use of a card accepted in retail outlets throughout the world: high-volume, relatively standard and focused operations. Other examples include a fixed menu restaurant (with no children's meals or deviations from the menu, for example) or a consultancy company that, while appealing to a wide range of industries, limits its operations to dealing with very specialised problems, such as installation of accounting software.

| Figure 2.7 | Focused operations for a narrow market |

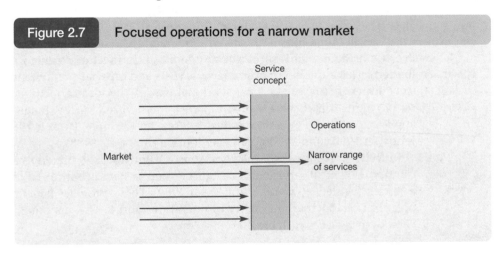

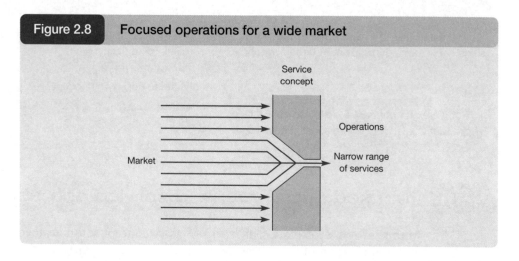

Figure 2.8   Focused operations for a wide market

In essence the service concept acts like a filter trying (not always successfully) to ensure that the right customers with the right needs and expectations will be drawn into the operation. In the case of providing a narrow range of services to a narrowly defined market, the service concept has to be tightly defined to restrict the number and type of customers to those few for whom the limited range of services is entirely appropriate. A key role for marketers is to understand the concept and find its market. A role for operations is to work out how to deal with those individuals who sneak through the filter for whom the service is not appropriate.

In the case of delivering a narrow range of services to a wide market, the concept attempts to attract as wide a customer base as is possible and appropriate and then filtering it into accepting a narrow range of services (Figure 2.8). A key role for marketers is to 'sell' this narrow service offering to as wide a market as possible. An issue for operations is to deal with the constant pressure to be flexible and widen its service portfolio.

These approaches allow for focused operations – highly efficient, repetitive, standardised services using a fixed mix of people, skills, equipment, materials and systems. The notion of focus was introduced into the manufacturing literature by Skinner in 1974 and it has now become one of the central pillars of manufacturing strategy (see, for example, Hayes and Wheelwright 1984, Hill 1993, Skinner 1985, Slack 1991). Skinner (1974) claimed that 'A factory that focuses on a narrow product mix will outperform the conventional plant which attempts a broader mission. Because its equipment, supporting systems, and procedures can concentrate on a limited task for one set of customers, its costs and especially its overheads are likely to be lower than those of a conventional plant.' The idea of focus – concentrating on providing a particular segment of customers with a narrow range of products – applies equally well to service industries (see, for example, Heskett 1986, Kimes and Johnston 1990a and 1990b, Van Dierdonck and Brandt 1988).

Indeed service focus makes good sense: 'Tight focus is imperative because you can't provide great service unless your business system is optimized to the needs of a certain segment' (Davidow and Uttal 1989). Focus provides benefits both to the organisation, such as simplicity of operation, and to the customer, such as high value at low costs (see Table 2.1).

Table 2.1 **The benefits of focus**

Benefits to the organisation	Benefits to the customer
Simplified operation	Ease of use
Predetermined service	Customers can select a service according to their specific needs
Dedicated operation	Low price
Dedicated facilities	
Tight process control	
Ease of training	
Lower costs	

2.5.2 Unfocused service operations

Through either a strategy of growth and development or strategic positioning many successful service organisations have unfocused operations, which deliver a wide range of services to either a narrow market segment or a wide market (see Figures 2.9 and 2.10). American Express provides a wide range of products and services for the international traveller. Coutts provides a full range of banking services but only for high-wealth individuals. On the other hand, organisations such as doctors, local authorities, governments, Disneyworld, supermarkets, hypermarkets, the internet, police services, leisure centres … all serve a very wide range of customers with a very wide range of services.

In the case of the narrow market, again the service concept has to act as a filter, filtering out those customers who are not appropriate for the services. Organisations use credit checks or income checks, while golf clubs may have handicap restrictions or require prospective members to be nominated by existing members, to try to ensure that the customers conform to the required specification. A key role for marketing is to understand the service's distinctiveness and find appropriate means of reaching appropriate customers. A key role for operations is to deliver something distinctive but involving a wide range of services.

The role of the service concept for unfocused operations appealing to a wide market segment is not necessarily to restrict the customer base – indeed many

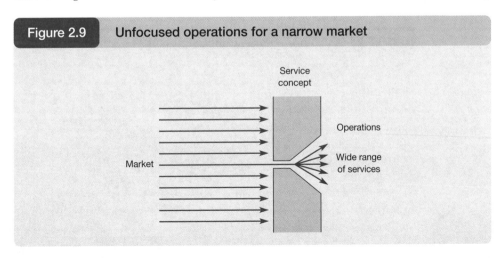

Figure 2.9   Unfocused operations for a narrow market

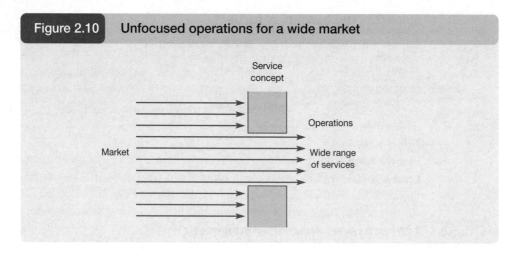

Figure 2.10   Unfocused operations for a wide market

organisations have little choice. State hospitals and government service providers, for example, have to deal with everyone who is in need of their services. The role of the service concept in these situations is more about education and information, explaining how long the service might take and the other alternatives, if any, that are available. A key role for marketers is to manage that information-giving process. The key role for operations is in trying to create as efficient an operation as possible while catering for diverse needs (see section 2.5.4)

At first glance it might seem that such unfocused operations could be inefficient. This is not necessarily the case; indeed in section 2.5.4 we explain how such organisations can make their operations as efficient as possible while still appealing to a wide market.

2.5.3   Four service concepts and changing focus

In summary, using the two traditional dimensions of focus – number of markets served and range of services provided (see Figure 2.11) – service concepts can be categorised into four broad types: service focused, market focused, service and market focused, and unfocused.

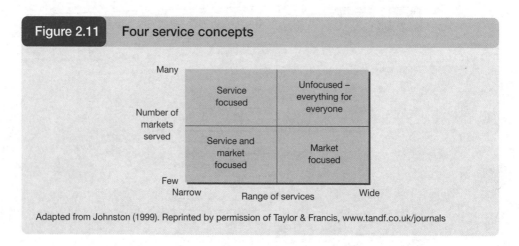

Figure 2.11   Four service concepts

Adapted from Johnston (1999). Reprinted by permission of Taylor & Francis, www.tandf.co.uk/journals

It is important to recognise that organisations are constantly changing and redefining their service concepts. Both Barclaycard and American Express, for example, are slowly changing their degree of focus.

Barclaycard's service concept is to provide credit facilities through the use of a card accepted in retail outlets throughout the world. It serves many markets with a single credit card service. However, Barclaycard has recently added more services to its portfolio, such as insurance. American Express, on the other hand, which traditionally provides a greater range of services than Barclaycard, such as Global Assist, a range of insurance services, travellers' cheques and airline tickets, is now trying to broaden the appeal of its card away from just the 'international traveller' (see Figure 2.12). Furthermore, internet banks, such as Egg, are focused on regular internet users and offer either one main product (service and market focused) or, as in Egg's case, a range of services including credit card, mortgages, loans and travel insurance. These banks are in a position to expand the number of markets they service as the use of the internet widens. Telephone-based credit companies such as Lombard Direct tend to be both service and market focused, with service concepts focused on clear market segments and providing a limited range of services. Through a 24-hour dedicated call centre Lombard Direct mainly provides unsecured loans from £800 to £15,000. These account for 90 per cent of its business. The organisation is in a position to consider expanding its product range. (More information on Egg and Lombard Direct can be found in Chapters 9 and 10.)

Cycle of proliferation and focus

There is a natural tendency for organisational growth to come by first increasing the range of services and then expanding the market, or by market expansion and then through product or service proliferation. Focus is then achieved by separating out the organisation into distinct operations or organisations focused on providing a particular service or on a particular market segment (see Figure 2.13). Indeed this is what has happened in the case of Lombard Direct, which is a subsidiary of National Westminster Bank.

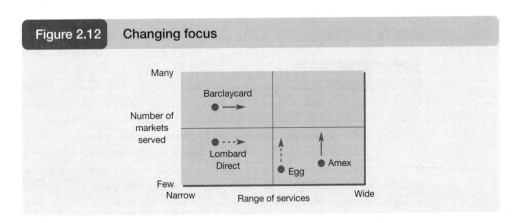

Figure 2.12   Changing focus

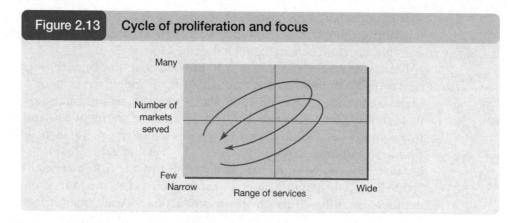

Figure 2.13 **Cycle of proliferation and focus**

Many

Number of
markets
served

Few

Narrow   Range of services   Wide

2.5.4 Achieving the benefits of focus in unfocused service operations

Many service organisations that have to provide a wide range of services can achieve the benefits of focus (such as simplicity and lower costs) in three main ways (developed from Johnston 1996):

- business focus
- operational focus
- encounter focus.

Business focus

If it is possible to split the market into segments with similar needs and expectations, the organisation may be able to split its businesses to deal with those different customer types (Figure 2.14). Holiday Inn's businesses are described in Box 2.7. The company is seeking to provide a whole range of services – long stay, short stay, full service and limited service – to a wide range of customers. It has developed several different businesses to focus on particular services for particular market segments – business focus. In essence it has split its activities into several distinct business units each focusing on a particular market segment.

Operational focus

For some organisations each business or site provides the same range of services to a range of customers and so they are unable to focus on particular services or segments at each site or business. Such organisations can gain the benefits of focus by splitting their operation into several parts so that each caters for a particular set of needs. Either customers then choose their channel and therefore their experience, or the organisation assists or makes the decision and thus designs fixed, but differing, delivery channels for its customers (see Figure 2.15).

Hypermarkets are unfocused organisations and provide 'everything for everyone' at each site – but few of their customers want 'everything'! Hypermarkets deal with

Figure 2.14	Achieving focus by splitting the business

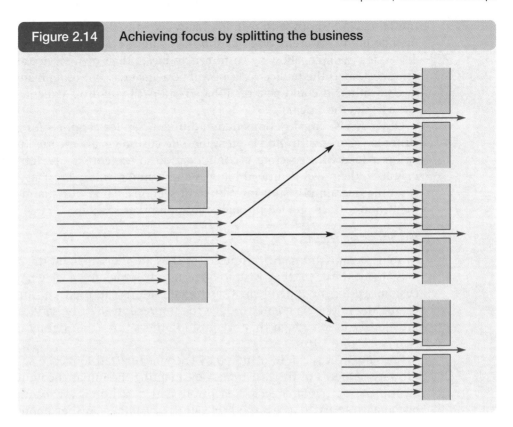

Holiday Inn

Box 2.7

Holiday Inn claims to be 'The World's Most Global Hotel Company' and has created several different business brands for a number of identified market segments. 'Our continued focus on guest preference has resulted in development of a range of brands, each serving a different market segment of the international hotel market . . . providing a variety of services, amenities and lodging experiences catering to virtually every travel occasion and guest need.'

Thus the service concept at Holiday Inn Express hotels focuses on value for money, offering competitive rates and limited service aimed at both leisure and business travellers. Holiday Inn Express provides, for example, a free continental breakfast bar, rather than table service, which reduces costs but meets the needs of guests wishing a light and fast breakfast. Holiday Inn's Staybridge Suites focus on the long-stay guest, providing a variety of suites (from studio to several bedrooms) together with a variety of on-site services, such as laundry rooms, library and breakfast room. Crowne Plaza Hotels and Resorts provide 'upscale lodging' to international discerning travellers, and the recently acquired Inter-Continental Hotels focus on providing five-star service and facilities.

Question

1 Summarise what you consider to be the concepts of Holiday Inn's different businesses. Assess the type of focus of each of them.

This illustration is based on material from www.basshotels.com

this by having 'shops-within-shop'. Many hypermarkets, or large shopping malls, include many different types of shops, retailers, cinemas and a range of eating places, for example, allowing customers to create their own service experience. For some customers the service concept will be a great day out using many of the facilities; for others it could be a retail-based 'shop-'til-you-drop' experience, or maybe just a trip to the cinema.

Other service organisations design different service channels for their different customer segments. In hotels premium-rate customers are escorted to their rooms and provided with spacious accommodation in 'executive' or 'club' rooms. They may have their own dedicated lounges and complimentary breakfast bars. In these cases the operation is split into different sections, 'shops' or channels and guests then choose, or are guided through, the appropriate sections.

Encounter focus

In some organisations the businesses or sites are the same and the delivery channels are identical, yet they wish to be seen to be providing a wide range of services customised for the individual. These organisations can use front-line staff to customise the initial experience to give the impression that the service is special for individuals, even though they are pushing them through a tightly focused operation (see Figure 2.16).

Encounter focus can be achieved by encouraging staff to recognise and deal with the varying needs of their customers by adapting the initial encounter to focus on customers' particular needs. Reception staff at a hotel, for example, could be encouraged to try to assess the needs of the customers as they approach the front desk. A business executive may appreciate a brisk service whereas a family may appreciate more time being spent explaining the facilities and where to find information about local attractions, for example. The facilities and indeed the remainder of the service may be identical for every customer, but the customers may feel their particular needs have been understood and 'delivered'. Business-to-business service organisations may employ account managers to provide the personalised touch to their key accounts, even though the operation may deliver the same range of services to all its clients.

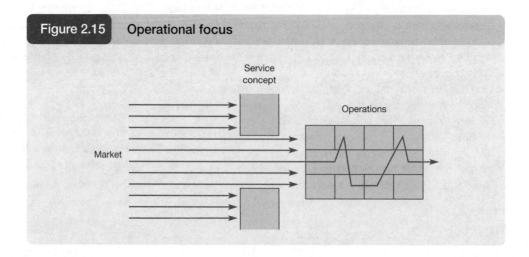

| Figure 2.15 | Operational focus |

Figure 2.16   Encounter focus

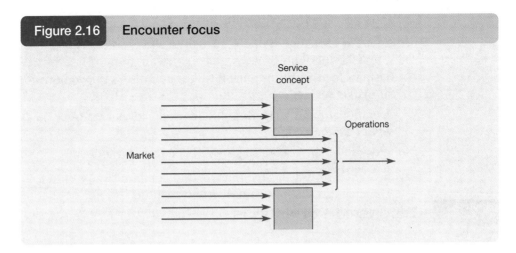

2.6 Summary

The service concept

- Customers 'buy' concepts.
- A service concept contains the 'organising idea' for the service.
- A service concept is more emotional than a business model, deeper than a brand, more complex than a good idea and more solid than a vision.
- A service concept is a shared understanding of the nature of the service provided and received, which should encapsulate information about the service experience, the service outcome, the service operation and the value of the service.
- A service concept should provide sufficient detail to make it clear what the organisation is selling/providing and what the customer is buying/receiving.
- The service concept acts as a 'service specification'.

The service concept as a strategic tool

- The service concept can be used to create organisational alignment by developing a shared understanding and making it explicit.
- Managers can assess the implications of design changes using capability mapping.
- Developing a service concept can create differentiated services and drive strategic advantage.

Focus and the service concept

- Focus means providing a particular segment of customers with a narrow range of services.
- There are four basic service concepts based upon levels of focus: service focused, market focused, service and market focused, and unfocused.
- The service concept acts as a filter and is the interface between the market and operations, determining the degree of focus required.

Unfocused service organisations

● Many service organisations are, by nature, unfocused, but they can gain the benefits of focus by adopting a:

 – business focus – splitting the business into distinct operations to serve particular market segments

 – operational focus – creating different operational channels to create different service experiences

 – encounter focus – adapting the initial encounter to focus on customers' particular needs.

2.7   Discussion questions

1 Select four service organisations and define their concepts and levels of focus. Evaluate the options facing them.

2 Select two service organisations offering similar but different services (a fast-food and a high-class restaurant, for example). Identify the key elements of the service concept and compare their profiles using the mapping tool illustrated in Figure 2.4.

3 Bernard Harrison, the chief executive of Singapore Zoo, is keen to continue developing the zoo: can you develop a new service concept for him?

2.8   Questions for managers

1 What is your organisation's service concept? How does this compare with your colleagues' view of its concept?

2 Profile your process and assess areas of weakness (non-alignment) and any opportunities to use it to drive strategic advantage.

3 Assess the ways in which your organisation achieves the benefits of focus.

2.9   Further reading

Fitzsimmons J. and Fitzsimmons M. (eds), *New Service Design*, Sage Publications, Thousand Oaks, Calif., 2000.

Jones, Robert, *The Big Idea*, HarperCollinsBusiness, London, 2001.

Meyer Goldstein S., Johnston R., Duffy J. and Rao J., 'The service concept: the missing link in service design research?' *Journal of Operations Management*, vol. 20, no. 2, 2002, pp. 121–34.

Normann R. and Ramirez R., 'From value chain to value constellation: designing interactive strategy', *Harvard Business Review*, July–August 1993, pp. 65–77.

2.10 References

Armstrong D., 'Thoughts bounded and thoughts free', paper to Department of Psychotherapy, Cambridge, 1991.

Booms B.H. and Bitner M.J., 'Marketing strategies and organisation structures for service firms', in Donnelly J. and George W. (eds), *Marketing of Services*, American Marketing Association, Chicago, 1981, pp. 47–51.

Campbell A. and Yeung S., 'Do you need a mission statement?' *Economist Special Report No. 1208*, Economist Publications, London, 1990.

Clark G., Johnston R. and Shulver M., 'Exploiting the service concept for service design and development', in Fitzsimmons J. and Fitzsimmons M. (eds), *New Service Development*, Sage Publications, Thousand Oaks, Calif., 2000, pp. 71–91.

Collier D.A., *The Service/Quality Solution: Using Service Management to Gain Competitive Advantage*, Irwin and ASQC Quality Press, New York, 1994.

Davidow W.H. and Uttal B., 'Service companies: focus or falter', *Harvard Business Review*, July–August 1989, pp. 77–85.

Dibb S., Simkin L., Pride W. and Ferrel O.C., *Marketing Concepts and Strategies*, 3rd edition, Houghton Mifflin, Boston, 1997.

Hayes R.H. and Wheelwright S.C., *Restoring our Competitive Edge*, Wiley, New York, 1984.

Heskett J.L., *Managing in the Service Economy*, Harvard Business School Press, Boston, Mass., 1986.

Hill T., *Manufacturing Strategy – Text and Cases*, Irwin, Homewood, Ill., 1993.

Johnston R., 'Achieving focus in service organisations', *Service Industries Journal*, vol. 16, no. 1, 1996, pp. 10–20.

Kimes S. and Johnston R., 'The application of focused manufacturing in the hospitality sector', in the proceedings of the Manufacturing Strategy Conference of the Operations Management Association, UK, University of Warwick, June 1990a.

Kimes S. and Johnston R., 'Four generic service concepts', in the proceedings of the Decision Sciences Institute Conference, USA, November 1990b.

Lovelock C.H., and Wirtz J., *Services Marketing: People Technology and Strategy*, 5th edition, Pearson/Prentice Hall, NJ, 2003

Lovelock C.H. and Wright L., *Principles of Service Management and Marketing*, Prentice Hall, NJ, 1999.

McCarthy E.J., *Basic Marketing: A Managerial Approach*, Irwin, Homewood, Ill., 1960.

Normann R. and Ramirez R., 'From value chain to value constellation: designing interactive strategy', *Harvard Business Review*, July–August 1993, pp. 65–77.

Prokesch S.E., 'Competing on customer service: an interview with British Airways' Sir Colin Marshall', *Harvard Business Review*, November–December 1995, pp. 101–12.

Skinner W., 'The focused factory', *Harvard Business Review*, vol. 52, no. 3, May–June 1974, pp. 113–21.

Skinner W., *Manufacturing: The Formidable Competitive Weapon*, Wiley, New York, 1985.

Slack N., *The Manufacturing Advantage*, Mercury, London, 1991.

Van Dierdonck R. and Brandt G., 'Focused factory in service industries', in Johnston R. (ed.), *The Management of Service Operations*, IFS/Springer-Verlag, Berlin, 1988.

Van Looey B., Gemmel P. and Van Dierdonck R., *Services Management: An Integrated Approach*, 2nd edition, FT Prentice Hall, Harlow, 2003.

Zeithaml V.A. and Bitner M.J., *Services Marketing*, McGraw-Hill, New York, 1996.

Lilliput Ltd

Reg Turner set up Lilliput as an offshoot of his carpentry business in 2000. Some years before he had been asked by a friend to provide his children with a playhouse for the garden. He made them a Swiss-style chalet covering an area of about 4 square metres. Within 12 months of its arrival in the garden Reg had received requests for 15 more houses from friends and neighbours. By 2002 Reg had designed 11 different styles, based on modular sections, which were easy to install. The business was located beside one of the large garden centres on the outskirts of the town. He employed three full-time carpenters, a driver and a sales assistant (his mother-in-law) to run the retail side of the business. Reg would not compromise on the quality of his playhouses. He would only buy good materials and he oversaw the construction of the houses himself. A carpenter would always accompany the delivery van and undertake the installation for the customer. Reg managed to keep his costs lower than most of his competitors by doing his own retailing and by keeping overheads low. He did not accept any credit cards. He priced his houses about 20 per cent below those of garden centres, although it was possible to find less expensive products. He explained, 'You can't forget how important children are in buying playhouses. It's not enough seeing pictures, they have to get inside and try them out. It is so important that we maintain a family-friendly feel to the business.'

By 2004 Reg had developed a reputation for quality and style and he decided to employ his daughter, Tiffany, who had recently finished art school and was showing an interest in the business. Her first task was to create a brochure for the business and he was delighted with the result. Although it wiped out last year's profit, the professional, full-colour brochure exuded quality and style. It displayed his range of houses with pictures of children playing in and around them. Other pictures showed the clean and tidy site and good parking facilities. The brochure provided useful information about sizes, styles, installation and maintenance, sources of timber and construction methods. Tiffany suggested that she should now set up a website and said that it was time the business investigated the possibility of developing an internet business, offering online ordering of a restricted range of houses.

Lilliput attracted many customers, particularly at weekends. Several people included a visit to Lilliput with a visit to the garden centre next door. Reg had developed a good relationship with the manager of the garden centre. They both believed they gained from each other. Reg also attracted buyers from some of the other garden centres, who were always keen to inspect his latest designs and assess his prices.

The site itself was causing Reg some problems. As he made all the houses on-site he had to keep an area fenced off from the customers for safety reasons. This was at the back of the site and necessitated delivery lorries moving through the display area. He explained: 'This site was only meant to be temporary. We had to demolish the building that was here before to make space. But it works well being next to the garden centre, so I think we might well stay here.' Reg knew he would need to lay a proper car park, as the existing one was just an open area with a rubble base and no markings. There were no signs except for one at the gate. Few of the houses had information, or even prices, on them – indeed it looked like they had been torn off.

The staff were friendly but the carpenters had little spare time to deal with the customers. However, the carpenters were frequently interrupted to discuss detail modifications requested by individual customers. Reg charged a small fee for these changes and felt that it was all part of the personal service he liked to give. Reg himself would often get personally involved in this design service, preferring to do this rather than concentrate on building the commercial aspects of the business.

Mavis Williams, Reg's mother-in-law, was based in the Portakabin office. She complained, 'I am rushed off my feet with people placing orders and calls for brochures. I hardly get out of the office. Some of the customers get cross because they have been kept waiting, but I have only one pair of hands.' By the end of 2004 the business was so successful that there were now at least five weeks between order and delivery. Reg asked Mavis not to make any promises on delivery dates for all new orders. Mavis replied with uncharacteristic anger, 'You just don't realise how difficult it is for me at the moment. How do you think the customers are going to react when I tell them I don't know when we can deliver and install the house? It's going to take me twice as long to deal with them now and I bet we lose a lot of sales. You have just taken advantage of me over the last three years and I have had enough.'

Reg felt that visitors to the site fell into a number of distinct categories and Tiffany carried out a survey to assess the number of customers in each of the categories. She found that at least 60 per cent of the visitors had decided they wished to purchase a playhouse and visited the garden centre next door to see what was on offer before visiting Lilliput. About 10 per cent of this group said they would eventually purchase from Lilliput. Some 25 per cent had no clear purchase intentions, but saw the houses on display and decided to investigate further. Only about 3 per

cent of this group made a purchase. The remainder were carrying out a more detailed review of the playhouse market before making a decision. These, more serious, potential customers were the most likely to purchase (about 30 per cent of those visiting the site).

Virtually all customers apart from the serious reviewers were heavily influenced by the personal touch, and the fact that their children were encouraged to 'try out' the houses. The third group (serious reviewers) were split almost equally into half. One part clearly took the children's experience into account; the second part had more or less made up their mind as to specification and were purchasing largely on price.

Reg was keen to grow the business and there was no shortage of interest in his product. He realised he now needed to focus his attention on the operation.

Questions

1 What are the service concepts currently delivered by Lilliput?

2 How would clarifying these service concepts assist Reg in deciding how to focus this service operation?

part two

Customer and supplier relationships

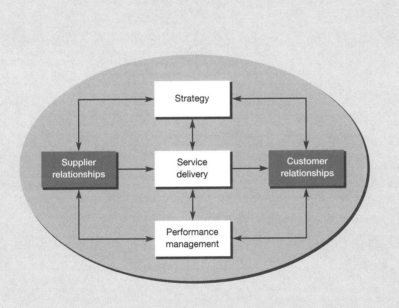

chapter three

Customers and relationships

Chapter objectives:

- to identify and understand different types of customer and discuss the operation's view of segmentation

- to recognise the benefits of retaining valuable customers and identify issues in the calculation of customer lifetime values

- to discuss the nature of customer relationships and some ways to manage them

- to discuss the nature of business relationships and some ways to manage them.

3.1 Introduction

It should perhaps be self-evident that a text on service operations should include an examination of customers and customer relationships. Indeed, in some organisations service is virtually synonymous with customer focus, ensuring that service design and delivery recognise the needs and desires of the customer. Sadly, this is often not the case. Organisations start with good intentions to recognise the customer, but often become somewhat arrogant in thinking either that they know best, or that they know what the customers want without having to ask. All companies need to review the way that they think about their customers, and be prepared to challenge any strongly held assumptions.

In this chapter we discuss relationships between service organisations and their individual customers, internal customers and business customers. We begin with an exploration of different types of customers and how operations can segment or group them. Just as service marketing will devote attention to segmenting customers in order to understand which groups are prime targets for the organisation, so service operations must be clear as to what is involved in delivering to each customer group. Also, service organisations have to build relationships with their customers, and we explain some ways of achieving this.

3.2 Customers and customer segmentation

When we use the word 'customer' it can mean very different things. We could be referring to individual consumers, users or clients, or internal customers or operations/units, or external organisations and their employees with whom service organisations do business. In the first sections of this chapter we predominantly, though not exclusively, focus on relationships with the individual consumer/client/user/customer (B2C, G2C and not-for-profit) and the internal customer. In the final section we focus specifically on business-to-business relationships.

3.2.1 Classifying customers

A first and critical step in understanding customers and then meeting their needs is to understand who the customer is. Customers can be classified in several different ways:

- external versus internal customers
- intermediaries versus end users or consumers
- stakeholders: payers, beneficiaries or participants
- valuable and not-so-valuable customers.

External versus internal customers

In many service sectors, particularly consumer services such as banks and restaurants, it is usually clear who is the customer. Customers are the individuals or groups of people, external to the organisation, who are receiving and often paying for the service. In many of these situations there is a clear time connection in the sense that service will be delivered on receipt of the required price, as in a fast-food restaurant or retail store. These customers are sometimes referred to as users, end users, or consumers, and they tend to be the people in mind when managers and employees talk about customers.

However, when we talk about customers, we are usually referring to both external and internal customers, and much of the material in this book can be applied to both internal and external customers. Internal customers are individuals or groups of individuals who are a part of the same organisation but from a different unit or operation. For example, the accountancy department, the personnel department and the IT department all in their own way provide services to the other parts of the organisation, just as they also require services from the rest of the organisation. The recognition of internal customers, and the need to provide them with services and information, is one of the key elements of many quality improvement programmes. These programmes are based on the important premise that the quality and cost of service provided to external customers depends upon the quality of the service provided to and by the network of internal customers.

Many organisations in recent times have recognised the value in refocusing their 'putting customer first' philosophies to 'putting employees first', realising that the level of external service is constrained by the level of internal service. While many organisations see their quality improvement activities (see Chapters 4 and 12) being about improving the quality for external customers, we believe that organisations should start by improving their levels of internal customer service. We often find that it is management's internal policies, procedures and practices that constrain the service providers' ability, and interest, in delivering good service to external customers.

Intermediaries versus end users or consumers

One of the design issues under debate for many service supply chains (see also Chapter 5) is the question of whether or not to use intermediaries – the 'middlemen' who sell a product or service to an end customer on behalf of one or more suppliers. Some financial services, for example, have recently removed the intermediary stage of independent insurance broker to set up their own direct operations. They have done this largely to reduce the transaction costs for commodity-type services such as car insurance, but also to gain ownership of the end customer. This has been possible to achieve as increasing customer knowledge about industry prices has forced companies and customers alike to re-evaluate the worth of the broker network.

The situation that many organisations face is the need to manage their direct customers, such as brokers or retailers, while at the same time being aware of the needs of the end consumer or user; therefore they have to encourage the intermediaries to give the desired service to their customers. In theory this should make perfect sense though, as GSV Software found, this is not always straightforward (see Box 3.1).

GSV Software   Box 3.1

Sara Sheppard, ITSMA, Europe

As a global software vendor with a well-established range of desktop software products, GSV Software had developed a largely channel-centric model to meet its broad range of customer technical services requirements. Service and support were allied to specific software products and were delivered by third parties. GSV put most of its service and support efforts into selecting the right intermediaries to deal directly with its user base, and also into providing any product training required to ensure that the intermediaries were effective. The advantage of this approach was that GSV had a limited number of support relationships to deal with.

This strategy to develop and support the channels to customers was supplemented by the provision of a limited range of direct technical services targeted at large accounts or provided to those few customers who wanted to come directly to the GSV for 'paid for' support at premium rates. Individual customers normally dealt with GSV's accredited agents or other partners such as value added retailers (VARs) for service and support.

This model worked well: the software applications were relatively simple and there was very little customisation or integration with other software products. However, as GSV's target market was moving towards 'enterprise class software', its service and support model needed to be revisited. Its software offerings were moving from largely standalone products to being part of a business solution, and enterprise class software implied significant amounts of customisation for each client. As a consequence, the ultimate support accountability for the performance of the solution, and type of technical support required, was becoming less clear.

In some cases a client would be acquired by one of GSV's agents and not unreasonably would expect a share of revenue. However, the support requirements for these 'enterprise' or bespoke systems could not be fully anticipated at point of sale, though it was recognised that some elements would be beyond the capability of GSV's agent. This was not an issue that could be just fixed behind the scenes as the possibility of 'flip flop accountability' (or nobody taking full responsibility) was becoming a major purchasing concern for major customers. It needed to be clearly articulated where responsibility lay, not least because these customers represented a significant part of GSV's business.

Customers were asking GSV to take 'more skin in the game'. This is an American term that means taking more business exposure themselves or shared risk – particularly in innovative business solutions that were using leading-edge technology. At the same time the GSV knew that its own business model, with a high commitment to continuing a channel-centric services model, would not support a heavy investment in a direct services business. There needed to be a hybrid model between a pure channel-based service and a direct-to-vendor model. It needed to be a way that improved customer confidence in the more complex solutions world: allowing GSV to encourage a healthy channel-orientated services business, and at the same time offering a way of improving customer satisfaction, with the level of responsibility being taken by GSV.

One of the solutions has been with 'leading-edge solutions' (which are seen to be breaking into new markets): the software vendor will commit to either taking the lead in the solution development or playing a significant role, alongside other channel partners. The role of the vendor is to transfer its superior knowledge of its software product into the solution being developed, and to pass this intellectual property on to the partners (which could also be the IT development group within a customer). This defined role then changes once the solution moves from the development and build stage to roll-out and management. The software vendor then plays a more 'behind the scenes' role, providing a back-up and escalation support route to the chosen third-party IT service provider, with contractually agreed service level agreements.

The customer sees GSV software playing a key role in the solution development, and therefore ensuring that the long-term supportability of the ultimate business solution is built into the design. Once the solution moves into roll-out stage, an IT service provider is selected with the appropriate competencies, but with a clear route back to the software vendor if required.

Questions

1 What are the implications for GSV in scaling this model to fit its large customer base?

2 What needs to be considered by the third-party IT service provider to ensure it can take accountability for the front-line service to the customer?

3 What does GSV need to provide to the IT service provider to ensure that the ultimate customer is satisfied with the service being provided?

4 How can GSV influence customer satisfaction with its software, and therefore its reputation as a global software provider (recognising that the important role of technical support is being provided by a third party)?

This illustration is used with permission from ITSMA Europe.

Stakeholders: payers, beneficiaries or participants

This categorisation explores the customers' extent of involvement with the service. In many services the customer participating in the service expects benefit from the service and also is required to pay for it. In the case of a restaurant, if there is a problem with the food or the service, customers are aware of it because they participate in the service, and care about the outcome because they are beneficiaries. Because they are also paying for the service, they are able to take appropriate action.

In many service situations, for example prisons, public health services and voluntary services, there may be a clear distinction between and indeed conflicts among payer, beneficiary and participant. This is the case not only in not-for-profit organisations. In business-to-business services, such as photocopier leasing, it is possible that the purchasing department may have cost reduction targets for its overall spend which may conflict with the need for high-copy quality in the user functions.

However, the links between purchaser and beneficiary become extremely difficult to understand when we consider public services. These are funded by taxpayers, but the budget is determined by politicians who (supposedly) represent the views and interests of their constituents. In the case of the police service, the beneficiary is again society at large, although the participants (criminals and offenders) may not see the actions of the police as a benefit! Even the most law-abiding citizens may be annoyed when stopped by the police for what seems to them to be a trivial matter.

As another example, the UK Benefits Agency is responsible for distributing money to the unemployed, those receiving disability benefit, etc. The Agency has invested heavily in improving its service standards for those who are out of work. This stems from a belief that all members of society deserve to be treated as human beings and also that better service will elicit a less aggressive response from individuals who may be under stress from their difficult circumstances.

This approach can be expanded. We can identify all the stakeholders of a service and understand their different perspectives. Box 3.2 describes the stakeholders for a prison service, and recognises that not all stakeholders will be willing participants. The value of this type of analysis is that it then allows the operations manager to identify the varying (and sometimes conflicting) requirements of each stakeholder group.

Valuable and not-so-valuable customers

The service marketing literature proposes that organisations prioritise service towards customers who can create the most value for the organisation (see, for example, Gummesson 1999, Payne et al. 1995, Reichheld 1996). Given that any operation has finite resources, it would seem sensible to ensure that any prioritisation safeguards long-term business interests. The problem is that what is meant by value is not always clear.

We define a valuable customer as one that is either of high value and/or valued. Note that we use the term valuable rather than loyal. While some customers are loyal, in the sense that they frequently use the organisation, they may also have other loyalties and may also not be very profitable or helpful to the organisation (see Reinartz and Kumar 2002).

The prison service
Box 3.2

The prison service provides an excellent example of the complexity of stakeholder requirements, to some extent reflecting the mixed task it faces. Society requires the service to carry out potentially conflicting activities:

- to ensure that 'dangerous criminals' are locked up for the safety of society
- to provide a regime that will punish wrongdoers as a means of payment for their crimes
- to support inmates, providing counselling and training to rehabilitate and reform them, to reduce the likelihood of re-offending.

The principal stakeholders and their requirements are as follows:

- *Government ministers* with responsibility for the prison service will be concerned to fulfil manifesto promises while meeting spending targets. At the same time they will be concerned about stories of prisoner escapes or drug abuse that may be damaging to their personal reputation, possibly forcing their resignation.
- *Prison governors* will seek to provide an appropriate environment for inmates, while keeping to strict operating budgets.
- *Prison officers* will be concerned to strike a balance between building a rapport with inmates and enforcing discipline.

- *Offenders* will have a wide range of requirements depending on the nature of the offence, length of term, desire to change, and so on.
- *Families of offenders* may wish to maintain contact with inmates.
- *Members of society* want to feel safe from criminals, but will also believe that some help should be provided for those who wish to reform.

The relationships between these stakeholder groups are often complex. Clearly, politicians ultimately report to those who elect them, including prison officers and families of offenders. Prison governors, with hopes of career advancement, may feel that they must satisfy the demands of the current party in power, which may be at odds with the requirements of other groups.

Questions

1 If you were a prison governor, what strategies would you adopt to find out about the needs of the various stakeholder groups?

2 What operational problems arise from having to manage this diversity?

- *High value* means that the financial value of the customer, over the long-term, is of value to the organisation. This view links with the idea of assessing the lifetime value of a customer (see section 3.3.1). For organisations that deal with many relatively small (in value) transactions it has been found useful to calculate the lifetime value. For example, a customer with a weekly supermarket spend of £100 represents annual revenues of £5,000 and lifetime revenue in excess of £250,000. Some service organisations claim that this understanding helps motivate managers and front-line employees to treat customers with respect – it certainly may help justify investment in customer service. Equipment-related services have been used to this approach for some years, since their customers understand the difference between lifetime cost of ownership as against the cost of acquisition. Indeed it is common in some industries for companies to make a loss on the sale of original equipment, knowing that 25 years of spares and service contracts would ensure long-term profitability.

The difficulty with this approach is that it is not always obvious as to who are the high-value and low-value customers. Again, business-to-business services may have a reasonable idea about customer value, perhaps represented by size of contracts; indeed, in some cases these organisations may have only one customer. Consumer services may have more difficulty. Financial services, for example, may be able to classify customers according to social economic groups, credit ratings or spending habits and make judgements accordingly. However, just because an individual is, for example, earning a relatively small sum today does not mean they will not be a millionaire in a few years' time, or indeed vice versa.

High-value customers are also those that tend to spend more than other customers, and whose spending increases over time. They may also be prepared to pay premium prices for the service.

- *Valued* customers are those individuals who are positively disposed to the organisation and are thus relatively easy to deal with (see Allies and Champions later). They appear to appreciate the service and interact helpfully and pleasantly with employees.

Valued customers are not only a pleasure to deal with, but they can also create financial value for the organisation. They could be involved in cost reduction by taking time to help the organisation and its staff by, for example, clearing tables after use, or reporting incorrectly functioning equipment. They are also usually cheaper to service since it can be costly to recruit new customers into an organisation. Valued customers can be involved in revenue generation by providing positive word-of-mouth advertising and by encouraging others to use or support the service. (Gremler and Brown, 1999, use the term 'loyalty ripple effect' to recognise the value of positive word-of-mouth encouragement.)

Valued customers are also supporters of the organisation and are ready and willing to help the organisation, maintain and improve its service, for example by completing questionnaires and providing suggestions. Valued customers also do not place undue demands on the service. For public sector organisations, such as a hospital, this might mean not using the service more than is necessary. For all organisations it might mean not asking for, or expecting, more than the service can provide.

In sum, valuable customers:

- are easy to deal with
- provide positive word-of-mouth advertising
- assist in service provision
- reduce operating costs
- increase revenues
- help the organisation maintain and improve its services
- do not place undue demands on the service
- generate long-term revenue streams (high lifetime values)
- spend more than other customers
- increase spending over time
- pay premium prices.

Operations managers need to:

- recognise the different types of customer
- understand the value of those different customer types
- understand the different nature of each group of customers (section 3.2.2)
- try to retain valuable customers (section 3.3)
- develop appropriate relationships with customers (sections 3.4 and 3.5).

3.2.2 Customer segmentation – an operations view

A clear understanding of segments is fundamental to service operations. It has long been true that a 'one size fits all' approach will not satisfy many customers, who wish to be treated as individuals. Segmentation is a first critical step in developing relationships with customers, whether those relationships are transactional or strategic. Transactional relationships (see also section 3.5.1) are one-off relationships we have with organisations, for example we may have several one-off relationships with supermarkets weekly or train companies daily, but not enough for us to consider it a 'relationship'. Here segmentation allows organisations to understand the needs of particular groups and amend the service offering to suit. Strategic relationships are more deeply embedded and have better levels of information exchange between the two parties, for example between patients and their doctor, or a client and their family lawyer. Segmentation may point to opportunities for up-selling or cross-selling other services to particular clients or customers.

Market segmentation

Marketing segmentation is traditionally based on customer characteristics. Thus organisations will focus on particular economic groups or target a geographic region. Other marketing approaches will consider lifestyles, family circumstances (for example single parents, empty-nesters or economising customers) or the reasons why customers buy a service (for example for its benefits, utility or in response to promotion).

Clearly, service operations managers must be aware of the emphasis behind the marketing approach adopted by the organisation. Not only does it make sense to target marketing effort on people most likely to buy the service, but market segmentation also helps operations managers design their facilities appropriately and deliver service in the appropriate way.

A restaurant provides a simple example. If the restaurant is targeting couples for romantic dinners for two, the design of seating and ambience will be rather different from a restaurant that considers families as its prime source of revenue. The type of food served and the way in which it is served – for example speed, manner and information provided – will be different. In the case of a family restaurant, easy-to-clean facilities with flexible seating will be required, together with value-for-money meals served efficiently. The romantic restaurant will require different furnishings, lighting, music, staff competencies and food. Clearly, a wide range of other decisions flows from this initial identification of the customer group to be served. Some restaurants manage to adapt to changing needs, providing classical music and reasonably bright lighting for early evening family groups and more elderly diners, moving to more upbeat music and dimmer lighting for younger couples as the evening progresses.

Thus decisions about market segmentation may define the target customers, such as families or romantic diners, and drive key decisions such as process and capacity management (see Chapters 6 and 8) and staff competencies (Chapter 7). However, once the operation is up and running, customers can be reclassified to allow the operations manager to identify issues critical to service delivery.

Customer types

We believe that operations managers and their staff need to develop an understanding of the nature of individual customers and their resultant behaviour, particularly when these customers are the direct recipient of the service delivery process, and may in fact be an integral part of it. The nature of the customer could significantly influence the type of service provided, how they need to be dealt with by staff, and their potential impact on other customers in the operation. Possible categories of customers classified by behaviour or attitude (see Figure 3.1) could include:

- *The Ally*. These valued customers usually arrive in a positive frame of mind, willing to help and give positive feedback to facilitate the service. The most helpful Ally is the customer whose opinion is respected by others. If the Ally is happy, then other customers will infer that the service must be good.

- *The Hostage*. These customers require service, but may be 'locked in' to a particular service provider contractually. An example is customers who must have their car serviced by the dealer appointed by the manufacturer. The service may cost rather more, but if an approved dealer is not used, their warranty will be invalid. These customers may not be in the most positive moods and will become very difficult whenever service performance deteriorates.

- *The Anarchist*. These customers dislike rules and systems. Indeed, notices suggesting what should and should not be done present a challenge. It is tempting to let the customer 'get away' with not following the system, but this may set up problems with other customers who feel that they have not been treated fairly.

- *The Patient*. These customers are very similar to the Hostage in that they are locked into the service, such as a hospital patient or a student at a school or university. These customers may be positively or unequivocally oriented towards the organisation and are willing to submit themselves to rules and regulations. However, unnecessary restrictions may turn them into a Hostage or Anarchist.

- *The Tolerant*. These customers may be passive, always waiting patiently for service providers to acknowledge their presence and deliver service. In fact they may be so patient that they become invisible to service staff and get ignored as a result. It may be dangerous to trade on their apparent goodwill.

- *The Intolerant*. These customers are seldom passive or patient, often causing stress and problems within the service for themselves, the service providers and other customers. Although initially they may be positively disposed to the organisation, without careful handling these people can easily turn into Terrorists.

- ***The Victim***. When something goes wrong in service organisations, some customers appear to attract bad luck. Some jobs seem to be dogged by ill fortune. Victims may react in a number of ways, perhaps blowing incidents up out of all proportion or alternatively becoming resigned to their inevitable fate.

- ***The Terrorist***. The Terrorist is the customer who mounts a damaging attack when you least expect it. An example might be the customer who declares their dissatisfaction loudly in the middle of a crowded restaurant, having said earlier how good the food was.

- ***The Incompetent***. Front-line staff should pay particular attention to these customers. It is possible that new customers may be confused by the organisation's procedures and, if not 'trained' by staff, may find the experience threatening, with the result that they do not return. It is possible, of course, that some customers are incapable of being trained.

- ***The Champion***. What all organisations want – valued customers who are not only supportive of their staff and its service delivery and helpfully participate in the process, but who also make a point of providing positive word-of-mouth about the organisation, its services and staff.

Creating Allies

Converting customers from the top left quadrant of Figure 3.1 into Allies is the easiest of the tasks. Allies are already positively disposed to the organisation but require engaging in the service delivery. Providing information, good communication and explanations and involving them in process development through soliciting feedback may easily convert these customers.

The negatively disposed victims in the bottom left quadrant may require counselling and support to turn them into Allies. The risk here is that even after considerable effort Victims can easily turn into Hostages or Anarchists.

Anarchists and Terrorists are the most difficult, yet most important, group of customers for the operation to deal with. Deselection (removal from the organisation) may be the best way out (see Chapter 7). On the other hand, if these activists can be employed to the good of the organisation by harnessing their negative energy

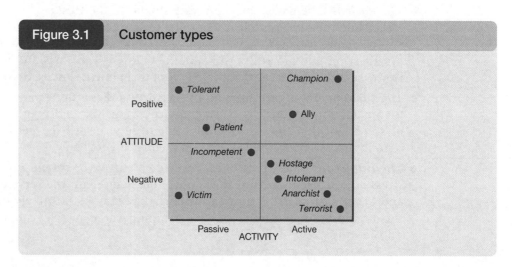

Figure 3.1 Customer types

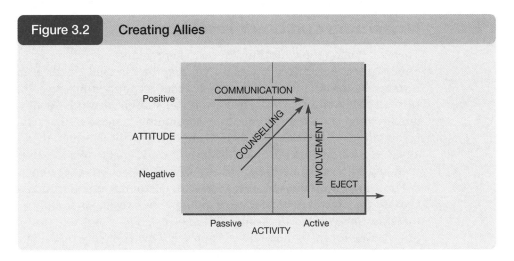

Figure 3.2 **Creating Allies**

through personal involvement in the organisation and its processes, they can make powerful Allies, or even Champions, for the organisation and its cause (see Figure 3.2).

3.3 Customer retention

A key task for some operations managers is retaining their valuable customers. It should be noted that retention may be of limited concern to some service organisations, such as local government services, housing associations, police, charities and health services, who may not be able to choose their customers, or whose customers have no or little choice. These organisations have to accept and deal with whoever 'comes through the door'. However, they still have to have relationships with them (see later) and manage those customers as well as they can (see Chapter 7).

As we explained earlier, retaining valuable customers provides significant benefits for many organisations. One key benefit for retaining valuable customers in for-profit organisations is in capturing the customer's revenue stream calculated as the lifetime spending of a customer (Reichheld 1996, Schlesinger and Heskett 1991). By building long-term customer relationships, which in turn encourage customers to be loyal and helpful, managers and marketers recognise the importance of retaining existing business rather than simply attracting new customers (see, for example, Buttle 1996, Gummesson 1994 and 1999, Payne *et al.* 1995).

A key problem in changing the emphasis to retention and/or building relationships with customers is that many organisations do not have adequate means of calculating the value of loyal and valuable customers. Few companies know the true cost of a lost customer, or even worse an upset customer who stays. If organisations could calculate these values they might be in a position to make more accurate evaluations of investments designed to develop relationships with customers. 'Unfortunately today's accounting systems do not capture the value of a loyal customer' (Reichheld and Sasser 1990).

3.3.1 Measuring customer retention

There are some simple measures of customer retention to put alongside sales or revenue figures. Retention, for example, may be assessed on an annual basis, for instance by tracking the number of customer accounts still 'active' during the year. In practice, of course, this is not always so straightforward. Retail customers frequently shop at more than one store, continuing to make regular purchases in each organisation. In this case the issue is more 'share of the wallet' than customer loyalty. Information systems linked to loyalty cards enable retailers to track trends in spending patterns to assess the 'loyalty' of various customer segments.

For some business-to-business services, customer retention is easy to measure because the organisation may have only one or two major accounts. Loss of a customer in these cases will mean that the business will probably not survive. This is not the case for many mid-range businesses. One company that supplied chemicals to a wide range of business customers appeared, superficially, to be healthy with reasonable annual sales growth. This hid the fact that of a nominal customer base of over a hundred business accounts, more than 20 per cent had not placed an order in the last 12 months and a further 15 per cent had reduced their order value in the last six months. This analysis prompted the organisation to re-examine the nature of its customer relationships in order to reverse what had become a trend that threatened the business's future profitability.

Calculating the lifetime value of a customer

Lifetime value of a customer is of particular interest to high-volume consumer services, for two reasons:

● It provides a degree of motivation for personnel who may deal with high numbers of short customer transactions each day. The customer who makes a regular £4 purchase may not seem that important in the grand scheme of things, but this viewpoint might be changed if this equates to £1,000 annual spend multiplied by the expected loyalty lifetime in years.

● Calculating the lifetime value gives focus to marketing activities.

As indicated above, there are a number of issues to be resolved when examining lifetime value. The first is to understand what 'lifetime' really means, and to what extent this can really help in marketing and delivering service. If the argument about lifetime value is followed to its logical conclusion, would this lead service providers to ignore all customers over a certain age? Clearly not, because the direct revenue gained is still valuable, and the value of word-of-mouth advertising and referrals is impossible to calculate.

For the purposes of employee motivation, it may be useful to calculate a value such as annual spend, which makes the point that this £4 transaction customer is someone worth looking after and at the same time does not make potentially exaggerated claims about worth.

Equipment-based service providers have for a long time calculated lifetime revenues based on the economic life of the piece of capital equipment, its original sales price plus expected service, maintenance and repair revenues. This has enabled them to create competitive original equipment-pricing strategies, and to understand that significant resources must be made available to support these revenue streams.

More recently, mobile phone service providers had to use customer value information more defensively. In the rapid growth of the mobile phone market, providers supplied handsets free or at a fraction of their manufacturing cost in a bid to gain a significant market share. They discovered that many customers were not paying line rentals for a sufficiently long period to enable the promotional equipment discount costs to be recouped. As a result, a wider range of tariffs and contracts was introduced to reduce this deficit.

When thinking about the value of the customer it is therefore useful to generate estimates of the following:

● Current and potential annual spend of customer segments, recognising that customers may use more than one service provider.

● The duration and durability of customer relationships. How long do customers remain loyal and is there potential for this to be extended?

● The number of points of contact with customers. How many different service products do they buy? Is there potential for cross-selling of service products?

● What is the current profitability of the customer? Is it costing more to keep this customer than we are likely to recoup?

Financial services providers are particularly sensitive to this type of analysis. Although the company may offer a number of products from loans and mortgages through to pensions and insurance products, many find that a typical customer only takes one product from the range. They find, though, that once a customer buys two or three products, they tend to stay loyal for rather longer than the single-product customer.

3.4 Managing customer relationships

Robust figures and good marketing alone, however, will not develop relationships with customers. The operation must deliver something of value to ensure loyalty and customer support. Loyal and valuable customers are created by providing a level of service that satisfies or even delights customers. It is important to note that there is a difference between relationship and loyalty and it is possible to confuse the two, particularly in high-volume services delivered to the mass consumer market. For organisations such as train companies, mass transit systems and even financial service providers, customers may be extremely loyal but not have a 'relationship' with the organisation.

Managing customer relationships (sometimes referred to as relationship marketing) is about establishing, maintaining and enhancing relationships with customers for mutual benefit. The emphasis in relationship marketing is on the requirement to develop relationships with individual customers – one-to-one marketing (Peppers and Rogers 1993) – and with groups of like-minded people – affinity groups (Gummesson 1999) – rather than see any and every service as a one-off transaction.

While the notion of relationship marketing appears to be very attractive, it is not appropriate in all situations. For example, in high-volume or commodity-based services, such as retail operations or mass transit systems, many customers may be more influenced by value for money than by a concept as intangible as a relationship. Indeed many customers do not wish for a relationship with some organisations and their staff. Despite this, there is no doubt that people often make decisions based on emotional or unconscious factors, even when they think that they have been driven totally by logic. Indeed some marketing professionals believe that brands and brand values far outweigh any other factor in customer decision making.

3.4.1   Three forms of customer relationships

To try to deal with this apparent mismatch we suggest that there are essentially two main forms of relationship: first, a relationship based on a portfolio of service products frequently found in higher-volume operations; and second, a personal relationship created between an individual customer and an employee, particularly prevalent in low-volume professional organisations. We also cover here temporary relationships, recognising the transactional, one-off nature of many services.

Product relationships

Product relationships involve the 'capture' of the customer using a variety of products. Banks, for example, work hard to establish a relationship with their customers by selling (and in order to sell) multiple products, such as current accounts, loans, house loans, insurance and executor services. This provides the customer with benefits such as a single point of contact for their product portfolio, discounts for new products bought, loyalty bonuses etc. The downside for customers who wish to switch is often the difficulty in untying themselves from the set of products. The benefits for the organisation are that product relationships provide higher-value customers, a longer-term revenue stream, opportunities to cross-sell other products or services to customers who are already engaged with the organisation, and also valuable information from and about that customer base.

Many service providers, such as retailers, airlines and restaurant chains, actively promote product relationships and loyalty on existing products and service through loyalty schemes such as frequent-flyer programmes or 'club' cards for supermarkets. Most of these are in essence discount schemes encouraging the customer to earn points by spending more money with a particular provider rather than the competition. Such providers are 'buying loyalty' rather than building relationships. However, the relationship can be developed by holding information about a customer's needs: for example, some hotels store information about their card-holding customers so that these customers are provided with a room that meets their requirements. Customers may also gain certain privileges: airline loyalty customers may be provided with access to executive lounges, free seat reservations, cheque-cashing facilities, company newsletters, opportunities to participate in special events and opportunities to provide information to the organisation. All these activities fall into the category of customer retention through the 'enhanced' transactional approach.

Harley Owners Group (HOG) Box 3.3

Harley-Davidson does not just make world-famous motorbikes – it sells a dream. From its start more than 100 years ago, Harley-Davidson has had a profound impact on the sport of motorcycling and the people who ride motorbikes.

From its humble beginnings in a small shed in Milwaukee where three friends turned out their first bike, the company now produces over 300,000 bikes a year. The company's turnover for the year ending 2003 was in excess of $4.6 billion (a 13 per cent increase on 2002), generating a gross profit of around $1.7 billion. Besides making its famous bikes, such as the Ultra Classic Electra Glide touring bike weighing over 370 kilograms with a twin-cam 1500 cc engine, the company also produces parts and accessories and a range of branded clothes and collectables. It is a global company, selling bikes all over the world; the fastest growth area in bike sales is currently Japan.

Not content with simply owning a bike, Harley owners wanted to have an organised way to share their passion and show pride in their bikes, so, in 1983, Harley-Davidson established the Harley Owners Group (HOG). By 2004 HOG had over 800,000 members, making HOG the largest factory-sponsored motorcycle organisation in the world.

HOG has a simple intent: 'To ride and have fun'. The organisation is split into local chapters where people who share the Harley passion come together. Each chapter is sponsored by a local dealership with events organised by the members. Membership (which costs around £25 in the UK) provides a range of benefits, including two magazines published by Harley-Davidson, *Enthusiast* and *Hog Tales*. A HOG handbook provides maps, dealer locations, climate information and riding laws for members planning long-distance trips. The local chapters organise member events, including national and international rallies, touring rallies, open houses and pit stops. In the UK there is almost one rally every weekend of the year for the UK's 1,500 members. There is also a members' website with details, dates and information about all HOG activities and events.

Questions

1 What are the benefits of membership for the members and the company?

2 How does HOG help develop a relationship between the company and the rider?

This illustration is based on information from www.harley-davidson.com and www.hog.com

The Harley Owners Group (Box 3.3) demonstrates that there is more than one way to build loyalty with customers who have some affinity with the company, its goods and services, and with each other. This case demonstrates that Harley-Davidson has clearly understood the breadth of the service concept, recognising that customers are buying rather more than a manufactured product. With this knowledge, Harley-Davidson has been able to capitalise on what has become virtually a cult of owners, each fiercely loyal to the brand.

Some customers hold several 'loyalty' cards – undermining the very concept! Indeed studies in the behaviour of supermarket customers (e.g. Knox and Denison 1992) have identified large segments of 'promiscuous customers' who switch loyalty to whichever provider is currently offering the best deal.

Personal relationships

Personal relationships exist in many professional and low-volume, high-margin services, where there is time and value in developing one-on-one relationships with clients or customers. These relationships, often using key account managers (see section 3.5.3), create multilayered or deep personal relationships with customers.

The objective on the service provider's part is to create a situation where the customer thinks first of one group of people when planning to place more business, in effect giving that service provider first opportunity to bid for the work. In B2B relationships there are advantages on both sides. The provider gets to know the customer's business well and this leads to a more effective service with a faster response, because providers do not have to go through another development phase.

Many B2B services take place over weeks, months and in some cases years. Management consultants may work alongside the client's employees and it is frequently critical that effective relationships are built in order to carry out the assignment. Technical expertise is clearly only part of the requirement for an effective consultant; the ability to build personal relationships with clients and clients' employees is also essential.

There are four key elements to a personal relationship between service provider and customer (see, for example, Mohr and Spekman 1994, Morgan and Hunt 1994):

- *Communication*. The extent to which there is two-way communication; the ability to deliver clear messages and the ability to listen carefully.

- *Trust*. The degree to which one partner depends on the work or recommendation of the other, without seeking extra justification or collaboration. In some cases, the partner may commit the other to work without prior consultation.

- *Intimacy*. The extent to which each partner shares their plans, strategies, profits, etc.

- *Rules*. A mutual acceptance of how this particular relationship operates: what is acceptable and desirable, and what is not.

Developing more personal relationships has often significant operational implications. In Table 3.1 we compare two organisations, one a professional service (business-to-business), the other a high-volume consumer service (business-to-customer), and identifies issues that must be dealt with by operations managers.

As we can see from Table 3.1, there may be considerable resource implications in adopting an approach based on broadening the relationship between customer and provider. Some of these implications are listed below:

- Processes and activities become less well defined and harder to predict.

- Capacity management is less precise and efficiency goals become harder to achieve.

- Processes must be more flexible in order to meet requirements that are ill-defined at the start of the relationship.

- Staff will require a different set of competencies.

Temporary relationships

High-volume consumer services often require the formation of temporary relationships, where customer connections are made quickly. Many sales processes depend on the ability of the salesperson to establish common ground with the prospective customer. When the customer is buying something that cannot be readily assessed, part of the purchasing process may include a conscious or unconscious assessment of the competence and honesty of the organisation's representative.

Table 3.1 Developing personal relationships

	Professional service: management consultant	*Consumer service: restaurant chain*
Communication	Two-way Free flowing Transfer of knowledge Relates to business possibilities as well as current contracts A significant amount of time is devoted to communication	Largely one-way – from provider to customer, apart from order-taking Formal communication Relates to formal service offer No budget for significant informal communication
Trust	Built between individuals (clients and consultants) in the course of the involvement May involve significant amounts of confidential and sensitive information	Built between customer and organisation largely by reliability (delivery to promise) Scope strictly limited to providing value-for-money meals in safe surroundings
Intimacy	Consultants become completely involved with the life of the client's organisation and are often regarded as semi-permanent employees Part of the team	Involvement between employees and customers may be limited to order-taking and basic service Customer intimacy is often linked to fortuitous discovery of common interests
Rules	May be developed as part of the initial relationship-forming process Negotiation as to who does what is often part of initial evaluation, but the brief may change as the relationship develops	Largely set by the organisation or service sector Based on established 'scripts', expected behaviour and assumed knowledge

A combination of perceived risk and lack of knowledge on the customer's part will mean that the possibility for a relationship will increase, given the need for reassurance on the customer's part. Examples might include purchasing a used car or a personal pension, where the customer is often incapable of making a totally informed decision.

These relationships might, at face value, appear relatively shallow, but there are clear implications for the service operation that recognises their value. The development of information systems to give customer history, training of customer contact staff and allocated time for each customer transaction (performance targets) are examples of areas that can be addressed. Some call centres have intentionally relaxed their 'talk time' targets to allow more space for these temporary relationships and have found that although each agent may talk to fewer customers, orders of higher value are being taken as a result of the effectiveness of the temporary relationship.

3.4.2 Risk and relationships

There is often a link between customers' perceived risk in purchasing or using the service and their desire for a type of relationship with the provider (see Table 3.2).

Table 3.2 Links between customer relationship and customer perceived risk

	Weak relationship (transaction based)	Strong relationship (partnership based)
High customer perceived risk	Opportunity	Protected
Low customer perceived risk	Buy loyalty	Familiarity

Where the customer does not feel that there is much risk, either in making the purchase or in receiving the service, there may be limited opportunity for relationship building. The majority of supermarket customers probably do not have any depth of relationship with Tesco or Wal-Mart, though they may have preferences as to which store they shop in. This reluctance on the part of supermarket customers to build a meaningful relationship with Tesco or Wal-Mart only applies, of course, when things are going well. If there is a significant service failure, customers may move quickly from low to high perceived risk. We will discuss this in more depth in the section on service recovery in Chapter 12. Where there is high customer perceived risk, but as yet a weak, transaction-based relationship, there is an opportunity for the organisation to build stronger links.

Where there are strong relationships in situations where the customer feels there is significant risk, the emotional switching costs for customers are high. It is likely that these customers will not move unless the relationship is significantly damaged in some way. An example of services of this type is a consultant who may have both a particular expertise and intimate knowledge of the client's company and markets. These relationships are most common in professional services and/or B2B services.

Of course, strong relationships may exist where there is low perceived risk, though they are probably rare in commodity services. In many cases these may be one-sided relationships where the customer has a stronger emotional bond to the company than is possible for any one employee to reciprocate. Again, we will return to these customers in our discussion of service recovery in Chapter 12, but it is sufficient to say that if there is service failure, these customers may feel let down, rather than merely angry that something has gone wrong.

It is important to recognise that in many cases the relationship is formed at the deepest level between individuals rather than with the organisation as a whole. This is particularly true with professional services. When a senior partner leaves to join another firm, their clients may follow them. The risk for the client in forming a relationship with an unknown quantity, even from the same organisation, may be too great.

In this instance, risk may also have an explicit or implicit cost dimension. The time spent on the client's behalf so that the professional can understand the issues fully in order to make informed judgements will represent a personal investment that will not be undertaken lightly. Cost is clearly not the only issue. If the process demands that client and professional work together for significant periods of time, personal chemistry may well be a significant factor.

3.4.3   Customer relationship management (CRM)

Customer relationship management (CRM) is a term given to the management of customer relationships in high-volume consumer services, with the objective of growing a more profitable business and trying to form some closer understanding of the needs of individual customers. The essential difference between CRM and other approaches to customer retention is that the identification and enhancement of customer relationships is facilitated by technology. CRM attempts to integrate the many communication channels between an organisation's units and its customers, for example recording information about customer preferences and then using the information to develop and strengthen the relationship and the profitability of the customer.

The aim of CRM is to collect data from all parts of the organisation to enable tracking and analysis of a single customer relationship, as well as the identification of more general trends. For example, until recently it was possible that a customer of a financial services company would have a number of the products – a mortgage, savings accounts and insurance. Each of these products would be handled by separate parts of the business, with no knowledge of the others. As a result, customers rarely felt that they had a relationship with 'the company'.

To redress this, many financial service organisations are turning to data warehousing. A data warehouse is an integrated source of data that collects, cleans and stores information about customers. Adolf *et al.* (1997) have termed this as 'information-based continuous relationship marketing'. Data warehousing allows the organisation to view relationships and profitability across the organisation.

Companies are now moving to integrated CRM solutions with the advent of e-commerce. Internet-enabled activity allows companies to give information to their customers and collect data from them in a much more structured manner than previously. A smaller version of the data warehouse is the data mart. This serves a division or department of the organisation and should ideally be integrated with the enterprise's data warehouse. Such integration avoids repetition of the original problem of invisibility of customer relationships across the company.

Finally, these data marts and warehouses are linked to the various forms of technology at the customer interface. Telephone call centres are rapidly being replaced by multimedia contact centres. Customers have a choice of routes into the organisation, whether by letter, phone or internet. Paper-based transactions have virtually disappeared from most organisations, though companies must guard against devaluing such transactions to the extent that insufficient attention is paid to them. An increasing number of transactions are carried out electronically. Computer telephony integration (CTI) allows the customer to browse the company website and make contact with a human agent only if required.

CRM is therefore aimed at both customer retention and relationship growth approaches.

Travelco Ltd

Box 3.4

Moira Clark, Director of the CRM Research Forum, Cranfield School of Management

Travelco is a large UK package holiday company that has experienced difficult times since September 11th, SARS and the Iraq War. Travelco's customer retention rate was around 20 per cent annually and its market was declining by 10 per cent annually. As a result of this the company had focused predominantly on a sales-led strategy and very little attention had been devoted to customer relationship management (CRM). However, this changed with the implementation of a comprehensive CRM strategy.

The company began with a thorough audit of its state of readiness for CRM. This included an assessment of its marketing strategy conditions, its culture and climate conditions and its IT system conditions (see Figure 3.3). These conditions are defined as follows:

- *Marketing strategy*. This is the set of management decisions concerning the definition and selection of target customers and the value propositions made for them. CRM will only work in situations where the target markets are homogeneous, distinct segments and the propositions are segment-specific.

- *Culture and climate*. The values of organisational culture must be aligned to the marketplace and be commonly held throughout the company, yet still remain flexible. Without these attributes, culture will hinder CRM progress. Similarly, the best CRM systems will fail if the organisational climate, that is the practices, procedures and rewards of the company, are not aligned to the organisation culture. In these circumstances tension will occur and a negative climate will lead to failures in CRM.

- *IT systems*. In effective CRM companies these include not just the software and hardware systems but also all data and information processes connected to customer contact and proposition delivery. They also include organisational structures and systems that support the IT process, such as internal intranets.

By applying these conditions to the company, Travelco identified that

- Its customer retention was weak and that while customer data from across the organisation was gathered and organised centrally, it was not analysed in such a way as to identify customer segments and value propositions. This analysis has since led to the development of meaningful customer segments and tailored value propositions for each of these segments in order to gain a single view of the customer.

Figure 3.3	Readiness for CRM

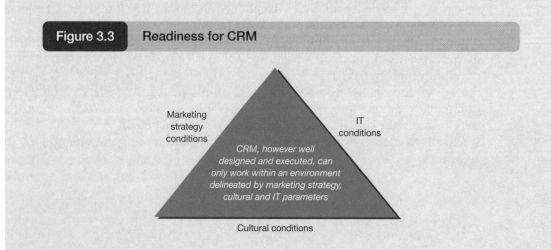

- Its culture and climate was not designed for developing customer retention strategies. The marketing strategy had traditionally focused on rewarding sales, leading to behaviour that did not support a customer-centric approach. As a result of this the company improved customer retention by adopting a complete cultural realignment. Training programmes were introduced and staff are now rewarded not only for acquiring customers but also for improvements in customer retention, cross-selling and customer satisfaction.

In summary, while there is no such thing as the 'perfect' CRM company, Travelco has gone a long way towards developing and maintaining long-term mutually trusting and profitable relationships with customers. It is now more focused in terms of selecting the right customers and developing tailored propositions for those customers. This has led to increases in customer satisfaction and its retention rate has now significantly improved.

Questions

1 What risks did Travelco face in adopting CRM?

2 Why was its approach successful?

CRM is defined as 'the management process that uses individual customer data to enable a tailored and mutually trusting and valuable proposition. In all but the smallest of organisations, CRM is characterised by the IT enabled integration of customer data from multiple sources' (Clark *et al.* 2002). Box 3.4 demonstrates that CRM demands much more than the introduction of an IT system, but also demands significant changes in the way the company operates. Not least, CRM requires the commitment of customer-facing staff to think behind the raw data from IT systems to apply insight to each customer transaction.

3.5 Managing business relationships

The work of the Industrial Marketing and Purchasing (IMP) Group over the last 40 years (see, for example, Ford *et al.* 2003) has demonstrated that building business relationships is different to building many consumer relationships. In essence business markets are often made up of a small number of powerful customers who are seeking solutions to problems. Many business relationships are close, complex and long-term, and each relationship is part of a network of relationships; others are short-term and adversarial in nature. Critically, inter-business relationships are created by the behaviours of a small number of individuals who form and hold the relationships by their words and actions. Also, as these players change, so does the nature of the relationship.

3.5.1 Types of business relationship

Business enterprises come in many shapes and sizes, such as contracts, partnerships, alliances, strategic/global alliances, partnering, joint ventures and networks. Each of these encompass slightly differing forms of relationship:

- *Contracts* are often non-equity agreements 'specifying the cooperative contributions and powers of each partner' (Stafford 1994), where greater power lies with usually the purchasing 'partner'.

- *Partnerships*, sometimes also referred to as alliances, may be contractual or informal, and tend to imply parity-type relationships built on equal input of both partners with shared goals and for mutual benefit (Mohr and Spekman 1994). Some partnerships are focused on short-term activities; others might be a prelude to a full merger of two or more companies (Moss Kanter 1994).

- *Strategic alliances*, sometimes also referred to as global alliances, are 'voluntary arrangements between firms involving exchange, sharing, or co-development of products, technologies or services' (Gulati 1998), though they tend to exist as asymmetric relationships since they often involve one party acquiring a partial stake in the other (Stafford 1994).

- *Partnering* is concerned with developing closer relationships between the partners in an environment of openness and trust.

- *Joint ventures* (JVs) are one form of alliance and involve the partners creating a new, separate body or subsidiary, jointly owned, to exploit a particular opportunity (Doz and Hamel 1998).

- *Networks* are structures of interconnecting partnerships, alliances or JVs, which can take many different forms (Håkansson 1997, Håkansson and Snehota 2002, Ford *et al.* 2003, Naudé and Turnbull 1998).

The critical point is that all of these forms involve relationships, ranging on a continuum from weak and distant to strong and close (Moss Kanter 1994). Recent work undertaken by Shape International, a consultancy specialising in business relationships, has taken this further and suggested that business relationships lie along one of two disconnected continua (see Figure 3.4) (Johnston *et al.* 2004). One continuum represents a range of transactional, one-off, relationships, and the second represents long-term strategic relationships, each with their own set of characteristics. As Box 3.5, illustrates, it is not easy moving from one type to the other.

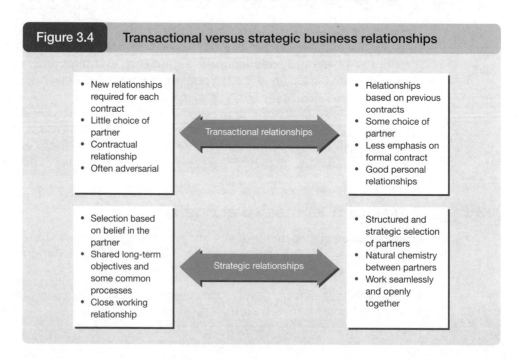

Figure 3.4 — Transactional versus strategic business relationships

National Grid Transco Group   Box 3.5

Roy Staughton, Shape International (www.shape-international.com)

Peter Roberts was the head of assets for National Transmissions and Trading within Transco, which is part of the National Grid Transco Group. Transco is a major player in the regulated industry and manages multi-million pound projects that create the infrastructure used to transport energy across the UK. Peter was responsible for the planning and construction, maintenance and ultimately decommissioning of the high-pressure gas pipelines and pumping stations within the UK.

Peter had some experience in developing strategic relationships:

A number of organisations want to move to having strategic relationships but they are struggling with how to do it. Strategic relationships call for a change in culture from an adversarial to a collaborative style. And that takes time – because it's a trust issue and trust is earned, not switched on overnight, and it quickly unpicks when things go wrong. People default back to type when under pressure, and that's a problem.

In a strategic relationship each party knows what turns the other party on, what is important to them and what they are trying to deliver. And they come together to agree how they can combine to meet each other's aspirations. There's a realisation that each party should provide added value and each party has a right to make a decent return. Such relationships can be quite hard for some clients because they are used to dictating to the supply chain exactly what they want. Part of a collaborative relationship is accepting that you've got to stop dictating and actually come together and look at what is best for the whole chain.

We did it by identifying which of our project managers had the mindset to move towards a collaborative way of working. We started to think about how we could bring the supply chain together in a spirit of trust and understanding. We had to stop dictating and start involving our contractors in important issues. We brought project managers and contractors together, outside a project context, to start to work collaboratively on things like policy and procedures for, say, health and safety and environmental issues. In that way both parties learned what collaborating involved, while working on issues that were important to the industry.

Peter believes that developing strategic relationships is not easy. He added, 'There isn't a hard and fast rulebook that works for everyone. It requires a leap of faith. If you think it's the right thing to do you should go with it and, if you've got any sense, you'll put some key performance indicators in place to help you and your partners.'

Using a process designed and facilitated by Shape International, Transco and one key partner agreed a jointly developed set of performance indicators, or metrics, to assess and develop their relationship. The process involved the key players from each party in identifying the things that make a difference to their relationship. These included a range of issues from the attitude of key players, to document quality and the nature of communications. Once this was agreed, Transco and each partner shared their two sets of independently developed characteristics to agree a joint set. Using descriptive anchored scales for each agreed characteristic, the two parties were then able to agree on their existing and desired current position.

Peter Roberts concluded: 'This process provided us with a jointly constructed set of weighted metrics that defined the relationship, together with agreement on the current and required performance for each one and a shared action plan to move things forward.'

Questions

1 What are the difficulties in developing strategic relationships?

2 Why is measuring relationships important?

3 Why is measuring relationships difficult?

While some of the issues and approaches contained in the previous section on customer relationships apply also to business relationships, there are three additional aspects to managing business relationships: measuring business relationships, using key account managers, and ways of developing personal relationships.

3.5.2 Measuring business relationships

One area that is of key concern to operations managers, yet has only limited coverage in the existing literature, is how to assess and measure relationships. This is an important area (see, for example, Ford *et al.* 2003, and Naudé and Buttle 2002). Ford *et al.* (2003), for example, state 'Regular assessment of a customer relationship is a prerequisite for conscious, purposeful intervention in it. Assessment is particularly valuable when any major change in the relationship is being considered, such as developing or adapting an offering or investing in operational capability for the relationship.' From an operational perspective, managers need to assess and measure relationships to understand where the deficiencies are, in order to work on them with their partners or to make decisions about which partners to use for particular contracts or purposes.

Transactional relationships – using SLAs

Managing highly contractual transactional relationships is often fraught with difficulty. This is particularly true where an aspect of the customer's business has been outsourced to a specialist provider. Examples of this lie in the area of facilities management or information technology support. Measurement tends to be concerned almost entirely with financial and hard measures of operational performance, such as price and on-time completion or delivery. Purchasers and suppliers tend to enter into service-level agreements (SLAs) – often imposed – to manage the relationship, or rather the contract (see also Chapter 5). Table 3.3 gives examples of key measures included in typical SLAs.

Table 3.3 Examples of service-level agreement measures

Help desk support	
Telephone response	95% within 3 rings
Problem resolution	65% through first-line support within 8 hours 35% through second-line support within 24 hours
Complaint escalation	To first-line manager after 8 working hours To senior manager after 16 working hours
Request for software fix	Initial response within 5 working days Outline proposal within 15 working days
Equipment maintenance	
Response to non-critical fault	2 working days
Response to critical fault	2 hours
First-time fix rate	95%
...ule adherence	95% within 2 working days
availability	95% within 48 hours 100% within 5 working days

The advantage of SLAs is that the measures provide a basis for review of how well the relationship/contract is working. The disadvantage is that it is impossible to describe all facets of service provision through an SLA. If the relationship deteriorates to a 'nit-picking' review of performance against an increasing list of measures, it is likely that it will not continue. Worse still, SLAs are sometimes used to exert undue pressure on suppliers. For example, if a supplier has performed very well against the agreed measures, instead of providing thanks and an extended contract the purchaser may try to reduce the price on the assumption that the supplier had more resources than necessary to meet the performance targets.

Strategic relationships – the need for jointly developed metrics

There are two common issues with measuring strategic business relationships. First, most organisations tend only to measure the financial and hard operational characteristics of the relationships. Indeed many operations managers would agree that it is difficult, if not impossible, to measure some of the softer, often more personal characteristics, such as attitude, communications and helpfulness. Yet it is usually these softer characteristics that are essential for the success of the relationship (Staughton and Johnston 2002). Second, the measurement activity is invariably one-directional, in that the 'purchaser' measures the performance of the 'supplier'. Whereas this might be appropriate for transactional relationships, it is not appropriate for organisations that are trying to work closely together in a long-term relationship and with mutual benefits in mind. We wholeheartedly agree with Ford *et al.* (2003) when they state:

> *We believe that it is only possible to make sense of what happens in a relationship by simultaneously studying both of the companies involved. Similarly it is only possible to manage a relationship by looking at it from the perspective of both companies rather than simply carrying out 'supplier-assessment' or 'customer-segmentation' alone.*

Box 3.5 demonstrates that progressive organisations are addressing this issue and provides some information about a process for jointly developing metrics of a relationship.

3.5.3 Key account management (KAM)

An approach appropriate for these situations where companies have a relatively small number of strategic customers is key account management (KAM). KAM recognises that these relationships are complex, with more than one channel of contact between provider and customer. Figure 3.5 illustrates the transition from a traditional ('bow tie') approach to buyer–supplier relationships, to the KAM approach represented by the diamond.

In the traditional approach, transactions are channelled through one point of contact, a sales or contract manager. As Figure 3.5 indicates, the weakness of this approach is that the relationship is only as strong as the link between a single buyer and the sales or contract manager. This relationship is vulnerable to changes in personnel, so some organisations regularly change their buyers in order to maintain 'arm's length' trading conditions. The danger for the supplier is that a change in a buyer might lead to a less favourable environment. The key point to note is that the relationship may be easily broken by competitors who manage to forge a strong contact with other influencers in the customer organisation.

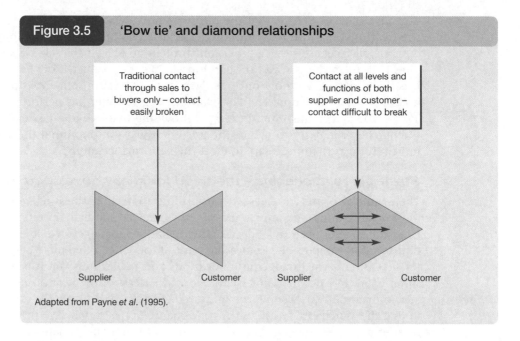

Figure 3.5   'Bow tie' and diamond relationships

Traditional contact through sales to buyers only – contact easily broken

Contact at all levels and functions of both supplier and customer – contact difficult to break

Supplier   Customer   Supplier   Customer

Adapted from Payne *et al.* (1995).

The aim of KAM is to turn the traditional 'bow tie' relationship into a much stronger 'diamond'. In this format, links are encouraged across the boundary between the two organisations. The role of the key account manager is now not to act as a conduit through which all communication must flow, but rather to act as an enabler for the relationship. If the customer has a particular need, KAM is focused on setting up the dialogue between the appropriate parties. Of course, the key account manager must monitor the effectiveness of these relationships to avoid the occurrence of problems that will damage the long-term business.

This approach is particularly useful for professional service firms that contain individuals or groups that are encouraged to be entrepreneurial in business development. It is not uncommon for customers to be approached by numbers of these, all from the same organisation, effectively in competition with each other for the same business, thus giving the customer the impression that the firm does not know what it is doing.

For B2B customers, the customer retention approach is so vital that it is almost a 'blinding flash of the obvious' to say that the organisation should focus on customer loyalty. A loss of a customer can threaten the existence of many of these services. The relationship growth approach has to be the main emphasis here, looking to build more links and broadening the base of business connection.

3.5.4   Building personal relationships

Enhancing business relationships can easily be overlooked by organisations that are operationally focused and busy delivering services, and also by organisations at the other extreme, which are market focused and intent on increasing their customer base. Business relationships can be established and enhanced in four key ways (Maister 1993, Payne *et al.* 1995):

- *Going the extra mile*. Providing higher than expected levels of service on a current project, such as providing enhanced documentation, analyses, explanations or even presentations, and/or greater accessibility to staff.

- *Increasing the amount of client contact*. Making frequent visits or telephone calls, creating contacts at different levels in the organisation, scheduling meetings and feedback/development sessions.

- *Building the business relationship*. Putting on special seminars for the client, helping them make other contacts, assisting with benchmarking, sending useful articles, even referring business to the client.

- *Building a social relationship*. Providing social activities and tickets for events, remembering personal anniversaries, etc.

In Box 3.6 the head of a global trading and shipping conglomerate explains how he tries to strengthen relationships with his suppliers and customers.

GP Group (Bangkok)　Box 3.6

The GP Group is a global trading and shipping company based in Bangkok. It is a family firm, which was established 125 years ago in Burma. It now has a turnover in excess of US$2 billion and comprises over 20 companies worldwide, specialising in commodity trading, ship chartering, ship management, rice production, seed research and production, manufacturing and exporting rubber products, chemicals, pharmaceuticals, jewellery and soya bean. It provides services such as property development, tour operations, plastic security cards, port management and project management.

Kirit Shah is the chief executive officer and owner of the Group, and he explained his role in the diversified business.

I am no longer personally involved in running any of my companies directly. All the companies have managing directors and they run the business on their own. I have good people. For the past 25 years I have been recruiting graduates from business schools. My typical day would involve meeting some of the directors and talking about what they are doing or working on a problem that they might have. I would meet a lot of their customers, their suppliers and their buyers, and I would typically host a lunch or dinner and meet them face to face to help them in their work.

The way I try to strengthen our business relationships is to have face-to-face meetings with people. I know this is very much against the trend, which is about global communications, mobile telephones and instant communication. But just think about it: if I can sit face-to-face with someone I can see their reaction, which on a fax or e-mail I cannot. As a buyer today you have a choice, the whole world wants to sell to you. So why me? Because you know me, because we had a meeting, had a drink, maybe our families know each other. It is the personal touch that I think is important in today's faceless world. We are all trying to get to a faceless situation but I don't think there is an effective substitute for personal interaction. And it's surprisingly easy to do, it's like an illusion. If you were in London and I was in London and I asked you for a meeting, chances are you would tell me, 'OK, let's meet next month', or you might not even accept my call. On the other hand, if I call you from Bangkok, chances are you will take my call as a priority over something else that you were doing. So if I said I was coming from Bangkok and I can meet you the day after tomorrow, chances are that you will see me faster than you would see a guy who is next door or in the next street. It's the perception that he is always there but the guy from Bangkok is not, so I must see him at a time convenient to him, not at a time convenient to me.

The downside is that we have to travel a lot more than we ever did. Now it's more intense than ever. Before, when I went on a trip it was for one week; now, because of frequency of flights, I go somewhere for one day. Even when I go to London I land at 6.00 in the morning and I take a flight back at 10.00 in the evening, having spent the day *there. With more direct flights we are all burning ourselves trying to get to the farthest point on the globe in the shortest possible time and get back.*

Questions

1 How does Kirit Shah go about strengthening his company's relationships with clients?

2 What are the advantages and problems associated with this approach?

3.6 Summary

Customers and customer segmentation

- Customers may be external, internal, intermediaries, end users, stakeholders, payers, beneficiaries, participants, and valuable or non-valuable.

- Operations managers need to develop an understanding of the nature of individual customers and the customers' likely attitude and behaviour.

- Operational categories of customers include the Ally, the Hostage, the Anarchist, the Patient, the Tolerant, the Intolerant, the Victim, the Terrorist, the Incompetent and the Champion.

Customer retention

- A key task for operations managers is retaining valuable customers.

- Customer lifetime values depend upon current and potential annual spend, the duration and durability of customer relationships, the number of points of contact with customers and the profitability of the customer.

Managing customer relationships

- Managing customer relationships is about establishing, maintaining and enhancing relationships with customers for mutual benefit.

- There are three main forms of customer relationship:
  - relationships based on a portfolio of service products, frequently found in higher-volume operations
  - personal relationships created between an individual customer and an employee, particularly prevalent in low-volume professional organisations
  - temporary relationships, which recognise the transactional, one-off nature of many services.

- There is often a link between customers' perceived risk in purchasing or using the service and their desire for a type of relationship with the provider.

- Customer relationship management (CRM) is used by some high-volume consumer services to try to grow more profitable business by better understanding the needs of individual customers.
- CRM attempts to integrate the many communication channels between an organisation's units and its customers.

Managing business relationships

- Building business relationships can be different to building many consumer relationships.
- Business markets often comprise a small number of powerful customers who are seeking solutions to problems. Many business relationships are close, complex and long-term and each relationship is part of a network of relationships; others are short-term and adversarial in nature.
- There are many types of business enterprise, such as contracts, partnerships, alliances, strategic/global alliances, partnering, joint ventures, and networks; each of these encompass slightly differing forms of relationships.
- Measuring business relationships is the key to improvement.
- Service level agreements (SLAs) are often used in contractual transactional relationships.
- Strategic relationships require jointly developed metrics.
- Key account management is helpful for organisations with a small number of strategic partners.
- Building personal relationships underpins many business relationships.

3.7　Discussion questions

1　How would you classify yourself and your colleagues/friends in terms of your customer attitude to a particular service? Could everyone be converted into Allies and if so, how?
2　Calculate your lifetime value for a supermarket, electrical retailer and bank. What are the problems in assessing lifetime values?
3　Assess the personal relationship you have with a professional service provider. How well is the relationship managed?

3.8　Questions for managers

1　Is your organisation pursuing a relationship approach? Is this what customers desire?
2　Have you considered the resources required for developing customer relationships?
3　To what extent do your processes take into account the differing needs of your target customer segments?

4 Do you understand the value of a customer? Is it possible to calculate the life-time revenue that each customer represents?

5 Can you identify different customer behaviours? Can you provide training and/or procedures to deal with these differences?

6 How important is customer retention to your business? How can the customer defection rate be reduced?

3.9 Further reading

Ford D., Gadde L-E., Håkansson H. and Snehota I., *Managing Business Relationships*, 2nd edition, Wiley, Chichester, 2003.

Gabriel Y. and Lang T., *The Unmanageable Consumer*, Sage Publications, London, 1995.

Olsen L.L. and Johnson M.D., 'Service equity, satisfaction, and loyalty: from transaction-specific to cumulative evaluations', *Journal of Service Research*, vol. 5, no. 3, 2003, pp. 184–95.

Payne A., Christopher M., Clark M. and Peck H., *Relationship Marketing for Competitive Advantage*, Butterworth Heinemann, Oxford, 1995.

Reinartz W. and Kumar V., 'The mismanagement of customer loyalty', *Harvard Business Review*, July 2002, pp. 86–94.

Yu Y.T. and Dean A., 'The contribution of emotional satisfaction to customer loyalty', *International Journal of Service Industry Management*, vol. 12, no. 3/4, 2001, pp. 234–51.

3.10 References

Adolf R., Grant-Thompson S., Harrington W. and Singer M., 'What leading banks are learning about big databases and marketing', *McKinsey Quarterly*, Summer 1997, no. 3, pp. 187–92.

Buttle F., 'Relationship marketing', in Buttle F. (ed.), *Relationship Marketing, Theory and Practice*, Paul Chapman Publishing, London, 1996.

Clark M., McDonald M. and Smith B., 'Achieving excellence in customer relationship marketing', *Cranfield Customer Relationship Marketing Research Forum Report*, October 2002.

Doz Y.L. and Hamel G., *Alliance Advantage: The Art of Creating Value through Partnering*, Harvard Business School Press, Cambridge, Mass., 1998.

Ford D., Gadde L-E., Håkansson H. and Snehota I., *Managing Business Relationships*, 2nd edition, Wiley, Chichester, 2003.

Gremler D.D. and Brown S.W., 'The loyalty ripple effect: appreciating the full value of customers', *International Journal of Service Industry Management*, vol. 10, no. 3, 1999, pp. 271–91.

Gummesson E., 'Making relationship marketing operational', *International Journal of Service Industry Management*, vol. 5, no. 5, 1994, pp. 5–20.

Gummesson E., *Total Relationship Marketing*, Butterworth Heinemann, Oxford, 1999.

Gulati R., 'Alliances and networks', *Strategic Management Journal*, vol. 19, 1998, pp. 293–317.

Håkansson H., 'Organisational networks' in Sorge A. and Warner M. (eds.), *The IEBM Handbook of Organizational Behavior*, International Thompson Business Press, London, 1997.

Håkansson H. and Snehota I., 'Analysing business relationships' in Ford D. (ed.), *Understanding Business Marketing and Purchasing*, 3rd edition, Thomson Learning, London, 2002, pp. 162–82.

Johnston R. Staughton R.V.W., and Putnam M., 'Developing a framework for analysing and developing business relationships', working paper, Warwick Business School, 2004.

Knox S.D. and Denison T.J., *Profiling the Promiscuous Shopper, Evaluating Shopper Loyalty*, Air Miles Travel Promotions Ltd, Sussex, 1992.

Maister D.A., *Managing the Professional Service Firm*, Free Press, New York, 1993.

Mohr J. and Spekman R., 'Characteristics of partnership success: partnership attributes, communication behaviour, and conflict resolution techniques', *Strategic Management Journal*, vol. 15, 1994, pp. 135–52.

Morgan R.M. and Hunt S.D., 'The commitment-trust theory of relationship marketing', *Journal of Marketing*, vol. 58, July, 1994, pp. 20–38.

Moss Kanter R., 'Collaborative advantage', *Harvard Business Review*, July–August 1994, pp. 96–108.

Naudé P. and Buttle F., 'Assessing relationship quality', in Ford D. (ed.), *Understanding Business Marketing and Purchasing*, 3rd edition, Thomson Learning, London, 2002, pp. 349–59.

Naudé P. and Turnbull P.W., *Network Dynamics in International Marketing*, Elsevier Science, Oxford, 1998.

Payne A., Christopher M. Clark M. and Peck H., *Relationship Marketing for Competitive Advantage*, Butterworth Heinemann, Oxford, 1995.

Peppers D. and Rogers M., *The One to One Future*, Currency/Doubleday, New York, 1993.

Reichheld F., *The Loyalty Effect*, Harvard Business School Press, Cambridge, Mass., 1996.

Reichheld F. and Sasser W.E., 'Zero defections: quality comes to services', *Harvard Business Review*, September–October 1990, pp. 105–11.

Reinartz W. and Kumar V., 'The mismanagement of customer loyalty', *Harvard Business Review*, July 2002, pp. 86–94.

Schlesinger L.A. and Heskett J.L., 'The service-driven service company', *Harvard Business Review*, September–October 1991, pp. 71–81.

Stafford E.R., 'Using co-operative strategies to make alliances work', *Long Range Planning*, vol. 27, no. 3, 1994, pp. 64–74.

Staughton R.V.W. and Johnston R., 'The "soft" dimension gap in business-to-business relationship management', in Tax S., Stuart F.I., Brown S.W., Edvardsson B., Johnston R. and Scheuing E.E. (eds), *Quality in Service: Crossing Borders*, University of Victoria, Canada, 2002, pp. 317–26.

The National Brewery   Case Exercise

Robert Johnston and Rhian Silvestro, Warwick Business School

The National Brewery has over 5,000 pubs in the UK, many of which used to be 'tenanted' houses, i.e. a tenant was appointed to run the pub and was overseen by an area manager. The area managers would pay regular visits to assess the pub's financial position, the success of recent activities and the licensee's plans for the future. Recent legislation, as a result of a Monopolies and Mergers Commission report that found an industry dominated by big brewers that were squeezing smaller real-ale brewers out of the industry, forced the big brewers, of which National was one, either to sell a proportion of their pubs or to release them from their tie to the brewery's products.

Some of the big brewers took their pubs back into management and therefore outside the jurisdiction of the legislation, while others sold off their chains of public houses to other companies. Both these strategies have had the effect of reducing the likelihood of the introduction of guest beers. National decided to change over 2,000 of its tenanted pubs to leased pubs and give the tenants the opportunity to purchase (usually) a 20-year lease. This was seen by many licensees as a golden opportunity to have not only security and control over their futures but also something of value that they could either pass on or sell in the years to come. National recognised that with each of these pubs becoming an independent business in its own right, away from the direct control of the parent company, it needed to create a new body to help and support these pubs in their growth and development. Thus a partnership approach was born through a specially created subsidiary, National Support Services (NSS).

To provide the new, extensive and comprehensive range of support and developmental services', National has done away with the area managers and appointed NSS managers (NSSMs) to work with licensees to help them develop their businesses. Many of them previously worked as area managers but over 50 per cent were new to the business. The services include sales promotions packages and beer discounts, which are delivered directly by the NSSM, together with advice on catering, property, security, financial matters, legal problems, quality standards and training on any aspect of the business, which are provided by NSS consultants. All these services are provided free to lessees. Information about the products is provided in glossy brochures available from the NSSMs.

One NSSM, Richard Jenkins, explained how things have changed:

> In the days before the lease agreements the then area managers had the right to require meetings with their licensees and to demand financial and promotional plans. Now, in the new spirit of partnership, the relationship is much more supportive. It is up to the NSSM to prove to the licensee the need for his or her support. This is achieved in all but a very few instances. However, it's OK for those who are doing well and using our services but what do I do if they then turn round and say that, apart from our beer and lager (which they are required to sell under the terms of the lease), they don't want to sell other National products?

> Should I continue to offer all the services or should I withdraw them? Also, what do I do for the lessee who is running a pub in a poor location? These licensees have not been overly receptive to many of the new possibilities – indeed, many of them just want us to reduce their rents, which we don't have the authority to do, or offer unlimited quantities of discounted or free beer for promotional purposes.

> You must realise that delivering the Support Services is not cheap. The payback for these costs comes from the enhanced rental income from our properties. This is achieved by having better-performing businesses because of the support provided by NSS. Some lessees have claimed that their rents have about doubled since the change in agreement. This increase in rents reflects, in part, the increased value that the licensees can now obtain from the premium on the assignment of their business, and their entitlement to take on guest beers.

National has three types of pub – the community pub, the tavern and the food pub – and it has put out to lease about equal numbers of each type. Examples of these pubs and a summary of their financial position are as follows:

- **The White Lion**, a 'community pub', is a male-dominated, traditional pub in a run-down area of Nottingham, where unemployment has been high for the past 20 years. There are several pubs of similar style in the area. The pub does not have a restaurant but offers bar snacks and sandwiches. The bar offers a limited product range and sells mainly beer. The pub was last refurbished 15 years ago and the decor is now somewhat the worse for wear.

- **The Oak**, a 'tavern', is located in a prosperous working-class suburb in Nottingham. It is a popular family pub, although there are a number of similar offerings in the area. The pub was refurbished at moderate cost five years ago. It remains in good condition and has a friendly atmosphere. The Oak has one restaurant offering a standard menu, and typical spend on food is around £8–9 per head. Pub lunches may be ordered from the bar.

There is an indoor family area and an outdoor play area for children.

- **The Castle**, a 'food pub', is a new pub located in an affluent, suburban location in a residential area in Nottingham. The pub is well differentiated in its locality, having a smart, fashionable, 'designer' feel to it, with bright, well co-ordinated furnishings and fittings. The pub targets the business community at lunch times. It is popular with 'yuppies' and 'dinkies' (double income, no kids) in the evenings. There is a 'wayside-inn'-style restaurant, which offers an extensive menu including traditional and ethnic dishes, where typical

spend on food is around £15–20 per head. Light meals can be ordered at the bar. Wine and cocktails are popular.

Questions

1 How will the lease change the relationship between the area manager/NSSM and the licensee?

2 Evaluate National Support Services from the point of view of their customers, i.e. the lessees.

3 How should the National Brewery go about developing its Support Services to meet the needs of all its lessees?

Table 3.4 End-of-year financial summaries

	White Lion	The Oak	The Castle
Trading square footage (front of house)	1,000	1,500	2,000
Mix of income (ex. Accomm.)			
Liquor sales	90%	83%	35.5%
Food sales	6%	14%	63%
Machine income net	3%	2%	0.5%
Other income	1%	1%	1%
Total annual income	£150,000	£320,000	£450,000
Margin			
Liquor margin	45%	53%	58%
Food margin	40%	54%	67%
Gross margin	43%	52%	63%
Cost ratios to total income			
Wages	11%	14%	17.7%
Fuel	2.8%	2.6%	2.9%
Trade expenses	1.8%	2.1%	3.4%
Equipment repairs	1.2%	1.3%	1.5%
Promotions	3.3%	2.8%	2%
Depreciation	2%	2.3%	3%
Rates, water, insurance	3.6%	3.4%	3.5%
Building repairs	2.3%	1.5%	1%
Overall costs	28%	30%	35%
House net profit	15%	22%	28%
Cumulative profit growth over three years not adjusted for inflation	5%	10%	19%

chapter four

Customer expectations and satisfaction

4

Chapter objectives:

- to understand customer satisfaction and service quality

- to discuss customer expectations and how they are created

- to define customer expectations using the service quality factors

- to describe means of finding customer expectations and assessing satisfaction

- to discuss how operations managers can manage perceptions during service delivery.

4.1 Introduction

The customer is an input resource for many service operations and thus not only do we need to know how to manage customers (Chapter 7) but also we need to understand what they expect from the operation. Most importantly, they are, in most cases, the final judge as to how well the quality of the service matches up to requirements, and, by their continued support, determine its long-term success. This should be more than sufficient motivation for operations managers to ensure that there is a match between expectations and service delivery in order to satisfy or even delight our customers.

Although the need to satisfy customers is something that 'goes without saying', this is precisely the problem with many organisations. Assumptions are made about what customers really want and, even if customers have been consulted, it may be such a long time in the past that this information is at best irrelevant, and often positively dangerous. Professional services, in particular, frequently suffer from an attitude of thinking that they know best, because they are the experts. This might be true, but this attitude can create blind spots when dealing with customers.

Understanding what satisfies and delights customers is something that must be continually addressed, using a variety of means to ensure that the answers do not fall into well-established patterns because the way the questions are asked do not vary sufficiently. Customer satisfaction is something that can be managed to some extent by influencing customers' perceptions and expectations of service delivery. This demands in-depth understanding of this subject.

It is no accident that many of those companies that have a reputation for excellent service spend time and money in listening to customers. Disney, for example, invented a new term for the activity of collecting information from customers. It is called 'guestology' – reflecting Disney's approach to treating its visitors as guests rather than mere customers.

4.2 Customer satisfaction, service quality and confidence

The purpose of trying to understand customers' expectations is to try to ensure that service can be designed and delivered in order to meet those expectations. If the operation meets the expectations, or indeed exceeds them, then customers are satisfied with the service. If they are satisfied they are more likely to become valuable customers who not only use the service again, but are positively disposed towards it and may even recommend it to others (we sometimes refer to this as their post-purchase intentions).

4.2.1 Customer satisfaction

In simple terms, satisfaction is the result of customers' assessment of a service based on a comparison of their perceptions of service delivery with their prior expectations (see Figure 4.1) (see, for example, Bitner and Hubbert 1994).

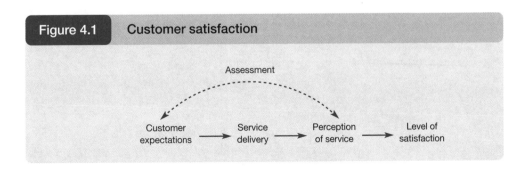

Figure 4.1   Customer satisfaction

If customers' perception of the service, the experience and outcomes matches their expectations then they should be satisfied (or at least satisficed). If their perception of the service exceeds their expectations then they will be more than satisfied, even delighted. If their perceptions of the service do not meet their expectations then they may be dissatisfied, even disgusted or outraged (Andreassen 2001, Schneider and Bowen 1999). (This is sometimes referred to in the consumer behaviour literature as the disconfirmation theory; see, for example, Oliver and DeSarbo 1988, Churchill and Surprenant 1982, Cadotte *et al.* 1987).

Satisfaction is the outcome of the consumer's evaluation of a service, which we sometimes refer to as perceived service quality, and can be represented on a continuum from delight to extreme dissatisfaction, which we have labelled from +5 to –5 (see Figure 4.2).

Thus expectations, and indeed perceptions, are key components in delivering a quality service. Operations managers need to understand and define expectations in order to:

● create a detailed service specification in line with the service concept
● design and deliver the appropriate service at the appropriate cost
● encourage marketers to try to influence customers' prior expectations so that those expectations can be delivered
● understand how to manage, indeed manipulate, customer perceptions during the service to achieve the desired level of satisfaction.

4.2.2 Excellent service and customer delight

Delivering excellent service does not necessarily mean exceeding expectations. Consumer research (Johnston 2001) has shown that excellent service is about doing two main things:

● *Delivering the promise*. This is about reliability: consistently doing what you promise and meeting customer expectations (and setting the right expectations in the first place); this is the subject of this chapter and Part 3 of this book.

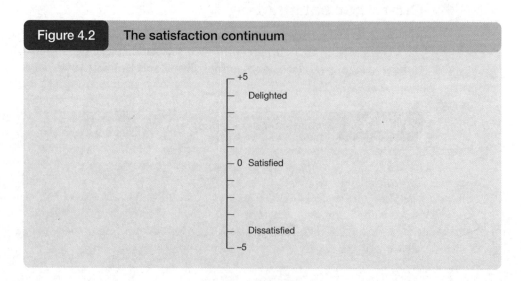

Figure 4.2 **The satisfaction continuum**

+5

Delighted

0 Satisfied

Dissatisfied

–5

- *Dealing well with problems and queries*. This is about service recovery and is covered in Chapter12.

And, where possible or appropriate:

- *Providing a personal touch*. This is about treating the customer as an individual.
- *Going the 'extra mile'*. This is simply about providing some small extra touches that the customer really appreciates.

It is important to realise that excellent service can be delivered by a full-service provider (see Box 4.1) or a no-frills provider (whether an airline, hotel or public sector organisation). Simply, customers can be delighted by organisations that do what they say, and, when something does go wrong, it is the company that sorts it out.

The Central Samui Beach Resort Hotel — Box 4.1

The Central Samui Beach Resort Hotel is the leading full-service resort hotel on Koh Samui, a tropical island paradise in the Gulf of Thailand. The hotel is located on the palm-fringed Chaweng beach, the longest and most beautiful beach on the island. The 'new colonial' style hotel has 208 rooms, which overlook the tropical gardens, swimming pools and beach. The hotel has excellent facilities, including swimming pools, tennis courts, fitness centre, spa and three restaurants.

David Good is the general manager of the hotel and he explained why guests choose this hotel.

There are three main reasons why our guests come here: location, space and service. Our location is ideal, a beautiful island with a superb all year round climate, but also we are located on Chaweng beach, which is the best beach with the best nightlife. Indeed I reckon we have probably the best piece of property on the best bit of the best beach on the whole island. Space, too, is important. Guests don't like to feel cramped. We have large gardens and common areas so that our guests are able to spread out. They really seem to appreciate that.

Finally there is our service, which is as good as you will find in the best hotels around the world. It is very traditionally Thai. Our staff are very good-natured and friendly and they provide genuine hospitality and warmth. This has a big impact on our guests. We receive

many thank-you letters and guests often send us the photographs they have had taken with the staff, asking us to pass them on with thanks. We also have a large number of returning guests, running at around 5 per cent, and growing, which is amazing given the short length of time we have been open.

The hotel provides an outstanding level of service and David went on to explain what this means.

First, we have very few problems or complaints. Indeed, I can honestly say we have no big issues that result in negative feedback. We do, like any hotel, have some minor issues, just small irritations. Right now, for example, we occasionally have problems with water pressure. Some people don't have quite as clear a sea view as they might have hoped, with some trees and bushes in the garden slightly obscuring their view. Some say the curry was a little too spicy.

Second, high quality service is about consistency. Consistency is important. When our guests come back they very much expect the same high level of service that delighted them the first time and that continues to delight them. The issue for us is to provide that same level of service – the smiles, the greeting, the helpfulness – day in, day out.

Thirdly, it's about the little things, personal touches, such as taking time with guests; a few minutes here and there to acknowledge people, or spend a few minutes talking with them. The guest-relations staff, for example, sometimes send small gifts to our guests if it's their birthday or if they are a returning guest or if they're on honeymoon or it's their anniversary. We try and track all these things – little surprises here and there. It's these small things that really stick in people's minds.

Questions

1 How does the Central Samui Hotel go about providing outstanding customer service?

2 By delighting customers on their first visit to the hotel, is David in danger of raising expectations so that they won't be delighted on subsequent visits?

4.2.3 Service quality

The term service quality is often used to mean different things. Some managers use the term to mean how the customer is treated. This is perhaps more accurately called quality of service, as opposed to service quality, which can mean the entirety of outcome and experience. It is a central theme of this book that service operations must be taken as a whole rather than simply concentrating on the points of contact with customers, important as they are. Other definitions of service quality include:

● satisfaction
● a relative impression of the organisation and its services
● quality delivered.

Satisfaction

Sometimes service quality is used to mean the same as satisfaction, i.e. perceived service quality.

A relative impression of the organisation and its services

Service quality is more often used as a more enduring construct, whereas satisfaction is situation and experience-specific (Oliver 1993). Satisfaction has to be experienced (Oliver 1993), whereas customers may have views about an organisation's service quality without ever having experienced the service. Bitner and Hubbert (1994) define service quality as 'the consumer's overall impression of the relative inferiority/superiority of the organisation and its services'. Recent empirical work would also suggest that there is an interactive relationship between satisfaction and service quality, i.e. each can have a moderating effect on the other, and therefore on post-purchase intentions (Taylor and Baker 1994). Patterson and Johnson (1993) suggested that satisfaction judgements decay into service quality – an overall attitude about the service.

Quality delivered

When we talk about service quality from an operation's perspective we usually mean the quality of the service we deliver, i.e. does it consistently meet the specification for that service? This, of course, may be different to how a customer sees the service (their perceived service quality), and thus there may be a mismatch between a customer's expectations of a service and their perception of its delivery. This mismatch could be the result of either a mismatch between expectation and delivery and/or a mismatch between delivery and perceptions (see Figure 4.3, which is a simplified version of the gap model developed by Parasuraman *et al.* 1985.)

There are several reasons why Gap 1 might exist. The service may have been inappropriately specified or designed, or there may be insufficient resources to meet expectations. It is also possible that the customer may have inappropriate expectations. An inappropriate specification or design of the service may be the result of a poor understanding of customer expectations by managers. Managers may have not put enough time and effort into either specifying the service concept and service delivery or getting feedback from customers about what they feel to be an appropriate level of service. Insufficient resources may be the result of a poor understanding of market requirements or demand profiles.

These 'internal' reasons often stem from a lack of determination to deliver consistently high standards. Managers consistently report a view that their organisation does not take time and trouble to understand what its customers want and therefore the service design process is flawed from the onset. This flows into poor or inappropriate service design and results in poor resource utilisation.

Inappropriate expectations may be the result of inappropriate marketing, promises made by the organisation that cannot be delivered, or inappropriate word-of-mouth referals or organisational image, which may be a result of poor service experiences in the past. Also, there are some customers who have quite unrealistic expectations of some service organisations and can cause a great deal of aggravation and nuisance as a result. These individuals either need their expectations reshaping before or during service delivery, or removing from the operation, if this is feasible (see Chapter 7).

Gap 2 may be the result of either incorrect delivery of a service or customers inappropriately perceiving the service. Incorrect delivery is not unusual in many service organisations. Service operations are often complex, human-based activities and things do go wrong. A mismatch as a result of poor delivery can be removed or at least reduced through service recovery (see Chapter 12). In service organisations we need to remember that 'reality' is what the customers perceive it to be, and that customers will perceive each service in their own personal, emotional and some-

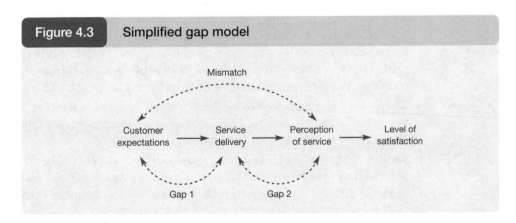

| Figure 4.3 | Simplified gap model |

times irrational way. Customers' perceptions of the quality of the service may not be the same as the quality of the service delivered, because humans tend to filter what they see and experience. They do this by:

- *Selective filtering*. Only noticing what is relevant to current needs.
- *Selective distortion*. Modifying and seeking information that supports personal beliefs and prejudices
- *Selective retention*. Remembering only those things that are relevant to needs and beliefs.

Ideally there should be a match between service quality (the quality of what the operation delivers) and the quality of the service as perceived by the customer. Table 4.1 summarises the reasons for the existence of the gaps and therefore dissatisfied customers.

Table 4.1 **Reasons for gaps**

	Gap 1	*Gap 2*
Internal causes	Lack of understanding of customer expectations Inappropriate specification Poor service design Insufficient resources	Incorrect delivery
External causes	Inappropriate expectations of the service experience and/or outcome	Inappropriate perceptions of the service experience and/or outcome

4.2.4 Downsides of the expectation–perception approach to service quality

While the expectation–perception approach to understanding service quality is extremely useful in focusing on the outcome of customer satisfaction and helps identify on mismatches between operational and customer views of quality, it does have some downsides (see, for example, Grönroos 1993):

- *Service could be perceived to be 'good' when it is 'bad'*. If customer expectations are particularly low (and indeed may have been deliberately created that way), poor service may be perceived as highly satisfying because expectations have been exceeded. This may look like a reasonable state, but is clearly one that makes for-profit organisations vulnerable to competitive threat from higher-quality providers, or may lead to government 'interference' in public sector organisations.
- *Service could be perceived to be 'bad' when it is 'good'*. Likewise, it is also possible that if expectations are high, due to over-promising, for example, then a good service may be seen as inadequate.
- *Service that was 'good' last time may only be 'OK' this time*. If a service was perceived to have been 'good' then the customers' expectations may be raised for next time; thus they may well be less satisfied on subsequent occasions, despite

the fact that the quality of the service has remained unchanged. This is a problem encountered by Disney. Visitors' first encounter with the Magic Kingdom is often so good, much better than expected, that subsequent visits are sometimes reported to be poorer in quality.

● *Satisfied customers may switch*. Even though a particular service may meet customers' expectations and customers are satisfied, customers may still switch suppliers, if there is a choice. Alternative service providers may offer a superior level of service, additional service features, or customers may be naturally disloyal or inquisitive. When it comes to measuring satisfaction, we need to remember to also measure the customers' post-purchase intentions; in particular, will they return? (Conversely, it is also important to remember that some dissatisfied customers will not switch and they may create particular problems for service employees!)

Nortel, the telecommunications company, surveyed its customers and discovered that those who scored up to 4 on a scale from 1 to 5 (1 = very dissatisfied, 5 = very satisfied) were vulnerable to switching. Only those scoring above 4.5 could be thought of as reasonably loyal. Avis Rent-a-Car tracks likelihood to repurchase alongside customer satisfaction. In the early 1990s it developed a 'customer satisfaction balance sheet', estimating the cost to the company in lost sales as a result of poor service.

These issues reinforce the need to link closely the creation of expectations in the minds of customers with the process that tries to deliver service, i.e. to communicate messages to set appropriate expectations and design and deliver service to meet them and manage them during the service process. We need to see the process of satisfaction formation as a dynamic process (this has been called quality dynamics – Ojasalo 1999).

4.2.5　Confidence

Before we spend time developing the notion of customer satisfaction through a better understanding of customer expectations and the formation of perceptions, we need to introduce the related but distinct notion of customer confidence.

Whereas satisfaction is an assessment by the customer following a service experience, confidence, or the lack of it, does not require previous contact with the organisation (Flanagan *et al.* 2004). This is an important notion for all organisations, and especially those with which people may have no or little contact, for example, social services, police, fire services, coroners' courts, hospitals, local schools and legal services.

Confidence is about having belief, trust or faith in an organisation, its staff and services. Our feeling of confidence in organisations such as the police will not only affect our feeling of well-being and our quality of life but importantly it may well influence how we interact with that organisation, i.e. our predisposition towards it. If we feel confident in the local police service, for example, we may, when caught for a minor offence, be more willing to co-operate with the police. Furthermore, if we feel confident in the police we may be more willing to provide assistance as a witness at an incident, or provide information about suspicious events, or even support officers attending incidents (or at least not making their jobs more difficult). All of which helps to improve the performance of the police service itself. Confidence may also affect our willingness to fund the police through local taxation.

For some organisations, understanding and measuring customer confidence may be more appropriate than customer satisfaction. Indeed some people might argue that customer satisfaction is a wholly inappropriate measure to be applied to some of the police service's customers (i.e. criminals).

Research by Flanagan *et al.* (2004) has shown that for post-purchase experience, the same factors that influence satisfaction affect confidence; however, pre-purchase confidence is influenced primarily by three things over which the organisation may have very limited control or influence:

- *Personal beliefs*. Beliefs held by the individual about that organisation.
- *Media*. For example television (news or even drama) coverage of the organisation.
- *Word-of-mouth*. The communicated experiences of others.

And three things that organisations have control and influence over:

- *Visibility*. Visibility of the organisation, its services and its employees.
- *Familiarity*. Familiarity with the organisation's employees, services or abilities.
- *Communication*. Knowledge of the service and its abilities.

By managing these factors, organisations can have an important impact on their potential customers and the efficiency and effectiveness of the service they deliver.

4.3 Customer expectations

Organisations need to understand expectations and, if appropriate, manage those expectations. Indeed it may be appropriate to try to rein-in customers' expectations in order to keep them at the right level that can be met or just exceeded by service delivery. This is a key challenge for service operations managers.

4.3.1 Levels of expectations

Expectations exist somewhere on a range or continuum, between ideal and intolerable (see Figure 4.4). An intolerable train journey may be one that arrives very late, or even not at all, where the carriages are filthy and the staff abusive. An ideal train journey might be clean, on time, very fast, and include chauffeur-driven transport at either end. The positioning of our expectations, i.e. what we believe to be likely, will vary depending upon which country we are in and the price we are paying, for example.

Some points on this continuum could be defined as follows (see, for example, Zeithaml *et al.* 1993):

- *Ideal*. The best possible.
- *Ideal feasible*. What should happen given the price or the industry standard.

| Figure 4.4 | Range of expectations |

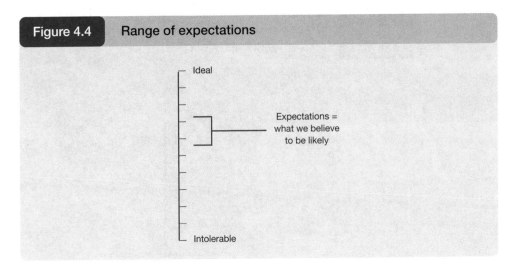

- *Desirable*. The standard that the customer wants to receive.
- *Deserved*. The level of performance that the customer ought to receive, given the perceived costs.
- *Minimum tolerable*. The minimum tolerable standards – those that must be achieved.
- *Intolerable*. The standards the customers should not receive.

It has been suggested that our expectations are not a single point on this scale but a range (see Figure 4.4) between what customers believe to be likely ('will' happen or predictive expectations) and what they believe 'should' happen (ideal feasible or normative expectations). Customers will also be able to differentiate between a 'should' expectation that may be formed as a result of little or no actual experience, and a 'will' expectation based on experience with the service.

The critical point here is that we should be careful when asking customers about their expectations. The following questions, for example, would each provoke a different response as they refer to different points on the scale:

- What would you like?
- What should be provided?
- What would be acceptable?

This range or zone of expectations, as shown in Figure 4.4, is usually referred to as the zone of tolerance (Zeithaml *et al.* 1993). This zone of 'acceptable outcomes' is shown in Figure 4.5.

The importance of this zone of tolerance is that customers may accept variation within a range of performance and any increase or decrease in performance within this area will only have a marginal effect on perceptions (Strandvik 1994). Only when performance moves outside of this range will it have any real effect on perceived service quality.

It has been suggested that the width of this zone of tolerance is inversely proportional to a customer's level of involvement and commitment (Johnston 1995a).

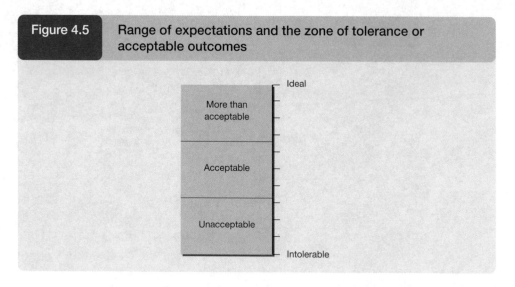

Figure 4.5 Range of expectations and the zone of tolerance or acceptable outcomes

This involvement refers to a customer's level of interest in a service, the importance they attach to it, and their emotional commitment to the service (see, for example, Dibb *et al.* 1997). For example, participants who have been sent on a training course, possibly against their will, may become hypercritical of details of training materials and course content because they have no real commitment to the objectives of the programme. Mature students, on the other hand, who are probably paying for a postgraduate business qualification, may be more supportive. This does not mean that they will necessarily accept poor quality, but the process by which they raise the issues and seek for a joint solution will often be quite positive. The fact that they have personally invested time and money in the course certainly changes their commitment to it and its success.

4.3.2 Fuzzy expectations

In some instances customers' expectations may be somewhat unclear and they may not be certain what they expect from a service provider, although they may have quite clear views about what is unacceptable. This vague idea about what is required has been called 'fuzzy' expectations (Ojasalo 1999). Ojasalo suggested that expectations, as a whole, are seldom fuzzy but 'that they usually include elements which are more or less fuzzy'. In some cases these expectations may be implicit and are not actively or consciously thought about by customers, but they may become explicit when expectations are either not met or exceeded.

Whether customer's expectations are fuzzy or crystal clear, operations managers have to be certain about the expectations they are trying to meet. They need to understand them, define them and then specify them to ensure that what they deliver meets that specification (this is what operations managers mean by service quality). In many cases this will require providing guidance to customer-facing staff to encourage them to ask questions to clarify the real needs of the customer, rather than to assume that what they are being asked for is actually what is required. Customers are often afraid of looking silly in front of other people (both customers and staff), and may ask for something quite inappropriate, leading to eventual dissatisfaction and defection.

In effect, service operations managers need to revisit the service concept (Chapter 2) to identify possible gaps between what is in the mind of the customer and what is in the mind of the service provider.

4.3.3 Influencing expectations

Customers' expectations will be influenced by many things (see Figure 4.6).

- *Price* often has a large influence on expectations. The higher the price, the higher up the continuum towards ideal are customers' expectations. Expectations of a customer flying tourist class from Paris to Chicago will be at a different level to customers flying business or first class. All three customers will have similar expectations about safety and timeliness, but expectations about legroom, quality of food, attentiveness of the service and ease of check-in may vary considerably. Price is perhaps one of the most important influences as customers are concerned not just about the service (outcome and experience) but also its value (see Chapter 2).

- *Alternative services available* will also help define and set expectations. If you have recently flown business class and the cabin attendants called you by name, you may expect this level of treatment on flights by other carriers.

- *Marketing* can have a considerable influence on expectations. Marketing, image, branding and advertising campaigns help set expectations, often at great cost to the organisation.

- *Word-of-mouth* marketing, which is less controllable, can have a profound effect on a customer's expectations. Indeed, in some situations, word-of-mouth may have a stronger influence than organisational marketing.

- *Previous experience* will help shape expectations, as prior knowledge makes them not only clearer and sharper but allows customers more accurately to position them on the scale. Previous experience also acts as a moderator on

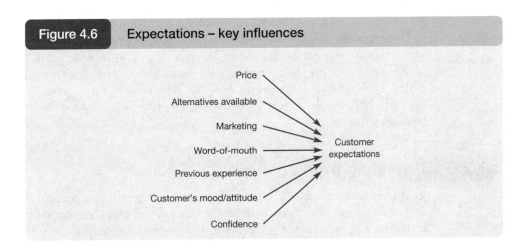

Figure 4.6 Expectations – key influences

marketing information either from the organisation or word-of-mouth. It is important to note that previous experience may not be of the service provider in question but other service providers. Our expectations for how we will be treated when we ring up our electricity supplier with a query will be influenced by our experiences with other call centres, such as utilities, retailers and financial services. This aspect is often forgotten by service organisations that continue to think that because they are as good as any other organisation in their sector, this is good enough. This is clearly not true.

- *Customers' mood and attitude* can affect their expectations. Someone in a bad mood or with a poor attitude to an organisation may have heightened expectations; someone less concerned and more tolerant may have a wider zone of tolerance and thus a wider range of expectations.

- *Confidence* about an organisation, even before we have used an organisation, will also influence our expectations. If we have confidence in our child's new school because of its reputation, for example, we may have a higher set of expectations as to how we and our child will be treated.

Expectations are dynamic. They are not fixed at a single point on a continuum between intolerable to ideal, and will change over time and indeed during the service itself. Customers are continually experiencing many service situations and consuming services. Their expectations are under continual review and change. What an organisation may have defined as adequate last month may be inadequate this month. As more and more organisations dealing with customer complaints, for example, try to resolve them by phone rather than letter, customers will start to expect similar treatment, whatever the industry

4.3.4   Expectations of a service never used

Because our expectations can be based on what we believe 'should' happen, we therefore do not need to have experienced a service to have expectations about it. People who have not experienced a funeral may have some clear expectations about the nature, mood and style of the event, and more fuzzy expectations about the actual series of events. These may be quite clear and explicit if they have, for example, witnessed such events, second-hand, on television or in novels, for example.

The problem for service operation managers is in trying to meet these unseen and unknown expectations, whose formation is to some extent out of the control of the organisation. The key tasks for operation managers are to know how to define expectations (section 4.4), how to discover what customers' expectations are (section 4.5) and then how to manage customers' perceptions during the process (section 4.6).

4.3.5   Providing service cues

Customer expectations are shaped from an early point in their contact with a service organisation. The careful use of service cues will allow the operation manager to influence expectations. For example, the customer entering a restaurant sees the way that it is set out and will draw conclusions about the level of service provided. If the tables and chairs are functional and there are no tablecloths or decorations, customers will be prepared to expect simpler service than one with comfortable seats, tablecloths and ornate decorations.

4.4 Defining expectations – service quality factors

A great deal of work has been carried out recently to help organisations understand the component parts of expectations. This allows them to operationalise expectations to design and deliver appropriate levels of quality, and also helps them to create instruments to measure customer satisfaction.

The service quality factors are those attributes of service about which customers may have expectations and which need to be delivered at some specified level. Several sets of factors have been identified (see, for example, Grönroos 1984, Parasuraman *et al.* 1985, Gremler, Bitner and Evans 1994 and Reynoso 1995).

Figure 4.7 provides 18 quality factors (Johnston 1995b and Silvestro and Johnston 1990) which try to capture the totality of service quality. These 18 may be consolidated into broader dimensions (see, for example, Parasuraman *et al.* 1985) and indeed may not capture every aspect of service quality for every organisation. However, are at least a starting point to help us define, deliver and measure service quality.

These factors have been defined as follows:

- *Access*. The physical approachability of the service location, including the ease of finding one's way around the service environment and clarity of route.

- *Aesthetics*. The extent to which the components of the service package are agreeable or pleasing to the customer, including both the appearance and the ambience of the service environment, the appearance and presentation of service facilities, goods and staff.

Figure 4.7	Service quality and its factors

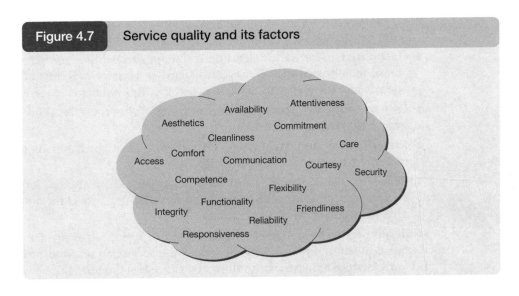

- *Attentiveness/helpfulness*. The extent to which the service, particularly contact staff, either provide help to the customer or give the impression of being interested in the customer and show a willingness to serve.

- *Availability*. The availability of service facilities, staff and goods to the customer. In the case of contact staff this means both the staff/customer ratio and the amount of time each staff member has available to spend with each customer. In the case of service goods availability includes both the quantity and range of products made available to the customer.

- *Care*. The concern, consideration, sympathy and patience shown to the customer. This includes the extent to which the customer is put at ease by the service and made to feel emotionally (rather than physically) comfortable.

- *Cleanliness/tidiness*. The cleanliness, neat and tidy appearance of the tangible components of the service package, including the service environment, facilities, goods and contact staff.

- *Comfort*. The physical comfort of the service environment and facilities.

- *Commitment*. The staff's apparent commitment to their work, including the pride and satisfaction they apparently take in their job, their diligence and thoroughness.

- *Communication*. The ability of the service to communicate with customers in a way they will understand. This includes the clarity, completeness and accuracy of both verbal and written information communicated to the customer and the ability to listen to and understand the customer.

- *Competence*. The skill, expertise and professionalism with which the service is executed. This includes the carrying out of correct procedures, correct execution of customer instructions, the degree of product or service knowledge exhibited by contact staff, the rendering of good, sound advice and the general ability to do a good job.

- *Courtesy*. The politeness, respect and propriety shown by the service, usually contact staff, in dealing with customers and their property. This includes the ability of staff to be unobtrusive and uninterfering when appropriate.

- *Flexibility*. A willingness on the part of the service worker to amend or alter the nature of the service or product to meet the needs of the customer.

- *Friendliness*. The warmth and personal approachability (rather than physical approachability) of the service, particularly of contact staff, including a cheerful attitude and the ability to make the customer feel welcome.

- *Functionality*. The serviceability and fitness for purpose or 'product quality' of service facilities and goods.

- *Integrity*. The honesty, justice, fairness and trustworthiness with which customers are treated by the service organisation.

- *Reliability*. The reliability and consistency of performance of service facilities, goods and staff. This includes punctual service delivery and the ability to keep to agreements made with the customer.

- *Responsiveness*. The speed and timeliness of service delivery. This includes the speed of throughput and the ability of the service to respond promptly to customer service requests, with minimal waiting and queuing time.

- *Security*. The personal safety of customers and their possessions while participating in or benefiting from the service process. This includes the maintenance of confidentiality.

These factors cover many aspects of a service, which we defined in Chapter 1, including:

- *Inputs*. For example, staff availability, friendliness, responsiveness, appearance, courtesy, competence and communication skills; the appearance, aesthetics, accessibility and comfort of the facilities; the functionality and reliability of the technology.

- *The service process/service experience*. For example, its reliability, friendliness and feeling of security.

- *Outcomes*. For example, the functionality and reliability of the outcome of the service.

4.4.1   Hygiene and enhancing factors

Although they will vary from organisation to organisation and also from customer to customer, the service quality factors can be divided into four groups. These groupings are defined in terms of a factor's ability to dissatisfy and delight: see Figure 4.8 (see, for example, Johnston 1995b, Silvestro and Johnston 1990).

- *Hygiene factors* are those that need to be in place: if they are they will satisfy, if not they will be a source of dissatisfaction. They are not likely to be a source of delight. For a bank, security, integrity and functionality, for example, are expected to be acceptable; if they are not acceptable they will dissatisfy. On the other hand, if these factors are over-specified they will not delight. A very large number of security checks will not delight customers; indeed they could dissatisfy them. Having all cash machines in perfect working order all of the time will not delight them either.

Figure 4.8	Delighting and dissatisfying factors

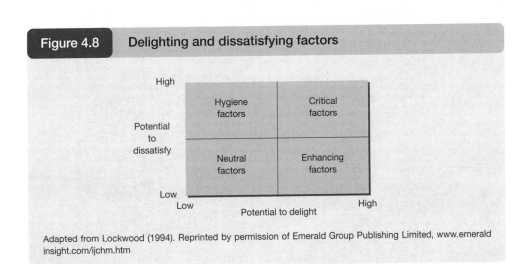

Adapted from Lockwood (1994). Reprinted by permission of Emerald Group Publishing Limited, www.emerald insight.com/ijchm.htm

- *Enhancing factors* have the potential to delight if they are present, but if they are not there they are not likely to dissatisfy the customer. Customers of a bank may be delighted with a warm caring approach by a member of staff or their flexibility in dealing with a problem; however, these things are not necessarily expected so, if they are not provided, their absence may not lead to dissatisfaction.
- *Critical factors* have the potential to both delight and dissatisfy. Responsiveness, communication and competence of bank staff and systems must be at least acceptable so as not to dissatisfy the customer, but if more than acceptable they have the potential to delight.
- *Neutral factors* have little effect on satisfaction. The comfort or aesthetics of a banking hall may play no part in customers' satisfaction or dissatisfaction (see Figure 4.9).

We believe that managers should not only be aware of the expectations of their customers but should also realise the importance and potential effect of the various factors. We need to know which factors will delight and which will dissatisfy in order to manage the creation of satisfaction during the service process (see section 4.6). How we can find these factors and identify the enhancers, hygienes and criticals is explained in the next section, 4.5.

While factors do not always neatly fall into one category or another, Figure 4.10 shows the relative frequency of mentions made of the factors in a study of UK banks (Johnston 1995b). What is striking is that the factors with the tendency to dissatisfy (hygienes and criticals) are systemic and concern the organisation's ability to deliver its core services: functionality, reliability, competence etc., whereas the factors with a tendency to delight tend to be the more interpersonal factors, such as attentiveness, friendliness, courtesy etc.

Care should be exercised in trying to identify neutral factors: in the research cited above the fact that few people mentioned security does not mean it is a neutral factor. It simply indicates that there were no instances of security having been the source of dissatisfaction or delight.

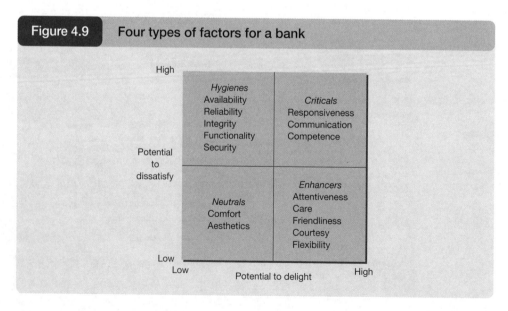

Figure 4.9   Four types of factors for a bank

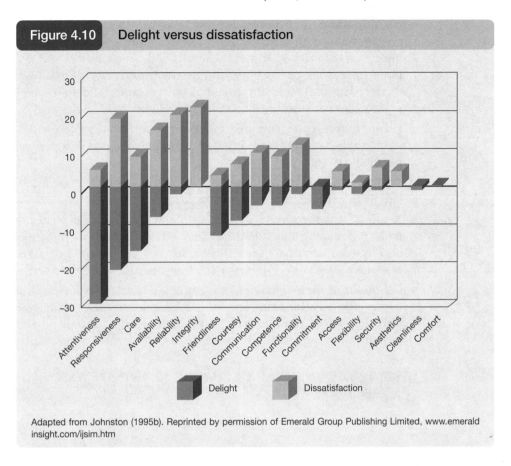

Figure 4.10 Delight versus dissatisfaction

Adapted from Johnston (1995b). Reprinted by permission of Emerald Group Publishing Limited, www.emerald insight.com/ijsim.htm

4.5 Finding expectations and assessing satisfaction

The 18 quality factors provide a base to help us understand and define customer expectations (whether internal or external), define appropriate levels, i.e. create the internal quality specification, and also measure customer satisfaction.

There are many different methods available to gather information (see Berry and Parasuraman 1997 for an evaluation). The methods broadly divide into those that are primarily used for understanding how customers are satisfied and those that are primarily used for assessing satisfaction.

4.5.1 Understanding how customers are satisfied

The first approach, which uses questionnaires and surveys, is the most quantitative approach and can be structured around all or some of the 18 quality factors and analysed by each factor. The other, more qualitative, approaches tend to collect descriptive data and provide the interpretation of events by customers in their own words. This creates more difficulties in analysis and interpretation in order to extract meaningful summaries. They do, however, have the benefit of providing ideas and examples that managers and employees can use and discuss to understand and improve their services.

- *Questionnaires and surveys*, written or verbal, can be a good means of soliciting opinions about an organisation's services and to identify what customers find important. Figure 4.11 shows the results of a questionnaire asking customers of a hotel (mid-week guests only) to rate the importance of various aspects of the service. The staff were also asked to do the same. There are several interesting mismatches between the views of staff and guests.

- *Focus groups* usually comprise groups of about 15 customers with a trained facilitator, brought together to discuss one or a few aspects of a particular existing or planned service.

- *Customer advisory panels* are similar to focus groups but are likely to meet regularly with a more structured agenda.

- *New/lost customer surveys* are very useful ways of finding out what attracts customers to the organisation and indeed why they left. While many organisations are now conducting exit interviews, the most successful rely heavily upon the direct involvement of senior managers to ensure appropriate access, information and action.

- *Complaint/compliment analysis* can be undertaken upon customers' voluntary contributions, although they tend to be more negative than positive. They do provide information about the extremes of delight and dissatisfaction. Box 4.2 explains how Singapore Airlines makes use of its complaints and compliments.

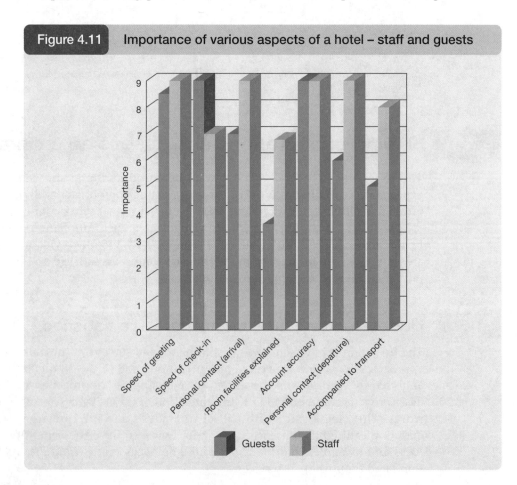

Figure 4.11   Importance of various aspects of a hotel – staff and guests

- *Critical incident technique* (CIT) attempts to identify the things that delight and dissatisfy customers. Critical incidents are events that contribute to, or detract from, perceived service or product performance in a significant way. The CIT instrument usually comprises two questions. The first question asks customers to think of a time when they felt very pleased and satisfied with the service/product received and to describe, in a few sentences, the situation and why they felt so happy. The second question requires customers to think of a time when they were unhappy and dissatisfied with the service/product they received and to describe, in a few sentences, why they felt this way.

- *Sequential incident analysis* combines CIT, walk-through audits and process mapping (see Chapter 6) (Stauss 1993). Customers are 'walked through' a pre-prepared process map of the service they have recently encountered and asked for their experiences of each stage or transaction in the process. This technique not only identifies critical situations but also potentially critical ones.

Singapore Airlines (SIA)　　　　Box 4.2

SIA employs varied and systematic methods to obtain information from its passengers, including quarterly passenger surveys and focused group work with its frequent flyers. The company also uses its magazine for frequent flyers, to ask for passengers' reactions to proposed new ideas. It also checks out the service for itself by conducting on-site audits with test calls to reservations, for example, to see how service is being delivered. Also when any members of staff fly in its aircraft they are asked to submit reports of their travel experiences. Senior staff members must submit a comment sheet on each flight with their expense account. SIA staff also monitor their competitors and often go and check out their services.

SIA takes both compliments and complaints seriously, indeed there is a vice-president with responsibility for complaints and compliments. Every letter has to be acknowledged, investigated and followed up, even letters of compliment. Lam Seet Mui, the senior manager for human resource development, explains:

We investigate all complaints. Then not only do we try to recover the customer or the situation, we will also use it as a learning lesson. If we don't learn something from a complaint then we've failed. We also take compliments seriously. Not only do we disseminate them so that people can share in the success, but we try to learn things from them too. They can help us understand what we need to do to excel.

Sim Kay Wee, the senior vice-president responsible for cabin crew added:

We do try to deal with problems at the time they arise. If a problem occurs on board the crew will try to recover immediately. Any follow-up or written complaint is overseen by the customer affairs department. However we do the investigation, we find out precisely what happened and report to them. We try to do it personally and quickly.

SIA also produces newsletters for particular groups of staff. *Highpoint*, for example, is aimed keeping its 8,000 in-flight personnel informed about the airline's latest offerings and its commitments to passengers. The newsletter has a regular feature page with about eight or nine extracts from letters – half compliments and half complaints. An example of each follows.

An example compliment:

I noticed the service, although in economy class, was professional and better than any flights I have ever been on. Miss Iris lee was the most hardworking amongst all the crew. She came round distributing newspapers, drinks, postcards, playing cards, amenities etc. As a director of travel and tours, I fly often and I have never come across such an outstanding cabin hostess ... She loves to fly and it shows.

An example complaint:

We were sitting close by the galleys and were able to observe the cabin crew at work throughout the flight, and the impression we gained was that they were unable to cope with a full load of passengers. There seemed also to be a lack of leadership and organisation – the cabin crew were rushing back and forth getting in each other's way – not the smooth activity which we have come to expect from Singapore Airlines.

Higher Ground is a bi-monthly newsletter aimed at the ground services staff, including ticketing, reservations and check-in, as well as baggage handling, logistics and transportation. *Higher Ground* also contains extracts from letters, usually two complaints and one compliment.

Example compliment:

I would like to pen a note of appreciation for the extra help your staff gave my aged parents when they took your SQ860 from Singapore to Hong Kong. They were told at the check-in counter to come back to see your staff. My brother accordingly brought them to the counter near the check-in time. Then one of your staff very kindly brought them into the restricted area, through immigration and right to the departure room. This was of great help to them as they do not understand the signs in English and may have had to look around or ask around for the direction to the departure room. Walking extra would also be troublesome for my mother who is recovering from a stroke. Thank you once again to your staff for going out of their way to assist my parents. I am indeed proud of our national airline.

An example complaint:

On 26 July we flew Singapore Airlines. Prior to the arrangement being made and also a few days before the actual flight, I reiterated the comment that my mother would require a wheelchair for both embarkation and disembarkation ... She had travelled last year by Singapore Airlines and had no trouble whatsoever. At [embarkation] a wheelchair was provided and we boarded the plane with no problems . . . On arrival ... we were not docked at a bridge, but parked in the middle of the airfield. I was then asked if my mother could manage to get down two external steep flights of stairs and to walk to a bus that would then take her to the terminal. As she had come on by wheelchair I would have thought it was patently obvious that this was totally impossible for her. We were told that it was our fault that [the airport] had not been informed. I explained that I had done as much as I could in informing [the station at departure], and they certainly knew she required a wheelchair to get on the plane and therefore, obviously, to get off the plane. It took an hour to get some means of transport to take her off the plane and into the airport terminal.

Questions

1 Evaluate the methods used by SIA to understand customer expectations and assess satisfaction.

2 What is the purpose of providing both complaints and compliments?

This illustration is based on a case study written by Robert Johnston, Warwick Business School, and Jochen Wirtz, National University of Singapore, 2004. The case was commissioned by the Institute of Customer Service as part of a study into service excellence. The authors gratefully acknowledge the sponsorship provided by Britannic Assurance, FirstGroup, Lloyds TSB, RAC Motoring Services and Vodafone. The authors would like to thank the interviewees for their participation in this project and also Jasmine Ow, National University of Singapore, for her valuable assistance.

4.5.2 Assessing satisfaction

Satisfaction can be assessed using some of the more qualitative approaches above, but is usually assessed in a more structured way, either using questionnaires and surveys or mystery shoppers.

- *Questionnaires and surveys* can be constructed using the 18 quality factors, or those that customers identified as being important in focus groups etc. One of the best-known instruments for assessing service quality is SERVQUAL, developed and refined by Parasuraman *et al.* (1988, 1991 and 1994). SERVQUAL is a concise multiple-item scale questionnaire that organisations can use to assess their customers' expectations and perceptions of their service and obtain a single figure for tracking and comparison. The instrument itself is a skeleton questionnaire that asks questions of customers about their expectations and perceptions of the services of a particular company. It uses five consolidated quality factors or dimensions (assurance, empathy, reliability, responsiveness, tangibles) with 22 items for perceptions and 22 for expectations, using a seven-point Likert scale. A perception gap score is then calculated for each pair of statements (expectations and perceptions), the difference being the SERVQUAL score. Different questions relate to the different dimensions, which can then be aggregated and averaged to identify perception gaps for each dimension. The scores can also be weighted by getting customers to add weights to each dimension. Repeated administration allows an understanding as to how customers' perceived service quality with each of the dimensions is changing over time (for detailed information see Zeithaml *et al.* 1990).

- *Mystery shoppers* are used by several organisations, in particular retailers, to assess the service that their customers experience. The mystery shoppers can be managers acting incognito but are usually provided by external agencies and work to an agreed script or scoring system. The problems encountered using this method include whether the expectations implied within the structure are appropriate, since they have been created by managers based on their understanding of what they think customers expect. A particular problem with mystery shoppers is that they are prone to becoming too 'professional' in their analysis. In other words, because they have become sensitised to service quality, they may highlight details that are largely irrelevant to the average consumer.

4.5.3 Problems with assessing customer satisfaction

Collecting information about customer satisfaction is something that many organisations now do. However, all too often there are either problems with the instrument and/or problems in the use of the data (see, for example, Piercy 1995).

Problems with the instrument

There are several common problems with customer satisfaction instruments:

- *Changing questions*. One of the most important benefits of collecting satisfaction data is to track trends over time. However, frequently changing the questions undermines this benefit.

- *Too many questions*. There is often a tendency by researchers and market analysts to ask every conceivable question. While it might be helpful to know about every aspect of the service, long questionnaires usually result in poor returns.

- *Missing the point*. The reason for measuring satisfaction is often to find out the impact of customer satisfaction, yet this is often missed out of satisfaction instruments; for example, will customers return, will they provide positive word-of-mouth?

- *Qualitative versus quantitative*. While a survey may be able to tell you that a service has scored 4.2, it will not help you understand what to change or how to change it. Likewise, focus groups may give you some ideas about what to do, but it will not be possible to assess the changes without quantitative data. There needs to be a combination of both qualitative and quantitative assessment of customer satisfaction.

- *Survey-weary customers*. Since so many organisations wish to know about our satisfaction, we often feel disinclined to complete them, especially if we have no confidence that the organisation will make the changes suggested or deal with the issues identified.

- *Analysis fodder*. In cases where respondents are not asked for any personal views but have to provide a large amount of data about an organisation and its services, customers feel that they are just being used to feed a data engine, either to keep analysts busy or help the organisation justify doing whatsoever it wishes.

Problems in the use of the data

- *Resource hungry*. Many organisations consume large amounts of resource in collecting, coding, analysing satisfaction data, and writing reports with lots of graphs and tables.

- *Little or no impact*. Far too many customer-satisfaction measurement exercises have little or no impact on the organisation or its performance.

- *Satisfaction versus success*. High satisfaction scores do not necessarily lead to organisational success. Just because customers say they are very satisfied does not mean that they are valuable customers, by, for example, providing a profitable revenue stream, or support for the organisation or frequently using the organisation. Indeed, 60–80 per cent of defectors claim they were satisfied before they defected.

- *Open to manipulation*. When organisations link the satisfaction measures to employee reward systems, people may manipulate the system to ensure a beneficial result.

In sum, a lot of customer satisfaction assessment is a waste of time and effort; it drives no discernable improvement, consumes valuable organisational resources and wastes customers' time. There are, however, some exceptions. In Chapter 2 we provided an illustration (Box 2.3) describing the work of the RAC. In Box 4.3 we describe how it goes about measuring customer satisfaction and what it does with the data.

RAC – Customer satisfaction is king | Box 4.3

Nigel Paget, the RAC's operations director, explains the importance of measuring customer satisfaction:

Customer satisfaction is absolutely the king here. Each patrol hands out a customer satisfaction card at the end of every breakdown and every month the patrols get their customer satisfaction index (CSI) for the customers they have dealt with. We not only measure the patrols' satisfaction rating but we also measure their personal response rate as a means of ensuring that they hand out the forms. We also measure all the other things that are important to our customers, such as technical ability, their fix rate and also if they solved the problem. For example, if they can't actually fix the fault, did they solve the problem for the customer, such as take the car to the dealer up the road? We want the patrol to take responsibility and go the extra distance to sort out the problem. Again it is all benchmarked and they receive a bonus for excellent performance.

Around 40,000 customer satisfaction cards are returned a month – that's about 400–500 per person. We know exactly what the customers the patrols served in the previous month actually thought of them. We compare this to their previous performance and to an aggregate score for everyone. We reward people as a result, and so if you are average you get your salary. If you perform above average, you get rewarded on top of that. So the incentive is to be better. Around 15–20 per cent

will get the top bonus, which equates to about 10 per cent of salary, but it's on a sliding scale.

Despite the central importance of customer satisfaction and the pressure on an individual's performance, the measurement of satisfaction is seen as a positive that is valued by staff. Managers recognise that sometimes there are customers who do not necessarily answer the questions with integrity, and that sometimes not every interaction with a customer is going to be perfect because someone is a trainee or is just having a bad day. So an individual's measures are compared not only with their previous performance but also with the average performance for everyone else. Nigel added:

They understand that one bad customer report out of 400 in a month is not going to have a disproportionate affect, but 30 or 40 out of 400 will. I find it hugely encouraging that when I sit down with people they will just ask me if I have any ideas as to how they might improve their CSI because they simply want to do better.

Question

1 Assess the advantages and disadvantages of the RAC's collection and use of satisfaction data.

This illustration is an extract of a case commissioned by the Institute of Customer Service as part of a study into service excellence. The author gratefully acknowledges the sponsorship provided by Britannic Assurance, FirstGroup, Lloyds TSB, RAC Motoring Services and Vodafone.

4.6 Managing perceptions

As we suggested earlier in this chapter, there should be a match between service quality (the quality of what the operation delivers) and the quality of the service as perceived by the customer. From an operation's view it can be all too easy to put aside customers' views or perceptions of the service and focus on operational service quality – i.e. delivery to the specification. We also suggested that managing quality should be a dynamic process and so here we show how perceptions can be managed during the process of service delivery.

4.6.1   Managing perceptions during the service process

Operations managers must become attuned to their customers and understand how perceptions of a service develop during the service process. Figure 4.12 combines Figures 4.2, 4.4 and 4.5 earlier (the levels of expectations and zone of tolerance, and the outcome of a service – the level of satisfaction and dissatisfaction), and looks at how expectations give way to a perception of satisfaction during the service process/experience (Johnston 1995a). The figure shows the zone of tolerance extending from expectations through the process to the outcome of satisfaction.

Figure 4.12 depicts something similar to a control chart, which managers can use first to identify customer expectations – what is acceptable, less than acceptable and more than acceptable (using approaches described earlier) – and then to assess during the service process/experience the impact of each stage or transaction in a single-service transaction or encounter or a series of service encounters. This helps managers understand how they can design their service to have the appropriate interventions at appropriate times to achieve the desired outcome – whether satisfaction or delight.

A number of suggestions have been made about the use of this model (Johnston 1995a). Take, for example, a patient with an appointment to see a doctor for a routine medical examination. We might consider there to be seven transactions here:

1 arrival at the clinic
2 reception
3 waiting for the doctor
4 introduction to the examination by the doctor
5 examination
6 discussion of findings
7 departure.

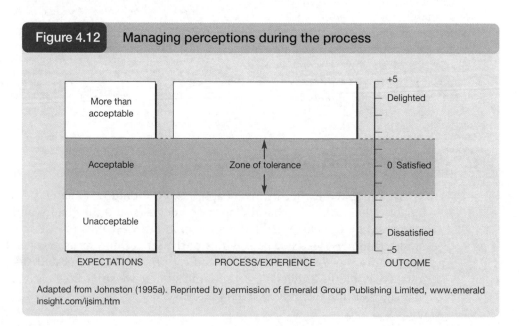

Figure 4.12   Managing perceptions during the process

Adapted from Johnston (1995a). Reprinted by permission of Emerald Group Publishing Limited, www.emerald insight.com/ijsim.htm

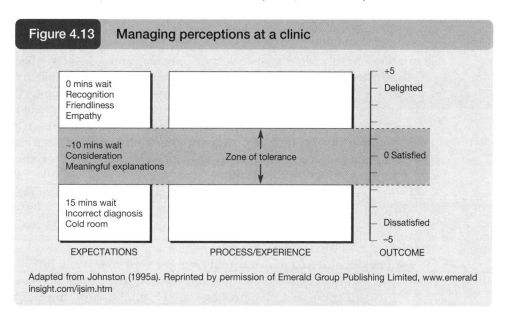

Figure 4.13 Managing perceptions at a clinic

Adapted from Johnston (1995a). Reprinted by permission of Emerald Group Publishing Limited, www.emerald insight.com/ijsim.htm

Expectations may have been managed by the medical practice through its code of conduct, for example, which informs patients that they should have to wait no longer than 10 minutes to see the doctor, that they will be treated with care and consideration, and that all medical facts will be explained to them in a meaningful way (see Figure 4.13).

A number of outcomes are possible

● Performance within the zone of tolerance results in satisfaction. Providing the customer's perceptions of the transactions are not greater or less than acceptable, the outcome will be a 'satisfied' customer with a 'score' somewhere within their outcome zone of tolerance (see Figure 4.14). It has been suggested that the quality of a performance within the customer's zone of tolerance may not be

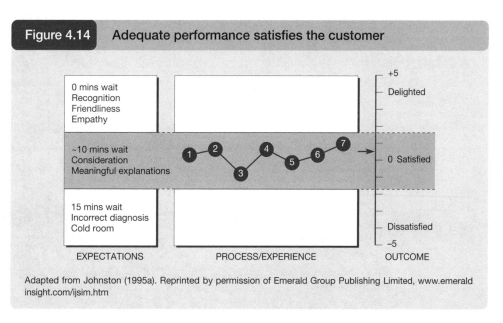

Figure 4.14 Adequate performance satisfies the customer

Adapted from Johnston (1995a). Reprinted by permission of Emerald Group Publishing Limited, www.emerald insight.com/ijsim.htm

consciously noticed, so for an organisation wishing to make an impact it will need to build-in positive (or maybe even negative) interventions.

● Sufficient incursions above the zone of tolerance threshold will result in a highly satisfying outcome (delight). By including one or more enhancing factors, the doctor's surgery may be able to delight the patient. For example, the receptionist greeting the patient by name and inviting them to take a seat and bringing them a coffee might be quite unexpected (at least on the first occasion) and delight the customer (see Figure 4.15). The outcome 'score' may not be a mean score, but delighting (and indeed dissatisfying) incidents may have the effect of skewing the resulting level of satisfaction.

● Sufficient incursions below the zone of tolerance threshold will result in a dissatisfying outcome. A delay of 12 minutes (a hygiene factor) may be forgiven, but this coupled with a brusque treatment and a cursory examination may well lead to dissatisfaction (see Figure 4.16).

● Some dissatisfying and satisfying transactions may be compensatory. Lack of spaces in the car park, resulting in a walk of 500 metres in the rain to the surgery, will count as a dissatisfying transaction, but a profuse apology from the receptionist coupled with particularly caring treatment by the doctor may compensate for the initial problems (see Figure 4.17).

● Several satisfying transactions will be needed to compensate for a single dissatisfying transaction. It could be that one dissatisfying transaction will require compensation by more than one delighting transaction (as above).

● A failure in one transaction may raise the dissatisfaction threshold. A dissatisfying experience may also have the effect of shifting the zone of tolerance upwards, and/or maybe reducing its width. For example, if patients have had to walk 500 metres in the rain their dissatisfaction with this transaction may be such as to negatively dispose them towards the rest of the service. This could mean that future transactions that might previously have been within their zone

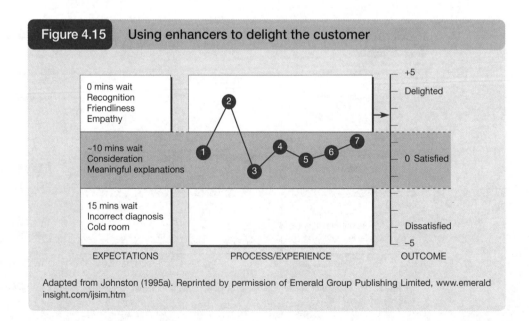

Figure 4.15   Using enhancers to delight the customer

Adapted from Johnston (1995a). Reprinted by permission of Emerald Group Publishing Limited, www.emerald insight.com/ijsim.htm

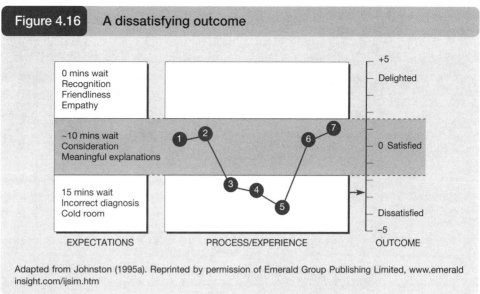

Figure 4.16   A dissatisfying outcome

Adapted from Johnston (1995a). Reprinted by permission of Emerald Group Publishing Limited, www.emerald insight.com/ijsim.htm

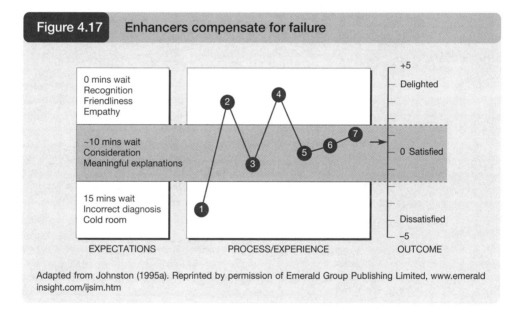

Figure 4.17   Enhancers compensate for failure

Adapted from Johnston (1995a). Reprinted by permission of Emerald Group Publishing Limited, www.emerald insight.com/ijsim.htm

of tolerance are now felt to be dissatisfying (see Figure 4.18). This shifting of the zone increases the likelihood of the outcome being a feeling of dissatisfaction.

● A delighting transaction may lower the zone of tolerance. Conversely an enhancing transaction may lower the zone of tolerance (and/or widen it) so that further transactions that might before have been within the acceptable range are now felt to be delighting. This has also been referred to as the 'halo effect' (Wirtz and Bateson 1995). Prompt treatment by the receptionist, a feeling of being expected and welcome, and all the forms ready to be signed, for example, may not only delight but positively dispose the patient to the rest of the service, increasing the likelihood of a delighting outcome (see Figure 4.19).

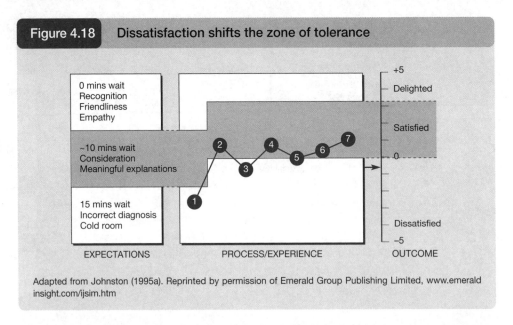

Figure 4.18   Dissatisfaction shifts the zone of tolerance

Adapted from Johnston (1995a). Reprinted by permission of Emerald Group Publishing Limited, www.emerald insight.com/ijsim.htm

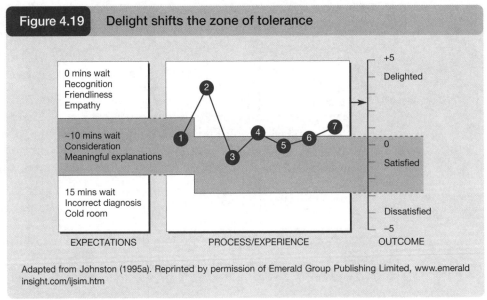

Figure 4.19   Delight shifts the zone of tolerance

Adapted from Johnston (1995a). Reprinted by permission of Emerald Group Publishing Limited, www.emerald insight.com/ijsim.htm

4.6.2   Design issues

It would seem sensible then for organisations wishing to satisfy the customer to ensure that there are no failures on hygiene factors throughout the process. Delighting transactions are unnecessary; the organisation is more likely to satisfy customers if their zone of tolerance can be made as wide as possible by appropriate marketing of the service.

For organisations seeking to delight their customers, a narrower zone of tolerance will increase the likelihood of delighting (and dissatisfying) the customer. Some delighting transactions are needed – ideally early in the process – to affect the level and possibly the width of the zone of tolerance. A delighting transaction at the end may also serve to put the icing on the cake. Although a delighting early transaction can have considerable impact, it has been shown that a build-up to a strong end of process results in higher perceived service quality (Hansen and Danaher 1999).

A final method of manipulating service perceptions is by making the intangible tangible.

Making the intangible tangible

In section 4.3.5 on expectations we explained how an organisation needs to ensure that early cues in the process/experience help set the right expectations for the service. Such cues can also be used to manipulate perceptions (see also Chapter 6). For example, the managers at the RAC (Box 4.3) recognise the importance of their patrols looking clean and tidy and having clean vans. Customers may associate these cues with professionalism and capability.

Such intangible factors are vital to many service experiences, and customer perceptions of them can be strengthened simply by trying to make them tangible at appropriate places in the service process/experience. The toilet paper folded into a point in the hotel bathroom is a tangible representation of less tangible cleanliness and care. A management consultant's cufflinks/jewellery or well-cut suit/dress and expensive car are tangible representations of reliability and professionalism.

4.6.3 Transaction satisfaction versus overall satisfaction

The above discussion has implied two levels of satisfaction: satisfaction with a single transaction during a service, and an overall, cumulative, satisfaction based on all the transactions. The question remains, how exactly do transaction satisfactions develop into an overall satisfaction with the service experience and outcome? There are two key approaches: a rational and an incident-based approach.

- *The rational approach*. The rational approach would suggest that customers consciously or unconsciously use a weighted average, so that a high score on one attribute or factor may offset a low score on another (Sasser *et al.* 1978) to arrive at a rational evaluation of the quality of a service. Indeed many satisfaction surveys, such as SERVQUAL, are based on the assumption that a reasonable way of calculating overall satisfaction is by allocating weights to the various factors of transactions (according to importance as perceived by the customer), multiplying the weight by the score (on a 1–5 scale for example) for each factor, and then cumulating them into an overall satisfaction rating.

- *The incident approach*. An alternative view is that customers are less rational and react more to individual incidents, as suggested in the above section. So any single incident – delighting or dissatisfying – could, despite the remaining adequate and satisfying transaction, result in a feeling of overall dissatisfaction or delight. Sasser *et al.* (1978) suggested that either a single factor would determine the outcome, all others receiving nominal or no consideration; or one attribute would determine the outcome, but certain attributes must achieve at least a minimum acceptable level.

The reality is likely to be some combination of these approaches, which means it is important to take care when constructing algorithms to assess customers' overall satisfaction with a service. It is certainly a mistake to assume that customers can identify with precision the reasons why they are satisfied or dissatisfied with a service. For example, on a training programme participants complained about the standard of the accommodation. It was only in discussion with the group that it emerged that the underlying dissatisfaction was with one of the presenters and that the accommodation, if not wonderful, was in fact satisfactory.

4.7 Summary

Customer satisfaction and service quality

- Satisfaction is the result of a customer's assessment of a service, based on a comparison of their perceptions of service delivery with their prior expectations.
- Service quality from an operation's perspective is about consistently meeting the service specification for that service.
- Excellent service entails delivering the promise and dealing well with problems and queries.
- There may be gaps between expectations, perceptions and service quality delivered.

Customer expectations

- Expectations exist somewhere on a range or continuum, between ideal and intolerable. Care needs to be taken when asking questions about expectations.
- Customers may accept variation within a range of performance, and any increase or decrease in performance within the zone of tolerance area will only have a marginal effect on perceptions.
- Many factors, including price, will affect an individual's level of expectations.

Defining expectations – service quality factors

- The service quality factors are those attributes of service about which customers may have expectations and which need to be delivered at some specified level.
- Neutral factors have little effect on satisfaction; hygiene factors will dissatisfy but not delight; enhancing factors will dissatisfy but may delight; and critical factors both dissatisfy and delight.

Finding expectations and assessing satisfaction

- There are many different methods for understanding how customers are satisfied and for assessing satisfaction.
- All too often there are problems with the instrument and/or problems in the use of the data.

Managing perceptions during service delivery

- A key role for operations is to manage customers' perceptions during the service process.

4.8 Discussion questions

1 What methods are most effective in identifying the influencers of customer satisfaction, given that some aspects of service may be unconsciously experienced by customers?

2 For a high-volume/low-variety service (business-to-consumer) and for a low-volume/high-variety service (business-to-business or professional service) identify potential gaps between customer expectation and customer perception of service delivery. What strategies would you suggest these organisations utilise to close these gaps?

3 Collect a few customer survey forms and evaluate them.

4.9 Questions for managers

1 When was the last time your organisation carried out a detailed study of customer satisfaction? Assess the methods used and the impact of the exercise.

2 Who compiled your customer satisfaction survey questionnaire? Have you checked with customers as to how relevant it is, or do you assume you know what customers want?

3 What are the reasons for gaps between customer perception of service delivery and customer expectation? How can they be closed?

4 Do you understand the zone of tolerance for your service delivery? Are customer expectations sometimes fuzzy? What guidance and/or resource is required to clarify these expectations?

5 What is the most effective method of assessing customer satisfaction? How widely have you communicated the findings of customer research?

4.10 Further reading

Johnston R., 'Towards a better understanding of service excellence', *Managing Service Quality*, vol. 14, no. 2/3, 2004, pp. 129–33.

Heracleous L., Wirtz J. and Johnston R., 'Cost effective service excellence – lessons from Singapore Airlines', *Business Strategy Review*, vol. 15, no. 1, 2004, pp. 33–8.

Olsen L.L. and Johnson M.D., 'Service equity, satisfaction, and loyalty: from transaction-specific to cumulative evaluations', *Journal of Service Research*, vol. 5, no. 3, 2003, pp. 184–95.

Schneider B. and Bowen D.E., 'Understanding customer delight and outrage', *Sloan Management Review*, Fall 1999, pp. 35–45.

Zeithaml V.A. and Bitner M.J., *Services Marketing*, McGraw-Hill, New York, 1996, pp. 75–32.

4.11 References

Andreassen T.W., 'From disgust to delight: do customers hold a grudge?' *Journal of Service Research*, vol. 4, no. 1, 2001, pp. 39–50.

Berry L.L. and Parasuraman A., 'Listening to the customer – the concept of a service-quality information system', *Sloan Management Review*, Spring 1997, pp. 65–76.

Bitner M.J. and Hubbert A.R., 'Encounter satisfaction versus overall satisfaction versus service quality: the consumer's voice', in Rust R.T. and Oliver R.L. (eds), *Service Quality: New Directions in Theory and Practice*, Sage Publications, Thousand Oaks, Calif. 1994, pp. 72–94.

Cadotte E.R., Woodruff R.B. and Jenkins R.L., 'Expectations and norms in models of consumer satisfaction', *Journal of Marketing Research*, vol. 24, August 1987, pp. 305–14.

Churchill G.A. and Surprenant C., 'An investigation into the determinants of customer satisfaction', *Journal of Marketing Research*, vol. 19, November 1982, pp. 491–504.

Dibb S., Simkin L., Pride W, and Ferrel O.C., *Marketing Concepts and Strategies*, 3rd edition, Houghton Mifflin, Boston, 1997.

Flanagan P., Talbot D. and Johnston R., 'Confidence – the development of a concept for assessing "satisfaction" with the police service', in Edvardsson B., Gustafsson A., Brown S.W. and Johnston R. (eds), *Service Excellence in Management: Interdisciplinary Contributions*, Karlstad University, 2004, pp. 106–15.

Gremler D.D., Bitner M.J. and Evans K.R., 'The internal service encounter', *International Journal of Service Industry Management*, vol. 5, no. 2, 1994, pp. 34–56.

Grönroos C., 'A service quality model and its marketing implications', *European Journal of Marketing*, vol. 18, no. 4, 1984, pp. 36–44.

Grönroos C., 'Toward a third phase in service quality research: challenges and future directions', in Swartz T.A., Bowen D.A. and Brown S.W. (eds), *Advances in Services Marketing and Management*, vol. 2, JAI Press, Greenwich, Connecticut, 1993, pp. 49–64.

Hansen D.E. and Danaher P.J., 'Inconsistent performance during the service encounter', *Journal of Service Research*, vol. 1, no. 3, February 1999, pp. 227–35.

Johnston R., 'The zone of tolerance: exploring the relationship between service transactions and satisfaction with the overall service', *International Journal of Service Industry Management*, vol. 6, no. 2, 1995a, pp. 46–61.

Johnston R., 'The determinants of service quality: satisfiers and dissatisfiers', *International Journal of Service Industry Management*, vol. 6, no. 5, 1995b, pp. 53–71.

Johnston R., *Service Excellence=Reputation=Profit: Developing and Sustaining a Reputation for Service Excellence*, Institute of Customer Service, Colchester, 2001.

Lockwood A., 'Using service incidents to identify quality improvement points', *International Journal of Contemporary Hospitality Management*, vol. 6, no. 1/2, 1994, pp. 75–80.

Ojasalo J., *Quality Dynamics in Professional Services*, Ph.D. dissertation no. 76, Swedish School of Economics and Business Administration, Helsingfors, 1999.

Oliver R.L., 'Cognitive, affective, and attribute bases of the satisfaction response', *Journal of Consumer Research*, vol. 20, no. 3, 1993, pp. 418–30.

Oliver R.L. and DeSarbo W.S., 'Response determinants in satisfaction judgements', *Journal of Consumer Research*, vol. 14, March 1988, pp. 495–507.

Parasuraman A., Berry L.L. and Zeithaml V.A., 'Refinement and reassessment of the SERVQUAL scale', *Journal of Retailing*, vol. 67, no. 4, Winter 1991, pp. 420–50.

Parasuraman A., Zeithaml V.A. and Berry L.L., 'A conceptual model of service quality and implications for future research', *Journal of Marketing*, vol. 49, Fall, 1985, pp 41–50.

Parasuraman A., Zeithaml V.A. and Berry L.L., 'SERVQUAL: A multiple-item scale for measuring consumer perceptions of service quality', *Journal of Retailing*, Spring 1988, pp. 12–40.

Parasuraman A., Zeithaml V.A. and Berry L.L., 'Reassessment of Expectations as a Comparison Standard on Measuring Service Quality: Implications for Further Research', *Journal of Marketing*, vol. 58, no. 1, January 1994, pp 111–124.

Patterson P.G. and Johnson L.W., 'Disconfirmation of expectations and the gap model of service quality: an integrated paradigm', *Journal of Consumer Satisfaction, Dissatisfaction and Complaining Behavior*, vol. 6, 1993, pp. 90–9.

Piercy N.F. 'Customer satisfaction and the internal market. Marketing our customers to our employees', *Journal of Marketing Practice: Applied Marketing Science*, vol. 1, no. 1, 1995, pp. 22–44.

Reynoso J., 'Towards the conceptualisation and operationalisation of internal service quality: an examination in UK hospitals', doctoral thesis, University of Manchester, 1995.

Sasser W.E., Olsen R.P. and Wyckoff D.D., *Management of Service Operations*, Allyn and Bacon, Boston, 1978.

Schneider B. and Bowen D.E., 'Understanding customer delight and outrage', *Sloan Management Review*, Fall 1999, pp. 35–45.

Silvestro R. and Johnston R, 'The determinants of service quality – enhancing and hygiene factors', QUIS II Symposium, St John's University, New York, July 1990.

Stauss B., 'Service problem deployment: transformation of problem information into problem prevention activities', *International Journal of Service Industry Management*, vol. 4, no. 2, 1993, pp. 41–62.

Strandvik T., *Tolerance Zones in Perceived Service Quality*, Swedish School of Economics and Business Administration, Helsingfors, 1994.

Taylor S.A. and Baker T.L., 'An assessment of the relationship between service quality and customer satisfaction in the formation of consumers' purchase intentions', *Journal of Retailing*, vol. 70, no. 2, 1994, pp. 163–78.

Wirtz J. and Bateson J.E.G., 'An experimental investigation of halo effects in satisfaction measures and service attributes', *International Journal of Service Industry Management*, vol. 6, no. 3, 1995, pp. 84–102.

Zeithaml V.A., Berry L.L. and Parasuraman A., 'The nature and determinants of customer expectations of service', *Journal of the Academy of Marketing Science*, vol. 21, no.1, 1993, pp. 1–12.

Zeithaml V.A., Parasuraman A. and Berry L.L., *Delivering Quality Service*, Free Press, New York, 1990.

The North County Breast Screening Unit — Case Exercise

Rhian Silvestro, Warwick Business School, and Marilyn Merriam

Breast cancer is the most common cause of death from cancer in women in the UK, and women with breast cancer form almost 1 per cent of in-patient admissions. England and Wales have the highest mortality rates for breast cancer in the world, making it a major public health problem, which is a national target area in the Government's Strategy for the Health of the Nation. The NHS Breast Screening Programme, set up in 1987, aims to reduce mortality from breast cancer, through early identification of the symptoms, by screening women aged between 50 and 64 every three years. It is possible that the age range will be extended to between 45 and 64 in future.

The North County Breast Screening Unit (NCBSU) was set up in 1989 and serves some half a million residents, with an uptake on invitations for screening of 77 per cent (compared to the national target of 70 per cent and an 'achievable quality standard' of 75 per cent). The NCBSU is part of a hospital trust. The Trust's mission statement is as follows:

We aim to provide high-quality acute and specialist services which:

- *are responsive to customer needs*
- *use leading-edge and effective medical technologies*
- *are at a cost that compares favourably with the rest of the NHS*
- *have motivated and properly trained staff.*

To this end the Trust supports a number of quality audit and improvement initiatives, including ISO 9000 and Investors in People. The NCBSU employs 32 members of staff, including part-timers. There are four radiologists, seven full-time radiographers, two breast-care nurses, and a number of receptionists and office staff. The unit is also supported by several part-time radiographers and visiting surgeons.

In 1999 a small patient satisfaction survey was conducted to obtain detailed feedback about patient expectations and perceptions of the service and to identify areas for improvement. Staff from the different functional areas were also interviewed, in order to identify any gaps between patient expectations and perceptions and staff perceptions of the quality of service provided.

Thirty-two patients were interviewed. These included 16 patients who had come to the NCBSU for screening and 16 patients who had been screened and had been called back to the NCBSU because they were diagnosed with breast cancer. Each patient was asked to assign the relative importance, on a 5-point scale, of a series of quality factors. They were then asked to rate, again on a 1–5 scale, their perception of the service levels delivered with regard to each factor. Table 4.2 lists the statements that were used to capture each quality factor and Figure 4.20 shows the mean values assigned for each factor by the staff and patients.

Staff were provided with the same list of factors and asked to rate on a scale of 1–5 how important they believed the factor to be to the patients, and what service level they believed the patients perceived themselves to be receiving. This would facilitate identification of any mismatches between staff and patient perceptions.

Questions

1 Evaluate the quality of service provided by the NCBSU.

2 What recommendations would you make for improvement?

Table 4.2 Statements used to capture each quality factor

Quality factor	Statements used
Access	Was the NCBSU easy to find? Were there transport problems in getting here?
Availability	Were you given as much time as you wanted with staff?
Care	Were you shown concern, consideration and sympathy? Were you treated with patience?
Communication	Were you provided with enough information in a way you could understand?
Competence	Were you impressed by the skill, expertise and professionalism of the staff?
Courtesy	Were staff polite and respectful? Were staff discreet and unobtrusive when necessary?
Functionality	Did the equipment seem adequate in delivering the service?
Reliability	Was the NCBSU reliable and consistent in performance?
Privacy	Were you given enough privacy?
Responsiveness	Was there much waiting and queuing?
Comfort	Was the unit comfortable?

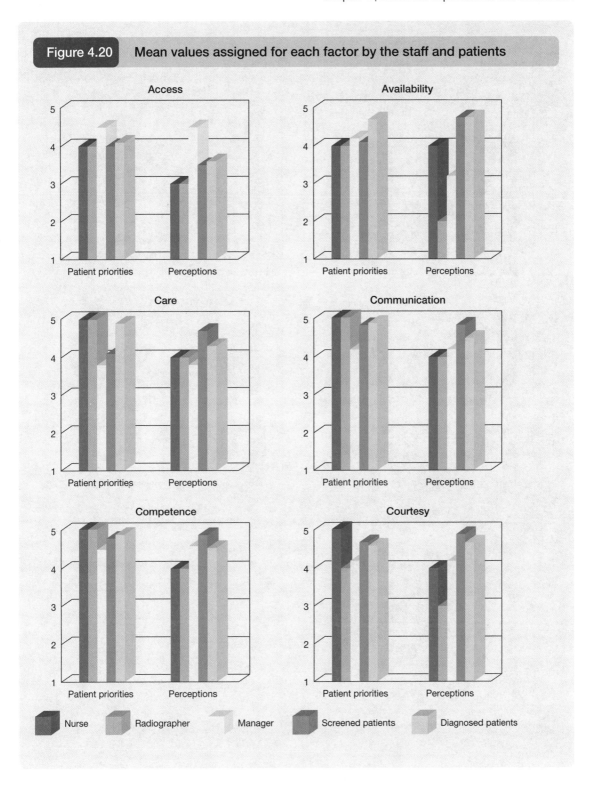

Figure 4.20   Mean values assigned for each factor by the staff and patients

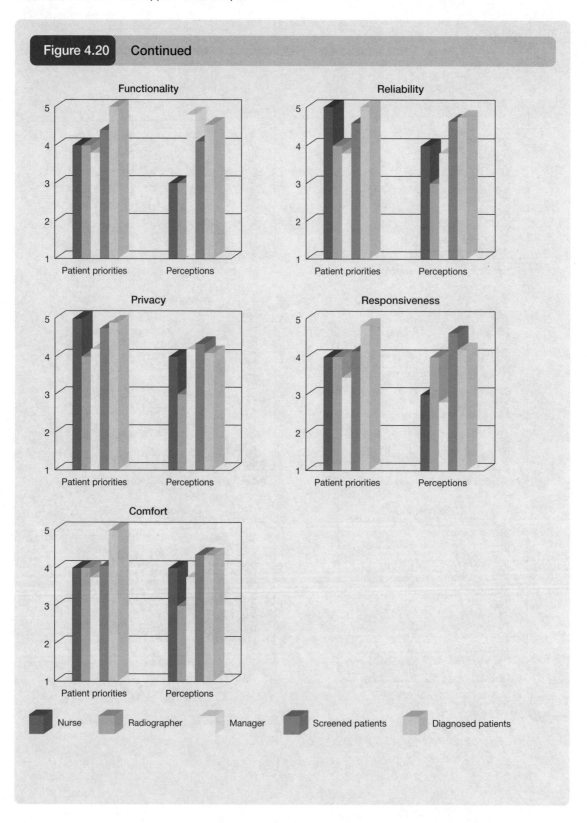

Figure 4.20 Continued

chapter five

Managing supply relationships

Chapter objectives:

- to identify the main types of supply relationships

- to define supply chains, explore service applications and discuss the main issues in supply chain management

- to understand the use and management of intermediaries

- to identify the main types of supply partnerships and how they can be managed effectively

- to evaluate the role of service-level agreements.

5.1 Introduction

This chapter describes the management of the relationships involved in service delivery to the end customer. It recognises that the chain or network of activities is frequently rather complex, involving numbers of interrelated participants, each with their own set of priorities and requirements.

Manufacturing companies have been developing their understanding of how to manage supply lines more effectively for many years. The supply chain management approach was born out of an understanding that in order to manage significant increases in product availability, combined with greater responsiveness without massive increases in inventory, the various elements of the chain need to operate in synchronisation. These ideas have great relevance for service organisations.

5.2 Types of supply relationships

This chapter deals with three types of supply relationships: 'simple' service supply chains, management through intermediaries and supply partnerships (see Figure 5.1).

5.2.1 The service supply chain

Here we address the issues faced by a service provider who wants to ensure that its own key suppliers meet cost and quality targets required for the effective management of service delivery to customers.

Figure 5.1 depicts a 'simple' supply chain where, for example, a pharmaceutical company (S2) makes drugs for an international distributor (S1), who delivers them to a chemist/pharmacist (P), who sells them to a customer (C). The reality is that most service operations are involved in complex sets of supply chains, usually referred to as supply networks, which include many streams of products and services.

A service provider, such as a supermarket for example, will have several chains of suppliers for services such as contract cleaning, legal services and auditing, as well as the various food items. Those food producers, for example, may be contracted to particular wholesalers or distributors, who are contracted by the supermarket to supply potatoes, organic beef, or regional wine, for example. (Sometimes organisations cut out the 'middleman' and deal directly with the producer; see disintermediation in the next section.) Likewise the producers themselves will have their own suppliers. The wine producer will have suppliers of bottles and corks, diesel for tractors, accounting and wine testing services.

The levels of suppliers and customers in this network are usually referred to as first-tier and second-tier suppliers (and so on), and also tiers of customers, until the final end user. In the case of the supermarket, the wine distributors would be a first-tier (S1) supplier and the wine producer a second-tier supplier (S2), and the cork producer the third-tier supplier.

Figure 5.1	Types of supply relationships

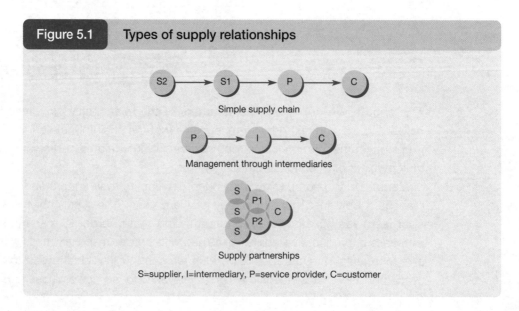

Simple supply chain

Management through intermediaries

Supply partnerships

S=supplier, I=intermediary, P=service provider, C=customer

5.2.2 Management through intermediaries

As in the case of the supermarket, some supply chains or networks involve 'middlemen': distributors, agents or dealers who take responsibility for managing a section of the supply chain, thus making managing the chain easier for the service provider.

Many financial service companies, for example, have chosen to sell through brokers, not seeing the customer contact as part of their core business. Car producers, likewise, do not see their role as selling cars to the public and often set up owned or franchised dealerships to deal with the consumer.

Disintermediation and outsourcing

A trend in many supply networks has been to circumvent or remove some of these intermediaries, an action referred to as disintermediation. This approach may bring benefits such as reduced costs and greater responsiveness, but may also increase the management task for the service provider (see section 5.3).

Where disintermediation reduces the size of the supply network, outsourcing expands it. Outsourcing, and the related off-shoring, is the splitting out of a part of an operation to a specialist company. Usually it affects a peripheral activity, such as purchasing or accounting functions or call centres, but occasionally a core activity is split off, such as equipment repairs. Organisations that do this believe there are financial and strategic benefits for letting a specialist supplier manage what used to be in-house tasks. Outsourcing and off-shoring is dealt with in more detail in Chapter 9.

5.2.3 Supply partnerships

A partnership or alliance may be formed to provide a jointly managed service delivery mechanism. These relationships may take the form of joint ventures or, in the retail world, 'in-plants' such as a branded shop within a larger retail store. Of course there are numbers of possible combinations, but for the most part they are variations on a theme and the principles described below cover the vast majority of situations.

5.3 Managing service supply chains

5.3.1 Supply chain definition

A supply chain is the link, or usually the network, that joins together internal and external suppliers with internal and external consumers. Supply chain management (SCM) is concerned with managing the network and the flow of information, materials, services and customers through the network.

The essential exchange mechanism is information. More accurate information about expected demand passed in appropriate format to upstream suppliers allows them to manage their production with minimum cost. The theory is then that the benefits of increased competitiveness will be shared equitably with the 'partners' in the supply chain. In practice this does not always happen when the organisations with 'muscle' or buying power dominate; however, there are numbers of examples of effective supply chains where purchasers have moved away from adversarial practices.

Figure 5.2 is a much-simplified version of a supply chain, concerned predominantly with the movement of materials, in this case pet food and its constituents. To make the whole supply chain operate smoothly and at minimum cost requires inventory of materials (raw materials, material in the supply chain and finished products), together with good information about customer demand from the supermarket. However good the information, there will always be a need for some inventory in the supply chain:

- Processes require work in progress to run. In Figure 5.2, the pet food factory will need several days' worth of inventory for its processes to operate effectively, rather than manufacture a tin at a time!

- Inventory is also put in place because the chain does not operate perfectly. For example, supermarkets require stock on the shelves because they cannot forecast

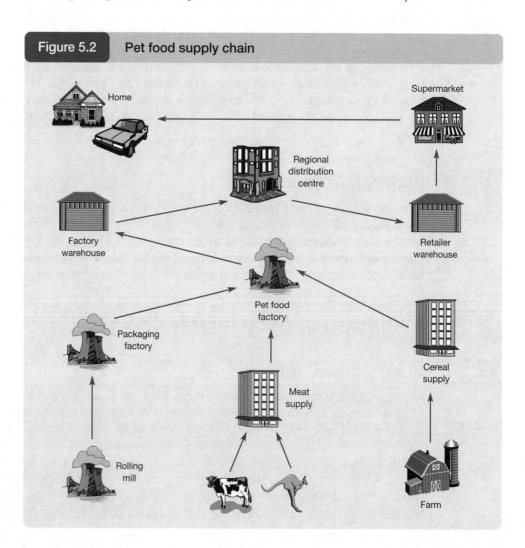

Figure 5.2   Pet food supply chain

demand with 100 per cent accuracy, and the pet food factory requires more than the minimum inventory because its processes may be inflexible or unreliable.

SCM is targeted primarily at reducing the second of these two reasons for increase in inventory, while simultaneously increasing both service level and responsiveness to changing market conditions.

SCM has direct relevance to services that include the provision of manufactured goods as a part of the service concept. For example:

- Retailers need to combine high levels of product availability with competitive prices and responsiveness to changes in market demand or fashion.
- Equipment service and repair companies, who are measured on 'time to fix', need to manage the logistics of spare part availability, frequently across a geographically dispersed network.
- An airline that outsources the production of meals for its passengers needs to manage information flows to ensure that customers receive the choice of meal they require without the airline holding too many extra meals.

Other service organisations need to manage their supplier base because there are significant cost savings to be made. For example, airlines will watch the price of fuel carefully because marginal savings here will impact the profit line directly. On a smaller scale, a local seafood restaurant will want to develop reliable sources of supply of fresh fish to serve to its customers.

Managing the supply chain or network is vital for 'pure' service providers who create their services by packaging together a set of other services. The holiday industry is a good example (see Figure 5.3). Travel agents traditionally sell holidays to customers through shops in town centres or shopping malls. The customers may be individuals or group travellers. The travel agents sell a range of 'products', or packages, created by a number of tour operators. These tour operators will each negotiate independently with a range of hotels, airlines, restaurants, entertainment activities and venues, and transportation companies, for example, to create a package holiday aimed at a particular market. Given the size of their operations they are often able to achieve substantial discounts and can hold, often on a call-off (or as required) basis, services for many months while the travel agents sell the packages.

This industry also provides a good example of disintermediation. Over the last few years, tour operators have been cutting out the travel agents and selling directly to the public, although they have had to incur additional costs of call centres or websites to sell and service their products (see Figure 5.3). Even greater disintermediation is visible as hotels, airlines, car rental companies etc. have made their services available and bookable directly through websites, thus cutting out both tour operators and travel agents (see Figure 5.3). The advantage might be greater control and sometimes lower costs for consumers, but certainly at the expense of considerably greater efforts from them.

The value of SCM is that it allows for the benefits of vertical integration without the long-term overhead and inherent inflexibility that comes from trying to manage all activities in a supply chain under the umbrella of one organisation. This allows organisations to continue to 'do what they are good at' and to form supply relation-

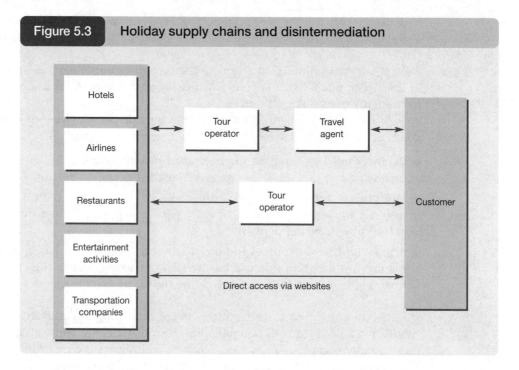

Figure 5.3   Holiday supply chains and disintermediation

ships that have sufficient duration to allow for the development of understanding of how to do things better (see Box 5.1). It is always recognised, though, that as the market demands change, some of these relationships cease to be effective.

Companies in the financial services sector have also become interested in the concept of supply chain management, but frequently what is meant in this context is a desire to gain control of the channels to market, a subject considered in more depth in section 5.4.

Sharnbrook Upper School   Box 5.1

Sharnbrook Upper School is located to the north of Bedford, some 70 miles north of London. The school has approximately 1,700 students between the ages of 13 and 18. The majority of the students come to the school through the three middle schools in the area, which teach children between the ages of 8 and 12 years. These 'feeder' schools are situated in the villages of Clapham, Harrold and Riseley. The combined annual intake for Sharnbrook Upper School is just less than 400 students, each of the feeder schools sending about 100 students each, with others joining from 'out of catchment' schools.

The three feeder schools are each in turn served by a cluster of lower schools for children from 4 to 7 years old.

There have been a number of attempts in the past to manage this 'pyramid' of schools, but without much tangible success. There has been a perception that Sharnbrook is the big school with all the resources and power, with the smaller schools not wanting to be controlled by their larger counterpart. One of the consequences of this three-tier system is that students moving from middle to upper school have little time to adjust to new subjects and a new school environment before they embark on coursework that contributes to the final marks for the national examinations (GCSE) held at age 16.

The group of four schools (upper and three middle) recognised the value of working together rather than as four independent units. They call this collaboration 'managing the pyramid', although it is in effect a service supply chain, with raw material being students rather than inventory. Following supply chain principles, the pyramid has recognised that it may be beneficial for the teaching (value-adding activity) currently carried out in one part of the pyramid to be reallocated to another. An example of this redistribution is that of language teaching. Some students who show particular talent for languages can be identified during their years in the feeder school, and these students might be able to study more languages if they started earlier. A fairly radical proposal is that language teachers from the upper school might spend time teaching in the feeder schools. This has the advantage of providing specialist skills not always available in the feeder school, and also developing a consistent approach across the feeder system that will facilitate more rapid progress once the students arrive at the upper school.

Other opportunities for managing the total pyramid more effectively include:

- collaboration in developing students' talents in a wider range of sports activities
- achieving greater utilisation of expensive media equipment at Sharnbrook.

This latest attempt to work together has been met with enthusiasm from headteachers and governing bodies of the schools involved. A significant amount of time has been spent in building relationships and it is encouraging to report that as well as 'top down' pressure from the upper school, there is now significant momentum from the three middle schools and each associated cluster of lower schools to manage the pyramid more effectively.

Questions

1 What are the major benefits and disadvantages for the upper school and its feeder schools in developing this approach?

2 What advice could you give to Peter Barnard, headteacher of Sharnbrook Upper School, as to how to deal with the key stakeholders in the pyramid? These include teachers, school governors, parents and the local education authority.

This illustration was developed with the assistance of Peter Barnard, headteacher of Sharnbrook Upper School, Bedfordshire, UK.

5.3.2 Supply chain management approaches

The basis of SCM lies in the development of strong buyer–supplier partnerships. Figure 5.4, from the work of Helper (1991), is a useful starting point to understand the approach.

Helper's work was based on research carried out with suppliers to the large automobile manufacturers in the USA. It is interesting because it views the partnerships from the standpoint of the relatively weak suppliers as opposed to that of the buyers, who tend to claim benefits not shared by weaker partners.

Helper categorised the relationships as follows:

- *Voice*. This equates to partnership sourcing. The partners share information on long-term activity forecasts and in some cases collaborate on research and development (R&D). This box is characterised by the expectation of long-term contracts, often linked to placing orders at an aggregate level some months ahead, to be firmed up with more detail as the due date approaches.

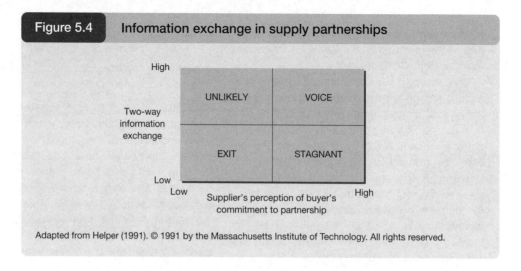

Figure 5.4   Information exchange in supply partnerships

● *Exit*. This is what has come to be termed 'traditional' or adversarial purchasing. Contracts are generally short and there is no sharing of long-term demand forecasts or assistance with process development. It is likely that contracts are placed almost exclusively on price, and buyers will continue to search for competitive bids in order to keep their suppliers in line.

● *Unlikely*. It is unlikely that a supplier will perceive that the buyer is committed to doing long-term business with them in the absence of two-way communication. Of course, it may be that the supplier also chooses to operate at arm's length, not wanting to become too dependent on the one purchaser.

● *Stagnant*. In this scenario, there is a strong sense of commitment, but this has not been turned into a relationship that realises its full potential.

The research was carried out over a period of ten years, during which time many of the automobile manufacturers had moved to just-in-time (JIT) manufacturing and purchasing. At the start of the period, the vast majority of suppliers felt themselves to be in the Exit box, with no real sense of enduring relationship with their customers. Ten years later, a large number of suppliers reported that they still felt that they were in the Exit box, but that the demands made on them in terms of more frequent delivery and self-certification of quality had increased.

However, there were a significant number of suppliers that reported a move to the Voice box. For these, there was evidence of sufficient confidence to make significant investment in process automation, with resulting improvements in both cost and quality. The conclusion that might be drawn from this is that a relationship approach is not always appropriate or possible. Certainly, one of the aspects of SCM is the reduction in numbers of suppliers, allowing the buyer to concentrate on a relatively small number of 'strategic' partnerships.

Benefits of supply chain management

The key elements of supply chain management include:

● the management of the supply chain in its entirety, using measures that assess the performance of the total chain

- the development of buyer/supplier partnerships with the expectation of sharing the benefits of increased co-operation over time
- the reduction of the number of suppliers in the chain, with an increase in single or sole suppliers, allowing resource to be focused on the strategic issues
- increasing interchange of information, possibly including long-term demand forecasts, financial costings, process improvements, and research and development
- the possibility of reallocating activities to the most effective position in the supply chain.

The benefits claimed for this approach are as follows:

- reduction in the total cost of inventory held by the chain as a whole
- reduction in administrative overheads involved in managing multiple relationships
- collaboration in scheduling and in process improvement, leading to higher service levels and quality improvement
- faster response to changes in market demand.

5.3.3 The purchasing or procurement function

The function traditionally responsible for managing the supply chain is the purchasing and supply or procurement department. This is an important activity found in all organisations – public, private, governmental and charities – and can be responsible for a large amount of spending. Spending by service organisations on, for example, materials, components, facilities, subcontract capacity, IT equipment and supplies, consumables, stationery, travel and insurance, can constitute a significant amount of money, often 30–60 per cent of an organisation's turnover (Croom and Johnston 2003).

Procurement is traditionally an internal service provided by a dedicated team of professionals. It typically operates at the interface between the organisation's external supplier marketplace and the organisation's operational processes. Procurement has many of the characteristics of the marketing function, although it faces the other direction in the supply chain. Procurement is usually responsible for the identification of (internal) customer's needs, translation of those needs into specifications, management of the delivery of goods and services and an assessment of the (internal) customer's satisfaction with those goods and services. The other elements of the process involve communication with suppliers – sourcing, requests for tenders, price negotiation, ordering, receipt and invoicing (Croom and Johnston 2003).

Unlike marketing, procurement is often seen as a 'Cinderella' activity in many organisations. Despite the economic value of this internal service, managers often see 'promotion' into the purchasing function as a retrograde step into an organisational backwater (Bales and Fearon 1996). It is often held in low regard by its internal customers who see the function as bureaucratic, difficult to deal with, sometimes remote and delivering poor service (Nolan 1999). Senior managers, too, often see it as a problem area where there is low compliance, with internal customers either abusing or circumventing the systems (Croom 2000, Gebauer and Segev 2001). It is also regarded as a high-cost activity where there is unnecessary paperwork, material costs and errors

(Lamming 1993, Hines 1994). However, good management applied to this area can have a significant impact on costs. A report by consultants PricewaterhouseCoopers suggested that just a 10 per cent reduction in purchase costs could easily lead to a 50 per cent rise in profit margin (Sheng 2002).

e-procurement

Electronic procurement systems are a form of disintermediation. In essence, e-procurement systems mirror the procurement process through the provision of two distinct, but connected, infrastructures – internal processing (via, for example, corporate intranet) and external communication with the supply base (via, for example, internet-based platforms) (Croom 2000). The critical difference is that such systems allow individual employees to order goods and services directly from their own PCs through the web. Requests and orders are channelled through various forms of 'hub' or database, which act as online catalogues of specifications, prices and, often, authorisation rules. Such systems allow individual employees to search for items, check availability, place and track orders and initiate payment on delivery (Croom and Johnston 2003).

Research by Croom and Johnston (2003) found that e-procurement provides three key benefits over traditional procurement:

- *Customer satisfaction*. Internal customers reported greater satisfaction with electronic-based procurement systems. Even though they had to undertake more work (searching, ordering and paying) themselves, they appreciated greater accessibility and availability of purchased goods and services, faster fulfilment of requests and much greater control over the process and their own budgets.

- *Process compliance*. E-procurement systems provided greater reliability than traditional systems and, because they were easy for individuals to use, there were less 'maverick' purchases made (for example small purchases that were then reclaimed on expenses). The processes tended also to be more transparent and afforded better control of the purchasing process.

- *Cost reduction*. Not only were there significant savings in the cost of purchasing, but because employees had greater control over the process, less 'emergency' or 'just-in-case' supplies needed to be kept.

An additional and important impact of e-procurement is that the traditional roles of the purchasing department, such as placing and managing orders, can now be done electronically. This leaves the purchasing function in a position where it can either be more easily outsourced or take on a more strategic role, such as evaluating the impact of e-procurement, advising on systems and policies, and driving savings across the whole organisation.

5.3.4 Supplier selection: multiple, single or sole suppliers?

One of the key decisions for a procurement function is the selection of suppliers, particularly for those who are to undertake critical elements of the supply chain. Some criteria for supplier selection, apart from cost, include:

- financial standing
- people management skills, including training and industrial relations record
- commercial awareness
- productivity
- quality management approach
- focus on continuous improvement activities.

A major consideration is the extent to which the buyer's requirements comprise a significant amount of the supplier's business. A supplier who is totally dedicated to one buyer may seem like a good idea at first sight, but may lead to complacency in the relationship. Many buying organisations set targets that limit the proportion of business to be transacted with any one supplier. This has a particular benefit in that if the buyer's business should decline in the short term, their supplier base is more likely to remain viable.

However, part of the approach to SCM includes the reduction in the number of suppliers. Concern has been expressed that if the organisation is dependent on a single supplier, that may leave the buyer exposed. Nokia has developed an approach to this issue that is typical of many organisations. Nokia has three types of suppliers:

- *Sole suppliers*. These are used for new technologies where there may be only one supplier capable of delivering to the required specification.
- *Single suppliers*. This is the preferred approach for many components. A supplier will be appointed to provide the organisation's total requirements of a component or family of components for a region or possibly globally. Nokia will have other suppliers who are capable of supplying these components in the event of a problem, but who are currently providing similar products.
- *Multiple suppliers*. These are used only when necessary, perhaps to develop a supplier's capability or to provide locally specific components.

Nokia's approach to SCM has enabled it to develop the flexibility it requires to meet the demands of a market that has the challenges of rapid growth and shortening product life-cycles.

5.3.5 One-stop shops

A consequence of organisations wishing to reduce their administrative overheads is the rise of the opportunity for service providers to sell a comprehensive package to customers. For example, facilities management organisations offer full maintenance for organisations that do not wish to employ their own staff to look after their buildings, i.e. they outsource buildings maintenance. The Building Services Limited illustration in Box 5.2 provides an example of a facilities management company needing to develop its own ability to manage suppliers in order to provide a more comprehensive service to its own customers.

Building Services Limited (BSL)

Box 5.2

Building Services Limited (BSL) was originally formed to provide basic building maintenance services to small to medium companies not wishing to employ their own maintenance team. BSL was able to employ area teams of mechanical and electrical building engineers to provide a fast response to immediate problems, in addition to routine maintenance activities. The speed of response to incidents and frequency of maintenance were laid down in service-level agreements.

BSL realised that it needed to develop new capabilities to manage its customer relationships, and appointed client managers for their largest and most profitable accounts. As a result, the business grew and some of its customers began asking if BSL could take on more of the customer's outsourced requirements. This meant that BSL would now be responsible for servicing more specialised areas, such as air-conditioning and clean rooms for semiconductor production.

As an organisation, BSL encourages its regional managers to be entrepreneurial and to develop new service offerings. Its provision of 'energy management' services had been introduced as the result of the initiative of an area team, which had seen the opportunity of making use of the information it held for its customers.

As the business grew, so also did the nature and size of the clients. BSL was now providing full facilities management services for national companies that wanted BSL to provide the same level and scope of services to all sites. At the same time, customers wanted BSL to act as a 'one-stop-shop' for all their outsourced services, including IT and office equipment service. BSL saw this as an opportunity to move into the provision of services that commanded higher premiums but recognised that in the short to medium term it would have to act as a services 'broker', buying these services from other service providers now acting as subcontractors to BSL, rather than the final client.

Questions

1 What are the challenges for BSL in taking on this new role of 'one-stop shop' for its customers' multi-site operations?

2 Should BSL continue to develop its own in-house capabilities or increase its own supplier base of 'associated service providers'?

This illustration is based on a real organisation although all names and places have been changed.

5.3.6 Supply chain improvement: lean thinking

Lean thinking is generally held to have originated through the work of Toyoda and Ohno at the Toyota Motor Company in Japan (Womack *et al.* 1990). The Toyota production system has been studied and copied by manufacturing companies throughout the world, who wish to reap the benefits of reduced costs as well as an organisational culture that believes in the possibility of continuous improvement throughout the supply chain.

The essence of lean thinking is to drive out *muda*, the Japanese word for waste, which is defined as anything that creates no value for the customer. Womack and Jones (1996) list five principles of lean thinking:

Specify value

Value must be defined by the ultimate customer. It is so easy to revert to a 'producer' mentality that assumes that because the provider thinks that the product is good, it must represent value. Womack and Jones use airlines as an example of organisations that have not always understood value in these terms, providing executive lounges and extra facilities on flights when what passengers really want is rapid, safe travel to their destination.

Identify the value stream

The value stream is the set of actions required to bring the product to the customer. The total supply chain from raw material through to final delivery and use by the customer must be understood in order to identify where activities at particular points in the chain in reality create no value for the customer, but have always been carried out because nobody had an overview of the total chain. When analysing the whole value stream, three types of activities can be identified:

- those that create value for customers
- those that create no value for customers but cannot be eliminated because of current technology or process constraints
- those that create no value and can be removed.

It should be noted that the second of these categories of activities, those that create no value but cannot be removed, must be closely examined to see if this assumption is, in fact, correct. It may be that the activity persists simply 'because we have always done it this way', and so the activity may be eliminated.

Telecom equipment providers such as Ericsson, Motorola and Nortel are working hard to become more involved in their customers' businesses. In order to do this, they must know more about how the customers – the network operators – manage their businesses, and also what the ultimate customers require. This increased customer focus leads to a shortening of the value stream, more focused research and development, lower costs and greater value for customers.

Create flow

The essence of lean thinking is that work flows continuously and smoothly through a 'pipeline' without stopping. In other words, the tendency to create batches of work that occur when the hand-offs from department to department are not well managed has to be reduced. These discontinuities in the flow of work create the possibility for errors, they slow down the response to customer demand, and create a requirement to manage the workload that could be avoided. Batched work creates queues, with the need to manage priorities and to expedite work that, as it gets later, becomes ever more urgent.

This work-flow thinking has been applied with great success to the back offices of many financial services companies, particularly as many have reorganised around customer processes and dismantled the traditional departmental or 'silo' mentality.

Pull not push

Traditional production systems produce in the hope of selling their wares. This creates *muda* in terms of overproduction and therefore excess cost. The challenge of lean thinking is to have operations schedules governed by demand pull rather than production push. Pull systems are essentially replenishment systems working on the basis of 'sell one, make one'. A good example is provided by McDonald's in the replenishment of burgers as customers buy them. The task for the organisation is to monitor and adjust the replenishment levels as demand patterns vary.

Pull systems require a major shift in operational culture since it means that work in progress is significantly reduced and there is not the comfort factor of piles of work in progress in the system. The challenge for the service organisation is to find ways to manage the total supply chain in similar ways to the manufacturing examples.

Strive for perfection

This fifth principle of lean thinking flows from the other four. As partners in the total supply chain apply the lean thinking philosophy, many of the problems are addressed, but, more importantly, a culture of both significant and continuous improvement develops.

Applying lean thinking to service operations

Ohno identified seven sources of *muda*:

- over-production ahead of demand
- waiting for the next process step
- unnecessary transport of materials
- over-processing of parts due to poor technology or process design
- excessive inventories
- unnecessary movement of employees
- defective production.

These all apply to many service operations, particularly those that have factory-like back offices, and those that have the supply of physical product as part of the concept. It is also worth applying Ohno's classification to the customer process, considering a customer as the unit of material. This would encourage thinking about the cost to the customer in time or money when dealing with a particular service provider. A reduction in cost for the customer would almost certainly equate to an increase in value, which is the essence of lean thinking.

5.3.7 Barriers to supply chain management implementation

Although SCM makes sense in many ways to organisations, there are a number of barriers to successful implementation:

- *Lack of systems capability*. SCM requires the ability to pass information about changing demand patterns through the chain. Not all companies have invested in the capability to achieve this.
- *Complacency*. Where industry sectors have been reasonably stable, organisations may not see the need for SCM and ignore it until a new entrant operates in a different mode. A more dangerous form of complacency exists when organisations feel that they have already fully implemented SCM and have lost the drive for continuous improvement.

- *Information used for a variety of conflicting purposes*. This relates particularly to demand forecasts, which may be used on the one hand to create an optimistic picture of the future to manage shareholder expectations, but on the other must be used for detailed planning activities. The former may bear no relation to reality, leading to over-investment in capacity.

- *Mistrust*. Previous, over-inflated estimates of demand may lead to suppliers reducing capacity allocations to levels less than required.

- *Power games*. Reorganisation along supply chain lines may be resisted by individuals whose power base will be diminished as a result. There may also be resistance on the part of suppliers who fear that they will be overwhelmed by a more powerful partner.

Many of the technical problems can be overcome to make the supply chain more effective. As with most significant change programmes, the major resistance comes from the people involved.

5.4 Managing through intermediaries

Many service organisations continue to use intermediaries for the selling process as well as for service delivery to the end customer or user. These organisations have continued to develop support networks of agents, dealers or franchisees for a variety of reasons.

Financial service companies have traditionally dealt through pensions or insurance brokers. This was in part to give the customer confidence that they were being given independent advice, for the same reason that Microsoft uses certified solution providers (see Box 5.3) . The problem with this approach is that it often leads to confusion as to who is the 'real' customer – the intermediary or the final consumer. Of course, the simple answer is that both groups are customers, but it would be wrong to suggest that satisfying both groups is an easy task.

Microsoft   Box 5.3

Microsoft chooses to sell and provide support for its software through a comprehensive worldwide network of partners and associated companies, rather than deal directly with customers. There are a number of channels for Microsoft to manage in order to ensure that its users receive the appropriate level of service.

One of these channels is managed by Microsoft under the Certified Solution Provider Programme. Microsoft providers are able to receive training, sales support and software, as well as priority information about the latest upgrades and software patches, to ensure that they are up to date and able to give their customers good service.

For the larger solution providers, Microsoft has introduced a Partner Programme. To qualify for this programme, the provider must demonstrate a number of attributes under the headings of commitment, significance, proactivity and effectiveness. To demonstrate their competence the partner must employ a given number of Microsoft certified systems engineers or solution developers. In return, the partner receives an

---

increased level of support and is allocated the assistance of a Microsoft business development manager. Microsoft requires ongoing evidence not only that their partners are technically competent, but that they have viable business plans.

The partners receive significant sales and marketing support. They are linked to the Microsoft.com home page for potential customers looking for solutions providers. In the Partner Network, they can search for potential collaborators. Partners receive priority notification of potential sales leads from Microsoft's telesales operation, and they have access to 'customer-critical' technical support.

Microsoft emphasises the independence of their providers and provider partners. They are able to sell and support solutions from other software developers. However, it is apparent that Microsoft offers every incentive to its partners to sell proactively and support its own solutions.

Questions

1 How much resource should Microsoft devote to auditing its partners' continuing ability to meet its criteria?

2 What are the costs and benefits for Microsoft in adopting this approach as opposed to developing its own network?

This illustration is based on material from the Microsoft website: www.microsoft.com

5.4.1 Why use intermediaries?

Armistead and Clark (1992) suggest the following reasons for the use of agents or dealers in the provision of customer support for products and systems:

- *Closeness to customer*. Many customers prefer to deal with an organisation that is physically close to them. This might be because they prefer to deal 'face to face', have not got access to electronic processes, or the nature of the service requires the presence of the service provider. For example, one of the major drivers for customer satisfaction in the ownership of cars is the ease of access to a recognised dealer for service and repair.

- *Local knowledge*. The parent organisation may have insufficient knowledge of local conditions and culture. In the development of global strategies, much emphasis is placed on 'thinking globally, acting locally'.

- *Focused expertise*. Microsoft (see Box 5. 3) has chosen to restrict its activities to software development rather than get involved in the creation and administration of a network of distributors and developers. This allows for a high degree of flexibility as service partners close to the market develop new solutions using Microsoft platforms.

- *Poor service margins*. The volume of service revenue may be too small in some geographical regions for the provision of a dedicated service unit. Capital equipment suppliers may sell only one or two units initially into a region, but must provide aftersales support. Rather than recruit and train service engineers for a few service calls per year, the company may use local service agents, who may also service competitors' equipment.

- *Insufficient capacity*. A strategy adopted by many call centres is to have 'subcontract' capacity available through providers set up explicitly for this type of activity. The information systems available to call centre agents enable them to act in such a manner that the customer is unlikely to detect any difference in service delivery.

5.4.2 Managing intermediaries

The central issue in dealing with intermediaries is that their objectives may not always coincide with those of the parent organisation. Figure 5.5 illustrates a 'military' model for aftersales customer support in which various service delivery mechanisms are outlined. This model suggests that intermediaries may be aligned to Mercenaries, fighting for the cause, primarily because they are being paid.

The key dimension in Figure 5.5 is that of in-house control. The trade-off that service organisations adopting the intermediary approach are making is between the potential quality cost of poor quality of service and lost customers, against the cost of forming and maintaining a distributed network of service units.

The reasons for maintaining high in-house control of service include:

- to increase the depth and breadth of a customer relationship
- to ensure that customer complaints are effectively dealt with and that rapid feedback for process improvement is facilitated
- to retain control over innovative goods and services for which there is limited resource.

The various service forms are as follows:

- *The Commandos*. These are highly trained service personnel, often used as 'hit squads' able to tackle most problems on their own with little or no management direction. They are typically used to support complex products such as process

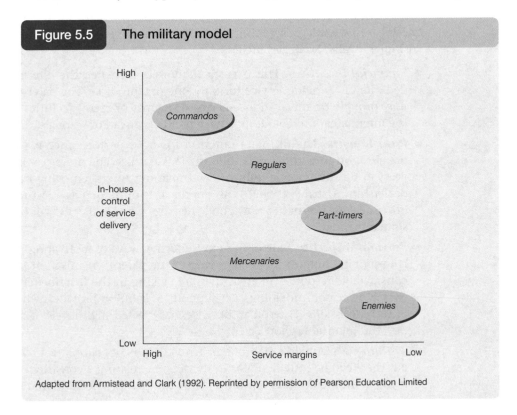

Figure 5.5 The military model

Adapted from Armistead and Clark (1992). Reprinted by permission of Pearson Education Limited

automation or innovative information systems. These service providers are often found in professional services, particularly those that provide support services for software or communication systems.

- **The Regulars**. Regulars are less comprehensively skilled than the Commandos and are less able to work without direction. The tasks they carry out tend to be more specialised and, of course, there are more of them. It is important to note that, because they are employed by the parent organisation, there is still a relatively high level of in-house control. This is diminished slightly by the fact that the Regulars are usually geographically dispersed by region or site.

- **Part-timers**. These service providers are the customers themselves, trained by the parent organisation to carry out service tasks for themselves. An example is provided by the photocopier companies that train key operators to change toner cartridges and free paper jams without using expensive service engineers (Regulars).

- **Mercenaries**. Mercenaries are not part of the parent organisation. The prime reason for fighting on the side of the main organisation is that they are being paid to do so. They may switch sides if there is sufficient incentive, and they do not share the culture of the parent organisation.

- **Enemies**. These are not on the same side. It may be that the parent organisation has decided not to provide service in all circumstances, particularly if the profit margins are small.

This chapter concentates especially on the management and motivation of the Mercenaries. The challenge is to provide such intermediaries with sufficient financial incentive while developing the customer service values required to generate customer loyalty. Strategies include:

- **Financial incentives**. This is particularly relevant when the intermediary is not dedicated to provide service for only one organisation. The parent organisation may provide financial inducements, discounts or credit facilities to encourage the intermediary to favour its service products ahead of its rivals.

- **Punishments**. The ultimate sanction for poor performance is for the parent organisation to withdraw its support. This has become more common in recent years in the automobile industry, with manufacturers removing franchises from dealerships. Usually, though, this approach is only used as a last resort, because other dealers, no matter how good they are, wonder if they will be treated in a similar manner.

- **Providing expertise**. One of the most effective ways of motivating intermediaries is to provide support for their business. The parent organisation frequently has considerable resources in areas that are lacking in the intermediary. In Box 5.3 we saw Microsoft providing sales support for solution providers who are stronger in technical skills. Caterpillar, likewise, has created high levels of dealer satisfaction through the support given.

- **Training**. McDonald's Hamburger University is occasionally a source of jokes, but there can be little doubt as to its value in creating a consistency of approach throughout the network of outlets, both company owned and franchisees.

● *Information systems and technology*. Provision of process technology will assist in ensuring consistency of delivery. A franchisee generally receives a package of standard equipment and operating procedures to deliver the core service in the manner laid down by the parent organisation. Both Caterpillar and Microsoft provide online technical support to their partners and dealers. This serves the dual purpose of ensuring high-quality technical support is given to their customers and also training their partners and dealers in the desired approach.

5.4.3 Selection of intermediaries

The recruitment and training of intermediaries are critical, particularly for those organisations choosing to operate through franchises. Franchisees operate under the company brand and any poor performer will seriously damage it. Criteria for selection should be at least as stringent as for the selection of suppliers, but should also include a review of the potential franchisee's commitment to the brand values of the parent organisation.

5.5 Supply partnerships

As the pace of competition quickens it has become increasingly common for organisations to enter into partnerships and alliances for a number of strategic reasons:

● to enter a new geographic region, where a partner may have a stronger market presence

● to provide a package of goods and services that require the joint expertise of the partners to deliver them

● to develop new expertise in association with others, sharing resources in order to gain joint benefits.

In Chapter 3 we described many types of business relationships, including partnerships, alliances and networks. In this section we want to focus on alliances that have been formed in order to collaborate in the development and/or delivery of a specific set of services.

5.5.1 Types of alliances

Faulkner (1992) identified three dimensions of alliances:

● *Focused or complex*. A focused alliance has clearly defined aims, and is set up under particular specific circumstances. Generally, the focused alliance deals with a subset of each of the partners' total activities. An example would be a telecommunications system's provider such as Ericsson or Motorola forming an alliance with a software company in China to market a specific communications solution. It is clear that this agreement does not go beyond these boundaries.

A complex alliance would involve a much more substantial part of both partners being involved, perhaps retaining separate brands and marketing identities, but operationally much more interlinked.

- *Joint venture or working agreement*. A major task for a partnership cannot be handled by semi-formal agreements. It is more likely to be dealt with by the formation of a joint venture company. A significant issue here will be the allocation of power between the two partners.

- *Partnership or consortium*. While many strategic alliances take the form of a partnership between two organisations, a complex task requiring a wide range of skills and knowledge may be handled using a consortium. The issues involved in the management of these projects are correspondingly more complex.

5.5.2 Conditions for success

Figure 5.6 describes some of the major factors to be considered in assessing the likely success of an alliance.

Criteria for assessing the likely success of an alliance include:

- The extent to which the strategic aims of the partners coincide, but do not overlap. If both partners want the same benefits, there is little point in pursuing the partnership.

- The extent to which the two cultures allow for effective working. Are the values, beliefs and general ways of working compatible?

- Are the two partners (A and B in Figure 5.6) able to let the venture work in its own way? The culture of the venture is likely to be different from those of both its 'parents' and may be viewed with suspicion.

- Has there been sufficient discussion and negotiation as to what are the likely benefits for each partner? Is it clear as to which partner is responsible for which activities?

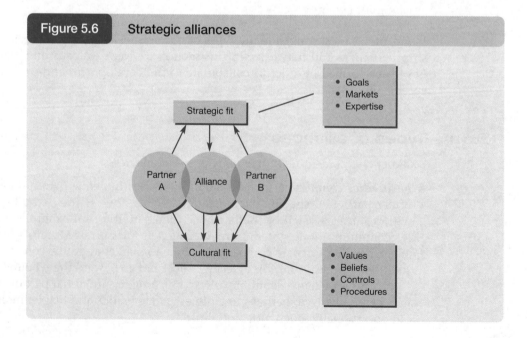

Figure 5.6 **Strategic alliances**

- Is there a dominant partner in the enterprise? Has this been agreed and is the less powerful partner happy with the arrangement?

- Is it clear how long the partnership will last and what are the terms of the dissolution of the partnership?

The experiences of alliances are many and varied. The key issue is the extent to which senior management is truly committed to the process, rather than paying lip-service to the idea. Hutt *et al.* (2000), in describing the creation of a co-branded service product between a telecommunication company and a financial service organisation, outline the impact of a 'clash of corporate egos'. Each partner was used to exerting its muscle since both were powerful in their traditional markets. The initial lack of compromise between the partners at senior level led to a series of disputes at the operational level, including conflicts about what company name would be used by customer service representatives.

The study carried out by Hutt *et al.* followed the alliance from inception into its second year. At the end of the first year the alliance was only moderately profitable, but was showing signs of improvement. Both partners found difficulty in generating mutual trust, having been used to adversarial negotiating stances in the past. The study found that this was a major problem in the early life of the project and staff needed continuing social contact to begin to break down barriers raised on day one. The illustration of Sussex Police in Box 5.4 demonstrates that significant amounts of time must be invested in order to generate the levels of trust required to move a partnership approach forward.

Sussex Police, UK   Box 5.4

Police services throughout the UK have undergone a major change in approach to their task in recent years. One obvious sign of this change is that the police is now known as a 'service' rather than a 'force', recognising the need to integrate more obviously into the society it serves rather than simply enforce law.

Sussex Police, in common with others, is facing the issue of dealing with rising levels of crime but with limited resources. Many issues in society today cannot be solved simply by putting more police officers on the streets, even if this were possible to do. Problems of drug dealing or racial unrest require co-operation between society at large, community leaders and other social agencies. The Sussex Police Way, launched in 1999, set out five policing principles to support the purpose of Sussex Police, which is 'to reduce the number of incidents which require an intervention by Sussex Police and/or from other social agencies'. The aim is to address the root cause of problems and to break the vicious cycle of responding to emergency calls in a wholly reactive manner. Principle 4 states: 'We will emphasise and develop the partnership approach. This will involve a wide range of official and voluntary agencies as well as the general public.'

One example of this approach is provided by Operation Columbus. Sussex has several language schools attracting students from many countries who are interested in studying English in a location close to the sea but near to London. These students may be vulnerable to attack either because they are naïve or because they provoke jealousy. Months of consultation between police, language schools and student bodies have resulted in a manual available to those involved in student welfare. It covers every aspect of student safety, from simple precautions to be taken by the students themselves through to advice for police officers in dealing with students, whether they be victims or offenders. This information is presented in multilingual documents, through posters featuring the adventures of Columbus, and through an attractive Operation Columbus website.

Questions

1 What benefits can be generated from this partnership approach? How would you justify the investment in time, effort and materials required?

2 In extending this approach to more sensitive issues such as drug taking or racial disharmony, what problems could be anticipated in generating the information flows required to build a partnership?

This illustration was compiled from information on the Sussex Police website (www.sussex.police.uk) and the Operation Columbus site (www.sussex.police.uk/columbus/index.html).

5.6 Service-level agreements

Service-level agreements (SLAs) are forms of contracts agreed between a service supplier and the service purchaser or user. These are usually found in a business-to-business context and often between internal suppliers and customers where a traditional contract is not felt to be appropriate. They are an important means of managing the relationship between partners in a supply chain.

Whether for internal use or external use, an SLA goes beyond the traditional remit of a contract, i.e. a statement of a service specification and the price that will be paid for it. While an SLA, like a contract, defines the nature of the goods or services and the level of quality to be provided, the idea of an 'agreement' is that it is a mutually agreed view of what can and will be provided, but also, and importantly, it exists for the mutual development of both parties. That is, an SLA is seen to be an integral part of the development of a relationship between a supplier and a customer – indeed the SLA attempts to formalise this relationship.

There are three key features of an SLA: setting a service specification, dealing with day-to-day, routine issues, and the development of the relationship.

Service specification

The core of an SLA is the development and agreement of the service specification. This will include:

● Agreeing the key dimensions of performance, such as response times, availability, accuracy etc. This allows for both customer and supplier to understand what is important about the service from both points of view.

● Agreeing how each dimension will be measured. Discussion and agreement about the measures to be used reduces the likelihood of disagreements at a later date about performance.

● Setting mutually agreed targets for each dimension. It is possible that standards set by one party may be too high for the needs of the other; clarity and agreement over what is needed and what is possible should lead to a feasible and achievable – and indeed low-cost – outcome.

- Defining where the responsibility lies for the measurement of each dimension. Unlike a traditional contract the responsibility for performance measurement may rest with either the supplier or customer, but such information is made openly available to both parties.

Routinised relationship

The routine part of the relationship formalised by the SLA concerns the day-to-day operation of the agreement. This may include:

- Providing a mechanism for reporting performance against standards at agreed intervals. Underpinning an SLA is the sharing of information, the purpose of which should not be unilateral action, as it might be in a traditional contract, but understanding and improvement.
- Setting out the procedures to be invoked if a failure against standard should occur. Routines for dealing with problems should be agreed in advance so that both parties understand their obligations and duties in such event. Failures should not be seen to be negative but as opportunities for supplier and customer to work together to solve each other's problems.

Developmental relationship

A key, though often ignored, element of an SLA is its role in developing a long-term relationship between supplier and customer. This involves:

- Providing a mechanism for routine discussion of the measures and targets and to share ideas for all-round improvements. This 'double-loop learning' activity formalises the need to regularly review the agreement, the measures used, the targets applied and the relationship between the parties.

5.6.1 Advantages and disadvantages

Clearly, SLAs require a considerable deal more input of time and effort by both parties than a traditional contract. They have to be tailor-made for each service with each supplier in the supply chain, they can be complex, and they need an investment of time and effort in the long term to secure the potential benefits.

However, they do have the potentially significant benefits of a closer working relationship and therefore better service between supplier and provider. They can reduce risk for the supplier and the purchaser or user, and they create loyalty and reliability by focusing on the development of people and systems rather than focusing on systems of 'punishment'. They also prevent unnecessary and expensive over-provision of quality by defining agreed standards.

5.6.2 Frequent mistakes in SLAs

Sadly, for many organisations, SLAs degenerate into a traditional contract, missing out on the real benefits that can be obtained. The usual mistakes that are made include:

- too few or inappropriate dimensions of performance
- no mutually agreed targets for each dimension
- responsibility for measures not identified
- no mechanism for reporting and discussion of performance
- no procedures to deal with problems
- mutual benefits not discussed or delivered
- no mechanism for discussion of measures or targets or to share ideas for improvement
- lack of commitment of managers from both parties to derive the benefits from the agreements.

5.7 Summary

Types of supply relationships

- There are three main types of supply relationships: service supply chains or networks, management through intermediaries, and supply partnerships.

Service supply chains

- A supply chain is the network that joins together internal and external suppliers with internal and external consumers.
- Supply chain management (SCM) is concerned with managing the network and the flow of information, materials, services and customers through the network.
- Some supply chains are contracting through disintermediation, others are expanding through outsourcing.
- Procurement tends to be a 'Cinderalla' activity and e-procurement is challenging the traditional procurement functions.
- The value of SCM is that it allows for the benefits of vertical integration without the long-term overhead and inherent inflexibility that comes from trying to manage all activities in the supply chain under the umbrella of one organisation.

Managing through intermediaries

- The main reasons for using intermediaries include closeness to customer, local knowledge, focused expertise, poor service margins and insufficient capacity.
- The main trade-off to be managed is between in-house control and profit margins.

Supply partnerships

- It is increasingly common for organisations to enter into partnerships and alliances.
- There are many forms of partnership, the three main dimensions of which are focused or complex, joint venture or working agreement, and partnership or consortium.

- Service-level agreements are forms of contracts agreed between a service supplier and the service purchaser or user.
- The three activities involved in managing SLAs are: setting a service specification, dealing with routine issues, and the development of the relationship.
- Many SLAs do not realise the potential benefits.

5.8 Discussion questions

1 Compare the approaches of two organisations in the same service sector, one choosing to operate through intermediaries, the other preferring to deal with end customers directly. What are the benefits and challenges of each approach?

2 How can supply chains be managed more effectively to provide more effective service delivery in order to increase customer satisfaction, while also increasing profitability for all the companies in the chain?

5.9 Questions for managers

1 Have you reviewed your supplier relationships recently? Are any of these relationships in the 'Stagnant' category? If so, what can you do about them?

2 Could you be more effective in reaching new markets by forming a strategic alliance? What would you require in such a partner?

3 Are you using the potential of e-procurement to manage your supplier base more effectively?

5.10 Further reading

Croom S. and Johnston R., 'E-service: enhancing internal customer service through e-procurement', *International Journal of Service Industry Management*, vol. 14, no. 5, 2003, pp. 539–55.

Faulkner D., 'Strategic alliances: cooperation for competition', in Faulkner D. and Johnson G. (eds), *The Challenge of Strategic Management*, Kogan Page, London, 1992.

5.11 References

Armistead C.G. and Clark G.R., *Customer Service and Support*, Financial Times/Pitman Publishing, London, 1992.

Bales, W.A. and Fearon, H.E., 'Presidents' perceptions and expectations of the purchasing function', report by the Center for Advanced Purchasing Studies, Tempe, Arizona. 1996.

Croom S., 'The impact of web-based procurement on the management of operating resources supply', *Journal of Supply Chain Management*, vol. 36, no. 1, 2000, pp. 4–13.

Croom S. and Johnston R., 'E-service: enhancing internal customer service through e-procurement', *International Journal of Service Industry Management*, vol. 14, no. 5, 2003, pp. 539–55.

Faulkner D., 'Strategic alliances: cooperation for competition', in Faulkner D. and Johnson G. (eds), *The Challenge of Strategic Management*, Kogan Page, London, 1992.

Gebauer J. and Seveg A., 'Changing shapes of supply chains: how the internet could lead to a more integrated procurement function', working paper, Haas School of Business, University of California, Berkeley, 2001.

Helper S., 'How much has really changed between US automakers and their suppliers?' *Sloan Management Review*, Summer 1991, pp. 15–28.

Hines P., *Creating World Class Suppliers. Unlocking Mutual Competitive Advantage*, Pitman, London, 1994.

Hutt M.D., Stafford E.R., Walker B.A. and Reingen P.H., 'Defining the social network of a strategic alliance', *Sloan Management Review*, Winter 2000.

Lamming R.C., *Beyond Partnership. Strategies for Innovation and Lean Supply*, Prentice Hall, London, 1993.

Nolan A., 'Purchasing's new power', *Director*, vol. 52, no. 7, 1999, pp. 46–9.

Sheng M.L., 'The impact of internet-based technologies on the procurement strategy', in the proceedings of the 2nd International Conference on Electronic Commerce, Taipei, December 2002.

Womack J.P. and Jones D.T., *Lean Thinking*, Simon & Schuster, London, 1996.

Womack J.P., Jones D.T. and Roos D., *The Machine that Changed the World*, Macmillan, New York, 1990.

The Regional Forensic Science Laboratory — Case Exercise

Robert Johnston, Warwick Business School, and Tay Ming Kiong, Department of Scientific Services, Institute of Forensic Science and Forensic Medicine, Singapore.

The Regional Forensic Science Laboratory (RFSL) provides a one-stop service to a range of professionals. These professionals include police officers investigating crimes, narcotics officers who want drugs analysing, fire officers concerned to find the cause of a fire, defence counsels who are trying to strengthen the legal case for their clients, hospitals wishing to identify the cause of cases of poisoning, and private individuals who might be considering taking civil action.

Michael Tay is the head of the RFSL and he explains how his unit operates:

> Forensic science is the application of science to the law and our role is to assist our clients in identifying suspects and victims, clearing innocent persons of suspicion and bringing the wrongdoer to justice. Our task is to provide accurate and objective information based on the evidence with which we are provided. We provide both written reports and verbal evidence in legal trials.
>
> We have seven laboratories here, all under one roof, though often exhibits may well be sent from one lab to another for different specialised examinations. The Toxicology Laboratory examines body fluids and organs to determine the presence or absence of drugs and poisons. The Drugs Analysis Laboratory examines exhibits for drug content and body fluids and hair for drug consumption. The Physical Evidence Laboratory applies the principles and techniques of chemistry and physics to identify and compare a wide range of crime-scene evidence: firearms, gunshot residues, tool marks, shoeprints, tyre prints, paints, fibres, explosives etc. The Biology Laboratory examines exhibits for biological material (dried bloodstains, semen, saliva and other body fluids) and identifies the source using conventional serology or DNA typing. The Document Examination Laboratory examines handwriting and typewriting on doc-

uments, some of which may be badly charred, for example, to ascertain authenticity and/or source. The Latent Prints Unit processes and examines evidence for latent fingerprints and identifies the source of lifted prints. And the Forensic Pathology Laboratory investigates sudden unnatural, unexplained or violent deaths to determine the cause of death.

I know this sounds quite straightforward and scientific but the reality is rather different – it is fraught with problems and confusion. All the police officers, fire officers and hospitals etc. will send exhibits directly to the appropriate lab. This is fine until that lab sends it to another lab and the client no longer knows who has their blood sample etc.

The sample they give us will have been given to them by someone else. It might have come from a crime scene, from a victim or a suspect or an eyewitness. Because it can take time to get the sample from the origin it means we are under tremendous pressure to undertake the analysis quickly in order to help them complete the investigation. Hospitals, for example, rely on speedy response from the Toxicology Laboratory to ascertain the cause of poisoning so as to be able to administer the right antidote or treatment quickly to save the victim. The other professionals are usually under very tight deadlines imposed by the organisations, such as courts, to which they are responsible.

Yet we have to be very careful to do a thorough and proper job because at the end of the day the real customers are the suspect, either exonerated or convicted, the families and sympathisers of the suspects, the victims and their families who may have suffered terribly, the public, and of course the press and the media. Forensic science carries a heavy weight in the legal system. The judge and jury generally view forensic evidence as objective and impartial when assessing the case against a defendant.

The forensic expert's testimony must be clear and comprehensible to lay persons. Prosecutors, defence lawyers, judges and juries often have little time or inclination to get to grips with highly technical forensic evidence. We have to provide it in an accessible way. Because we have to make the information accessible and understandable, defence lawyers will use it to try to undermine the quality of the forensic science laboratory, our processes and even our staff. Their job is to interpret the evidence in favour of their clients and so they will look for weaknesses in the forensic findings to discredit the evidence or render it inadmissible.

We also have a problem with the evidence that is sent to us. We rely on the people, at the scenes of crime for example, to collect the right type and right amount of evidence. There is also the problem of which evidence to believe – it is possible that it may have been 'planted'.

Furthermore, like many forensic services, our laboratories face significant staff turnover and shortage, which affect capacity, result in loss of expertise and disrupt client relationships. As a result our delivery times can be quite long. The situation is made worse by new technologies that not only are expensive but require a substantial investment in training. Also the people we have are from scientific backgrounds and may be excellent in technical skills but lacking in business sense and customer awareness.

At the end of the day, members of the public want to see justice done, and the criminal punished. They are alarmed when the criminal and judicial processes are unsuccessful in identifying and convicting the criminal. The public expects the correct culprit to be quickly apprehended and dealt with. Mistakes in the criminal justice systems have a wide-ranging impact on the community, victim, victim's family, falsely accused person, investigators, the investigation process, the forensic community and the judicial process. In capital punishment cases, the mistake cannot be corrected because the sentence is irreversible. Justice must not only be done, it must be seen as done, and we have a vital role to play in this. Unfortunately, I sometimes feel that the system is against us and we are not doing all that we should.

Questions

1 Summarise the problems faced by Michael Tay and the other professionals involved in the collection, analysis and use of forensic evidence.

2 How could a supply chain approach overcome some of the problems?

part three

Sevice delivery

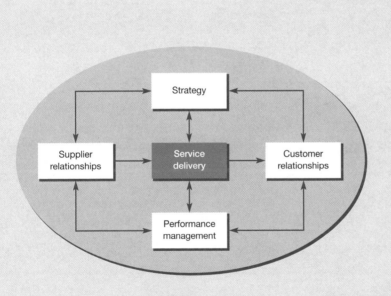

6

Service processes

Chapter objectives:

- to define service processes and their importance

- to understand the nature of service processes

- to provide some tools to help 'engineer' service processes

- to understand how to control service processes

- to explain how to reposition service processes.

6.1 Introduction

Processes are the lifeblood of the service operation. Rather like DNA provides the pattern for a living organism, a good process ensures that service is delivered consistently, time after time. Process design describes and prescribes the procedures to be followed in service delivery and also how they will use or interact with other resources such as materials or equipment. For example, call centre agents in a telephone bank are given clear guidance as to how to speak to the customer, what questions to ask, and what performance standards are expected. The agents also have access to screens on their computers to prompt them to ask particular questions or to help them answer routine enquiries. Finally, the information system will guide the agents through the customer data requirements to be filled in during or immediately after the call.

Moving to a macro level, process managers and designers have to pay attention to how the various activities or sub-processes link together to provide the whole service. In the telephone bank the service is not simply that delivered by the agent but also involves loan application processes, credit card issuing processes, international funds transfer processes and so on. The whole interrelated chain of processes needs to be carefully designed, managed and controlled to deliver value to customers and to the organisation.

However, designing and then managing service processes is not easy. Processes are as varied as the service organisations of which they are a part. Some are extremely flexible, able to meet a wide variety of customer requirements using the same set of resources. Some management consultants, for example, are able to utilise a wide range of approaches in developing customised solutions for their clients. Other processes, such as many call and contact centre operations, are much more closely defined in order to achieve benefits of consistency and efficiency. In a similar manner, some processes depend a great deal on the skill, knowledge and expertise of individual employees, such as medical doctors in general practice, while other processes employ resources such as technology or information systems to reduce the dependence on individual skills, thus enabling the service organisation to deal with greater volumes and to grow geographically.

6.2 Service processes and their importance

Excellent service – which satisfies the customer and meets the strategic intentions of the organisation – is usually the result of careful design and delivery of a whole set of interrelated processes. These processes not only 'process' customers but they also process materials, information and even staff. Many service processes are therefore quite complex, involving many interrelated processes, departments, people, decisions and activities. One of the most complex service organisations is a hospital, and in Box 6.1 we describe the process taken by an acutely ill patient.

Although the service process is only one element of the service operation, it is the 'glue' that holds the rest – the customers, staff, equipment and materials – together. And it is the part that creates the customer's experience and results in the service outcomes.

It is important to note that when we are talking about processes we are not simply referring to the point where the customer receives the service. Service providers that consistently meet both cost and quality targets manage the chain of processes from start to finish (often designated end-to-end, or e2e, processes) rather than simply the final stage of delivery to customers. It is also crucial to remember that services frequently fail because they have been inadequately designed and executed. The service process is central to this design activity.

6.2.1 The service process: creating the service experience

A holiday consists of many different activities: flights, hotel accommodation, meals and tours, for example. While these are the elements that come together to create the holiday, it is the way the customer, information and materials are processed and how they link together that creates the experience. Key elements of the experience may involve being met off the plane and being led to transfer coaches, the checking-in at the hotel, the way the reps provide assistance and information, and so on. The service experience or process is not just the elements of the holiday but also how they link together as the holiday unfolds. Some processes will be highly visible to the customer, such as check-in, while others may be, at least in part, invisible to the customer, such as computerised booking and reservations, cooking and cleaning at the hotel. Some processes will process customers, such as the transfer coaches; some processes deal with information, such as reservations systems; and some processes will process materials, such as catering services. (See Box 6.1 for a detailed example of another service process.)

The acute patient's journey | Box 6.1

Paul Walley, Warwick Business School

When an acutely ill patient needs to be treated urgently, the whole healthcare system has to respond in a co-ordinated manner. For example, if a patient attends a general practitioner's (GP) clinic with abdominal pain and the GP assesses this as a probable acute appendicitis, the patient needs to be admitted to hospital for surgery immediately. First the GP might phone a house officer at the local general hospital to agree the probable diagnosis, so that the patient can be 'surgically accepted' by the hospital. An ambulance will be immediately requested, to take the patient to hospital. However, the target response times may be breached if the ambulances in the area are allocated to other emergencies.

When an ambulance arrives to take the patient to hospital, the GP usually gives the paramedic a letter of admission to take with the patient. This contains any immediate patient information that the hospital staff may find useful, including drugs that have recently been prescribed for pain relief. Ideally, ambulance paramedics should be given the same information so that they know what treatment has already been given, to avoid duplication. This does not always happen, especially if the doctor is unable to meet the ambulance crew themselves.

When the ambulance arrives at the hospital, it is normal for the patient to be taken to either the accident and emergency (A&E) department or to a specialist 'surgical assessment unit'. First, the patient will have to be booked into the system by a receptionist and the ambulance staff will not be allowed to leave before this is done. This is to ensure that accurate information about the patient's condition is given to the hospital staff receiving the patient. The booking procedure needs to establish the patient's identity accurately, so that the correct patient's notes can be retrieved from the hospital's archives. Other details, such as the patient's next of kin, are also required, so that relatives can be informed, particularly if the patient is extremely ill. The patient's arrival will be cross-referenced with the call to surgically accept the patient.

Once the patient has been booked in, they will be assessed for the urgency of their condition. This 'triage' will usually be performed by a senior nurse or doctor. A house officer, supervised by a senior house officer, will then hopefully provide an accurate diagnosis. The first steps in the diagnosis will usually involve basic blood tests and X-rays. Most hospitals have their own emergency X-ray units attached to A&E, staffed by radiographers. These often become very busy with patients, especially where specialist fracture clinics share the resource. Each X-ray needs to be assessed by a radiologist and a report typed up by a medical secretary. When blood is taken, the most common tests might be analysed using small testing machines located near the A&E department. Most samples are sent to central pathology labs, where they are processed alongside the hundreds of routine samples that each lab has to perform each day. Skilled pathology technicians operate the equipment and ensure that the results are accurately obtained. Pathologists assess the results, which are usually reported on a computer printout. Urgent results are sometimes telephoned through. Only a few departments have electronic reporting of this type of information.

Often one of the biggest hurdles for the patient is to be found a bed within the hospital. This is the responsibility of a specialist team of bed managers. Wards are divided into medical and surgical units with male- and female-only wards. Given that most hospitals in the UK work with 90 per cent or more occupancy of beds, finding a space for up to 50 acute admissions per day can be a real challenge. Acute admissions typically comprise 30 per cent of all admissions and so emergencies compete with elective cases for bed space. The space available partially depends upon the surgical lists that drive the elective admissions. Commonly, Mondays and Wednesdays see most elective surgery and so these are frequently the most difficult days for unplanned admissions. In many hospitals, medical wards overflow at times. This can result in patient 'medical outliers' being placed on surgical wards, further restricting space. One bed manager highlighted other problems:

Requests for beds should come through us. This does not always happen, as patients can be admitted via the 'back door' by consultants etc., without telling us. It can be confusing when we think we have free beds but we haven't. We continually monitor where beds are available on the computer and by doing a ward round. We conduct a census on wards to find free beds not recorded on the computer.

When a patient needs urgent surgery, a theatre slot needs to be found. This can be complicated as the theatres usually have particular elective clinical specialism booked for each half-day session, with just a few slots reserved for emer-

gencies. Theatres are not all equipped in the same way: theatres specialising in orthopaedics, for example, need specialist pieces of equipment. There are also issues to address when assembling the most appropriate surgical team of surgeons, anaesthetists, nurses and support staff, since not all staff are multiskilled or available. Staff time taken by emergency surgery inhibits other activities such as ward rounds. The theatres also have to ensure that there is a readily available stock of sterilised equipment, and it usually takes 24 hours for used equipment to be cleaned and resterilised.

Patient welfare is also enhanced by the array of support services. The catering services need to provide patients with three meals a day. Cleaning services need to ensure that all areas are kept as clean as possible. This is a difficult task because they must not interfere too much with the daily workload. The traffic of thousands of staff, patients and visitors bring in dirt and waste incessantly. Cross-infection caused by poor hygiene requires a massive co-ordinated, preventive programme.

Hospitals also need efficient discharge procedures. If patients are discharged later in the day, they may occupy the bed unnecessarily. Delays can be caused by poor co-ordination with pharmacy, as patients wait for take-home drug prescriptions to be prepared for them. If these are not ready by 5.00 p.m., pharmacies often close for the day, forcing patients to stay an extra night on the ward. Other delays can be caused by waits for porters or transport. Relatives often only pick patients up in the evening, once they have come home from work, causing a bed blockage.

Questions

1 Map the patient's journey (see section 6.4.1).

2 Which do you think are the unnecessary delays and/or steps in the process?

3 Why is the process for treating a patient with appendicitis so difficult?

As Box 6.1 shows, a service process comprises many interrelated processes, some of which predominantly process customers, others information and others materials. Some tasks and activities may be located in the back office remote from customers, while other tasks or activities take place in the presence of the customer. These front office processes may be performed in a number of locations: in the organisation's facilities or in the customer's home, for example. Together, these processes – in an appropriate sequence – create the service experience and deliver the service outcomes. Figure 6.1 shows a simplified diagrammatic representation of some operations processes (see also Armistead and Clark 1993).

Front office processes

Front office processes deal directly with customers and may be visible to them. These might provide personal interaction with service employees (face-to-face or by telephone), or interaction through technology such as the organisation's website.

The customer often plays an important role in front office processes and is an operational resource (Figure 6.2). Customers fulfil many roles, providing themselves and others with service, collecting materials and providing information to staff, for example (for more details see Chapter 7). Indeed some processes depend on the customer to be an integral part of the operation, for example in service partnerships (section 6.3.3) such as management consultancy or development. The 'selection' and 'training' of these 'customer employees' (see Chapter 7) will be critical for the operation's success. The presence of the customer may have benefits in terms of providing an additional resource and better communication, but also disadvantages because the presence of the customer may inject unpredicted variations into the service process.

Figure 6.1	Simplified service processes

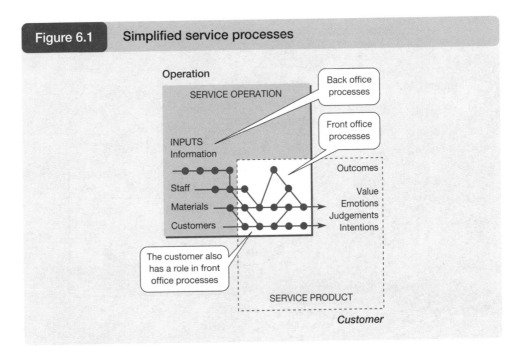

Examples of front office processes include:

- a management consultant working with a client to develop a diagnosis of the problem to be solved
- a nurse administering prescribed drugs to a patient
- a call centre agent answering a customer's query about the progress of a mail order shipment
- a prospective customer navigating the website of a electrical goods retailer in order to select and order a computer.

This demonstrates that there is a wide range of possible front office processes; some have well-defined routines, as in the call centre enquiry process, whereas others depend almost entirely on the skill, knowledge and expertise of the service provider, such as the corporate lawyer. In the case of the management consultant, there may be a preferred approach to problem diagnosis, but this process is likely to be extremely flexible. (We will develop these issues in section 6.3.)

The final example in the list illustrates a growing trend for the service designer to shift the activity from provider to customer. Indeed some service organisations are trying to encourage the customer to do more (see Figure 6.2). We are encouraged to use the internet to buy tickets or find out information about holidays and train or plane times, thereby reducing costs for the organisation (and sometimes the costs to ourselves) but usually at the cost of much greater time and effort on the part of the customer. In this case the service designer has developed a clear process to

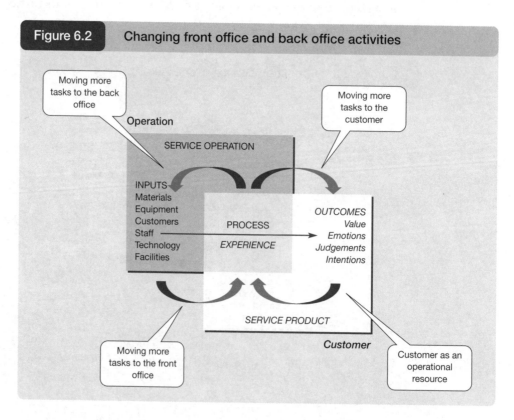

Figure 6.2   Changing front office and back office activities

guide the customer through the company's internet site. This demands greater investment in process design and technology, but yields benefits for the provider in lower transaction costs and for the customers in greater access to information and freedom to shop at their own convenience.

All front office processes have a common problem: the unpredictability of the customer. In the example of the management consultant, the competence and willingness of the client to understand and communicate the true nature of the problem to be studied and solved will have a major impact on the effectiveness of the consultancy process. This variability is also present to some degree in high volume business-to-consumer services such as fast food chains. However much the customer is 'trained' to ask for a standard product in a standard manner, there is likely to be a significant percentage of customers who want something different or who disrupt the carefully designed service process by asking for advice or help beyond the expected level.

Back office processes

Back office processes operate at a distance from customers and are largely invisible to them. These processes do not have the complication of the customer's presence and are frequently more efficient as a result. Customers tend to inject a greater degree of variability of demand when they are able to interact with the people involved in the service production process. Examples of back office process include:

- cheque-clearing processes for a retail bank
- computer repair processes
- preparation of food in a restaurant
- most manufacturing processes.

Some organisations are shifting activities from the front office to the back office (see Figure 6.2). Many retail banks, for example, have removed many administration processes from their branches (front offices) and combine them in high-volume and efficient centralised (back office) processing centres (such as a cheque-processing centre). There are several reasons why organisations might wish to move activities from the front to back office:

- Common back office processes serving a variety of customer-facing processes provide cost and consistency benefits. An example would be the company managing a portfolio of restaurant brands, each with a different style, but using food menus with a considerable degree of overlap. Consolidation of common processes such as recipe development, purchasing and inventory management yields major benefit for the company, leaving the individual brand managers to concentrate on the service differentiation issues.

- Moving processes from front office to back office reduces the need for immediate response to customer requests. Providing capacity in the front office to respond to the variations in customer demand (both content and timing) is enormously expensive. Generally, the trade-off in this case is that the customer expects more restricted service and slower response in return for lower prices.

- Expensive technology may require scale to justify its purchase. In this case, the business may operate from a number of locations close to customers, which take orders and deal with other customer service issues, while the bulk of the work is carried out more cheaply at a remote location. In this case longer customer lead-times are traded off against lower costs/prices to customers.

Conversely, some organisations are moving some tasks from the back office to the front office (Figure 6.2). Some services recognise that customers need access to technical experts who may, traditionally, be back office employees, rather than deal through an intermediary such as an account manager or front-line consultant. However, some technical experts have little interest or aptitude in customer service and are best employed at a suitable distance from customer contact!

In some situations, technology has enabled what were back office processes to be moved to the front office. A good example of this is photo processing. For a number of years, large film processing laboratories provided a reasonably rapid service at lower cost to customers. The advent of affordable mini-labs means that customers can take their films or digital camera memory cards to a convenient location, the service is rapid and reasonably priced, and precious films are not subject to the uncertainties of the postal system.

6.2.2   The service experience

The service experience is the customer's direct experience of the service process and concerns the way the customer is dealt with by the service provider. It is affected by how customer-facing staff interact with customers and also the customer's experience of the organisation and its facilities. The interactions may be:

- *Face-to-face*. Here a customer deals directly with a service employee, as in a restaurant or in the branch of a retailer in a shopping mall. These encounters may be an essential element of the service product and contribute directly to customer satisfaction. A positive interaction between customer and the restaurant's serving staff may make a major contribution to the enjoyment of the meal.

- *Telephone*. Telephones are typically employed by call centres to provide advice, complaint handling or order-taking activities. The advantage of these experiences/processes over face-to-face experiences/processes is that they may be provided by a central resource and may therefore be provided at lower cost. The advent of broadband technology has facilitated the relocation of these activities to low-labour-cost economies, providing still further efficiency improvements. As customers become more remote, however, there is a much greater possibility of misunderstandings occurring, and service employees missing cues that would be obvious if the customer were physically present.

- *E-service and other remote interaction*. Internet-based services enable still further efficiency savings to be made. E-service provides access for customers at all times and enables them to request information or to order goods and services as and when they wish. Other remote service processes include contact through letters or mailings, or through automated service processes such as bank automated teller machines (ATMs).

In each type of experience/front office process it is imperative that the impact of the service design on customer perception is recognised. It is all too easy for the process to be designed for the benefit of the service provider and virtually to ignore the customer requirement.

Clearly some experiences/front office processes are generally more intense in nature for provider and customer alike, as Figure 6.3 illustrates. An aspect of variability in the service encounter is the extent to which the customer perceives some degree of risk or uncertainty.

This risk may take a number of forms:

- *Financial risk*. In some situations, it may be difficult for the customer to assess the extent of the risk. The purchaser of a used car does not know how reliable the vehicle will prove to be. In the same way, purchasing a pension plan may feel like an extremely risky activity, particularly for someone who is unfamiliar with financial matters.

- *Physical risk*. Going on an adventure holiday or flying in an aeroplane clearly entails some physical risk. In the former, it could be reasonably expected that customers choosing such a holiday have made some assessment of the risks involved and will see them as part of the expected experience. With an airline flight, although the risk to life and limb is small, it does create a degree of discomfort for many people.

- *Psychological risk*. This type of risk may arise from a number of sources. It may come from the customer's lack of confidence or competence. Anxious customers are likely to prove difficult in the service encounter, not because they are intentionally obstructive, but rather because they channel energies into distracting their thoughts from their concerns. Furthermore nobody likes to feel inferior or incompetent. It is possible that service organisations may make assumptions as to the competence of their customers. If this is combined with a very public display of ignorance, the customer may become either very quiet or very noisy. Finally, a significant number of people find the presence of large numbers of people in close proximity a trial in itself. For some of these 'private' people, any form of social encounter can be painful. This may be in stark contrast to the customer-facing employee who may have chosen this role in large part because of its high degree of customer contact.

Figure 6.3	Customer perceived risk and social interaction

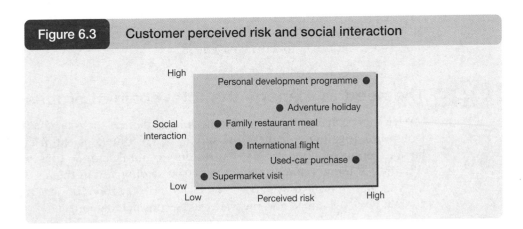

Figure 6.3 illustrates the extent of social interaction in a routine service encounter for a number of service situations. Each of these has implications for the extent of desired and possible customer relationship, as discussed in Chapter 3. For example, in the supermarket visit there are limited opportunities for anything more than superficial conversations, whereas a meal in a restaurant where the customers and staff know each other reasonably well might lead to interaction that goes beyond the baseline of ordering food.

It should be noted that social interaction is often linked in some way to a mechanism for managing risk. In evaluating the riskiness of the used-car purchase, the customer is frequently judging the trustworthiness of the salesperson. The busyness of the cabin crew on a long-distance flight provides a distraction for those who might be tempted to dwell on the risk of flying, and allows the crew to keep an eye on those who might be suffering from extra anxiety.

There is also a wide range of customer variables that will complicate the service experience. Some of these are listed below:

- *Customer mindset*. The nature of the service may be reflected in the state of mind of the customer. A customer complaint process will probably not have the customer in the most helpful mindset! On the other hand, customers who are going to a theme park or to a family celebration in a restaurant are more likely to be predisposed to having a good time.

- *Customer mood*. This is somewhat linked to customer mindset, in that people who complain might be expected to be angry, while people going to a celebration might be expected to be in a happier frame of mind. The message here is that it is extremely dangerous to make assumptions about individual customers. Customers who were in a bad mood because they were under pressure or rushed on a previous occasion may turn out to be model customers the next time.

- *Personality clashes*. Some people simply do not get on. They seem to take an instant dislike to each other, or there is something about the other person that reminds them of another difficult or disliked character. Psychologists call this 'transference', which describes the situation when attributes of a previous relationship are transferred to a current relationship. A common example relates to authority figures. If some aspect of the service provider reminds the customer of a hated figure from the past, it is unlikely that this transaction will be successful.

All these factors must be taken into account both in designing the experience/process, and in its day-to-day management.

6.2.3   The need to manage the total chain of processes

Service operations managers need to be able to manage the total chain of processes, which link together to deliver the service to customers or end users. Most of us have experienced poor service that results from a lack of co-ordination between activities, a simple example being the person serving you in the restaurant promising you that your meal will arrive in a few minutes without understanding that the kitchen is overwhelmed and the wait will be considerably longer.

Failure to manage end-to-end (e2e) processes leads to inefficiencies across the organisation or chain of organisations that comprise the service supply chain, leading to lack of consistency, poor reliability in terms of quality and lead-times, and increased cost. We worked with a major technology provider that operated its processes in functional 'silos', with little or no co-ordination between them. The result of this was that some functions were laying off staff one month and rehiring the same staff in the following month. This was clearly damaging to quality, delivery performance and efficiency. When this organisation moved to manage and co-ordinate its processes on an e2e basis, operational performance improved dramatically.

In Chapter 5 we describe the challenges in managing supply chains which, though simple in concept, prove to be much more complex in application. Service managers must not only deal with the individual issues in managing the back office and front office processes, including managing the customers, but also deal with the challenge of integrating activities across the chain. For the technology provider discussed above, many of the individual process steps required the undivided attention of large numbers of highly qualified engineers. The end result was that artificial barriers were erected between functions, tasks were ill-co-ordinated and activities duplicated. Customer satisfaction ranked rather low in the list of operations priorities, with resultant poor performance. On a smaller scale, the conference hotel that does not co-ordinate the activities of room preparation, food service, and greeting and directing course delegates on arrival will not survive in a market that demands both high service standards and competitive pricing.

Managers, including operations managers, have a tendency to draw a boundary around their processes that coincides with the physical or geographic boundary of their responsibility. The problem faced by many customers is at the interfaces between the many back office and front office processes that together create the total chain of processes. A hospital, for example, comprises many departments: some back office departments such as cleaning, administration, finance and personnel, and front office processes such as reception, patient wards, nursing and treatment. While each one may appear to be efficient in its own right, problems are often felt, usually by customers, when they attempt to use the service that requires co-ordinated action between all of them. For example, problems can include:

- There is a desire for prompt treatment, but the general practitioner's notes have been delayed or are unavailable.
- A request for medicines or equipment is held up because of the paperwork.
- A request is made to turn up on time for an appointment, but there is insufficient car parking spaces outside.

By assessing and designing service processes from the point of view of the 'thing' being processed, whether it is the customers themselves, or a file, or information, such as a loan application, we can expose the interface problems. The objective of good service design is to achieve an efficient process from an operations perspective and seamless service for the customer. Dr Michael Shulver from Warwick Business School provides the following 'tests' for seamless service:

Customers (or their files, requests, etc.) should:

- flow smoothly through the service
- experience no discontinuity.

Staff should:

- take ownership of processes
- take ownership of individual customers (or their files, requests, etc.).

Managers should:

- take a process not a functional perspective
- understand whole processes
- understand how they fit into the processes
- work in cross-functional teams to assess and improve the design.

6.2.4 The process environment – the servicescape

We cannot ignore the fact that a service experience/process takes place in an environment that will affect the customer's perception of the experience/process itself. Bitner (1992) coined the term 'servicescape' to describe the physical surroundings of the service operation. We use it here to include both the physical and informational environment in which a service is both created and delivered: it is the environment for both staff, back office and front office, and customers. The servicescape of a hospital, for example, comprises the car parks, the buildings, the décor and the arrangement of seats in a waiting room or staff canteen. An internet-based servicescape may include the appearance, user-friendliness and accessibility of an organisation's website.

As such the servicescape can:

- affect the customer's experience
- influence the behaviour of customers
- influence employees.

Affecting the customer's experience

When operations managers buy or build their facilities they need to ask about more than the size, type, number and location of those facilities but also their impact on the customer's experience. Hard chairs without arms, set out in clinical rows in a waiting room provide one type of experience, whereas clusters of armchairs with coffee tables and magazines provide quite a different one. The choice and style of facilities should therefore be in tune with the desired service experience (based on the service concept). That is not to say that all chairs, for example, should be comfortable. Those in fast-food restaurants may be designed to provide adequate support and comfort for leaning forward and eating but are less comfortable for leaning back and relaxing at the end of a meal, thus creating an experience at the end of the meal that 'encourages' the customer to leave.

The location of a building, its size, structure and décor will contribute to the service experience. Indeed customers are adept at decoding the emotional and symbolic importance of environmental clues (Gabriel and Lang 1995). The type of office furniture and the nature of décor in the office of an accountant, engineer, public servant or charity will give particular clues about their trustworthiness, success, profligacy and the cost of the service.

The hard or soft architecture and other environmental clues, such as dress, furniture and décor, are an important means by which organisations can establish or reinforce their desired image and create a particular service experience. The distinctive uniforms of Singapore Airlines flight attendants, the classic styles of Caesar's Palace or Bellagio's in Las Vegas, the memorabilia of Hard Rock cafés, all seek to create a particular experience for the customer and in many cases differentiate the service from the competition.

Influencing customer behaviour

Customers' behaviour, and thereby their experience, can be, to some extent, determined by the servicescape, its ambience, lighting, décor or indeed the music (see, for example, Milliman 1982). A warm bar may encourage customers to drink more, while the tempo of background music in a shop can influence the pace of shopping and the amount spent by customers.

A number of studies have addressed the issue of environmental design effects (sometimes referred to as aesthetic atmospherics) upon psychological and behavioural responses of consumers in shopping centres, retail outlets and other service encounters (see, for example, Botschen *et al.* 1999, Kaplan 1987, Kotler 1973). Clean, clear and well-lit food cabinets, for example, lead customers to perceive that that the products are fresh.

The servicescape also influences the nature of the interaction between customers and between customers and employees (Bitner 1992). Seating arrangements or the amount of background noise, for example, may encourage or discourage conversation and/or interaction.

The existence of queues, whether a physical queue or a queue on a telephone for example, provide physical or informational evidence that influences customers' behaviour. The simple existence of a queue, in some countries, encourages customers to modify their behaviour: they will wait in turn, physically position themselves relative to others waiting, and, up to a point, be prepared to accommodate a delay in service. A queue, like other environmental clues such as temperature and lighting for example, may also generate 'approach' or 'avoidance' behaviour (Mehrabian and Russell 1974). Mehrabian and Russell suggested that individuals react to environments with two general and opposite forms of behaviour: they are either attracted to it or repulsed by it. For some people a queue to enter a restaurant, for example, may signal 'a place to be seen' or a 'popular destination worth trying'; to others it may represent 'crowded and trendy' and may act as a deselection device.

The design of equipment or information interfaces will also have an effect on customers' behaviour, in particular their ability to interact with and obtain service from remote service providers such as organisations using the internet, remote cash machines or ticketing machines. Fast, easy and user-friendly interfaces will lead to approach behaviour, whereas slow and difficult may well lead to avoidance.

Influencing employees

Just as the physical and informational aspects of a service environment influence customers, they also influence employees and affect their experience of their organisation. It has been suggested that an appropriate environment results in approach rather than avoidance behaviour by employees and as a result they are more committed to the organisation, stay longer, and are more able to carry out their roles effectively (Bitner 1992).

In Box 6.2 we can see how the design of a new headquarters for British Airways created an informal working environment and encouraged communication between staff.

6.3 Understanding the nature of service processes

Processes, whether front office or back office, whether they process customers, material or information, need to be 'engineered' (section 6.4) and controlled (section 6.5). To do this effectively we need to understand the nature of service processes. We can do this by asking three key questions:

- How much service product variety does the process have to deal with?
- What type of process is it, in terms of the volume and variety that it can handle?
- Where is the value-added for the customer?

6.3.1 Service product variety

In simple terms a car servicing shop might be seen to have one end-to-end process, which includes sub-processes or tasks, such as customer greeting and discussion of the job to be done, initial diagnosis, parts procurement, car service, customer

---

British Airways, Waterside   Box 6.2

In 1998 British Airways opened its new head office, Waterside. The aim of the new building was not only to reduce the high costs of managing 14 offices scattered around Heathrow airport and in the centre of London, but also to encourage teamwork and open communication between its employees.

The idea was to create a 'village' atmosphere. A central enclosed 'Street' links all the buildings and makes them feel a part of a whole. The informal atmosphere is created by trees and fountains, coffee shops and restaurants surrounded by glass-walled offices, walkways and lifts. There are no direct lifts linking the underground car park with offices, so forcing employees to use the Street and meet each other. Not only is this a place for managers and administrators but it also brings together cabin crew and customer service staff by combining an office block with training rooms (including a mock-up of a Boeing 747), together with staff facilities such as video dispensers, fitness rooms

and hairdressers. To facilitate communication Waterside's offices are open plan, with many small 'club' areas where employees can work informally in lounge areas.

'As a result the atmosphere is informal and transparent,' explained BA's chief executive. 'People can see and meet others who work in different departments. In the old building it was different. People worked in their own rooms and had their own space. If you went to visit them it was like going on to someone else's territory. The way we operate here is not only more transparent, it is more efficient.'

Questions

1 Is this approach suitable for all service organisations?

2 What key ingredients of the British Airways servicescape might be translated into smaller organisations?

This illustration is based on material in *The Times*, 20 July 1998.

billing and car return. Yet through this one process may flow a variety of types of jobs: some may be routine, such as a 10,000-mile oil change; others may be less routine but still standard activities, such as a gear box repair; others may be non-standard activities that happen infrequently and can be more difficult to predict how long or how many resources they will require, such as an intermittent electrical fault. The first step in designing and managing service processes is to understand the mix of these 'runners', 'repeaters' and 'strangers' (a classification first used by Lucas Industries) which the process has to deal with.

Runners

Runners are standard activities predominantly found in high-volume operations, such as the request for the balance of a bank account made to a telephone call centre. From an operations point of view, runners:

- are often relatively predictable, allowing the operations manager to match resources to forecast demand with reasonable accuracy
- lend themselves to efficient operations through tight process control or automation.

Repeaters

Repeaters are also standard activities, possibly more complex than runners, but which occur less frequently. Repeaters may be created by default rather than by design, when an organisation significantly expands the range of services it offers. This may mean that processes that were designed to handle relatively few standard activities must now deal with much greater variety. Banks have experienced this problem, having moved from providing one or two standard deposit or chequing accounts to offering 'personalised financial packages'. As a result:

- repeaters often absorb more resource than an equivalent runner because lower volumes cannot justify process automation
- there may be some degree of relearning or readjustment of a process required for each reoccurrence of the repeater activity if the previous occurrence was some time in the past.

Strangers

Strangers are non-standard activities, perhaps associated with a one-off project or activity. New service introduction may give rise to stranger activities in the first instance, which usually will migrate to repeaters or runners as service volumes increase. Strangers are the least efficient and indeed the most difficult processes for operations managers to deal with because:

- it may be more difficult to forecast demand
- the resources required to deal with demand may be less certain
- they are least well defined in terms of resource requirements.

However, an organisation that is used to dealing with strangers will be much more flexible and adaptable than one that is used to dealing with repeaters or runners.

Managing runners, repeaters and strangers

Table 6.1 gives some examples of these three types of activities in three different organisations. The problem is that all three can and sometimes do exist within the same organisation, such as the car servicing shop described earlier.

Table 6.1 **Runners, repeaters and strangers**

Service	Runners	Repeaters	Strangers
Car service	Standard oil change and maintenance Replacement of brake pads etc.	Body panel replacement Gear box repair	Intermittent electrical fault Product recall
International airline	Passenger check-in Baggage handling In-flight service Maintenance Scheduling	Aircraft overdue or replacement required 'Serious' customer complaints	Special charter for VIPs
Hospital	Patient records Standard operations Recovery and rehabilitation Domestic services	Surgery with 'complications' Dealing with difficult or distraught patients and relatives	New surgical procedures

Importantly, the relative mix of these activities will suggest the most appropriate type of service process. In addition, the type of service process may limit or restrict the variety of activities that can be carried out. A car service shop that accepts a wide range of jobs will need to have a more flexible process than one that focuses totally on doing oil changes. It will also need more flexible and skilled mechanics and will not have as high a throughput. The oil change specialist may have a high throughput, will need less skilled mechanics but will also need to turn away the potentially higher margin jobs that are outside its area of competence.

This takes us back to the typology of service processes we introduced in Chapter 1: the key parameters of volume and variety.

We will also return to the idea of runners, repeaters and strangers in Chapter 8, where we will examine the problems posed for resource management when the mix of service requirements changes faster than the processes. For example, if the mix of surgical procedures in the hospital changed so that there were fewer complex or new operations, and more simple, routine procedures, this might mean that some of the more highly qualified (and paid) surgeons would be surplus to requirements and that there might be insufficient junior doctors to carry out the more mundane activities. A possible short-term solution might be to employ the higher-paid consultant surgeons on routine work. This would dramatically affect the cost base and would no doubt seriously reduce the morale of the surgeons!

6.3.2 Types of process: volume and variety

In this section we start by providing more detail of the key differences between the extremes of high volume/low variety and low volume/high variety, and capability and commodity processes. We then go on to describe processes that do not lie

Figure 6.4	Volume–variety matrix

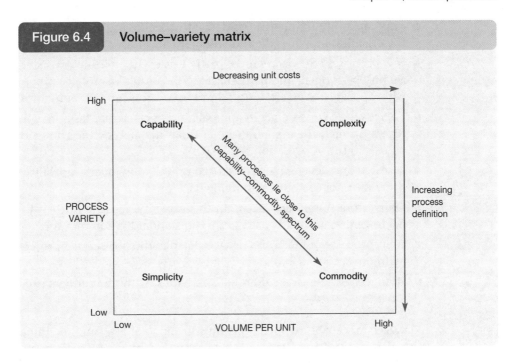

between these extremes, off-diagonal processes. In section 6.6 we discuss the issues in managing process transitions.

Capability processes

Processes that lie in the top left-hand corner of the volume/variety matrix (Figure 6.4) are typically focused on providing a capability for their customers or users, rather than a 'pre-prepared' service. As such they do not have the clarity of service concept that characterises high-volume consumer services, but they have much more flexibility to change service outcomes, service experience and service delivery processes. These processes are more suited to managing strangers than runners. Examples of this type of service include:

● traditional professional services, such as lawyers or accountants, particularly those small firms that deal with a wide variety of work for their clients

● companies that sell their creative ability, such as advertising agencies, software developers and engineering design consultants

● organisations that adapt their capabilities to satisfy a wide range of customer needs, such as consultants, counsellors and management development providers.

A key task for all these organisations is to ensure that they maintain their skill base. The firm of lawyers must ensure that it retains its capability to deal with employment or patent law, just as the business school must employ professors of the major management disciplines. This points to a number of attributes that generally apply to this type of service operation:

● The service concept is based on the provision of a particular skill set or knowledge base.

- This capability frequently resides with specific individuals, and may be lost to the organisation when the individual leaves.

- Few processes are documented, partly because there is no consistency in types of activity performed, and partly because the individual service providers may resist what appears like an attempt to impose controls on their autonomy.

- There is little consistency in approach to tasks. Similar tasks may follow different routes through the organisation, at times dictated by the whims of certain individuals in the organisation.

- Research and development is centred on the individual's capability to deal with a wider range of customer requirements.

- Many professional services are in this category, moving further down the diagonal towards commodity as volume and standardisation increase.

- Such processes tend to be service partnerships or service projects (see KDAM matrix in section 6.3.3).

- Strangers and repeaters dominate activities, with few runners except in support functions.

Managers of capability operations must be good at assessing the impact of an additional task on an existing workload. So, for example, a firm of management consultants must be able to negotiate with a new client as to when a new assignment can be carried out without adversely affecting existing assignments. This is a major issue because, as we will discuss in Chapter 9, the firm's real capacity will alter rapidly as assignments call for differing areas of expertise. This is complicated still further by the fact that the level and nature of expertise may not be fully understood at the point where contracts are signed.

Commodity processes

Commodity processes are ideal for runners. These operations are exemplified by the high-volume consumer services such as fast-food restaurants, general insurance providers and retailers. The service concept for these organisations is of necessity clear and relatively rigid. This particularly applies when service must be delivered across several service locations, by a wide variety of service employees.

Whereas the capability operations offer 'solutions' to their customers, commodity operations are much clearer in their definition and marketing of the service concept. They will tend to compete on their ability to provide consistent quality at a competitive price. One of the most significant service dimensions will frequently relate to the availability of service, through the absence of physical queues or through rapid telephone response. Examples of these service operations include:

- multi-site services, such as restaurant chains, supermarkets or other retail operations

- centralised communication-based services, such as 'direct' insurance, telephone banking or catalogue-based selling

- equipment repair services based on simple replacement processes, such as car tyre and exhaust centres, domestic appliance repair or computer service.

Central tasks for the majority of these operations include:

- maintaining consistency of service delivery to ensure that customer expectations are met across all encounters
- managing standard service in such a way that individual customers still feel that they are not just a number
- providing an appropriate level of service and managing resource productivity to tight targets.

Contrasts with the attributes of capability services are as follows:

- The service concept is translated into a series of tightly controlled processes, with little opportunity for deviation from standard activities.
- Customer-facing employees are likely to be relatively junior staff and poorly paid.
- The organisation depends on focused training, often of a few days' or weeks' duration for its customer-facing staff, as compared to several years' professional training for key staff in capability operations.
- Capacity is generally well defined, with an emphasis on developing flexibility to deal with rapid changes in demand.
- The operational focus is typically that of the service factory or DIY service (see KDAM in section 6.3.3 below).
- The types of service that lie in this area are mass services and mass service shops.
- Activities are typified by runners, with an increasing proportion of repeaters as the organisation seeks to differentiate through mass customisation.

In contrast to capability operations, the central task of managers in commodity operations is to create a planned environment where the various activities of its constituent parts can be carried out as efficiently and consistently as possible. Managing the fast-food restaurant supply chain requires forecasts and schedules to be given to all suppliers in a timely fashion, with as few last-minute changes as possible. Thus capability managers may strive to get better at reacting to changes, whereas commodity managers strive to get better at reducing unforeseen variances to plan. This is important to note as we discuss later in this chapter the challenge of moving along the capability–commodity spectrum. It may be possible to change the process design, but certainly harder to change the behaviour of process managers!

Profiling processes

Figure 6.5 summarises key points from the preceding sections in the form of a chart (capability–commodity profile) to assist operations managers to locate their existing processes on the capability–commodity spectrum and to determine whether action needs to be taken to make appropriate adjustments. The figure illustrates the profile for a motor insurance provider, showing the difference between its direct operation, providing policies to individual users, and its support for insurance brokers.

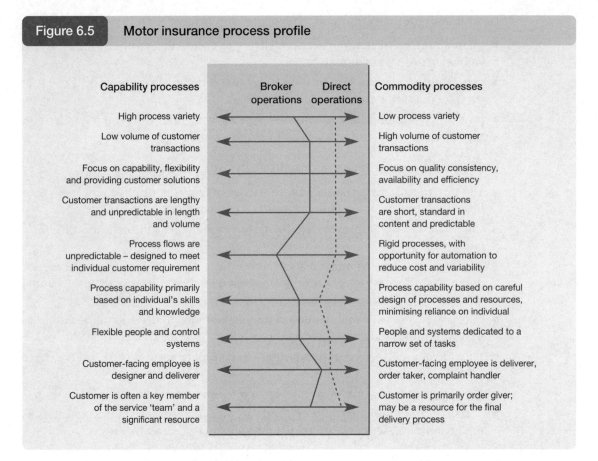

Figure 6.5 Motor insurance process profile

Capability processes	Broker operations	Direct operations	Commodity processes
High process variety			Low process variety
Low volume of customer transactions			High volume of customer transactions
Focus on capability, flexibility and providing customer solutions			Focus on quality consistency, availability and efficiency
Customer transactions are lengthy and unpredictable in length and volume			Customer transactions are short, standard in content and predictable
Process flows are unpredictable – designed to meet individual customer requirement			Rigid processes, with opportunity for automation to reduce cost and variability
Process capability primarily based on individual's skills and knowledge			Process capability based on careful design of processes and resources, minimising reliance on individual
Flexible people and control systems			People and systems dedicated to a narrow set of tasks
Customer-facing employee is designer and deliverer			Customer-facing employee is deliverer, order taker, complaint handler
Customer is often a key member of the service 'team' and a significant resource			Customer is primarily order giver; may be a resource for the final delivery process

Use of this profiling approach identifies the potential mismatches to be addressed by service managers. These frequently arise because the service task has changed, whereas the delivery processes have not evolved to meet the new requirements adequately. For the insurance company in Figure 6.5, a shift from broker operations to direct operations may well mean that the processes are more flexible than necessary and some staff may be overqualified for their new duties.

This move would almost certainly mean a significant change in management style and, of course, a change in the priorities among the key performance indicators utilised. The direct operation would probably concentrate on fast response and low cost, while broker operations would place more emphasis on flexibility and personal service.

It should be understood that using the volume–variety matrix or the capability–commodity profile to compare and contrast processes in totally different service sectors is of limited value. It is almost meaningless to compare a small firm of corporate lawyers (capability) with a restaurant chain (commodity). It is more helpful to compare different process types within the same sector, as in Figure 6.6.

Hernia operations (see Figure 6.6) are now standard procedures, although there was a time when they were in the 'pioneer' category. There are many advantages to being in this commodity area, as the Shouldice Hernia Hospital demonstrates (Heskett 1983). Hernia operations here are carried out most cost effectively, with

| Figure 6.6 | Depicting different surgery processes |

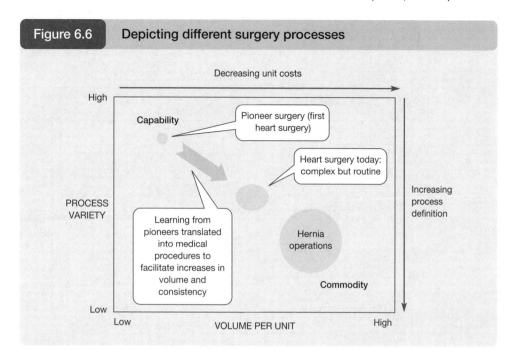

the lowest amounts of 'rework' and with high levels of patient satisfaction. This focused approach has now been replicated across the world and extends to similar surgical procedures. In this case, the move from capability towards commodity does not deskill the surgeon, but it does mean that surgeons may become increasingly specialised and less able to revert to more general surgery.

Off-diagonal processes

The 'line of best fit' between capability and commodity is in reality rather wider than it was portrayed at the start of this section. More flexible processes, better support systems and better training for employees will mean that the 'effective area' can be extended (Figure 6.7). However, operations may sometimes find that their processes are operating suboptimally because there is not an exact fit between existing processes and market requirements.

Operating in the complexity area

Processes in the top right-hand corner of Figure 6.7 are attempting to provide high-volume services that are capable of great flexibility. Processes in this area, sometimes referred to as 'mass customisation' (Hart 1995, Pine 1993), attempt to provide the customer with whatever they want, however they want it and wherever they want it at an affordable price. One example of this is telephone and internet banking which, although not providing the complete range of banking services, provide a wide range of service, 24 hours a day, every day of the year, accessible from any telephone or computer, and at little cost.

Any operations wishing to push their processes in this direction need to think very carefully about the technology and skills required to operate effectively, and profitably, in this area. We will return to this area at the end of this chapter.

Figure 6.7	Off-diagonal processes

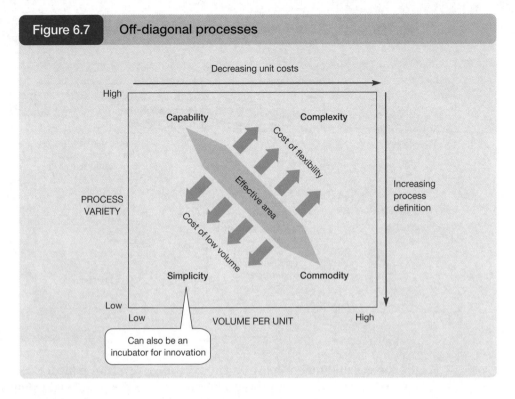

Operating in the simplicity area

The issue here is that the operation is unlikely to be operating as efficiently as it might because it has low volume. This could mean that either resources are under-utilised or the organisation is unwilling at this stage to invest in process technology to decrease its unit costs. However, this position could suit a small niche player, such as a microbrewery that produces very small quantities of a single beer for consumption in one or two outlets, or a corporate lawyer with just one or two clients. It is likely that the margins earned by these niche players far outweigh any operational inefficiencies.

However, this position (in the left-hand bottom corner of Figure 6.7) could be employed by large or small organisations as a pilot or as a start-up operation, hence its alternative description as the 'incubator'. Box 6.3 illustrates the challenge of managing processes in this area.

6.3.3 Adding value for the customer

In operations we must be careful to recognise where value is added, or perhaps more accurately where value should be added. We are sometimes guilty of not being sufficiently clear in our definitions and therefore the analysis of added value becomes muddled. The categories of value introduced in Chapter 1 were:

● Customer value: what the customer recognises and pays for.

● Brand value: aspects of the service that communicate the style that the organisation would like to display.

Data Warehouse Services (DWS)

Box 6.3

DWS is part of a large electrical retailing group whose businesses are predominantly focused on consumer markets. As with most high-volume consumer services operating through multiple outlets, the group seeks to compete largely through providing low prices and rapid delivery. Its senior operations managers tend to adopt similar approaches across the group.

DWS provides data-mining services for large retailers. It takes the information collected by loyalty card schemes and electronic point-of-sale systems (EPOS) in order to track trends in consumer spending and identify profitable lines of business and valuable customer segments.

DWS is unusual in that it operates solely in the B2B market with its customers being its own parent group and other retail companies (though not its direct competitors). Despite this difference, much of the operations are relatively high volume and standardised; however, there are some activites that do not fit so easily into the classification of processes that DWS and its parent organisation understand.

DWS has recently launched a customer training service. This has the potential to grow into a significant revenue stream, but although this is acknowledged by the business, the management is becoming impatient with its apparent lack of immediate success. At the same time, DWS has employed a group of people who are interested in providing consultancy services related to customer relationship management (CRM). It is not envisaged that this service will be provided to many customers but it is hoped that this will be a profitable activity for DWS.

Questions

1 How would you assess the performance of the operations managers responsible for both the training operation and the consultancy service? How would this differ from DWS standard operations?

2 Given the preferred approach to process design and management in both DWS and its parent, what recommendation would you make regarding the training operation?

- Financial contribution: earning revenue for the organisation.
- Organisational contribution: aspects of operations that currently do not fall readily into the previous categories but are deemed to be essential for the organisation's current or future success.

When we receive a level of service that is beyond our expectations, we sometimes term this added value, though might more accurately be described as a high perceived level of service. The service process designer must be clear in these definitions in order to avoid solving the wrong problem. Take a bank, for example. We as customers, and even the bank's staff and management, may say that personal interaction between customers and the bank's staff is important, and indeed it is. But from an operations perspective the bank is essentially a big factory that processes millions of financial transactions every day, most of which we do not see or even think about, such as maintaining standing orders and direct debits (unless there is a problem!). The bank certainly has to get its customer interaction right but the main value it provides is in handling our accounts and in managing financial movements.

It is therefore important to view service operations in their entirety, i.e. the multiplicity of interrelated processes, both front office and back office, and recognise where the bulk of the value-adding activity lies.

Identifying the key decision areas

The key decision area matrix (KDAM) (see Figure 6.8) provides a means of categorising service processes. This matrix helps us understand where the prime value is added and therefore what should be the key focus of attention for operations managers. The figure identifies four types of decision area (the area within the dotted line) in the relationship between C–F–B (customer, front office and back office), for runners/repeaters and strangers/repeaters depending upon the level of customer involvement.

Before exploring this matrix further, it is necessary to define customer involvement. By this we mean the extent to which the customer is an intrinsic part of the service delivery process, and thus can be thought of as a resource for the organisation (see also Chapter 7). There is a difference therefore between customer contact and customer involvement. For example, if you stay in a luxury hotel, the service operation can be described as having high customer contact rather than requiring high customer involvement. Customers directly experience the facilities of the hotel, and there are large numbers of staff to attend to their every need. The hotel would move higher on the customer involvement scale if you were required to make your beds and cook your own meals!

The service factory

A service factory is a high-volume, low-variety operation dealing in runners and occasionally repeaters, with low customer involvement. Examples include high-volume consumer services, such as retail operations, restaurant chains and many financial services. The key decision area for these services is in the back office, where the prime task is efficient and consistent, high-volume operations. For example, if a bank wishes to offer a faster cheque-clearing service to its customers, it will examine the capability of the back office first and foremost. These operations will place as much of the value-adding activities as possible in the back office.

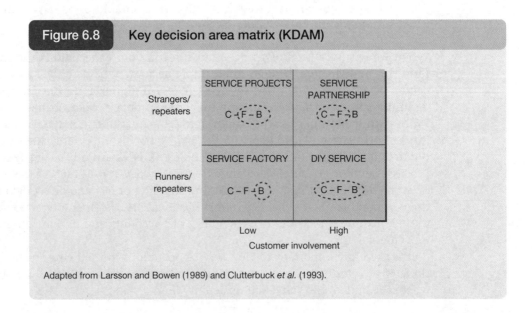

Figure 6.8 Key decision area matrix (KDAM)

Adapted from Larsson and Bowen (1989) and Clutterbuck *et al.* (1993).

This is not to say that there is not a role for the front office staff. The front office's role is to make this service factory seem friendly and to give the impression that each customer is valued and special. The front office, however, has no ability to offer significantly different services to individual customers. These organisations may look to provide a degree of personalisation in the front office, but without encouraging customers to make too many special requests, which tend to reduce the efficiency of the operation as a whole.

There is also a role for customers in the service factory. Customers are 'trained' to fit into the service delivery system, filling in the right forms, standing in the correct queues and not making non-standard requests.

The service factory is potentially efficient and consistent (particularly across multi-site operations), but may feel impersonal to customers. There may also be significant problems with low morale in the front office as staff deal with mismatches in customer expectations compared to service delivery.

Do-it-yourself service

DIY services are high-volume, low-variety processes, with runners and repeaters but with high levels of customer involvement. We find examples of this type of service in the leisure industry, in tourism and in sports and fitness clubs. Self-service retailing is also moving from the service factory towards the DIY service quadrant. It could be argued that many internet-based retail services are also found in this quadrant.

We have drawn the key decision area around the total customer, front office and back office chain. This reflects the fact that these services have to balance decisions in all areas. Significant effort lies in the design work for the initial set-up of facilities and networks. Amazon.com has devoted much design time to its internet service and in setting up back office distribution activities to fulfil customer orders. The capability of the customer must also be included in the design brief to ensure that the service runs smoothly. In the case of Amazon.com, the front office decisions regarding the design of the website and its ease of access and use by customers are also critical.

Some of these internet-based services rely on significant customer capability in terms of both expertise and equipment. The music sites that allow the customers to download album tracks, creating their own customised collection, currently require a level of sophistication beyond many potential users.

Service projects

Service projects utilise processes that are predominantly repeaters and strangers, with limited customer involvement. A good example of this type of service is provided by a market research company. There is frequently an intensive initial diagnosis/specification phase carried out with the customer by front office personnel. The second phase consists of research work carried out by staff in the back office without the presence of the customer. There is usually a final stage where results are presented and discussed.

In many small market research firms, of course, the front and back offices are one and the same, although this becomes less common as the organisation grows. The principle remains, however, that service project organisations must have much closer links between front office and back office than is necessary for the service factory, not least because they will be dealing predominantly with strangers and some repeaters, rather than runners, with resultant variability in demand volumes and process type.

The front office staff must have more skill and flexibility than in a service factory. When face to face with a potential customer, front-line employees or service professionals must be able to demonstrate considerable technical as well as interpersonal skill. They must have considerable knowledge as to both capability and capacity of the combined front office/back office, often making commitments on behalf of the organisation based on their diagnosis of the customer's requirements.

Service partnership

Service partnerships involve highly customised service processes with high customer involvement, dealing in either strangers or repeaters. The key decision area is around the customer (or client)–front office partnership. The theme is very much one of co-development, where the service provider is intimately involved with the client. An example is provided by the sort of consultant who works with a management team in the process of strategy development, where there is an expectation that part of the service outcome is that the consultant will mentor management team members as part of their personal development. In this case, the customer is an integral part of the service process.

Because customer and service provider are so directly linked, the effectiveness of this service is often a function of the personal chemistry between the individuals involved. In small consultancies one of the guiding principles is often that consultants will only work with people they like, on the basis that a good working relationship is fundamental in developing a satisfactory outcome.

The challenge for these organisations is to manage the communication link between front office and back office. The back office often provides administrative support and may be perceived to be of lower status than the 'professionals' in the front office.

A mix of decision areas

The challenge for larger, complex service organisations is that all four types of key decision areas may be represented in their operations. To take the example of a bank:

- Service factory: retail banking for consumers – high volume, standard accounts.
- Service projects: business loans for entrepreneurs.
- Service partnership: managing investment portfolios for large corporate clients.
- DIY service: internet and telephone banking.

It is important to recognise and manage this diversity. It is increasingly true that 'one size fits all' is not appropriate. Each operation will require different performance criteria, technology, management style and, ideally, different processes and people.

Task allocation

Operations managers must make the decision as to which tasks are carried out in the front office, back office, or by the customer. As the service concept extends or changes, it is likely that the positioning of the service, as described in Figure 6.9, will also change and so too will the allocation of tasks. Figure 6.9 illustrates some examples of task re-allocation, which are described below.

Figure 6.9	Changing task allocation

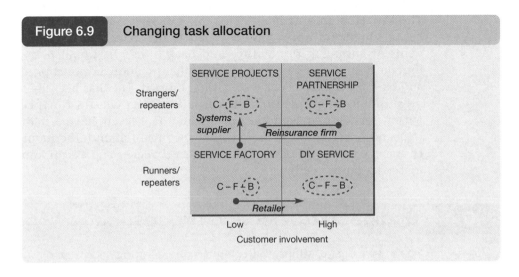

- *A **reinsurance firm*** operating in the City of London has traditionally based its business on cultivating strong personal client relationships, but is under increasing pressure to demonstrate value and to deliver cost reductions, moving from a service partnership approach to a service project environment. The firm realised that the time spent with individual clients was becoming less effective and contributed to the retention of an ever-decreasing number of clients. This shift required a major culture change to reduce the time spent with clients, and to develop standard ways of working. It also required a significant investment in information systems to support this change.

- *A **retailer*** is moving from a physical presence in a shopping mall to also providing internet-based shopping. This represents a move from an organisation largely focused on back office functions, such as purchasing and logistics, to one that must add to this the ability to design systems that enable the customer to play an increasing role in the delivery system. These systems require a greater sophistication on the part of the customer, perhaps forcing the service provider to give greater thought to the implementation of new technology in terms of initial customer training.

- *The **systems supplier*** has largely been concerned with the provision of telecommunications and computer 'boxes'. Its operations have been focused on the production of these systems as efficiently as possible in the back office. As product margins have decreased through competition, the company has recognised the need to provide more customised 'solutions' to its customers. The front office role has moved from being a sales order-processing activity to providing applications consultancy. The major changes for this organisation involve moving expertise that has traditionally been located in a back office role (remote from customers), to a front office activity with significant customer interaction. It is also vital for front office and back office to create more integration in their processes to ensure that greater variation in customer requirements can be dealt with effectively.

The key decision area matrix (KDAM) can give an insight into the impact of changes in service concept as they relate to the changing role of the three components of customer, front office and back office. It should be noted that the introduction of new services may mean that traditional distinctions between front and back office may become somewhat blurred. This has been the experience of organisations implementing multimedia contact centres to replace person-to-person service or telephone call centres. The result has been that customers frequently have access to areas within the organisation hitherto 'protected' from customer contact. This clearly poses both a challenge and a significant opportunity for service process design.

6.4 'Engineering' service processes

Few service organisations, unlike their manufacturing counterparts, employ specialist service engineers or use service laboratories to help them design, test and evaluate their service processes (Shostack 1987). Because of the intangibility of service, process design is often an ad hoc trial-and-error activity rather than a formal, even proceduralised, management activity. Most faults and problems are effectively 'designed in', albeit inadvertently, and as a result customers experience poor service and the processes are inefficient.

The key to good service design is about taking a customer perspective and understanding the whole service process. This may seem obvious, yet in many organisations managers and their staff simply get used to seeing – and therefore ignoring – poor processes, or see them from an internal perspective, thus missing the experience from their customers' perspective. Several tools and techniques have been developed to help 'engineer' service, i.e. to design new service processes, or assess and improve existing ones:

- process mapping (for front and back office processes)
- walk-through audits (for front office processes)
- service transaction analysis (for front office processes).

6.4.1 Process mapping

Process mapping is the charting of a service process in order to assist in the evaluation, design and development of new or existing processes. There are many types of charting methods in use. However, the essence of mapping is to capture all the activities and their relationships on paper, which normally requires a team of people who understand the various aspects of the process. It is perhaps not surprising that this activity is incredibly time-consuming but it can yield some significant results – the first of which is usually the emergence of a shared view and understanding of a process by all those involved in it, and thus a realisation of their role in the end-to-end process.

Gaining maximum benefit from process mapping involves two issues, mapping and mapping tools, and turning the map from a descriptive into an analytical tool.

Mapping and mapping tools

The first question to be considered at the start of a mapping activity is the level or degree of detail. Process maps can be used at a macro level, depicting major activities and their relationships, or at a micro level, mapping all the detailed tasks involved in a process or a part of a process, or indeed somewhere in between. The minimum level depends upon the use to which the maps are to be put but is usually that which exposes the overall process and where the main elements are visible. More detailed individual maps can be created if and when required. It is also important to agree mapping symbols and structures. The traditional operations symbols are shown in Figure 6.10 (Slack *et al*. 2004).

Different symbols may be appropriate to use in other circumstances and may be more visual and meaningful for the people developing the map, such as a picture of a computer for a computer interface, a queue of people to depict a queue, an in-tray to depict a pile of files in an in-tray. The symbols chosen should be appropriate, but should be common and understandable with a single meaning (for more information see, for example, Johnston 1999, Shostack 1987, Kingman-Brundage 1992).

The lines on the chart may be coloured to depict flows of different materials – blue for customers and green for information, for example – or to depict different volumes or routings, such as standard processes versus non-standard processes.

The example in Figure 6.11 shows a simplified process for a loan application, depicting customer activities, front office activities (the customer service agent – CSA) and back office activities (the computer). We only identified key information flows in this case to provide an overview of the process. A potential pitfall of process mapping is that too much detail is shown, obscuring the issues and opportunities for improvement.

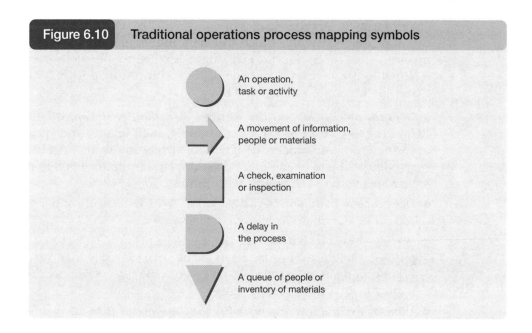

| Figure 6.10 | Traditional operations process mapping symbols |

An operation, task or activity

A movement of information, people or materials

A check, examination or inspection

A delay in the process

A queue of people or inventory of materials

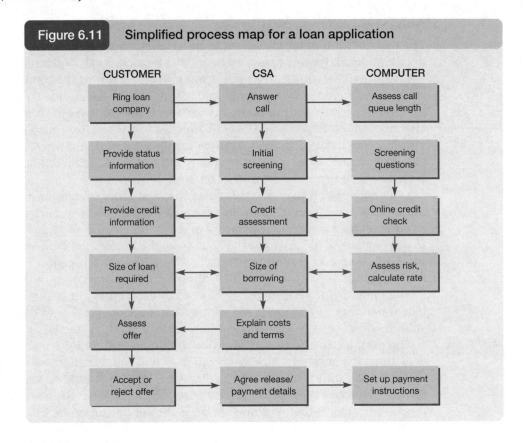

Figure 6.11 Simplified process map for a loan application

Analysis of process maps

Process mapping in itself can be a very time-consuming task with little benefit gained. By itself, a process map is of only limited benefit, but it can help communicate the complexity of a process or help individuals agree or realise the steps involved in a process. Process mapping is essentially a descriptive activity: what is required to derive maximum benefit from a process map is to ask key questions that help turn it into an analytical tool:

- *Does the process support the strategic intentions of the operation?* If the operation is expected to provide, for example, high-quality and speedy service to customers, is the process designed in such a way so that decisions are made speedily, that end-to-end process performance is minimal and that quality controls are in place at all points in the process?

- *Does each activity provide added value?* Which elements of the process do not add value? Can they be removed or redesigned?

- *Is the process 'in control'?* For the key elements or maybe every element in the process, what measures and targets are in place to ensure that particular element is performing as expected? Who is responsible for overseeing, controlling and improving that particular element?

- *Who 'owns' and has responsibility for the process?* How many different individuals and/or departments are responsible for parts of the process? Who in particular, or which group of people, is responsible for the design, delivery and improvement of the whole process?

- *Is the level of visibility appropriate?* The process map can be used to identify those activities that involve and/or are visible to the customer, thus differentiating between back office and front office tasks. Should or could any of the activities or tasks be re-allocated? Can any of the elements be moved to the back office and away from the customer, which might lead to greater efficiencies? Are there elements that could be made more visible to the customer, which might lead to a greater sense of involvement and ownership and quality?

- *How efficient is the process?* By adding times, distances and resources used, such as numbers of staff, to the various tasks in the process map, the efficiencies of the whole process and various parts of the process can be calculated and bottlenecks identified and removed.

- *How can the process be improved?* What are the likely or main fail-points in the process? What procedures are in place to deal with these? Does everyone who is involved in the process understand their role in the whole process and the effect of their actions upon it?

6.4.2 Walk-through audits

As most service organisations process customers, a walk-through audit (Fitzsimmons and Fitzsimmons 1997) undertaken by staff, managers or independent advisers, acting as surrogate customers, can help evaluate and improve the service. The audit should be based on a checklist of questions that guide the 'customer's' assessment of the complete service (see, for example, Figure 6.12).

The key requirement for this approach lies in the choice of attributes to assess, and the scales on which the assessment will lie. As the name of the technique

Figure 6.12	Walk-through audit of an electrical store

	No spaces			Plenty of spaces	
1. How easy was it to park the car?	1	2	3	4	5

	Disgraceful			Very clean/tidy	
2. How did the store look?	1	2	3	4	5

	Uninviting			Very attractive	
3. How attractive were the displays?	1	2	3	4	5

	15 mins+	10–15 mins	0–5 mins		
4. How soon were you assisted?	1	2	3	4	5

implies, it should be developed to identify the critical elements of the customer experience from first contact with the service operation through to exit. It is crucial that this audit is not developed solely by people who know the service well, since they are prone to miss detail that they think is irrelevant but customers are affected by. The advantage of this type of approach is that it allows the manager to carry out regular service checks on key aspects of delivery, possibly comparing performance at different times of day between service units.

6.4.3 Service transaction analysis

Service transaction analysis (STA) (for more information see Johnston 1999) is a development of the walk-through audit and combines the service concept, the service process, transaction quality assessment, and service 'messages' and emotions felt by the 'customer' in order to provide a simple but powerful tool to assess and improve the customer's experience of a service process. This tool, an example of which is contained in Figure 6.13, can also be used as the basis of a walk-through audit.

STA comprises five key stages:

- The service concept needs to be agreed and specified. This alone is often a useful exercise to gain agreement between the employees on the nature of their service offering (see Chapter 2).

- Mystery shoppers, independent advisers or consultant-customers then walk through the actual process (not the process map) to assess how customers

Figure 6.13 Example of STA for an estate agent

SERVICE TRANSACTION ANALYSIS

Organisation:	Estate agent	Service concept
Process:	Buy house	Prestige properties with excellent
Customer:	Purchaser	service for the discerning purchaser

Transactions	Score + 0 −	Message/Emotions
Good location		We are accessible and available
Good facilities		Expensive but competent
Ignored		You are not worth the trouble
Introduction		We want to help you
Fill in forms		You are just another punter
No pen		We don't really care
Nothing available		What business are they in?
Go on mailing list		Try somewhere else

Overall evaluation: Poor service design. Little thought for purchasers. Company is not customer-orientated. Poor service.

Adapted from Johnston (1999). Reprinted by permission of Emerald Group Publishing Limited, www.emerald insight.com/msq.html

(might) assess each transaction. Each transaction is briefly described in the left-hand column and an assessment of it in terms of delighting (+), satisfactory (0) or unsatisfactory (–) is noted in the middle columns.

- The interpretation as to why the customer or surrogate customer arrives at this evaluation is entered into the right-hand column, which describes the deliberate and the symbolic and subtle messages given off by the service. For example, an open door may provide an 'inviting' message, while a telephone operator unwilling to deviate from a set script may provide an 'unhelpful and unnecessarily bureaucratic' message to the customer. This section can also record the emotions felt by the customer, such as respected, helpless or frustrated.

- The assessments of +, 0 and – are joined to give a very visible profile of the transaction outcomes and an overall evaluation is entered at the foot of the table.

- Working from this sheet, service designers, managers and staff can begin to understand how customers might interpret the service process and then to discuss the improvements that can be made. The exercise can be repeated with a revised process and the profiles readily compared.

Unlike all other existing service process analysis tools, STA seeks to identify the reason for the outcome of each service transaction so that appropriate improvements can be made. Its key advantages are:

- It requires managers and employees to think about, and express in words, their service concept. This in itself creates an opportunity for healthy debate, and even disagreement, about what the intentions of the organisation actually are.

- It forces managers and employees to see the process from the point of view of the customer, increasing their level of customer orientation.

- It asks directly and explicitly what each transaction means to the customer and, importantly, what gives them this impression.

- It assesses the physical, tangible issues as well as the service scripts, and it also asks what messages these give to the customer and captures the resulting emotions.

- It attempts to bring a systematic evaluation of a complete service process. It does not rely upon individual complaints or initiatives but analyses and evaluates a process, step by step, from the customer's point of view.

STA is a simple yet very effective analytical tool that can easily be employed by managers to increase the level of customer orientation of staff and can lead to speedy and easy improvements in service processes.

6.5 Controlling service processes

A key operational performance objective is to achieve consistency of outcome for customers. Most service organisations report that reliability is one of the most significant factors in influencing customer satisfaction – in other words, 'saying what you do and doing what you say'. This section considers two aspects of control: assessing the capability of a process, and the role of quality systems, such as ISO 9000.

6.5.1 Capable processes

The quality management concept of building capable processes is helpful here. This is a fundamental principle of quality management and is at the heart of the Deming philosophy, requiring 'evidence that quality is built in' (Deming 1986). Many service operations utilise the statistical process control (SPC) methodology to assess the extent to which a process is capable, or in control.

Figure 6.14 shows the distribution of sample means measuring the performance of two hotels (A and B), which deliver breakfast trays to guests' rooms. In each case, the hotel offers guests a choice of times for delivery of their breakfast tray. Both hotels have chosen 10-minute 'windows' in the belief that this is what customers require. Figure 6.14 shows the distribution of the breakfast tray delivery times for a particular 10-minute window. Hotel A has put in place the processes and capacity to ensure that it consistently keeps its promises, whereas Hotel B appears unable to do so. The former is an example of a capable process whereas the latter is a process out of control. If the promise of meeting this time window is a key element of the 'contract' between provider and customer, the customer satisfaction ratings for Hotel B will be under threat.

Hotel B has two basic strategies that its management might consider:

- to invest in the delivery process to ensure that it can meet its process specification consistently
- to relax the process specification, in this case increasing the duration of the 'time window' offered to guests (perhaps 20 minutes instead of the current 10 minutes).

Of course, this can only be implemented once customer research has indicated the importance of this aspect of the service offer.

SPC (see, for example, Oakland 1992) is based on the production of process control charts. It is normal practice to take a series of measurements and then to plot the mean of the sample readings. This is because under the central limit theorem,

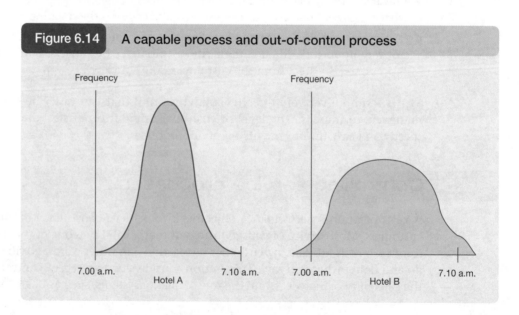

Figure 6.14   A capable process and out-of-control process

the distribution of the sample means tends towards a normal distribution, even if the underlying distribution is not normal.

Processes can be plotted on to a control chart, such as Figure 6.15, to give a visual picture of their state of health.

Figure 6.15 shows a plot of sample means taken at random, possibly depicting the times breakfast was delivered in the hotel from the previous example. The chart shows the process mean (x bar); warning limits set at ± two standard deviations (2σ); and action limits at ± three standard deviations (3σ). The value of process control charts lies in the removal of a temptation to 'meddle' in the process. A number of readings (5 per cent) will be expected to lie between the warning and action limits. The general advice if a reading is taken in this zone is to take another reading before doing anything. Premature adjustments may take the process out of control.

Figure 6.15 shows a process initially in control (the first six readings are a normal pattern), but then showing signs that the process mean has shifted as a run of points are all moving in the same direction as opposed to the normal scattering of readings. As process managers spend time understanding these processes, it is frequently possible to identify causes of variation. These can be divided into those causes that may be avoided, perhaps through automation or better training, and those that are unavoidable. An example of the latter might be the impact of bad weather on a breakdown service.

SPC has been used extensively to control and improve 'runners' in high-volume, standard processes. Examples include:

- accuracy of cheque transactions in a major retail bank
- computer service response times
- sickness and absenteeism in a call centre
- numbers of customer complaints per thousand transactions.

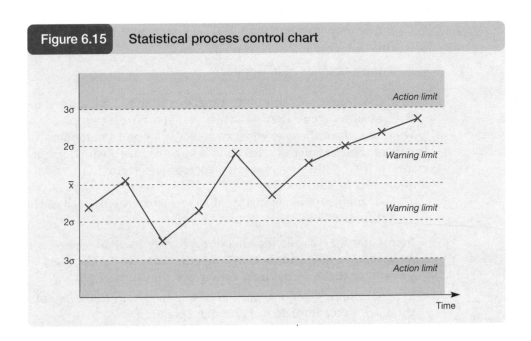

Figure 6.15 Statistical process control chart

It would be wrong to give the impression that SPC is easily applied to all service processes. It is clearly applicable to factory-like processes where measures such as response times may be accurately assessed, but it is also valuable to apply the technique to attributes such as the number and intensity of customer complaints. As is often the case, the value may come from the discipline of thinking about the process as much as from the monitoring of the control chart.

6.5.2 Quality systems

Some industries have had a long history of quality assurance, usually for reasons of health, hygiene or safety. Many manufacturing companies have been required to produce evidence of quality plans, schedules of inspection and records of quality checks being carried out. This activity has frequently been viewed somewhat negatively by operations managers, considering it as something that does not add value to the operations activity, and indeed stifling innovation and change.

It is unfortunate that this quality assurance activity should be viewed as a 'police officer' operating in a somewhat negative way, preventing poor quality but not actively encouraging good quality. The British Quality Standard BS 5750 (now BSEN-ISO9000) and then the International Standard ISO 9000, and their associated standards, aim to correct this biased view of quality assurance.

High-volume 'commodity'-type services whose processes tend towards runners lend themselves most naturally to the quality systems approach. This is because processes can be mapped, and clear, consistent standards can be established and monitored throughout service production and delivery. For example, many hotels have used standard operating procedures (SOPs) for a number of years covering aspects of service delivery such as the way that housekeeping cleans and prepares a room. This activity lends itself to checklists:

- Has the floor been vacuumed?
- Have the complimentary soaps and shampoos been replenished?
- Has the bed been made and turned down?
- Have the waste bins been emptied?

These SOPs translate readily into processes that can be audited for compliance under a quality system. They deal with relatively tangible outcomes rather than less tangible aspects of the customer experience. Call centres attempt to measure these aspects of the customer experience by using checklists, which might include statements such as 'Did the agent use the appropriate greeting?' or 'Did the agent thank the customer for the order?'

The advantages of using quality management systems such as those related to ISO 9000 are as follows:

- Incorporating critical elements of service delivery in a process that has been mapped, described and measured in such a way as can then be audited develops a discipline that may not have existed previously.
- External auditing and recognition of this success in the award of a certificate is good for internal morale and external reputation.

- The better quality management systems include a formal review process, which prompts the organisation to consider what needs to be done differently in order to improve.

- The process of preparing for external accreditation requires the organisation to document its processes and should be used as an opportunity for process redesign before application.

In recent years, the ISO 9000 approach has been totally revised and relaunched as ISO 9000.2000. The emphasis here is on the development of a quality management system that has the objective of creating processes that reflect customer requirements and are sensitive to changing market conditions. The previous criticism of these systems was that they evaluated process adherence rather than looking at whether or not the process was appropriate for the service task. ISO 9000.2000 now concentrates more helpfully on creating the management system to deliver quality targets.

6.6 Repositioning service processes

Many service processes are under pressure to change. High-variety/low-volume capability operations dealing with strangers may be under pressure to increase volumes and/or drive down the high costs of operating such processes. Low-variety/high-volume commodity-type processes dealing primarily with runners may be under pressure to become more flexible and customise their service for customers (see Figure 6.16).

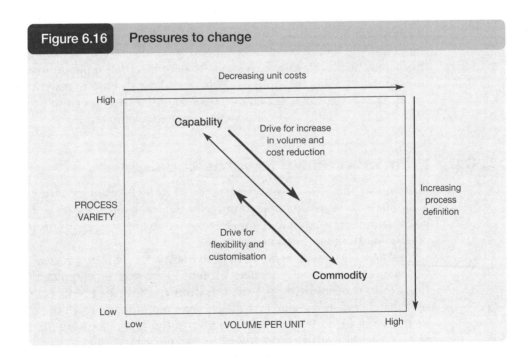

Figure 6.16   **Pressures to change**

6.6.1 From capability towards commodity

Many innovative organisations have a requirement for growth. The small firm of consultants that has built up a local or national practice may seek to become internationally recognised. Within a global company it may be that an innovative solution developed for an individual customer can be 'packaged' and sold to a much wider range of clients internationally. To do this, a number of issues must be addressed:

● Customers may require greater levels of consistency across service transactions carried out by different providers across locations. For example, a technical consultancy working for a multinational customer must be able to provide the same solution in all locations, probably at the same or similar price.

● Larger organisations tend to be extremely conscious of their image, which may entail setting stricter guidelines for their staff as to the scope and style of work carried out.

● The 'capability' of the organisation, previously reliant on the skills and knowledge of specific individuals, must be replicated through more specialised resources, tighter process management and specific training if the organisation's growth is not to be limited by scarce resources.

● To sustain growth, it is likely that the organisation may have to develop more competitive sales and marketing activities. In some sectors, this might take the organisation into previously non-experienced cost competition.

Perhaps the most significant aspect of this type of transition is the impact on the individual service providers. Many of the individuals in capability organisations will have joined for the professional autonomy that they offer. It is common for these individuals to enjoy the creativity that frequently is part of their role. As the organisation grows, however, these individuals will not be as motivated to turn their creativity into developing consistent and efficient processes. At the same time, the management task will be changing to become rather more positive in providing direction for the organisation as a whole and for its employees. The Ku-Ring-Gai Vet Hospital (see Box 6.4) demonstrates the increasing pressure for a move from generalist to specialist that comes with increasing volume.

6.6.2 From commodity towards capability

Examples of this type of shift may be found in high-volume consumer services. To avoid the trap of becoming a commodity service, competing on price alone, these organisations may extend the range of services on offer, perhaps providing a degree of customisation for individual customers.

Of course, it may be possible to design a service delivery process that delivers a wide range of commodity services without increasing the complexity of the operations task, thus allowing the organisation to move in the direction of the top right-hand corner of Figure 6.16. This is covered in more depth in later sections on flexibility but may frequently be similar to the manufacturing idea of 'mass customisation' incorporating the following two principles:

Ku-Ring-Gai Vet Hospital — Box 6.4

The Ku-Ring-Gai Vet Hospital is situated in Sydney, Australia. Opened in September 1966, it is one of the largest veterinary hospitals in the world. Dr Greg Ross, one of the partners, is quoted as saying that their aim in building this hospital was to set a standard for all vets in Australia to follow.

The hospital is on three levels, with seven consulting rooms, three operating theatres, two dental stations, two radiology suites and an intensive care department. The hospital also has a 'grieving room' for distraught owners who wish to be with their pets when they are put to sleep.

This hospital challenges the traditional idea of the local vet dealing infrequently with a wide variety of tasks and yet building strong client relationships with pet owners. The vet specialist is increasingly the model being adopted, as veterinary science follows its human equivalent. Young vets are fast acquiring specialist qualifications, and older vets are being forced back to college to learn new skills.

Despite the 'high-tech' nature of the facilities, the pet owners have not been forgotten in the design process. Glass partitions give visibility for visitors to see what is going on, allaying fears that their pets may not be humanely treated once out of sight of their owners.

The three partners are the veterinarian equivalent of general practitioners. They are able to call on a cluster of specialists, which include small animal practitioners, dermatologists and a behavioural psychologist. Just about every part of a pet that can go wrong now has a specialist attached to it.

Questions

1 How well do you think the hospital has been able to cope with the increase in volume of transactions? What are the potential disadvantages for customers and how could they be avoided?

2 What is the impact of increasing volume on the vets? How far has the hospital moved from being a capability service towards commodity?

This illustration is based on material from A. Musgrave, 'Old dogs, new bones', *The Australian Magazine*, 30 November–1 December 1996.

- *Develop standard 'modules'*. Companies may develop 'menus' of standard services, which may then be arranged in appropriate combinations to provide a degree of customisation for individual customers. The customisation therefore lies in the management of the combination rather than in the development of new services. An example of this type of mass customisation is provided by holiday resorts that allow customers to choose a limited number of activities from a predetermined list.

- *Postpone customisation until the latest possible stage*. In this approach the delivery process is standardised for all stages until the last. This allows the service operation to gain all the efficiency and consistency benefits of a high-volume/low-variety process. Courier services are adopting this approach by using their basic distribution networks for all customers but using different mechanisms to deliver the package to its final destination.

A major transition occurs when the number of service delivery processes increases significantly. This transition takes the process mix from a few runners to several repeaters. Significant changes in the operations task frequently include the following:

- Shifting the focus of the operation from managing back office operations consistently and for maximum efficiency towards building front office flexibility.

- Requiring customer-facing staff to give informed advice as to the best service for an individual customer. Moreover it has become unacceptable for front-line staff in these organisations to act merely as a 'post box', taking requests from customers for advice but being unable, themselves, to give an immediate response.

- 'Upskilling' the front line through a combination of greater staff training and the provision of information systems that allow the service provider to act 'as if' an expert.

- Making processes more flexible, often allowing greater discretion on the part of the employee to make choices as to which service commodity will be most appropriate for the customer.

As with the previous case, there are major implications for the service provider and for the role of management. There is far greater onus on front-line staff to possess both technical and interpersonal skills. The service transactions are likely to be longer and more intense in nature. If the customer transaction includes a high degree of diagnosis of customer requirements and the extent to which the various services on offer match these expectations, the front-line employee will require excellent listening and consultative skills.

The second major area for change might be that 'specialist' employees who hitherto had been distanced from the customer, and were able to work in back office functions now may have direct contact with customers. This is particularly true in call centre or help desk situations where the customer wishes to deal directly with someone who has the expertise and authority to give a decision or advice on complex issues. (This may be less of an issue when more transactions take place electronically through the internet or through television-based applications.) Of course, not all technical experts have customer-handling skills.

The role of management changes from being the 'enforcer' of the service concept and process owner to ensuring that the service employees are developed and retained. Many jobs in commodity organisations are low paid and need very little training, often a few days or weeks. Commodity organisations that are seeking to become more flexible may find that they need to invest several months' training in front-line staff, meaning that employee retention becomes a major focus for management attention.

6.6.3 Strategies for change

The majority of service operations, of course, do not lie at the extremes of the diagonal. For those in the centre of the spectrum, between capability and commodity, there are four basic strategies to deal with transition at whichever point they lie. These are illustrated in Figure 6.17. Few organisations are able to manage these changes without some degree of disruption and the directions for change illustrated in Figure 6.17, therefore, may not be what was planned or desired, but describe what actually occurred.

1 *Building capability through systems and training*. Here the organisation may be wishing to move towards offering solutions for its customers rather than a relatively narrow range of well-defined services. The mechanism for this (preferred)

Figure 6.17	Strategies for change

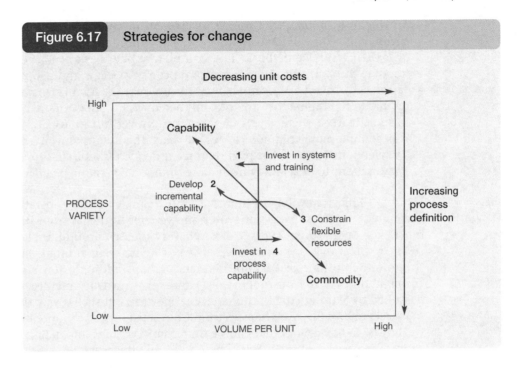

approach is to invest heavily in more powerful information systems, while also expanding the role of the front office staff. The benefit of this approach is that the organisation is then well placed to deal with the new challenge. The downside is that there may be significant upfront investment, which may not give the desired return.

2 *Building capability through incremental development.* In this case the organisation may take what appears to be a less risky approach to building capability. It effectively takes on activities or client assignments that are outside its normal sphere of action, but which it believes can be fulfilled by 'learning' from experience. This process is inherently inefficient and, unless any mistakes are confined to the internal workings of the organisation, potentially damaging to future customer relationships. This is particularly sensitive because capability operations must often work quite closely with customers, in a rather more intimate manner than commodity operations. This clearly means that any deficiencies are not easily hidden.

3 *Moving to a commodity by constraining flexible resources.* An example of this would be a gourmet chef being asked to work in a fast-food, limited-menu, restaurant. Although it is possible that the chef would be able to cook burgers and fries, they would be over-qualified, too expensive, and after the first meal or two would not be motivated to continue to cook to what will seem a rather repetitive and limiting process. Moving in this direction poses significant challenges for management, employee morale, and in the development and provision of appropriate cost and quality control systems. If these are not in place, the organisation will rapidly become uncompetitive as other organisations manage mass production more effectively.

4 *Moving to a commodity through investment in process capability*. In this case the organisation will have identified a market need for a high-volume version of an existing service or possibly a completely new service. Rather than try to 'muddle through' with inappropriate processes, systems and people, the organisation will invest in a similar way to direction 1. Again, this approach will require initial capital investment, and therefore may appear more risky. However, in some markets there is very clearly a 'first mover' advantage and this approach is becoming more common. In recent years, the investment in a greenfield site for telephone banking has paid significant dividends, not least in allowing these organisations to break away from more traditional banking practices.

Figure 6.18 illustrates the position that many complex service operations may find themselves in after a period of evolution: we refer to this as from start-up to starburst. The operation at start-up is often very focused around a relatively simple task, e.g. the provision of one 'runner' service. The original intent may have been to grow the volume of this one service, perhaps adding a few similar services through time as the business grew. However, in a way not dissimilar to that described by Skinner (1974), the service range grows in such a way that operations managers must deliver the full spectrum from capability to commodity.

The case in Box 6.5 illustrates how a simple task can grow into quite a complex challenge over a period of time. This is not to say that this is wrong – the point for us to consider is the impact on service operations managers. The network provision and management activity for British Telecom (BT) was conceived as a low-cost, commodity service handling large numbers of standard transactions (position 1 for a very short time during start-up, moving rapidly to positions 1a and 2 in Figure 6.18). However, as BT supported the full range of customers from the domestic household with one telephone line to the major corporate requiring advice as to how to integrate voice and data services (position 5), it can be seen that a major management challenge developed.

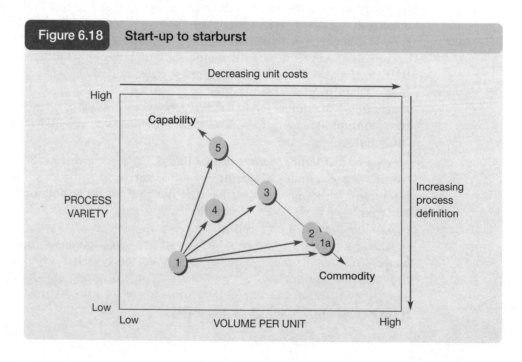

| Figure 6.18 | Start-up to starburst |

BT Wholesale

Box 6.5

BT Wholesale is part of the BT (British Telecom) group. Its role is to build and manage the central telecommunications network across the UK. BT Wholesale's customers are other telecoms providers and it has a statutory obligation to provide the same level of service to all companies operating in this market. In other words, BT's customer-facing company, BT Retail, receives no advantage over its competitors.

With the proliferation of telecommunications products, what might be thought of as a fairly straightforward activity very soon became extremely complex. BT continues to support older technologies such as telex as well as being commited to an aggressive installation programme for broadband.

Two more factors combine to make a potentially standard activity rather the opposite. The first is the 'engineering culture' of the organisation. Engineers may take the opportunity of a new customer requirement to create a completely new approach rather than adapt an existing one. The size and complexity of the organisation contributes to this. The second factor is that two customers requiring a similar service will frequently have different operational requirements. For example internet service providers (ISP) will not accept a standard broadband offer. The Markets Division therefore works with major customers such as the ISPs, corporates who require private circuits, and mobile operators such as Vodafone and T-Mobile, in order to engineer a cost effective solution for each.

With the advent of broadband, BT Wholesale was determined not to fall into the same pattern of too much process variety, frequently self-inflicted. The organisation was facing tough targets in terms of reduced customer lead-times as well as productivity improvements. It has identified a handful of process families, termed service process lines, and broadband is one of these. Some of the most senior managers in the organisations have been appointed as service process line owners, to demonstrate BT's commitment to this approach. Each process line is now managed end to end, with a shift from a task focus to a customer focus. Early results suggest a major performance improvement.

Questions

1 What are the process management principles that BT Wholesale is adopting as it attempts to improve service (faster response) and reduce costs?

2 Using the volume–variety matrix, plot BT Wholesale pre and post the change to service process lines. What are the management challenges in making this change?

As indicated in Box 6.5, the engineering mindset of the organisation has tended to mean that the customised activities appear more interesting and may attract more management attention than the need to create efficient and consistent volume services. This aspect of a dominant company culture can lead to some problems in matching service and process. Frequently, companies consider themselves as operating towards the capability end of the spectrum, whereas they need to operate the majority of their activity towards the commodity end in order to reap quality consistency and efficiency benefits. For example:

● A financial services company considers itself a 'professional' service provider. It thinks of itself as moving towards providing tailored solutions for its customers. The problem with this is that while it promises a great deal to its customers and, at first, contact is very friendly, the company fails to deliver a consistent service, continuing to use labour-intensive, inefficient processes.

- A software company values innovation in its products. However, most of its senior managers have been software developers at some point in their careers and do not understand the processes required to distribute and service its products to a mass market. As a result, these activities are under-resourced and ineffective, jeopardising the future health of the organisation.

6.6.4 Managing the gap between market position and operations

In the previous section we indicated that there may often be a divergence between the market position and the operations approach. In selling the benefits of a particular service it is common to find that companies emphasise customer flexibility – providing a personal service – while continuing to operate on a mass-production basis. Figure 6.19 illustrates this effect. This is often a very effective strategy. The main danger is that customer satisfaction will fall if the gap is too great between what is offered and what is delivered. To counteract this, organisations may adopt several strategies to 'manage the gap':

- *Customer service departments*. In many consumer services customer service departments frequently act as 'sweepers' to deal with customer complaints and to provide a relatively cheap human interface between the customer and the service factory of the back office.
- *Named personal contact*. Named contacts provide some personalised attention for the individual. Customer are allocated a specific individual to give confidence that they are not solely numbers in what may feel like a factory-type process. An unusual but appropriate example is in hospitals where nurses, nurs-

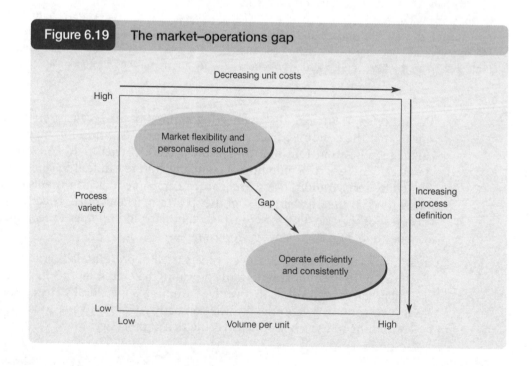

Figure 6.19 The market–operations gap

ing auxiliaries and volunteers provide the individual care valued by patients but not always delivered by a medical system that is focused on maximising utilisation of scarce resource (doctors and consultants).

- *Account or client managers*. Business-to-business services may use account or client managers to provide the point of contact for their customers. In some cases these may operate in a similar manner to the named contact described above. Where there are multiple relationships between individuals or functions/departments in the client and supplier organisations, there is great value in maintaining an overview. Account managers may also play a role in ensuring that the client perceives a level of customisation that is not always as great as it is presented.

- *Change the nature of the service*. Here process is repositioned: from service partnership to DIY, or service factory to service project, for example. The provision of internet-based services, for example, while offering the customers the opportunity to request service at their own convenience, may also become a means whereby customers 'do it themselves' rather than wait for the organisation to respond.

- *Change customer expectations*. All organisations need to try to align customer expectations with the nature of the service. If it is a high-volume, low-touch process it is important to educate customers not to expect personalised service.

Unfortunately, some service organisations adopt the approach of 'hoping for the best', taking no special action to manage the gap between customer expectation and actual service experience. This is a potentially disastrous strategy, with the organisation running the risk of long-term damage to its reputation and relationship with its customers.

6.7 Summary

Service processes and their importance

- A service process is the set of interrelated tasks or activities that together, in an appropriate sequence, create the service.
- 'Good' service processes not only create satisfied customers but also reduce costs, enhance value-added and underpin financial performance.
- Processes must be understood and managed end-to-end in order to provide the desired outcomes and experience for customers.
- The servicescape is a key ingredient of service process design and has a significant impact on customers and employees.

The nature of service processes

- Runners, repeaters and strangers help identify the extent of variety to be dealt with by the process.

- Value may be added in the front office or back office or both, with varying degrees of customer involvement.
- The volume–variety matrix helps identify the key attributes of service processes, and the implications of attempting to deal with a wide range of tasks with one process.
- Process profiling can help identify what needs to be changed to reposition a process.

Tools to 'engineer' service processes

- It is important to identify and manage end-to-end processes.
- Three tools that are effective in helping 'engineer' service are process mapping, walk-through audits and service transaction analysis.

Controlling service processes

- Reliability and consistency are important to most service operations and their customers.
- Capable processes can be created through the implementation of statistical process control.
- Quality systems should not only provide process definition, but should also be the catalyst for quality improvement.

Repositioning service processes

- There are pressures on many processes to change their nature.
- Organisations must manage the gap between what is marketed and what is delivered.
- There are four main ways in which service processes can be repositioned:
  - building capability through systems and training
  - building capability through incremental development
  - moving to a commodity by constraining flexible resources
  - moving to a commodity through investment in process capability.

6.8 Discussion questions

1 What examples can you give of capability and commodity service operations? What are the operations management challenges of each type?

2 Undertake a service transaction analysis of a service operation, identifying the critical points for management attention.

3 Analyse the servicescape of your favourite restaurant/eating place. What aspects encourage the 'right' behaviours in the customers and employees? Are there any aspects of the servicescape that you would change?

6.9   Questions for managers

1 To what extent are the traditional roles of front office and back office in your organisation changing? Has your management approach changed in line with the new task? What are the implications of customers potentially penetrating to the heart of the organisation through mechanisms such as internet-based access?

2 What is the basic culture of your service management approach? Is it capability or commodity based? Are there any people and activities that do not fit with this culture? How well are they managed?

3 Is there a mismatch between the current performance requirements of your service processes and the task for which they were designed? Have you identified future requirements before attempting to redesign your processes?

4 Carry out a walk-through audit of your service processes, looking at them through the eyes of the customer.

5 How many of your customer-critical processes are in control? Do you have statistical evidence of this fact?

6.10   Further reading

Fitzsimmons J. and Fitzsimmons M. (eds), *New Service Design*, Sage Publications, Thousand Oaks, Calif., 2000.

Gouillart F.J. and Sturdivant F.D., 'Spend a day in the life of your customers', *Harvard Business Review*, January–February 1994, pp. 116–25.

Schmenner R.W., 'Service businesses and productivity', *Decision Sciences*, vol. 35, no.3, Summer 2004, pp. 333–47.

6.11   References

Armistead C.G. and Clark G.R., 'Resource activity mapping: the value chain in service operations strategy', *Service Industries Journal*, vol. 13, no. 4, 1993, pp. 221–39.

Bitner M.J., 'Servicescapes: the impact of physical surroundings on customers and employees', *Journal of Marketing*, vol. 56, April 1992, pp. 57–71.

Botschen M., Koll O. and Rigger W., 'The attraction of aesthetic atmospherics', in Hildebrandt L. and Plinke W., (eds.), *Marketing and Competition in the Information Age*, in the proceedings of the 28th Annual Conference of the European Marketing Academy, Berlin, 1999, (available on CD-ROM).

Clutterbuck D., Clark G. and Armistead C., *Inspired Customer Service*, Kogan Page, London, 1993.

Deming W.E., *Out of the Crisis*, MIT Center for Advanced Engineering Study, Cambridge, Mass., 1986.

Fitzsimmons J.A. and Fitzsimmons M.J., *Service Management for Competitive Advantage*, 2nd edition, McGraw-Hill, New York, 1997.

Gabriel Y. and Lang T., *The Unmanageable Consumer*, Sage Publications, London, 1995.

Hart C.W.L., 'Mass customization: conceptual underpinnings, opportunities and limits', *International Journal of Service Industry Management*, vol. 6, no. 2, 1995, pp. 36–45.

Heskett J.L., 'The Shouldice Hospital', Harvard Business School Case Study (9-683-068), 1983 (revised June 2003).

Johnston R., 'Service transaction analysis: assessing and improving the customer's experience', *Managing Service Quality*, vol. 9, no. 2, 1999, pp. 102–9.

Kaplan S., 'Aesthetics, affect, and cognition', *Environment and Behaviour*, vol. 19, January 1987, pp. 3–32.

Kingman-Brundage J., 'The ABCs of service system blueprinting', in Lovelock C.H., *Managing Services*, 2nd edition, Prentice Hall International, New Jersey, 1992, pp. 96–102.

Kotler P., 'Atmospherics as a marketing tool', *Journal of Retailing*, vol. 49, no. 4, 1973, pp. 48–64.

Larsson R. and Bowen D., 'Organisation and customer: managing design and the coordination of services', *Academy of Management Review*, vol. 14, no. 2, 1989, pp. 213–33.

Mehrabian A. and Russell J.A., *An Approach to Environmental Psychology*, Massachusetts Institute of Technology, Cambridge, Mass., 1974.

Milliman R., 'Using background music to affect the behaviour of supermarket shoppers', *Journal of Marketing*, vol. 46, Summer 1982, pp. 86–91.

Oakland J.S., *Total Quality Management*, 2nd edition, Heinemann, Oxford, 1992.

Pine B.J., *Mass Customization*, Harvard Business School Press, Boston, Mass., 1993.

Shostack G.L., 'Service positioning through structural change', *Journal of Marketing*, vol. 51, January 1987, pp. 34–43.

Skinner W., 'The focused factory', *Harvard Business Review*, vol. 52, no. 3, May–June 1974, pp. 113–21.

Slack N., Chambers S. and Johnston R., *Operations Management*, 4th edition, FT Prentice Hall, Harlow, 2004.

Computer Services Limited (CSL)   Case Exercise

Computer Services Limited (CSL) was set up in the 1980s to provide a low-cost repair service for the customers of one of the large computer manufacturers. It was one of the first third-party or independent maintainers to compete directly with the service function of the original equipment manufacturer (OEM).

Because CSL had lower overheads, it was able to compete effectively on price. It drew its workforce from ex-employees of the OEM's service function and was able to find more than sufficient business from customers in the London area. At this stage, product life-cycles were relatively long and CSL was able to grow and sustain this business without a significant increase in complexity. It realised fairly quickly that it would be able to provide a similar repair and maintenance service for other makes of computer. However, this did mean the implementation of more sophisticated control systems to manage a growing workforce of service engineers and to ensure the purchase and provision of spares for a wider range of computer products.

The OEM realised that it was losing a significant amount of profitable business. Original equipment margins were being squeezed and the aftersales market represented an important source of long-term revenue as well as an opportunity to build customer loyalty. The OEM responded to the threat of the independent maintainers by setting up its own service divisions, sometimes repairing competitors' products at lower cost. CSL was being forced to compete on more than price.

At the same time, customers were asking for a 'one-stop shop' where CSL would undertake to maintain all equipment in a given area of the customers' business. This might include computers, peripherals, and other office equipment such as photocopiers. CSL did not have in-house expertise for all this equipment and so developed alliances with service organisations, who provided the equipment maintenance while CSL managed the customer relationship.

As computer equipment became more reliable, the revenue from repair and maintenance activities (sometimes called break/fix) fell, although customers still required CSL to provide this service as part of the total package delivered. On the hardware side, CSL is called upon to provide a rapid response to its business customers to ensure high service levels. As CSL has grown, its customer base has extended from the London area alone to provide cover across the UK. At the same time, its customer base contains a number of national organisations that expect consistent service standards across a number of locations in the UK.

To sustain this growth, CSL's operations have changed in several aspects, including:

● Service engineers now deal with a much broader range of equipment.

● CSL offers standard service-level agreements (SLAs) to major accounts, offering consistent response to all customer sites across the UK.

● CSL has invested heavily in control systems and IT to co-ordinate service engineers from its central contact centre in North London.

● To improve response and increase the efficiency of its service engineers, CSL has established help desks with tight targets to solve an increasing percentage of customer problems without the need for a site visit.

● Some CSL engineers have developed expertise to advise users on basic software problems, though as yet this is not included in the standard service offer. CSL is generating some revenue from this source, although it is unclear as to its profitability.

CSL needs to consider both the risks and benefits as it continues to grow and extend its portfolio of services. There is a danger that CSL will stray beyond its current operational competence, but because the changes have been incremental it may be that CSL is incurring more cost than is sensible because it has been somewhat reactive to its customer demands. In particular, CSL must consider how to deal with the increasing complexity of service provision.

CSL is also facing competition from larger organisations providing outsourced IT services to major companies. Despite diversification, CSL continues to face both lower volumes of business from each customer and erosion of its margins. Until recently this has been offset by the acquisition of new customers, but this rate of growth is also slowing.

It has been suggested that CSL enter the IT solutions market. This would be attractive to some of CSL's major accounts, who are hoping to invest in significant IT solutions in areas such as enterprise resource planning (ERP) and customer relationship management (CRM).

Questions

In order to identify the issues for CSL:

1 Compare and contrast the operational challenges CSL would face in delivering IT solutions as opposed to its traditional business.

2 How would you recommend that CSL develop the required operational capabilities to deliver IT solutions?

chapter seven

Service people

Chapter objectives:

- to understand the pressures on service providers

- to describe a number of means by which operations managers can manage and motivate their staff

- to describe how customers can be managed to fulfil their roles and display the 'right' behaviour.

7.1 Introduction

If you ask operations managers what is the activity that they spend most time on or that gives them the most problems, many of them would tell you that it is managing their people. Most service organisations employ large numbers of people, both customer-facing (front-line) employees and back office employees who support (and thus provide service to) the customer-facing staff. They may be, for example, customer service agents in a bank, or computer specialists staffing a help line, or HR professionals providing recruitment and training services to their colleagues.

From a customer perspective, the difference between a mediocre and an excellent service experience lies more often than not with the person who serves them – their immediate point of contact. This person embodies the service and the customer's perception is influenced to a large extent by the way they view this interaction. It is possible for a service organisation to invest in meticulous process design and expensive technology but having failed to invest in its people it will not achieve the expected levels of customer satisfaction. This is only the tip of the iceberg, because employees will not be motivated to own and improve service processes to deliver required levels of quality and productivity.

Managing service providers is an important task because:

- These people, individually and collectively, have a crucial role: they are responsible for delivering service to their customers (whether internal or external).
- In most services, the providers form a significant element in the service experience.
- Employees represent significant resource for many service businesses, and frequently represent the largest variable cost to the organisation.
- The essence of professional services, in particular, lies in the skill, capability and knowledge of the people. Professionals 'are the service', in the sense that it is these people – a blend of their expertise and chemistry with the client – that the customer is buying.

An additional 'service provider' are the customers themselves. In service organisations customers often play an active part in the process of service delivery so, just like employees, they are an organisational resource that needs to be carefully selected, trained and supported to do their 'job'.

The chapter deals primarily with the leadership and motivation of service employees and customers as they relate to service delivery, rather than addressing aspects of terms and conditions of employment contracts.

7.2 Understanding the pressures on service providers

Delivering service minute after minute, day after day, year after year is not easy. For many people this may be a rewarding, fulfilling and enjoyable task; for others it is, at best, a daily struggle and, at worst, a nightmare. All service providers face two distinct but often equally difficult pressures: pressure from their managers (organisational pressures) and pressure from their customers (customer pressure) (see Figure 7.1).

7.2.1 Organisational pressures

The nature of the service task will present challenges for the employee. Some tasks are inherently more stressful. There are some challenging tasks faced by the staff in the Housing Association described in Box 7.1, where staff face large numbers of desperate customers and do not have enough resources to keep some of them off the

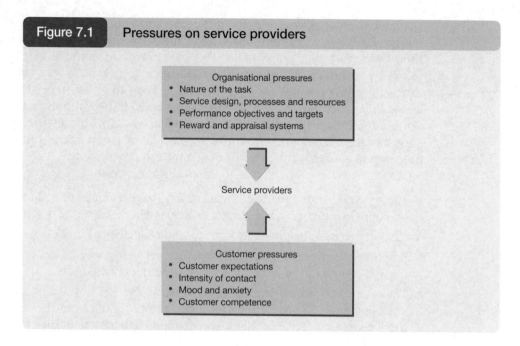

Figure 7.1   Pressures on service providers

Organisational pressures
- Nature of the task
- Service design, processes and resources
- Performance objectives and targets
- Reward and appraisal systems

Service providers

Customer pressures
- Customer expectations
- Intensity of contact
- Mood and anxiety
- Customer competence

streets. Likewise, the surgeon who performs life-saving surgery may feel more anxiety than a supermarket checkout employee, since the consequences of mistakes are more serious. It has to be noted, though, that reaction to pressure is very much an individual response, which results in some fairly relaxed surgeons and some extremely tense checkout operators! This might seem a trivial point, but organisations that are often under pressure (see the coping zone in Chapter 8) now recruit individuals who are better equipped to deal with stress.

The service design and the design of processes and the use of operational resources can have a significant impact on the employees. For example, service engineers who work from home may well find that their journey times to customers are reduced, but that they miss out on the support of colleagues they might receive if working from a central location. Many companies have a reception area for visitors staffed by an employee who also operates the telephone switchboard. This creates an inevitable conflict as the employee must make a decision as to who is most important: the customer on the telephone or the visitor in front of them.

Almost all organisations set increasingly demanding performance targets. Because these targets are aimed at performance improvement, they frequently conflict. For example, the call centre agent may have to meet a productivity target of average call handling time (ACHT), while maintaining service quality targets of accuracy and courtesy. This may not be always possible, particularly when demand outstrips capacity and the service organisation enters the coping zone, as discussed in Chapter 8.

Finally, reward and appraisal systems may be the source of pressure as employees struggle to maintain performance standards that ensure maximum payments.

7.2.2 Customer pressures

Customers bring another set of pressures (see Box 7.1). Some of the significant issues for service employees resulting from customer expectations include:

- The constant presence of customers in high-contact services. Serving staff in restaurants are constantly 'on show' and cannot relax.
- Customers like to think that the service transaction they receive is special for them. For the service employee it is likely to be just one of many.
- Customers may have expectations of the service beyond the design specification based on experiences of other service providers.
- Some customers may have totally unrealistic expectations of service delivery.

New Islington and Hackney Housing Association | Box 7.1

New Islington and Hackney Housing Association is a registered social landlord and a registered charity that owns and manages 6,500 properties in London and Essex in the UK. Employing around 650 people with a turnover of around £42 million it is one of a number of quasi government bodies that provide housing and associated services in areas of significant social deprivation and social exclusion. Fifty per cent of its customers are from black and minority ethnic groups, over 20 per cent have English as a second language and nearly 90 per cent are in receipt of some form of government benefit. Many of these people are unemployed and nearly 50 per cent have no qualifications.

These customers have little or no choice. There is a serious undersupply of housing accommodation in London so the alternatives for these customers include the very expensive private rented sector, short-term hostel accommodation or living rough on the streets.

In the main, these people are grateful to the Association for providing them with quality, affordable accommodation, although often they do not directly contribute to the rent unless they find work. There is, however, a minority of customers who are difficult and on occasions abusive and threatening. Bob Heapy, the Association's operations director, explained some of the problems he and his staff face:

I would describe most of our customers as good customers; however, some customers are very difficult to manage. This is sometimes due to their expectation of service levels being in excess of what we are required to provide or indeed can provide for them – often we find that this is because they don't understand what we can or can't do. There are clear service standards expressed in our tenancy agreements (our contracts) with our customers and a key task for us is to assist our customers to understand these standards. This can make our dealings with our customers difficult; customers can be frustrated, anxious, demanding and occasionally aggressive to customer-facing staff. As a result staff require specific skills to manage these customer interactions. We took the view, when we reviewed our customer-contact staffing groups, that we required excellence in 'soft' skills, so we undertook to employ staff from the retail sector, who appeared to demonstrate these competencies, and provided intensive training for 'technical' housing-related skills.

The staff do a fantastic job. They are professional and dedicated and they often choose to work in the not-for-profit sector through a sense of social purpose. We provide our customer-facing staff with good physical conditions of work, and good employment conditions, including rewards and pay all incentivised through a bonus scheme, which is also linked to the individual's performance reviews and appraisals. These appraisals and reviews are undertaken quarterly by line managers, including updating of key personal performance targets. The performance targets are driven by the Operational Plan, which in itself is driven by the overall Organisational Business Plan. In our view this gives a sense of perspective of where an individual fits within the business and how their performance impacts on our business as a whole.

We undertake regular training and development of employees. Another key issue for us is the continuous improvement of the services responding to our customers' needs. Recently we have identified that communication issues were preventing certain groups accessing services, so the provision of community languages became a key requirement. We have been able to include in our recruitment requirements a second language for customer-facing staff. We now have 12 community languages spoken in our customer contact section.

Questions

1 What are the customer pressures that the staff of the Association face?

2 What effect do you think this has on the staff?

3 How does the Association try to deal with these pressures?

The intensity of the service encounter may contribute to the pressure on service employees. It is likely that the average customer at the supermarket checkout is less demanding than a participant on a management training programme – for two reasons. First, the transaction at the supermarket is completed in a few minutes, whereas the training programme might take place over several days. The extended contact time brings a degree of pressure, but probably more significant is the meaning of this event for the customer. The management training programme may represent a promotion opportunity for the participant/customer and the resulting anxiety may be easily transferred from customer to provider.

The mood of the customer is clearly a major factor in the equation. Many leisure services have a built-in advantage here, because customers are generally in a positive mood and may be more co-operative with service employees as a result. On the other hand, diners at a special celebration meal in a restaurant may be more demanding as they want this occasion to go without any problems. At the other end of the scale, 'customers' of the prison service (inmates) may be less friendly and less co-operative!

Finally, the competence of the customer may have a significant impact on the service provider. Regular airline passengers know the various steps of the check-in process and know where to find flight information. Infrequent fliers slow up the process because they do not know what to do, and they ask more questions for clarification or reassurance. There is also a category of customer that poses yet more challenges for the service provider: the customers who think they know what to do but in reality do not and may cause significant disruption as a result.

Front-line service employees may find themselves playing a wide variety of roles; some of these form part of their formal job description, while others are perhaps unexpected but must be dealt with to some degree. These include:

● *Order taker*. The front-line staff form the interface between customer and organisation.

- *Advice giver*. The customer is often looking for 'inside' knowledge as to what is particularly good or what is not worth purchasing.
- *Image maker*. The brand is delivered by service employees.
- *Service deliverer*. The front-line staff may be the final point of contact for customers.
- *Complaint handler*. The most effective point of service recovery is at the point of delivery. Many informal complaints are dealt with here.
- *Therapist*. For some customers, any human contact is an opportunity to offload problems and to seek support and advice.
- *Trainer*. Front-line staff must be able to deal with both competent and incompetent (possibly new) customers.
- *Coach*. Many customers need confidence building and coaching to ensure a good service experience.

This section has given a very brief introduction to the issues relating to the diversity of customers and their expectations of service providers. Clearly, these pressures are felt most immediately by service employees in customer-facing roles, but are soon transmitted through the system to those in back office activities, and further on to suppliers and partners.

7.2.3 Resultant issues for service providers

If not managed well, these frequently conflicting forces of organisational and customer pressures result in problems of motivation and stress, for example, causing increased costs, damaged staff and poor service (see Figure 7.2).

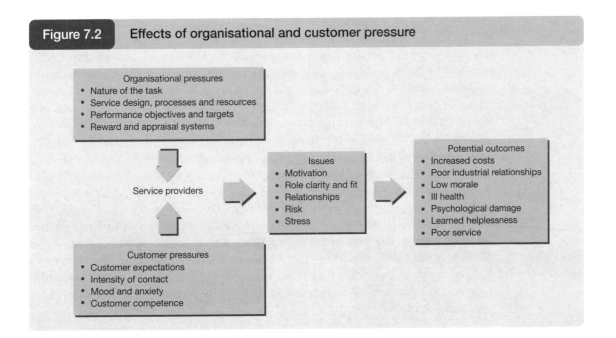

Figure 7.2 Effects of organisational and customer pressure

Organisational pressures
- Nature of the task
- Service design, processes and resources
- Performance objectives and targets
- Reward and appraisal systems

Service providers

Issues
- Motivation
- Role clarity and fit
- Relationships
- Risk
- Stress

Potential outcomes
- Increased costs
- Poor industrial relationships
- Low morale
- Ill health
- Psychological damage
- Learned helplessness
- Poor service

Customer pressures
- Customer expectations
- Intensity of contact
- Mood and anxiety
- Customer competence

- *Motivation*. Many of us have experienced the pressure of continually trying to satisfy groups of people with conflicting demands. For a relatively short period this may give you an 'adrenaline rush' as you work at superhuman rates, balancing all the various needs. After a while, though, enthusiasm may be replaced by apathy, particularly if you feel that you are working harder than others, and that the management does not seem to worry that you are overstretched. In some situations the very nature of the task itself may represent a challenge for employee motivation. Some tasks are rather repetitive, frequently constrained by information systems or other technology requirements to improve productivity and consistency. This relative powerlessness may be a significant factor in poor employee morale.

- *Role clarity and fit*. This issue applies particularly to customer-facing roles and often relates to the situation where the service provider is torn between providing the service that the customer requires or adhering to the level of service laid down, even when there seems to be no logic in so doing. Service organisations frequently report the problem of customer-facing staff becoming more aligned to customer needs than organisational requirements. Although it might seem that it is a good thing for staff to put the customer first, this is not the case when providing extraordinary service effectively costs money!

  Role fit is a particular problem for high-volume services with many employees. The organisation may have the correct headcount but the personalities do not always match the roles. For example, in the call centre on a shift that is difficult to staff, it may be that there are insufficient experienced agents to deal with complex enquiries. Less experienced people must often do their best, attempting to satisfy the customer without the necessary skills or training. Needless to say, customers may not be happy, and the employee may be demotivated as a result – and may not be as willing to help in future.

- *Relationships*. A continuing question for many service organisations is 'do customers have a relationship with the organisation, or are customers more influenced by a particular employee?' The answer, as ever, is 'it depends'. For many professional service firms, the customer is loyal to an individual provider first and to the firm second. In consumer services, however, rapid staff turnover and shift patterns mean that customers rarely encounter the same employee twice. In this case, any 'relationship' between employee and customer is somewhat limited. Despite this, many customers seem to expect a degree of personalisation that they would not experience in their everyday relationships.

- *Risk*. Most activities contain a degree of risk. Some service roles contain obvious elements of risk, such as the risk of violence encountered by officers or health professionals. For others, it may be more subtle, such as the gradual build-up of abuse experienced by some schoolteachers. Risk can be taken to mean that which is encountered directly by the employee, or some aspect of consequence for customers in the event of service failure. Again, some aspects of risk will be obvious, such as the physical risk of a train or plane crash, while others are more hidden, such as the potential damage to a student's future career if not well taught. For a more detailed discussion of risk and anxiety in service operations see James and Clark (2002).

- *Stress*. Stress is experienced where the requirements and challenges of the situation exceed an individual's perception of their ability to meet them, as a result of their own abilities, the training provided, or the organisation's unhelpful or difficult systems, procedures or policies. Stress may also result from providers being overloaded for long periods of time. The results of stress include robot-like service delivery, becoming overly focused on unimportant details, and ill-health.

Potential outcomes

Feeling of frustration, demotivation, lack of control and stress can have serious consequences for the organisation, the service provider and the customer. For the organisation it can mean increased costs of cover for absent staff, high attrition rates and poor industrial relationships. For the service provider it can mean low morale, ill health, psychological damage and, of course, poor service delivery. Indeed one common manifestation of stress is organisation-induced and/or customer-induced 'learned helplessness' (Overmier and Seligman 1967, Bowen and Johnston 1999). A poor working environment induces employees to display passive, maladaptive behaviours, for example to act immaturely, uncreatively and passively, and to be unhelpful to customers and managers. This learned helplessness can be so deeply ingrained that even when changes are made this passive maladaptive behaviour may continue. The outcome from the customer's point of view is poor service and uninterested and unhelpful staff.

7.3 Managing and motivating service providers

Service managers must employ a range of approaches to help service providers deal with the negative aspects of being between the opposing pressures of organisation and customer (see Figure 7.3). These approaches to managing and motivating service providers include:

- providing inspirational leadership
- harnessing the power of teams and teamwork across the organisation
- clarifying the roles of service providers
- using scripts appropriately
- defining and enabling appropriate levels of employee discretion
- establishing effective communication to employees
- involving employees in performance improvement
- encouraging ownership of customer and process.

Applying these approaches (as discussed below) and protecting employees from some of the pressures can lead to:

- inspired and involved employees
- responsive and responsible employees
- process and customer ownership
- employee commitment and retention

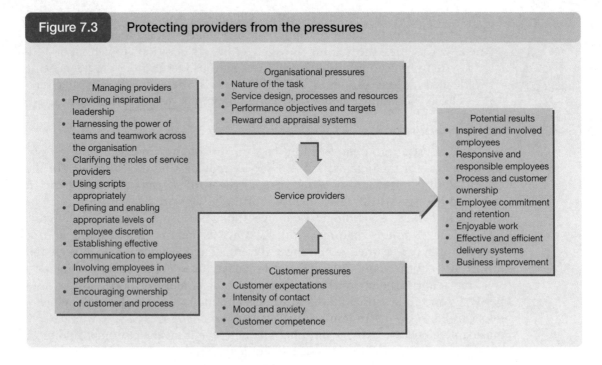

Figure 7.3 Protecting providers from the pressures

- enjoyable work
- effective and efficient delivery systems
- business improvement.

7.3.1 Providing inspirational leadership

'Leadership is the privilege to have the responsibility to direct the actions of others in carrying out the purposes of the organisation, at varying levels of authority and with accountability for both successful and failed endeavours' (Roberts 1989). When we discuss 'leadership' with managers and executives they usually point to the top of the organisation. We point out that all managers, at varying levels of authority, have a leadership role and need to develop and display leadership qualities.

Leadership is thus often categorised as transformational or transactional (see, for example, Kakabadse and Kakabadse 1999). The essential difference between the two is that transformational leaders develop and project a vision of the future, having energy and influence to encourage others to contribute to this new direction. Transactional leadership, often described as the ability to deal with the day-to-day management of operations, is equally important in the effective running of a service organisation.

Transformational leadership, as is implied by its name, is required at times of significant change. Many of the companies with a reputation for increasing the quality of service delivery and customer care have done so with the support and leadership of a chief executive who actively demonstrated their personal commitment. Examples of these include:

- Jan Carlzon, the renowned chief executive of the airline SAS who was credited with transforming the airline at a very difficult time during its history. He popularised the notion of service encounters as 'moments of truth' for the service organisation. He is quoted as saying that there were 50,000 'moments of truth' for SAS each day: points of contact between customers and the airline, which will either enhance or detract from the service experience. His 'recipe for success' has been emulated many times since by CEOs across the globe.

- Sir Tom Farmer of the tyre and exhaust chain Kwik Fit, who took every opportunity to preach the importance of customer service for business success and who changed the mission statement of the organisation from 'our aim is 100 per cent customer satisfaction' to 'Our aim is 100 per cent customer delight' (see Chapter 12).

What is interesting about these and similar leaders is that they are able to communicate a vision in such a way that it motivates the people in their organisations to performance levels significantly greater than might have been expected.

Different situations and different settings may require differing leadership qualities. These quantities might include (Roberts 1989 and Johnston 2001):

- accountability
- anticipation
- competitiveness
- courage
- credibility
- decisiveness
- dependability
- desire
- empathy
- in touch
- into the detail
- loyalty
- not complacent
- openness
- passionate
- responsibility
- self-confidence
- stamina
- stewardship
- tenacity
- timing
- trusting.

Bennis (1999) lists four competencies of great leaders:

- *The management of attention.* The ability of the leader to capture the hearts and minds of people through communicating a focus of commitment and a compelling vision.

- *The management of meaning.* This relates to the importance of bringing substance to the vision in such a way as to make it clear to those following. This is particularly important when dealing with the type of service that contains a high degree of intangibility. Indeed, it could be argued that the translation of service product-focused delivery into what is achieved in the perception of the customer needs this type of management of meaning. It is very understandable that the person serving in the fast-food restaurant may become overly focused on the number of burgers or pizzas sold per shift, but creating the customer experience requires a rather different focus, which can be provided by clear leadership.

- *The management of trust.* One of the key attributes of leaders is consistent reliability. In the same way that customers value reliability of service delivery, employees look to leaders to provide the same degree of security. They do not want messages and programmes that change on what seems like a whim, but to understand what has to be done well. Clearly, lining up actions with words is part of this attribute.

- *The management of self.* Bennis says that great leaders know their strengths and weaknesses. More specifically, he states that the best leaders do not seem to be easily defeated by mistakes or problems, nor do they start blaming their employees. In a service organisation this is particularly important – enabling employees to listen to customer complaints and institute non-defensive recovery routines.

Each of these attributes has particular application to the leadership of service operations. Of course, not all service organisations are undergoing radical change at all times – although it may frequently feel like it! It is here that transactional leadership is relevant. Some writers have downplayed the importance of this style of leadership, equating it with a mundane form of management that is little more than routine administration of a well-defined concept and its associated processes. This is particularly dangerous in the context of service delivery, which depends to a large degree on the example of front-line leaders.

However, these first-level managers, supervisors or team leaders have the prime responsibility for providing the day-to-day leadership of a service unit, which may make the essential difference between a robot-like service delivery and one that has life to it. Larkin and Larkin (1996), when discussing the communication of change, state that most employees prefer to hear about change from their immediate supervisor, particularly if senior management is felt to be remote and prone to changing approaches with alarming frequency. There is little doubt that these front-line 'role models' have a major influence on shaping the attitudes and behaviours of those who work with them.

Finally, individual employees may be capable of a form of service leadership as they exercises discretion over the service delivery process, potentially developing new ways of interacting with customers or more productive procedures. This is aligned with developing what psychologists term 'an internal locus of control'. More simply, the aim is to develop a sense of service process ownership in the hearts and minds of the employees. This theme is developed further in a later section on empowerment and employee discretion.

7.3.2   Harnessing the power of teams and teamwork

A critical design decision is the extent to which opportunities for teamwork may be built into the service delivery process. Many of the total quality management (TQM) programmes of the 1980s and 1990s evolved into teamwork programmes, as processes were redesigned to reflect the need to become more customer responsive. Several financial services organisations, for example, have restructured their customer-facing activities in such a way that a team handles all transactions from sales to service. This has frequently led to increases in both quality of service and productivity, as team members develop a greater ownership of customer and delivery process.

Most of the writers on teams (for example Katzenbach and Smith 1998) rightly point out that teams are not appropriate in all situations. For a group of individuals to become a team there must be a real requirement for them to work together because their roles interrelate in some way. In other words, if there is no obvious benefit for the individuals to work together, they remain a group rather than a team. It is important to distinguish here between working in a group and working as a team. Many organisations may claim to be doing the latter, but unless there are real synergies created from the individuals' work together, we would suggest that they are, in fact, simply working as a group of individuals.

Katzenbach and Smith (1998) provide the following benefits of what they term 'high-performance teams':

- Complementary skills and experience exceed those of any one individual. This facilitates a more effective response to demands for innovation and customer service.

- As teams work together to develop clear goals and to improve the processes in which they are involved, they also develop more effective means of communication, which allow them to respond more flexibly to changing customer needs.

- As team members work together and overcome significant challenges, people build trust in others and in others' capabilities. Again, this builds towards a more effective service delivery system.

- Close and collaborative working not only leads to team success but high-performing teams often enjoy their work and have more fun than others. This communal sense of humour can be very powerful in dealing with the stress of intensive customer transactions.

A particular point to note for service design is that in some cases the customer is an integral member of the team (see section 7.4). This is particularly relevant for professional services where the customer's presence and input are essential for service development and delivery. A firm of management consultants must often work alongside their clients in order to carry out their work. Part of the service might be for the consultants to provide mentoring and development for the client's employees.

While there has been a certain amount of research into the formation of management teams (see, for example, Belbin 1981), there is relatively little comparable work on the formation and management of teams involved in the day-to-day running of manufacturing processes or service delivery. Katzenbach and Smith (1998) again provide some useful principles for developing successful teams:

- Setting a demanding performance challenge is more effective in creating a successful team than the use of team-building exercises or appointing team leaders with 'ideal' profiles.

- Organisations need to pay attention to 'team basics'. These include such things as team size, purpose, goals, etc.

- Organisations that emphasise individual performance over team performance erect barriers to team success.

- Teams are a natural unit for integrating performance and learning.

Many team initiatives fail because not enough attention is paid to team design and team processes (see the First Mortgage Direct example in Box 7.2). In other words, just saying 'let's be a team' is not sufficient to create one. There must be a genuine requirement for a team to operate together if it is to be a success.

Osburn and Moran (2000) report the results of organisations that have redesigned their operations to move towards 'self-directed work teams'. They give examples of teams that have increased productivity and quality. Shenondoah Life is quoted as processing 50 per cent more applications and customer services requests, with 10 per cent fewer people, by using work teams. A powerful example of the impact of teamwork is provided by the Experian consumer service centre in Texas. In 1994 it had all the typical ailments of call centres: low morale, high employee turnover, fragmented service delivery systems and poor quality compliance. A redesign, which included investment in new technology and integrating service functions, combined with a team approach, turned this poor service operation into a benchmark site for call centre operations.

First Mortgage Direct

Box 7.2

A call centre within the First Mortgage Group was organised into a number of teams. Team leaders had a range of objectives:

- to organise and co-ordinate the team
- to update training plans
- to produce weekly performance reports
- to monitor and record holidays
- to deal with queries
- to review sickness.

The issue for Mike Walker, the newly appointed manager, was that there was no consistency or co-ordination across teams. In other words, there was no teamwork at team-leader level. Each team operated independently, creating 'mini-call centres' within the unit. This resulted in poor performance, duplication of work and resistance to implementing improvements originating from other teams.

Mike's approach was to clarify the broader vision of the call centre for his team leaders. His objective was to get them to see their role as contributing to the success of the call centre as a whole, rather than simply leading their team. Mike involved his 'team of team leaders' in putting the detail to the vision. This was achieved through brainstorming sessions, benchmarking visits, using advice from the National Society for Quality through Teamwork (NSQT) and focus groups formed from call centre staff.

A number of audits were carried out. A skills audit revealed that there were training and development needs for team leaders to take on more people-focused roles. A task audit showed that team leaders were concentrating on clerical activities to the detriment of less quantifiable tasks such as coaching team members. As a result of this analysis, the team leader role was redefined so that it was expected that 60 per cent of time should be spent in coaching, and only 10 per cent in call handling.

The call centre was reorganised, with an operational support unit dealing with many of the clerical activities previously handled by team leaders. This enabled team leaders to concentrate on performance improvement in line with the vision. Some of the benefits realised by this initiative included:

- more effective team management, despite increases in team size of up to 50 per cent
- 35 per cent increase in productivity
- improved customer service
- increased innovation and proactivity
- fewer ineffective meetings
- a saving in team-leader time of 1.5 days per team leader per week.

Mike Walker reports that the creation of a culture of encouragement and the facilitation of learning has provided a solid platform for future change.

Questions

1 Do you think that all the team leaders would be happy with the changes made by Mike Walker? How would you deal with this?

2 Why do you think this approach has been successful for First Mortgage Direct?

This illustration is based on material from M. Walker, 'Empowering your team leaders', *International Journal of Call Centre Management*, vol. 1, no. 2, 1998, pp. 91–8.

Osburn and Moran (2000) agree that not all situations are suitable for teams, and provide a helpful checklist for feasibility:

- Are the work processes compatible with self-directed teams?
- Are employees willing and able to make self-direction work?
- Can managers master and apply the hands-off leadership style required by self-directed teams?
- Is the market healthy or promising enough to support improved productivity without reducing the workforce?
- Will the organisation's policies and culture support the transition to teams?
- Will the local community support the transition to teams?

The writers also provide a useful insight into the transition process, pointing out that the organisation is unlikely to be able to move from a situation without teams to the autonomy and employee maturity required for self-directed teams in one step. The required change in leadership style and employee discretion is covered in following sections.

The role of team leaders

Recent research into the role of team leaders (Betts *et al.* 2004) has shown that the team leaders play a critical role in the success of teams. And just like all service providers they, too, feel squeezed between the pressure of the organisation pushing for business results and the team members looking for support and care. This feeling is exacerbated in some organisations where the team members see them as managers but managers often see them as part of the team.

The research identified six key attributes of a team leader. They should be:

- approachable
- empathetic
- supportive
- organised
- knowledgeable about the role of the team members
- knowledgeable about the business.

An additional and interesting finding was the value of having a team of team leaders. There was unanimous agreement that having a team of team leaders provided for stronger collective responsibility, better communication between teams, more effective use of resources and sharing of best practice.

7.3.3 Clarifying the roles of service providers

Most people work more effectively when they have a clear understanding of their role, what is expected of them, and how they will be assessed. Research into the effectiveness of service encounters suggests that role conflict and role ambiguity should be minimised if customer-facing employees are to be motivated to provide good service:

- *Role conflict.* In many organisations, service providers may have a number of responsibilities, yet it may be impossible to carry out each role simultaneously. An example is provided by the call centre employee who is charged with reducing queue lengths and also with trying to persuade customers to purchase more services, a task that requires more time to be spent on each transaction. Role conflict may occur when the basic service design is in error, as in the example above, or when the demands of the job are in conflict with the individual's personal view of how much status is conferred on the role. In the UK, for example, service jobs are often seen as rather demeaning, with perhaps some feeling that they are similar in nature to the role of servants to the 'lord of the manor'. This feeling of inequality and lack of value may be detected when employees call customers 'Sir' or 'Madam' in a somewhat sarcastic tone of voice.

- *Role ambiguity.* Role ambiguity occurs when the person is unsure of the requirements of the role (Katz and Kahn 1978). A cause of this for service providers might be that there is a lack of clarity about the guiding philosophy or strategy of the organisation. This is frequently a result of poor leadership both from senior management and from first-line supervisors.

Both role conflict and role ambiguity may occur as the organisation grows and develops. What was carried out by committed individuals in the early stages of the organisation's existence may be taken over by people who have been recruited more recently. In theory this should be an opportunity to formalise roles and responsibilities, but this may be resisted since it may be felt to be contrary to the entrepreneurial spirit of the original vision.

Service designers must take into account these issues in order to manage all aspects of service delivery, but must pay particular attention to the roles of customer-facing employees. If these people are experiencing role stress of any nature, their ability to create the required service experience is likely to be significantly diminished.

7.3.4 Using scripts appropriately

Many mass service companies employ the use of scripts as a technique for providing both consistency and efficiency in service delivery. In addition, as we shall discuss later, scripting may also provide a sense of security for customers and employees alike. A familiar script may allow customers to relax because they understand the 'rules' by which the encounter will be played out.

Tansik and Smith (2000) suggest 11 functions for using scripts in service delivery:

- *To assist the service employee to find out what the customer wants or needs*. The script should be designed to encourage customers to describe their needs in such a way as to allow the employee to diagnose them accurately and offer the appropriate service.

- *To control the customer.* The script should help the employee guide the customer through the system with minimal disruption. This is particularly important where customisation is actively discouraged. 'Can I suggest our special two-course offer?' enables a rapid decision, although there may be a danger of closing off opportunities for selling more profitable services in the cause of an efficient order-taking process.

- *To establish historical routines that may be relevant to the service encounter*. Frequent customers will often become pre-programmed to carry out the necessary actions in the service process without prompting. An example is provided by airline passengers who have packed their luggage in the most appropriate cases, who anticipate the check-in questions, and who have their documents in order before approaching the check-in desk. Tansik and Smith suggest that the service designer should provide the appropriate triggers to what Schank (1980, 1982) termed memory organisation packets (MOPs), which allow the customer to move into what may often be unconscious routines, which may lead to early involvement in the service delivery process. There may be a danger of changing scripts in order to make a differentiation between service providers: this may cause confusion rather than build service quality.

- *To facilitate control of workers*. Scripts may provide the means of increasing consistency across multiple sites and multiple servers. This has the particular benefit of ensuring that the appropriate customer script is activated, and that all the required questions and prompts are given. Scripts have particular value in the process of cross-selling, as for example in a call centre selling direct insurance that encourages the employee to use 'sub-scripts' such as 'Are you sure you have sufficient cover for your house contents?' or 'Can we help you with any other insurance worries?'

- *To legitimise organisational actions*. Here the script informs the employee as to what behaviours and attitudes the management believes customers expect. The restaurant chain TGI Friday encourages staff to display high energy levels in their interactions with customers, whereas gourmet restaurants might prefer staff to encourage a rather more sedate and relaxed form of delivery.

- *To serve as analogies*. Scripts learned by a worker in a previous employment may be used as the basis for developing new scripts in later, similar situations.

- *To facilitate organised behaviour*. Scripting may allow for the smooth running of a team engaged in interdependent activity. Tansik and Smith provide the example of a surgical team, where the actions of team members are choreographed and rehearsed beforehand. Developing routine medical procedures means that individual team members may change, provided that others can perform their roles. Scripting facilitates this interchangeability.

- *To provide a guide to behaviour*. Scripts set expectations as to what will happen next in a service encounter. Because customers have experienced this or similar service organisations before, there is no need to provide explanation as to why things are done this way or why certain information is requested before the service may be delivered. It is also suggested that scripts may be used to explain service 'fairness'. Most patients in a casualty clinic will tolerate another patient being seen earlier than their turn if the condition is clearly more serious than their own.

- *To buffer or exacerbate role conflict*. A script may deflect difficult questions such as 'Why do I have to give this information?' by the use of scripts such as 'I'm sorry but it's company policy', or 'The financial services regulations require us to gain this information'. Scripts may help when the employee is faced with giving unwelcome or unpopular information to customers.

- *To provide a basis for evaluating behaviour*. Scripts can be used as a checklist for management to evaluate an employee's behaviour. This is commonly used in telephone call centres where supervisors may routinely monitor large numbers of calls. It is particularly relevant where supervisors may be looking for evidence of specific behaviours, such as the generation of sales as well as simple order taking. Scripts such as 'Have you considered . . . ?' may be useful here.

- *To conserve cognitive capacity*. Scripts allow the employee to work on a number of activities simultaneously because the script may be performed as if on 'automatic pilot'.

As can be seen from the list above, scripts can play a valuable part in service design and delivery. Carefully designed scripts can provide opportunities for early involvement of the customer with the organisation and its employees. Scripts can provide both conscious and unconscious means of support for customers and employees alike. They assist in the management of customer expectations, and may facilitate the smooth passage of the customer through the service delivery system because there exists a good understanding of what will happen and what is required of the customer at each stage to enable this to occur.

There are, however, a number of problems with using scripts in the delivery of service:

- *They may become too inflexible*. Customers who do not make the appropriate responses to fit the script may provide inexperienced or poorly trained employees with too great a problem to deal with.

- *They may lead to a customer perception of robot-like behaviour*. The standard restaurant script that prompts the server to ask 'Is everything all right for you?' is frequently greeted with the expected response 'Yes, it's fine, thank you', which is often not a comment about the food, but more a way of getting rid of an intrusion as quickly as possible. Because this script is used too often, without the perceived sincerity that would suggest that there is genuine interest in the response, the possible impression is of someone going through the motions of service with none of the personal attributes of warmth or customer responsiveness required.

- *They may lead to defensive behaviour*. Standard scripts may become a two-edged sword. While they may have a useful role in providing employees with a clear form of words to deal with difficult situations, it may be rather too easy to use a scripted response when the situation requires something rather different.

7.3.5 Defining and enabling appropriate levels of employee discretion

It is neither desirable nor possible to create a script for every service situation, so most service organisations give some degree of discretion to their service providers. This lines up with a general trend in organisations to tap into the brainpower and creativity of all employees, and not exclusively the senior management team. A move to self-directed or semi-autonomous teams and flatter organisations may build on the need to give more people more autonomy in the workplace.

We refer here to discretion rather than empowerment, because most people are 'empowered' – the critical question is how much discretion they have (see Bowen and Lawler 1992 and 1995). It is generally accepted that giving clear indications of the limits of an employee's autonomy is more helpful than providing no guidance at all. Empowerment in this context means that these limits are extended for employees. An interesting aspect of empowering employees is, of course, that their managers are to some extent 'disempowered' because they must step back from activities they have previously undertaken.

Kelley (1993) summarised the work of earlier writers such as March and Simon (1958) to develop three types of employee discretion:

- *Routine discretion* means that the employee has discretion regarding how the basic task is performed rather than what task is undertaken. The range of routine discretion may be extended with the complexity of the task. The more complex the task, the less it is possible to describe each step in a rigorously controlled procedure document. Kelley uses the example of an investment adviser who draws on a wide range of information sources in order to make the appropriate recommendation to each client. In the same way, customer-facing employees will make changes in the way that they deal with each service encounter.

- *Creative discretion* is exercised by those who develop both what and how they do things. This may relate to people who do not have a tried and tested formula for doing things, but nonetheless have some training and experience that allows them to make informed judgements as to what to do. At the extreme end of this spectrum might be those creative people who are involved in the innovative activities of the organisation, as in new product design or in the development of strategies that represent a significant shift from what has been the accepted norm.

- *Deviant discretion* differs from routine and creative discretion in that it is generally not approved by the organisation, whereas the other two types are recognised and approved by it. In the service context, Kelley gives the example of the retail salesperson who gives a customer a refund contrary to company policy. This may gain increased customer satisfaction for this individual, but not be approved by senior management. Deviant discretion is potentially disruptive since it usually involves individuals acting on their own authority, rather than on behalf of the organisation. Such people may earn the reputation of mavericks or being 'just plain awkward'. Indeed, an organisation made up of people who operate in this way would be interesting, but rather chaotic! However, an organisation without such people might easily become rather stagnant, without challenge to the status quo.

Figure 7.4 provides a framework for exploring some of the issues around developing or restricting employee discretion (see also Armistead and Clark 1993). The key dimensions are as follows:

- *Organisational style*. Fluid organisations are those who must change their structure relatively frequently. Project-based organisations, such as consultancies, may organise around expertise. The consultant who is the expert provides the lead, possibly providing direction for employees with greater seniority. As the clients' needs shift, so may the requirement for different skills/knowledge sets change, prompting further changes in organisational structure and processes.

- *Perceived individual employee discretion*. This will be discussed in more detail below, but it is important to recognise that the issue is frequently how much discretion employees 'feel' that they have. We will discuss this from the employees' point of view. Some employees may not realise and 'grow into' the discretion they have been given; others may feel that their freedom to act has been curtailed. Clearly this aspect might also be analysed from the manager's perspective, and it is worth considering the issues arising from differences of opinion between managers and employees.

The compliant organisation

The complaint organisation is frequently found in the high-volume/low-variety service operations discussed in Chapter 6. Compliant organisations have the following characteristics:

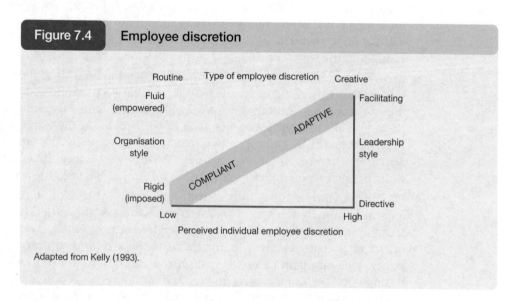

Figure 7.4 Employee discretion

Adapted from Kelly (1993).

- Their focus is on consistent service delivery, often across multiple locations and with many servers.

- Such operations have well-developed process documentation, with training for employees as to how they should behave in each situation.

- High volumes and consistent processes lend themselves to automation and/or the employment of relatively low-cost labour.

- The management style employed is frequently somewhat directive, often because employee turnover is such that employees are relatively inexperienced (and with low motivation).

- Performance measurement often relates to short-term indicators such as response times or orders taken.

As Figure 7.4 suggests, the problem for these organisations is that the service delivery process feels as if it is imposed by management. The process has been designed by head office staff, who then carry out periodic audits to ensure compliance to the predetermined design. Local innovations are not desired or encouraged, since this might create customer expectations that may not always be fulfilled in every location and will lead to potential increases in unit costs.

The problem therefore for the compliant organisation is that front-line (and often junior) employees lack the motivation or ownership of either the service concept or the customer to bring life to a rather mechanistic style of service delivery. The challenge for service managers is to engender both ownership and a spark of creativity in a workforce that might otherwise appear like robots.

In so doing, the aim is to change the emphasis from compliant to process ownership. The objective here is for the employees to take ownership of service delivery, rather than to feel that it is imposed on them. How this may be achieved is covered more fully in the chapters on service culture and continuous improvement (Chapters 12 and 14), but broadly the approaches utilised are as follows:

- *Communication*. Good communication is given from management as to how well the company is performing and the reason for future strategies. Also, it is useful to open lines of communication from customer-facing employees to senior management in order to facilitate the passage of invaluable customer feedback.

- *Involvement*. Inclusion in process improvement projects is encouraged as and when possible. The aim here is to foster a sense of ownership of both process and customer, because employees have had a hand in process design. Many service organisations have found that continuous improvement activities such as *kaizen* or six sigma have been very beneficial in this area (see Chapter 12).

- *Celebration*. A major problem for the motivation of staff in customer-facing roles is that they are frequently on the receiving end of complaints and abuse and rarely receive praise from customers. Indeed, some customer service functions are set up with the explicit task of dealing exclusively with complaints. Some service organisations counteract both the potential boredom of routine transactions and the deadening effect of dealing with customer complaints by creating rituals of celebration of success.

● *Teamwork*. Organising customer-facing staff into teams may help engender a sense of purpose, and also provide opportunities for job rotation, support and motivation.

All these approaches have one thing in common: they create a sense that the organisation values the contribution of even the most junior employees. Without this, it is unlikely that service encounters will be anything more than adequate, and will probably not build customer loyalty.

The adaptive organisation

The adaptive organisation is more often found at the high-variety/low-volume end of the spectrum, which we described as capability organisations in Chapter 6. Many people in professional services such as management consultants or legal advisers might fit into this category. The characteristics of adaptive organisations are:

● There are high degrees of creative discretion in developing both product and process.
● There is frequent dependence on key individuals' skill and knowledge.
● There is a resistance to the generation of standard processes, leading to inconsistency in approach.
● There is an emphasis on innovation.
● Research and development activities are often focused on the professional development of the people in the organisation as opposed to the development of service brands and products found in commodity organisations.
● The management style is likely to be 'facilitative', focusing on ensuring that the skilled individuals are able to work to their full potential.
● Performance measures are likely to be rather more long term in nature than is the case for the compliant organisations. Marketing, for example, may have targets that include the development of a number of new service products over a period of months, while an academic is required to develop new material for teaching next year's course.

The challenge of these organisations is to ensure that a reasonably consistent approach is adopted to service delivery. In many professional service organisations, client relationships are managed by the individual provider, leading to potential inefficiencies. Another weakness here is that individuals are reluctant to share their knowledge with others because this might weaken their position in the organisation. This may cause major problems when key individuals leave, often taking their portfolio of clients with them. Management may need to focus its attention on the following:

● Motivating key individuals, by providing opportunities to extend their skill and knowledge.
● Emphasising situations that require individuals to collaborate in order to carry out their tasks.
● Developing multiple links with clients to ensure that these relationships are not severed when individuals leave the organisation.

Managing transitions

Figure 7.5 illustrates two common conditions that describe what may happen when an organisation decides to increase or decrease the nature and amount of discretion given to individual employees:

- compliant to adaptive: the anxious zone
- adaptive to complaint: the frustrated zone.

Compliant to adaptive: the anxious zone

Service organisations may wish to increase the amount of discretion given to customer-facing employees. This is particularly relevant if the strategy is to increase the range of service options available to customers. In this case, individual service providers may be asked to take more decisions and to carry out a greater proportion of the service delivery process.

In many cases, of course, the implementation of this change is well planned and executed. Typically, this will involve investment in training and information systems, but no matter how well this is managed, individuals change at different speeds, which are dictated by their individual personality and history. Thus, in this case, the individual employees are being moved from what might feel like a reasonably 'safe' environment where they are provided with a clear structure and process to follow, to one where individual decision-making is required.

This may be summed up as 'being empowered but not feeling it'. The individuals involved want the challenge but are either unsure of their own ability or are uncertain as to how much real discretion the organisation is willing to give them. In this transition, individuals may well not perform immediately to the level of their capability and, indeed, may be written off by the management as not being up to the new task.

In reality, with support and training, large numbers of staff may be able to deal with the added responsibility of increased discretion. There is often a rich vein of talent for continuous improvement activities and the opportunity to build ownership of the service delivery process. It is important to note, though, that

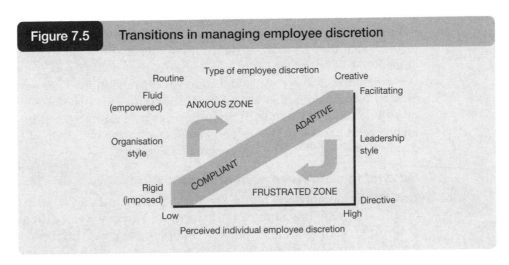

Figure 7.5 Transitions in managing employee discretion

customer-facing employees in the anxious zone will probably not always deliver service to the new (usually more demanding) design standards.

Adaptive to compliant: the frustrated zone

Organisations may want to restrict the degree of discretion of some or all of their employees. A common reason for this would be that as a consequence of actual or desired growth, systems and processes are standardised, reducing the opportunity for individuals to develop their own approach to service. This is particularly relevant to professional services seeking to provide consistent services to national or multinational business clients.

For these 'professional service shops', the implementation of management by process will result in a reduction in autonomy on the part of the individuals in the organisation. A good example is provided by the larger consultancy firms who may seek to develop solutions that may be adapted for a wide range of clients. In this scenario, although consultants may have some discretion to adapt the basic solution to their individual client, the basic design work has been carried out by other people in the firm. This philosophy will clearly change from firm to firm, as will policies regarding brand management and standardisation of approaches to client relationships.

The characteristics of the frustrated zone are as follows:

- Individuals resist the implementation of standard processes (an imposed system), claiming that the system prevents them from operating in the most effective way in delivering solutions to their customers.

- These individuals are frequently extremely vocal about these perceived or real restrictions.

- As can be see from Figure 7.5, employees in the frustrated zone often perceive that they still have high degrees of discretion, despite the standard processes being implemented. The result is that these employees feel that they are 'above' the system, that it does not apply to them and that they can circumvent its requirements in order to 'get the job done' in the way that they think best.

The problem here is that individuals who have become used to high levels of perceived discretion find it particularly difficult to work in an environment where they feel that their freedom is restricted. They may 'comply' with the system if the alternative is that they lose pay or status in the organisation, but they find the system difficult to accept and are likely to become disaffected as a result.

It is important to recognise the concerns of these individuals because they frequently possess skills that are essential to retain. This may be achieved in some cases by providing them with opportunities for personal development through involvement in activities that do not conflict with the objectives of the more standardised service delivery processes being implemented.

Balancing empowerment and control

The illustration provided by the Open Door Church (Box 7.3) demonstrates how organisations in the same service sector may have very different operating philosophies. Individuals who were happy in one organisational culture may struggle in another. It is important to note that when an organisation wishes to

Open Door Church, St Neots, UK   Box 7.3

The Open Door Church is only a few years old, but is growing rapidly where other, more traditional, faith groups appear to have reached a plateau, or are declining in numbers. There are a number of possible reasons for this success. A fundamental aspect of the Open Door Church is its vision statement of 'Open to God, open to you', which makes the point that church is not supposed to be the exclusive domain of those who are rich and talented. It is for anyone, including those who may be deemed less acceptable by society at large.

The Open Door Church meets on Sundays in a local school, but in reality the organisation is a cluster of small groups or 'cells'. These meet formally on a weekday evening but are encouraged to build relationships internally and with friends and neighbours. The volume of official meetings is much lower than many churches, to give space for life outside, and for members to be a real part of the community. Although the basic format of Sunday services for the whole church, with small groups meeting in homes on weeknights, looks similar to other churches, the underlying emphasis is entirely different. Traditionally, in other churches, the focus is on

Sunday services with a small percentage of members meeting in homes during the week. In the Open Door Church, the focus is on the development of cells with their ongoing relationships. These cell groups come together on Sundays, and attendance at the weeknight meetings is frequently higher than that at the Sunday services.

Tony Thompson, the first leader of the church, comments: 'The growth of many churches has been limited by the availability of experienced and talented leaders. We've taken a different approach, encouraging people who are relatively new members to become cell leaders.' This has meant that many more people have the potential to become group leaders, and this in turn has allowed room for growth.

These new cell leaders are given a great deal of support, including training and an 'apprenticeship' as an assistant cell leader. Cell group meetings are quite structured, with a recognised format and detailed notes provided by the church leadership team. John and Janet Lloyd were asked to lead a cell after a short time in the church. 'We were worried that we wouldn't be able to cope with leading the group. We thought we might have to deliver a "second sermon", but

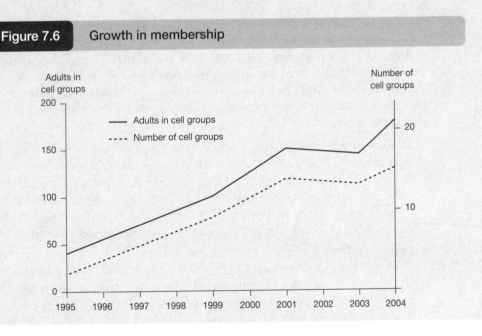

Figure 7.6   Growth in membership

the church leaders give us plenty of support and guidance week by week.'

Some people joining the church from more traditional denominations have taken time to adjust to this approach. If they have been group leaders before, it may feel like the role of the cell leader is more defined, possibly lacking freedom. Tony Thompson's response is:

We have made it easier for people to grow quickly into the cell leader role. It used to be so daunting that few people would volunteer for it. As soon as a cell has a stable member-ship of about 16 members, we're looking for it to become two cells of eight members. This multiplication may happen as quickly as six months and so we need a lot of leaders to sustain our growth.

The statistics shown in Figure 7.6 indicate the speed of growth. Increasing from three cells in 1995 to 15 in 2001 has required the identifica-tion, training and support of nearly 30 leaders and assistant leaders. This was no mean feat,

given that a sizeable proportion of the church's new members were not just new to the church but also new to Christianity.

In 2004 there were nearly 200 adults meeting each week in cell groups. The rate of growth has been more significant than the graph suggests because between 2001 and 2002 50 adults left the Open Door Church to found new ventures in St Ives and Luton. The second group included Tony Thompson, his place being taken by Martin Tibbert, an existing member of the leadership team.

Questions

1 How does the Open Door Church's approach to leadership differ from that adopted by more traditional organisations?

2 What are the challenges it faces in sustaining the rate of growth experienced so far?

This illustration has been developed from discussions with Tony Thompson, the first leader of the Open Door Church in St Neots, Cambridgeshire, UK, and with his successor, Martin Tibbert.

make significant changes, individuals must be treated as such, recognising that some will welcome more empowerment or discretion, others will be happiest in more prescribed roles, whereas others will take time and support to grow into a larger role.

As we have seen previously, the dilemma is to know how and by how much indi-vidual employees can be 'empowered'. Situational leadership theory (Hersey and Blanchard 1982) suggests that a key issue is the maturity of the 'followers': the extent to which they are both willing and able to take more responsibility.

Simons (1985) suggests there are four control organisational systems that assist the service manager in moving towards employees taking more ownership of their service processes:

● **Diagnostic control systems**. These are the standard performance measures of the organisation and include indicators such as sales per employee, response times and so forth. Managers may watch these indicators and allow employees to decide how they are to be achieved. Simons maintains that the danger here is that there may be pressure to 'massage' the figures in order to demonstrate ability. Thus, these measures are not sufficient in themselves to give management control.

● **Beliefs systems**. These convey the key values of the organisation. We discuss more of these in Chapter 14 on service culture; Kwik Fit's mission to provide '100 per cent customer delight' would be a good example. At worst, these state-ments appear to be simply following the latest trend but, at best, they can inspire employees to look for opportunities to contribute and do things better.

- *Boundary systems*. These are best described as systems that state minimum standards or express the rules that govern acceptable behaviour in terms of what is done or not done.
- *Interactive control systems.* Diagnostic control systems detect when the organisation is failing to meet performance standards. Interactive control systems are focused on detecting in what way the environment and therefore the task of the organisation might be changing. Strategic reviews and customer focus groups might form part of an interactive control system.

Simons asserts that managers need to use all four of these levers together, in order to provide an environment in which employees may operate more effectively.

7.3.6 Establishing effective communication to employees

Many service providers do not appreciate being kept in the dark about the organisation, its current activities and plans for the future; indeed, many service providers appreciate being involved in the process of development and often have important contributions to make. Communication is the key to success and its importance is recognised by some outstanding organisations (see Box 7.4)

Organisations use a variety of mechanisms to communicate and listen to their service providers. These include:

- briefings by managers
- annual meetings
- roundtable meetings
- question and answer sessions
- intranet-based information and updates
- informal meetings and gatherings
- company newsletters.

Box 7.4 describes the variety of mechanisms used by First Direct.

First Direct   Box 7.4

First Direct was the first bank in the UK to offer banking services exclusively over the phone. It was launched in 1989 by Midland Bank, which was acquired by HSBC. Peter Simpson was one of the original members of a working group set up to develop a new approach to banking in 1988. He has been First Direct's commercial director since 1991. He explains why First Direct was launched:

We had to find a way to differentiate ourselves from all other banks. Customer satisfaction with banks in general was low and customers felt the banks were all as bad as each other. The existing notion was that a bank required the customer's physical presence. We decided upon the radical idea of a purely telephone operation. Telephone was the obvious channel because just about everybody had a telephone in their house or access to a telephone at work. We went live at midnight on Saturday 1 October 1989. Making a Sunday as our first day of trading made it clear that we were very different and out to provide the customer with a service that they had never experienced before. We took around about 200 calls on the first night and since that day we have never closed.

Matthew Higgins, the manager with responsibility for planning and research, added: 'We now take something like 45,000 calls a day but increasingly we are getting more and more web traffic. We launched internet banking back in 1997 and around 400,000 of our customers are now using internet banking in addition to the telephone service.'

Although the customer is likely to speak to a different person each time they call, consistency of response is important. This is ensured by each representative having all the caller's details on the screen in front of them, including information about the customer's last call and any issues or problems they may have encountered. Each call is concluded with the operator asking if there is anything else they can do for the customer. However, the bank goes well beyond providing these traditional ingredients of good service. First Direct is a bank with personality. As Matthew explains:

The difference is how people feel when they finish talking to us. They go away with a feeling that they have had a good conversation with a friend. It is taken for granted that what they have asked to be done has been done. If they have asked to pay a bill, it has been paid. If they have asked for a balance, they have got a balance. But it is the extra bit. It is the attitude our people have and their sense of humour. They will also take the initiative. We like our staff to be proactive and to do this they need to feel both competent and confident and be good communicators willing and able to make decisions.

Although staff are incentivised through sales targets they are focused on providing excellent service. They manage this otherwise potential conflict by having good information about their customers. Matthew explains:

The more information we have about specific customers the more we can target better. So we don't, for example, make the mistake of trying to sell somebody a credit card or mortgage if we know they already have one. By talking to our customers we can understand them better and so serve them better and by doing so build up a relationship built on mutual trust.

What is important for us is that a person answers the phone – you don't get a voice that says press one for this and two for that. We want to be there for the customer. We want our staff to use their own style and personality. Obviously we have to ask for security details but, strange as it might seem, our people ask for it in many different ways. It makes it a much more human experience.

There is a balance between giving operators a script and getting them to be themselves. The downside is that mistakes get made, but this is a small price to pay. Mistakes are OK – we don't go around blaming people, otherwise they would want to go back to hiding behind set scripts with no personality or feeling and we don't want that. We accept mistakes and help people learn from them. Mistakes are about support, not blame. If somebody makes a mistake or if someone sees someone else making a mistake we expect them to be very open about it and do something about it straight away. The critical thing is that they tell somebody, their team leader or someone else in their team. We want people to be open and to learn from what they do. The team leaders will happily sit with them and help them sort it out. We don't say 'Don't press that button' or 'Press that button', but we would say 'Is this the one you want?' We try to point them gently in the right direction and even have a bit of a laugh about it as well.

In essence I think we are about 'sorting it with attitude'! We don't just want to sort out paying a bill, for example, but we want to do it with a particular personality and style. It's not written down anywhere – it's just what we do – we all know that. This idea is shared through senior management presentations, team presentations, marketing presentations and in direct discussions one-to-one with team leaders or managers and also through our TV advertising – which is not just aimed at potential or existing customers but also at our staff.

We spend a huge amount of time communicating. But that's the very soul of this organisation, so if you don't spend time communicating you might as well pack up and go home. If you can't communicate within the organisation, how can you communicate to customers? Communication has always been our strength.

Peter Simpson added: 'First and foremost we are a communications organisation. Second we are a bank selling financial products. The products are of course important, but it's about the way we do it. Without that we are the same as everyone else.' Matthew explains:

A couple of times a year the chief executive does a round of big presentations explaining the goals and plans for the following six and twelve months. This is done in groups of about 200 at a time so it takes a while to get around all 4,000 staff. One of the things that I have always found very refreshing is the amount of often quite confidential information that is shared with absolutely everybody. We trust our staff. The sessions often include question time with a panel of people – we get some very challenging questions!

First Direct's core values of openness, respect, contribution, responsive, right first time and *kaizen* reflect the way its employees behave to customers – and indeed how they hope and expect customers will behave towards them. The company believes in treating its internal customers in the same way as its external customers. According to Matthew Higgins:

Our values are basically commonsense values. They are just there to remind us about how we should operate. We don't ram them down people's throats, otherwise they might lose their meaning. They are just embedded in the way we do things. There is also belief that you would not treat anybody internally any differently from how you would treat a customer. It is about dialogue and information exchange but it is also about treating people as equals.

The board of directors takes the findings of their customer research very seriously. They are concerned about what their customers think. They are also concerned about what their employees think too. Board members would not hesitate to wander round the floor and talk to people to get their ideas and reactions to new ideas and initiatives or problems. Matthew added:

We were talking about service recovery yesterday and the chief operations officer arranged several sessions with a range of people, including people on the phones. Another director, following a particular incident, asked for people's suggestions. Senior managers make a point of listening and responding to the staff. They understand that the people on the phones not only know what is going on but may have many good ideas too because they are talking to customers all day. The directors not only understand the strategic issues but they understand the tactical issues as well.

Questions

1 What are the key aspects of management style or leadership that ensure that customers 'go away happy' from First Direct?

2 How important is the recognition that First Direct must be a communications company first and a financial services organisation second?

The case was commissioned by the Institute of Customer Service as part of a study into service excellence. The author gratefully acknowledges the sponsorship provided by Britannic Assurance, FirstGroup, Lloyds TSB, RAC Motoring Services and Vodafone.

Quirke and Walters (2003) describe four communication responsibilities for leaders. These have been developed by Synopsis, a consulting firm specialising in communication. These responsibilities are summarised in the FAME model:

- *Focus*. Leaders must set a clear focus with relatively few priorities, which are repeated and reinforced consistently. Leaders should identify what they want employees to think, feel and do to help.
- *Articulate*. Leaders must be able to turn management speak into plain language, and to make the messages memorable.
- *Model*. Leaders must champion company values, lead by example and challenge unacceptable behaviour.
- *Engage*. Leaders must make the connection between the organisation's agenda and the individual's agenda. They must be able to listen, facilitate, ask effective questions and handle any difficulties that may arise when employees speak up.

Many managers believe that they are effective communicators, but Kotter (1995) suggests that a significant reason for the failure of many change processes is 'under-communicating by a power of ten'. Quirke and Bloomfield (2004) therefore suggest that communication must be carefully planned to avoid contradiction, repetition, overload of trivia and insufficient communication of key issues.

7.3.7 Involving employees in performance improvement

We will discuss this in more detail in Chapter 12, but it is important to emphasise here that actions that build the self-esteem of employees will provide an antidote to the pressure they experience. At the most basic level, it is common sense to involve the people who are closest to any task in its improvement, given that they probably know most about it. Service designers who are remote from routine service delivery may sometimes create processes that are not always 'employee friendly'. Involvement of service employees may create wins for both employee and organisation.

This will inevitably mean that the organisation has some investment to make in terms of time, training and management support, but most organisations report benefits from these activities.

7.3.8 Encouraging ownership of customer and process

This has been discussed in some detail in section 7.3.5 above. However, it is worth emphasising that in the same way that customers like to feel that they have a degree of control over their own destiny, so also employees like to feel that they too are able to exercise some influence over what happens to the customer they are serving, and the processes they follow.

Encouraging ownership of customers largely comes from the example of managers. If the manager/leader is seen to champion the cause of individual customers, following through on problems and questions, employees will follow. Likewise, giving employees responsibility for processes builds ownership, and the sense of being in control of the process rather than the process controlling them.

7.4 Managing customers

This chapter has focused so far on employees as service providers. However, in many service organisations the customers too fulfil some provider roles. We would argue that, just like employees, managers need to understand how these 'temporary employees' should be managed so that they fulfil their required roles and display the desired behaviours (see also Bowen 1986, Johnston 1989, Mills and Morris 1986).

7.4.1 Customer roles

Customers perform a surprising variety of functions in the service delivery system. Their precise role will depend on the nature of the activity and the approach determined by the service designer. These roles include:

- *Service provider*. In many organisations the customer provides themselves – and sometimes other customers – with a service. An obvious example is the task we fulfil in supermarkets, taking items off the shelves, taking them to the cashier, bagging the items and taking them to the car. Less obvious are the roles we play in faith organisations, syndicate or work groups that rely on the involvement of all to create the service (and benefits) for each other. Another role customers provide, to other customers, is that of providing the atmosphere in a restaurant or place of entertainment. By being quiet or joining in the fun customers help set the tone or mood for others to enjoy and/or follow.

- *Service specifier*. In most services the customer must provide clear information about requirements before the appropriate service product can be selected and delivered. This may be relatively straightforward in consumer services where the service product is well defined and customers may have wide experience of the scripts (see section 7.3.4). It may not be as straightforward, however, in customised service, such as many of the professional services, where in many cases the customer has little relevant knowledge or experience.

- *Quality inspector*. Many service organisations will use the customer as a quality control inspector. Organisations may provide formal feedback mechanisms such as focus groups or questionnaires, or may encourage a wide range of comments from customers. Some organisations appear to rely on the customers to bring errors to their attention rather than ensure zero defects.

- *Trainer/role model*. In some organisations customers are used to help other customers know what to do and how to behave. By being seen to stand in an orderly queue or talk quietly in a restaurant, existing customers define the roles and behaviours for new customers. They may even take it upon themselves to admonish transgressors through a reproachful look or even active intervention.

7.4.2 Benefits of customer involvement

There are many benefits from encouraging the customers to fulfil the desired roles, for example:

- *Inclusion*. Customers who become actively involved in the service delivery process often develop an increased sense of loyalty. Having started the process, these customers are less likely to stop and find another provider in the short term.

- *Resource productivity*. If the customer is carrying out some of the tasks, the service operation requires fewer resources of its own to run. Self-service restaurants and supermarkets provide a simple example (see also Johnston and Jones 2003).

- *Customer control*. A major advantage for customers who become part of the service process is that they may feel that they have more personal control over what happens to them. This is one of the attractions for the internet-based services where customers may access the service at times to suit themselves and also may exit the service at any stage if they so wish.

7.4.3 Customer management issues

Since customers are significant components of service delivery both as recipients and as co-producers of the service experience, it would seem to be sensible to 'manage' customers as if they were employees. However, it can be harder to manage and control customers than employees! Managing customers entails some or all of the following:

- *Defining customer competence*. One of the changes in the service concept that may redefine the way things are done relates to the extent to which the service organisation assumes it is dealing with competent or incompetent customers. For example, telecommunications equipment suppliers formerly dealt exclusively with competent customers – national network operators. The advent of mobile networks and increased competition means that they may now be dealing with entrepreneurs rather than engineers. This opens up possibilities for the development of new services, as well as presenting challenges to accepted ways of working.

- *Customer selection*. Most organisations will be clear as to which market segments they are targeting. This has a particular relevance for some services, particularly those where the service experience is made up in part by the other customers. For example, the theatre experience is affected by others in the audience. Some restaurants insist on a strict dress code, sending a clear message as to what types of customer are welcome and what type of behaviour is acceptable. Center Parcs, the holiday company, will not take bookings from large, single-sex groups (particularly young men), because it does not want its reputation as a family-focused holiday to be damaged by too much 'inappropriate' behaviour.

- *Customer training*. To develop the customer resource, time must be set aside for training. Although this may incur set-up costs, it may pay dividends in the long run. A security alarm company discovered that many of the service calls it received were avoidable, but tied up expensive resource in answering them. It embarked on a programme of training key personnel in its customers' organisations. The result was significantly fewer false alarms, which improved productivity and customer satisfaction.

- *Customer motivation.* Service organisations may devise rewards for 'good' customer employees. Sometimes this can be achieved by customer-facing staff using their discretion to give more than was requested to customers who have been helpful. Many organisations assume that customers will want to be helpful. Moving to the front of a queue in a fast-food restaurant, you are encouraged to present your order in the 'approved' style and are rewarded by prompt service. Financial incentives might be given to customers who use the internet to book holidays or theatre tickets. Alternatively, service organisations may devise 'penalties' for customers who do not conform, such as fines for late return of library books, or speeding.

- *Customer removal.* As a last resort, service organisations will remove customers. This is particularly important in social situations where one group of customers may damage the experience for the majority.

7.5 Summary

The pressures on service providers

- The organisation is a source of pressure for service employees requiring them to deliver to certain levels of quality and productivity.

- Customers are a source of potential pressure for all service providers: through unrealistic expectations, customer incompetence and anxiety.

- These pressures may lead to issues of motivation, poor customer relationships, anxiety and stress.

Managing and motivating service providers

- Clear leadership is essential for counteracting the pressures on service employees.

- Teams and teamworking can provide a powerful mechanism for support and also for building ownership of service processes.

- Well-designed service scripts serve a number of purposes in service design, enabling consistency and providing useful prompts for employees.

- Good service is facilitated by reducing role conflict and ambiguity, and increasing role clarity.

- Defining the degree and type of discretion required for each role is essential, and provides insights for the manager in dealing with operational transitions.

- Internal and external communication is a powerful element in building commitment from customers and employees.

Managing customers

- Like employees, customers are often service providers.

- The key roles taken by customers include service provider, service specifier, quality inspector and trainer/role model.

- The key issues in managing customers include defining customer competence, customer selection, training, motivation and removal.

7.6   Discussion questions

1 Provide an example of a scripted response. Describe and discuss the advantages and disadvantages in using this script.

2 What are the advantages and disadvantages of using teamwork in student assignments?

3 Evaluate and assess your role as a customer in a supermarket, internet-based travel agency and university/college course.

4 From your observation of managers in shops and restaurants, what behaviours assist their staff in dealing more effectively with the pressures they experience, and what actions increase this pressure?

7.7   Questions for managers

1 Are you aware of the pressures on your staff? What should you do about this?

2 How well are you managing staff in transition? Are they anxious or frustrated?

3 Has your organisation realised the full benefit of teamwork? Are the teams progressing towards being self-directed?

4 What is the impact of stress on service delivery? Is there anything you can do to deal with the causes of this stress in the medium term, and alleviate its impact in the short term?

5 What style of leadership is appropriate for the individuals/groups you manage? How much discretion do your staff feel you give them?

6 What actions can you take to build ownership of customers and processes? How effective is your communications strategy in achieving this?

7.8   Further reading

Bowen D.E. and Johnston R., 'Internal service recovery: developing a new construct', *International Journal of Service Industry Management*, vol. 10, no. 2, 1999, pp. 118–31.

Bowen, D.E. and Lawler, E.E., 'The empowerment of service workers: what, why, how and when', *Sloan Management Review*, vol. 33, no. 3, 1992, pp. 31–9.

James K. and Clark G.R., 'Service organisations: issues in transition and anxiety containment', *Journal of Managerial Psychology*, vol. 17, no. 5, 2002 pp. 394–407.

Tansik D.A. and Smith W.L., 'Scripting the service encounter', in Fitzsimmons J. and Fitzsimmons M. (eds), *New Service Design*, Sage Publications, Thousand Oaks, Calif., 2000, pp. 239–63.

7.9 References

Armistead C.G. and Clark G.R., *Outstanding Customer Service: Implementing the Best Ideas from around the World*, Irwin Professional, Homewood, Ill., 1993.

Betts A., Clark G.R. and Johnston R., *Creating the Effective Team Leader*, research report, Institute of Customer Service, Colchester, 2004.

Belbin R.M., *Management Teams: Why they succeed or fail*, Butterworth-Heinemann, Oxford, 1981.

Bennis W., *Managing People is like Herding Cats*, Executive Excellence Publishing, South Provo, Utah, 1999.

Bowen D.E., 'Managing customers as human resources in service organisations', *Human Resource Management*, vol. 25, no. 3, Fall 1986, pp. 371–84.

Bowen D.E. and Johnston R., 'Internal service recovery: developing a new construct', *International Journal of Service Industry Management*, vol. 10, no. 2, 1999, pp. 118–31.

Bowen D.E. and Lawler E.E., 'The empowerment of service workers: what, why, how and when', *Sloan Management Review*, vol. 33, no. 3, 1992, pp. 31–9.

Bowen D.E. and Lawler E.E., 'Empowering service employees,' *Sloan Management Review*, Spring 1995.

Hersey P. and Blanchard K.H., *Management of Organizational Behavior: Utilizing Human Resources*, Prentice Hall, Englewood Cliffs, NJ, 1982.

James K. and Clark G.R., 'Service Organisations: issues in transition and anxiety containment', *Journal of Managerial Psychology*, vol. 17, no. 5, 2002, pp. 394–407.

Johnston R., 'The customer as employee', *International Journal of Operations and Production Management*, vol. 9, no. 5, 1989, pp. 15–23.

Johnston R., *Service Excellence=Reputation=Profit: Developing and Sustaining a Reputation for Service Excellence*, Institute of Customer Service, Colchester, 2001.

Johnston R. and Jones P., 'Service productivity: towards understanding the relationship between operational and customer productivity', *International Journal of Productivity and Performance Management*, vol. 53, no. 3, 2003.

Kakabadse A. and Kakabadse N., *Essence of Leadership*, International Thompson Business Press, London, 1999.

Katz D and Kahn R.L., *The Social Psychology of Organisations*, 2nd edition, John Wiley, New York, 1978.

Katzenbach J.R. and Smith D.K., *The Wisdom of Teams*, McGraw Hill, London, 1998.

Kelley S.W., 'Discretion and the service employee', *Journal of Retailing*, vol. 69, Spring 1993, pp. 104–26.

Kotter J.P., 'Leading change: why transformation efforts fail', *Harvard Business Review*, March–April 1995, pp. 59–67.

Larkin T.J. and Larkin S., 'Reaching and changing frontline employees', *Harvard Business Review*, May–June 1996.

March J.G. and Simon H.G., *Organizations*, Wiley, New York, 1958.

Mills P.K. and Morris J.H., 'Clients as "partial" employees of service organisations: role development in client participation', *Academy of Management Review*, vol. 11, no. 4, 1986.

Osburn J.D. and Moran L., *The New Self-Directed Work Teams*, McGraw Hill, New York, 2000.

Overmier J.B. and Seligman M.E.P., 'Effects of inescapable shock upon subsequent escape and avoidance learning', *Journal of Comparative and Physiological Psychology*, vol. 63, 1967, pp. 28–33.

Quirke W. and Bloomfield, R., 'Developing a consistent planning approach', *Strategic Communication Management*, vol. 8, no. 3, April–May 2004, pp. 14–17.

Quirke W. and Walters D., 'What every manager should know about communication', *Strategic Communication Management*, vol. 7, no. 5, August–September 2003, pp. 26–29.

Roberts W., *Leadership Secrets of Attila The Hun*, Bantam Press, London, 1989.

Schank R.C., 'Language and memory', *Cognitive Science*, vol. 4, 1980, pp. 243–84.

Schank R.C., *Dynamic Memory: A Theory of Reminding and Learning in Computers and People*, Cambridge University Press, Cambridge Mass., 1982.

Simons R., 'Control in an age of empowerment', *Harvard Business Review*, March–April 1985.

Tansik D.A. and Smith W.L., 'Scripting the service encounter', in Fitzsimmons J. and Fitzsimmons M. (eds), *New Service Design*, Sage Publications, Thousand Oaks, Calif., 2000, pp. 239–63.

The Empress Hotel Group

Case Exercise

Robert Johnston and Bridgette Sullivan-Taylor, Warwick Business School

Davina McColl had just taken over as personnel director at the Empress Hotel Group, a major international five-star hotel chain with its headquarters in Hong Kong. Her task in the previous hotels in which she had worked involved setting up systems and procedures, updating the standard operating procedures, and running customer service training departments that provided and coached scripts, encouraged teamwork and allocated roles and duties. She had personally trained senior hotel managers in leadership and motivation. This hotel chain, she realised, was going to be rather different.

The Empress Hotel Group's chairman and chief executive was Bob Beaver, an evangelical American whose dream was to create 'the most perfect hotel chain in the world'. He felt that the standardised approach to five-star hotels was not appropriate for the discerning international traveller, who wanted a taste of local culture and traditions, not a 'McDonald's experience'. He wanted his hotels to be run by the local management teams, not by head office. He felt the hotels should use local furniture and furnishing and decorations, create local menus and use local produce. He thought the uniforms should be different from hotel to hotel and reflect the local culture and climate, and that the service should be warm and spontaneous.

Davina, like most of the hotel's management, had come from other mainstream chains, which were extremely different. The HR department's role was to create manuals spelling out exactly what should be done, by whom and how. The role of the operations managers was to implement these procedures, and if they were not sure of anything they always knew they could find the answer in one of the manuals that covered one wall in their office.

It surprised Bob, but did not surprise Davina, that the amount of discretion applied by managers in the hotels was, in practice, small. Indeed her predecessor had worked with them to provide systems and procedures, for which he was sacked. Bob was determined to bring about his vision and Davina was instrumental in this.

All the staff were paid slightly above the industry average and Empress Hotels were seen as *the* place to work. As Bob ruefully pointed out, 'It is not necessarily seen as *the* place to stay. We need to put my vision into practice.' Davina's job was to persuade both hotel managers and the staff, from front-of-house to pot washers, to use the discretion they really had to make Empress Hotels the best place in the world to stay.

Davina had to deal with the hotel's facilities, food and service, and she decided to start with the service. On her way out to see her mother in Germany she stopped for a night at the group's highly rated hotel in Dubai, and stayed in the Seychelles on the way back.

She realised she had her work cut out. At check-in both hotels 'processed' her very efficiently but there was no warmth or colour. She asked both receptionists, who were not busy, about local attractions and was told 'See the concierge' (Dubai) and 'There are some leaflets in your room' (Seychelles). Davina also asked the difference between the guestroom she had booked and an executive room and was told '350 dirham' (Dubai) and 'They are on the fifth floor with breakfast included' (Seychelles). At dinner in the hotels' restaurants she was not offered a dessert, although in Dubai she was asked if she would like a coffee.

Back in Hong Kong Davina set herself objectives in three areas:

- Reception – to try to make the service more spontaneous.
- Staff training – to encourage the staff to focus on the needs of the guests and not on the procedures.

- Hotel managers – to help them assess their staff in terms of good service rather than compliance and encourage their staff to do a good job rather than what they have always done.

Davina explained her approach:

It's about mixing discretion with professionalism. We need to get away from standarisation and focus on the customer and let the local colour and culture come out. Training staff is going to be the key, but its going to be hard when we can't define or specify what they have to do. They will need to have the right skills, be highly motivated and willing to go the extra mile. We just have to bring it about!'

Question

1 What would you suggest Davina should do to encourage the staff to exude warmth and spontaneity when their natural instinct is to seek security from procedures and routines?

chapter eight

Resource utilisation

8

Chapter objectives:

- to explain how service operations can get the most out of their fixed resources – capacity management

- to explain how operations try to ensure that each customer gets what they want, when they want it – operations planning and control

- to describe how to manage bottlenecks and queues

- to show how operations can deal with capacity peaks – when they enter the 'coping zone'

- to suggest ways in which operations can improve their resource utilisation.

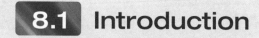 **8.1 Introduction**

Making the most effective use of operational resources is at the heart of service operations management. Most managers spend a significant proportion of their time and energy in working out how they can serve more customers, improve choice and flexibility, while at the same time cutting costs. Ensuring that resources such as materials, staff, equipment and process technology are utilised to the right level has a major impact not only on the efficiency, and therefore the costs, of the operation but also upon customer satisfaction. To add complexity to this challenge, the customer frequently plays a significant part in service delivery and must be thought of and managed in a similar way to internal resources.

For example, the managers of the hub for a large parcel delivery service are responsible for the movement of hundreds of thousands of packages each day, from collection, transportation, sorting, despatching and tracking, to timely and accurate delivery to the customer. The resources they manage on a day-to-day and week-by-week basis include not only the packages but also the hundreds of trucks and drivers, the system of conveyors, and the people and processes employed in sorting out the parcels at the hub, not forgetting the information technology behind it all. In many cases, customers act as a resource for the company, too, when they enter collection details via the website. Like all operations managers, the parcel service managers need to make the best use of their resources while at the same time ensuring they meet customer and organisational requirements.

In this chapter we assume that the organisation's structure – its networks, technology and information systems, for example – are fixed (these issues are dealt with in Chapter 9). We are focusing on short- and medium-term capacity management, which relates to the management of existing resources rather than the development of new capacity. Short-term capacity management might include the development of weekly staffing schedules for a call centre or a monthly air crew roster for an airline. Medium-term capacity management might require the recruitment and training of new staff, or the hiring of subcontract staff to deal with anticipated summer peaks, for example.

8.2 Capacity management

Managers are concerned with ensuring that the service process has sufficient resources to deal with the anticipated levels of customer demand in such a way that quality of service meets pre-set targets in the most cost-effective manner. This is a delicate balancing act because both underutilised and overstretched resources can be disadvantageous.

Underutilising resources has the potential to damage the long-term success of the organisation in a variety of ways:

- Expensive resources not earning revenue lead to poor financial results. The airline that fails to achieve a high load factor on its planes will struggle to survive.

- In many services, customers are suspicious of services that appear to be not busy. Banks and similar financial institutions find that customers are not happy about using an empty branch, and many diners prefer the 'buzz' of a busy restaurant.

- Service employees may become demotivated if underutilisation persists. Boredom and concern for their long-term employment may lead to poor service attitudes, which again lead to reduced customer satisfaction and lower profitability.

Conversely, resources that are overstretched also lead to problems for the success of the organisation:

- Overloaded resources mean that many aspects of service delivery suffer. A sudden surge of customers into a shop means that waiting times increase and staff cannot devote the amount of attention to customers that is desirable.

- Staff that are continually overloaded make more mistakes and, in the longer term, may decide to leave the organisation in search of less stressful employment.
- To deal with overload, staff may be drafted in to carry out tasks with which they are unfamiliar or for which they are only partially trained. The potential for increased error rate is high and, again, stress levels may be intolerable for some members of staff.

The task of capacity management is to try to achieve a balance between too much and too little resource utilisation, within the constraints of the networks and facilities of the operation. Capacity management is concerned with putting a plan in place that makes the best use of resources, given the forecasted or expected demand for services.

8.2.1 Defining service capacity

Service capacity is defined as the maximum level of value-added activity over a period of time that the service process can consistently achieve under normal operating conditions (Slack *et al.* 2004). We can define and measure capacity relatively easily at the process level. For example:

- the number of calls a customer service agent can handle in the course of a shift
- the number of meals served by a restaurant during the lunchtime period
- the number of repair calls made by a computer service engineer during an eight-hour day.

It is important to note the words 'under normal operating conditions' and 'consistently'. It may be possible, in some cases, for an individual employee to exceed the throughput rate for a short period. If call centre employees handle 120 calls over 8 hours (15 calls per hour), it may be possible for them to achieve as many as 30 calls in one of these hours, but this rate is not sustainable over any length of time.

As we will see later, in section 8.5, overloading resources may appear to increase output. Indeed, if analysed solely in terms of numbers of customer transactions completed in a given period, this may seem to be the case. However, there may be an impact on the nature of the service, the service concept and also the quality of the service provided. Service organisations must take particular care to ensure that the service concept is not changed in the search for greater productivity. For example, a restaurant may decide to encourage customers to leave their table having completed their meal, in order to fit in a second sitting for dinner. On the face of it, the restaurant has doubled its capacity, but customers may feel that the nature of the service has changed and the level of service has deteriorated. Of course there are strategies that the restaurant can adopt to manage this sensitively, but the operations manager must be certain that in increasing productivity the desired service concept (outcome and experience) is maintained.

8.2.2 Measuring capacity

To manage capacity, we must be able to measure it. A simple measure is the amount of demand in a specified time period. The parcel delivery service may have an overall measure of capacity in terms of the total number of parcels that can be processed overnight; however, this overall measure is not very helpful in managing the day-to-day operation. It is necessary to develop a measure of capacity that is sufficiently detailed to give a 'good enough' estimate of capacity. For the parcel delivery company, some of the key aspects to be considered include:

● The size, weight and value of the parcels to be moved – a package that is small but valuable will provide more revenue per truck movement than something less valuable that takes up a large amount of space.

● The geographical locations served by the company – rural districts have greater travel times, and many inner city areas suffer from traffic congestion.

In determining capacity, a number of factors make the assessment of service capacity difficult:

● *Service product mix*. If the service product mix is made up of high volumes of 'runners' (see section 6.3.1), the capacity calculation is relatively straightforward. However, once the product mix becomes more complex, incorporating fluctuating volumes of 'repeaters' and 'strangers', the calculation becomes more complex. The customer service agent may be able to handle 120 'normal' calls in a shift; however, if some of the calls are complex enquiries or serious complaints, for example, the number of calls handled will drop significantly.

● *The impact of location*. At first sight, the measure of capacity for a computer service engineer or a telephone engineer would seem to be relatively straightforward. However, if we consider the difference between an engineer operating in a major city and another engineer dealing with rural communities, it can be seen that calculating capacity on the basis of calls completed alone would be inaccurate, since it would take no account of travel times.

● *The extent of intangibility in the service product*. Service products with low degrees of intangibility are relatively easy to deal with. The number of short transactions per hour in a fast-food restaurant is relatively consistent. However, the customer-facing staff in a gourmet restaurant may have greater discretion as to how to carry out their task. They may perhaps spend time with customers in 'building relationships', with the result that the individual's capacity becomes more difficult to define. This calculation becomes more complex when dealing with knowledge workers, who must combine short-term revenue generating activities with long-term research and development. Capacity in this case is linked more to the individual service provider. As a manager, it may be almost impossible to know when someone is working to capacity when output is so variable.

● *The ease of identification of resource constraints*. The capacity of a process is determined by resource constraints or bottlenecks. In the Karolinska Hospital example (see Box 8.2), it was clear that the resource constraint was the operating theatre. Finding ways to increase the effective utilisation of this space was relatively straightforward. For more complex systems, the identification of the key resource constraints may be rather harder. An information systems provider may require a wide range of technical skills relating to different applications and programming languages, but the precise requirements may not be known until part way into the contract.

There are three basic short-term capacity strategies, although, as we will discuss, many organisations employ a mixture of all three (see Box 8.1). These strategies are:

- *Level capacity*. In this case scarce or expensive resources are maintained at a constant level, and the organisation must manage the consequential issues for service quality.
- *Chase capacity*. The service organisation attempts to match supply to demand as much as possible by building flexibility into the operation. The prime objective is to provide high levels of service availability or fast response, in the most efficient manner.
- *Demand management*. Rather than change the capacity of the service operation, the organisation influences the demand profile to 'smooth' the load on the resources.

Alton Towers — Box 8.1

Alton Towers is an award-winning theme park in the UK, with over 100 rides and attractions aimed at every member of the family. Alton Towers' mission is to 'Create magic for everyone' by providing an inclusive package of magnificent surroundings, historic heritage, fun and fantasy to suit all ages and tastes.

The park is perhaps best know for its white-knuckle rides, such as the Runaway Mine Train, Corkscrew, Black Hole, Nemesis and Oblivion. Oblivion, for example, was the world's first vertical-drop roller-coaster. The ride lasts 160 seconds and reaches speeds of up to 100 kph while pulling a G-force of 4.5 – NASA astronauts only experience 3G at take-off!

The park is open from March to November. Demand peaks at about 50,000 visitors on Easter Bank Holiday Monday and usually runs at about 35,000 throughout the summer. The busiest times are usually during the week. Fridays and Saturdays during the peak season tend to be relatively quiet. The various activities in the park reach peak demand at different times. The peak time at the gate is 10.30–11.00 a.m. and for the restaurants is 12.30–1.00 p.m. The major rides are very busy all day, with queues reaching their longest in the early afternoon.

Alton Towers employs around 350 full-time and 1,200 seasonal staff. The majority of staff lives within a 30-kilometre radius. To help cope with unexpected fluctuations in demand, a pool of staff is available for work at short notice. Most of the operators are trained to operate several rides.

Alton Towers provides comprehensive information on its website about when the park will be busy and encourages visitors to pre-plan their visit. It is possible to obtain fast-track tickets for the most popular rides, which offer visitors an allocated time slot. This means that the time spent physically waiting is much reduced. These tickets can be purchased in advance for a small fee.

Questions

1 Which capacity strategies are used at Alton Towers?

2 What are the implications of its choices?

This case is based on material from the Alton Towers website, www.alton-towers.co.uk, and other published material.

8.2.3   The level capacity strategy

The prime objective of this strategy is to maximise utilisation of expensive fixed resources. An airline seeks to fly planes that are as full as possible with passengers paying the highest fares. The key operational measure is the 'load factor', with the airline knowing that if it is exceeding a certain figure (about 80 per cent for an international airline), it will be making profit.

To achieve this level of utilisation, the service organisation may have to make a number of trade-offs, most notably around quality of service. Figure 8.1 illustrates the situation in a hospital clinic. Here, the task is to make the most of the medical consultant. The clinic has to solve the problem of always having enough patients for the consultant to work on, with the added difficulty of there being a high percentage of 'no-shows'. The clinic has chosen to overbook appointments, and believes that it is better to upset a few patients rather than lose valuable consultant time.

To deal with the no-shows problem, the clinic has made four appointments at the start of each 15-minute period, estimating that one in four patients do not arrive and that the consultant will require 5 minutes per patient. If all goes to plan, the first patient will be seen immediately, the second within 5 minutes and the third within 10 minutes, but it should be noted that they each had the same 2.00 p.m. appointment. In practice, some of the 2.00 p.m. appointments will still be waiting when the next 'batch' arrives for a (supposed) 2.15 appointment.

Some general principles and issues can be drawn from this example about the level capacity strategy:

- Resource utilisation goals are frequently achieved at the expense of service quality.

- Customers may receive inconsistent service levels (those with 2.00 p.m. appointments fare better than those with later appointments).

Figure 8.1	Level capacity strategy in an out-patients' clinic

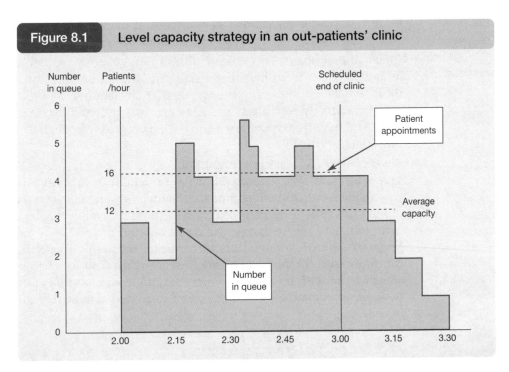

- Customers (patients) accept (or suffer) this poor level of service because the service is valuable to them and there may be no or few alternatives.

- There is a danger that the service provider may become complacent and not make attempts to cut the emotional cost of waiting for the customer, making it potentially vulnerable to competition (in this case private healthcare).

To overcome this problem of variable service levels, the service provider may use yield management or queue management approaches (described later).

Examples of organisations that use the level capacity strategy as its dominant approach include:

- Airlines, which need to maximise the revenue from their most expensive resource (planes). The prime objective is to have planes flying as frequently as possible, preferably full of passengers. This may mean that passengers do not always receive the service they anticipated.

- Professional services, who may have a recognised expert in a specialised field. It is frequently the case that the overall workload will not sustain another professional, leaving clients with a choice as to whether they wait or find an alternative provider.

- Popular restaurants, which may intentionally not expand capacity in order to maintain exclusivity. Having to book days, sometimes months, ahead in order to ensure a table may enhance the service concept.

Examples of approaches adopted under the level capacity strategy include:

- *Promoting off-peak demand*. This is often combined with a pricing strategy to encourage customers to switch. The organisation must be careful that this does not bring about a change in service concept. A restaurant encouraging customers to move to less popular times may institute a 'happy hour' with cheap drinks, which may damage the restaurant's reputation with existing customers.

- *Queue management*. This is dealt with in more depth in section 8.4.2, but it is important to point out here that making an assumption that customers will continue to queue can be dangerous. It is, after all, sending the message that their time is relatively worthless, and they are only prepared to wait because they anticipate that the service they receive will be valuable enough to make the wait (lost time) worthwhile.

- *Booking systems*. Making forward bookings is obviously a form of queue management. It allows the organisation to schedule capacity ahead, and for customers to utilise queuing time for themselves. Supermarkets have successfully utilised this system for their delicatessen counters, issuing customers with numbered tickets to ensure that people are served in order, and allowing customers to judge whether they have time to continue shopping before their number is called. As with the physical queue, customers may not want to wait and so go elsewhere. Indeed, if the organisation has the reputation that customers need to book ahead, it may lose potential sales if customers assume that there is no point in trying.

8.2.4 The chase capacity strategy

This strategy is usually adopted by high-volume consumer services, since a major aspect of their competitive strategy is the provision of ready and rapid access to service. For these services, capital resource utilisation is rarely a prime goal, although cost reduction will be very important. To explain this further, consider the following statements concerning a fast-food restaurant:

- A key objective is to maintain short queue lengths. This is managed by staffing tills and kitchen in line with expected demand.
- If the queues are too long, customers go to another fast-food outlet.
- The premises are not fully utilised: there are only about six hours out of the possible 24 hours when the facilities are 100 per cent utilised.

The challenge of these high-volume standard services is to develop volume flexibility (see section 8.6.2). In other words, the operation must be able to cope with wide ranges of customer demand, providing consistent service standards at minimum cost. Figure 8.2 shows the demand pattern for a fast-food restaurant, with a crew roster to show how the restaurant manager schedules the staff to deal with the variation in demand.

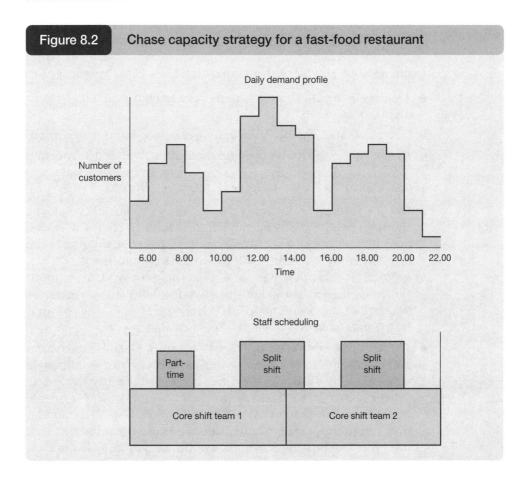

Figure 8.2 Chase capacity strategy for a fast-food restaurant

In this restaurant, the staff are organised into three categories: those on one of the core shift teams, those working split shifts, and those working part time. The split shifts allow the manager to schedule staff for the forecast demand peaks. There will probably be a weekly rotation between the core shifts and the split-shift personnel. In this example, the early morning peak load is covered by employing part-time labour. In addition, the manager will have a pool of labour to be contacted at short notice to cover absenteeism or an unexpected rise in demand. A common strategy is to extend the length of the split shifts, with some organisations operating a 'compulsory overtime' policy as part of their conditions of employment.

General principles and issues for the chase capacity strategy are:

- Most organisations operating the chase strategy must develop a high degree of volume flexibility. In other words they must be able to respond to changing demand profiles. In most cases this is achieved through employing staff on flexible contracts, allowing the operations manager to decide working hours as required.

- Although a principal objective is to ensure that customer service targets such as availability or response times are achieved, many of these service organisations fall into the commodity category (high-volume/low-process variety). In contrast to the organisations employing the level strategy, they frequently have relatively little means of differentiation and are therefore rather price sensitive. The challenge in adopting the chase strategy, therefore, is to ensure that costs are strictly controlled and that flexibility is not achieved at any price.

Examples of organisations that employ the chase capacity strategy include:

- Retailers that need to deal with extremely high demand at weekends and after normal office hours.
- Direct insurance companies operating extended hours through call centres.
- Theme parks, which may open up more attractions as demand grows.

Typical approaches to the chase capacity strategy include:

- *Flexible staffing levels.* Some organisations use flexible employment contracts, allowing the operations manager to decide when staff will be working. In some cases staff will work a standard core time, but in many retail organisations staff may not know when they will be working beyond the next few shifts. Another approach is to employ part-time staff who must work 'compulsory' overtime as and when needed. Although this gives flexibility, the operations manager must be aware of the possibility of staff resentment at having to work inconvenient hours, and the knock-on effect of poor customer service.

- *The use of subcontractors or temporary staff.* Organisations may use temporary staff or subcontractors to deal with short-term overloads. Although these workers may be readily available, they may not be sufficiently trained or motivated to deliver service in the style of the organisation. However, some organisations report that their temporary staff may be more responsive and less complacent than long-service staff. Some call centres use organisations that specialise in what is called 'peak lopping'. Excess calls are automatically routed to the organisation and they are answered in such a manner that customers are unaware of the switch.

- *Making use of customers*. Many service operations may have the option of changing the service process to utilise customers as temporary employees. In effect this is again changing the service concept. Some regular customers may be very happy to be included in the service process – clearing tables, or even serving other customers as well as themselves.

8.2.5 Demand management strategies

Most companies operate a mixed approach to capacity management. Whether adopting a principally chase or level strategy, most service organisations also operate some degree of demand management. Examples of this approach include:

- *Pricing strategies*. This typically takes the form of offering price incentives to encourage customers to move to off-peak times. The 'happy hour' in the pub or wine bar is a good example.
- *Restricted service at peak times*. The philosophy here is similar, though taking the form of a disincentive. In this case the service may provide a limited service at peak times, again encouraging customers to move to less busy times. Some restaurants operate this policy, providing a limited menu at these times.
- *Specialist service channels*. Rather than provide a general service at all times, the provider may choose to segment the demand and to allocate specific times for special needs. Doctors' surgeries are a good example, with advertised times for services such as immunisations, mother and baby clinics, and counselling provision. This allows the surgery to schedule specialist resources to restricted times, often making better use of scarce resources.
- *Advertising and promotion*. Increasing public awareness of the service and informing customers of special offers will stimulate demand. Bookshops not only advertise, but will also stimulate demand by arranging sessions for authors to autograph their works. A particular problem with advertising is that it tends to increase the inaccuracy of any forecasting model used by the business. Although it is possible to track the effectiveness of advertising in stimulating demand, it is often difficult to pre-judge the likely impact of a new campaign.

8.2.6 Putting the strategies together

Most complex service organisations use both of the major capacity strategies in different parts of their operations, depending on the respective underlying cost models. Some examples are shown in Table 8.1.

The prime objective of the airline is to maximise 'load factor' on flights, the utilisation of its most expensive assets. It employs a number of strategies to ensure that it makes the maximum revenue on each flight, using sophisticated yield management techniques (section 8.6.1) to help adopt the optimum pricing strategy to sell unsold seats as departure time approaches. The airline may simply oversell seats in the belief that there will be a number of 'no-shows'. Passengers who are then not able to obtain

Table 8.1 Capacity strategies

	Level capacity strategy	Chase capacity strategy	Demand management
International airline	Ensure that planes are flying with maximum payload as frequently as possible	Schedule staff reservations department to meet demand to ensure bookings can be made	Promote off-peak demand Try to maximise revenue from each flight (yield management)
Insurance company	Protect back office experts (actuaries and investment specialists) from variations in customer demand	Schedule direct sales operation (call centre) to provide maximum access for customers	Influence selling cycle so as not to coincide with policy renewal peaks
Restaurant chain	Keep manufacturing of basic food materials as close to 'level' as possible Maintain high utilisation of process plant	Draw up staff rosters to reflect anticipated demand Use part-time staff to manage peaks Call in staff for demand surges	Use promotional activity to stimulate demand in quiet periods Devise special offers to allow for bulk-purchasing discounts

the seat they thought they had booked need to be compensated in some way, although unless managed well that can significantly affect customer satisfaction.

To maximise the opportunity for customers to book seats, the airline employs a chase strategy in its sales department using relatively cheap resource (as compared with planes), scheduling staff to meet forecast demand patterns. It is better to suffer slightly reduced productivity here rather than lose potential seat revenue.

The insurance company uses a level strategy for its actuarial staff (back office), in part because they are relatively expensive, but more because they are often in short supply. The lead-time to recruit and train an actuary is measured in years rather than weeks and therefore it makes no sense to attempt to chase demand.

Similarly the restaurant chain will operate a level strategy in its manufacturing function because it has relatively fixed capacity: although it can increase capacity marginally by overtime, significant increases can only be achieved by investing in another kitchen or restaurant.

8.3 Operations planning and control

In the previous section we discussed how the operations manager decides a capacity strategy, thus creating a capacity plan. This sets the broad parameters within which this capacity may be allocated to specific customers and/or tasks in order to meet customer service and productivity targets. This section looks at the mechanisms that may be deployed to micro-manage this plan as effectively as possible. Operations planning and control is concerned with the sequencing, allocation and control of capacity and ensuring the flow of resources to meet the schedule.

8.3.1 Sequencing and allocation of capacity

Most operations have rules or policies regarding the allocation of capacity. Sometimes these rules are relatively informal, developed over time in such a way that most customers are satisfied. Other operations, usually those with more volume and/or complexity, tend to have more formal allocation systems.

For example, most leisure centres have one large space or sports hall, which can be used for a number of activities. It might be configured for two five-a-side football pitches, four badminton courts or one tennis court. To create the short-term plan, often referred to as a schedule or timetable, the leisure centre manager must carry out the following tasks:

- Decide the proportion of time that the sports hall will be configured for each of the activities.

- Ascertain the optimal schedule for these activities based on customer preference. For example, badminton clubs may prefer Thursday evenings while five-a-side football may be more popular on Fridays.

- Check the schedule for ease of transition between activities. It may be relatively easy to move from tennis to circuit training because there are relatively few changes to make, but changing from badminton to football might require more staff to move and set up equipment.

- Create a booking schedule for the various slots to allocate capacity (times) to specific customers.

This schedule is required because the leisure centre does not have infinite resources. It is clearly impossible to satisfy all possible customer demands and remain a viable service organisation. The way that operations deal with this issue is to create sequencing rules in order to manage the prioritisation of allocation. Here are six examples of sequencing rules:

- *First in, first out (FIFO) or first come, first served*. This is the approach used by many consumer services. The leisure centre may allow customers to book up to two weeks ahead for badminton for the Thursday evening time slots of 6.00–7.00 p.m., 7.00–8.00 p.m. and 8.00–9.00 p.m. and will take requests in order until all the courts are full. This scheduling rule is simple and has the advantage of being perceived to be fair to all potential customers.

- *Last in, first out (LIFO)*. There are rare occasions when this rule makes sense. The sequence of loading a delivery truck would follow LIFO scheduling so that the first call would be to deliver the goods closest to the tailgate of the lorry.

- *Most valuable customer first*. The leisure centre may allow the local football club to have early access to certain parts of the forward schedule and to 'block book' capacity for training. If the club needs to have the use of the hall on every Friday for training, this represents steady income for the leisure centre, though may be the source of annoyance for other, smaller organisations that are excluded from using the hall for single occasions.

- *Most critical first*. Emergency services adopt variants of this rule, grading the nature of each demand between critical and non-essential. Clearly, life-threatening situations call for immediate action and these demands tend to override all other activities.

- *Least work content first*. In situations where demand far outstrips supply, this rule allows more customers to be satisfied quickly. Airline check-in desks sometimes operate a version of this rule, providing faster service for those passengers with hand baggage only. This means that the total queue is reduced and fewer customers wait. The problem with this rule is that some customers wait far longer than they would under FIFO and are potentially more dissatisfied.

- *Most work content first*. With activities that have long process lead-times it might seem prudent to schedule the tasks with the longest time requirement first. This may not always be helpful because, once started, these tasks may become lost in among other 'work in progress' and not progress as fast as they could. Using this rule alone does not usually produce the best performance against customer requirement dates.

Different rules may be applied in different circumstances. Where customers arrive together, they generally expect to be treated equally and therefore FIFO will tend to be applied. However, this is not always the case. At the Alton Towers theme park in the UK, it is possible to buy priority passes that enable customers to bypass the queues of customers who pay standard prices. This obvious privilege can cause high degrees of ill feeling among 'standard' customers.

Back office processes frequently deal with longer lead-times than front office processes and may apply a number of scheduling rules. In the more complex situations it is possible to use a simple algorithm similar to that used in manufacturing shop floor control, called critical factor calculations. In this approach a comparison of estimated work content against requirement date allows for a calculation of an urgency factor. Each stage in the process is provided with a list of the most urgent jobs, enabling prioritisation. A spin-off from these calculations is a spot check of the performance of the process. If all tasks fall into the 'most urgent' category, clearly significant action is required to avoid major customer dissatisfaction.

8.3.2 Control systems

Control systems for managing capacity allocation range from comprehensive, complex and expensive to extremely simple.

At the complex and expensive end of the spectrum are the ERP (enterprise resource planning) systems. These software-based systems, sold by companies such as SAP and Baan, offer the capability to integrate a number of functions across the organisation. For example, sales order processing systems can provide direct input into operations control, and then into supplier management/procurement systems.

At the other extreme, many control systems are basic, but effective nonetheless. Examples of these simple systems include:

- An appointment book at the car servicing workshop, providing space for a given number of standard services and more complex jobs.
- A table plan for the restaurant – as bookings are received, tables are allocated, giving an instant picture of the loading for any given time period.
- A school timetable that shows where every pupil, and member of staff, should be at any time of the day – and what they should be doing.

An effective control system can be a significant source of competitive advantage. The ability of the organisation to provide an immediate response to the question 'When can you do this?' is a major factor in building customer confidence. In recent years, retailers have been able to interrogate logistics systems so that customers can negotiate a delivery slot for their purchase of furniture or electrical goods, with some confidence that this promise will be fulfilled.

8.3.3 Ensuring that resources flow to meet the schedule

The schedule is the operating plan that enables the various aspects of the operation to be co-ordinated. The Karolinska Hospital operating theatre (Box 8.2) provides a good example of the benefits of a robust schedule. A robust schedule should include:

- *A clear customer flow*. The schedule provides the opportunity for customers to be 'flowed' through the system to arrive at the right time and place. We might compare customers in this way to the work-in-progress (WIP) inventory in a manufacturing process. If WIP is minimised, customer delays are reduced, there is less disruption, and costs kept to a minimum. An organisation that encourages customers to arrive early because it is unable to manage its schedules may have to invest in larger reception (customer-holding) areas, or suffer a major decline in customer satisfaction.

- *Ensuring supporting resources are available to meet the schedule*. Once the schedule has been established making best use of the availability of scarce resource, all other resources must be scheduled to meet this plan. For the hospital operating theatre this will involve the scheduling of people (operating theatre staff and surgeons), and of course physical inventories such as blood, bandages and surgical instruments. Restaurants, likewise, will match inventories of food to expected customer demand.

- *Creating schedules for interlinking activities*. The bottleneck schedule allows the operations manager to create a realistic plan for the service as a whole. In some organisations this is termed the master schedule. This then facilitates the production of supporting schedules for all the resources that feed this master schedule, using a variety of scheduling rules matched to each situation.

- *Creating schedules for suppliers*. Good information provides a sound basis for negotiation with key suppliers. This gives rise to the potential for managing day-to-day activity more accurately with less waste (see Chapter 12 on operational improvement).

8.3.4 Managing short-term, medium-term, and long-term schedules

The detail of schedules will increase as 'time now' approaches customer requirement dates. To return to the leisure centre example, tomorrow's schedule will tell us exactly which customers have booked a badminton court, and at what time. Moving further forward, the manager will be interested only in which evenings are allocated to specific activities.

It is essential to know the time period ahead within which it is impossible to change the schedule. A restaurant may be able to deal with changes in customer mix almost up to the last minute, whereas the operating theatre in Box 8.2 will require more notice of change in detail schedule. We will return to this topic later in this chapter when we consider resource flexibility, which aims to reduce the period ahead where the schedule must be fixed.

8.4 Managing bottlenecks and queues

Bottlenecks – the parts of a process that constrain or restrict capacity – and the resulting queues of customers or their orders, are features of many service operations. Managing these well can have a significant impact on both capacity utilisation and customer satisfaction.

Karolinska Hospital, Stockholm | Box 8.2

Karolinska Hospital faced a crisis as the pressure on operating budgets was rising. This prompted an investigation as to how well expensive resources were being utilised. It was soon identified that operating theatres were not being used effectively. In fact, surgeons, operating theatre staff and of course the theatres themselves were idle for more than 50 per cent of the time. It soon became clear that the schedule of patients through the theatre needed to be managed more carefully. The scarce resource was time in the theatre itself, so the management looked at ways to reduce the time that patients spent in the theatre. A significant step forward created a separate patient preparation area allowing this activity to be carried out in parallel rather than in sequence with surgery.

Further investigation revealed that some delays were caused because anaesthesiologists were called away to other parts of the hospital. Adding anaesthesiologists formally to the operating room staff team and creating an anaesthesia clinic to evaluate pre-operative patients also improved the efficiency of the system.

Having increased the throughput through the bottleneck, more operations could be carried out in the same time frame, and waiting times were dramatically reduced. The unforeseen benefit was that it was now possible to create a much more reliable schedule because the lead-time between diagnosis and surgery was dramatically reduced. Patients were happier because they were treated faster and there were fewer 'no shows', which had happened when lead-times were much longer. A consistent theatre schedule meant that any tests required prior to surgery could be arranged with more certainty. Previously, these tests had been frequently repeated as surgery dates had been delayed.

For Karolinska then this approach to scheduling has paid off in a number of ways. The theatre carries out more operations per day, costs are reduced and patients are seen more quickly. Operating rooms were reduced from 15 to 13, while the number of operations per day was increased by 30 per cent.

Questions

1 What impact do you think that this approach to scheduling would have on the surgeons and operating theatre staff?

2 Why do you think that it took so long for this to be adopted?

This illustration is based on material from the video, *Time Based Competition* from Harvard Business School 1993, and from healthcare industry sources.

8.4.1 Bottleneck management

All organisations need to understand their key resource constraints. A clear understanding of these constraints or bottlenecks provides greater clarity as to what is a realistic estimate of capacity. To return to our example in section 8.3, the key resource constraint of the leisure centre is likely to be the central sports hall. All other resources, such as other facilities and staff, are likely to be linked to the most effective use of this space.

Bottleneck management, or the theory of constraints, is generally well understood in manufacturing organisations. It is seen to be important to manage the bottleneck – the stage in any process with the lowest throughput rate and which therefore determines the effective capacity of the whole operation (see, for example, Goldratt and Cox 1984).

In the same way, it is important for service operations managers to understand where the bottlenecks exist in service processes. For example, a company providing loan finance needed to increase the standard of service provided to its customers, while also increasing productivity of its risk assessment process. The management was given the task of meeting increasing demand without increasing resources. Initially, it was not clear how this could be achieved, but when the process was mapped it became obvious that a problem lay with the actuaries. Figure 8.3a shows a simplified version of the original process flow, with all proposals passing through an actuary's hands for sign-off.

As can be seen from Figure 8.3a, the original capacity was constrained by the throughput of the actuaries at 15 proposals per hour. It was recognised that many proposals did not require actuarial sign-off because the credit scores indicated a clear accept or reject decision, which could be taken by more junior, less expensive staff. The initial processing took slightly longer, but in the revised process (Figure 8.3b) only 50 per cent of the proposals needed to be seen by an actuary. The capacity of the process therefore rose by nearly 50 per cent to 22 proposals per hour.

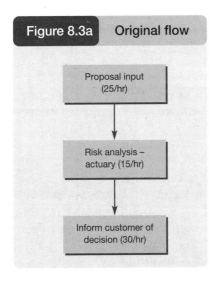

Figure 8.3a Original flow

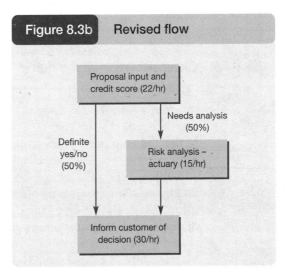

Figure 8.3b Revised flow

This improvement was achieved simply by monitoring the activity levels within the process and then deciding whether the current resource constraints were really bottlenecks or not. Once the assumption that all proposals must be seen by actuaries had been questioned, it became possible to improve response times and productivity simultaneously.

There are some general rules for managing bottlenecks:

- Ensure that only essential work passes through the bottleneck.
- Be ruthless in taking away non-essential activities from the bottleneck.
- Ensure that no substandard work passes through the bottleneck.
- Once you have established where the bottleneck is, devote proportionally more management attention to it to ensure maximum throughput and therefore maximum effectiveness for the process.

And finally, if you have a complex system, Goldratt and Cox (1984) suggest that you should not attempt to move the bottleneck. It may be difficult to manage but at least you know where it is!

One way to identify a bottleneck is to observe where the queues of work or customers form in the process. In simple processes, this is probably as good a test as any, but it is as well to be wary. Queues may form much earlier in the process because people operating feeder activities may work at a slower rate than is theoretically possible because they believe there is no point in working flat out if the customer or the jobs will have to wait at the subsequent bottleneck. Indeed, service operations might well decide to limit the number of customers accepted into the process because of the potential dissatisfaction caused for customers who have to wait much longer than anticipated.

It is also important to distinguish between long-term and short-term bottlenecks. Long-term, or fixed bottlenecks, provide the best estimate of the capacity of the operation and the basic capacity management approach can be determined as a result. However, short-term bottlenecks may frequently occur, giving rise to the need for immediate response. For example, a key member of a call centre may be unexpectedly absent, which may mean that capacity to deal with particular enquiries is dramatically reduced.

8.4.2 Queue management

Queues occur in most service activities. Indeed, for any operation using a level capacity strategy queues are 'designed-in'. Furthermore, no capacity strategy is perfect and queues are almost inevitable. Queues may be lines of people visible to both the customer and employee, or they may be invisible to one and/or the other, for example a queue of callers to a switchboard or a list of customers awaiting a repair engineer.

While queuing theory can be used to calculate the number of servers required to meet forecast demand, resource constraints and forecast inaccuracy invariably mean that operations managers need to look for other ways to minimise the impact of queuing on their customers. It has been shown that not only does dissatisfaction with the wait increase with waiting time (Katz *et al.* 1991) but also dissatisfaction with the service as a whole (Davis and Vollmann 1990).

Given that perceived waiting time is greater than actual waiting time (Katz *et al.* 1991), the answer is to try to reduce perceived waiting time, which can also be a great deal cheaper than employing more servers! Ten principles of waiting have been suggested (1–8 by Maister 1985; 9 by Davis and Heineke 1994; and 10 by Jones and Peppiatt 1996).

1   *Unoccupied time feels longer than occupied time*. It is a good idea to try to provide customers with something to do or forms of distraction so that the time passes more rapidly for them. Some services show promotional videos while waiting in a physical queue. Waiting areas for lifts often have mirrors to enable the customer to check their appearance. Telephone call centres or help desks frequently play music while 'on hold', although this is not universally welcomed.

2   *Pre-process waits feel longer than in-process waits*. Once customers feel that they have made a start inside the service process and that something, however trivial, is happening, they tend to feel happier. A simple acknowledgement by a server that they have been noticed can have a significant impact. Also using pre-process time in some way, such as completing a form or making choices about the service, can reduce the perceived waiting time.

3   *Anxiety makes the wait seem longer*. Sometimes customers do not know whether they have been forgotten or not, which can be allayed by giving them numbered tickets to demonstrate that they are part of the system. Also, the nature of the service will have a significant impact. If the customer is worried about flying or going to the dentist the wait may seem interminable, possibly giving rise to some tense behaviour with service providers. Customer-facing employees should be trained to observe the effects of anxiety and to find ways of giving reassurance.

4   *Uncertain waits are longer than known, finite waits*. Customers are generally more happy to wait if the expected duration is known, and if there is a good reason for it. If the duration is unknown, research suggests that customers become restless much more quickly. Theme parks frequently position markers at known points in the queue informing customers how long they should expect to wait. Of course, the real wait time is usually a little shorter than this, with customers pleased that they did better than expected!

5   *Unexplained waits seem longer than explained waits*. Being provided with a plausible explanation of a delay reduces uncertainty for the customer. It also gives the impression that the organisation knows it should not take the customer for granted.

6   *Unfair waits are longer than equitable waits*. Generally, customers expect that those who arrive first should be seen first. Many organisations have replaced the multiple queue/multiple server system with a single queue/multiple server approach because of the perceived unfairness of being stuck in a slow-moving queue. This approach also eliminates the anxiety as to which queue to join. In some cases, such as a hospital casualty department, there may be a good reason why some customers are seen out of turn, but there still needs to be an explanation rather than for the provider to assume that other customers will understand.

7 *The more valuable the service, the longer customers will wait*. The more complex the service, and the more it is customised to the needs of the individual, the more likely it is that customers may be prepared to wait. It should be noted, however, that this should not be assumed.

8 *Solo waiting feels longer than group waiting*. The realisation that others are also feeling the pain may reduce the customer's anxiety of thinking that they have made the wrong choice. If others think it is worth waiting, it confirms the customer's decision to wait. Also, people tend to talk to each other, providing a distraction from the length of the wait.

9 *Uncomfortable waits feel longer than comfortable waits*. By making queuing conditions as comfortable and indeed as distracting as possible, the wait time will be perceived to be much shorter. Uncomfortable conditions sensitise customers to the time and poor service.

10 *New or infrequent users feel they wait longer than frequent users*. Frequent users of a service may be attuned to a wait and they may be more relaxed because they know what to expect. New or infrequent users are likely to be more anxious and uncertain, so operations should consider trying to identify them and provide them with information and reassurance.

Booking systems are a queue of sorts, with the advantage to customers that they do not have to physically queue for the service. The advantage for the service provider is that the operations manager is better able to manage resources to meet demand. Alton Towers (Box 8.1) has in effect created a 'virtual queue' through its fast-track system. Visitors to the park are given time slots to return to a pre-booked ride which allows them to use their time more effectively. Supermarkets that operate a ticket system at their delicatessen counters are using the same principle. In both cases, the service provider has found a way to ensure equity of treatment for its customers and has enabled customers to make better use of time otherwise spent queuing.

8.4.3 Queuing theory and simulation

Management scientists and mathematicians have studied the behaviour of queues, producing statistical models to predict queue length and so on. Fortunately, few of us need to understand the detail of these models, as there are a number of computer simulations available to help us predict the implications of operational decisions.

Simply put, there are three key parameters to queuing theory: the arrival rate for customers, the server rate, and the number of servers or serving positions available. The arrival rate and server rate must be further understood in terms of their variability. Even if the average server rate and arrival rate are the same, queues will still form if there is variability in these rates. Figure 8.4 illustrates this situation.

The example in Figure 8.4 demonstrates the impact of variability in arrival rates and process rates. In this case, the process time is reasonably constant – perhaps because it is a standard process, possibly determined to a large extent by automation or standard scripts – while customers arrive in a more random pattern. In this simple system, there may be up to four customers in the queue, the first being served and three waiting. The longest wait time for customers is therefore 20 min-

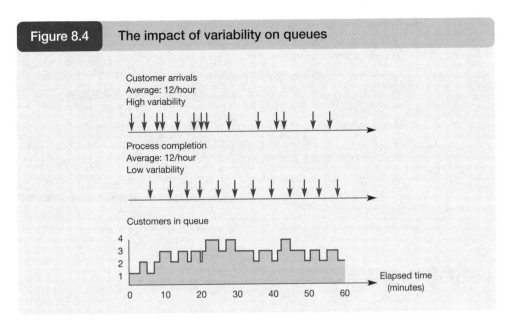

Figure 8.4   **The impact of variability on queues**

utes (4 × 5 minutes), which perhaps is surprising when we know that average process time matches the average arrival rate. The average queue length is about 2.5 customers, implying an average wait time of 12.5 minutes.

Computer simulations now provide invaluable information to the service operations manager. In a more complex situation than that described above, it would be impossible to model the likely outcomes, but a simulation can identify the impact of different queue designs, priority rules and so on. Whether the situation is complex or simple, the key question remains: 'How long is an acceptable waiting time?'

We do not provide a detailed analysis of queuing theory here. Fitzsimmons and Fitzsimmons (2004) give a useful summary of the key elements of the mathematical theories that underpin this topic (see also Slack *et al.* 2004). Useful terminology includes:

- *Calling population*. This describes the customer base. In many cases, the calling population may consist of a variety of groups, each requiring different things. For example, customers contacting the computer company's call centre may enquire about billing, delivery, faults, purchase of service contracts, and so on. A key element of queuing theory is the size of the calling population. Consumer services have so many customers that the calling population is thought of as infinite and the probability of the arrival of a specific customer is unaffected by recent events. If, however, the calling population is relatively small, as exemplified by potential callers to an internal computer help desk, the probability of new callers is reduced if significant numbers have already called.

- *Arrival process*. It is clearly essential to understand the arrival pattern for customers. Fitzsimmons and Fitzsimmons state that many arrival patterns follow an exponential distribution. Intervals between customer arrivals in a retail store in a busy period might follow this distribution, with the majority of intervals being rather short, and long intervals being somewhat rare.

- *Queue configuration*. This describes the number of queues and their location. In many retail operations there has been a shift from multiple queues linked to multiple servers, because some queues seem to move faster than others, leading to customers moving between queues and possible ill-feeling as customers believe they have been treated unfairly. A single queue leading to multiple servers has the advantage of demonstrating equity of treatment.

- *Queue discipline*. Management will choose the rule to determine who gets served next from the queue. The most common rules are discussed earlier (section 8.3.1), though first come, first served is the most popular with physical queues.

- *Balking*. A key measure for service systems is the number of customers who leave when confronted with a long physical queue, or who have been asked to wait for a call centre agent to become available. Balking is the queuing theory terminology for customers who abandon their wait for service.

8.5 Managing the coping zone

There is usually a point at which service managers find it difficult to cope with increasing demand (the break point: see Figure 8.5). This is when managers and staff enter the 'coping zone'. At these levels of resource utilisation things are just too busy – staff become stressed, everything becomes a problem and importantly perceived quality, i.e. customer satisfaction, declines along with revenues per customer (see Clark and James 1997, Armistead and Clark 1994).

For example, in a restaurant operating at high levels of resource utilisation, in the coping zone:

- Customers have to wait a long time for service.
- There is increasing likelihood of 'stock-outs' (items removed from the menu).
- Customers feel rushed and under pressure not to ask too much from busy serving staff.
- Staff feel under pressure and are less likely to give courteous responses or the personalised service expected.

This break point is usually reached before full or 100 per cent utilisation for two reasons. First, it is often not possible to run any single resource at full capacity for any period of time; staff in a restaurant for example simply cannot work 'flat out' all the time. Second, several resources may be involved and while staff might be working 'flat out', only 80 per cent of the tables might be in use.

Interestingly there may be problems at times of low utilisation, too, which affect both staff and customers. In the case of the restaurant:

- The perception of the overall quality of service experience is low because the restaurant is 'dead'. There is no buzz of conversation, often with prolonged silences.
- Service may be slow, because although there are not many customers, the kitchen may not be working at maximum effectiveness.
- In the same way, serving staff may be less attentive than might be expected, because again they may not be busy enough to be fully tuned in to customer needs.

Figure 8.5 illustrates the profile of customer perceived quality against resource utilisation and illustrates how quality may suffer through both too many and too few customers in a high-quality restaurant.

The shape of the profile, the break point and the size of the coping zone will vary between organisations. Figure 8.6 illustrates the relationship between customer perceived quality and resource utilisation in a nightclub. Here customers may not enjoy the atmosphere until the place is crammed with bodies! Still, at some point the club's resources will start to struggle with the demand placed upon its resources – bouncers, toilets and bar, for example – as it enters the coping zone.

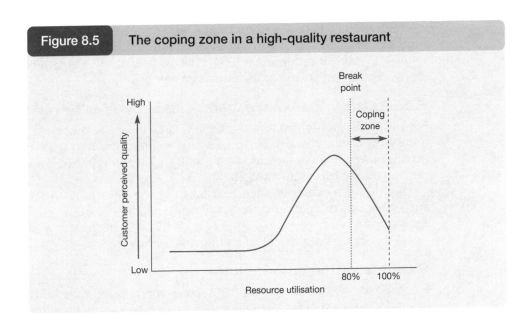

Figure 8.5 The coping zone in a high-quality restaurant

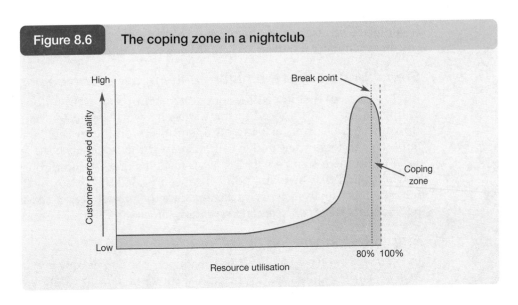

Figure 8.6 The coping zone in a nightclub

8.5.1 How to manage the coping zone

There are seven steps in building up this profile and managing the coping zone.

Step 1 Identify the service concept

Underpinning the service concept of a high-quality restaurant is the belief that customers may book a table for the whole evening. They will not be rushed to vacate their table since the restaurant has no intention of selling the space twice in an evening. It is intended that the service experience should be relaxed, with staff able to converse with customers and make recommendations about food and wine, where appropriate.

This is a very different concept from a restaurant wishing to create a high-energy situation, often with staff rushing around, and with the customers encouraged to eat up and leave. It is important to be clear as to what the designed or desired service concept is, particularly as the restaurant gets busy.

Step 2 Determine how resource utilisation is to be measured

For the high-quality restaurant, the best measure of resource utilisation is the number of tables, and also chairs, that are occupied during the evening. To some extent, other resources such as serving staff or kitchen capacity can be adjusted to the busyness of the restaurant area.

The unit of measure is often best taken at the lowest level that the business analyses or controls performance. A call centre might look at the average loading of a customer service agent on an hourly basis throughout the day, whereas a professional service firm might look at an individual's case load.

Step 3 Draw the outline profile

Figure 8.5 shows the relationship between customer perceived quality and resource utilisation as it exists for the majority of customers on the majority of occasions. This does not represent all customers at all times. Some customers, for example, prefer the empty restaurant and would rank it as high quality at low utilisation. For others, the occasion and their mood will have a significant influence on where they would place themselves on the profile. This data can be captured from aggregating customer satisfaction indices and comparing it to utilisation at the time.

Step 4 Understand the nature and impact of the coping zone

While we accept that low utilisation is as much of a problem for quality of service as high utilisation is, indeed in some ways it's worse because revenue is also low. However, here we are focusing on operations working in the coping zone. It is important to recognise the signals that suggest this zone has been reached and be sensitive to them. Tempers flaring, customers looking around or queues appearing may all signal that breaking point has been passed. It is also worth undertaking some financial analysis to try to demonstrate the impact between passing the break point and its effects on costs and revenues, for example.

Step 5 Determine the 'ideal' operating area

In Figure 8.5 we have identified the break point at 80 per cent resource utilisation. At 100 per cent utilisation, in the case of the restaurant, it would be impossible to seat any more customers. There are two broad approaches that can be adopted:

- Operate at 80 per cent resource utilisation. Operating at this point would suggest that the restaurant could be losing potential revenue. It is true that it might receive lower short-term revenues, but it may also upset longstanding customers by appearing to be greedy, squeezing as many people as possible into every available space. It is critical to understand the difference between customer satisfaction at 80 per cent and at 100 per cent, and to what extent this significantly reduces the customers' likelihood of returning.

- Operate at 100 per cent resource utilisation. Generally speaking, this is a short-term cash-generating strategy. It is more appropriate to theme restaurants that are the 'place to be seen' for a period, before those customers that are concerned about fashion move on to the next 'in' place. This strategy might also be appropriate for restaurants in holiday resorts, which do not expect high levels of customer returns.

Our example restaurant depends on long-term customer retention and word-of-mouth advertising. As a result, it targets its operations at the 80 per cent point. To manage this, the owner has removed some of the tables to give a less crowded feel to the area, only replacing them on particularly busy occasions.

As a result, the owner has made the 80 per cent a 100 per cent effective capacity. In other words, at this point, the restaurant is making sufficient revenue to meet its short-term financial goals, and is giving a high level of customer satisfaction to safeguard its future business. It is worth noting that because there is a gap between 100 per cent effective capacity and 100 per cent potential capacity, it is possible for the restaurant to be working at greater than 100 per cent utilisation on some occasions. For many managers this is the norm in their businesses!

Step 6 Understand why coping happens

Clearly it is impossible to maintain the capacity balance on 80 per cent resource utilisation at all times. Even if the restaurant has a booking policy, there is always the possibility that one of the most valuable customers will book at the last minute and the owner will be reluctant to turn this business away.

In other situations, the launch of a new product or periods of faster than anticipated growth may put parts of the business into 'coping' mode. This has been seen recently in the customer service departments of mobile phone network providers and banks following product launches. In some cases, some of the coping might have been avoided if the company had carried out some forecasting, or had simply communicated internally.

A key point here is to recognise that all but the extremely resource-rich organisations will be in the coping zone sometimes. If the coping zone is never entered, the inevitable conclusion is that the organisation has too much resource.

Step 7 Develop coping strategies

Most organisations cope after a fashion. In the restaurant, all the diners are given food, but perhaps not with the greatest service experience. Likewise, on the crowded flight, all passengers get a meal and a drink, though those that are served last may have limited choice and little time to eat before the aircraft starts its descent.

Left to their own devices, customer-facing staff will find their own ways of coping. Some of these informal coping strategies will be entirely appropriate and innovative, using interpersonal skills and intuition to judge how to handle each customer. Others might be less satisfactory, typified by the following examples:

- Waiters who becomes overly focused on one task, making it impossible for customers to attract their attention to make yet more demands.
- Doctor's receptionists, faced with a crowded waiting room, become extremely efficient in their dealings with patients, to the point of rudeness.
- Retail assistants who 'forget' to offer a customer a range of products, knowing that if the customer chooses one of these, their work load will increase.

Operations managers develop coping strategies based on one or more of the following:

- Giving more information to customers alerting them to possible difficulties. An example is the electricity company that after a major storm placed a recorded message on its help line to say 'If you're calling about loss of power in this district, we should be able to restore it within two hours'. This reduces the load on overworked telephone lines and operators.
- Intentionally reducing the service on offer, perhaps using a limited menu at peak times in the restaurant.
- Being clear to staff about what really matters most for customers: concentrating on the 'must dos' rather than the 'nice to dos'.
- Building resource flexibility by bringing staff from a lightly loaded area to assist with the overload. Call centres manage this by switching calls to other centres, whereas Disney brings managers from back office functions to assist with customer-facing operations on busy days. It is important to note that some of this resource may not be as efficient as the normal workforce.

There is a very strong link between prolonged overload and employee stress (see Chapter 7). It is relatively easy for providers to deal with short-term, predictable overloads. If we know we're going to be busy for a week or two, we can prepare for it, and many people get a 'buzz' from working together to cope with a crisis. The real problem with coping comes from protracted periods of overload, without hope of a let-up in the foreseeable future. Management support and appreciation becomes extremely important at this stage.

If the operation is in the coping zone for prolonged periods, it may be necessary for managers to give their staff 'licence to underperform'. For example, nurses in a busy accident and emergency department may not be able to carry out all their duties in the way in which they were trained. If this persists for any length of time, this will lead to stress and possible burnout. Part of the coping strategy, therefore, is to agree which bits of the service are 'must dos' and which bits can be safely left for the time being.

8.5.2 Coping: key questions

We have devoted a lot of space to coping because understanding how the organisation deals with this area may give clues as to where capacity management must be strengthened. The key questions to address are:

- What does the customer perceived quality/resource utilisation profile look like for your service or services?
- How does this vary by service process and by customer group?
- What measures or early warning signals tell you that you are about to enter the coping zone (as opposed to measures like lost customers or increased complaints which tell you that you *were* in the coping zone)?
- What suffers for customers when you enter the coping zone?
- What suffers for employees when you enter the coping zone?
- How could you manage the coping zone better to reduce the impact on customers and employees?
- How could you avoid being in the coping zone as much?

Of course, coping will affect every part of the organisation, in areas where both chase and level strategies are operating, although coping is perhaps more obvious in operations that are employing a chase strategy. In effect, chase becomes level in the short term because the organisation is not capable of adding another unit of capacity quickly enough to deal with an unexpected surge in demand. Coping is perhaps more sensitive here because, as we have noted, organisations employ this strategy when fast response or high levels of availability to customers are particularly important. These customers are not usually prepared to wait, either because the service is not particularly valuable to them, or because there are alternatives available to them.

8.6 Improving resource utilisation

There are four important additional ways of trying to improve resource utilisation:

- yield management
- building flexibility
- reducing capacity leakage
- getting organisational support for resource utilisation.

8.6.1 Yield management

Yield management is employed extensively by hotels and airlines to deal with the fact that their capacity is perishable (see Box 8.3). In other words, if the hotel room is not sold tonight, the contribution from that potential sale is lost for all time (see, for example, Fitzsimmons and Fitzsimmons 2004, Kimes 1989, Jones and Hamilton 1992).

Yield management is focused on determining the maximum revenue to be obtained from the various segments served by the capacity at hand. Thus the airline estimates how many full-fare-paying (business-class) passengers will book for any given flight, and adjusts the remaining capacity for economy-class passengers and other discount, pre-booked customers. As departure time approaches, the

The Kowloon Hotel, Hong Kong — Box 8.3

Sheryl E. Kimes, Cornell University

Yield management, the notion of charging higher prices when demand is high and offering discounts at times of low demand, has traditionally been applied in reservations-based industries such as airlines, hotels and car rental agencies. Managers at the Kowloon Hotel in Hong Kong felt that it might offer them the solution to improving their restaurant revenues.

The Kowloon Hotel on Nathan Road in Hong Kong is well known for its sumptuous all-day buffet. The buffet, which includes a selection of sashimi, oysters, salads and desserts, is open from midday to midnight. As is typical with most restaurants, customers only wanted to dine at particular times of day, and the restaurant was often empty in the late afternoon and late evening. To deal with this problem, the Kowloon Hotel's managers decided to move away from a single price for its buffet and charge different prices depending on when customers arrive.

When guests arrive (check-in) they now receive a 'buffet zone pass'. The cost of the pass varies depending on their arrival time. At noon, the price is HK $118, but increases to $128 at 1.00 p.m., but then drops back to $118 at 2.00 p.m. The 3.00 p.m. price is even lower ($108), but then progressively increases from $128 at 4.00 p.m., to $168 at 5.00 p.m., $208 at 6.00 p.m. and $248 at 7.00 p.m. Following this peak, the price gradually decreases back to $138 at 10.00 p.m. and to only $98 at 11.00 p.m.

Not only has this new pricing system resulted in a 33 per cent increase in revenue – which was attributed to a fuller utilisation of the restaurant space, hence an increase in revenue per available seat hour (RevPASH) – it has also proved to be a hit with customers, with extremely positive customer reaction. As a result, the management has decided to continue the time-of-day pricing for an indefinite period.

Question

1 What are the advantages and disadvantages of this approach for the organisation and the customer?

airline may release some capacity to discount travel shops and, as a last resort at the very last minute, to stand-by passengers.

Service managers must be aware, however, of the potential damage to the service concept in using this approach. Full-fare-paying customers may be unhappy to discover that the person in the seat next to them is flying for a fraction of the price. This may give the impression that the airline is merely after every last dollar of revenue, with customer satisfaction of minor importance. The Kowloon Hotel appears to have overcome this particular objection by creating a completely new concept where the charging policy is clear and unambiguous. Customers can therefore make their choice of eating time, knowing that they will be treated equitably.

8.6.2 Building flexibility

There are four basic forms of operational flexibility. It is critical to define carefully the type and extent of flexibility required in order to develop effective capacity management plans:

● *New product flexibility*. This is the requirement of the service operation to introduce new services into an existing mix. It will be necessary to define how frequently this might occur and the extent to which the operation will require new capabilities to achieve it. For example, mortgage companies are continually introducing new products with varying interest rates and repayment terms. In this case the frequency of new product, introduction is extremely high, but the requirement for new capability is low.

● *Product mix flexibility*. This is the ability of the operation to deliver more than one service product. A hotel may provide a number of services simultaneously dealing with business people, holiday travellers, conferences and wedding celebrations.

● *Delivery flexibility*. This is the capability of the operation to change the timing of the activity. Courier organisations are increasing this form of flexibility, offering different speeds of delivery and a range of pick-up and delivery times.

● *Volume flexibility*. This form of flexibility is required by many consumer services operating a chase strategy. It refers to the ability of the organisation to change its level of output to cope with fluctuating demand. Thus the call centre may deal with 6,000 telephone transactions on a normal day, but may have to cope with twice that amount following an advertising campaign or a new product launch.

Figure 8.7 demonstrates the notion of minimum effective lead times – the time it takes to respond to a change in demand. If an unexpected surge of demand occurs, the call centre manager can increase capacity by 50 per cent in four hours. This is accomplishes by asking staff to stay on after their normal shift, calling in off-duty staff, and by bringing in other staff from the organisation to man the phones. It should be noted that this is very much a 'first' or emergency response as some of the staff will not be fully trained and productivity levels will probably suffer as a result. Within eight hours the call centre manager can bring on line more capacity, perhaps from other call centres if the increase in demand is sustained.

This is a valuable tool in assisting operations managers to plan for the foreseeable contingencies. In addition to specifying the type of flexibility required, the service manager must also consider the following:

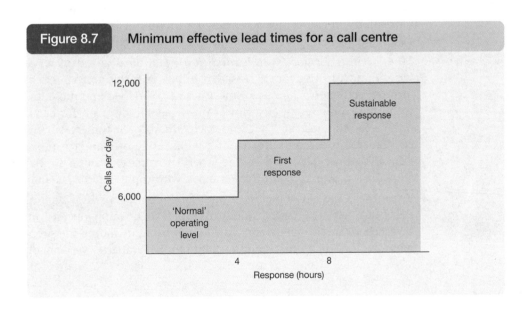

Figure 8.7   Minimum effective lead times for a call centre

- *Range*. How much flexibility is required? Does the call centre need to move from 6,000 calls to 12,000 calls or only to 8,000 calls per day? How many new products will be introduced and how frequently?

- *Response*. How quickly must the change be made? Can the call centre change from 6,000 to 12,000 calls in four hours or will eight hours be good enough? Clearly the faster the response, the more expensive it is likely to be.

- *Effectiveness across the range*. Most processes have an optimal range. It is unlikely that they will be equally productive across the potential range, and are likely to strain at the extremes.

- *Cost of providing the flexibility*. What is the premium resulting both from the change in output level itself, and in providing the capability in the first place? For example, providing training so that more staff are multiskilled represents a significant investment.

There are a number of approaches to building flexibility. These include:

- *Flexible employment contracts*. Employees may be asked to work a given number of hours per week, month or year. In this way, staffing levels may be more easily matched to expected demand. Flexibility in this area may extend to the requirement for staff to move between functions to cover fluctuating workloads. It is important to recognise that these staff may not be as effective when carrying out tasks that are less familiar to them.

- *Overtime*. Asking staff to work longer hours is a common short-term measure for building volume flexibility. However, it is generally accepted that using overtime in the longer term does not give the required increase in output as employees simply expand the work to fit the extra time available. In this event, overtime is a poor approach, costing a great deal in extra salary and creating employees who are overtired through being at work for long periods.

- *Short-term outsourcing*. The development of relationships with other service providers who can deal with short-term peaks in demand is a common practice, particularly in call centre activities. This requires some pre-qualification of suppliers, but can provide flexibility at relatively low cost.

- *Menu-driven service (standardisation)*. Standardisation of service offers provides opportunities for increased volumes of fewer activities. This creation of 'runner' activities (Chapter 6) smoothes the workload and provides opportunities to provide a degree of customisation or personalisation for customers. This is often referred to as the 'Dell' approach, whereby customers can create their own configuration of computer from a wide range of standard modules on offer. Education providers, such as the Open University, adopt a similar approach in allowing students to tailor their courses, within pre-determined constraints.

- *Teamwork*. The development of multifunctional teams allows a group of employees to deal with fluctuating workloads rather than simply operate on an individual basis. There are several benefits to this approach, including the support that group members give each other, and the ability to 'flex' capacity very rapidly.

8.6.3   Reducing capacity leakage

Many operations managers carefully plan their capacity in ways we have discussed in this chapter; however, sometimes managers are surprised to find they do not have as much capacity as expected. Here are some possible explanations:

- *Labour sickness and absenteeism.* Prolonged periods of overload and compulsory overtime usually prove counterproductive, with staff taking time off to recover. Alternatively, the organisation may need to look at its management style, placing more emphasis on team building rather than 'command and control' approaches.

- *Labour underperformance.* It is extremely common to find that call centres may have the right number of 'heads' but they may be ineffective because there has been insufficient investment in training. Alternatively, employee churn means that experienced staff leave just at the point they are becoming effective.

- *Scheduling losses.* There are times when staff are idle with too much capacity for the demand, whereas at other times there is too much demand for the capacity to deal with. This often arises because demand profiles are not understood or are too volatile, or where staff preferences for work patterns do not fit with the business need.

- *Costs of complexity.* The more the organisation deals with a broad range of services, the greater the possibility that staff deal with a greater percentage of tasks that may not be part of daily routine. This potential 'relearning' may give rise to inefficiencies and rework.

- *Quality failures.* The need to deal with quality failures is clearly lost capacity. Of course, part of the role of the call centre may be to deal with poor quality generated elsewhere in the organisation. It is essential that the extent of this rework is understood and charged to the appropriate location.

8.6.4   Organisational support for resource utilisation

The challenge for operations managers is to understand resource utilisation in the context of a changing world. Many of the issues need to be resolved by the organisation as a whole, rather than simply confined to the management of service delivery processes. Aspects of this organisational support include:

- *How is the service concept changing?* To what extent do operations managers have 'visibility' in the future strategic direction of the organisation? Without this inclusion in the strategic development process it is unlikely that capacity planning and resource utilisation and development will be effectively carried out. Often resource managers are left to develop capacity plans that have little relevance because the concept has been changed. For example, many product service companies providing repair and maintenance support for information technology have changed the emphasis of their service concept away from servicing equipment towards supporting customers. The nature and length of customer transactions have changed beyond recognition and require a link between this change in strategic direction and resource planning for it to be implemented.

- *How well are the internal interfaces managed?* A key role for the operations manager is to manage the internal relationships as well as customer relationships. Co-ordination of marketing promotions and new product introductions are vital, as well as getting to the root of quality failures and long-term quality costs. Successful organisations are often those that manage the internal relationships well. This does not necessarily mean that everyone always agrees, but that there is valuable internal debate. In fact, it could be asserted that an organisation without some degree of conflict will not learn and move forward.

- *How important is resource management in the culture of the company?* In some sectors, resource management is seen as a low-level task. The 'stars' of the company are often seen as those who deliver the latest deal or solve the latest crisis. Resource management needs a different type of 'hero' who is able to plan longer term and persuade the organisation to think differently about resource management.

8.7 Summary

Capacity management

- It is essential to be able to define the capacity of each service process, identifying the expected output for customers in the relevant service period.
- Capacity is influenced by a range of factors including product mix, location, intangibility and resource constraints.
- Most organisations adopt a mixture of capacity strategies: level, chase and demand management. The mixture should reflect the strategy of the operation.

Operations planning and control

- Capacity must be allocated to specific tasks for specific customers, using appropriate rules or algorithms.
- Control systems range from expensive ERP (enterprise resource planning) systems to simple appointment lists. The operations manager must choose the most appropriate mechanism.
- Capacity may be managed more effectively by ensuring that resources flow to meet the schedule.

Managing bottlenecks and queues

- Key constraints (bottlenecks) define the capacity of the service process. It is critical to devote management attention to these aspects of operations.
- Queues are inevitable in service operations. Developing 'waiting line' strategies will reduce potential customer dissatisfaction.
- Queuing theory and computer simulations provide valuable means of understanding complex queuing situations.

Managing the coping zone

- Almost all service operations experience a point where demand outstrips supply: customers may perceive a fall in quality, and staff feel under increased pressure. This is known as the coping zone.
- We recommend that organisations develop coping strategies, given that all operations will be there sometimes.
- It is important to develop actions to avoid being in the coping zone too much. This usually requires organisation-wide approaches.

Improving resource utilisation

- Yield management techniques enable services with perishable capacity (hotel rooms, airline seats) to maximise revenues.
- It is critical to define the nature of flexibility required to meet market demand in terms of range and response. Techniques to build flexibility include flexible employment contracts, overtime, outsourcing, developing menu-driven service products, and teamwork.
- Capacity leakage may impact significantly on the ability of the operation to meet its demands.
- Understanding and developing the organisation's support for resource management is an important task for operations managers.

8.8   Discussion questions

1 Select four service organisations and suggest how they might measure capacity, outlining the problems in so doing.
2 What capacity strategies might be used by an insurance broker, an internet retailer and a cruise ship company? Explain why they are appropriate.
3 Describe the last time you were in a queue. Apply the principles of queuing to assess your waiting experience.
4 What is meant by the coping zone? What are the implications for staff and customers of a supermarket when the operation enters this zone?

8.9   Questions for managers

1 How important is resource utilisation to the success of your organisation? What interest do senior managers take in this aspect of operations?
2 How well is the capacity strategy matched to the financial model of your organisation? Could a significant increase in customer satisfaction be achieved by an increase in relatively inexpensive resource?
3 Do you know where the bottlenecks or scarce resources are in your processes? How effectively are they managed?
4 What is the impact of the coping zone on your staff and customers? What strategies do you have in place to manage this more effectively?
5 What are the major causes of capacity leakage? Are they avoidable?

8.10   Further reading

Johnston R. and Jones P., 'Service productivity: towards understanding the relationship between operational and customer productivity', *International Journal of Productivity and Performance Management*, vol. 53, no. 3, 2004, pp. 201–13.

Klassen K.J. and Rohleder T.R., 'Combining operations and marketing to manage capacity and demand in services', *Service Industries Journal*, vol. 21, no. 2, April 2001, pp. 1–30.

Pullman M.E. and Thompson G., 'Strategies for integrating capacity with demand in service networks', *Journal of Service Research*, vol. 5, no. 3, 2003, pp. 169–83.

8.11   References

Armistead C.G. and Clark G., 'The "coping" capacity management strategy in services and the influence on quality performance', *International Journal of Service Industry Management*, vol. 5, no. 2, 1994, pp. 5–22.

Clark G. and James K., 'The "coping" zone: stress and quality', in Ribera J. and Prats J. (eds), *Managing Service Operations: Lessons from the Service and Manufacturing Sectors*, IESE, Barcelona, 1997, pp. 385–90.

Davis M.M. and Heineke J., 'Understanding the roles of the customer and the operation for better queue management', *International Journal of Operations and Production Management*, vol. 14, no. 5, 1994, pp. 21–34.

Davis M.M. and Vollmann T.E., 'A framework for relating waiting time and customer satisfaction in a service operation', *Journal of Service Marketing*, vol. 4, no. 1, 1990, pp. 61–9.

Fitzsimmons J.A. and Fitzsimmons M.J. *Service Management*, 4th edition, McGraw-Hill, New York, 2004.

Goldratt E.M. and Cox J., *The Goal*, North River Press, New York, 1984.

Jones P. and Hamilton D., 'Yield management', *Cornell HRA Quarterly*, vol. 33, no. 1, 1992, pp. 88–95.

Jones P. and Peppiatt E., 'Managing perceptions of waiting times in service queues', *International Journal of Service Industry Management*, vol. 7, no. 5, 1996, pp. 47–61.

Katz K.L., Larson B.M. and Larson R., 'Prescription for the waiting-in-line blues: entertain, enlighten, and engage', *Sloan Management Review*, Winter 1991, pp. 44–53.

Kimes S.E., 'Yield management: a tool for capacity-constrained service firms', *Journal of Operations Management*, vol. 8, no. 4, 1989, pp. 348–63.

Maister D.A., 'The psychology of waiting lines', in Czepiel J.A., Soloman M.R. and Surprenant C.F. (eds), *The Service Encounter*, D.C. Heath & Company, Lexington, Mass.,1985, pp. 113–23.

Slack N., Chambers S. and Johnston R., *Operations Management*, 4th edition, Financial Times/Prentice Hall, Harlow, 2004

Medi-Call Personal Alarm Systems Ltd | Case Exercise

Medi-Call provides personal alarm systems to the elderly and infirm. Customers are principally those people who live alone, preferring to stay in their own homes rather than be looked after in some form of institutional care or with family.

The customer has a small transmitter/receiver, which can be worn as a pendant or on the wrist like a watch. If the customer has a problem they press the button on the pendant, which activates a base station located at the customer's telephone. The base station calls Medi-Call's contact centre, which provides 24/7 cover to ensure maximum reassurance for its customers. Medi-Call's agent will attempt to establish contact with the customer. Because the transmitter is so sensitive, it is possible to carry out a conversation up to 50 metres away from the base station. Medi-Call's staff are trained to provide immediate reassurance to the caller, who is likely to be confused and frightened.

Each customer provides a number of contact numbers, including neighbours and immediate family. If there is a problem, as for example an elderly person having fallen and not being able to get up, the normal procedure is for Medi-Call to alert the closest neighbours, asking them to visit and call back. If required, Medi-Call will alert emergency services and also contact family members if appropriate.

The call centre deals with a wide range of demands:

- **Emergency calls.** These result in Medi-Call agents being on the phone for an average of 30 minutes. This time may be spread over a number of calls to the customer, neighbours, family and so on. Each emergency call requires an average of 8 minutes administration time to ensure records are kept up to date – this is normally completed immediately after the call is completed, and definitely before the agent completes their shift.

- **Technical enquiries.** These calls normally come from new customers, unsure about the function of the equipment. The average duration of these calls is 5 minutes, with 1 minute associated administration time.

- **Reassurance calls.** Medi-Call encourages customers to ring the call centre about once a month to check that the equipment is working properly. Many elderly customers spend long periods by themselves at home and see this as an opportunity to have a rather longer conversation than is strictly necessary. Medi-Call considers this as part of the service it provides. The average reassurance call lasts about 6 minutes, with 1 minute associated administration time.

A typical morning in the call centre has the profile in Table 8.2.

Table 8.2 Call profile

Time	Staff numbers	Emergency calls	Technical calls	Reassurance calls
0000-0100	6	4	0	2
0100-0200	6	5	0	5
0200-0300	6	5	0	7
0300-0400	6	4	1	5
0400-0500	6	5	0	7
0500-0600	6	7	0	5
0600-0700	10	12	2	11
0700-0800	10	11	4	15
0800-0900	10	13	3	15
0900-1000	10	9	8	12
1000-1100	10	8	8	12
1100-1200	10	10	1	13

Medi-Call estimates that its employees are effective for about 80 per cent of the time that they are on shift, and this forms the basis of its staff scheduling system. This figure allows for short comfort breaks, and also recognises that not all staff are fully competent. Medi-Call provides thorough induction training and continuing staff development, but annual turnover of staff is in the order of 20 per cent, and it takes upwards of six months for staff to be fully trained.

The majority of calls are handled by the member of staff who is the first point of contact. In less than 10 per cent of calls, the agent handling the call may ask for assistance from a more experienced colleague or the supervisor.

Questions

1 When does Medi-Call's call centre enter the coping zone? What is the likely impact of this overload on customers and staff?

2 What strategies do you recommend that Medi-Call adopts in busy periods? What actions would you need to take to implement them effectively?

3 Do you agree with Medi-Call's philosophy on reassurance calls? What do you recommend?

chapter nine

Networks, technology and information

Chapter objectives:

- to describe how networks, technology and information are transforming service

- to discuss the management of physical and virtual networks

- to discuss the management of technology and information

- to introduce an approach for integrating and assessing networks, technology and information.

9.1 Introduction

For the service operations manager, this chapter is concerned with some of the most exciting changes in service delivery in recent times. Here are some examples:

- Couriers have constructed global networks to guarantee delivery of urgent documents to any centre of business in the world within 48 hours.
- Telecommunications technology means that calls to telephone numbers in one part of the world can be answered in a completely different country and time zone. This opens up the possibilities of 24-hours-a-day-for-7-days-a-week (24/7) access to service, as well as the obvious benefits to the organisation of much reduced labour costs.
- It is possible for a hotel to market its accommodation globally through the web so that potential customers can take a 'virtual' tour of the facilities.

This chapter is about finding new and innovative ways to deliver service, enhancing service products and increasing productivity by managing networks, technology and information. It describes how organisations have been able to devise completely new services and to change the way that we live. All this poses some challenges for the service operations manager. It forces us to think and plan longer term to ensure that future investment delivers the significant improvements in performance that will be essential for survival.

It also forces us to think more globally about service delivery. Thinking globally for service operations has until recent times consisted largely about how companies might grow by moving into new geographical markets, being concerned as to how service concepts might translate from one national culture to another. Even the ubiquitous McDonald's has made changes in its offerings to reflect local requirements. Today, technological advances mean that elements of service operations that were location specific can be carried out almost anywhere in the world. 'Virtual' teams mean that experts can work on client projects wherever they are, rather than have the expense and time of physically assembling the team on the client's premises.

9.2 How networks, technology and information are transforming service

Recent years have seen major changes in the nature of service. Networks, technology and information have enabled both better operations management and have also been able to create some entirely new services. These developments fall into four, overlapping, categories:

Integrated information provision

Information technology, coupled with technologies such as satellite tracking, has enabled operations managers to make decisions based on more complete and real-time information. An obvious example is the parcel business. Both managers and customers are able to track the location of parcels sent by courier. A less obvious example is the police service. In the past if you rang the police emergency phone number asking for assistance, the operator would make a note of the call and pass it to the local duty officer who would put a radio call out asking for the location of nearby units and send the nearest to the scene. Police call centres now have integrated technologies, which provide more information to the police and allow a more effective and appropriate response. Even before your call is answered the duty officer in the centralised incident room will have the location of the telephone being used, its caller's call history, a map of the area, whether the house has a registered firearm, the location of all registered firearms and offenders in the area, and the location of available officers and other specialist resources, all visible on the map on the screen.

Integrated services

Networks, technology and information allow distinct but related services to work together to create many new possibilities. One example of this is the Octopus card – see Box 9.1.

Octopus

Box 9.1

Nearly every one of Hong Kong's 6.75 million inhabitants carries an Octopus card. The Octopus card is a rechargeable smart card and is the answer to carrying small change. The card was originally lanched in September 1997 as a ticketless fare collection system for the city's mass transit rail system (MTR). Now the card is used as electronic cash, with most transactions being for relatively small sums, often less than HK $20. Eric Tai, chief executive of Hong Kong's Octopus Cards Ltd, explained: 'We're not out there to get the larger payments market. We see ourselves as a micropayments operator.' The card can be used for almost any small payments, including 7-Eleven stores, McDonald's, Starbucks, supermarkets, parking meters, buses, trains and ferries.

The Octopus card is simple and easy to use. Indeed it does not even have to come into contact with the scanners: it does not need to be taken out of a wallet or purse. At the rush hour people simply waft their bags over the scanners as they rush to catch their train. According to Eric Tai, this contactless system takes only 0.3 seconds to register a payment, compared with one or two seconds for a contact card, not counting insertion and extraction time.

This has become one of the most successful electronic cash (e-cash) systems in the world. There are around 8 million Octopus transactions each day in Hong Kong, worth around HK $48 million. The card is used by more than 95 per cent of the population. While trials and early-stage deployments of similar systems have been made in Japan, Singapore, Rome and elsewhere, no major market has replicated the breadth or depth of Hong Kong's Octopus experience. Eric Tai explained, 'Every city is different. We are blessed with a number of different ingredients that have made us successful.' One critical ingredient is the fact that most people in Hong Kong use the citiy's public transport network, which provided the platform for adoption and growth.

The Octopus system was created by AES ProData (Hong Kong) Limited, a member of the ERG Group of Companies, based in Perth, Western Australia. AES ProData is responsible for the design, build, operation, maintenance and financing of automated fare collection in the Octopus system. MTR stations in the city sell Octopus cards, which cost HK $150. $50 of that is a refundable deposit on the card; the remaining amount is the credit available for spending. Top-ups are available in add-value machines located in all MTR stations. Every transaction is settled by the end of the day, with Octopus Cards Ltd netting around 1 per cent of the transaction amount.

The optional personalised Octopus card acts as a security device, providing access to offices and main entrances to housing estates. This card can also be linked to a bank account to provide automatic payment and top-up functions. It also has the option of a lock-out to prevent unauthorised use should the card be lost. An Octopus watch has also beeen launched, which contains the smart chip so users can just wave their arm over a sensor. And in a city with a very large proportion of mobile phone users, Nokia has introduced an Octo-phone with the chip embedded in the cover.

The Octopus card appears to have only one disadvantage – just like cash, if you lose it, its gone!

Questions

1 What are the advantages and disadvantages of the Octopus card?

2 Why has the implementation of such a card been less successful in other cities?

This illustratiion is based on information from www.octopus.com and http://en.wikipedia.org/wiki/Octopus_card

Service on demand

Information technology has transferred some of the work to the customer but also put them in greater control of the service and its delivery. From our computer at work we can order our own stationery and computer peripherals, changing the role of the traditional purchasing department (Croom and Johnston 2003) (see also Chapter 6). From our home computer we can order our weekly groceries or train tickets or cinema tickets, or move money between bank accounts and pay bills. As a result, many customers now expect immediate service and 24/7 access. In the UK the Government has developed NHS Direct to provide 24/7 access to health workers, who provide first-line advice and grade calls and direct appropriate resources (see Box 9.2).

NHS Direct   Box 9.2

The National Health Service (NHS) set up NHS Direct (NHSD), a call-centre-based operation in the UK, to provide access to healthcare information and advice more rapidly than the local doctor's surgery. Part of NHSD's role is to relieve pressure on these hard-pressed resources, though hoped for reductions in emergency calls and visits to accident and emergency departments in hospitals have not been realised. There are 22 call centres distributed across the country, each managed by an NHS Trust. In total, over 3,000 staff deal with 500,000 calls a month.

Each call is answered by a call handler who is not medically qualified but who is able to complete some calls, or transfers callers to either the Health Information queue (non-symptomatic information) or to the First Advice queue (symptomatic health advice). If health advice is required, the call is handled by nurses who are able to give advice within specified guidelines and to initiate a response if appropriate (such as call an ambulance to transfer someone to hospital).

The NHSD strategy is based on increasing access for the public largely through the call centre, but also through the internet. NHS Direct Online receives some 500,000 web-based enquiries a month. The internet service provides a comprehensive medical encyclopaedia and general advice for patients who have already received a medical diagnosis. NHSD is continuing to develop access to the public, including an interpreting service for non-English speakers, Type Talk for the hard of hearing, information

points linked to the website, and interactive digital TV.

The call centre operation depends to a large extent on an effective information strategy and the development of robust procedures to deal with each situation. Training and recruitment of staff is fundamental to the success of NHS Direct, not least because those calling are frequently in some distress and need the reassurance of people who demonstrate competence.

NHS Direct has seven key aspects in its management approach:

- *Clinical audit*. A random audit of 1 per cent of calls ensures that the information provided by staff is accurate. In addition, each employee has three calls reviewed per month (by self, peer and supervisor).

- *Clinical risk management*. Policies have been developed to give guidance to call handlers and nurses, and NHSD invests heavily in staff training in this area.

- *The use of information*. NHS Direct recognises the need to give accurate information, and to develop its information systems to develop its service.

- *Staff and staff involvement*. Staff are fully involved in quality audits, service development and process improvement.

- *Education and development*. All employees have personal development plans linked to every aspect of clinical and operational performance. There is an NHSD Competency Framework for every staff group.

- *Patient and public involvement*. This is facilitated through patient forums and through the investigation of complaints. Public and patient involvement groups are also used to market NHSD services.

- *Clinical effectiveness*. Performance data are compared to the National Audit Office's 'Best Practice' to ensure value for money and also clinically effective advice.

The formation of NHS Direct has met with mixed reactions. Some doctors and patients remain sceptical about the use of technology. Others see the benefits of shifting some work from hard-pressed local surgeries. A positive benefit is that NHS Direct is creating information systems that enable the service to be run more effectively, so creating an understanding of how resources may be used more effectively in the future.

Questions

1 What is the service concept of NHS Direct (refer to Chapter 2)? How does this differ from more traditional healthcare?

2 In what way does NHS Direct enable the NHS as a whole to operate more effectively?

This illustration was written with the assistance of J.J. De Gorter, Medical Director of NHS Direct, Thames Valley, UK, and from material from www.nhsdirect.nhs.uk

Intelligence networks

A major development in recent years has been the construction of intelligence networks. By this we mean the links between computers and networks that facilitate communication and the transmission of data between individuals within organisations and between organisations. A simple example is provided by company intranets. Information about customers, products, company procedures and training programmes, as well as e-mail, can be accessed by all employees. Links can be provided to personal development activities, with the possibility of sharing improvement activities to avoid duplication of effort. Advances in networking technology have opened major possibilities for changes in location and mobility of intelligence across and between organisations.

Sawhney (2001) suggests four strategies for profiting from intelligence migration:

- *Arbitrage* allows intelligence to be moved to locations where the cost of maintaining it is lower. The shift of call centres and software development to India, Eastern Europe and Latin America provide good examples.

- *Aggregation* combines isolated elements of infrastructure intelligence into one large pool of shared infrastructure. Software companies providing suites of inter-related applications are examples of this.

- *Rewiring* allows organisations to co-ordinate processes more tightly across many participants, and indeed across organisations. A simple example is a tracking device that alerts police when a high-value car has been stolen, and then provides information to recover the vehicle and offenders.

- *Reassembly* enables information from a variety of sources to be consolidated into a personalised package for customers. Blackboard.com (Box 9.6) brings together a variety of aspects of university life in one package for students.

9.2.1 Operations challenges

The critical lesson for operations managers is to recognise that service concepts (see Chapter 2) are changing rapidly and new service providers may be providing better value for customers by taking advantage of changes in networks, information and technology. More positively, it would seem that there are many possibilities to provide better service at lower cost by integrating services and information provision and by harnessing the power of intelligence networks.

The pace of change provides both opportunity and challenge to the service operations manager. These include the need for:

- investments in future-proof technologies
- sophisticated but reliable technology
- large, reliable and up-to-date databases
- more centralised operations
- technology-competent staff
- involving users in the development of 'unknown' services
- maintaining a personal relationship with the customer, despite limited personal interaction.

NHS Direct (Box 9.2) provides some insight into these and other challenges. Some information-based organisations see opportunities for developing advanced services following, for example, the creation of databases based on the original service. In such cases the potential rate of innovation may be quite rapid, which in itself presents significant challenges for the operations manager.

9.2.2 Flexing the structure of operations

In the past the structure of the operation acted as a constraint to operations. Today, through the use of technology, information and the creation of global, physical and virtual networks, constraints can be removed, and new services and operational capabilities created.

Structure versus infrastructure

The usual way of describing the two main clusters of operational tasks are those decisions concerned with managing the structure and the infrastructure of the operation (Hayes and Wheelwright 1984). The structure of an operation is akin to a human body – it is the skeleton, organs and muscle structure, which create its shape and define its ability. For an operation the structure includes the technology, facilities, buildings and their location, and the supply network. These hard structural parts of an organisation define its overall shape and architecture, and in the past have constrained its abilities. A restaurant with only 30 seats, for example, constrains its activities, just as the capacity of a telecommunications device, measured in kilobits, may constrain the type and speed of information flows. Structural decisions include the location, capacity (size), capability and the resilience or flexibility of the various physical or virtual parts of the operation.

An organisation's infrastructure, on the other hand, comprises the decisions that affect how the structure is used – the organisation, planning, control and improvement of its processes, staff and customers, for example – and decisions about how performance is measured and improved.

Much operations decision making has taken structure as a given, or at least as a very expensive resource. This means that operations mangers have concentrated on infrastructural decisions, such as process design, people management and resource allocation (Chapters 6–8). Today operations structures are much more fluid through the use of networks, technology and information, and they can provide the key to new services and new levels of productivity and customer service. There are two aspects for operations managers to consider here:

- managing physical and virtual networks
- managing technology and information flows.

9.3 Managing physical and virtual networks

A network is a configuration of resources linked through physical, virtual or other forms of information transfer, which combine to provide the possibility of new or enhanced service offers and greater operational performance. While networks per se are not new – indeed all organisations have a portfolio or network of relationships with suppliers, customers, financial institutions, etc. (Ford 2002, Turnbull 1990, Håkansson 1997, Håkansson and Snehota 1995) – developing networks, physically or virtually, can create new opportunities. Here are some examples:

- Courier companies have created 'hub and spoke' networks to move parcels and packages first between sorting offices (hubs) and then by delivery routes (spokes) to their final destination.
- Distribution companies link national and regional warehouses to minimise inventory holding and transportation costs while improving service levels.
- Global airlines plan routes and times to allow for maximum opportunities for passengers to interconnect and reach their destinations.
- Utilities build physical networks to transmit electricity, gas or water to customers, linking together production facilities or reservoirs to ensure continuity of supply to all customers.
- Telecommunication technology has allowed call centres to be located in low-labour-cost areas, frequently providing greater service at much lower cost. Call centres around the globe may be linked to facilitate capacity management.
- The internet provides the opportunity for universities to develop new modes of learning, providing more flexible access for students in terms of timing and location, and also enabling teaching professionals to work more effectively.

A hub and spoke network is perhaps the commonest form of physical network, employed by airlines and distribution companies. A simple parcel distribution network, with a central hub connected to secondary distribution centres, is illustrated in Figure 9.1.

| Figure 9.1 | Hub and spoke network |

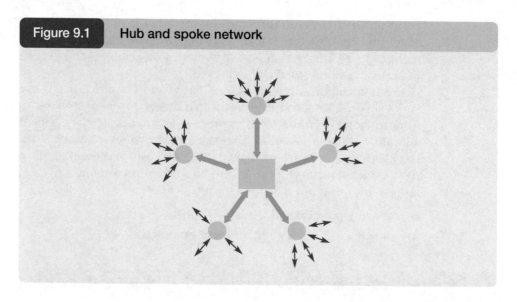

This physical network allows for the efficient and timely movement of parcels between hubs. Because the volumes are relatively high, it is possible to invest in technology at the hubs to ensure that packages are rapidly sorted into those packages that will be transferred to another hub in the chain and those that will be allocated to each of the local delivery routes. Some key operational decisions can be readily identified:

● The location of each hub must be carefully chosen to provide maximum access to customer destinations.

● The capacity of each hub must be linked to some estimate of future demand, possibly allowing for incremental increases as the market grows.

● Information flows must be identified and managed to ensure that the material flow between hubs and delivery routes are managed within specified service levels.

● The design of the network should allow for future geographical extension, adding hubs and delivery routes as required.

These decision areas are described in more detail in section 9.3.2.

Other forms of networks, either physical or virtual, include ring networks, which are used in particular by the internet and utilities, and hierarchical networks, which are found in many supply chains (see Chapter 5). These are illustrated in Figures 9.2a and 9.2b.

Virtual networks comprise a combination of physical sites and/or computer sites linked by communication technologies via cable, satellite and fixed lines. They involve the creation of several systems, which combined, electronically rather than physically, can provide a particular service or range of services. The electronic parts include computer systems (from stand-alone systems to the web), networks such as an organisation's intranets or the internet, software systems and applications; while end nodes of the networks, which are accessed by customers, include phones, faxes, televisions and computers.

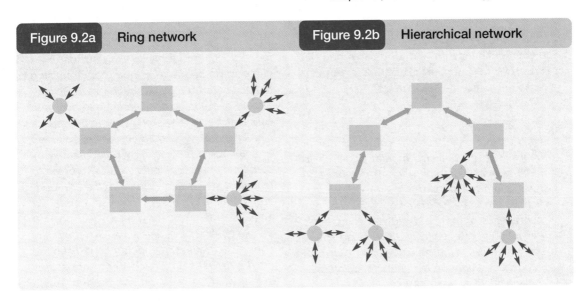

Figure 9.2a Ring network

Figure 9.2b Hierarchical network

The organisation may be entirely virtual (see adabra.com, Box 9.3) or primarily a physical structure with some virtual elements.

adabra.com | Box 9.3

adabra is a new internet company that has created a virtual network to access, supply and service its customers with a wide range of products, covering categories including home and garden, sports and leisure, and office and communication. Products sold include cameras, televisions, microwave ovens, telephones, golf clubs and computing equipment. adabra.com specialises in community buying. By linking with interested customer groups, such as over-50s portals, sports and leisure clubs or individuals through its website, it encourages people to come together and gain discounts from bulk buying. By offering the latest branded products at a range of prices, depending upon the number bought within a certain time-frame, its customers can save up to 30 per cent on normal retail prices. Vincent O'Farrell, the company's consultant operations director, summarises the service: 'This is not "auction buying" where consumers compete against each other and drive the price up. adabra is about co-buying, or community buying, which is about consumers working with each other to drive the price down.'

The company is not a 'bricks and mortar' organisation but a value network, comprising carefully constructed and managed partnerships to create a new, fun and interesting service for its customers. The network of partners provides products, sales, logistics, customer service, and product servicing and repairs.

The organisation has to make decisions about which are the right products, opting solely for premium brands. By developing partnerships with suppliers, adabra can negotiate not only numbers of products but also the discounts it can offer for a variety of sales volumes, and also have items pre-allocated to speed delivery to customers.

The company's 'front end' is its website, with information about the products on offer and explanations of how to buy. Access to markets is provided through several channels. While its website is available direct, most traffic will be driven through other major gateway partner sites such as Egg's site – egg.com – and other specialist community websites. Such channels not only provide good access to appropriate markets but also provide co-branding, which gives customers confidence in the company and its services as well as minimising traditional business-to-consumer marketing costs.

Vincent explains:

The key activities for the company have included not only the technical development of the website but also market research to identify what customers want. We have to think about the amount and type of information we provide – for example the number and consistency of product images, because this impacts on both quality and download speed – and the provision of a consistent level of information about products made as interesting and interactive as possible.

Distribution is subcontracted to major package-handling companies. adabra uses Securicor as its main delivery partner and a number of other third-party suppliers to deal with large specialised products. Some items, such as washing machines, are delivered directly by the manufacturers.

Vincent described adabra's customer service:

Customer service involves dealing with customers' queries or problems. We are currently facing several issues here as we start to ramp up sales. Should customer service be an internal bricks-and-mortar operation or should it be outsourced? Either way we need to ensure that the right image is created by customer service. What are acceptable turnaround times for responding to e-mails? How standardised can e-mails be made without compromising the ability to provide a personalised service? Should there be an answerphone to deal with calls that cannot be taken by customer service agents and, if so, should customers be asked to call back or should they be contacted by outbound agents? Should calls be rerouted to technical specialists? What are the appropriate opening hours? However good our website and products are, we will not get people coming back unless we can create the right customer service operation. We need to build a robust structure that can consistently deliver what we need but also has the flexibility to deal with unknown volumes, timings and preferred access routes, for example.

Product servicing and repairs are outsourced to companies specialising in this work. 'One key issue we have in managing this network is consistency,' explained Vincent. 'Each of our partners has different ways of working, for example delivery lead times and availability. adabra needs to create its own consistent service to shape its brand.'

Question

1 Identify and assess the problems and benefits of the network that adabra has created.

9.3.1 Comparisons between physical and virtual networks

Although there are clearly similarities between physical and virtual networks, it is important to identify key differences in network design and management (Table 9.1).

So far we have presented networks as being either physical or virtual. In reality of course, many service organisations combine both physical and virtual networks to provide a flexible and efficient response to customers. For example, the global consultancy firm has a number of relatively fixed assets (consultants in a region) and these consultants may be redeployed to provide a physical response to clients. The firm may develop a more flexible physical network, by forming links with associates who may provide capacity to meet excess demand. The consultancy firm's capability may be further enhanced by developing the virtual network, enabling the locally based consultant to tap into the global network of expertise. The firm's expert in, for example, customer relationship management, need not now be physically at the client's location but may be included in service delivery.

Table 9.1 Comparing physical and virtual networks

	Physical networks	Virtual networks
Examples	Logistics and physical distribution Couriers Airlines Electricity generation and transmission Telecommunications	Global design teams Software design and development Loose networks of associate consultants Web-based study groups
Service product	The product is normally clearly defined and its cost fixed; for example, the cost to transfer a package from A to B in a given time frame would be known and quoted to customers	The product is often less well defined, with price linked to access to the network, rather than necessarily a fixed outcome
Network ownership	The network is frequently owned by one organisation, or a few partner organisations; examples are alliances between airlines or agreements between electricity generating companies	Who owns the network is less defined: a number of organisations may 'own' the physical structure (e.g. telecoms links) but the strength of the informational links between individuals and organisations is less clear and is continually changing
Capacity	The capacity of the network is relatively easy to determine and manage as material flows are relatively tangible; it is defined by physical resources such as trucks or pipelines	The capacity of the network is hard to determine as its structure may change rapidly as new links are established; bandwidth will constrain capacity
Flexibility	Physical networks are determined by their structure, pipelines, and delivery routes; they are relatively inflexible	Virtual networks may be extended relatively quickly by adding informational links
Central issues	A major concern for network managers is the movement of goods or people across the network and also the physical security of the network	Transmission of data is a key issue for virtual networks, but this is frequently overshadowed by issues of access and connectivity to the network and between its constituent parts; security is also an issue but extremely difficult to manage

9.3.2 Managing the network

Whether the network is physical, virtual or a combination, there are four key decision areas for operations managers: location, capacity, capability and resilience.

Location decisions

Location is the geographic positioning of a facility or facilities. Location decisions are often expensive and may have a significant impact not only as an investment cost but also on operations costs, since location may be affected by local wage rates and business rates, for example. Location may also have an impact on revenues, particularly when the operation involves physical contact with customers. For operations that do not require direct physical contact with customers, such as call centres and internet service providers such as health or benefits advisory services, location decisions can be made to minimise the physical costs of the buildings and the running costs of the operation. For operations that need direct access to customers, expensive town-centre or out-of-town shopping malls may be essential.

Location decisions are a balancing act between supply-side factors and demand-side factors (Slack *et al.* 2004). Supply-side factors are those that influence the costs and difficulties of a location decision. The demand-side factors are those that influence revenues. Not all the factors below will apply to every location decision but they are an indication of those factors that may need to be taken into account.

Supply-side factors include:

- land costs – the costs of acquiring the land
- labour costs – wage costs, employment taxes, welfare provisions etc.
- energy costs – the cost of energy or the availability or even the consistency of the supply of energy
- transportation costs – the costs of getting resources to the site and of transporting materials to customers
- government factors – local taxes, capital restrictions, financial assistance and political climate, and planning restrictions
- social factors – language and local amenities
- working environment – the history of labour relations and labour supply.

Demand-side factors include:

- convenience to customers – the site's accessibility for customers, including transport network, parking, distance from markets
- labour skills – the availability of particular talents, skills, accents and cultures
- characteristics of the site – the intrinsic and maybe aesthetic appeal of the site
- image – the reputation of the surrounding area and the extent to which there are complementary services in the vicinity.

Virtual networks frequently enable more choice of location for the operation. Some telephone workers may work from home rather than travelling to the call centre itself. Professionals may provide a global service based at a single location.

Capacity decisions

Another key question is: how big should the facility be? For the package distribution operation, some estimate of volumes to be sorted in a relatively short time window each night will be required. Likewise, when deciding the size of a supermarket, call centre, airport, surgery or cinema the costs need to be weighed against forecast demand – not only short-term demand, but also long-term demand, because the cost of changing facility size can be expensive and sometimes difficult.

The two interrelated issues for operations managers are:

- facilities can usually only be added in large – and expensive – chunks
- capacity needs to match demand.

Adding new facilities usually requires the organisation to commit significant amounts of capital. This can be a risky business because long-term demand can rarely be predicted with any great certainty. If necessary break-even volumes are not met, the facility will not pay for itself. In some cases, such as a theme park where having sufficient customers creates the atmosphere, the service may not be as good as it should be if volume targets are not achieved. If volumes are exceeded, there may be significant localised problems for customers, resulting in customer dissatisfaction and lost business. Given that the majority of forecasts will be wrong, operations managers will invariably suffer from the consequences of over or under-capacity.

Many airports have suffered from the latter problem; furthermore, owing to the length of time it takes to design a new runway or terminal building, and to go through the planning process and build the facility, volumes may again exceed capacity as soon as the new facility is opened. Southwest Airlines (see Box 9.4) owes its success to a careful capacity expansion approach.

Southwest Airlines   Box 9.4

Southwest Airlines has been consistently successful as a service operation because of two aspects of the way it operates. Southwest is often quoted as the 'fun' airline, with cabin crew encouraged to be creative about the way they carry out their duties, sometimes playing games with the passengers during the flight.

Southwest could deliver what became known as its 'luv' strategy because it was founded on sound operational principles, an emphasis on tight cost control, and careful expansion of the network. Each time Southwest acquired a new plane, a decision had to be made as to whether it would be directed to an existing route, where

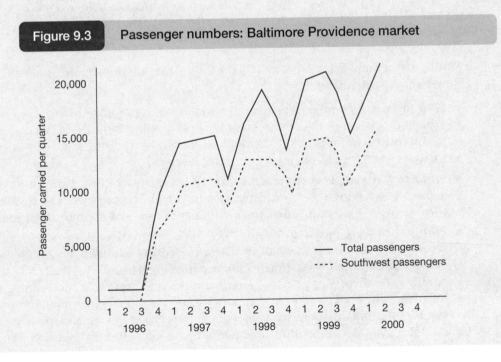

Figure 9.3   **Passenger numbers: Baltimore Providence market**

demand volumes were predicted to rise, or to develop the network, by adding a non-stop service between cities previously requiring passengers to take more than one flight.

The airline's pricing strategy has been a key factor in influencing the volume of demand on any given route. Southwest made a policy of pricing against the cost of ground transport, not against other airlines. This could lead to total demand for air transport increasing as much as four or five times the level prior to Southwest's entry. As Southwest grew, so this pattern of market growth was repeated many times over. This allowed the route planners to develop a simple demand growth model to indicate the level of capacity growth required over time.

The entry of Southwest into a market could be expected to stimulate a significant demand, which then drops back to a sustainable level. In the early 1990s Southwest expected to become the sole carrier after two or three years. As the other airlines responded to Southwest's approach, the airline could no longer be guaranteed this total dominance, but as the sample figures from the Baltimore Providence market demonstrate, both growth and market share are impressive. From entry in 1996 passenger numbers increased from just over 1,500 per quarter to over 21,000 per quarter in 2000 (see Figure 9.3), and from the beginning Southwest's share has been approximately 70 per cent of the market.

Another factor in making capacity expansion decisions was the number of expected flights per day. Investment in a new destination required investment in departure gates. Although prepared to commence operations with ten departures a day, Southwest wanted to expand rapidly to 20 departures a day to use two gates effectively. Another important criterion in Southwest's route strategy was the availability of people to fit in with Southwest's distinctive culture. Southwest found that this aspect of location decision making had a significant impact on its success.

Questions

1 What type of competitive action would have a significant impact on Southwest's forecast market growth curve?

2 Which would be the limiting factor in Southwest's growth: availability of routes or availability of people to fit into Southwest's culture?

This illustration is adapted from material contained in Harvard Business School's case *Southwest Airlines: 1993 (A) 9-694-023*; Harvard Business School's case *Southwest Airlines in Baltimore 9-602-156*; and from industry sources.

Similar to medium-term capacity (Chapter 8), there are three main strategies for long-term capacity planning:

- *Plan to exceed demand forecasts*. This strategy is appropriate where there is an expanding market or the cost of building a new facility is inexpensive compared to the cost of, or problems that would be created by, running out, such as electricity or water supply, or air traffic control facilities.

- *Build to forecast*. This approach would balance the likelihood of not having enough and having too much capacity and is appropriate where the costs and consequences of exceeding demand are similar to those for not meeting demand.

- *Plan not to meet forecast demand*. This is an appropriate strategy where it is acceptable not to meet demand or where the cost of capital is very high compared to the costs and consequences of not meeting demand. Football clubs may be able to do this, using price premiums and revenues from television companies to balance the books and even set money aside for future expansion. The problem for some organisations that follow this strategy, such as supermarkets, is that it might give the competition time and income to pursue an aggressive expansionist strategy.

Developing a facility strategy involves steps that are easy to describe but difficult to implement:

- establish a measure of capacity
- develop demand forecasts, ideally several forecasts including optimistic and pessimistic, identifying the assumptions on which each is based
- identify alternative means of dealing with the forecasts
- undertake an assessment of the risk involved
- evaluate the alternatives.

Capacity in a virtual network refers to both physical and informational transfer capacity between nodes or elements and the size of the nodes themselves. In Box 9.3 adabra uses several types of distribution support: Securicor, other major package-handling companies, and the manufacturers for very large items. Information transfer is limited by the capacity of the links between the nodes, usually a digital network. Existing digital phones, for example, can transfer around 10 kilobits per second, while emerging technologies will allow the transfer of over 2,000 kilobits per second. The network capacity is also limited by the capacity of any single node. Often internet companies find their capacity constraints associated with the more traditional parts of their structures, such as customer service and logistics. In Box 9.3, adabra's current sales were starting to be limited by its customer service capacity.

Capability

It seems obvious that any new facility should be capable of doing what is required, but this is not as easy as it sounds. There are some airports whose runways are too short to accommodate some of the larger aircraft. A decision taken years ago on the length of a runway when planes were smaller creates constraints on operations now. Doctors' surgeries, too, have changed significantly over the last few years, as doctors form larger practices to share growing administrative costs and ease the burden of 24-hour cover. Surgeries also provide many more facilities than previously, such as well-person clinics and routine surgical operations, for example, putting stresses on facilities designed for a different way of working.

Network capability depends not only upon the capabilities of the individual elements of the network but also the ability to co-ordinate and control the whole network. As the complexity increases with the number of nodes or the number of interlinkages, the difficulties escalate. The problems experienced by adabra, for example, were concerned with consistency of service as it linked together more and more organisations with differing service standards.

A key problem we face is in forecasting both demand and also the nature of that demand and thus the nature of the services that have to be provided in the future. It is little wonder that many operations management problems stem from the size and nature of the facilities at their disposal.

Resilience or flexibility

Although forecasting the size and nature of demand and future services is difficult, if not impossible, the only thing an operations manager can do, besides keeping their finger on the industry's pulse, is to try to ensure that their facilities have some degree of resilience or flexibility.

Physical network resilience can be created through either structural flexibility or developing the potential of the infrastructure. Building flexibility or resilience into a facility can be done in many ways:

- buying extra land to facilitate any possible future expansion
- having a flexible internal structure, with open-plan offices and movable walls
- using flexible equipment, such as cordless telephones or desk-sharing schemes
- adopting different methods of working, using more home-based workers
- developing contingencies – railway companies, for example, may plan to use different routes if one route fails.

Resilience in virtual systems is similar to flexibility in physical systems. Ring network structures, for example, can provide different routing for information access or input if one route should fail. The more flexible the network, the greater its resilience should one part fail. The choice of network structure is critical here. The structure chosen will also affect how easy it is to add or remove nodes or other facilities as the demand for service expands or contracts. By linking with very large subcontractors, adabra is able to ensure there is sufficient capacity to cope with the growth that the company hopes will follow.

9.3.3 Developing a global network strategy

Because the combination of network design and information technology present many opportunities for developing competitive advantage, the service operations manager must develop a more considered approach to network design, particularly when wishing to manage in the global context.

Figure 9.4 brings together motivations for extending a global network and the key issues to be addressed in managing it. The major reasons for developing the global network include:

- *Market-seeking motives.* The organisation may have a desire to move into new (geographical) regions. Examples would include the spread of fast-food chains such as McDonald's and Burger King across the globe, and the establishing of national offices for major consultancies such as Accenture or CapGemini.

- *Resource-seeking motives.* More resources may need to be acquired in order to grow more rapidly. This motive is frequently associated with the market-seeking motive as an organisation may take over a competitor in order to move into a new market.

- *Strategic asset-seeking motives.* In this case, the network expansion might have as one of its goals the acquisition of key assets. This might relate to individuals with particular knowledge, or access to strategic customers.

- *Efficiency-seeking motives.* The transfer of service operations to low-labour-cost economies has become extremely popular as telecommunications technology has enabled processes to be outsourced or 'off-shored' in a way that was only thought possible for manufacturing a few years ago (see next section).

Figure 9.4   Global network strategy

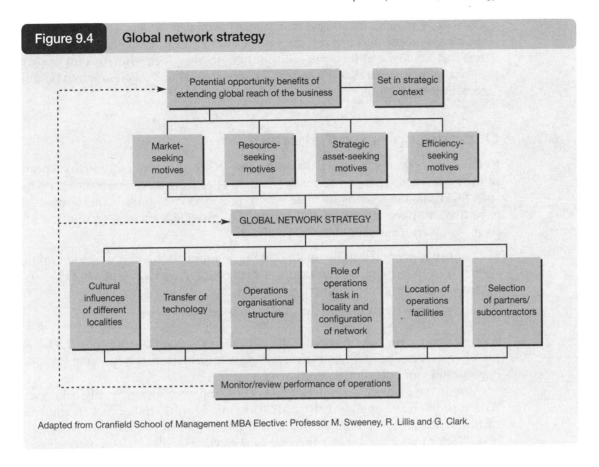

Adapted from Cranfield School of Management MBA Elective: Professor M. Sweeney, R. Lillis and G. Clark.

The operation of the global network must take into consideration some of the factors indicated in the lower part of Figure 9.4:

- *Cultural differences.* By this we mean the differences in national culture rather than organisational culture. Even McDonald's, renowned for the consistency of its products, has adapted its service offer, notably in Islamic cultures.

- *Technology transfer.* Technology transfer is frequently thought of as transferring 'hard' processes such as automation or process documentation. It is generally now recognised that the transfer of 'soft' technologies, which influence the organisation's culture, may present a more significant challenge to the network manager.

- *Operations organisational structure.* A key decision here is linked to the degree of local autonomy versus central control. Local units frequently feel that the centre exerts too much influence and stifles local responsiveness to customers.

- *The role of each unit in the network.* A global network strategy should bring clarity to each operational unit. In other words, each unit should understand its mission, whether it be to be the lowest cost operation or to provide access to local markets. The key performance indicators (KPIs) should then be developed according to the unit's specific mission.

- *Location decisions.* The unit's location will be decided after its specific role has been clarified.

- *Choice of partners and suppliers.* For many service providers, the choice of key suppliers and partners is a key strategic decision. This is particularly true in services that involve significant amounts of new or emerging technologies. The pace of change is so rapid that it is virtually impossible for one organisation to be able to deliver a total solution.

9.3.4 Outsourcing and off-shoring

In recent years there has been a major increase in organisations outsourcing aspects of their operations that can be managed more effectively (and more efficiently) by specialist companies. Many of these service providers have built upon a particular expertise and have repositioned themselves to provide a package or solution for their customers. Examples include:

- Companies who used to maintain building equipment, such as air conditioning or lifts, now provide a total facilities management service, replacing the customer's site maintenance function.
- Information systems support, including help-desk functions.

A key reason for the effectiveness of the outsourcers is that they can offer the benefits of economies of scale and investment in information systems that provide opportunities for operational effectiveness.

Outsourcing frequently involves a transfer of employees from the original organisation to the new supplier. This is particularly true in the public sector and this shift in culture from public service to commercial operation has proved to be a major factor in the success or otherwise of the activity. Gill (2001) reports on outsourcing experiences in the public sector in New Zealand and suggests four factors that distinguish between success and failure:

- Service centres that build an immediate relationship with their clients based on service were more successful in establishing a viable client base than those who were more interested in maintaining tight controls of transactions.
- Good operational performance builds client loyalty. Poor performance is a major reason for clients to choose new providers.
- Market size is critical to provide the economies of scale required to realise the efficiencies to provide margin.
- A major factor is the ability of senior management to move from a bureaucratic style, somewhat remote from stakeholders, to a more open style and a closer relatiopnship with customers and shareholders.

The manufacturing sector has been able to shift work to low-wage economies for many years. The advent of powerful telecommunications technology has enabled the recent rise of 'off-shoring' of service activities, not just of low-skilled jobs but also some requiring advanced skills, such as computer programming and medical diagnosis. One commonly off-shored activity is call centre work. India, for example, has become the prime destination for call and contact centres off-shored from the USA and the UK (see Box 9.5). As competition and pressures to reduce costs force services abroad, there will be a need to create new jobs in services in their place. However, if both low- and high-skill work is migrating to other countries, there is a question as to what might be left, apart from services requiring personal contact, should the trend continue.

Some organisations are facing a backlash from their customers and shareholders who are questioning the need to off-shore jobs. Other organisations believe there is a benefit to making a point of not off-shoring services. Nationwide Building Society is a case in point. The Society cited 'concern for its customer base' as the reason it decided to invest in its existing UK centres rather than transfer business to India. According to Stuart Bernau, Nationwide's commercial and treasury director, 'We don't have shareholders so our two stakeholders are our employees and our customers, and we wanted to invest in the communities where our business comes from. We'd have to have incredibly good reasons to make the move, and we don't believe the short-term cost-savings of off-shore are proven.'

Norwich Union call centre, Delhi — Box 9.5

EXL runs the Delhi-based call centre for Norwich Union, the UK's largest insurance company. The call centre employs around 900 call executives, and is clean, spacious and air-conditioned. It has a busy but pleasant atmosphere, not unlike some of the better call centres in Europe.

Vikram Talwar, from EXL, explains:

Demand has grown substantially over the last six to nine months. We have about one company a week come and visit us. There are two particular reasons. One obviously is cost. It saves approximately £20,000 per person that they move to India. But there is also the area of quality and productivity. We have only graduates working for us which means that the minimum standard qualification an employee must have to answer a call in India is a university degree.

Although an Indian call centre agent may only earn as much as one-sixth of the salary of their English counterpart, it is double what the average graduate earns in India. The staff also receive many benefits, including free meals in a well-appointed canteen, free healthcare, a gym, and transport to and from work.

The agents, however, are from a different culture to their customers, who may have different expectations, more aggressive attitudes – and strong regional accents. Vikram adds:

Indians understand the UK better than you might think. The relationship India has with the UK has in fact helped us to deliver a quality of service to the UK customer that would not necessarily be true if you were operating out of other places where the UK influence has not been as great as it has been in India.

In addition to customer service training, employees are given additional training in the UK culture, norms and behaviours and in understanding particular regional dialects.

While some customers are surprised and others are annoyed that they are dealing with a call centre in India, EXL believes that providing they deliver the service required, Norwich Union's customers are happy.

Questions

1 What are the advantages and disadvantages of off-shoring call centres?

2 What other services could be off-shored?

This illustration is based on material from the BBC's *Brassed-off Britain* series, first transmitted in June 2004.

9.4 Managing technology and information flows

Technology, either sophisticated or simple, is an intrinsic part of the operations structure. Information and information flows provide the glue that holds the structure – physical or virtual – together and facilitates infrastructural decisions. Technology and information strategies are therefore central requirements for service development in the majority of organisations. The implementation of a new information system or the introduction of a revolutionary new technology can transform the competitive or working environment. Electronic point-of-sale systems (EPOS), for example, have revolutionised the retail sector, enabling retailers to track consumer spending and to streamline their supply chains so that high levels of product availability have become the norm.

Investment in information systems is likely to be the major expenditure for many service organisations, both at the initial set-up of the operation, and also at frequent intervals as the industry moves forward and adopts similar technologies. Some services are built on the provision of information. In terms of the service concept, the outcome of the service is that the user is provided with information as to where to buy particular goods or obtain service.

Yellow Pages provides a good example of a service built solely on the provision of information for users that has changed its means of operation significantly over the time of its existence. Yellow Pages operations now exist in many countries across the world, providing users with information about how to contact businesses from abattoirs to zoos. In the UK this operation was set up by British Telecom (BT) in 1966, with the aim of increasing the use of telephones. For a number of years it was advertised with the slogan 'Let your fingers do the walking', encouraging users to phone possible suppliers rather than pay them potentially wasted visits.

In 2004 Yellow Pages UK was visited some 38 times a second. There were over 475,000 advertisers who were the paying customers for the service. As the service has grown, so Yellow Pages has adapted its format as new technologies have become available. The original operation was based on the delivery of paper directories to every home in a geographical region. In 1988, the company launched Talking Pages, a telephone-based service, and this was joined in 1996 by yell.com, an internet site.

In common with many services, changing technologies increasingly mean that the organisation deals with customers in many different ways. Behind all this lie two customer requirements, which are fast defining qualifying levels for service delivery:

- *Immediate and comprehensive access*. Customers now expect to be able to make contact with the service provider in person, by phone or by internet, 24 hours a day, seven days a week.

- *Control*. Customers want to feel that they are valued and important, rather than simply another piece of material to be processed. Technologies such as the internet allow the customer much more perceived control over what happens. They can browse through the online retail store, making choices at their own pace. In many cases they feel able to ask more questions than they might have done if they were in a store. Customers are able to compare prices between suppliers before making a purchase. There is no immediate pressure to buy imposed by the presence of a salesperson, or other customers waiting to be served.

This section deals with three key issues in managing technology and information flows:

- the roles for technology
- the internet and service operations
- knowledge management.

9.4.1 The roles for technology

The aim of this section is to discuss the role of technology in service delivery, recognising that information systems and the development of facilitating technologies will continue to be areas of key decision-making for the foreseeable future. We will not describe each technological advance in detail, but provide a framework for thinking about implications for the development of the service concept. Berry (1995) has provided a helpful set of roles to aid the development of a service strategy. These roles are:

- multiplying knowledge
- streamlining service
- customising and personalising service
- increasing reliability
- facilitating communications
- augmenting the service.

To which we would add:

- reducing cost
- increasing customer control.

Reducing cost is often closely linked with the second of Berry's roles, that of streamlining service, but is worthy of separate consideration.

Multiplying knowledge

There are a number of ways that technology can bring both flexibility and an extension to the service concept by leveraging and multiplying knowledge.

- *Leveraging knowledge about customers*. Information systems that ensure that customer-facing employees have all relevant information about the customer available during the service transaction present a more professional image, and allow the core transaction to be conducted more efficiently. When First Direct, the telephone banking service, was conceived, a fundamental requirement was for an information system that allowed any customer to talk to any service employee at any time. Some hotels keep comprehensive records of regular guests regarding their likes and dislikes, which room they prefer, and what are their dietary requirements. At a simple but effective level an airport hotel courtesy bus radios ahead as to which customers are on board so that they can be greeted by name when they arrive. This latter example demonstrates that technology does not need to be complex or expensive to achieve a significant impact.

● *Leveraging knowledge about the service product.* Service organisations that are moving away from offering a standard service may need to up-skill customer-facing staff. A greater choice for customers may require greater knowledge about the product in order to give appropriate advice. Information systems may allow the customer-facing employees to act 'as if' they were experts. Again, these systems vary from extremely complex to very simple. At one end of the scale, an expert system may harness all the knowledge of recognised experts and specialists. At the other extreme, a simple checklist on a computer screen may deal with many customer enquiries without the need to refer to expensive technical help. Many computer or software help lines operate on this principle, with on-screen diagnostic routines to aid the customer service agents.

● *Multiplying knowledge about the customers' use of the product.* This is an extension of the previous use of technology, and normally constitutes a change in service concept. Instead of simply selling a product, the service provider seeks to understand how the customer uses it and provides assistance or advice in how to use it more effectively. Truck manufacturers, faced with increased competition, moved the emphasis of their aftermarket operations away from simply selling spares to truck operators. To develop customer loyalty they invested in understanding how truck operators might manage their fleets more profitably. This knowledge was then disseminated through the manufacturers' dealer networks by means of an information system, rather than positioning a fleet profitability expert in each location.

Streamlining service

In this case, technology is used to eliminate steps in the service process. It is particularly valuable when applied to activities that have a direct bearing on the customer experience. Car rental companies have understood that business customers in particular do not want to spend large amounts of time either filling in paperwork to collect their car or waiting to return it. Smart cards automate the pick-up procedure, and staff with hand-held terminals waiting in the car return lanes speed up the drop-off process. The return process is particularly sensitive as far as the customer experience is concerned because at this stage the customer has effectively obtained all the value they required from the service. The processes from this stage on are perceived to be purely for the benefit of the rental firm, not for the customer, and therefore need to be as efficient as possible.

Many telephone-based operations use a customer database to call up addresses sorted by postal code. Rather than ask the customers to give addresses on the telephone – a lengthy process, prone to error – all that is required is a postcode that locates the street name, and then the house number or name within that locality. This relatively simple information system improves service times and reduces error rates.

Customising and personalising service

Supermarket loyalty cards are an example of this use of technology. Tesco, through its loyalty card, has built up a database of customer preferences. As a result it is able to target promotions to particular customer groups.

Increasing reliability

Technology has a major role in automating routine processes, the 'runner' processes described in Chapter 6. Customer information can be made immediately available to all parts of the business without the errors that occur when details are transmitted manually.

The performance of some physical products can now be monitored remotely. This is still relatively expensive but is valuable for customer-critical applications. For example, the service provider might monitor the performance of the customer's computer system. Any degradation in performance will trigger a service call to prevent complete failure of the system. In many cases the customer will be unaware that there has been any reduction in performance, or indeed that there has been a service visit.

Facilitating communications

The convergence of voice and data communication systems presents many opportunities for service providers to communicate with customers. A challenge here is to ensure that older technologies are adequately supported. Telephone call centres are being transformed into multimedia customer contact centres, with major opportunities for improvements in communication. However, it is possible that basic operations management principles are not observed in the rush for new technologies. There are many traditional telephone call centres that have insufficient capacity to deal with the increase in demand brought about by greater ease of communication.

Augmenting the service

Technology may allow the service provider to carry out more for the customer. In the 1990s bar-coding and electronic point-of-sale systems allowed some food manufacturers not simply to supply goods to retailers, but also to manage the customer's shelf space and inventory for them. Part-time degree courses can be made available globally through the use of electronic conferencing and 'groupware' systems.

Reducing cost

Technology may facilitate the removal of wasteful or repetitive steps in the service process. The resultant reduction in lead time from customer order to fulfilment is in itself likely to yield fewer errors and therefore lower costs. Financial services, traditionally operating through a network of local branches, are able to reduce the cost of their operations by dealing centrally through the telephone or internet.

Increasing customer control

When there is little or no obvious differentiation between service providers in a given sector, the 'feel good' factor is essential to build customer loyalty. A significant ingredient is the sense that a customer has of being valued by the organisation, and of not being merely another account number or statistic. Information systems allow the organisation to respond in ways that build a perception that the customer is important to the organisation. This is enhanced if customers feel that they can influence the service delivery process in some way, rather than being 'processed' in something akin to an assembly line. As has been described earlier, internet systems give this sense of customer control.

Blackboard.com

Box 9.6

Education providers around the world are moving into electronic learning (e-learning). This can mean many different things, and, to some extent, may be resisted by traditional academics who view the classroom as the most effective place for learning. This suspicion as to the value of e-learning is further fuelled by lack of understanding of the opportunities offered by the technologies available.

Blackboard.com has become one of the preferred suppliers of e-learning solutions, with a wide range of clients drawn from schools, universities and corporate development functions. Professor Penny Boumelha, Deputy Vice-Chancellor of the University of Adelaide says:

> Our goal is to become adept at taking advantage of the technological changes that will lead to major advancements in teaching and research. Blackboard will enable us to facilitate a flexible approach to distance and multilingual course delivery for remote and overseas students.

Blackboard.com offers a wide range of applications, which include those directed towards knowledge sharing, others that facilitate online interaction, and a further group that provide administrative support ranging from assessment recording through to payment systems. Part of Blackboard's appeal is the ease of interaction between systems. The Blackboard Learning System has been adopted by over 2,000 institutions and enables students and teachers to manage their portfolios, facilitates content sharing, assessment management and collaboration through free-form chat, chat lectures, question and answer chats, whiteboarding, class tours and group web-browsing.

It is the experience of the vast majority of Blackboard's clients that they have been taken by surprise by the rapid growth in the use of the system after introduction. The University of Durham, UK, launched Blackboard in September 2000, hoping to have 20 modules and three departments online by December 2000. In the event, more than 300 modules and 21 departments were online by March 2001. This was driven in no small part by student demand, as evidenced by the fact that more than 79 per cent of students enrolled in economics modules signed into their module site during the winter holiday.

Durham seems to be achieving two major objectives in this area: to enhance the student experience and to support new technologies in the learning environment. Dr Barbara Watson, learning technologies team leader, said: 'The university wanted a virtual learning environment (VLE) that was flexible enough for advanced staff to customise and easy enough to make less experienced staff say, "Even I can do this."'

As part of the feasibility study, Watson realised that other universities were also investigating VLEs. As a result, four universities in the north east of England created a joint taskforce to assess the commercial offerings available to educational institutions. This resulted in the purchase of Blackboard applications: key criteria being ease of use and integration with other systems.

For the student, there are many advantages, not simply access to course materials. All students have access through one system to a summary of their own course of study, assessment history, e-mail, and even their social diary.

Questions

1 What are the major benefits to universities arising from implementing systems such as Blackboard?

2 What must Blackboard do to ensure successful implementation of its applications?

3 What possibilities might exist for universities and similar institutions to create new learning environments for both students and faculty?

Implications of technological advances

Blackboard (Box 9.6) offers universities and other institutions many of the opportunities discussed above. In particular students are given more control over their learning through easier access, the transfer of knowledge may be facilitated through careful design of materials and forms of interaction, and the university may be able to provide more courses at lower cost as staff/student ratios may fall. An equally compelling argument may lie in the fact that the current and future generations of students will see e-learning as a core requirement in their choice of programmes of study.

9.4.2 The internet and the service operation

Many organisations are restructuring their operations to provide electronic-based services for their customers and/or suppliers. Electronic commerce (e-commerce) is challenging traditional business models and is creating new ways of accessing customers. It is also giving customers much more control as information, such as prices and services offered, become much more transparent (Voss 2000). Commerce is also challenging traditional structures and removing intermediaries (Voss 2000) as customers can create and then purchase their own customised products and services via the web, for example holidays, CDs, books and stock trading (see also Gunasekaran *et al.* 2002, Zhu *et al.* 2002, Croom and Johnston 2003).

E-commerce is also having a major impact on the cost of doing business, though the costs will vary from organisation to organisation. Thames Water in the UK has identified the costs of various types of transaction for its business (see Table 9.2).

Web-based organisations, either 'brick' (businesses with a physical presence in shopping malls, for example, with additional web channels) or 'click' (internet-only organisations), have created, almost overnight, multimillion-pound industries in many countries, providing instant, innovative, customer-controlled competition for the traditional procedure and service providers. With the rapid availability of the internet in both business and homes, e-mail and web-based commerce has become a key way of doing business. The vast majority of businesses have e-mail and internet communications, and during the first few years of the twenty-first century most homes will gain access to the web, at ever increasing speed as broadband technology becomes widely available.

Table 9.2 Comparison of transaction costs for letter, telephone and web

Process	Unit cost	% of telephone cost
Letter	£8.30	451
Telephone	£1.84	100
Web		
Query that requires agent response back to customer	£0.92	50
Automated billing query with occasional operator intervention	£0.18	10
Fully automated billing query	£0.09	5

Source: Voss (2000). Reprinted by permission of the Institute of Customer Service.

Following the dotcom boom and bust of the 1990s, internet services are now much better organised. Many combine a website for customer ordering with physical distribution for order fulfilment. The logistics operation frequently received little attention compared to the desire to present an attractive website to customers; the bookseller Amazon.com took several years to move into profit before sufficient volume was generated to support the supply chain needed to satisfy customers.

E-service

E-service is the delivery of service using new media such as PCs but also via other technologies such as digital TV, mobile phones and PDAs (personal digital assistants). Many e-service providers are well established, but new start-ups are happening every day, providing competition for traditional service providers and also creating new services (see adabra.com in Box 9.3).

E-services exist across most of the service sector: for example banks (Egg and FirstE), retailers (Amazon, Nortstar, LastMinute), airlines (Ryanair and easyJet), information (Scoot, Yahoo!) and utilities (Utilities.com). Job hunting, car purchasing, grocery buying, stock trading, community purchasing and auctioning can all now be carried out via the web.

For customers this means greater choice, with shopping and information gathering available from home or office. For business-to-business customers it means a more transparent market, with transparent pricing, accessibility to more suppliers, the ability to track deliveries and undertake electronic trading such as web-based purchase orders, invoices and payments. The principal advantages for service providers include:

- *Immediate access for customers*. Customers can visit websites at any time of day. The websites do not have to be staffed for 24 hours a day, and 365 days a year, but there is the opportunity for customers to make contact at any time.

- *Local business becomes global*. An advertisement for IBM showed an American couple visiting an Italian shop supplying olive oil. The image was of a poor business, struggling to survive, while the couple were running a successful business at home. The couple were amazed to find that, through the internet, this business was supplying customers in the USA, and had a wide range of global customers. Small businesses can now compete globally without the investment in physical sales networks.

- *Opportunities for building brands*. Customers form an impression of an organisation from its website. The messages it conveys, the information it contains, and practical issues such as how easy it is to navigate, present opportunities to support the brand position.

- *Giving perceived control to customers*. Customers can browse websites at their own discretion. In an online retail operation customers can decide at their leisure what goods they wish to purchase, without hassle from sales assistants wanting to boost their commissions, or from other customers in a queue.

- *Making information available to customers*. Websites allow the organisation to make vast amounts of information available for current and potential customers. Again, the advantage is that the customer can choose what to view and what to leave. The organisation does not need to bombard the customer with junk mail, which is frequently seen as both wasteful and intrusive.

- *Linking services.* Opportunities exist to build links between websites of complementary service providers. This creates the ability to form service alliances to increase the range of choice for customers or to create virtual 'one-stop shops'.

Operations implications

The movement to e-service has many important implications for operations management, including how the web can add value, the changing nature of customer relationships, changing service quality factors, and the importance of website design:

- *Value-added service.* For many organisations e-service will lead to a reappraisal of what adds value in services and indeed what constitutes a service. The support provided by travel agents, for example, may no longer be required by some customers, whereas easy access to operators providing a highly customised service may be of significant value. Music shops providing racks of CDs may be seen to be of less value than in-store or even in-home technology that will allow downloading of preferred tracks to create individualised CDs. Education will need to reassess its teaching role and look at opportunities for web-based learning. From an operations perspective it is likely that there will be a shift to front-line activity becoming a predominantly high value-adding activity focused on the more difficult interactions, with routine and maybe new services provided more cheaply and directly via the web.

- *The changing nature of customer relationships.* The nature of the relationship with customers will change as a result of e-service. Instead of the traditional and often specialist outward-facing customer service role providing the interface between the customer and the organisation, web-based services will allow the customer to infiltrate right inside the organisation. As a result the nature of customer relationships may have to be redefined, as will new ways for more people dealing directly with the customer (see Box 9.7). Operations will need to consider new ways of tracking customer needs and preferences, and of assessing customer satisfaction and retention. Key questions include:
  - Which customer segments will use web channels?
  - What are the transaction costs?
  - What is the nature of the customer relationships?
  - How will they be maintained?

- *Changing service quality factors.* The attributes of service, the service quality factors, may also change. New delivery channels lead to new expectations. Recent research has identified the quality factors for web-based transactions (Voss 2000):
  - *Fast response.* This includes both acknowledgement and service provision, from days or weeks in post-based business to hours and indeed minutes in e-service business.
  - *Automatic response.* Instant acknowledgement of e-mails to reduce anxiety and uncertainty.

Egg.com

Box 9.7

On 11 October 1998 Prudential launched Egg, a new internet bank, based in a purpose-built communications centre at Pride Park in Derby. Egg's services are available seven days a week, 24 hours a day by internet, telephone and post. Sir Peter Davis, chief executive of Prudential Corporation, said, 'Egg is part of Prudential's strategy for the UK to provide a broad range of products through a wide range of distribution channels. The launch of Egg anticipates the projected growth in direct distribution and electronic commerce.' The initial services provided by Egg included savings, loans and mortgages. Within its first week of operation Egg's website had received 1.75 million hits, plus around 100,000 telephone enquiries. By 2000 its services had expanded to credit cards, travel insurance, investment services, and web-based shopping. Mike Harris, Egg chief executive, said, 'Already Egg has made electronic trading a reality in UK personal finance. The internet is now set to play an increasingly important role in financial services in this country'.

Egg was the outcome of 12 months of research among 5,000 consumers to determine their financial product and service preferences. According to Mike Harris:

One of the key points to emerge from our research is that customers want to be recognised as individuals – to be seen as a person, not a number. They want a relationship with someone who can help them to make the choices that affect their lives, rather than being 'sold' to. We were talking to people (in one of our pre-launch market research panels) about the digital revolution. One woman said 'You know your revolution? It is similar to what Emma Goldman, the early twentieth-century American anarchist, said: "If I can't dance, I can't come to your revolution".' In other words, she was saying that she wanted to deal with an organisation that had a bit of happiness in it, that wasn't austere and dry, but that was an organisation dancing with its customers. We talked to real dancers. And we found they work in three ways. First is interaction when they are dancing – that's what we do on the phone. Second is preparation – so we started to explore just what kind of preparation we could do. Third is sensation – they try to create a response when they dance, so we looked at whether you could have a phone conversation that made people feel good . . . If the customer wants to joke, joke; if the customer wants to go quickly, go quickly.

Customers are provided with a named customer relationship contact, trained in the art of listening rather than selling skills. By developing a close relationship with customers through its customer relationship management (CRM), Egg is able to gain insights into meeting each customer's individual needs. Every conversation and interaction with a customer tries to set up the opportunity for the next – this creates the opportunity for the relationship to develop as the customer's financial and lifestyle needs change, for example when moving house, having children or retiring. Egg aims to understand the individual relationships its customers need, and the degree to which they want Egg to be proactive/reactive in their financial affairs. Egg aims to be head and shoulders above its competitors as a result of its attitude to 'the customer experience' and 'relationship marketing'.

Questions

1 Visit Egg's website (www.egg.com) and assess how the company provides a value-added service.

2 Evaluate the design of Egg's website.

This case is developed from material from www.egg.com and Voss (2000).

- *Customer communication*. The provision of information about length of the queue, for example, or how long before a response or delivery is likely.
- *Choice of phone follow-up*. The option to communicate person-to-person with the company in case of unresolved queries or concerns.
- *Ability to check status*. The ability to check location of goods, or the status of an order, the latest estimated time of arrival of an engineer, or a bank balance.
- *Links to FAQs*. The ability to see frequently asked questions (FAQs) to deal with obvious queries.

● *Website design*. Design of websites will be crucial in attracting customers and keeping hold of them long enough to interact with the site. Good navigability and speed of downloading will be crucial. Customer's trust of the site is also a key concern that will encourage consumers to use electronic transactions. The entry of big players and major brands will encourage use. Lesser-known brands can also establish themselves by using links through major portals such as internet service providers (ISPs). Key characteristics of good websites include (Voss 2000):

- *Responsiveness*. This includes both speed of downloading information on to the screen and also the response by the organisation to a customer's request.
- *Ease of navigation*. This includes limited information on each page, developing a logical and intuitive structure to the pages, and a consistent approach throughout the site. Ease of navigation was found to be a major determinant of customer satisfaction with a website.
- *Effectiveness*. This includes the time required to perform the tasks on the web and the speed and satisfaction with the service outcome (the delivery of goods or the provision of service).
- *Experience*. Customer satisfaction with the experience of the site may not simply be limited to the above points but may also include the enjoyment of the experience itself, which will encourage customers to return to the site. A range of supportive opportunities and features such as games, music, other links, or additional information, may enhance a customer's experience of a site.

Strategies for change

Professor Chris Voss (2000) has identified several key steps in developing an e-service strategy:

● *Upgrade the current service interaction*. Improve existing web-based service by improving response times, automatic acknowledgements, improving navigation of sites etc.

● *Understand customer segments*. Identify likely users and the services that can be best offered to them via the Web.

● *Understand customer service processes and interactions*. Identify service processes, activities, costs and value to help make decisions about the best services or parts of services to make web-based.

● *Define the role of live interaction*. Identify the tasks best suited to live interaction and those best for automation.

- *Make the key technology decisions*. Just because technology is moving rapidly, do not put off purchase decisions rather than investing now, since doing so may improve competitive position but may lead to implementation problems.

- *Deal with the tidal wave*. Be prepared to deal with the significant increase in customer interaction that is associated with web-based services.

- *Customer training*. Develop ways to encourage customers to use the appropriate channels for the appropriate services.

- *Channel choice*. Make decisions about 'brick versus click': a variety of channels of communication or web only, or telephone and web, for example.

- *Web relationships*. Exploit the web experience to build relationships with customers and convert them from browsers into buyers.

As this is written, early in the twenty-first century, internet businesses are still in their infancy. One of the pioneers, Amazon.com, the book and gift retailer, has just started to make a profit. Numbers of dotcom businesses have been floated on the stock market to be initially oversubscribed, but then to drop in value as investors begin to worry as to when the promised return will be realised. There is clearly a difference here between businesses that are essentially new services built around the opportunity presented by the internet, and those that have adapted existing services to capitalise on the internet channel. Many of the latter continue to operate in more traditional formats, using the internet to provide greater channel choice for their customers. Some of the dangers of which internet services must be wary include:

- *Building high expectations*. The immediacy of internet access has many benefits. With online retail operations, customers may place their order in minutes but then wait weeks for delivery.

- *Creating a limited service offer*. Some internet services offer limited choice in order to make the customer process less complex. This may result in compromises, such as the supermarket offering only one brand of a particular category, then only in one size.

- *Focusing on the website at the expense of operational structures*. It can be too easy to focus on the more intriguing and interesting front-end systems for interacting with customers. There is still a need to put in place operational structures to deal with logistics and customer service, for example. The complex problems of moving vast numbers of goods to potentially huge numbers of end destinations, or the control and copyright protection of digital information, cannot be ignored. Likewise it is easy to underestimate the high demand for person-to-person interaction to support internet services as individuals wish to make personal contact with the organisation. While new users may need help and reassurance, both old and new users will need to be able to voice and have heard their complaints.

- *Not managing service recovery*. Internet-based services must develop new strategies for managing customer complaints. As a general principle, service recovery is usually seen to be more effective when there is genuine contact between service provider and customer, often with named people involved from the service organisation. Service organisations must work hard to create that personalisation as a feature of their service recovery mechanisms.

9.4.3   Knowledge management

As organisations grow and compete in maturing markets, competitive advantage is to be found in intangible aspects of their operations. The management of these aspects is grouped under the term knowledge management (KM). The 'know-how' that certain employees have in their heads may be an essential part of the service process, which is not written in any process definition, but its importance becomes apparent when certain employees are absent.

As a simple example, the experienced server in a restaurant will be able to assess the progress of each set of customers and almost unconsciously plan activities in such a way that customers are served efficiently and to maximum satisfaction. A new member of staff may not be able to achieve this and will be in more reactive mode, responding to customers' prompts or complaints.

At a more complex level, organisations may recognise the concept of 'causal ambiguity' – they may be good at what they do, but are not entirely sure how they achieve it. This aspect of competitive advantage is often linked with organisational culture (Chapter 14).

A common reason for the introduction of knowledge management is the desire to ensure that knowledge held by key individuals is replicated and made available to the organisation as a whole. This is particularly relevant for organisations comprising large numbers of professional staff. A corporate lawyer may build a strong personal relationship with a client and develop a deep understanding of the client's business. If the lawyer leaves the firm, the client is frequently lost to the firm as a whole. Apart from the desire to protect its business, the organisation might be more effective if information is made more widely available in order to tailor its approach to its clients more efficiently. It is not unusual to find that clients receive approaches from several staff from the same firm. This is clearly not efficient and, worse still, may not present the firm in the best light to potential clients.

Marr (2003) identifies six groups of knowledge assets in an organisation:

- *Stakeholder relationships*. Agreements, contracts and partnering agreements.
- *Human resources*. The skills, competence, attitude and loyalty of employees.
- *Physical infrastructure*. The information and communication structure, including databases and intranets.
- *Culture*. The values of the organisation and its management style.
- *Practices and routines*. Formal procedures and tacit rules.
- *Intellectual property*. Patents, designs, trademarks, copyrights and brands.

The challenge for all organisations is to ensure that these various aspects of knowledge are maintained, and not lost when key people leave. More positively, making knowledge available to the wider organisation should provide the basis for improved performance and also the opportunity for growth, particularly globally. For example, executive search organisations are now able to operate globally, drawing on their worldwide database of managers.

Approaches to knowledge management vary, but fall broadly into two categories:

- *Codification of information*. This is useful where there are discreet elements of data to be shared throughout the organisation. A good example of this approach is provided by customer relationship management (CRM) systems. CRM systems collect data about customer demographics and spending patterns in order to tailor individual approaches to customers. Financial services have invested heavily in these systems and the informational infrastructure required to support them. For the organisation there are clear benefits to be realised. All points of contact with an individual customer should be equally well informed about customer history and value. The CRM system can provide 'prompts' as to which of the company's services are likely to be most attractive, giving opportunities for more proactive selling. Critics of such systems suggest that they may be too mechanistic and fail to capture essential elements of knowledge.

- *Personalisation*. Organisations that rely on this approach tend to believe that knowledge requires a high degree of individual provider interpretation, which does not lend itself to input due to the restrictions of a database approach. This school of thought is frequently found in professional services where the idea that any employee can deal with any client, given the right information, will meet with resistance.

The Centre for Business Performance at Cranfield School of Management identifies three views on knowledge creation (Marr *et al.* 2003):

- *Autopoetics*. This group believes in the individual interpretation of knowledge and therefore sharing will be extremely difficult.

- *Cognitivists*. This group believes that collection and codification of information is the central activity in knowledge development. The core belief is that knowledge therefore can be relatively easily transferred.

- *Connectivists*. This group believes that knowledge resides in the connections between individuals in a (local) team. For example, the knowledge created by the operations management faculty in a business school is dependent to some extent on the relationships within the team.

This identification of different approaches to knowledge creation is helpful as it provides an insight into the problems experienced by organisations in implementing more formal knowledge management systems. Implementing a cognitivist approach in an organisation whose employees hold an autopoetic view is doomed from the start!

9.5 Integrating networks, technology and information

This section describes an approach to understanding how the various operational resources may be configured or reconfigured to deliver service. Armistead and Clark (1993) proposed that the development of a resource activity map of the service organisation provides an opportunity to take an overview of where resources are currently deployed in order to identify opportunities for investment, either to reduce cost or to enhance the service offering. We have adapted this approach to identify the contribution of networks, technology and information. To these we have added the other operational resources of people and materials.

It is important to note that this technique may be used to review a self-contained activity within one service organisation, or to look at the key elements of a supply chain. The example below of a domestic appliance retailer includes the design and manufacturing activities of a key supplier.

The process of developing the resource activity map follows these stages:

- Identify the main stages in service delivery.
- Allocate the activities under each major heading to the five resource categories.
- Identify the major cost drivers and places where the organisation 'adds value' for customers. Question whether the cost/value relationship is satisfactory.
- Identify links between resources: those links that are working well, those that could be developed further, and those that currently do not exist.
- Search for opportunities to improve the effectiveness of the total map, recognising that an increase in cost in one area might reduce overall cost.

Figure 9.5 shows an outline resource activity map for the service and support activities of a retailer of domestic appliances. The map identifies the major resources employed by both the retailer and its principal supplier. It identifies the strong links (those that are working well), the missing links (which may represent opportunities for improvement), and missing resources (which are under consideration for investment).

Inspection of Figure 9.5 identifies a number of issues to be resolved by the company:

- There is a strong link between service history and manufacturing schedules. Good communications and congruence of planning approaches between the service planners and the supplier's production planning activity mean that there is high availability of spare parts, critical to maintaining fast response times and high first-time fix rates.
- There is a missing link between service engineers and product designers. Experience of engineers in the field is not being captured to feed back for design improvements. Investment in hand-held terminals for engineers could perform a number of roles, including the facility to pass customer feedback to both the retailer's sales staff and the supplier's designers.
- Although customers can use the service telephone call centre, it has been identified that there are a number of potential advantages to creating a company website. This would facilitate management of customer support requests, it would provide data for customer management, and also open another channel for customer feedback for design. Although this retailer does not yet have an online sales operation, the possibility is under serious consideration.

We have shown only a few of the possible links within this particular resource activity map. Many more exist, and the map can be used as a brainstorming tool for a service development team to identify possible projects to investigate. It is worth asking two key questions in relation to a resource activity map:

Figure 9.5	Resource activity map for a domestic appliance retailer

	Supplier		Retailer			
	Design	Manufacture	Sales	Service	Logistics	Customer support
Networks		Component manufacture in China	National store network	Regional engineering territories	National distribution centre	Website
Technology	CAD system	Machines CAM system		Call monitor PDAs		Diagnostics equipment
Information	Customer and competitor information	Schedules Quality systems	Customer database	Service history Call tracking	Schedules Routes	Support diagnostics
People	Designers	Production staff	Sales staff	Engineers	Drivers Warehouse staff	Engineers Support staff
Materials	Drawings	Raw materials Work-in-progress	Product in store	Spares	Product Spares	

——— Strong links   ------ Missing links   ⬭ Missing resource

- Is it possible to save cost for the map as a whole by investing in resource in one area? In Figure 9.5, investment in information to track trends in product failure enabled manufacturing to schedule spares into its master schedule in order to reduce inventory levels and increase service levels.

- Would investment create added value, resulting in increased competitive advantage? Again in Figure 9.5, the website will not be justified on cost saving, although there are possible savings to be made. It will be justified on the basis of providing better access for the customer to obtain service and support.

This process is, like strategy development (see Chapter 13), an iterative procedure. It is important to be honest in identifying what is and what is not working well, in order to find ways of improving the total resource activity map. This is particularly valuable when considering the contribution of the whole supply chain.

9.6 Summary

Networks, technology and information are transforming service

- Networks, technology and information have enabled better operations management and have also been able to create some entirely new services.
- These developments include integrated information provision, integrated services, service on demand and intelligence networks.

Managing physical and virtual networks

- A network is a physical and/or virtual configuration of resources.
- Key decisions in managing the network include location decisions, capacity decisions, capability and resilience.
- Issues concerning the development of global networks include cultural differences, technology transfer, organisational structure, the role of each unit in the network, location decisions and the choice of partners.
- Outsourcing and off-shoring involve specialist companies managing particular operational tasks.

Managing technology and information flows

- Technology and information strategies are central requirements for service development in the majority of organisations.
- There are three main issues in managing technology and information flows: the roles for technology, the internet and service operations, and knowledge management.

Integrating networks, technology and information

- Operational resources may be configured or reconfigured to deliver service using a resource activity map.
- Such maps provide an overview of where resources are deployed and identify opportunities for investment, either to reduce cost or to enhance the service offering.

9.7 Discussion questions

1 Describe the network structure of two organisations of your choice and discuss the differences between the two.
2 Assess the physical and virtual networks of a university/college in terms of its location, capacity, capability and flexibility.
3 Select an e-service provider and assess its website and service.
4 Select a major service provider in your locality, such as an airport or supermarket. Explain the reasons for its location and assess its capability.

9.8   Questions for managers

1 What are the key problems you face in managing your networks and how are they addressed?

2 What opportunities exist for outsourcing or off-shoring your services, internal or external?

3 What is, or could be, the impact of e-service on your operations?

4 Apply the resource activity map to your operations and identify any missing links and resources.

9.9   Further reading

Gunasekaran A., Marri H.B., McGaughey R.E., and Nebhwani M.D. 'E-commerce and its impact on operations management', *International Journal of Production Economics*, vol. 75, no. 1–2, 2002, pp. 185–97.

Voss C., *Trusting the Internet: Developing an Eservice Strategy*, Institute of Customer Service, Colchester, 2000.

9.10   References

Armistead C.G. and Clark G.R., 'Resource activity mapping: the value chain in service operations strategy', *Service Industries Journal*, vol. 13, no. 4, 1993, pp. 221–39.

Berry L.L., *On Great Service*, The Free Press, New York, 1995.

Croom S. and Johnston R., 'E-service: enhancing internal customer service through e-procurement', *International Journal of Service Industry Management*, vol. 14, no. 5, 2003, pp. 539–55.

Ford D. (ed.), *Understanding Business Marketing and Purchasing*, 3rd edition., Thomson Learning, London, 2002.

Gill J., 'Some New Zealand public sector outsourcing experiences', *Journal of Change Management*, vol. 1, no. 3, 2001, pp. 280–91.

Gunasekaran A., Marri H.B., McGaughey R.E. and Nebhwani M.D., 'E-commerce and its impact on operations management', *International Journal of Production Economics*, vol. 75, no. 1–2, 2002, pp. 185–97.

Håkansson H., 'Organisational networks' in Sorge A. and Warner M. (eds), *The IEBM Handbook of Organizational Behavior*, International Thompson Business Press, London, 1997.

Håkansson H. and Snehota I., *Developing Relationships in Business Networks*, Routledge, London, 1995.

Hayes R.H. and Wheelwright S.C., *Restoring our Competitive Edge*, Wiley, New York, 1984.

Marr B., 'Consider the culture when benchmarking KM processes', *KM Review*, vol. 6, no. 5, November/December 2003, pp. 6–7.

Marr B., Gupta O., Roos G. and Pike S., 'Intellectual capital and knowledge management effectiveness', *Management Decision*, vol. 41, no. 8, 2003, pp. 771–81.

Sawhney M., 'Where value lies in a networked world', *Harvard Business Review*, vol. 79, no. 1, January 2001, pp. 79–87.

Slack N., Chambers S. and Johnston R., *Operations Management*, 4th edition, FT Prentice Hall, Harlow, 2004

Turnbull P., 'A review of portfolio planning models for industrial marketing and purchasing management', *European Journal of Marketing*, vol. 24, no. 3, 1990, pp. 7–22.

Voss C., *Trusting the Internet: Developing an Eservice Strategy*, Institute of Customer Service, Colchester, 2000.

Zhu F.X., Wymer W., Chen I., 'IT-based services and service quality in consumer banking', *International Journal of Service Industry Management*, vol. 13, no. 1, 2002, pp. 69–90.

The North Island Hospital

Robert Johnston, Warwick Business School, and Elaine Palmer, University of Auckland, New Zealand

Rod Dowling is the chief executive of the North Island Hospital (NIH) in New Zealand. His clinical directors had just submitted a report for some new laser technology that treats kidney stones. This would require a capital outlay of NZ $1,500,000, for equipment that would only be needed two and a half hours per week. While this seemed to make little financial sense, the medical case was compelling.

Lithotripsy is the diagnosis and treatment of kidney stones. The traditional treatment involves radiography to locate precisely the stone or stones in the patient's kidney and then surgical removal under a full anaesthetic. Both these treatments are not without risk and require four to eight days' post-operative recovery. However, these operations can be carried out routinely using the existing theatres, urologists, nursing staff and equipment.

The new laser treatment represents a significant advance on previous treatment. It is non-invasive and in essence 'explodes' the kidney stones through precisely directed laser beams. The resultant particles are then small enough for the patient to pass with their urine. The procedure does not require any anaesthetic. After treatment patients need to be observed for an hour or so in a post-operative area and then spend three hours in a day unit, where they are encouraged to drink quantities of water. Patients can go home the same day. The specialist laser equipment needs to be operated by a technician.

Current numbers of patients requiring treatment for kidney stones at the NIH are running at just less than 100 per year. The hospital charges its patients for treatment as per Table 9.3, with the average costs for removal of kidney stones being around NZ $8,500 (UK £2,600). (The theatre charge is a standard charge, which covers the use of the facilities and equipment depreciated over three years.)

Although the new laser equipment is compact, theatre space is at a premium at the NIH and Rod Dowling is already under pressure to build a new theatre (at an estimated cost of NZ $500,000). Rod is aware that the four other hospitals on the Island are using the traditional treatment for kidney stones. (The five hospitals lie around the perimeter of the Island at about 320-kilometre intervals.) Rod starts to wonder if he could provide laser treatment to all patients on the North Island – maybe he could zap patients by internet or use 'star wars' technology?

Table 9.3 Charges to patients

Traditional treatment

Radiography services	15 mins @ $500/hr
Use of operating theatre	60 mins @ $1000/hr
Anaesthetist	60 mins @ $900/hr
Urologist	60 mins @ $1100/hr
Theatre nursing	90 mins @ $100/hr
Post-op care	6 days @ $900/day

Laser trreatment

Laser technician	60 mins @ $500/hr
Use of operating theatre	60 mins @ $1000/hr
Theatre nursing	90 mins @ $100/hr
Post-op care	4 hours @ $900/day

Questions

1 Assess the advantages and disadvantages of investing in the new technology for the hospital and its patients.

2 What advice would you give Rod?

part four

Performance management

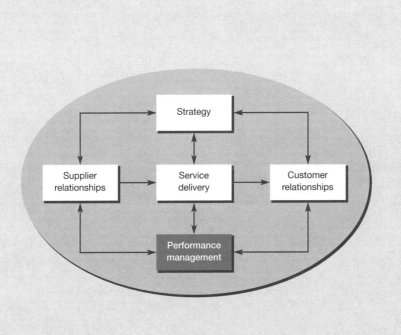

chapter ten

Performance measurement

Chapter objectives:

- to identify the purpose of performance measurement and ensure it is being met

- to encourage the use of a balance, or mix, of measures in measuring performance

- to investigate the relationships between the various types of measures and the link with strategy

- to identify different types of targets and their link to improvement and rewards

- to discuss benchmarking and how it can be undertaken.

10.1 Introduction

Some organisations have turned performance measurement into an industry. They have created measures and systems that require extensive management time and effort but provide little benefit in terms of controlling or improving their performance. This chapter provides some simple but powerful tools and frameworks, which have been used to great effect in many service organisations, to assess and develop performance measures and systems that help create action and drive organisational improvement.

The art of performance measurement has moved apace recently. Indeed, we would suggest that it is becoming more of a science as managers – in particular, operations managers – try to understand the effect of their decisions. For example, before pulling one lever they need to know, with some degree of certainty, how it will affect not only their operation, but also their customers, their staff and indeed the financial state of the organisation. Although we still have a long way to go, some organisations are starting to get to grips with these linkages and also ensuring that the information they have on performance measurement is not just collected for its own sake but leads to appropriate action.

10.2 The purpose of performance measurement

Performance measurement is costly. Few organisations have calculated just how much time and energy they spend on measuring their performance. Even fewer have calculated if all their systems, procedures and person-hours spent on performance measurement provide them with value for money.

Two useful tests of a performance measure are, first, what is its purpose and, second, what systems are in place to support or achieve that purpose.

10.2.1 Purpose

There are four main purposes or reasons to take measurement: communication, motivation, control and improvement.

Communication

By measuring something the organisation is saying that it is important; conversely, by measuring everything it is implying that nothing is important! A measure therefore informs employees as to what the organisation requires them to strive for and indeed what they as an individual or a department may be accountable for. It is also an important means of communicating and implementing strategy (see Chapter 13). By measuring speed of response in answering telephone calls, for example, an organisation is saying this is important, and it is implied that employees are expected to strive to meet targets or improve the speed of answering.

Motivation

The measure, or set of measures, used by an organisation creates a particular mindset that influences employees' behaviour. If speed of response is measured but not the quality of the interaction, employees may find themselves, albeit subconsciously, compromising quality for speed. It is important therefore to have the right mix or balance of measures (see section 10.3 below) and also a set that supports the strategic intentions of the organisation (see Chapter 13).

Control

One key purpose of performance measurement is to provide feedback so that action can be taken to keep a process in control. This requires a complete control loop, with measures, targets, a means of checking deviation, feedback mechanisms and means to take appropriate action if the process is not meeting the target. This may be used to ensure consistent performance not only within an organisation but also across organisations, such as government health and safety regulations or discrimination legislation.

Improvement

Performance measures can provide a powerful means of driving improvement. Often simply by communicating a measure, improvements can be obtained. By linking measures with rewards (such as bonuses) and/or punishments (such as no job), they can motivate individuals to improve performance – assuming the individuals have control over what is being measured. Information about what pushes the process on or off target can also help individuals and organisations learn how to manage better the process involved.

10.2.2 Systems to achieve the purpose

Having established the purpose for any measure, the acid test then is to check that there are systems or procedures in place to support the achievement of that purpose. We often find that although a manager purports that a certain measure is there to help improve the performance of the organisation, there is only a flimsy and indeed sometimes non-existent process in place to drive improvements. Similarly for the purposes of control, the vital part of the control loop that is frequently missing is action to put the process back on target.

Motor Finance Company | Box 10.1

Motor Finance Company (MFC) is a subsidiary of a major bank that provides car loans. MFC deals directly with car dealers rather than the public so that when dealers are faced with customers buying a car, they are able to arrange a loan. The dealer will take down the purchaser's details and then ring MFC direct who will give them an immediate decision on a loan. The dealer is paid a commission by MFC.

Sean Williams is the senior manager at MFC, leading its performance measurement evaluation team. He explained:

The team is currently evaluating seven key performance measures that form part of our quality index. We have two key measures for controlling the operation, same-day funding (whether the loan is agreed on the day it was requested) and proposal turnaround time (how long it takes us to generate the paperwork for an agreed proposal). The volumes of loan requests we receive on a daily basis, all of which are by telephone, are very variable and so we plot turnaround time on an hourly basis. We then use statistical process control (SPC) to help identify trends and the effect of any process changes. This helps us avoid any unnecessary reaction to normal variation within the process. Same-day funding is essential to help us ascertain if targets are being met. The measures are known for each team and area and collated into a departmental measure. Feedback is provided on a daily basis to team leaders and team members. Meeting targets is linked to the bonus scheme.

We have five measures that are used to try to improve our performance: telephone response times, calls not answered, commission amendments, monies collected and recruitment lag time. Telephone response times are collected daily by the department, though not broken down by area or teams. This helps us identify the speed of service. There are no targets used for this measure, as it is simply needed to raise awareness. Two managers have access to this data. The same is true for calls not answered, though we are thinking about linking it to bonus payments.

Commission amendments can exist for many different reasons, so at a high level this gives us a useful overview of the whole commission process, though in fairness there is little we can do to change things. We have been measuring monies collected recently and it has certainly raised awareness in the Collections Department. In the past we just measured how many cases each person was dealing with. Monies collected seems to be much more useful. While there is no systematic use of

recruitment lag time to improve the process, just the communication of this measure has helped people understand how we are doing. I reckon this has resulted in vast improvements.

Although this is early stages, we have put considerable effort into the development of the individual measures, which are believed to be robust and informative. On reflection it seems that some are used systematically whereas others are merely reported; maybe we need to give more attention to the purposes of measures and the systems to support them.

Question

1 How well do you think the measures used by MFC meet its desired purposes?

This illustration is based on a real organisation, although all names and places have been changed.

Displaying performance measures

One important way of using measures to achieve their purpose is to have a means of displaying the measure. While most managers recognise that displaying only a small number of measures is helpful, the way in which data is provided can be a key means of helping achieve its purpose.

Figure 10.1 shows a display for a single (important) performance measure – errors in a process – which includes four quadrants. Rather than simply showing the figure (in this case percentage errors) for this month (February), the chart (top left) provides a clear view of the trend and the associated target, thus allowing changes over time to be seen. The top right quadrant provides an analysis of February's data to identify the most frequent source of errors. As a result of the analysis, the bottom right quadrant reports on the actions to be taken to try to deal with the most common errors, who will be responsible for taking the action and by when they should report. The final quadrant provides an implementation record that checks the impact of previous action plans: who was supposed to do what, by when, and the effect that it had. The chart also displays the purpose or objective of the measure in the centre, with the person responsible for the measure and follow-up actions top right.

We would suggest that performance measurement reports should include only a small number of key measures and that for each measure there should be a display of:

- the purpose/objective
- the person responsible
- trends over time
- performance against target

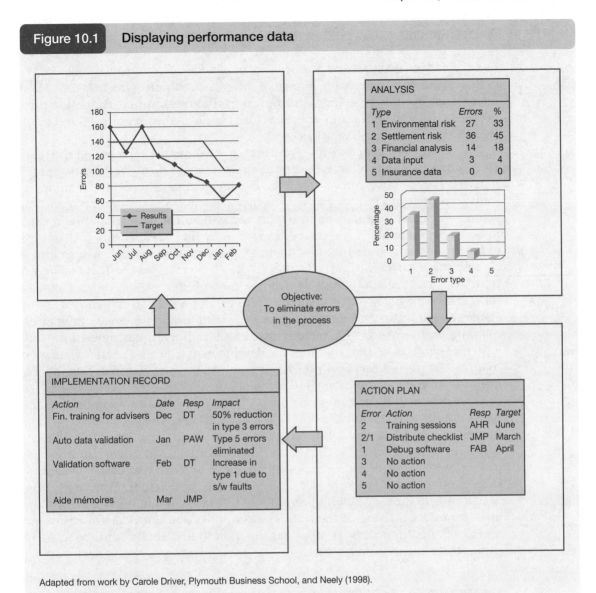

Figure 10.1 Displaying performance data

Adapted from work by Carole Driver, Plymouth Business School, and Neely (1998).

- supporting data and analysis
- identification of causes/problems
- action to be taken, by whom and by when
- an assessment of action taken.

10.3 A balance of measures

Just as companies compete on a wide range of dimensions, so organisations need to evaluate their performance on a range of measures, not purely financial or indeed operational. Section 10.4 deals with how organisations can understand the links between these various measures; this section considers the mix of measures available and the need to strike a balance.

The 'traditional' concerns for performance measures are represented in Figure 10.2. Senior managers tend to be most concerned about financial (F) performance measures – share price, return on capital employed, costs and profits. At an operations level the concern is perhaps for operational issues and measures (O), such as speed, productivity, equipment utilisation and staff absenteeism. The activities and indeed language of these two groups, supported by the measures they use, create a chasm of understanding that middle managers have traditionally tried to bridge (Johnston and Fitzgerald 2001). In the middle of the organisation these managers try to reconcile operations measures from below with financial needs from above – for example, the requirement to increase revenue or decrease costs is parried by the statement 'but we are already at full capacity'. Additional pressures arise from external data and measures (E), such as market share figures, customers lost, and customer satisfaction data, and from the development (D) needs of an organisation to learn, change and develop through, for example, training, research, communication, and problem identification and problem solving.

These often conflicting pressures and performance measures have been recognised and frameworks developed to help managers cope. The results–determinants framework (Fitzgerald *et al.* 1991) identifies that these pressures are of two different types: the determinants and the results. There is little use in driving an organisation only by knowing what the results (financial and external data) are because there is no means of knowing what is determining those results. Conversely, driving an organisation by determinants alone (operational and development data) gives no understanding of the results of actions taken. Both determinants and results are needed at all levels in an organisation to help understand the relationships between action and results.

Figure 10.2 Traditional performance measurement structure

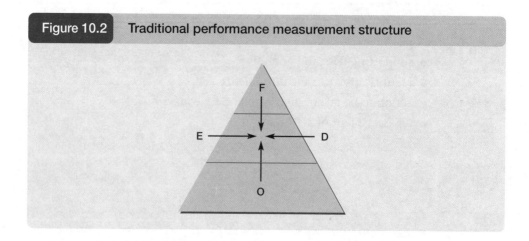

The best-known framework that encourages the use of a mix of measures is the balanced scorecard (Kaplan and Norton 1992) (see Figure 10.3).

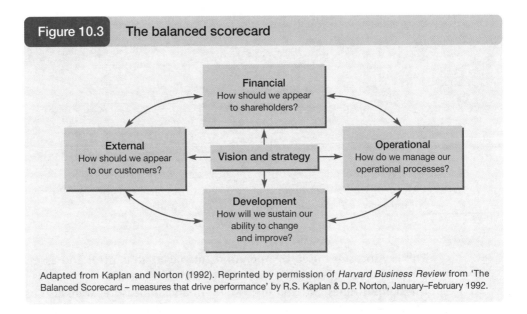

Figure 10.3   The balanced scorecard

Adapted from Kaplan and Norton (1992). Reprinted by permission of *Harvard Business Review* from 'The Balanced Scorecard – measures that drive performance' by R.S. Kaplan & D.P. Norton, January–February 1992.

This framework has had a huge impact over the last few years in encouraging managers at all levels to invest in moving to a more balanced set of measures. The framework (see Figure 10.4) changes the shape of the performance measurement structure and exposes all managers to measures of both results and determinants. This is the first stage in starting to understand the links between them (see section 10.4) and helps create a structure of performance measurement that links strategy with operations.

Research (by Brignall *et al.* 1999) into the performance measures used in service operations in the UK found that there was a reasonable balance, overall, in the mix of measures used (see Figure 10.5).

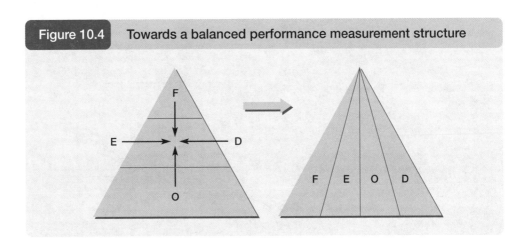

Figure 10.4   Towards a balanced performance measurement structure

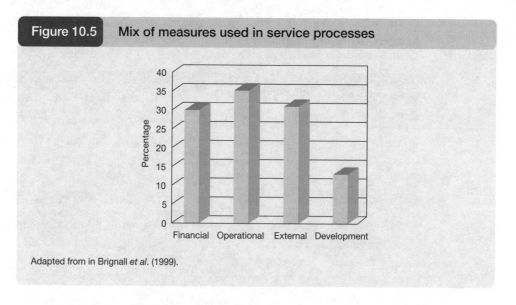

Figure 10.5   Mix of measures used in service processes

Adapted from in Brignall *et al*. (1999).

The key measures used by operations managers to control and assess their service processes were primarily internal operational measures, such as productivity, throughput times and volumes. Many financial measures were also used, for example costs and revenues. Customer-based measures such as satisfaction and market share were also in evidence. However, there was only limited evidence of the use of the fourth balanced scorecard measurement 'perspective': development, learning and growth.

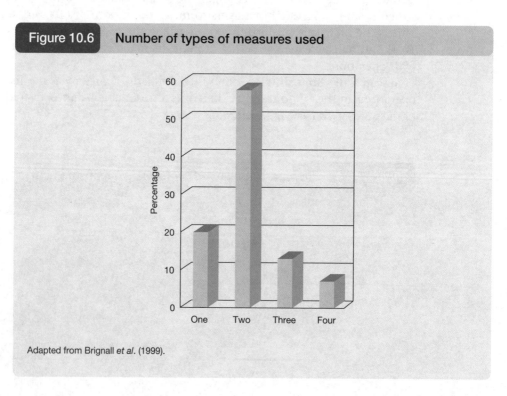

Figure 10.6   Number of types of measures used

Adapted from Brignall *et al*. (1999).

This overall picture, however, disguises the true state of affairs, as can be seen in Figure 10.6. Most operations managers were using only two types of measures (predominantly financial and internal measures). Only 15 per cent used three measures and only 7 per cent used all four types.

10.3.1 Performance measures for service operations managers

Operations managers need to ensure that they have a mix or balance of measures to communicate their intentions, motivate their workforce, control and improve their processes. Figure 10.7 provides a selection of measures that might be used, or developed for use, by service operations managers.

Customer-based measures

External data are important to allow operations managers to know how effective their actions are, yet often the measures they use to assess their processes miss out on a customer perspective. An interesting question to ask is: looking at the set of measures used by an operation, would its customers measure its performance in the same way? Measuring what is important to customers can easily be overlooked by organisations. Whereas they may well measure customer satisfaction, they may ignore, or overlook, measures of performance that are important to their customers and thus concentrate on the more comfortable and familiar operations measure of performance. Jan Carlzon, for example, when he was chief executive of SAS, noted that its cargo operations were measuring the wrong things:

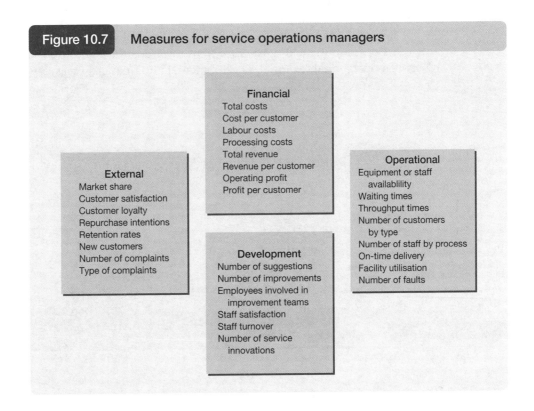

Figure 10.7 Measures for service operations managers

Financial
Total costs
Cost per customer
Labour costs
Processing costs
Total revenue
Revenue per customer
Operating profit
Profit per customer

External
Market share
Customer satisfaction
Customer loyalty
Repurchase intentions
Retention rates
New customers
Number of complaints
Type of complaints

Development
Number of suggestions
Number of improvements
Employees involved in
    improvement teams
Staff satisfaction
Staff turnover
Number of service
    innovations

Operational
Equipment or staff
    availablility
Waiting times
Throughput times
Number of customers
    by type
Number of staff by process
On-time delivery
Facility utilisation
Number of faults

We had caught ourselves in one of the most basic mistakes a service-oriented business can make [their cargo customers wanted prompt and precise cargo delivery] . . . yet we were measuring volume and whether the paperwork and packages got separated en route. In fact, a shipment could arrive four days later than promised without being recorded as delayed. (Carlzon 1987)

Several tools that can be used to help identify, and then measure, what is important to customers were provided in Chapter 3.

10.4 Interlinking

Having got a mix of measures in place, some organisations are now starting to try to understand the relationship between the various measures (see Figure 10.8) so that they can improve their decision making. This has been called 'interlinking' (Collier 1994).

By using knowledge about the relationships between operational, financial, external and development performance measures, organisations can become systematically smarter. Managers will begin to understand, with greater certainty, the likely effect of making resource decisions, which helps them set appropriate targets and better support the strategic intentions of the organisation. Indeed, we believe that tomorrow's leading-edge organisations will be those that understand and exploit these relationships. In Chapter 11 we will investigate the relationships between measures in more detail and look at how to create models to investigate and understand the relationships between the operational decisions and business performance.

In Box 10.2 Sean Guilliam, the head of Lombard Direct's call centre, explains how his operation is taking the first steps towards understanding the relationships between operational, external, developmental and financial measures.

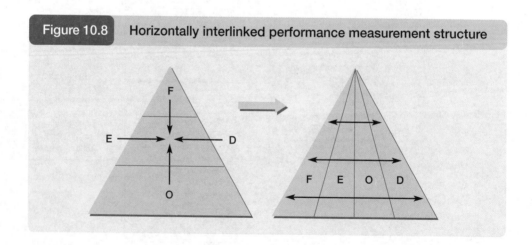

Figure 10.8 Horizontally interlinked performance measurement structure

Lombard Direct

Box 10.2

Lombard Direct must have one of the best-known telephone numbers in the UK, 0800 2 15000, which is based on their slogan 'loans from 800 to 15,000 pounds'. Lombard Direct is a subsidiary of Lombard Bank, part of the National Westminster Bank group. Unsecured loans over the telephone constitute about 90 per cent of the company's business, other products including insurance on loans, house, contents and motor insurance, savings and a credit card.

The main call centre, in Rotherham, South Yorkshire, is a 24-hour operation that operates every day of the year. The centre handles over 2 million calls a year. Monday is a typically busy day, when around 6,000–7,000 calls are received. The call centre has around 200 seats (for the customer advisers – CAs) and employs around 250 full-time equivalent staff, with a large contingent of part-timers. Callers are asked a number of questions to rate their creditworthiness and are allocated into a band. This risk assessment, together with the size of the borrowing requested, determines the rate of interest to be charged.

Sean Guilliam is the head of the call centre and he judges the performance of its CAs on six key performance measures. He explains:

We use the following measures:

- *Telephone availability – the time an individual is available to take calls.*

- *Insurance sales – because we want to encourage the people who take out loans with us to take out our insurance cover on the loans.*

- *Media and product code accuracy – it is very important for our marketing people to know where the customers heard of us. However, our systems are a bit lacking in this area and sometimes the CAs have difficulty finding the right code – there are so many!*

- *Call conversion – where we calculate the number of successful loans sold compared to the number of calls taken.*

- *CATS (Customer Adviser Technical Skills) – procedural accuracy, such as giving the right advice and adhering to data protection requirements.*

- *Call analysis – an assessment of the interactions with a customer and compliance with the correct procedure.*

We have four 'spot' levels and CAs are reviewed every three months. Each level has a set of criteria based on the six key measures. If someone attains a higher level for two assessments they go up one spot level; if they perform less well over three periods they will go down. Each level is worth about an extra £1 per hour, so it is quite significant. Also they need to get to Level 2 before we will offer them a permanent contract, though I think we need to remove this barrier and put everyone on permanent from the start to bring us in line with the industry.

At a call centre level I also monitor loan volumes, utilisation, talk time, service levels and abandon rates. Service level refers to the percentage of calls answered within 10 seconds. Utilisation is total talk time divided by total pay time (including training time and maternity, for example). Talk time is the time each operator spends talking to customers. When you compare this to telephone availability you have to be careful. Yes, you want high productivity, i.e. lots of talk time when available, but too much talk time could indicate either we need more staff because operators could be busy and we could be losing calls, or an individual spends too much time talking to customers. Similarly, when I compare loan conversions and insurance sales, although we want a good ratio of insurance sales to loans, too high a ratio might mean that staff could be doing too hard a sell. We don't want customers put off from using us again. The problem is in balancing flexibility with control! Especially when a 1 per cent increase in insurance sales can contribute a quarter of a million to the bottom line.

One of the big problems in staff schedul-ing is that call volumes are partly dependent upon marketing spend. And, just to make things interesting, volumes are also affected, as you might expect, by weather, holidays and sporting events, for example. We use the volume expectations from marketing spend to create a volume forecast, we then pro-rata this to forecast the volumes of calls we expect individuals to be dealing with: this determines the number of CAs I need and therefore the costs of the operation. I also monitor 'people measures' such as attrition, absenteeism and staff morale. It can be all too easy to trade-off volumes for morale. We have a great atmosphere here and morale is very high.

To help my planning we have created a corre-lation model that has looked at the relationships between volumes, utilisation, service levels, abandon rates, costs and 'people measures'. I can see the effect of a change in volume on all my key statistics. I want to get high utilisation, high service levels, low abandon rates, low costs and high morale. When we look at our perform-ance data we are now trying to look across the rows and not up and down. It's a new develop-ment but it's about how things link together. It helps us understand the relationships between the key variables and also helps us ask the right questions.

Questions

1 Categorise the measures used by Sean. How 'balanced' are they?

2 What are the advantages and disadvantages of the correlation model he has developed?

10.4.1 Linking measurement to strategy

A key objective of performance measurement systems and the control systems in which they are embedded is that they should link strategic planning and day-by-day operations (Brignall *et al.* 1999). Whereas interlinking helps us understand the interrelationships between variables, managers also need to ensure that they are consistent with the organisation's strategy.

Organisations that can translate their strategy into their measurement system are far better to be able to execute their strategy because:

- they can communicate their objectives and their targets (Kaplan and Norton 1996)
- they create a shared understanding of the organisation's strategic intentions
- managers and employees can focus on the critical drivers (Kaplan and Norton 1996)
- investment, initiatives and actions are aligned with accomplishing strategic goals (Kaplan and Norton 1996)
- operations managers can communicate with and influence strategic decision makers.

Based on their work with many clients around the world, performance manage-ment consultants 2GC (see www.2gc.co.uk) and Kaplan and Norton (2000) have found one of the best ways of linking measurement to strategy is using strategic linkage models (or strategy maps, Kaplan and Norton 2000). This approach, some-times referred to as second generation scorecards, tries to ensure that the objectives of all the different parts of an organisation support higher level objectives that sup-port the organisation's strategy.

Strategic linkage maps provide operations employees with:

a clear line of sight into how their jobs are linked to the overall objectives of the organization, enabling them to work in a coordinated, collaborative fashion toward the company's desired goals. The maps provide a visual representation of a company's critical objectives and the crucial relationships among them that drive organizational performance. (Kaplan and Norton 2000)

In strategic linkage models it is not the measures that cascade down the organisation through linked scorecards, but the objectives, leaving managers in the various parts of the organisation to develop their own and appropriate measures and targets to ensure they deliver their objectives. This approach not only helps to align all organisational and operational activities with strategy but also reduces the amount of unnecessary measurement and reporting that first generation scorecards and other measurement systems tend to encourage.

In Figure 10.9 we provide a simplified example of a strategic linkage model for a firm of consultants. The example depicts some of the objectives at just three levels in the organisation – head office, local office and the individual consultant – for the four main measurement areas associated with the balanced scorecard. The organisation's strategy is contained in the oblong at the top of the diagram, the objectives are contained in the ovals, and the arrows show major linkages.

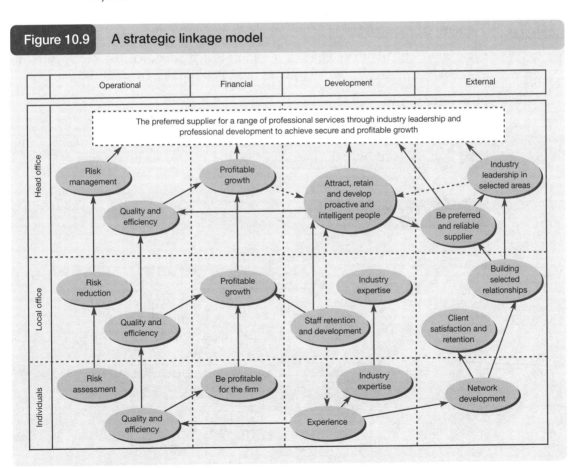

Figure 10.9   A strategic linkage model

This objective-driven approach to performance measurement has emerged as best practice from years of development around the world, because:

● they are more flexible, and easier to develop, communicate, maintain and 'cascade'
● they have been proven across a wide range of industries and functions.

10.5 Targets and rewards

While not all measures will have targets associated with them, targets can be a useful means to control performance, judge improvements, motivate employees and communicate the speed and size of the change required. Indeed, target-setting is a key element of driving performance improvement. There is evidence to suggest that performance improves when clear, defined, quantitative targets are provided (Berry *et al.* 1995). Operations managers need to decide how targets will be set for their measures to support process improvement, control communication and stimulate motivation. This section considers types of targets, the use of stretch targets, the impact of involving employees in target setting and the effect of linking targets to rewards.

10.5.1 Types of targets

There are essentially three types of target, or benchmarks, against which performance can be compared: internal, external and absolute (see Figure 10.10).

Internal targets

Internal targets are the basis of internal benchmarking. Such targets may be based upon the past performance of the process under consideration (process-based). The target is usually similar to the previous period's target, or slightly greater or lower in

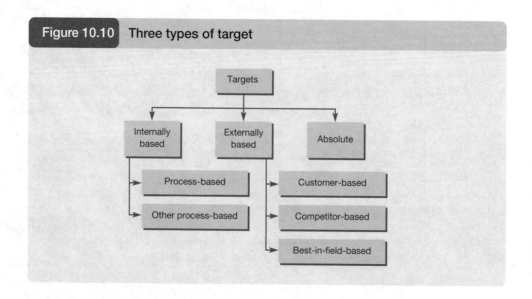

Figure 10.10   Three types of target

order to drive gradual improvements in the process. The key disadvantage of using the process itself as the base for comparison, while undoubtedly encouraging improvements in performance, is that it only provides information as to whether the operation is getting better over time rather than whether performance is satisfactory (Slack *et al.* 2004).

The targets may be based upon the performance of other similar internal processes (other process-based). This encourages comparisons across processes and the sharing of practices between them to try to meet the performance of the best. Comparison with other internal processes has the additional advantage that it provides a relative position for each process within the organisation.

External targets

External benchmarking uses targets based upon comparison with other organisations, using either competitor-based targets and/or 'best-in-field' benchmarks. Competitor-based targets are based on the performance of similar operations in other similar, competing organisations. Best-in-field benchmarks are based upon the performance achieved by organisations that may or may not be in the same industry but where the performance is considered to be outstanding.

An important, though often overlooked, external target base for service operations is customer-based targets (just as customer-based measures, too, are easily overlooked), i.e. for a particular activity, what level of service do customers consider to be appropriate?

Absolute targets

Some processes need to be operated with absolutely no defects or 100 per cent adherence to standard. It is unacceptable for life-support machines or stock-market computers or national defence systems to fail; although they do occasionally fail, with serious consequences, their operational targets are absolute.

10.5.2 Stretch targets

A critical question to ask is: by how much should the target be above the current level of performance? Essentially, this depends upon the size of the change in performance required, on the assumption that it is feasible and desirable that such a change can be made.

Internally based targets are appropriate for operations wishing to improve their performance continually and incrementally (Johnston *et al.* 2001). This would target performance improvements relative to their historical achievements. Often organisations using a continuous improvement strategy, or *kaizen* (see Chapter 13), tend to be both successful and competitive: they may have already outperformed competitors or be the best-practice leader focusing on building upon their existing strengths (Ruchala 1995).

Organisations undertaking radical change of a process should set stretch targets. These are likely to be based on external benchmarks because of the need to improve performance dramatically in relation to that of competitors (Johnston *et al.* 2001). Reference to external sources for targets, such as competitors, brings both legitimacy and a sense of urgency to those faced with the need for radical change.

Research (Johnston *et al.* 2001) has shown that few operations are actually using externally based targets to drive changes. In a study of about 40 operations in the service sector undergoing improvement, out of the 141 measures in place to help drive those improvements less than 20 per cent used externally based targets (see Figure 10.11).

In the study the researchers expected that those organisations seeking radical changes in process improvement would be predominantly using external benchmarks whereas those seeking gradual and continuous change would be using internally based targets. Although they found that most gradual changers did indeed use predominantly internally based targets, the radical changers still used external targets less than anticipated (see Figure 10.12). Perhaps many organisations, especially those seeking significant improvements, are not using externally based targets as much as they might.

10.5.3 Employee involvement in target setting

To motivate employees to try to reach a target level of performance it is essential that operators have some control over the variables that affect the performance, and also it helps if they have had a role in negotiating what that target would be, i.e. what they think is achievable. This is what one would expect to find for all processes undergoing continuous, *kaizen*-type, improvement as employee involvement and participation are central to the philosophy of *kaizen*. This approach encourages employees to address questions such as:

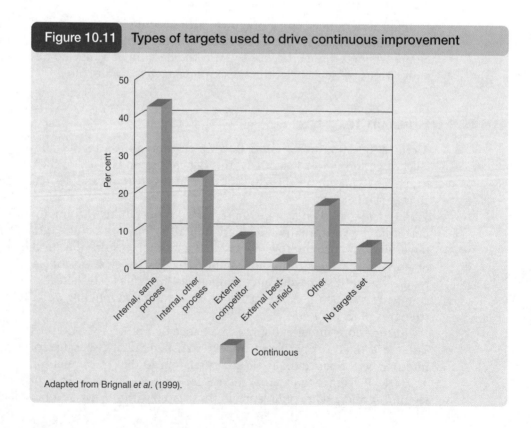

Figure 10.11 Types of targets used to drive continuous improvement

Adapted from Brignall *et al.* (1999).

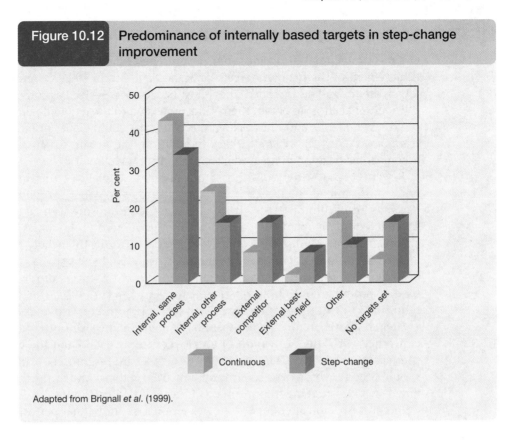

Figure 10.12 Predominance of internally based targets in step-change improvement

Adapted from Brignall et al. (1999).

- How can you improve what you are doing?
- How can you improve the process by which you are doing it?
- How can you improve the way in which you interact with other people?

This in turn requires the encouragement, support and authority (empowerment) to propose and implement these improvements, backed by a supportive organisational culture and a 'team' approach to problem-solving and improvement (Imai 1986). Because of this philosophy of empowerment, participation and involvement, where the responsibility for process improvement rests with employees rather than quality specialists for example, targets should be set through a process involving employees. The employees would decide what might be achievable over a period of time, as it is they who have the responsibility for change and the authority to carry it out.

For organisations undergoing more radical change targets may be imposed by the senior managers overseeing the change programmes on a command-and-control basis. In radical change programmes, therefore, overall responsibility may rest with senior management champions who devote a substantial amount of their time and effort to both the design and implementation of process change.

10.5.4 Linking targets to rewards

Organisations need to decide what rewards/penalties will be associated with the achievement of their chosen targets (Fitzgerald and Moon 1996). If rewards linked to targets are to work as intended, they must be clearly perceived as sufficient to justify the additional effort to obtain them, directly related to the required performance, perceived as equitable, and must take into account the complexities of individual versus team-based effort (Berry *et al.* 1995). In addition, the reward structure must also be accompanied by appropriate feedback mechanisms (Mullins 1989).

Rewards take a variety of forms, from purely financial to a mixture of financial and non-financial, such as achievement awards and other forms of recognition (Ezzamel and Willmott 1998). To be effective the rewards need to be tailored to the specific requirements of the performance improvement programmes in use within an organisation. Whilst we would would expect to find financially based rewards applied in all forms of change programmes, we would suggest that non-financial, and therefore less threatening and more encouraging, forms of reward would be used to promote continuous change. Ittner and Larcker (1995), for example, contend that continuous improvement strategies require 'reward systems that place greater emphasis on quality and team-based performance' since they are specifically concerned with the motivation of employees (Juran 1989) and the elimination of the fear of job losses (Deming 1986). Processes undergoing continuous change should therefore base their rewards on a mix of financial and non-financial rewards targeted at encouraging improvements in team-based performance.

In contrast, radical change strategies emphasise individual performance, so the performance measurement system 'should measure the location of specific results and individual employee performance' (Hall *et al.* 1993). Given the higher costs and risks associated with step-change improvements, we would expect rewards associated with such changes tend to be primarily financial in nature.

10.6 Benchmarking

A benchmark is a reference point: it was originally a surveying term for a mark cut in a building used as a base point for measuring altitude (*Concise Oxford Dictionary*). As implied in section 10.5.1, benchmarks are targets against which performance can be measured. Benchmarking is therefore the measuring of a process or an organisation against some target, whether an internal target (internal benchmarking) or an external target (external benchmarking).

However, many people use the term benchmarking to mean external, best-in-field benchmarking. Because the purpose of benchmarking is to search for the best practices that will lead to the superior performance of the organisation (Camp 1989), this usually implies seeking out best possible practices whether they are within or outside the industry.

The advantage that benchmarking provides over target setting is that by benchmarking practices against other organisations managers can gain an insight as to how the desired level of performance has been achieved by other organisations, thus suggesting how it can be achieved in their own organisation.

Benchmarking can help organisations:

1 assess how well they are performing

2 set realistic performance targets

3 search out new ideas and practices

4 stimulate creativity and performance innovation

5 drive improvement through an organisation.

The critical purpose – driving improvement (point 5) – can easily be overlooked in an organisation's desire to undertake benchmarking. Indeed, often the benefits attained get no further than 1 and sometimes 2 above. The real benefits obtained through 3, 4 and 5 are often not achieved. The reason for this is that many benchmarking activities become concerned and then bogged down with metrics – the establishment of good comparators of performance between operational processes so that an organisation can (as in 1 above) assess how well a process is performing. This tends to be a very difficult task because organisations measure things in different ways and collect different data, and so a great deal of time and effort can be spent on trying to establish a base by which performance can be compared. Once this is achieved, it is possible to evaluate the targets used and set realistic and indeed possibly stretch targets. This hopefully will lead to improvements in performance (point 5 above). This process of 'metric benchmarking' is shown in Figure 10.13.

While metric benchmarking fulfils the desire to know whether performance is relatively good or bad, it does not necessarily help managers understand how they might go about improving their own processes. Conversely, practice benchmarking (which can actually be carried out without knowing how good or bad the respective processes are) is an attempt to search out new ideas and practices and stimulate creativity and performance innovation (points 3 and 4 above). This involves seeking out ideas and practices that might be adapted for the benefit of the organisation (see Figure 10.14). It is important to recognise that this approach is further removed from the strict definition of benchmarks (creating a reference point) and much more concerned with the purpose of benchmarking: trying to achieve superior performance.

While metric benchmarking is essential for establishing whether the performance of a particular process is relatively better or worse and therefore by how much a process can be improved, practice benchmarking is important in understanding how the process can be improved. There are dangers with each approach. While the metric approach can get bogged down in discussions about 'apples' and 'pears',

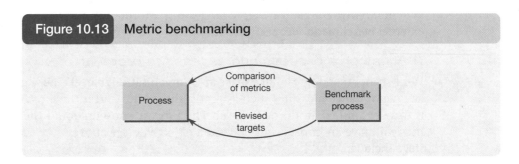

Figure 10.13 Metric benchmarking

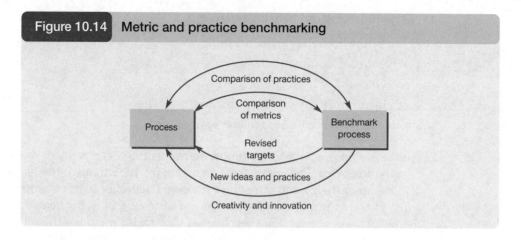

Figure 10.14 Metric and practice benchmarking

practice benchmarking can easily fall into the trap of 'industrial tourism', where managers enjoy looking at other processes and operations although those experiences may not lead to improvements. The acid test for benchmarking is whether it leads to improvement. We would recommend that organisations undertake practice benchmarking to obtain an understanding of other processes and to benefit from quick gains, and then follow this with metric benchmarking once a relationship and mutual benefits have been obtained. It is essential to keep an eye on the continuous improvements that need to be obtained from such an activity.

Benchmarking has developed into a structured and proactive process to improve operations processes (see, for example, Camp 1989). From our experiences we would suggest that there are six key steps to benchmarking.

1 Define the objectives and select type of benchmarking

It is essential to undertake benchmarking with clear objectives, to bring about not only improvements in a process, but clarity about the nature of changes required and the speed of change.

The nature of change required is a function of the organisation's strategy. Does the organisation wish to pursue a strategy of lowest price, or highest quality, or speediest delivery, or most able to customise? While all of these might be desirable at once, there is a need to concentrate on specific performance criteria to be improved and this then limits the type of organisations that might be chosen for benchmarking.

The rate of change required might also affect the benchmarking activity. The desire for continuous and incremental improvements might only require internal benchmarking. For radical step-changes in performance one might expect to use external benchmarks (see section 10.5.2).

2 Focus on a process and assess the process

While benchmarking can take place at an organisational level – i.e. a comparison of key performance measures such as profit, share price and turnover – benchmarking is usually applied at a process level. The process chosen should therefore be one that will have an impact on the desired objectives (see above). Key activities at this stage include:

- select an appropriate process
- define the process and its objectives
- map the process
- assess the process
- identify and define all the measures and targets used
- assess the measures and targets
- determine current performance and practices
- involve the people involved in the process.

3 Select a method of benchmarking

There are several ways of going about benchmarking. This may involve a one-to-one relationship between two organisations and indeed two particular departments. Alternatively, benchmarking data and round-table discussions may be facilitated by a third party, such as a benchmarking club or an industry body. Or benchmarking may be part of a large-scale assessment activity such as that by the European Foundation for Quality Management (EFQM) (see Chapter 11), where one organisation's performance is compared to many other organisations and questions raised that may lead to changes in practice. Other benchmarking mechanisms specifically designed for service organisations have been developed recently including Service Probe, national customer satisfaction barometers/indices, and one dealing specifically with complaints – the Complaints Management Excellence Programme.

- *Service Probe.* This is a well-developed, refined and tested instrument that benchmarks service organisations against a database on many aspects of the drivers and results of business performance. With over 100 questions, it provides organisations with a detailed understanding as to how they stack up against other service organisations, in total and by sector, on a wide range of criteria, such as management style, service culture, employee management, service quality, service design and development, delivery system and processes, service effectiveness, service recovery and business performance. The questionnaire is administered by the Confederation of British Industry (CBI) in London, England.

- *National customer satisfaction barometers/indices.* The first national customer satisfaction index for domestically purchased and consumed products and services was established in 1989 – the Swedish Customer Satisfaction Barometer (SCSB) with an original database of 130 companies from Sweden's largest industries (Fornell 1992). The American Customer Satisfaction Index (ACSI) was introduced in 1994, and other barometers have been introduced more recently in Europe, New Zealand, Austria, Taiwan and Korea. These instruments all use multiple survey items to operationalise quality, satisfaction, loyalty and other constructs as latent variables within a drivers–results model.

- *The Complaints Management Excellence Programme.* This is a detailed benchmarking instrument with over 200 questions assessing many different aspects of complaint management. It is based on a drivers–results model and provides detailed feedback, positioning participating companies against a database in terms of their employee practices and attitudes, complaint processes, customer satisfaction and financial benefits, for example. The programme is administrated by the Customer Service Network, in Cheddar, UK.

4 Select partner(s) (for one-to-one benchmarking)

The type of organisations selected for benchmarking will in part be determined by the level of benchmarking selected and the performance objectives for that particular process. For best-in-field benchmarking it is important to 'think outside the box' and to move away from traditional sources of comparison to seek out truly different and challenging good performance.

5 Deal with the partner(s) (for one-to-one benchmarking)

It should be remembered that benchmarking is not a one-way activity, and that both partners can and should gain a great deal from it. Indeed it is through benefits going both ways that a benchmarking activity will stay alive and purposeful. Some key points for dealing with benchmarking partners are the following:

- look for win-win outcomes
- start with practice benchmarking
- discuss step 1 above with partners to ensure there is comparability of objectives
- help partner undertake step 2
- set up regular meetings to discuss practice and methods of improvement
- evaluate relative performance through joint definition and agreement of measures and performance levels
- focus on improvement.

6 Improve performance

Given the intricate and often difficult tasks outlined above, it is understandable why the improvement objective can be missed – so much time and effort is involved in the process of benchmarking. This sixth stage is the most critical, and indeed there should be performance measures in place to assess the benchmarking activity and these should be about improvements created. The UK school performance or 'league' tables described in Box 10.3 highlight some of the problems of providing comparative performance data, and question the benefits of this activity.

Some key activities that can help realise improvements as a result of benchmarking include:

- assess differences
- focus on improvement – the 'how'
- focus on the rate of improvement
- focus on action
- develop stretch targets, coupled with action plans to achieve the targets
- draw up improvement plans
- adapt not adopt
- assess results against objectives (step 1 above).

School performance tables
Box 10.3

Since 1996 the UK Government's Department for Education and Employment has published performance tables for schools. Tables for secondary schools present statistics on such things as examination performance and the extent of unauthorised absence. These tables appear to be very useful for parents wishing to find out which school to send their child to, rather than having to rely on a school's reputation in the area or trying to make a judgement based on meeting the headteacher.

One of the prime measures for a school teaching 16-year-olds, the school leaving age, is the percentage of students achieving good grades in nationally recognised qualifications. These are the General Certificate of Secondary Education (GCSE) and General National Vocational Qualification (GNVQ). Performance statistics are produced for each school, showing the trend in its achievement for recent years, its position against other schools in the same local education authority, and comparison with national statistics.

These statistics have great appeal for government ministers, not least because the current tables at national level show a continuing rise in the percentage of students achieving good GCSE/GNVQ grades. It is clear, however, that not everyone is happy with these tables. In an article published on BBC News Online in 1998, Dr Keith Devlin of St Mary's College, California, said that it was very dangerous to take numbers developed to deal with the inanimate world and apply them to the world of people with all of their imprecision and unpredictability.

The need to be aware of the impact of chance is confirmed by others. Professor Ted Wragg of Exeter University, also reported by BBC News, suggested that there were not enough children in the individual schools to make the figures statistically significant, although clearly the national statistics are not a problem. A senior teacher commented that schools that are in prosperous catchment areas perform relatively consistently, but those in poorer areas seem to oscillate, having alternate good and bad years. He said that this 'yo-yo' effect can be very demoralising to staff who feel that they are judged on statistics that, to some extent, may be outside their control.

Some teachers feel that the statistics may be positively dangerous. This may be in part due to the reluctance of professionals to be measured by an external agency, but teachers are also concerned that reducing the performance of a school to a limited set of statistics may mislead parents. The figures, for example, do not demonstrate how well the school has developed the gifted student, the one who would perform well in almost any circumstance, nor do they indicate whether genuine learning has taken place as opposed to good preparation for examinations.

There is also concern that the statistics may be used to remove underperforming teachers, using information which could be flawed. As a result, some teachers spend time ensuring that their figures are presented in the best possible light, knowing that unhelpful conclusions may be drawn if the school is seen to be failing using this set of statistics. There is frustration that so much emphasis is placed upon school performance tables, particularly since they do not appear to present a fair and rounded picture of the school.

There is growing interest in the concept of value-added, which would measure the progress of the child from entry to exit. This would undoubtedly put some of the schools in poorer areas in a higher position in the league table than they currently occupy. Professor Ted Wragg has suggested that the adoption of the value-added concept would send shock waves through the education system, not least because some schools, traditionally seen as excellent performers, might slip down the rankings because they were working with good 'material' (students) in the first place. There are signs that this approach is gaining support, with education authorities placing more emphasis on the process of learning rather than simply examination success.

By undertaking benchmarking, success is not guaranteed. Indeed benchmarking can be a very slow and costly activity. It requires a culture that supports learning and improvement, together with the necessary investment and allocation of staff to undertake the work.

10.7 Summary

Purpose of performance measurement

- Performance measurement is a costly activity and should provide value for money.
- Performance measures can be assessed in terms of their ability to facilitate communication, motivation, control and improvement.

A balance of measures

- A balanced set of measures includes operational, financial, external and developmental measures.
- Having a balanced set of measures is the first step towards understanding the relationships between them and corporate strategy.

Interlinking

- Interlinking is about using knowledge about the relationships between operational, financial, external and development performance measures.
- Tomorrow's leading-edge organisations will be those that understand and exploit these relationships.

Targets and rewards

- Target setting is a key element of driving performance improvement.
- There are three main types of targets, or benchmarks, against which performance can be compared: internal, external and absolute.
- To link rewards to targets requires the rewards to be seen as sufficient to justify the additional effort required, be directly related to the required performance, be perceived as equitable, take into account individual versus team effort, and be accompanied by appropriate feedback mechanisms.

Benchmarking

- Benchmarking is the measuring of a process or an organisation against some target: an internal target (internal benchmarking) or an external target (external benchmarking).
- Benchmarking can help managers:
  - assess how well they are performing
  - set realistic performance targets
  - search out new ideas and practices
  - stimulate creativity and performance innovation
  - drive improvement through an organisation.

10.8 Discussion questions

1 Key measures used by some call centres are speed of response and call abandonment rate. Assess these measures as drivers of improvement.

2 A tour operator specialising in holidays for young people is concerned about the quality of service provided. Each month the marketing manager reports on the number of complaints received. How could this be better reported to help the firm improve its service?

3 Select a process you are involved in, such as being taught, cooking, cleaning etc. What might be the benefits of benchmarking this process and with whom could you compare your performance? How would this lead to the benefits identified?

10.9 Questions for managers

1 Assess the purposes, and systems to deliver the purposes, for your key measures.

2 Evaluate the mix of measures used at various levels in your organisation. What are the implications of this?

3 Evaluate some of your operational targets. How could benchmarking help?

10.10 Further reading

Cobbold I. and Lawrie G., 'The development of the balanced scorecard as a strategic management tool', paper presented at the PMA Conference Boston, 2002, available at www.2gc.co.uk

Johnston R., Brignall S. and Fitzgerald L., 'Good enough performance measurement: a trade-off between activity and action', *Journal of the Operations Research Society*, vol. 53, no. 3, 2002, pp. 256–62.

Kaplan R. and Norton D., 'Having trouble with your strategy? Then map it', *Harvard Business Review*, vol. 78, no. 5, September–October 2000, pp. 167–77.

Neely A., *Measuring Business Performance*, The Economist Books, London, 1998.

10.11　References

Berry A.J., Broadbent J. and Otley D. (eds), *Management Control: Theories, Issues and Practice*, Macmillan Press, Basingstoke, 1995.

Brignall S., Fitzgerald L., Johnston R. and Markou E., *Improving Service Performance: A Study of Step-change versus Continuous Improvement*, CIMA, London, 1999.

Camp R.C., *Benchmarking: The Search for Industry Best Practices that lead to Superior Performance*, ASQC Quality Press, Milwaukee, Wis., 1989.

Carlzon J., *Moments of Truth*, Ballinger, Cambridge, Mass., 1987.

Collier D.A., *The Service/Quality Solution: Using Service Management to Gain Competitive Advantage*, Irwin and ASQC Quality Press, New York, 1994.

Deming W.E., *Out of the Crisis*, MIT Center for Advanced Engineering Study, Cambridge, Mass., 1986.

Ezzamel M. and Willmott H., 'Accounting, remuneration and employee motivation in the new organisation', *Accounting and Business Research*, vol. 28, no. 2, 1998, pp. 97–110.

Fitzgerald L. and Moon P., *Performance Measurement in Service Industries: Making it Work*, CIMA, London, 1996.

Fitzgerald L., Johnston R., Brignall T.J., Silvestro R. and Voss C., *Performance Measurement in Service Businesses*, CIMA, London, 1991.

Fornell C., 'A national customer satisfaction barometer: the Swedish experience', *Journal of Marketing*, vol. 56, 1992, pp. 6–21.

Hall G., Rosenthal J. and Wade J., 'How to make re-engineering really work', *Harvard Business Review*, vol. 71, no. 6, 1993, pp. 119–31.

Imai M., *Kaizen: The Key to Japan's Competitive Success*, McGraw-Hill, New York, 1986.

Ittner C. and Larcker D., 'Total quality management and the choice of information and reward systems', *Journal of Accounting Research*, vol. 33 supplement, 1995 pp. 1–34.

Johnston R. and Fitzgerald L., 'Performance measurement: flying in the face of fashion', *International Journal of Business Performance Measurement*, vol. 3, nos 2/3/4, 2001, pp. 181–90.

Johnston R., Fitzgerald L., Markou E. and Brignall S., 'Target setting for evolutionary and revolutionary process change', *International Journal of Operations and Production Management*, vol. 21, no. 11, 2001, pp. 1387–403.

Juran J.M., *Juran on Leadership for Quality, an Executive Handbook*, Free Press, Homewood, Ill., 1989.

Kaplan R.S. and Norton D.P., 'The balanced scorecard – measures that drive performance', *Harvard Business Review*, January–February 1992, pp. 71–9.

Kaplan R.S. and Norton D.P., *The Balanced Scorecard*, Harvard Business School Press, Boston, Mass., 1996.

Kaplan R. S. and Norton D.P., 'Having trouble with your strategy? Then map it', *Harvard Business Review*, vol. 78, no. 5, September–October, 2000, pp. 167–77.

Mullins L.J., *Management and Organisational Behaviour* (2nd edition), Pitman, London, 1989.

Neely A., *Measuring Business Performance*, The Economist Books, London, 1998.

Ruchala L., 'New, improved or re-engineered?' *Management Accounting*, December 1995, pp. 37–41.

Slack N., Chambers S. and Johnston R., *Operations Management*, 4th edition, FT Prentice Hall, Harlow, 2004.

The Squire Hotel Group   Case Exercise

The Squire Hotel Group (SHG) runs a chain of 20 hotels, with between 40 and 120 bedrooms, in locations that include Oxford, Warwick and Southport. SHG sees itself in the three-star market, with hotels that have their own personality and style, providing high-quality food and service at an affordable price. The majority of mid-week guests are commercial clients. The normal mid-week occupancy rate is about 80 per cent. Weekend occupancy is about 30 per cent, comprising mainly weekend-break packages. The company does not have any major expansion plans but is trying to strengthen its existing market position.

Squire's managing director, Justin Palmer, believes that it has a high degree of customer loyalty in the commercial sector. He explains:

The hotel managers are expected to integrate with their local community through Chambers of Commerce and Round Tables, primarily to gain visibility but also to demonstrate a local and caring attitude. The image they try to create is a good-quality, small and friendly hotel that local business can rely upon for their visitors. The hotel managers are expected to work hard to develop personal relationships with local firms and may also try to promote other hotels in the chain for any 'away' visits. We get most of our repeat bookings because of the reputation we have developed for the quality of our food and attentive and courteous service.

The Squire Hotel Oxford has 41 bedrooms and is situated close to Magdalen College. The entrance lobby is small but pleasantly decorated. The room is dominated by a grandfather clock and an elegant mahogany desk. 'I do not like the traditional counter arrangement', explained Charles Harper, the hotel's manager. 'I like a simple, open and friendly situation with a clear desk to demonstrate our uncluttered and caring attitude. Even our computers are kept in a small room just off the lobby, out of sight. I want my guests to feel that they are

important and not just one of the 70 that we are going to deal with that evening.'

SHG's hotel managers are totally responsible for their own operations. They set staff levels and wages within clear guidelines set by head office. Although pricing policy is determined centrally, there is scope for adjustment and they can negotiate with local firms or groups in consultation with head office. Charles Harper added: 'Every year, each hotel manager agrees the financial targets for his own operation with head office, and if the manager does not reach his target without good reason, he may well find himself out of a job. I believe that it is my job to be constantly improving and developing this business. This is naturally reflected in the yearly profit expectations.' The hotel managers report performance to the group monthly on four criteria: occupancy, profit, staff costs and food costs. The information provided allows senior managers to drill down to the costs of individual people and meals.

Charles Harper explained:

My job is to try to get and maintain 100 per cent occupancy rates and keep costs within budget. During the tourist season Oxford has more tourists looking for beds than it has beds, so in the peak season, which is only two months long, we expect to achieve 100 per cent utilisation of rooms. Indeed, I am budgeted for it. This has been a bad year so far. The high value of the pound has kept many American tourists away and our occupancy has sometimes been as low as 90 per cent. In the off-season our occupancy drops to 60 per cent – this is still very good and is due to our excellent location. In the peak season we charge a premium on our rooms. This does not cause any problems, but our guests do expect a high standard of food and service.

We get very few complaints. Usually these are about the food, things like the temperature of the vegetables, though recently we had a complaint from two elderly ladies about the juke-box in the bar. We don't have any formal means of collecting information about quality. Head office may come and check the hotel once or twice a year. We always know when they are coming and try to look after them. We don't use complaints or suggestion forms in the bedrooms because I think it tends to get people to complain or question the service. However, I do try to collect some information myself in order to get an indication from guests about how they feel about the quality or the price. I don't document the results, but we know what is going on. Our aim is to prevent complaints by asking and acting during the service.

I have 40 staff, most of whom are full-time. Ten work mainly on the liquor side, 20 on food and 10 on apartments. There is a restaurant manager and a bar manager. Staff turnover is 70 per cent, which compares very well with most hotels, where turnover can be as high as 300 per cent. In general the staff are very good and seem to enjoy working here.

The restaurant at the Squire Hotel in Oxford has 20 tables with a total seating capacity of 100. The restaurant is well used at lunchtime by tourists and visitors to the local colleges and by local business people. However, there are several excellent and famous restaurants that tend to draw potential customers and even hotel guests away from the hotel restaurant in the evenings.

The restaurant managers have considerable discretion in menu planning, purchasing and staffing, providing they keep to the budgets set by head office. These budgets specify, for example, the food and staff costs for an individual breakfast, lunch and dinner. Overall food costs and staff costs are reported weekly to the hotel manager. The style of restaurants in the hotels varies considerably from carvery to à la carte, with the decisions made on the basis of the type of hotel and the requirements of the local community. Elizabeth Dickens, the restaurant manager, explained:

My job is concerned with keeping to food and staff budgets, and so most of my time is taken up with staffing, purchasing and menu planning. At lunchtime, for example, I provide four items, three traditional and one vegetarian, and these change weekly. We aim to serve a main course within 15 minutes of taking an order. I am constantly looking for new ideas for our menus and better ways of serving but I am constrained by continually tightening budgets from head office. I think we have now reached the point where we are starting to lose many of our established customers. We really do need to respond to the changing demands of our customers in terms of speed of service, particularly at lunchtimes, and changes in diet together with the desire for a greater and more interesting range of meals. I think head office is out of touch with reality.

Questions

1 Evaluate the performance measures in place at the Squire Hotel Group.
2 What improvements would you suggest?

chapter eleven

Linking operations decisions to business performance

Chapter objectives:

- to discuss the need to understand cause–effect relationships between operational decisions and business performance

- to develop a framework – the service performance network – to try to capture these relationships

- to identify the key stages in developing a network

- to define world-class service and its key characteristics.

11.1 Introduction

It is important that operations managers understand the impact of any changes they make to their delivery system. Although we can usually calculate or estimate the costs associated with any particular change or initiative, we are often much less certain of their impact on the organisation's wider business performance, for example an increase in customer satisfaction, retention, revenues, market share and profit.

Many management decisions are simply an act of faith, based upon a well-intentioned belief that actions and decisions will be to the benefit of the business. We believe that most managers have little evidence to support their actions. This chapter, therefore, sets out to identify the relationships between operations actions and business performance, and demonstrates that world-class performance is achieved through understanding and exploiting these relationships.

11.2 The relationship between operational decisions and business performance

In most organisations the cause–effect relationships between operational decisions and business performance are extremely complex, involving many factors with inherent lags and delays in their relationships. This complexity is enough to put off many managers, who retrench into 'seat-of-the-pants' management. We believe that leading-edge organisations are now moving beyond intuition-based management and are working at understanding the links between their operational drivers and business results (Figure 11.1).

For example, as a result of data collection and analysis some organisations understand the relationships between their operational drivers of service delivery performance, such as employee involvement, or improved complaint management systems, or customer management, and the resulting impact on customer satisfaction, retention and profit.

The Sears company, for example, has made great strides in understanding these relationships in an initiative driven by its chief executive, Arthur Martinez. In Box 11.1 two Sears vice-presidents, Anthony Rucci and Steven Kirn, and a past vice-president, Richard Quinn, explain the organisation's understanding of the relationship between some of the key variables.

Figure 11.1	Linking results and drivers

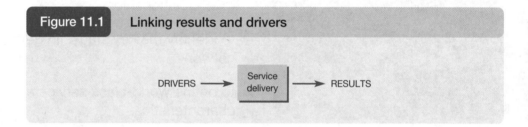

Sears, Roebuck and Co.   Box 11.1

R.W. Sears Watch Company, founded in Minneapolis in 1886 by Richard Sears, has developed into one of the largest stores and mail-order businesses in the USA – Sears, Roebuck and Co. Although the company was one of the early pioneers of mail-order shopping, in 1925 it branched out into retail stores. By 1997 Sears operated 833 department stores and 1,325 furniture, hardware and car parts stores. In addition, Sears sells appliances, hardware and car parts through 1,384 independently owned stores. Sears continues to provide home shopping and other home services. The company's turnover in 1998 was over $41 billion.

The company is known for its innovation and creativity. Back in 1906 Sears was facing significant operational difficulties following the opening of its new 3 million square feet mail-order plant (the largest business building in the world at the time). After a good deal of experimentation the mail-order executives introduced a system that involved scheduling of individual orders through the plant to the shipping of goods. This was facilitated by an intricate system of belts and chutes. This method of controlling and transporting items around the plant system led to a ten-fold increase in volumes handled. The operation became a sort of 'seventh wonder' of the business world and Henry Ford is reported to have visited the Chicago plant to study the assembly-line technique used in the system.

More recently, creativity has been applied to understanding the linkages between employee policies and profit. Two vice-presidents, Rucci and Kirn, and a past vice-president, Quinn, explain: 'The basic elements of an employee–customer–profit model are not difficult to grasp. Any person with even a little appreciation in retailing understands intuitively that there is a chain of cause and effect running from employee behaviour to customer behaviour to profits.' Many companies do not have a grasp of these relationships, but Sears claims that it does, as a result of data collection, analysis and modelling. Rucci, Kirn and Quinn add:

We understand the several layers of factors that drive employee attitudes, and we know how attitudes affect employee retention, how employee retention affects the drivers of customer satisfaction, how customer satisfaction affects financials and a great deal more. We have also calculated the lag time in any of those metrics and a corresponding change in financial performance, so that when we see a shift in, say, employee attitudes, we know not only how but also when it will affect our results.

Questions

1 What are the benefits of understanding the links between the variables mentioned above?

2 What do you think the problems are in trying to understand the links between the drivers and results?

This illustration has been developed from material from www.sears.com and Rucci *et al.* (1998).

11.2.1 Chains of cause and effect

We believe managers need to try to understand the chains of cause and effect between their operational drivers and business performance so that they know how to get the right response – and the most effective one – from their limited resources. What is needed is a method or framework to help managers do this. Over the last few years several tools have been developed to try to give managers a better understanding of these relationships, such as the balanced business scorecard (Kaplan and Norton 1996), the service profit chain (Heskett *et al.* 1997), the results determinants framework (Fitzgerald *et al.* 1991), the performance pyramid (Lynch and Cross 1991), return on quality (Rust *et al.* 1995) and the business excellence model (EFQM 1999).

11.2.2 Awards for excellence

The use of such tools and frameworks has been spurred on by the interest in, and proliferation of, quality awards, so much so that many organisations are incorporating such cause–effect frameworks into their decision-making structures.

There are awards for quality in many countries in the world, supported by local quality foundations or governments that recognise outstanding organisations: the European Quality Award and the Malcolm Baldridge Award (in the USA), for example. The European Foundation for Quality Management (EFQM) was founded in 1988 by the presidents of 14 major European companies, with the endorsement of the European Commission. The European Quality Awards are presented to organisations that 'demonstrate excellence in the management of quality as their fundamental process for continuous improvement' (EFQM 1999).

Figure 11.2 EFQM excellence model

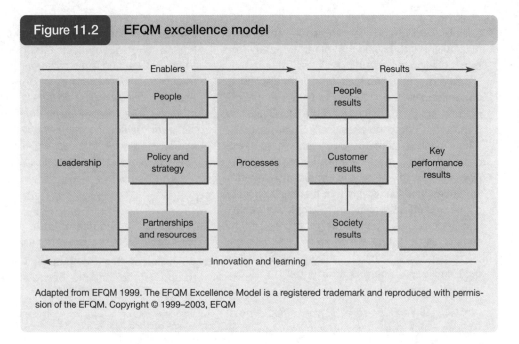

Adapted from EFQM 1999. The EFQM Excellence Model is a registered trademark and reproduced with permission of the EFQM. Copyright © 1999–2003, EFQM

The quality awards are usually based on a cause–effect model. Figure 11.2 provides the model that underpins the EFQM award. This model depicts how customer satisfaction, people (employee) satisfaction and impact on society are achieved through leadership that drives policy and strategy, people management, partnerships, resources and processes, and which ultimately leads to excellence in business results. The enablers, or drivers, are concerned with *how* the results are achieved and the results are concerned with *what* the organisation has achieved. Innovation and learning feed back to the other parts to enable a continuous cycle of improvement and development.

11.3 The service performance network

Simply stated, cause–effect thinking maintains that there are direct and strong relationships between service delivery (as a result of service design, employee management, customer management and infrastructure management), an organisation's financial performance (such as reduced costs and/or increased revenues) and broader aspects of business performance (such as improved customer satisfaction, retention and attraction).

What managers need to know is how these variables are related to one another so that they can have greater confidence in their decisions, certain that by spending £X on making decision Y there will be a return of £Z. (A return is defined as what is financially important to the organisation – for a charity this might mean greater donations; for a public-sector organisation it might mean a reduction in costs; for a for-profit organisation it might mean profit or return on capital employed.) These relationships may not be linear and so by simply spending more and more on certain aspects of service delivery, there may actually be diminishing returns: we need to be able to find the optimum points.

This section develops a network that sets out the possible relationships and then the following section goes on to explain how we can start to understand the relationships between the variables in any given organisation.

11.3.1 The service performance network

The service performance network is the combination of two networks: the interrelated set of results (the results network) and the interrelated drivers (the drivers network), and the relationships between them. At the centre is service delivery, which concerns the value of the service (experience and outcomes) as perceived by customers and/or the organisation. This service performance network can be used by both for-profit and not-for-profit organisations to help understand the relationships between operational drivers and business results.

11.3.2 The results network

The impact of service delivery on financial and broader business performance, particularly between service quality and profit, was highlighted by the PIMS study (profit impact of market strategy) (Buzzell and Gale 1987). Many ensuing studies have explored and confirmed the relationships between various elements in the network (see, for example, Georgiades and Macdonell 1998, Loveman 1998, Reichheld and Sasser 1990, Reichheld 1996, Rust *et al.* 1995, Heskett *et al.* 1997, Schneider and Bowen 1995, Schneider 1980, Anderson *et al.* 1994, Rust and Zahorik 1993, Voss *et al.* 1997, Voss and Johnston 1995, Anderson *et al.* 1997, Jones and Sasser 1995).

Drawing on all these studies, we have identified all the main results of service delivery and the relationships between these aspects of business performance (see Figure 11.3).

Service delivery → financial performance

A change in service delivery, resulting in an improved service experience and/or service outcome for the customer, may well represent a cost to the organisation and therefore have a negative impact on financial performance. Improving processes,

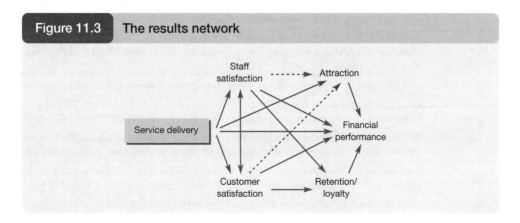

Figure 11.3   The results network

increasing staff, redesigning jobs, increasing capacity, improving quality, for example, are all likely to incur costs. On the other hand, improvements may reduce costs in the longer term. For example, an investment in an improved process, although requiring initial investment, may allow for reduced staffing levels, or improved quality may reduce the need for resources committed to dealing with problems.

Operations managers need to understand not only the balance between short-term costs and longer-term financial benefit, but also the wider-scale impact of changes to the delivery system that can have significant beneficial impacts on financial performance. Knowing these relationships moves service operations management from an act of faith to a co-ordinated and controlled activity.

Service delivery → customer satisfaction

Improvement in service delivery should result in improved perceptions of performance leading to increased customer satisfaction (this part of the chain was covered in Chapter 4). It should be noted that what satisfies customers is not just quality of the service but the perceived value of that service, including, for example, its quality, reliability, dependability, flexibility and cost.

Customer satisfaction → financial performance

Improved customer satisfaction can have a direct and positive impact on financial performance. A charity that raises its profile by increasing its impact through improved use of its resources may lead to existing donors being more satisfied with its work and willing to give more than they might have done previously. In for-profit organisations happier customers may also be willing to spend more, as Lord Marshall, chairman of BA, points out: 'Many service companies (even at the lower end of the scale) ignore the fact that there are plenty of customers ... who are willing to pay a little more for superior service' (Prokesch 1995).

Also, more satisfied customers means less dissatisfied customers, and therefore less money needs to be committed to dealing with dissatisfied customers.

Customer satisfaction → retention and loyalty

There is no shortage of evidence that customer satisfaction, both transaction-specific and overall satisfaction, has a measurable and positive impact on customer retention (see, for example, Anderson *et al.* 1994, Loveman 1998, Rust and Zahorik 1993, Rust *et al.* 1995). If existing customers are more satisfied because they have experienced a better service than before and/or better than that provided by alternative or similar suppliers, they are more likely to become repeat buyers and be more loyal. This is sometimes referred to as defensive marketing (see, for example, Rust *et al.* 1995).

The nature of the relationship between satisfaction and loyalty depends upon the nature of the organisation. Jones and Sasser (1995) conducted research between customer satisfaction and customer loyalty in 30 different organisations in five service industries and found clear but differing relationships between satisfaction and loyalty. These relationships varied from a very low propensity to switch, whatever the customer's level of dissatisfaction, to an increasing propensity to switch as satisfaction with the service declined (see Figure 11.4). In some organisations where the customers had, for example, no choice over supplier, their loyalty and repur-

| Figure 11.4 | Relationship between satisfaction and loyalty |

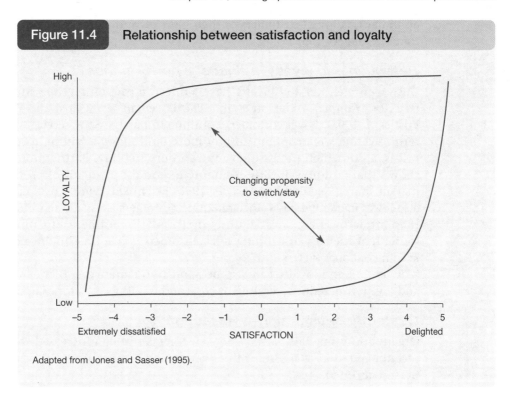

Adapted from Jones and Sasser (1995).

chase intentions were high whatever the level of satisfaction or dissatisfaction with the organisations' services. In the more competitive organisations, highly dissatisfied customers switched and delighted customers stayed. Interestingly, those customers who were just 'satisfied' were significantly less loyal than completely delighted customers. Xerox's 'totally satisfied' customers were six times more likely to repurchase Xerox products over the next 18 months than its satisfied customers. Merely satisfying customers who have the freedom to make choices is not enough to keep them loyal. The only truly loyal customers are totally satisfied customers (Jones and Sasser 1995).

The degree to which the customer is free to choose or is 'locked-in' to the service primarily depends on the nature of the organisation, switching costs and substitutability. The freedom to choose will vary considerably between monopolistic organisations or institutions, where the customer has absolutely no choice, and organisations operating in highly competitive environments. Switching costs include not only the financial costs or penalties involved in moving from one service provider to another, but also the time and effort required. Some financial institutions, for example, sell multiple products, such as current banking, loans, house loans and insurance, and so the customer may feel it is too much trouble or too difficult either to untie an individual service or to transfer all of them. Other switching costs might include an emotional tie, such as a legal firm that one's family has used for years, or where the partner is a friend of the family. Services that are easily substituted can be more easily changed. More commodity-like services, such as food, clothes and mobile telephone providers, for example, may be more easily exchanged than diagnostic, professional-type services that are based on an understanding of customers or their business and where services have been cus-tomised to meet their needs.

Retention and loyalty → financial performance

Customer retention and loyalty have a direct impact on revenue and profitability (see, for example, Anderson *et al.* 1994, Loveman 1998, Rust and Zahorik 1993, Rust *et al.* 1995). Loyal customers continue to purchase the service, generate long-term revenue streams, tend to buy more, and may be willing to pay premium prices, all of which increase revenue and profitability. Furthermore, it has been shown that customer loyalty is a more important predictor of profitability than market share (Reichheld and Sasser 1990, Reichheld 1996). Loyal customers may also lower marketing costs since retaining customers is usually significantly cheaper than attracting new ones. A study by the US Department of Consumer Affairs found that the cost of winning new customers is five times more expensive than keeping old ones (Peters 1987).

Retention and loyalty can also be applied to employees. Higher staff retention and loyalty will reduce recruitment costs and training costs, for example.

Customer satisfaction → attraction

Organisations may also attract new customers through increased word-of-mouth recommendation as a result of delivering good service to its existing customers (Rust *et al.* 1995).

Service delivery → attraction

Organisations are likely to be able to attract new customers as a result of improved or superior service delivery and their ability to advertise these improvements. This is often referred to as 'offensive marketing' (Rust *et al.* 1995). Charities known for their effective delivery systems, which have minimal overhead costs or are fast at moving into conflict areas, for example, may find it easier to attract new donors. Similarly, public-sector organisations may find it easier to attract funds if they have a reputation for good service delivery.

Attraction → financial performance

Attracting new customers may mean increased revenues and an increased market share, and, providing the services sold are profitable, this will lead to increased profit.

Service delivery → staff satisfaction

If employees perceive that service delivery is effective and/or improving, they may become more satisfied with the organisation. Fewer failures and problems and fewer complaining customers should result in a feeling of greater control over the work situation and thus less stress (see, for example, Matteson and Ivancevich 1982). In turn, less stress tends to be associated with greater job satisfaction and organisational commitment, and better job performance and health (Fox *et al.* 1993, Motowidlio *et al.* 1986).

Customer satisfaction ↔ staff satisfaction

Greater staff satisfaction leads to greater customer satisfaction as the positive and supportive behaviour of staff leads to more satisfied customers, just as greater customer satisfaction leads to greater staff satisfaction, i.e. happy staff results in happy customers which results in happy staff. This virtuous cause–effect relationship between customer and staff satisfaction has been called the 'satisfaction mirror' (Heskett *et al.* 1997). Several studies have shown a high correlation between these two variables (see, for example, Schneider 1980, Heskett *et al.* 1997, Schneider and Bowen 1995).

Staff satisfaction → retention and loyalty

Higher levels of staff satisfaction result in less stress, attrition and absenteeism and greater staff loyalty and retention.

Staff satisfaction → financial performance

High levels of staff satisfaction should have a direct impact on financial performance, through reduced absenteeism and the costs associated with this. Happier staff tend to be more productive, again reducing costs.

Staff satisfaction → attraction

Positive word-of-mouth by staff about their organisation and its services, and success at improving those services may well lead to the attraction of new customers and indeed new high-quality staff.

Understanding linkages

Not all the linkages will apply to every situation and to every organisation but by trying to unravel these linkages, managers can start to understand the direct impact of changes they make to the service delivery on the organisation's financial and broader business performance.

11.3.3 The drivers network

The drivers are the levers operations managers can apply to gain an anticipated result (see Figure 11.5). The key operational drivers are:

- process (Chapter 6)
- people, both employees and customers (Chapter 7)
- resources (Chapter 8)
- networks, technology and information (Chapter 9).

Several organisational variables have a significant bearing on the operational drivers of performance. Much of this can be summarised under the popular description of 'the way we do things around here' – what is expected, what things are rewarded and so on. Leadership is generally recognised as a key driver of sustainable success, being the ability to command attention and influence people in such a way that challenging performance objectives are achieved (see, for example, Deming 1982 and 1986, Feigenbaum 1986, Bennis 1999).

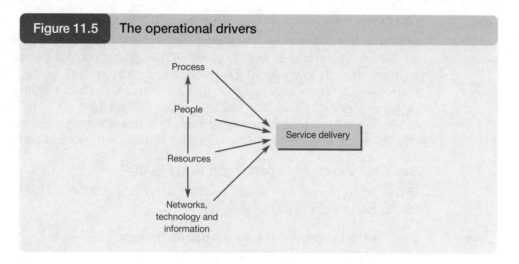

Figure 11.5   The operational drivers

To achieve these performance objectives, leaders develop, own and communicate a clear vision for the organisation. This sets the context and provides meaning for all the other activities of the organisation, its people and functions. The overarching vision of what type of organisation the leadership envisages can then be matched against the current and potential service concepts, recognising that leadership may be required to change people's perceptions as to what it is that customers are really buying. Leadership, too, is required to take an organisation into uncharted waters where a strategy cannot be formulated by rational analysis of undisputed facts alone. It is here that the vision and character of leadership are tested, as the dream is translated into tangible commitments in terms of resources and actions.

Finally, to return to the influence of culture on organisational decisions, and thence to service delivery, it is important to remember that organisational culture has a dynamic quality to it. It shifts and changes with successes and failures, and as people in the organisation interpret key decisions. They observe what is valued by leadership and then make choices as to their own actions and decisions. It is important to recognise therefore that organisational culture can and should be influenced in order to develop the required attitudes and actions. An extremely powerful means of influencing is for leaders, be they senior or junior managers, to act as role models for the desired behaviour. Including these variables completes the service performance network (see Figure 11.6).

Leading-edge research by Georgiades and Macdonell (1998) has demonstrated significant relationships between all the main variables in the network. They found high correlations between leadership, vision and culture with management practices – what we have referred to here as the operational drivers – that are correlated with staff satisfaction, customer satisfaction and profit.

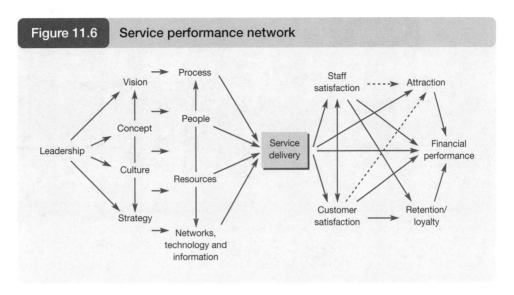

Figure 11.6   Service performance network

11.4   Key stages in developing a network

While high positive correlations have been demonstrated between the variables in the network for particular organisations or types of organisations, the strength of the individual relationships may vary considerably from organisation to organisation. For those organisations wishing to know the relative power or strength of any particular operational driver compared to another, or to create a particular effect, such as increasing the number of new customers/supporters/donors or increasing spend of existing customers or having a major impact on cost reduction, they need to understand the nature and strength of the relationships for themselves. This, at a simple level, involves three main stages: create a model, collect data, analyse the data.

11.4.1   Create a model

It is unlikely that organisations in the early stages of understanding relationships within the network will be able or willing to investigate all the possible relationships. It would seem sensible therefore to start with what are considered to be the key variables and, over time, expand the network model to a more complete model of the business.

The existing models, such as service profit chain (Heskett *et al.* 1997), service organisation profile model (Georgiades and Macdonell 1998), and the EFQM business excellence model, all use particular features and can be used directly or adapted for a particular situation. Each model takes a particular thread or threads through the service performance network. For example, an organisation wishing to focus on the effects of teamwork on staff satisfaction, customer satisfaction, and retention and profit, could take that particular thread through the network (see Figure 11.7). The limitations are clearly that only part of the variance will be explained or captured by the relationships.

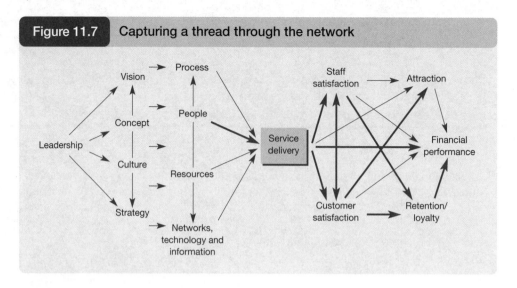

Figure 11.7 Capturing a thread through the network

11.4.2 Collect data

For many larger organisations the problem will not be data collection but finding the data within the organisation. The information on culture change, staff satisfaction, levels of empowerment, process changes, customer satisfaction, costs reductions and profit, for example, may all be collected but may be held in different parts of the business. This activity should therefore be undertaken as an organisation-wide initiative requiring top-level commitment and widespread organisational support.

Other organisations may have to start collecting data. We would recommend that considerable time be put into the planning stages of this because the longitudinal strength of the model created can be undermined by frequently changing the collection instruments.

11.4.3 Analyse the data

Simple regression analysis and graphical representations are powerful enough to permit a basic understanding of the relationships. Other, more complex methods, such as structural equation modelling (see Hoyle 1995 and Maruyama 1997, for example) and data envelopment analysis (see Norman 1991, Johns *et al.* 1997 and Andersson 1996, for example) may be considered.

The critical point is that data must be collected over time and regression analyses must be undertaken at intervals, because relationships may not be linear. It may be important to identify optimum points in the relationships between variables so that effort can be moved from one driver, whose power is waning, to one that might have an increasing effect.

Box 11.2 shows how one organisation, BUPA, has gone about understanding the relationships between some of its drivers and profit.

BUPA

Box 11.2

In 1947 17 British provident associations joined together to provide high-quality private health-care for the general public. The result was the British United Provident Association, or BUPA. Over 50 years later, BUPA is still the UK's leading independent healthcare organisation and is a major international organisation. It has nearly 4 million members in 180 countries worldwide, and has offices in Hong Kong, Ireland, Saudi Arabia, Spain, Thailand and the UK.

As a provident association, BUPA has no shareholders to pay. This means that any money it makes is invested back into the business. BUPA is best known for its private medical insurance; how-ever, it now owns and operates many associated facilities. BUPA has 36 hospitals in the UK and one in Dublin, owns and runs 34 health-screening centres, operates 221 care homes and 54 retire-ment home developments, and runs home care and nursing services. BUPA also owns Sanitas, the leading private healthcare organisation in Spain. BUPA's services also include travel, dental, disability and critical illness cover.

Catrin Weston is a senior manager in the Organisation Development Department at BUPA. She has worked closely with Dr Nicholas Georgiades of consultants TLC Ltd in attempting to validate aspects of the service value cycle which is based upon the Harvard Business School service profit chain (see Georgiades and Macdonell 1998). She describes what happens:

What we've done so far is to establish significant correlations between the results we get from our annual staff survey, our customer surveys and the profit for each of our 36 hospitals in the UK. We have been tracking the staff satisfaction score, the customer loyalty indicator and the profit for each hospital. We have calculated these correlations twice now and we will be repeating it again this autumn.

Our staff opinion survey, the service organisation profile (SOP), was developed by Dr Georgiades and TLC Ltd. They run this for us each year, which is quite a big job because around 12,000 employees and 1,000 managers

are currently involved in the survey. The SOP is an empirically developed staff opinion survey based upon the Burke Litwin model of organisation performance. The SOP provides us with a valuable way of mapping the performance of business units, departments and individual managers in the organisation. It is easy to understand and communicate and not only provides a measure of current performance but also helps managers put together action plans to work on critical issues in their work groups. The questionnaire covers ten key factors: leadership, customer service mission, adaptive culture, management practices, group climate, group tension, job satisfaction, role overload, role ambiguity and career development.

Each year we ask our staff to complete the questionnaire confidentially, and return it to TLC Ltd. TLC undertakes the analysis at an aggregate and individual manager level, so every manager gets their own feedback about how their team sees them as a manager. It also provides information about staff perceptions about BUPA as a whole – its leadership, the organisation's commitment to customer service and its prevailing culture.

When the managers receive their feedback they are charged with sitting down with their team to have an open discussion to explore the key issues. They then agree an action plan to deal with these issues. These plans are then reviewed to check progress at subsequent meetings. Some managers are good at this, others less so!

Some of the issues can't be dealt with at team level because they relate to organisation-level concerns, so every manager sends me a copy of their action plan and I go through them to identify what needs to be done at an organisational level. As a result you get a good idea what influences staff opinions.

Dr Georgiades and I have been working to test the validity of the service value cycle in the 36 BUPA hospitals. The model suggests that employee motivation, loyalty and commitment drive customer loyalty and satisfaction and that in turn customer loyalty and satisfaction drive profitability.

We took the total score on the SOP (averaged for each hospital) as the measure of motivation, loyalty and commitment, and related that score to each hospital's customer loyalty score (taken from consumer opinion surveys) and the profitability measured against target. The evidence was sufficiently strong to suggest that pursuing the goal of improving staff satisfaction, loyalty and commitment was not just a liberal 'good employer – nice thing to do' but had real, tangible results for our customers and for BUPA's profitability.

We are at an early stage in our research at the moment but it is very exciting and has already provided us with some invaluable information.

Questions

1 Identify the threads through the service performance network captured by BUPA.

2 Evaluate Catrin Weston's attempts to understand the relationship between staff satisfaction and profit.

11.5 World-class service

World-class service organisations have superior business performance that is the result of best-practice service management, i.e. superior process management, people management, resources management and management of networks, technology and information (Heracleous *et al.* 2004). In turn these behaviours result from a clear vision, a clearly articulated service concept and strategy, and an appropriate culture driven by good leadership. World-class organisations tend to have gone beyond the intuition stage and not only understand the relationships between their operations decisions and business performance but also use this understanding to tremendous effect.

11.5.1 Relationship between results and drivers

Figure 11.8 shows the relationship between an aggregated drivers score against an aggregated results score for over 100 UK service organisations. The strong positive correlation demonstrates that, overall, the better an organisation manages its drivers – such as process, people, resources, and networks, technology and information – the better will be its results, including market share, customer and staff satisfaction and profit.

Those organisations at the top right are considered to be world-class organisations, closely followed by contenders for world-class status and some promising organisations (see Figure 11.9).

Figure 11.10 shows the percentage of organisations in each of the above categories based on two studies undertaken in the UK and the USA (Voss and Johnston 1995 and Voss *et al.* 1997). Although UK service organisations have fewer world-class organisations than the USA, the USA appears to have a longer tail of poor performers (additional information can be obtained from www.severn-trent.com/usdocs).

| Figure 11.8 | Relationship between drivers and results |

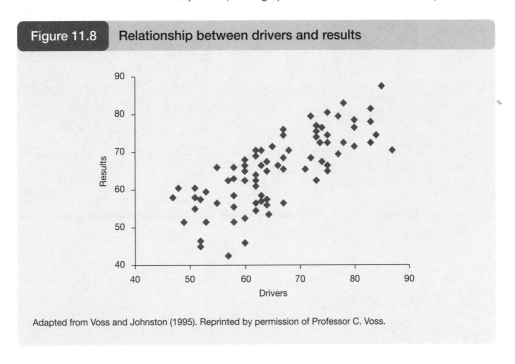

Adapted from Voss and Johnston (1995). Reprinted by permission of Professor C. Voss.

| Figure 11.9 | Categorising organisations by performance |

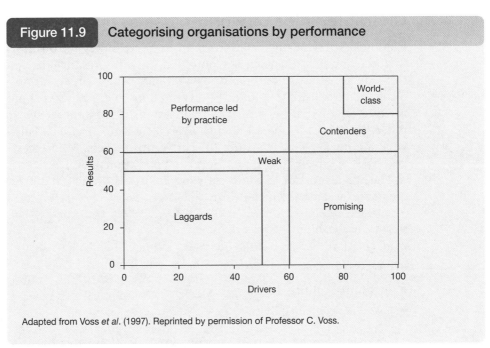

Adapted from Voss et al. (1997). Reprinted by permission of Professor C. Voss.

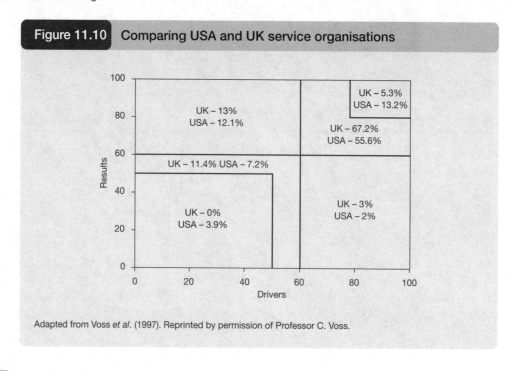

Figure 11.10 Comparing USA and UK service organisations

Adapted from Voss *et al*. (1997). Reprinted by permission of Professor C. Voss.

11.5.2 Characteristics of world-class service organisations

World-class service organisations tend to have impressive business results, both financial and non-financial. The non-financial measures include employee satisfaction, customer satisfaction and market share. These organisations are generally recognised by customers, industry organisations and business commentators. They are often quoted as benchmark organisations, their approaches are imitated by others, and they accumulate a range of accolades and service and quality awards. So what are the key characteristics that drive this success? We suggest that there are two types of drivers, at corporate level and operational level.

The characteristics of world-class organisations (Johnston 2001 and 2004) at a corporate level usually include:

- great leadership
- clear vision
- clarity of concept
- supportive culture
- a well-developed strategy.

At an operations level, world-class organisations (Johnston 2001, 2003 and 2004) are set apart by their:

- willingness to listen to customers
- continuous process development
- consistency of service

- responsiveness
- 'can do' attitude
- big and little thinking
- supportive and committed staff
- excellent performance management
- lack of complacency.

Box 11.3 describes how Singapore Airlines illustrates many of these world-class characteristics.

Great leadership

The key to great service is 'genuine service leadership at all levels in an organisation' (Berry 1995, p. 7). Clear and purposeful leadership right from the top of the organisation is needed to develop and sustain a world-class organisation. Furthermore, that purpose and the organisation concept must be continually emphasised and enacted. A willingness to listen encourages communication up and down the organisation. Good leadership is also characterised by a belief in and investment in people, systems, training and the delivery of outstanding service (see, for example, Georgiades and Macdonell 1998, Roberts 1989).

Clear vision

Service vision is more than simply having clarity about where the organisation is going; it is also an ability to communicate enthusiastically to others. Vision, created by great leaders, provides employees with something to believe in and something that challenges them; it provides the emotional energy required to deliver outstanding service and it generates commitment to the provision of service (Berry 1995).

Clarity of concept

'Excellent service companies define their business in strikingly clear terms' (Berry 1999, p. 238). In world-class organisations the service concept is well defined, communicated and well understood by employees and customers. This brand image is well known in the marketplace and the organisation is known to be a market leader. Other organisations may try to emulate and reproduce the concept but are continually outrun by the organisation that invests in continuous process development.

Supportive culture

Great service in world-class organisations is delivered by employees who do not need to be defensive in their dealings with customers. A positive attitude is generated by an organisational culture consistent with the declared competitive strategy, and that values the contributions of all members. A supportive culture is self-renewing, not looking back to the 'good old days' but encouraging the development of new ways of thinking and acting. For a good overview of cultural effects on service provision, see Georgiades and Macdonell (1998).

Well-developed strategy

World-class organisations have clear plans in place that set out how they will achieve their goals and their vision. The vision is not pie-in-the-sky but something concrete that employees feel is both achievable and desirable. The strategy communicates how this will be achieved and defines the employees' part in the activity. An essential attribute of a well-developed strategy is that it has been formulated with the ownership and buy-in of all levels in the organisation.

Willingness to listen to customers

World-class organisations take great efforts to listen to their customers. They use many methods of listening (see Chapter 4) and take all comments very seriously. Customers' views are used to drive developments, although the need to be financially and commercially viable is never forgotten. The nirvana that world-class service companies seem to have found is in meeting, without compromise, both customer needs and their own criteria for financial success. For world-class service organisations, these two requirements, so often at odds, seem to go hand in hand.

Continuous process development

World-class organisations try continually to develop their service. This is not just redesign but requires more fundamental questioning that leads to 'reinvention' of their services (see Chapters 2 and 12). This vigorous search for distinctive service can only be undertaken in an organisation that is confident in its ability to ask and deal with difficult questions. World-class service organisations firmly reject 'me-too' service. Any changes they make are usually based on detailed research, but they also take risks and sometimes 'take a flyer' when it feels right. They are equally willing to drop an idea, despite the investment cost, if an innovation is not seen to be working. They also see service delivery boundaries as flexible and carefully manage overlaps with other service providers.

Consistency of service

David Good, the general manager of the Central Samui Beach Resort Hotel we described in Chapter 4, made the point that high-quality service is about consistency. World-class service organisations do not just deliver outstanding service – they do it routinely and consistently. World-class service providers may surprise their customers with their level of service, their willingness to deal with an issue, their ability to recover the customer after a problem and the speed of their service. World-class service organisations, however, go beyond making the customers say 'wow' about the service by getting customers to say 'wow' the next time because it was like that again. 'Great service companies ... couple the basics of service with the art of surprise' (Berry 1995, p. 78).

Responsiveness

Customers of world-class service organisations find that not only are they listened to, but the organisation is happy and able to respond to reasonable requests for service. Customers are not greeted with a mechanistic response such as 'I'm sorry, we don't do that', but staff are encouraged to try, within reasonable limits, to satisfy customers. A cliché in hotel receptions is the standard response, 'No problem'. For world-class service organisations, this is reality. Another test of a world-class service organisation is to ask yourself, after making a request, 'Do I feel that I have been heard and that the organisation will deal with my request, or do I feel that my request has disappeared into a black hole?'

'Can do' attitude

World-class service organisations are concerned with the longer-term relationships between customer and provider and try to find ways to please the customer. Berry and Parasuraman (1991) summed this up as 'purposely treating customers personally'.

Big and little thinking

Lord Marshall, chairman of British Airways, referred to this as 'Nothing too big. Nothing too small' (Prokesch 1995). World-class service organisations never lose sight of the 'big picture', keeping strategy, concept and vision at the forefront, while at the same time, however, paying close attention to the detail. David Good, the general manager at the Central Samui Beach Resort Hotel, said, 'It's about the little things, personal touches, such as taking time with guests; a few minutes here and there to acknowledge people, or spend a few minutes talking with them'. Getting the detail right makes outstanding service providers stand head and shoulders above the rest. It is through the detail that the customer confronts excellence.

Supportive and committed staff

Excellent service is delivered either directly or indirectly by employees. World-class service organisations use approaches such as empowerment or self-directed work teams appropriately rather than implement these ideas because they have seen them work elsewhere. Staff are committed to the organisation and to the service concept because they are involved in the process of service development – they are encouraged to own the service delivery process, to look for ways of improving it, and they are motivated by the right mix of recognition and reward.

Excellent performance management

Performance measurement is an important driver of world-class success. Key drivers are measured, service is carefully quantified and targets set in key areas of the business. Results, both financial and operational, are shared throughout the business. Targets are based not only on what was achieved in the past but also on the activities of competitors and other excellent organisations, perhaps not even in the same field. World-class organisations have a good understanding of the rest of the industry and regularly, and systematically, check out their competitors' services, not just for the sake of comparison but to promote learning and development and growth. Furthermore, world-class organisations 'celebrate excellence' (Berry 1995, p. 244). Measuring performance and knowing what is excellent is only one step – recognising the people who have achieved excellence and then regarding it through a mixture of financial and non-financial ways validates those achievements, motivates others and sustains excellence.

Lack of complacency

One key trait that seems to separate the outstanding from the very good is a lack of complacency. World-class organisations never accept they have reached their goals – they always need to stretch the organisation and its staff. Indeed it is this continual questioning of boundaries and encouragement of talent that keeps such organisations forging ahead. In the study of UK and US service organisations mentioned earlier (Voss and Johnston 1995 and Voss *et al.* 1997) a clear link was found between the performance of organisations and their assessment about how well the organisation's managers believed it was able to compete with the best of its competitors. The resulting 'complacency index' shows that managers who viewed their organisations as strong compared to their competitors had below-average performance, whereas those who viewed themselves as 'having a good deal to learn and not as good as their competitors' turned in the best performances (see Figure 11.11).

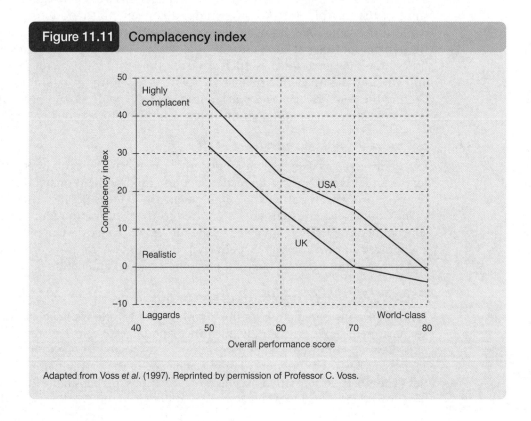

Figure 11.11   Complacency index

Adapted from Voss *et al.* (1997). Reprinted by permission of Professor C. Voss.

Singapore Airlines (SIA)

Box 11.3

Singapore Airlines (SIA) is recognised as one of the world's leading carriers. With one of the most modern fleets in the industry, its route network spans 90 cities in 40 countries across five continents. Singapore Airlines was the pioneer of in-flight services, including free drinks and complimentary headsets, in-flight telephones and interactive entertainment systems. Today it is still setting industry standards. It has the most advanced in-flight entertainment system, providing a wide range of audio and video programmes 'on demand', enabling passengers to pause, fast-forward and rewind any programme at their convenience. It was the first airline to provide an in-flight e-mail service, and e-mail check-in and text-message flight alerts notifying customers of plane arrivals and delays. For first and business class passengers who want to choose their own menus there is a 'book the cook' service, and on some long-haul routes a cleverly designed flat bed that takes up little more room than a conventional seat. SIA is also, consistently, one of the most profitable airlines in the world.

SIA's mission statement is 'A global company dedicated to providing air transportation services of the highest quality and to earning good returns for shareholders'. This is underpinned by six core values: pursuit of excellence, safety, customer first, concern for staff, integrity and teamwork.

Having an international reputation for service excellence makes delivering excellent service a continuous challenge. Yap Kim Wah, SIA's senior vice president responsible for product and service, explained:

We have a high reputation for service and that means that when someone flies with us they come with high expectations. But still we want them to come away saying 'Wow! That was something out of the ordinary'.

We need to give our customers a great experience and good value. It is important to realise that they are not just comparing SIA with other airlines. They are comparing us against many industries, and on many factors. The new ball game for SIA is not just to be the best of the best in the airline industry but to work at being the best service company.

Dr Goh Ban Eng is the senior manager responsible for cabin crew training. She explained:

Excellent service is really attentive and very personalised service with great attention to the little details. We want the passenger to feel that they don't have to ask for anything. We want to anticipate their needs and at the same time be very warm and caring. And if anything should go wrong they know they will be well taken care of. There is a mutual trust and respect between customers and our staff.

SIA has very elaborate feedback mechanisms to help its staff not only listen to customers but also understand them better. Information is collected from a random sample of customers on about 10 per cent of SIA's flights. SIA also listens to its staff. Yap Kim Wah added:

Our crew are very important people because they are very intimately in contact with our customers. So for every flight that we operate we listen sincerely to our crew. They know that the management takes their feedback very seriously. If they gave us feedback and we didn't do anything about it, they would be disheartened.

Training is central to SIA's goal of continuous improvement. SIA's chief executive officer, Chew Choon Seng, stated, 'Training is a necessity, not an option. It is not to be dispensed with when times are bad. Training is for everybody. It embraces everyone from the office assistant and baggage handler to the chief executive officer.'

SIA's latest service excellence initiative, called transforming customer service (TCS), involves staff in five key operational areas – cabin crew, engineering, ground services, flight operations and sales support. The programme is about building team spirit among staff in key operational areas to make the whole journey as pleasant and seamless as possible for passengers.

Although SIA is totally focused on the customer and providing continually improving service, managers are well aware of the need for profit. Kim Wah Yap explained how they meet these dual yet potentially conflicting objectives:

> *First, it's about what we call 'ownership'. We are very cost conscious; it is drilled into us from the day we start working for SIA that if we don't make money, we'll be closed down. Singapore doesn't need a national airline. Second, the company has made a very important visionary statement that says 'We don't want to be the largest company. We want to be the most profitable.' That's very powerful. And third, we have a rewards system that pays bonuses according to the profitability of the company. It's the same for all of us, the same formula from the top to the bottom. As a result there is a lot of* informal pressure *from everybody. Everyone is quite open and they will challenge many decisions and actions.*

SIA is a visionary company and its senior managers talk about 'globalness' and strategy. However, according to Yap Kim Wah:

> *You would be surprised that many of our senior people, as well as our departmental heads and managers, go down to detail like a hawk. And, when there is a need, we will hover and if necessary swoop. It can be very painful for the department involved, but the reality is that we are in a very competitive environment and we cannot afford to be soft.*

Despite its success, managers at SIA know they cannot afford to be complacent. Every opportunity is taken to develop their staff and systems, to deliver great service – and to re-invent the service by anticipating the potential needs of customers and by benchmarking SIA both inside and outside the industry.

Question

1 What makes SIA a world-class service provider?

This illustration is based on a case study written by Robert Johnston, Warwick Business School, and Jochen Wirtz, National University of Singapore, 2004. The case was commissioned by the Institute of Customer Service as part of a study into service excellence. The authors gratefully acknowledge the sponsorship provided by Britannic Assurance, FirstGroup, Lloyds TSB, RAC Motoring Services and Vodafone. The authors would like to thank the interviewees for their participation in this project and also Jasmine Ow, National University of Singapore, for her valuable assistance.

11.6 Summary

The relationships between operational decisions and business performance

- Understanding the chains of cause and effect between operational drivers and business performance helps managers make efficient and effective decisions.
- Leading-edge organisations are working at understanding the links between their operational drivers and business results.
- There are several frameworks that help us understand the chains of cause and effect.

The service performance network

- The service performance network documents many of the cause–effect linkages between operational drivers and business results.

Key stages in developing a network

- The key stages in developing a network are: create a model by capturing several threads through the network, collect data, and analyse the data to understand the relationships between the variables.

World-class service

- World-class service organisations have superior business performance and understand relationships between their operations decisions and business performance.
- The characteristics of world-class organisations at a corporate level include:
  - great leadership
  - clear vision
  - clarity of concept
  - supportive culture
  - a well-developed strategy.
- The characteristics of world-class service at an operations level include:
  - willingness to listen to customers
  - continuous process development
  - consistency of service
  - responsiveness
  - 'can do' attitude
  - big and little thinking
  - supportive and committed staff
  - excellent performance management
  - lack of complacency.

11.7 Discussion questions

1 Compare and contrast the EFQM business excellence model and the service performance network.
2 Apply the characteristics of world-class service to an organisation of your choice.
3 Can a world-class operation exist within a run-of-the-mill organisation and vice versa? Explain your answer and provide some examples.

11.8 Questions for managers

1 How well does your organisation understand the links between drivers and results?
2 Evaluate the relationships between some of your key drivers and results.
3 How does your organisation stack up against the characteristics of world-class organisations and operations?

11.9 Further reading

Bates K., Bates H. and Johnston R., 'Linking service to profit: the business case for service excellence', *International Journal of Service Industry Management*, vol. 14, no. 2, 2003, pp. 173–83.

Berry L.L., *Discovering the Soul of Service*, Free Press, New York, 1999.

Georgiades N. and Macdonell R., *Leadership for Competitive Advantage*, Wiley, Chichester, 1998.

Heracleous L., Wirtz J. and Johnston R., 'Cost effective service excellence – lessons from Singapore Airlines', *Business Strategy Review*, vol. 15, no. 1, 2004, pp. 33–8.

Heskett J.L., Sasser W.E. and Schlesinger L.A., *The Service Profit Chain*, Free Press, New York, 1997.

Silvestro R. and Cross, S. 'Applying the service profit chain in a retail environment: challenging the "satisfaction mirror"', *International Journal of Service Industry Management,* vol. 11, no. 3, 2000, p. 244.

Wirtz J. and Johnston R., 'Singapore Airlines: what it takes to sustain service excellence – a senior management perspective', *Managing Service Quality*, vol. 13, no. 1, 2003, pp. 10–19.

11.10 References

Anderson E.W., Fornell C. and Lehmann D.R., 'Customer satisfaction, market share, and profitability', *Journal of Marketing*, vol. 58, July 1994, pp. 53–66.

Anderson E.W., Fornell C. and Rust R.T., 'Customer satisfaction, productivity, and profitability: differences between goods and services', *Marketing Science*, vol. 16, no. 2, 1997, pp. 129–45.

Andersson, T.D., 'Traditional key ratio analysis versus data envelopment analysis: a comparison of various measurements of productivity and efficiency in restaurants', in Johns N. (ed.), *Productivity Management in Hospitality and Tourism*, Cassell, London, 1996, pp. 209–26.

Bennis W., *Managing People is like Herding Cats*, Executive Excellence Publishing, South Provo, Utah, 1999.

Berry L.L., *On Great Service: A Framework for Action*, Free Press, New York, 1995.

Berry L.L., *Discovering the Soul of Service*, Free Press, New York, 1999.

Berry L.L. and Parasuraman A., *Marketing Services: Competing through Quality*, Free Press, New York, 1991.

Buzzell R. and Gale B., *The PIMS Principles: Linking Strategy to Performance*, Free Press, New York, 1987.

Deming W.E., *Quality, Productivity and Competitive Position*, MIT Center for Advanced Engineering Study, Cambridge, Mass., 1982

Deming W.E., *Out of the Crisis*, MIT Center for Advanced Engineering Study, Cambridge, Mass., 1986.

EFQM European Foundation for Quality Management, www.efqm.org, 1999.

Feigenbaum A.V., *Total Quality Control*, McGraw-Hill, New York, 1986.

Fitzgerald L., Johnston R., Brignall T.J., Silvestro R. and Voss C., *Performance Measurement in Service Businesses*, CIMA, London, 1991.

Fox M.L., Dwyer D.J. and Ganster D.C., 'Effects of stressful job demands on physiological and attitudinal outcomes in a hospital setting', *Academy of Management Journal*, vol. 36, 1993, pp. 289–318.

Georgiades N. and Macdonell R., *Leadership for Competitive Advantage*, Wiley, Chichester, 1998.

Heracleous L., Wirtz J. and Johnston R., 'Cost effective service excellence – lessons from Singapore Airlines', *Business Strategy Review*, vol. 15, no. 1, 2004, pp. 33–8.

Heskett J.L., Sasser W.E. and Schlesinger L.A., *The Service Profit Chain*, Free Press, New York, 1997.

Hoyle R.H. (ed.), *Structural Equation Modeling*, Sage, Thousand Oaks, Calif., 1995.

Johns, N., Howcroft, B. and Drake, L., 'The use of data envelopment analysis to monitor hotel productivity', *Progress in Tourism and Hospitality Research*, vol. 3, no. 2, 1997, pp. 119–27.

Johnston R., *Service Excellence=Reputation=Profit: Developing and Sustaining a Reputation for Service Excellence*, Institute of Customer Service, Colchester, 2001.

Johnston R., *Delivering Service Excellence: The View from the Front-line*, Institute of Customer Service, Colchester, 2003.

Johnston R., 'Towards a better understanding of service excellence', *Managing Service Quality*, vol. 14, no. 2/3, 2004, pp. 129–33.

Jones T.O. and Sasser W.E., 'Why satisfied customers defect', *Harvard Business Review*, November–December 1995, pp. 88–99.

Kaplan R.S. and Norton D.P., *The Balanced Scorecard*, Harvard Business School Press, Boston, Mass., 1996.

Loveman G.W., 'Employee satisfaction, customer loyalty, and financial performance: an empirical examination of the service profit chain in retail banking', *Journal of Service Research*, vol. 1, no. 1, 1998, pp. 18–31.

Lynch R.L and Cross K.F., *Measure Up! Yardsticks for Continuous Improvement*, Blackwell, Oxford, 1991.

Maruyama G.M., *Basics of Structural Equation Modeling*, Sage, Thousand Oaks, Calif., 1997.

Matteson M.T. and Ivancevich J.M., *Managing Job Stress and Health*, Free Press, New York, 1982.

Motowidlio S.J., Manning M.R. and Packard J.S., 'Occupational stress: its causes and consequences for job performance', *Journal of Applied Psychology*, vol. 71, 1986, pp. 618–29.

Norman M., *Data Envelopment Analysis: The Assessment of Performance*, Wiley, Chichester, 1991.

Peters T.J., *Thriving on Chaos: Handbook for a Management Revolution*, Harper and Rowe, New York, 1987.

Prokesch S.E., 'Competing on customer service: an interview with British Airways' Sir Colin Marshall', *Harvard Business Review*, November–December 1995, pp. 101–12.

Reichheld, F. *The Loyalty Effect*, Harvard Business School Press, Cambridge, Mass., 1996.

Reichheld F.F. and Sasser W.E., 'Zero defections: quality comes to services', *Harvard Business Review*, September–October 1990, pp. 105–11.

Roberts W., *Leadership Secrets of Attila The Hun*, Bantam Press, London, 1989.

Rucci A.J., Kirn S.P. and Quinn R.T., 'The employee–customer–profit chain at Sears', *Harvard Business Review*, January–February 1998, pp. 83–97.

Rust R.T. and Zahorik A.J. 'Customer satisfaction, customer retention, and market share', *Journal of Retailing*, vol. 69, no. 2, Summer 1993, pp. 193–215.

Rust R.T., Zahorik A.J. and Keiningham T.L., 'Return on quality (ROQ): making service quality financially accountable', *Journal of Marketing*, vol. 59, April 1995, pp. 58–70.

Schneider B., 'The service organisation: climate is crucial', *Organisational Dynamics*, Autumn 1980, pp. 52–65.

Schneider B. and Bowen D.E., *Winning the Service Game*, Harvard Business School Press, Boston, Mass., 1995.

Voss C.A. and Johnston R., *Service in Britain: A Study of Service Management and Performance in UK Organisations*, Severn Trent plc, Birmingham, 1995.

Voss C., Blackmon K., Chase R., Rose B. and Roth A., *Achieving World-class Service*, London Business School/Severn Trent plc, Birmingham, 1997.

Superstore plc

Dr Rhian Silvestro, Warwick Business School, and Stuart Cross formerly a postgraduate at Warwick. Stuart Cross is now head of strategy development, Boots the Chemist

The UK supermarket industry is dominated by four leading chains, with all others competing in the second tier. The four main players have all diversified into the non-food sector; now, at the end of the economic recession, with a slow-down in price-based competition, the emphasis has shifted to competition based on customer loyalty and quality.

Superstore is one of the big four supermarket chains in the UK and operates a chain of hundreds of stores, which retail in excess of 40,000 product lines, including food products and non-food items like music, personal care products, clothing and pharmaceutical products. Superstore has positioned itself as a family store offering good value and, like many of the large super-stores, the company has introduced loyalty card technology and a self-scanning service with a view to improving customer loyalty.

In a recent annual report the company's chief executive stated that customer satisfaction and loyalty were the real drivers of the company's profit and growth, and that these were influenced by how its people felt about their work, their rewards and their manager. This was also a central theme in the company's management training programme.

To test out this contention Julie Carroll, a senior officer in the Personnel Department, collected together some existing performance data. The data was a mixture of internal measures, based on the performance of 15 stores, and a survey of customer and employee perceptions based on six stores (see Table 11.1).

One particular measure calls for some explanation: store operating ratio is a ratio of actual to planned working hours. This was considered by the company's management to be an indicator of the quality of working life at a store because, as the ratio of planned to actual working hours increases, it was believed that the workplace became more stressful and that therefore the quality of working life diminished.

Julie calculated the correlation coefficients between the various data sets and her results are shown in Table 11.2. The correlations entered in

Table 11.1 Performance data

Internal data:

    Profit margin
    Sales per square foot
    Employee turnover
    Employee absence
    Operating ratio

Customer/employee survey data:

    Service delivery value – customers' perceptions of the value of the service delivered by the store
    Share of grocery budget spent at the store
    Average basket size (i.e. value of the average basket)
    Customer referral – customers' willingness to refer the store as a good place to shop
    Customer satisfaction with the store
    Employee referral – employees' willingness to refer the store as a good place to work
    Overall employee satisfaction
    Employee satisfaction with the style of supervision

Table 11.2 Correlation coefficients between the various data sets

	Sales per square foot	Employee turnover	Employee absence	Operating ratio	Service delivery value	Share of grocery budget	Average basket size	Customer referral	Customer satisfaction	Employee referral	Employee satisfaction	Satisfaction with supervision
Profit margin	**0.77**	0.18	−0.35	**−0.75**	**0.88**	**0.91**	**0.88**	**0.86**	0.70	−0.25	**−0.87**	−0.63
Sales per square foot		−0.10	−0.04	**−0.65**	**0.92**	**0.95**	**0.60**	**0.91**	0.59	0.03	−0.61	−0.36
Employee turnover			−0.36	−0.27	−0.09	0.02	0.30	0.06	−0.35	0.34	0.10	0.73
Employee absence				0.25	−0.60	−0.51	**−0.58**	−0.57	0.24	−0.44	0.13	−0.22
Operating ratio					**−0.97**	**−0.96**	**−0.80**	**−0.93**	**−0.86**	0.36	0.76	0.46
Service delivery value						**0.98**	**0.94**	**0.98**	**0.86**	−0.21	−0.64	−0.26
Share of grocery budget							**0.91**	**0.99**	0.78	−0.24	−0.69	−0.33
Average basket size								**0.89**	0.72	0.05	−0.60	−0.34
Customer referral									**0.82**	−0.22	−0.62	−0.18
Customer satisfaction										−0.53	**−0.83**	−0.19
Employee referral											0.61	0.42
Employee satisfaction												**0.82**

bold indicate a significance at the 95 per cent level or higher. (The minimum value of the calculated correlation coefficient necessary for 95 per cent confidence was 0.51 when the sample size was 15 stores, and 0.81 when the sample size was six stores.) Julie was not sure what to do next.

Questions

1 What conclusions could Julie draw from the data?

2 What are the issues and implications for the store?

chapter twelve

Driving operational improvement

12

Chapter objectives:

- to describe a range of incremental and radical approaches to operational improvement: total quality management, six sigma, business process re-engineering, lean thinking and benchmarking

- to assess service recovery and discuss how it can be used to drive improvements

- to consider how service guarantees can drive improvement.

12.1 Introduction

One important aspect of performance management is performance improvement. This chapter considers some ways in which improvements to operations are not simply encouraged but are used to drive change through organisations.

While processes, people, capacity, technology and culture (Chapters 6–9 and 14) can promote and indeed inhibit operational improvements, there are many ways in which operations managers can make significant improvements to their operations. Performance measurement, with its focus on improvement, was dealt with in the previous two chapters. This chapter focuses on a range of service management tools and approaches that have also been used to great effect in the drive for operational improvement.

All improvement processes focus on two key elements: what adds value for customers and the organisation, and how to mobilise service employees to contribute to the improvement process. Ensuring that process improvement is driven by the need to raise the customer's perception of service outcome and experience might seem self-evident, but examples of organisations improving aspects of operations that are unimportant to customers are commonplace. Of course, we are not just interested in customer satisfaction – improvements in resource utilisation are also valuable in terms of reduced cost and/or increased profitability.

A thread that runs through much of operational improvement is the need to involve all employees. Indeed, this involvement of itself will have an impact on the motivation of employees, frequently bringing about improvements in operational performance, as was implied in the famous Hawthorne studies (Roethlisberger and Dickson 1939). However, this involvement in itself is insufficient to sustain improvement, unless there are substantive changes in process design, resource allocation, and reward and recognition systems. What cannot be denied is that there is a continual need for organisations to improve operational performance. Customer requirements are continually changing and service providers must guard against becoming complacent. Likewise, stakeholders and/or shareholders are looking for confidence that the operation is well managed and that their investment has been a good one.

12.2 Approaches to operational improvement

Having recognised that there is an ongoing need for operational improvement, we need to consider the amount and speed of change required. Change strategies are traditionally split into two types, which represent different and, to some extent, opposing philosophies (see, for example, Imai 1986, Slack *et al.* 2004, Tapscott and Caston 1993, Venkatraman 1994). These two philosophies are continuous, incremental change and radical, step-change.

12.2.1 Continuous incremental and radical change strategies

Continuous improvement, often referred to as *kaizen*, is an evolutionary approach to operational change and is synonymous with the concept of total quality management. Radical change, in contrast, is a revolutionary approach concerned not with amending processes but totally reinventing them. Table 12.1 summarises the key differences between these approaches.

Continuous change involves modest but continual changes to an existing process, whereas step-change seeks radical changes – indeed the total redesign of existing processes coupled with a significant improvement in performance. The benefits from small, successive continuous improvements are expected to be attained over a long period of time, unlike radical change which aims to create major improvements in the short to medium term. Continuous incremental improvement involves everyone in an organisation and the changes are driven by them, thus requiring little senior management time and effort, unlike radical change which is usually driven by a senior management champion requiring

Table 12.1 **Key differences between continuous and step-change strategies**

	Continuous change	Step-change
Existing process	Little change	Redesigned
Improvement expected	Modest	Substantial
Benefits attained	Long-term	Short-term
Change driven by	Employees	Senior management
Senior management time/effort	Small	Substantial
Business risk	Small	High
Capital expenditure	Small	Substantial
Use of information technology	Little	Significant

Adapted from Brignall *et al.* (1999).

substantial senior management time and effort. Senior management involvement is required because the risk involved in the total redesign of cross-functional processes is often high, and capital expenditure, often involving the use of IT, can be substantial (see, for example, Hammer 1990, Imai 1986, Brignall *et al.* 1999, Slack *et al.* 2004, Tapscott and Caston 1993, Venkatraman 1994).

The following sections outline five of the most common forms of continuous and radical operational change: total quality management, six sigma, business process re-engineering, lean thinking and benchmarking.

12.2.2 Total quality management (TQM)

Total quality management (TQM) is one of the best-known approaches to continuous improvement and has had a major impact on organisations by putting the customer at the heart of quality decisions and improvements. TQM was developed in the 1950s by Armand Feigenbaum, although it has lost some of its cachet over the last few years as employees and managers have become unhappy about what some people see to be a 'flavour of the month' approach to management thinking.

It should be made clear, however, that TQM is not a 'programme' or an activity with a definitive start and end, but simply good management practice; however, it does require a thought revolution in management (Ishikawa 1985). The main sources of inspiration for the TQM approaches are the quality gurus, such as Deming, Juran, Ishikawa and Crosby. The two foundation stones of TQM are customer focus and total involvement:

- *Customer focus.* The TQM philosophy is centred on customers, meeting their expectations in order to retain those customers and capture others, thus enhancing profitability and meeting the strategic needs of the organisation. This necessitates identifying which customers the organisation wishes to serve, understanding their expectations and ensuring that all systems, procedures, activities and culture are focused on meeting those needs.

- *Total involvement.* The main difference between the more traditional approaches to quality and TQM is the word 'total' (Slack 1991). TQM is based on a culture of continuous improvement, which is shared and enacted by everyone in an organisation, all working with a single purpose of improving what they do.

TQM as a continuous improvement activity has a great deal to offer service organisations; many of its elements are now traditional activities of many organisations, though not necessarily parading under the banner of TQM. The key elements are expressed diagrammatically in Figure 12.1.

The three corner-stones of TQM concern people, systems and culture (covered in more detail in Chapters 6, 7, 8, 9 and 14). People, i.e. employees, are responsible for and capable of driving change in the systems and this is encouraged by an appropriate people-centred, supportive and improvement-based culture. Employees are given the responsibility for improvement, and have an understanding of the systems and processes to which they contribute. To support this there is training in the use of quality tools and techniques, for example process mapping and statistical process control (see Chapter 6). Measurement systems provide feedback on actions taken and information is provided at the level of the operator (see Chapter 10). Top-management commitment is essential to the successful implementation of TQM because it requires changes organisation-wide and a supportive and appropriate culture (see Chapter 14).

12.2.3 Six sigma

Motorola Inc. is generally credited with the invention of six sigma (Barney 2002). Bill Smith, an engineer in Motorola's Communications Division, introduced the concept in order to deal with increasing warranty claims. This continuous improvement approach was then championed by Bob Galvin, the CEO of Motorola, and six sigma has become part of the company's culture, to the extent that the Motorola University provides training programmes as a major part of its activities. Alongside Motorola, Jack Welch and GE have become major advocates of the six sigma philosophy. The GE website proclaims: 'Six sigma has changed the DNA of GE, it is now the way we work, in everything we do and in every product we design' (www.ge.com/sixsigma).

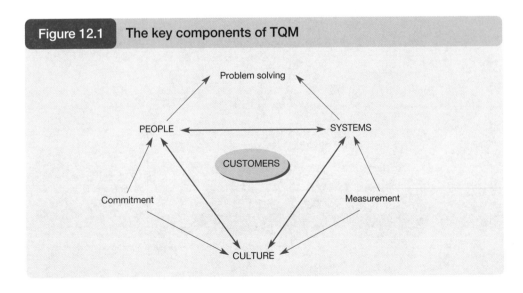

Figure 12.1 The key components of TQM

In essence, six sigma is focused on reducing variance in processes. The six sigma target is 3.4 DPMO (defects per million opportunities). Imagine you are running a call centre with 6,000 customer transactions per day. With what seems like a low problem rate of 1 per cent, you will be upsetting 60 customers a day. At the six sigma rate, in theory you would upset just over one customer a year! The statistical basis for these figures is covered thoroughly in specialist publications, but summarised in Figure 12.2.

Each process may have a specification. For example, a hotel may promise a room service breakfast will be delivered between 7.00 a.m. and 7.15 a.m. rather than exactly at 7.10. This allows for variability in the process and fluctuations in supply and demand. A three sigma process (Figure 12.2) means that the distribution of outcomes only just fits the process specification. In practice, this is not enough, as the process distribution shifts, perhaps as new items on the breakfast menu are added, or new staff are employed. This explains the move to the six sigma target, because changes in the process are much less likely to impact on customers.

Clearly there are some questions to be answered. It may not be technologically or physically possible to meet the six sigma ideal. Critics of six sigma suggest that it is not economically viable in many cases. That said, the approach is worth considering for customer-critical processes – those activities that have a significant impact on customer satisfaction. Service operations that have used this approach tend to be those with large volumes of standard transactions, such as back office functions in financial services.

On the face of it, six sigma is a set of tools and techniques aimed at understanding and improving processes. It has become a major industry in its own right, with clearly defined structures and training courses. It claims to be more oriented to

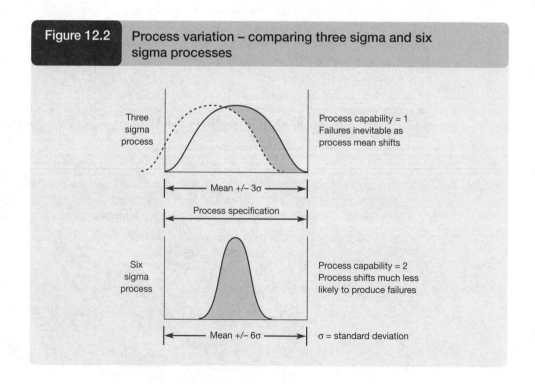

Figure 12.2 Process variation – comparing three sigma and six sigma processes

business results than TQM, and is facilitated by those who have been through accredited training programmes to become master black belts (expert consultants who have completed a number of six sigma projects), black belts (who have completed at least two projects and have leadership and process training), and green belts (who are part-time project members, trained by the black belt).

Six sigma is clearly more than a statistical process control approach. Motorola now refer to it as a 'four step high performance system to execute business strategy' (Barney 2002). These four steps are:

1 *Align*. Six sigma projects must be aligned to business priorities driven by a balanced scorecard approach, focused on the organisation's bottom line.

2 *Mobilise*. Customer-focused project teams are empowered to take action, sponsored by senior managers acting as process champions.

3 *Accelerate*. Project teams are coached and encouraged to ensure that their projects meet specified milestones, rather than allowing them to drift.

4 *Govern*. Leaders actively sponsor projects and share best practice with other parts of the organisation.

GE's philosophy is somewhat similar, emphasising how customers define quality, the need for customer delight, the need to understand the business from the customers' perspective, and leadership commitment demonstrated through training, employee motivation and investment in project teams.

Whatever one's view on the effectiveness of six sigma, most people who have experience of it recommend the DMAIC approach to continuous improvement. This acronym outlines the six sigma approach:

- Define the business problem.
- Measure the current state against the desired state.
- Analyse the root causes of the business gap.
- Improve the process using six sigma tools.
- Control the long-term sustainability of the solution.

A final quote from GE gives an insight into the value of six sigma and similar approaches for service operations:

> *Often, our inside-out view of the business is based on average or mean-based measures of our recent past. Customers don't judge us on averages, they feel the variance in each transaction, each product we ship. Six sigma focuses first on reducing process variation and then on improving the process capability. Customers value consistent, predictable business processes that deliver world-class levels of quality. This is what six sigma strives to produce.*

The Queensland Police Service

Box 12.1

Bruce Millett, University of Southern Queensland

The Queensland Police Service (QPS), with around 12,000 employees and responsible for the policing of one of Australia's largest states, is committed to high standards of performance, in part through continual evolution of operational procedures and staff attitudes towards their role and community co-operation. In geographical terms, the Queensland community covers over 1.7 million square kilometres, is seven times the area of the UK and five times the size of Japan. The population is approaching 4 million, and Queensland is the most decentralised state in Australia.

In the past few years, there has been an increasing focus on performance, with a strong emphasis on seeking greater accountability for performance from regional and district officers. When a new commissioner was appointed in November 2000, he established priorities for the service, focusing on professionalism, partnerships, people and performance. The commissioner, Bob Atkinson, identified the need to develop a system that could focus overall performance across the organisation and provide strong leadership in communicating the service's strategic direction, key operational priorities and the impact these had on the Queensland community

Communication about the issues of performance management within an organisation with such a dispersed workforce and community presented a significant challenge up through the command structure, as well as down through the operational centres. For the new commissioner, operational performance reviews (OPRs) offered a way to address these issues and focus the dialogue on constructive feedback and action.

The opportunity to introduce OPR was provided by the information systems developed during the 1990s. As Commissioner Atkinson states: 'The Queensland Police Service is recognised as a lead agency in the area of information technology within the Australian law enforcement arena. This achievement is something which we as a police service are very proud of.'

The OPRs also offered the opportunity to refine and use the service's statistical collection for operational purposes. There are a number of models of operations performance review systems, which have their genesis in the computer comparison statistics process, known as Comstat, introduced within the New York Police Department (NYPD). The aims of the NYPD Comstat programme are to:

- ensure managers are paying sufficient attention to crime in their geographic areas
- ensure that the tactics and strategies to attack problems embrace three aspects: traditional reactive investigative policy, prevention and problem solving and creativity, and initiatives particularly relevant to the local circumstances
- follow-up on events from the previous meetings to demonstrate consistency and stay focused on the objectives
- ensure that all departmental and external resources that could be brought to bear on a problem are co-ordinated and available
- provide an ongoing teaching/learning situation to all in attendance at the meetings on how to develop strategies and assess their impact
- review results.

At the centre of these review systems are meetings that focus the attention of accountable officers on crime trends and police responses to these trends. They are therefore dependent on good information systems that can provide the levels of analysis required. In the QPS, the commissioner conducts the meetings, together with other senior executive members. From the outset, the commissioner established five priority areas as the focus of the initial reviews:

- public safety
- property crime
- calls for service
- major planned and unplanned events
- unique district issues.

Comparison between crime rate figures for the period July to December 2001 and the same period in 2002 revealed that in 2002:

- homicide decreased by 14 per cent
- other homicide decreased by 27 per cent, including an 18 per cent drop in attempted murder, a 67 per cent drop in conspiracy to murder, a 2 per cent drop in manslaughter, and a 53 per cent drop in driving causing death
- robbery decreased by 27 per cent, including a 38 per cent drop in armed robbery and a 17 per cent drop in unarmed robbery
- unlawful entry decreased by 8 per cent, including a 6 per cent drop in unlawful entry to dwellings, a 13 per cent drop in unlawful entry to shops and a 10 per cent drop in other unlawful entries
- arson decreased by 15 per cent
- other property damage (including offences associated with graffiti and vandalism) decreased by 30 per cent
- motor vehicle theft decreased by 6 per cent
- other theft decreased by 4 per cent, including an 8 per cent drop in stealing from dwellings,

a 2 per cent drop in shop stealing and a 4 per cent drop in stealing from vehicles
- fraud decreased by 11 per cent
- there was no increase in the rate of assault.

Officers of the OPR unit make the point that although they cannot establish causality between the OPRs and these results, they believe that they are having a considerable impact on crime and the quality of life in the community. There is some support for this view. While there has been considerable debate over the impact of Comstat on New York's downward crime trends, which for a time appeared to be matched by similar trends across the US, according to figures published in July 2003 New York still appears to be experiencing a downward trend, while many other States have seen an increase.

Questions

1 Evaluate the approach used by the Queensland Police

2 What advice would you give the commissioner?

This illustration is based on internal documents developed by officers of the Queensland Police Service.

12.2.4 Business process re-engineering (BPR)

A well-known radical approach to improvement and change is business process re-engineering (BPR), a concept introduced into the literature in 1990 (Hammer 1990). BPR is about 'the fundamental rethinking and radical redesign of business processes to achieve dramatic improvements in performance'.

The main principles of BPR involve the following:

- *A cross-functional approach.* BPR recognises the need to take a cross-functional approach to improvement, since most processes cut across traditional functional boundaries. It is therefore only through the creation of cross-functional teams working together on their processes that these processes can be radically redesigned.
- *Out-of-the-box thinking.* BPR is meant to be radical and so requires radical thinking. To do this, traditional beliefs and views need to be challenged – indeed put aside – to allow total redesign starting with a clean sheet of paper. BPR is about rejecting the conventional wisdom and received assumptions of the past to create something new and very different.

- *Simplification*. BPR attempts to discard wasteful activities and focuses on simplicity and logical ordering. However, the often significant use of IT to enable radical changes can create a source of complexity that can undermine improvements.

Implementing BPR (see, for example, Harrington 1991) requires the formation of a high-level team with a champion to co-ordinate action. It requires a clear understanding of current processes, facilitated by process mapping (see Chapter 6). Redesign is then a key activity for the team, involving both visioning and detailed concern for measurements and control, to ensure not only the efficacy of the new process but also its improvement.

BPR is clearly a risky activity, both because current processes are rejected and also because of the high capital expenditure required and frequent reliance on IT. It is not surprising, therefore, that many BPR activities – as many as 70 per cent (see, for example, Hammer and Champy 1993 and Macdonald 1995) – fail to meet their original objectives. Another key factor in their failure is that, because of their emphasis on business processes, systems and structure, the 'people factor' tends to be overlooked, ignored or underestimated (Clark 1995). Indeed, because of the job losses incurred in such radical change, BPR has become synonymous with downsizing.

12.2.5 Lean thinking

The principles of lean thinking are covered in more depth in section 5.3.6. However, it is appropriate to highlight its importance in a chapter on improving operational performance. Lean thinking, or lean operations (or even lean six sigma!), has become another 'banner' under which a cluster of improvement activities can take place.

The essence of lean thinking is to clarify what adds value for the customer and/or organisation and to strip out all other activities. The objective is to ensure that the customer, or the task being carried out on behalf of the customer, flows through the system as quickly as possible, without non-productive waits, thus reducing cost and improving customer satisfaction.

A home loan provider employed this approach to good effect. The existing end-to-end process was mapped from the time the customer requested a loan to the point that the transaction was completed. It was found that the total elapsed time was nearly eight weeks, compared to the 'value-adding' time of just under two hours. Clearly there were periods where the company could not do anything itself – for example when it was waiting for surveys or for solicitors to act; however, this investigation spurred it into action. The home loan/house buying process also raises many anxieties for customers. The numbers of enquiries about the progress of the loan rise exponentially as time goes on. If the time is reduced, with an equivalent increase in dependability, there will be fewer customer enquiries and fewer employees devoted to this expediting process. By applying the principles of lean thinking (section 5.3.6) the home loan provider reduced the end-to-end time to four weeks, with a value-adding time of just over an hour.

Similar benefits may be experienced by a broadband provider, for example using the lean philosophy to manage the process from customer request to installation, dramatically cutting lead-times.

The main benefits of lean thinking include:

- reduced process times and/or lead-times
- reduced processing costs per item/customer through increased productivity
- increased customer satisfaction, leading to repeat business and word-of-mouth advertising
- reduced costs resulting from a higher completion rate (some customers get part-way through a process and leave because they perceive that the provider is too slow)
- better communication with all the parties in the chain
- reduced customer anxiety
- reduced costs resulting from lower levels of complaints or enquiries.

12.2.6 Benchmarking and improvement

In Chapter 10 we explained how benchmarking could and should be used to drive operational improvements, although this objective is sometimes forgotten in practice. One additional point we stress here is about the use of targets. Section 10.5.2 on stretch targets argued that processes undergoing continuous improvement are likely to employ internal benchmarks based on their past performance or the performance of similar processes within the same organisation (Brignall *et al.* 1999). Conversely, organisations undertaking radical change of a process are more likely to adopt external benchmarks for setting performance targets because of the need to improve performance dramatically in relation to that of competitors.

12.3 Service recovery

Despite best efforts to design operations well (Chapter 6) and to try to improve their performance through continuous or radical improvement strategies, things go wrong. This is not surprising because service operations are usually complex, human-based systems involving concurrent provision of many customer experiences and outcomes, with both employees and customers taking part in the process. Errors, mistakes or failures are inevitable, leading in many cases to complaining customers. And, without doubt, the numbers of customers who are complaining are on the increase. In recent years organisations such as holiday firms, train companies, police services, health services and local government have reported increases in complaints, from between 8 per cent and 40 per cent per annum.

There are several possible reasons for this growth. Perhaps the quality of service has declined, or more likely the perceived quality of service has declined, as customers become increasingly service aware and more intolerant of poor service. This might have been brought about by greater pressures on time and/or on available money, making consumers – and indeed businesses – much more concerned about value for money. Second, there has been a recent growth in consumer movements and government initiatives, which have not only alerted people to their rights and the obligations of organisations but have also made customers more aware that organisations are trying to satisfy them! Whatever the reasons, service recovery is becoming an increasingly important task for service organisations.

12.3.1 Types of failure

Failure and problems are not always 'service' failures, i.e. problems with the service process – they could be the result of faults in the goods, equipment or facilities, or often they are faults due to the customers themselves (see Figure 12.3).

Service failures include process problems such as a late-running doctor's surgery or a computer error resulting in an airline 'losing' a passenger. Other problems with a service might include lack of availability of goods and services, unresponsive service, and poor or inappropriate treatment being given to customers.

Equipment failures may also cause problems in the service process. The failure of computers, automatic doors or air bridges in an airport will disable parts of the process and cause problems for staff and customers.

It is interesting to note that the majority of failures are customer failures. Customer failures can be divided into two types: those caused by 'problem customers' and those caused by customers who make mistakes (Johnston 1998). Problem customers are those individuals who are involved in serious offences such as staff abuse or drunkenness (Bitner *et al*. 1994, Lovelock 1994). Customers who make mistakes, on the other hand, make simple and often inadvertent errors, such as forgetting something or turning up at the wrong time or wrong place (Johnston 1998).

From a customer's point of view, a failure is any situation where something has gone wrong, irrespective of responsibility (Johnston 1995). Even if a customer is late for a plane and the airline may consider it the passenger's fault, the passenger may have been late due to rail strikes or road works; whatever the reason, they will be likely to blame the airline for not holding the plane. Importantly, each failure, again irrespective of responsibility, provides the organisation with an opportunity to recover.

12.3.2 Defining service recovery

The key purpose of service recovery is not to satisfy the customer per se, (i.e. recover the customer – although this may be important), but to use the information gleaned

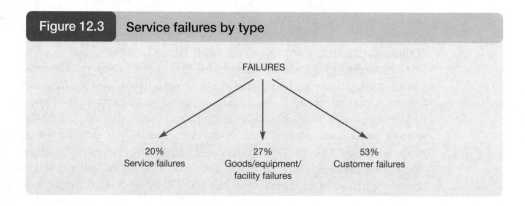

| Figure 12.3 | Service failures by type |

FAILURES

20%
Service failures

27%
Goods/equipment/
facility failures

53%
Customer failures

from the failure and its consequences to drive improvements continuously through an organisation by focusing managerial attention on specific problem areas (Van Ossel and Stremersch 1998, Tax and Brown 1998, Tax *et al.* 1998). If the focus of service recovery is solely to satisfy the complaining customer, its potential to prevent the problem recurring – and thus prevent more dissatisfied and lost customers and reduced financial performance – is lost. However, research shows that this is too often the case. 'Customers are often fobbed off with money or promises that the system has been changed for the future, but they are often left with the feeling that they, the customers, have basically expected too much, and any action is a goodwill gesture on the part of the service provider' (Armistead and Clark 1994).

One of the first definitions of service recovery, used in British Airways' 'Putting the customer first' campaign back in the 1980s, was 'to offset the negative impact of a screw-up' (Zemke and Schaaf 1989). While dealing with the customer after something has gone wrong is without doubt an essential ingredient of recovery, we would argue that an additional and indeed critical benefit of service recovery is that of driving improvements in business performance. Sadly, many organisations do not obtain these benefits and view service recovery simply as a means of trying to pacify and mollify a dissatisfied customer.

We therefore define service recovery as the action of seeking out and dealing with failures in the delivery of service in order to improve delivery performance. This definition expands service recovery away from complaint management by another name to the activity of finding failures and potential failures – preferably before the impact of such failures has been felt by the customer – and putting them right, i.e. driving improvements to operational processes. The act of recovering from a failure should also lead to satisfied, even delighted, customers. This should lead to higher retention rates and therefore all the financial benefits this provides (long-term income streams and reduced costs, etc.) as well as positive word-of-mouth recommendations. Reduced costs may also be an outcome of improved processes, just as improved processes may attract more customers and themselves lead to increased revenue. Improved processes should lead to greater staff satisfaction, retention and possibly easier attraction (see Chapter 11).

12.3.3 The four acid tests of service recovery

We suggest that four acid tests (Johnston 2001) can be applied to an organisation's service recovery process to assess its success:

1 Does it lead to increased customer satisfaction (at least for those customers that the organisation wishes to retain)?
2 Does it improve retention rates?
3 Does it drive process improvements?
4 And, as a result of the above, does it improve financial performance?

Customer satisfaction

When things go wrong, organisations have a chance to demonstrate what they can do for their customers. Indeed for some organisations, such as utilities, the occurrence of a failure or a problem is one of the few times that the organisation's staff may come into direct contact with customers. While employee unwillingness to recognise and deal with problems is known to be a driver of dissatisfaction (Bitner *et al.* 1990), it is known that good service recovery is a key source of delighted customers (Johnston 1995). In a study of critical incidents (Johnston 1995) it was found that over half of delighted customers felt so because of something having gone wrong and the organisation dealing well with them and the problem.

Customer retention

Satisfied customers may not be enough – some customers who are satisfied still switch organisations. For the financial benefits to be gained, customers need to be not only satisfied but also retained through recovery. Recovery can lead to retention for two reasons: first, good service recovery can generate high levels of satisfaction (see above), which increase the likelihood of the customer staying, and second, the principle of reciprocity applies. Because the organisation has been seen to go out of its way to sort out a difficult situation for a customer, customers may feel obliged to reciprocate this by not only staying but also becoming a champion for the organisation (see section 3.2) and so not only being more supportive of the organisation during service delivery but also acting as an advocate of its staff and services. In their book on breakthrough service, Heskett *et al.* (1990) stated: 'Mistakes are a critical part of every service ... errors are inevitable. But dissatisfied customers are not. A good recovery can turn angry, frustrated customers into loyal ones.'

The potential of failures and service recovery to retain customers has not been lost on British Airways. Chairman Lord Marshall explained how BA changed the nature of its complaint department: 'We have transformed customer relations from a defensive complaint department into a department for customer champions whose mission is to retain customers' (Prokesch 1995).

Process improvement

What seems to make customers annoyed, even angry, after a failed service recovery, is not so much that they were not satisfied but that they feel the system has not been changed to prevent the problem from arising again. They often feel fobbed off with excuses or empty promises. We believe one acid test, failed by many organisations, is their ability to take problem data from customers – or even staff – and turn it into real improvements. Little time or effort is put into creating systems or procedures to facilitate this – indeed some organisations make it particularly difficult by setting up remote and disconnected customer service centres, whose role is to pacify customers while not disturbing the rest of the organisation and letting it get on with its 'real' task. Some organisations just let their staff soak up the pressure resulting from their inadequate service systems, leading not only to dissatisfied and disillusioned customers but also to stressed and negatively disposed staff, who feel powerless to help or sort out the problems. This helpless feeling (known as learned helplessness – see, for example, Martinko and Gardner 1982) encourages or rather induces employees to display passive, maladaptive behaviours, such as being unhelpful, withdrawing or acting uncreatively (Bowen and Johnston 1999). The employee alienation associated with this helplessness will be compounded when employees feel that management does not make efforts to recover them from this helpless state.

Information from customer complaints and from other failure or problem situations can provide organisations with the means (and motivation!) to improve what they do and make things better for the future – not only for their customers but also for their staff, who may experience on a regular basis what might seem one-off failures to customers. TNT, the international distribution and logistics company, has achieved some astonishing advances after it used the results of its complaint information (see Box 12.2).

Financial performance

An effective service recovery process should lead directly to enhanced business performance for the organisation. There should be increased revenues from higher levels of retention and from positive word-of-mouth from delighted customers, and reduced costs through higher retention levels, and from continuous operational improvements and reducing costs (financial and emotional) in dealing with dissatisfied customers.

Indeed, defined in this way, service recovery and complaint management could be viewed as profit centres; sadly, for many organisations they are seen as a necessary evil and a sunk cost. To understand better these relationships and to understand the relationships between complaints/recovery and financial performance, organisations need to collect and analyse the data to help them exploit the value of service recovery for the organisation.

TNT   Box 12.2

TNT is a subsidiary of TPG, a publicly listed company, with its headquarters in Amsterdam. TNT is a leading global express distribution, logistics and international mail company, which moves documents, consignments and business mail. TNT serves 200 countries and carries over 2 million consignments per week, which pass through its 969 depots and 85 international mail distribution centres. It has 50,000 employees and a 17,000-strong vehicle fleet, plus 40 aircraft dedicated to its operations.

TNT's philosophy focuses on the customer and aims 'to be your business partner, devising solutions for all our customers' distribution needs by combining our core capabilities to create new products and services'. The organisation is serious about complaints and works hard to derive improvements from problems and complaints. It uses a worldwide reporting system to identify all failures in detail, without exception, and then weekly in-depth root-cause analysis is used to identify and solve problems. Indeed, by focusing on complaint data, TNT has improved its performance dramatically, including a 96 per cent improvement in on-time delivery and missed pick-ups down by 78 per cent. This has resulted in less problems and hassle for staff, which has reversed the company's employee turnover figures and led to significant reductions in absenteeism. The impact on financial performance has also been evident, with profit before tax up by 81 per cent over two years.

Question

1 Visit TNT's web site, www.tnt.com, and evaluate the organisation's methods of collecting feedback from customers.

This illustration was developed from material from www.tnt.com and Barlow and Møller (1996).

Part Four | Performance management

12.3.4 Consumer behaviour

Before identifying what makes a good recovery system, it is important to understand how customers react to service failures. How they react will be dependent on the type of person they are and their attitude to complaining, the perceived likelihood of successful redress, and age and sex (see, for example, Blodgett *et al*. 1993, Day 1984, Landon 1977, Oliver 1997). We believe one key driver of consumer reaction is the level or intensity of dissatisfaction (see Johnston 1998 and Prakash 1991).

By scaling consumer dissatisfaction (see the satisfaction continuum in Chapter 4) from 0 to –5, where 0 is not dissatisfied (i.e. satisfied), through extremely dissatisfied, to customers who feel absolutely furious, we can obtain a picture of their likely responses to failures given their level of dissatisfaction (see Figure 12.4). (It should be noted, however, that many other connections are possible – an extremely dissatisfied customer, for example, may exhibit only a mild reaction and vice versa – but in most cases the outward display of reaction may be the only means of assessing a customer's level of dissatisfaction.)

The more dissatisfied customers are, the more extreme and more types of complaint behaviour they will exhibit (Johnston 1998).

For some people a problem or failure may have little effect – they may be tolerant or expect poor service. Others, level – 2, may just store up a black mark for future recall when something else goes wrong. Others may make a fuss – not quite a complaint, more of a verbal warning: 'I'm not complaining but ...' Complaining formally, verbally or in writing, is the next level which, like all the others, will not necessarily be mutually exclusive (some customers may exhibit several behaviours!). Dissatisfied customers may tell friends and colleagues, indeed may go further and actively dissuade them from using the service again. Others may go to the extreme of becoming a terrorist and campaigning against the organisation by

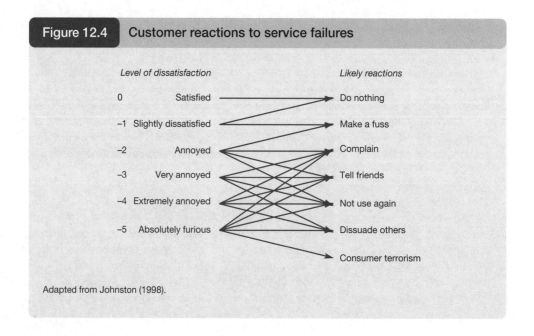

Figure 12.4 Customer reactions to service failures

Adapted from Johnston (1998).

putting up signs, taking out newspaper advertisements, seeking legal redress and sometimes illegal acts.

While figures abound about how many people a dissatisfied customer will tell, it has been shown (Johnston 1998) that the number they tell will depend upon their level of dissatisfaction. Slightly dissatisfied customers told on average three other people, whereas extremely annoyed customers told over 15 each, and absolutely furious customers usually exceeded 25.

Why this is important in the design or assessment of service recovery and complaint systems is that the type of response to a customer may need to take into account the level of dissatisfaction of the customer. There is little sense – indeed it could be counterproductive – to offer a furious customer a small token gesture.

12.3.5 Service recovery ingredients

Service recovery, as defined at the start of this chapter, implies more than just dealing with customers who have experienced a failure; likewise service recovery as an activity must do more than this. Service recovery has three essential ingredients:

- designing-out failures to prevent them happening in the first place
- excellent complaint handling
- proactive service recovery – seeking out problems and potential problems.

Designing-out failures

The best way of preventing complaints and eliminating the need for service recovery is to prevent problems happening in the first place. While Chapter 6 dealt with service design, we would like to add one extra approach here, which is specifically designed to prevent failures – failsafing.

Failsafing (Chase and Stewart 1994) is one means of trying to reduce the likelihood of failures in service processes. This idea is called *poka yoke* in Japan (from the Japanese *yokeru*, meaning to prevent, and *poka*, inadvertent errors) and was advocated by Shigeo Shingo (1986). *Poka yoke* are simple failsafe automatic devices that can be designed into a service to prevent many inevitable mistakes becoming failures. *Poka yoke* usually have the dual advantages of cheapness and simplicity, and are used to prevent both staff and customers doing the wrong thing.

Poka yoke can be used to reduce customer failures by encouraging customers to do the right thing. Simple but effective examples include airline lavatory doors that need to be locked to have the light come on. Electronic tags on goods in a store ensure that they are not inadvertently or intentionally taken out of the store. Computer disks can only be inserted the right way round, thus ensuring there are no (or at least fewer) problems in accessing data.

From an operations perspective *poka yoke* can be used to ensure that staff adhere to procedures in order to reduce or eliminate service failures. Some computerised procedures, for example, will not allow operators to move to the next screen until all the information has been provided on the previous screen. The 'dead-man's handle' on a train will automatically stop the train unless a driver is holding the handle down.

Equipment failure can be prevented or the consequences minimised by making them literally failsafe: automatic doors that can only fail when open, traffic lights whose fail mode is amber in all directions. Parallel wiring or having back-up components or systems can dramatically reduce the likelihood of equipment failure.

There are five key steps in failsafing:

1 Identify the potential or actual weak points in a process. This can be done using either process engineering tools (process mapping, walk-through audits or service transaction analysis – see Chapter 6) or the results of analysis of complaints data.

2 Identify the type or nature of the failure(s) (service, equipment, or customer).

3 Focusing on the type of failure, brainstorm various ways of reducing or preventing errors.

4 Select, design and implement the most appropriate *poka yoke*. If the failure is not preventable, ensure good complaint handling procedures are in place (see the next section).

5 Monitor and evaluate the effect of implementation and repeat the above steps if necessary.

Excellent complaint handling

A good deal has been written over the last few years on the 'ingredients' of recovery (see, for example, Armistead and Clark 1994, Bell and Zemke 1987, Bitner *et al.* 1990, Hart *et al.* 1990, Johnston 1995, Johnston and Fern 1999, Johnston and Mehra 2002).

Essentially, excellent complaint handling consists of three key operational activities: dealing with the customer, solving the problem for the customer, and dealing with the problem within the organisation.

Dealing with the customer involves five key activities:

- *Acknowledgement*. Acknowledge the problem has occurred. For some customers, if staff are dismissive of the problem it can create a good deal of dissatisfaction and bad will.

- *Empathy*. Following from acknowledgement, try to understand the problem from a customer's point of view.

- *Apology*. For many people, certainly at dissatisfaction levels –1, –2 or –3, an apology may certainly satisfy the customer and is all that might be required. Some organisations may have difficulty in saying sorry because they may be concerned that it implies fault, opening the way for litigation. In such circumstances, words similar to 'I am sorry this has happened to you' may do the trick. A written apology or a verbal follow-up call from management may delight customers at the lower end of the dissatisfaction scale but may be expected by customers at the highly dissatisfied end.

- *Own the problem*. If a member of staff gives the customer some confidence in the system and the outcome by getting hold of the problem and assuming clear ownership – and reinforcing this to the customer – the sense of relief felt by a customer may become an outpouring of support that creates a positive cycle and bond between customer and employee.

- *Involve management*. For more severe cases (customer dissatisfaction levels –3 and less), customers often expect that a more senior person will deal with their problem. This should be part of the system, even if the original employee is perfectly competent to deal with the problem.

Solving the problem for the customer involves two key activities:

- *Fix the problem for the customer*. The key here is at least to try – or appear to try – to fix it. For customers who are –3 and less on the dissatisfaction scale staff may need to be seen to be putting themselves out to fix a problem and 'jumping through hoops'. At the higher end of the scale the fixing may need to be seen to be done or at least overseen by someone in higher authority.

- *Provide compensation*. Some organisations seem overly keen to dispense compensation or tokens, assuming that this alone will appease customers. Often customers simply want the problem fixed and dealt with so that it does not happen again (see below). Token compensation may be unnecessary for level –1 and appreciated by level –2; levels –3 and –4 may require equivalent compensation – refund and making a token gesture; whereas level –5 customers may need 'big gesture' compensation – either monetary, goods or services, or acts of contrition by management.

Dealing with the problem within the organisation involves three essential steps:

- *Find the root cause*. There should be clear operational responsibility to deal with the opportunities identified by customers. Root-cause analysis should identify the real causes, being careful to put aside blame, which can destroy such processes.

- *Solve the problem*. If it is felt to be appropriate to solve the problem, this needs to be done. If it is deemed too expensive or inappropriate for other reasons, a procedure needs to be put in place to ensure staff know how to deal with the situation should it occur again.

- *Provide assurance*. For customers at level –3 or beyond, it may be appropriate to provide them with assurance that the problem has been/will be sorted and should not occur again. For level –4 and –5 customers a written explanation about the investigation that was carried out, its outcome and the steps being taken may be expected.

Proactive service recovery

Unfortunately the majority of customers do not complain. The proportions vary significantly between organisations and also depend on the nature of the person involved – and indeed the seriousness of the complaint and intensity of dissatisfaction felt. Williams (1996) suggested that 49 per cent of dissatisfied customers in a restaurant will not complain. In stores this is about 44 per cent, whereas for a council with monopoly control over local services only 30 per cent of customers complain when dissatisfied.

Unfortunately many customers tell others about poor service rather than tell the organisation's staff, who might be able to recover the customer and fix the prob-

Table 12.2 **Reasons for not complaining**

Reasons for not complaining	Percentage citing those reasons
Did not think anything would change	50
Too much effort	17
Did not want to cause trouble	17
Too busy	8
Too stressful	8

Adapted from Johnston and Fern (1999).

lem. Research suggests that customers often feel that complaining is just not worth the effort and, more significantly, that if they did, the organisation would not actually change anything (OFT 1990, Johnston and Fern 1999) – see Table 12.2.

To encourage feedback, complaints and helpful suggestions from customers, organisations need to deal with the root causes of this problem. This involves making it easy for customers to provide feedback and ensuring – and assuring them – that things will change, that the organisation takes the feedback seriously and then acting on it. The MTR in Hong Kong goes to great lengths to solicit customer feedback (Box 12.3).

Mass Transit Railway Corporation (Hong Kong) Box 12.3

The four lines of the Mass Transit Railway (MTR) Corporation – Kwun Tong, Tsuen Wan, Island and Tung Chung Lines – cover over 40 kilometres connecting 38 stations in Hong Kong. The trains move around 2.5 million people every weekday, making it one of the most heavily used mass transit systems in the world. Besides running a mass transit system the Corporation is also actively involved in the development of key residential and commercial projects above existing stations and along new line extensions. In 1998 its turnover was close to HK $7 billion, with a profit of nearly HK $3 billion.

'The MTR Corporation's key mission is to be the best mass transport company in the world for customer service, and recent benchmarking studies have confirmed that the MTR is one of the world's finest railways for reliability, customer service and state-of-the-art technology', explains Jack C.K. So, the chairman. To meet this aim the interval between peak-time trains is less than 2 minutes, with dwell time at stations around 30 seconds. All the trains and underground stations are air-conditioned and are kept scrupulously

clean. The Corporation has recently embarked on an HK $8 billion five-year capital works programme to continue improving its stations and trains. Improvements to stations include better entrances, more lifts and escalators, new concourses, and platform screen doors to improve platform management and make it easier to maintain comfortable environmental conditions on the platforms.

Customer service is one of the Corporation's three core values and it strives to provide the highest standards of service and reliability. To help it understand how it can better meet the changing needs of passengers, the Corporation makes enormous efforts to listen to its customers' concerns and needs. Its staff undertake annual passenger surveys, home interview surveys, biannual customer service surveys, and focus group discussions. They also run a customer telephone hotline, have station suggestion boxes, and even hold station coffee evenings and the occasional radio phone-in. The MTR is obsessed with how customers feel and with developing its services and facilities to meet their needs. 'We listen, we act', said Nancy Pang, marketing and communications manager.

Questions

1 What are the benefits of using several different methods of listening to customers?

2 What do you think are the effects of the MTR's efforts to obtain customer feedback on its customers, staff and financial performance?

This illustration was developed from material from www.mtrcorp.com, and Tocquer and Cudennec (1998).

There are a variety of methods for encouraging feedback. These include:

- *Comment cards*. The feedback sought should allow customers the chance to air their views (What did you like? What went wrong?), ask how the customer thinks the service could be improved and ascertain information about whether they will return (Will you use us again?) as well as provide other ways of dealing with their complaint if comment cards are not felt to be appropriate (e.g. free-phone customer service numbers). Some organisations also use incentives, such as prizes, to encourage positive and negative feedback.

- *Notices*. Notices are useful in explaining to customers the process for making a comment or complaint. Freephone numbers may help encourage those who would otherwise not provide feedback. A small number of organisations are trying to demonstrate how seriously they take feedback and involve senior managers or sometimes even the chief executive (see Box 12.4).

Kwik-Fit   Box 12.4

'What differentiates us from the competition', explained Kwik-Fit's customer services manager, Kenny King, 'is that we actually entice people to call us or write to us.' Indeed Sir Tom Farmer, chairman and chief executive, has his picture all over Kwik-Fit's corporate literature, exhorting customers to do just that.

From the opening of the first Kwik-Fit Centre in Edinburgh in 1971, the Kwik-Fit Group is now one of the world's largest automotive parts repair and replacement specialists, providing and fitting tyres, exhausts, brakes, shock absorbers, batteries, oil filters, wiper blades and child seats. It operates around 2,000 centres across Europe, with plans to open further centres in other countries. Over 9,500 repair centres (which include recent acquisitions of Speedy and Pit-Stop) in England, Scotland, Wales, Ireland, Holland, France, Belgium, Germany, Spain and Switzerland now service the needs of almost 7.5 million motorists a year.

Sir Tom Farmer believes that the growth of this company, now with a turnover of over £500 million, has been due to its aim to deliver 100 per cent customer delight. Alongside his image can be found Kwik-Fit's freephone number and customers are encouraged to ring it. An operator will take down details of the problem and pass the information on to the area manager with responsibility for the centre involved. After talking to the centre, the area manager will call the customer to discuss the problem and also what needs to be done. On occasion, if it is necessary, the area manager will also visit the customer in person. The area manager then takes the appropriate action and prepares a report for the centre involved. Kwik-Fit aims to have all complaints resolved within three days.

Not only does Kwik-Fit encourage customers to call it with comments, it also actively solicits them. Kwik-Fit's customer survey unit calls several thousand people each evening and solicits information that may not have been serious enough to warrant a complaint but still made the customer unhappy or concerned.

Sir Tom Farmer is well aware that as well as making customers happy, this philosophy makes sound financial sense. Kenny King explained: 'If a customer is in the position where he or she thinks, "Well, I wasn't satisfied earlier, but I am now", they're more likely to blow Kwik-Fit's trumpet'. Car servicing is just the sort of conversation that crops up in the pub and Kwik-Fit's approach to customer service provides it with service champions and converts.

Sir Tom Farmer added, 'At Kwik-Fit, the most important person is the customer and it must be the aim of us all to give 100 per cent customer satisfaction 100 per cent of the time. Our continued success depends on the loyalty of our customers. We are committed to offering them the best value for money with a fast, courteous and professional service.'

Questions

1 What are the disadvantages of encouraging customer comments?

2 Evaluate the impact of the chief executive's involvement in soliciting feedback.

This illustration is based on material from www.kwik-fit.com and British Institute of Management (1998).

- **Websites**. While the number of 'unofficial' websites is increasing (where terrorist customers are providing others with an opportunity to voice their opinions about organisations), other organisations are taking the proactive step of capturing feedback via the web. TNT Express Worldwide is one company that has done this (www.tntew.com).

- **Staff feedback**. Front-line staff are often the people who pick up the small comments or grumbles and are usually in a position to provide feedback to managers. Sadly, few organisations seem to harness this information stream by having formal or informal feedback and improvement mechanisms, whether unit meetings or paper-based systems.

Preventing issues becoming failures

Front-line staff have a critical role to play not only in complaint management and staff feedback, but also in spotting something before it goes wrong or before dissatisfaction escalates. Employees who are 'tuned-in' to customers and are observant, caring and thoughtful can have a significant impact on preventing issues becoming failures. There are several ways in which employees might do this:

- be sensitised to customers' body language, mood, looks, sighs, expressions
- look for potential fail-points and deal with them
- check if everything is OK and mean it
- catch problems early, when they are still just grumbles, to prevent escalation
- if something goes wrong, tell customers before they find out
- take action in response to failures, not just complaints.

12.4 Service guarantees

Like service recovery, service guarantees are an important means of driving change through a service organisation and improving its service processes. Indeed, service guarantees are an extension of service recovery. A service guarantee – a promise to recompense a customer for service that fails to meet a defined level – makes clear for customers what they should expect to receive should the service fail. And for some organisations (see Box 12.5), service guarantees are a key part of a customer-focused strategy.

Guarantees require an organisation to formalise the service recovery process. A service guarantee includes the setting up of a clear and inviting mechanism for customers to trigger the guarantee, as well as training and empowering employees to

---

Zane's Cycles   Box 12.5

Zane's Cycles is a bicycle store in Branford, Connecticut. The store has a sales area of around 3,000 square ft (340 square metres) which includes not only a large selection of adult and children's mountain bikes, road bikes and hybrids, a range of accessories and clothing but also a large coffee bar (with free coffee) and a children's play area. In 2004 the company sold around 4,000 bikes and had a turnover of around $1.8 million from its retail division, plus $4.5 million from 25,000 bikes sold through its special markets division.

Chris Zane is the company president. He described the company's policy:

We provide a lifetime free service guarantee, so we will service the bike for free while ever you own the bike. We also provide a lifetime warranty, covering not only the bike but anything else you might buy in our store – helmets, pumps or clothes – and also a 90-day price protection policy that says if you see the same bike for less elsewhere within 90 days we will refund the difference. We added on the 90-day protection policy after feedback from our customers who told us that if we provided lifetime free service and lifetime warranty we must be expensive. So the 90-day price protection policy gives them confidence that not only do we have the best warranties but that we are also competitive.

Chris Zane founded Zane's Cycles in October 1981 when he was 16 and still at school. He had been running a bike repair business from the age of 12 in the family's garage, and also working in a bike shop in the summer holiday. When the owner of the shop decided to liquidate the inventory because of high operating costs, Chris, after a lot of difficulty convincing his parents to let him run the business and another relative to put up a guaranteed loan, purchased the operating business for the cost of the inventory. His first year's turnover was $56,000.

Zane's Cycles guarantees include:

- **Guaranteed for life**. Every bicycle purchased from Zane's Cycles comes with our exclusive 'Zane's Cycles lifetime free service and lifetime parts warranty'. Anytime your bicycle needs service, a full tune-up or just a quick adjustment, we will make those necessary adjustments for free as long as you own your bicycle.

- **90-day price protection**. We guarantee you will never overpay at Zane's Cycles. If you find any item you purchased in stock for less anywhere in Connecticut within 90 days, we'll gladly refund you the difference plus 10%.

- **30-day test ride**. To guarantee you have purchased the correct bicycle, ride it for 30 days. If during that time you are not completely satisfied, please return the bicycle for an exchange. We will gladly give you a full credit toward your new selection.

Chris explained:

> *I know a lifetime free service guarantee may sound expensive but it really is not. The products are so well made these days that they actually don't need a great deal of service and a lot of bikes don't get ridden too much anyway. We know most of our customers are going to use their bike for eight to ten years, then want to trade up to a new bike. So we use the guarantee as a tool to help us develop a relationship with the customer.*
>
> *We don't use lifetime free service to sell the bike. Well, OK it's a sales tool to get the customer through the door for the first time, but then it's a relationship tool to help sell the second and third and fourth bike. And, then that customer will tell their friends that this is the place to buy a bike. For example, someone comes into the store four years after they bought the bike, and they say the gears are slipping, so we service the bike and they come and pick it up and it's actually free. From that point forward they have a completely different relationship with us at a different level and they know we are a trustworthy operation. They become our apostles, promoters of our business. They tell all their friends, 'Hey I went to Zane's, I had the bike four years and they didn't charge me to have the wheels straightened'.*

Always with an eye on the long-term Chris's philosophy is to 'give away the first dollar'.

He added

> *I decided a long time ago to develop programmes that are good for the customers first and then figure out how to make the long-term relationship profitable. I didn't want to 'nickel and dime' my customers. Many companies profit on the small parts and pieces that are hard to find. I, on the other hand, believe a retailer, for pennies, can secure even more profitable long-term customer relationships. At Zane's Cycles, we don't charge for anything under $1. Often a customer comes in for a small part needed to solve a frustrating problem. The master link on his child's bike has broken, and the child is upset because he can't use his bike. Or, while changing a flat tyre, a customer loses an axle nut. We give customers the small parts they need for free. By the way, this programme costs less than $100 a year – the equivalent of one bad print advertisement that no one ever mentions seeing.*

Questions

1 What is the main purpose of Zane's Cycles guarantees?

2 What are the benefits and disadvantages of Zane's Cycles guarantees?

This illustration is based on material from www.zanes.com and from discussions with Chris Zane.

deal with invoked guarantees (Hart 1993a). It should also specify the compensation for the failure (Wirtz 1998). The guarantee can also be used proactively: for example, a pizza restaurant developed explicit recovery procedures, which included front-line staff invoking the guarantee on behalf of the customer if the pizza was late, apologising and immediately presenting the guest with a voucher for a free pizza (as promised in the guarantee) (Wirtz 1998).

12.4.1 The four acid tests of service guarantees

The same four acid tests of service recovery can therefore also be applied to a service guarantee:

1 Does it lead to increased customer satisfaction?

2 Does it improve retention rates?

3 Does it drive process improvements?

4 And, as a result of the above, does it improve financial performance?

Customer satisfaction

A restaurant that promises to serve a lunch to customers within 10 minutes of order not only focuses the organisation on what is important to customers, reduces the risk for them and provides them with a positive attitude towards the service, but also provides a mechanism for dealing with any dissatisfaction:

- *Focusing on satisfying the customer.* A guarantee helps to focus an organisation and its employees on satisfying the needs of a customer. It sharpens them and acts as a constant reminder of the need to satisfy customers.

- *Reducing perceived risk.* For the customer a guarantee may reduce any risk in the purchase, which is important since many services cannot be assessed until experienced. A service guarantee can reduce risk by clarifying the standards of performance the customer can expect, promising high-quality performance in those service elements that are perceived as important by the consumer, and by the promise of a pay-out and/or rework should the service fail.

- *Creating a positive attitude.* According to the theory of reasoned action, an increased strength of the belief that buying the service will lead to a favourable outcome induces the customer to form a more favourable attitude towards buying, which in turn leads to a stronger behavioural intention towards buying (Wirtz 1998). This strengthening of behavioural intention has a positive impact on customer beliefs, attitude, purchasing intentions and the number of customers actually buying.

- *Dealing with dissatisfaction.* A well-designed guarantee provides customers with clear standards against which to assess a service performance (Wirtz 1998). The guarantee also promises the customer a meaningful compensation if guaranteed standards are not met. This therefore encourages complaining, indicating that it is acceptable – indeed encouraged – and provides staff with mechanisms to deal with dissatisfaction. This in turn increases the chance of recovery and therefore customer satisfaction.

Customer retention

Not only customer satisfaction but also customer retention is increased when complaints are resolved (Gilly *et al.* 1991) and/or guarantee pay-outs are made (Berry 1995, Hart 1988). Also by providing a guarantee organisations may retain customers who might otherwise switch because of a perceived increased risk of purchasing elsewhere. Furthermore, well-designed service guarantees have a high communications quality in themselves and may induce customers to talk about them (Heskett *et al.* 1990).

Process improvement

Service guarantees, just like service recovery, help identify fail-points in an organisation. As Hart (1993a) expressed it, service guarantees turn up the pressure, and like turning up the pressure on a garden hose, leaks become more apparent. Often in the design stage of a guarantee, the organisation is forced to confront its delivery systems and support systems to try to ensure that it will meet the required standards (Hart 1993b). Indeed Hart (1993a) found that many companies actually re-engineer their processes from top to bottom in order to bring quality up to the requirements of their guarantees.

When invoked, service guarantees provide data on poor performance, track errors and thereby help organisations identify and remove fail-points. By their existence, they also reinforce the need for employees to provide error-free service.

Financial performance

Service guarantees, well designed and well applied, should therefore lead to customer satisfaction, which drives retention and long-term revenue streams. Reduced perceived risk in the purchase of the service not only helps satisfy existing customers but will help attract new customers to the organisation. Improved process performance should also help retain existing customers as well as attract new ones. Improved performance may also help reduce both the costs of the process and the costs of losing customers or rework. Significant cost savings can emerge, even though they were not the initial motivation for the introduction of the guarantee (Firnstahl 1989, Hart 1993a).

An additional cost, however, is the cost of the compensation specified in the guarantee. This may not be insignificant if the guarantee is to have any meaning for customers, although at least this puts a clear internal cost on failure, which the organisation can seek to reduce. Furthermore, services are real-time performances and cannot be executed 100 per cent failure-free all of the time, i.e. occasional service failures are unavoidable. Given the more positive attitude of dissatisfied consumers towards complaining and invoking the guarantee, pay-out costs will be incurred (Maher 1991) and overall expenses increased.

However, since the perceived probability of a favourable outcome is increased and the potential negative consequences are reduced, the expected value of a service is enhanced, and therefore consumers are likely to be willing to pay a price premium for the service (Hart *et al.* 1992). Guarantees may also reduce employee costs. After Hampton Inns introduced a service guarantee, employee surveys showed that the guarantee increased employee morale. This was also reflected in a drop of employee turnover from 117 per cent to 50 per cent within three years (Greising 1994).

12.4.2 Downsides of guarantees

Service guarantees do, however, have their downsides. They imply that the service may well fail – thus the existence of a guarantee will sensitise customers to the performance of the service and maybe even make them look for poor service. Conversely, the standards set in the guarantee may be higher than customers need or even expect, thus unnecessarily increasing the costs of the service.

A frequently quoted concern is that customers may cheat. It has been known for students to order a pizza with a guaranteed delivery and then to barricade doors and corridors to ensure it is late and therefore free! Research by Wirtz (2004) found that despite the reluctance of many organisations to provide them, full money-back guarantees will be abused no more than smaller pay-outs. He also suggested that guarantees are best targeted at repeat customers because customers intending to use the service again tend not to cheat.

12.4.3 Design of a guarantee

There are three key aspects to the design of a service guarantee: the design of the promise, the design of the procedure to invoke the guarantee, and using the resultant information to improve systems and procedures.

Design of the promise

There are five key elements in the design of the promise (Hart 1988):

- *Meaningful*. The promise needs to be based on customers' expectations and to cover what they regard as being the critical determinants of success or failure. If an organisation guarantees something that is of little consequence, the guarantee will have little value. Before embarking on guarantees organisations should conduct market research to understand customer needs.

- *Easy to understand*. A guarantee should be simple to understand and communicated in a clear way. Guarantees that involve pages of fine print will be regarded with scepticism. Indeed guarantees that include constricting conditions, which are only revealed on close inspection, might be regarded as misleading and lead to dissatisfaction with the service in particular and the organisation in general.

- *Explicit*. The most powerful form of guarantee is one that is explicit – it is quite clear about what is being guaranteed and what the pay-out will be for failure. Some organisations, particularly professional service organisations, may use implicit guarantees, where it is implicit that any problems will be dealt with (in an unspecified way). Federal Express was the first express company to offer a money-back guarantee – its guarantee states 'on time delivery or your money back' (www.fedex.com).

- *Unconditional*. The most powerful promise is one that guarantees satisfaction without conditions (see Box 12.6). Less powerful, though sometimes expedient, are guarantees that offer pay-outs with conditions attached. Airlines providing guarantees of punctuality may not cover instances when the delays are not their fault. The aircraft may be late due to typhoons or air traffic control problems.

- *The pay-out*. The service promise needs to have an appropriate level of pay-out. Too high a level – for example £1,000 for a late delivery of a pizza – may encourage cheating or may even put customers off claiming their rights. Inappropriately small pay-outs (£0.01 for a late pizza) may be deemed to be insulting and not worth informing the organisation of the problem (which was part of the intention in the first place!).

Design of the procedure

The procedure to invoke or use a guarantee needs to be simple and easy. If the customer is expected to fill a set of forms in triplicate and get signatures from all parties involved as well as a written statement from a third party, the guarantee

Radisson Hotels Box 12.6

Radisson Hotels Worldwide is a world leader in the hotel industry and operates, manages and franchises hotels and resorts. It has over 385 hotels, providing around 92,000 guest rooms throughout the USA and around the world, including North America, Europe, the Middle East, Latin America and Asia/Pacific.

The company pursues a strategy of combining global brand strength with local market expertise and service delivery, provided by its partners and franchisees. At all levels the company is committed to providing personalised, professional guest service and genuine hospitality at every point of guest contact. The company's vision is centred on quality of facilities and services, 'beginning with the guest in mind'. The company's chief mission is to create loyal, satisfied customers who will return to Radisson.

Radisson has many initiatives in place to try to provide total guest satisfaction, including training programmes in marketing, operations, training and public relations, computerised reservations, sales and service, and a sophisticated global reservations system.

Radisson also highlights its hotel employees' 'genuine hospitality' with an advertising campaign – 'The difference is genuine'. The campaign focuses on Radisson hotel employees' proactive efforts to provide high-quality service to the guests, not because of training or operating procedures, but because of the spirit of hospitality, which puts the guest first. This philosophy is underpinned by a guest relations training programme called 'Yes, I can!' This programme tries to instil in staff the need to act positively in all customer interactions, and the company believes that this makes its service distinctive.

Furthermore, in 1998 Radisson implemented a 100% guest satisfaction guarantee as part of the brand's worldwide initiative to achieve total guest satisfaction with every guest stay at each hotel, and build long-term guest loyalty. The guarantee, found in every room and on all guest keycard holders, states: '100% Guest Satisfaction Guarantee. Our goal at Radisson is 100% guest satisfaction. If you aren't satisfied with something, please let us know and we'll make it right or you won't pay.'

Questions

1 What are the benefits of offering this guarantee?
2 What are the disadvantages?

This illustration is based on material from www.radisson.com

loses all its credibility and all its potential. The system should be easy, non-threatening, clear and known.

Improving systems and procedures

A final and critical design aspect often lost in the marketing hype of service guarantees is that one of their key purposes – and the most important – is to help drive improvement through the organisation. If the guarantee simply proceduralises a system of pay-outs without providing information to the organisation about failures and encouraging improvement, we believe it is of limited value.

Datapro Singapore

Box 12.7

Jochen Wirtz, National University of Singapore

Datapro Information Services provided IT and telecommunications information and consulting services around the world. It employed over 400 analysts and consultants. Although having sold its pre-packaged information services in Asia for many years, Datapro only started offering consulting services throughout South-East Asia in 1993 via its Singapore office. Being confident about the high quality of its work, but at the same time somewhat lacking the brand equity other providers of similar services enjoyed, Datapro decided to become Asia's first IT consulting firm that explicitly guaranteed its services. Every proposal would contain the following guarantee in the last section just before the acceptance form:

Datapro guarantees to deliver the report on time, to high-quality standards, and to the contents outlined in this proposal. Should we fail to deliver according to this guarantee, or should you be dissatisfied with any aspect of our work, you can deduct any amount from the final payment which it deems as fair, subject to a maximum of 30%.

In the event Datapro should fail to deliver the commissioned report in its entirety at the end of the period, you will have the option to deduct 10% off the price of the study for each week the said study is overdue, subject to a maximum of 20%.

We are able to offer this guarantee as we are confident about the good quality and professionalism of our work. We have secured a large number of blue-chip clients who have been completely satisfied with our services. Our clients in the last 12 months have included: British Telecom, Fujitsu, Sony, Hewlett-Packard, Philips, Intel, etc.

The guarantee was introduced by Datapro in 1994. Datapro had ideally wanted to provide a 100 per cent money-back guarantee, but at the same time wanted to limit the potential financial risks inherent in the introduction of such guarantees. These risks were considerable, with typical projects exceeding a value of well over US $100,000. The guarantee contained a full-satisfaction clause, as well as concrete promises, such as on-time delivery. This mixed design has been shown to be considerably more effective than either full-satisfaction guarantees or other specific guarantees alone (see Wirtz 1997).

The marketing impact was dramatic. Clients were delighted that Datapro was willing to stand by its word and guarantee deadlines as well as content quality – especially as deadlines were a thorny issue in Asia's rapidly growing IT markets, and clients were often promised the sky during the proposal stage, only to be confronted with late deliveries subsequently. The guarantee allowed Datapro to promise credible delivery dates, which otherwise might have been discounted by its clients. Datapro's management felt that the guarantee was an effective marketing tool that helped to sell a number of projects, and Datapro's consulting unit was extremely successful, with a revenue and profit growth of around 100 per cent per annum for a number of successive years.

On the operations side, the guarantee pushed Datapro to keep up its quality. For example, it did not have a single late delivery after the introduction of the guarantee, mainly for two reasons. First, case leaders were cautious not to promise delivery dates they knew they could not keep. Second, in the case of unforeseen problems or delays, case leaders would move heaven and earth to bring the case back on track. A similar pressure was on the case teams to keep their clients happy, as a dissatisfied client could mean a significant reduction in revenue and profit for that case, resulting in a steep reduction in staff bonuses.

Datapro was very successful, especially in breaking into the high-growth telecommunications consulting market, and was taken over at the end of 1997 by the Gartner Group, the world's largest IT consulting firm.

Question

1 Evaluate the guarantee provided by Datapro.

12.5 Summary

Process improvement

- Process improvement demands a focus on what adds value for customers and the organisation, and emphasises greater responsiveness as well as cost reduction.
- Successful improvement approaches involve employees to gain expertise and to promote ownership.
- Approaches such as total quality management, *kaizen* and benchmarking are more suited to short-term, continuous change, while business process re-engineering, six sigma and lean thinking may result in longer-term, major change.

Service recovery

- Things go wrong, so all organisations need to have recovery procedures in place.
- Service recovery is the action of seeking out and dealing with failures in the delivery of service.
- Service recovery should lead to increased customer satisfaction and retention, process improvements and improved financial performance.
- Service recovery has three essential ingredients:
  - designing-out failures to prevent them happening in the first place
  - excellent complaint handling
  - proactive service recovery – seeking out problems and potential problems.

Service guarantees

- A service guarantee is a promise to recompense a customer for service that fails to meet a specification.
- Service guarantees should lead to increased customer satisfaction and retention, process improvements and improved financial performance.
- There are three key aspects to the design of a service guarantee: the design of the promise, the design of the procedure to invoke the guarantee, and using the resulting information to improve systems and procedures.

12.6 Discussion questions

1 What are the significant differences between the various approaches for operational improvement?

2 What is the difference between a service guarantee and service recovery?

3 Explain why some organisations' service recovery procedures, though intent on satisfying customers, tend to lead to dissatisfaction.

4 Select a guarantee provided by a service organisation. Discuss its strengths and weaknesses.

5 Design a guarantee for a particular service. Explain how it would work, its benefits and any difficulties in its implementation or use.

12.7 Questions for managers

1 Have you established an approach for operational review and improvement? Does it matter which approach you use?

2 Evaluate your recovery processes. How could they be improved?

3 What would be the impact of offering a guarantee on the service that *you personally* provide?

12.8 Further reading

Barlow J. and Møller C., *A Complaint is a Gift*, Berrett-Koehler, San Francisco, 1996.

De Feo J.A. and Barnard W.W., *Juran Institute's Six Sigma: Breakthrough and Beyond*, McGraw-Hill, New York, 2004.

DeWitt T. and Brady M.K., 'Rethinking service recovery strategies', *Journal of Service Research*, vol. 6, no. 2, 2003, pp. 193–205.

Johnston R. and Mehra S., 'Best practice complaint management', *The Academy of Management Executive*, vol. 16, no. 4, November 2002, pp 145–55.

Lidén S.B. and Skålén P., 'The effect of service guarantees on service recovery', *International Journal of Service Industry Management*, vol. 14, no. 1, 2003, pp. 36–58.

Wirtz J. and Kum D., 'Consumer cheating on service guarantees', *Journal of the Academy of Marketing Science*, vol. 32, no. 2, 2004.

12.9 References

Armistead C.G. and Clark G., 'Service quality and service recovery: the role of capacity management', in Armistead C.G. (ed.), *The Future of Services Management*, Kogan Page, London, 1994, pp. 81–97.

Barlow J. and Møller C., *A Complaint is a Gift*, Berrett-Koehler, San Francisco, 1996.

Barney M., 'Motorola's second generation', *Six Sigma Forum Magazine*, May 2002.

Bell C.R. and Zemke R.E., 'Service breakdown: the road to recovery', *Management Review*, October 1987, pp. 32–5.

Berry L.L., *On Great Service – A Framework for Action*, Free Press, New York, 1995.

Bitner M.J., Booms B.H. and Mohr L.A., 'Critical service encounters: the employee's viewpoint', *Journal of Marketing*, vol. 58, October 1994, pp. 95–106.

Bitner M.J., Booms B.H. and Tetreault M.S., 'The service encounter: diagnosing favorable and unfavorable incidents', *Journal of Marketing*, vol. 54, January 1990, pp. 71–84.

Blodgett J.G., Granbois D.H. and Walters R.G., 'The effects of perceived justice on complainants' negative word-of-mouth behavior and repatronage intentions', *Journal of Retailing*, vol. 69, Winter 1993, pp. 399–428.

Bowen D.E. and Johnston R., 'Internal service recovery: developing a new construct', *International Journal of Service Industry Management*, vol. 10, no. 2, 1999, pp. 118–31.

Brignall S., Fitzgerald L., Johnston R. and Markou E., *Improving Service Performance: A Study of Step-change versus Continuous Improvement*, CIMA, London, 1999.

British Institute of Management, 'Satisfaction guaranteed', *Management Today*, April 1998, p. 92.

Chase R.B. and Stewart D.M., 'Make your service fail-safe', *Sloan Management Review*, Spring 1994, pp. 35–44.

Clark J., *Managing Innovation and Change: People, Technology and Strategy*, Sage Publications, Thousand Oaks, Calif. 1995.

Day R., 'Modelling choices among alternative responses to dissatisfaction', in Kinnear T. (ed.), *Advances in Consumer Research*, vol. 11, 1984, pp. 496–9.

Firnstahl T.W., 'My employees are my service guarantee', *Harvard Business Review*, July–August 1989, pp. 28–32.

Gilly M.C., Stevenson W.B. and Yale L.J., 'Dynamics of complaint management in the service organization', *Journal of Consumer Affairs*, vol. 25, no. 2, 1991, pp. 295–322.

Greising, D., 'Quality: how to make it pay', *Business Week*, 8 August, 1994.

Hammer M., 'Re-engineering work: don't automate, obliterate', *Harvard Business Review*, July–August 1990, pp. 104–12.

Hammer M. and Champy J., *Re-engineering the Corporation: A manifesto for business revolution*, Harper Collins, New York, 1993.

Harrington H.J., *Business Process Improvement – The Breakthrough Strategy for Total Quality, Productivity, and Competitiveness*, McGraw-Hill, New York, 1991.

Hart C.W.L., 'The power of unconditional service guarantees', *Harvard Business Review*, July–August, 1988, pp. 54–62.

Hart C.W.L., *Extraordinary Guarantees – A New Way to Build Quality Throughout Your Company and Ensure Satisfaction for Your Customers*, Amacom, New York, 1993a.

Hart C.W.L., 'The power of guarantees as a quality tool', *CMA Magazine*, July–August 1993b, p. 28.

Hart C.W.L., Heskett J.L. and Sasser W.E., 'The profitable art of service recovery', *Harvard Business Review*, July–August 1990, pp. 148–56.

Hart C.W.L., Schlesinger L.A. and Maher D., 'Guarantees come to professional service firms', *Sloan Management Review*, vol. 33, no. 3, 1992, pp. 19–29.

Heskett J.L., Sasser W.E. and Hart C.W.L., *Service Breakthroughs: Changing the Rules of the Game*, Free Press, New York, 1990.

Imai M., *Kaizen: The Key to Japan's Competitive Success*, McGraw-Hill, New York, 1986.

Ishikawa K., *What is Total Quality Control? – The Japanese Way*, Prentice Hall, Englewood Cliffs, NJ, 1985.

Johnston R., 'Service failure and recovery: impact, attributes and process', *Advances in Services Marketing and Management: Research and Practice*, vol. 4, 1995, pp. 211–28.

Johnston R., 'The effect of intensity of dissatisfaction on complaining behaviour', *Journal of Consumer Satisfaction, Dissatisfaction and Complaining Behavior*, vol. 11, 1998, pp. 69–77.

Johnston R., 'Linking complaint management to profit', *International Journal of Service Industry Management*, vol. 12, no. 1, 2001, pp. 60–9.

Johnston R. and Fern A., 'Service recovery strategies for single and double deviation scenarios', *Service Industries Journal*, vol. 19, no. 2, 1999, pp. 69–82.

Johnston R. and Mehra S., 'Best practice complaint management', *Academy of Management Executive*, vol. 16, no. 4, November 2002, pp. 145–55.

Landon E.L., 'A model of consumer complaint behavior', in Day R. (ed.), *Consumer Satisfaction, Dissatisfaction and Complaining Behavior*, Indiana University Press, Bloomington, Ind., 1977, pp. 31–5.

Lovelock C.H., *Product Plus*, McGraw-Hill, New York, 1994.

Macdonald J., 'Together TQM and BPR are winners', *TQM Magazine*, vol. 7, no. 3, 1995, pp. 21–5.

Maher D., 'Service guarantees: double-barrelled standards', *Training (TBI)*, vol. 28. no. 6, 1991, pp. 27–30.

Martinko M. and Gardner W., 'Learned helplessness: an alternative explanation for performance deficits', *Academy of Management Review*, vol. 7, no. 2, 1982, pp. 195–204.

OFT, *Consumer Loyalty*, Office of Fair Trading, London 1990.

Oliver R.L., *Satisfaction: A Behavioral Perspective on the Consumer*, McGraw-Hill, New York, 1997.

Prakash V., 'Intensity of dissatisfaction and consumer complaint behaviors', *Journal of Consumer Satisfaction, Dissatisfaction and Complaining Behavior*, vol. 4, 1991, pp. 110–22.

Prokesch S.E., 'Competing on customer service: an interview with British Airways' Sir Colin Marshall', *Harvard Business Review*, November–December 1995, pp. 101–12.

Roethlisberger F.J. and Dickson W.J., *Management and the Worker*, Harvard University Press, Boston, Mass., 1939.

Shingo S., *Zero Quality Control: Source Inspection and the Poka-Yoke System*, Productivity Press, Stamford, Conn., 1986.

Slack N., *The Manufacturing Advantage*, Mercury, London, 1991.

Slack N., Chambers S. and Johnston R., *Operations Management*, 4th edition, FT Prentice Hall, Harlow, 2004.

Tapscott D., and Caston A., 'The demise of the IT strategic plan', *Information Technology Magazine*, January 1993.

Tax S.S. and Brown S.W., 'Recovering and learning from service failure', *Sloan Management Review*, vol. 40, no. 1, Fall 1998, pp. 75–89.

Tax S.S., Brown S.W. and Chandrashekaran M., 'Customer evaluations of service complaint experiences: implications for relationship marketing', *Journal of Marketing*, vol. 62, 1998, pp. 60–76.

Tocquer G.A. and Cudennec C., *Service Asia*, Prentice Hall, Singapore, 1998.

Van Ossel G. and Stremersch S., 'Complaint management', in Van Looey B., Van Dierdonck R. and Gemmel P., *Services Management: An Integrated Approach*, Financial Times Pitman Publishing, London, 1998, pp. 171–96.

Venkatraman N., 'IT–enabled business transformation: from automation to business scope redefinition', *Sloan Management Review*, Winter 1994.

Williams T., *Dealing with Customer Complaints*, Gower, Aldershot, 1996.

Wirtz J., 'Is full satisfaction the best you can guarantee – an empirical investigation', in the proceedings of the 8th Biennial World Marketing Congress 1997, Kuala Lumpur, Malaysia, *Journal of the Academy of Marketing Science*, vol. 8, 1997, pp. 416–18.

Wirtz J., 'Development of a service guarantee model', *Asia Pacific Journal of Management*, vol. 15, 1998, pp. 51–75.

Wirtz J., and Kum D., 'Consumer cheating on service guarantees', *Journal of the Academy of Marketing Science*, vol. 32, no. 2, 2004.

Zemke R. and Schaaf R., *The Service Edge: 101 Companies that Profit from Customer Care*, NAL Books, Beltsville, Md, 1989.

Gold Card Protection Service

Case Exercise

Executive Bank plc is a bank that attracts premium customers, usually international travellers. As part of its exclusive, and expensive, Gold Chargecard Service it offers its customers the opportunity to join, for a small additional annual fee, its card protection scheme, the Gold Card Protection Service.

The card protection scheme simply provides insurance against the theft and misuse of its customers' charge and credit cards (the cards may be issued by any bank, credit company or store). In addition, this service also provides a wide range of benefits that are not dissimilar to the card protection schemes run by other companies. These include:

- a 24-hour worldwide freephone number
- a single call to cancel all cards and order replacements
- £1,000 insurance against misuse prior to notification
- unlimited cover after notification
- £1,250 interest-free emergency cash if the customer is stranded abroad
- a lost key and luggage retrieval service
- help in the emergency replacement of driving licence and passport
- payment of emergency hotel bills up to £500
- emergency airline or ferry tickets up to £1,000
- emergency car-hire assistance.

The Gold Card Protection Service boasts that it provides a 'friendly, efficient and thorough service to all its customers' and that it will 'answer calls within an average of 10 seconds, generate loss reports to the card issuers, by fax or telex, within 20 seconds after the call, and always send prompt confirmation of action taken'.

The following is a letter sent by a customer after having experienced the service.

6 February

Mr Daniel Payne
Customer Services Manager
Gold Card Customer Services
Executive Bank plc
London

Dear Mr Payne

I am writing to express my profound dissatisfaction with the service provided by your organisation.

At 9.30 a.m. on 17 January I was robbed whilst entering a bus near Warsaw railway station on the way to Warsaw airport. My wallet, containing all my credit and charge cards and a number of personal items, was stolen. I reported this loss to your Gold Card Protection Service at 11.00 a.m. on my arrival at Warsaw airport. I greatly appreciated the opportunity to make a reverse charge call.

I was told that all my cards would be stopped immediately and replacements requested. The operator asked if there was any cash in the wallet. I told her that there was about £20 in the wallet. She asked me if I had cash with me and I confirmed that I had. The operator asked for a number where I could be contacted that evening. This was provided.

I was impressed by the arrival of my replacement Executive Gold Card on 19 January.

By Wednesday 24 January all the replacement cards had arrived with the exception of my Standard Bank Cashline Card. This was an important card as it was my main means of obtaining cash. Having been without the card for a week, this was becoming a problem!

On returning home from work at 8.00 p.m. on 25 January I found that the card had still not arrived. I rang the Standard Bank's telephone banking service to ask when I should expect to receive my card. I was told that the card had been stopped but no replacement ordered. I was told they would notify my branch, but that I should ring the branch the following day. I then rang your organisation to try to discover why the replacement card had not been ordered. I spoke to James Creek who informed me that the Standard Bank did not accept orders for replacement cards from anyone but the customer and that I should contact my bank directly. I complained that I had not been told this – indeed one week had gone by during which I had assumed it was on its way. James apologised and said the operator should have told me. I then asked James if the small amount of cash that I had in my wallet was also covered. James told me it was and he offered to send me a claim form. I asked why the operator had not checked this with me at the time. James said she should have done so and again apologised and promised to send me a claim form immediately. I felt very dissatisfied with your service at this point. One of my card issuers had sent me, with their replacement card, information about their card protection scheme which I noticed provided free cover for family members. I pointed this out to James and asked him to send me information about your card protection scheme so I could make a comparison. He agreed to do this and also offered me free cover for my spouse for one year to make up for the inconvenience I had suffered. James told me that he would contact my bank to try to sort out the replacement. He sincerely apologised for all the errors.

On 26 January I rang my bank to check that a card had been ordered. My branch confirmed that a replacement had been ordered by your organisation and it would arrive about 30 January. I would then have to return the confirmation slip and when they received it the card would be operative (over two weeks after it had been stolen). I complained that it was my only means of getting cash. I was told there was nothing that could be done, though I could speed the process by taking the confirmation slip to my branch as soon as I received it. I suggested that might be difficult as I had a full-time job.

On 30 January my Cashline Card arrived and I returned the confirmation slip by post. There was no material from your organisation. I rang and spoke to you and you apologised for the incidents. You agreed that the material should have arrived by now, since stationery orders are processed overnight. I agreed to wait a few more days.

Today is 6 February. I have just received the PIN number for my Cashline Card and have managed to use it – nearly three weeks after the robbery. I am still without the promised material from your organisation.

I would be grateful if you could answer the following questions:

1 Why did the operator not tell me that my Cashline Card would not be replaced unless I contacted my bank?

2 Why did the operator not tell me that the cash in my wallet was also covered by your scheme and volunteer to send me a claim form?

3 Why did the operator not ring me in the evening to tell me about the problem with the Cashline Card or to confirm that all the instructions had been carried out? I would have very much appreciated this reassurance.

4 Why could James order a replacement on 25 January but the initial operator could not do so on 17 January? Did I need to contact the bank or not?

5 Why did James not ring me a few days later, on 27 January for example, to check that I had received the material he promised and that everything was now all right?

6 Why did I not receive the material?

7 Why do you wait till the customer is so fed up and has to ask you to sort something out? I have now made five telephone calls and written this one letter. I have not yet received any call or correspondence from yourselves. I can only conclude that you just don't care.

8 Why do you only do what appears to be the minimum possible to deal with an aggrieved customer?

9 Please would you tell me why I should continue to pay the large annual fee for the Executive Gold Card and the additional cost for the Gold Card Protection Service for this appalling lack of service?

Yours sincerely

David Smith

Question

1 How would you respond to this letter?

part five

Managing strategic change

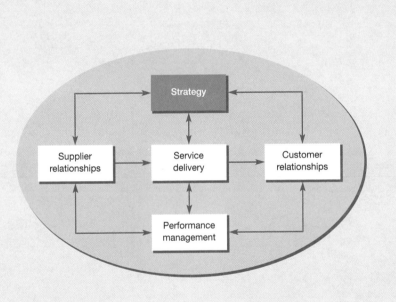

chapter thirteen

Service strategy

Chapter objectives:

- to define what is meant by a strategy and identify its key components

- to discuss the use of service as a competitive weapon

- to explain how performance objectives are turned into operations priorities

- to describe strategy formulation and development

- to explore the issues involved in sustaining a strategy.

13.1 Introduction

'All great service companies have a clear, compelling service strategy. They have a "reason for being" which energises the organisation and defines the word "service"' (Berry 1995). By having a clear strategy managers know what initiatives to approve and those to reject, customers know what to expect, employees know what to provide and operations knows how it has to deliver the service. If employees do not know what the organisation's strategy is, or each person has their own view, success is going to be hard to achieve.

A service strategy (or a manufacturing strategy) provides the intellectual frameworks and conceptual models that allow managers to identify opportunities for bringing value to customers (Normann and Ramirez 1993) and for delivering that value at a profit or within budget. The role for service operations managers is to help create and deliver that value by contributing to the strategy debate and by developing the operation, its resources, people and processes, to provide for the future success of the organisation.

A strategy is only as good as its implementation. The organisation needs to call on a wide range of abilities in order to create an effective strategy, from the visionary thinker at director level, through the interpretation of this strategy into policies and plans by senior and middle management, to the involvement in and ownership of service delivery by front-line staff. It is not the purpose of this book to describe the strategic process in detail. We are concerned with the creation and implementation of strategy insofar as it has direct relevance to service delivery. In this sense, the three major components of strategy – market and competitive analysis, strategic choice, and implementation – are very important issues for the service operations manager.

13.2 Service strategy

Research into strategy development asserts that effective strategies generally are evolutionary rather than revolutionary (Quinn 1978, Bailey and Johnson 1992; see also Mintzberg *et al.* 1998). Quinn suggests that although there is often refined strategic analysis embedded in strategic formulation, the real strategy evolves as internal decisions and external events combine to form a widely shared consensus for action among key members of the management team. Today, we would suggest that key contributors to strategy development must include those in constant contact with market requirements: the customer-facing staff.

These employees, often rather junior and poorly paid in many consumer services, have a key role in strategy development. They often have advance information as to customer likes and dislikes, and about the way that customers' tastes are changing. Crucially, these staff have the task of 'living the strategy'. If they are not committed to the goals and objectives of the organisation, it will be plain for all to see. The old adage that strategy should be 'top down and bottom up' has much to commend it.

13.2.1 Defining service strategy

Service organisations, like all businesses, need to have overarching strategies in place to try to prevent non-aligned and disjointed activities and decisions (Lovelock 1994, Senge 1993). A strategy is usually seen in market terms as an organisation's plan to achieve an advantage over its competitors. Some organisations, however, may not wish to achieve advantage but see their role as maintaining their position in the marketplace. Others operate in non-competitive situations and wish to ensure that they are able to adapt to their own changing environments. Service

strategy is therefore defined as the set of plans and policies by wh
organisation aims to meet its objectives.

Strategy: harnessing five elements

A strategic plan will harness the various aspects of an organisation and ensure that they support each other and are consistent with the direction indicated by the drivers of change. Five critical elements of strategy are: the creation of corporate objectives, an understanding of the environment, the development of an appropriate service concept, the identification of appropriate operations performance objectives, and the development of an appropriate operation – see Figure 13.1 (see also Johnston 1988 and 1989, Heskett 1986, Heskett *et al.* 1990):

- *Corporate objectives*. These provide the targets or goals for the strategy. If a strategy is a set of plans or policies to meet objectives, there needs to be a statement of those objectives. In part the objectives provide the motivation for change, but they also set out the size and speed of change. Such a statement is an important step in making the change 'public' so that employees are made aware of what is expected of them. In essence the objectives set out the parameters for change.

- *Environment*. All organisations operate in a context and that environment needs to be understood to assess not only the opportunities that it might afford but also the likely response of other organisations and the reaction of customers to change.

- *Service concept*. This identifies the proposed nature of the business – the service in mind that the organisation wishes to create. The service concept helps the organisation focus on the value that it can provide to customers.

- *Performance objectives*. These provide the means by which a strategy is translated into operations language, setting out the priorities for the operation. Together with the service concept they specify the task for operations.

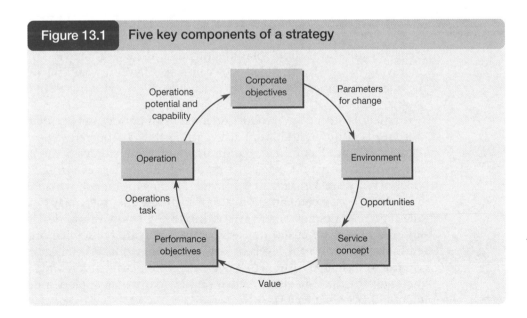

Figure 13.1 **Five key components of a strategy**

on. People, processes, structure, performance measurement systems, chains etc. – the operation – may have to be developed and changed to ent the strategy. Also the operation may provide the impetus for change its current, or potential, capability.

ative and continuous process

an iterative process. The key components, objectives, environment, service concept, performance criteria and operations all need to be aligned in the delivery of service and the achievement of the strategic objectives. This requires a constant checking of all the elements to ensure that objectives can be met.

Strategy formulation is also not a one-off activity. Organisations need to respond to the two main forces of change that operate upon them: the external and internal environments. As a result, a strategy requires continuous assessment and, if necessary, amendment.

13.2.4 Planned or emergent strategies

Strategies may be intended, formal and planned; alternatively, they may either emerge from an intended strategy that was not realised, or emerge independently of a formal planning process (see, for example, Mintzberg 1998 and Mintzberg *et al*. 1998). The creation of intended strategies tends to be a top-down approach, starting with either a statement of corporate objectives or an evaluation of the environment and market opportunities. Emergent strategies tend to be bottom-up processes, often starting with an idea for a new service concept or the emergence of new operational capabilities. Both types of approaches may be at work in successful organisations (Burgelman and Grove 1996).

13.3 Service as competitive advantage

Many organisations, both manufacturing and service, are recognising that by improving the service provided they can make significant and sustainable gains in the marketplace. Service and service delivery can be, and increasingly are, a competitive weapon.

For manufacturing and product-oriented organisations, service may be an important means of differentiation, particularly if they are operating in markets where there is little product differentiation or where product development is slow, difficult, expensive or short-lived. The nature of the services available and the way in which services are delivered may provide a means to competitive success.

Service-oriented companies are also recognising that there may be a need to provide high levels of customer service. Increasing competition, declining sales and more service-aware customers are putting pressure on service organisations to rethink and improve the levels of service that they offer. The effect of good service on creating valuable customers, increasing customer retention and loyalty, and on attracting other customers, as well as on the financial position of an organisation is important (see Chapter 11).

In addition, for organisations that compete on cost, service has a role to play in ensuring right-first-time delivery and low operational costs.

13.3.1 Competing on outcome and/or experience

Some service organisations compete on their service outcomes and others on the experience, while some manage to compete on both (see Figure 13.2).

As Figure 13.2 suggests, there are a number of positions that the service organisation may take up when compared with the competition. This analysis can also be applied by public-sector and not-for-profit organisations, since they, too, are in a form of competition for resources. Civil service departments compete for a larger slice of the country's budget, and charities compete for donor funds.

The five positions suggested by Figure 13.2 are as follows:

- *Failing*. The organisations' outcomes are below industry specification, and their customer service is poor. Traditional services that have failed to move with market trends find themselves in this position. Some years ago in the fast-food market Wimpy found that it was left behind by McDonald's in terms of higher food standards and faster service.

- *Complacent*. In these organisations the service outcome is excellent, but the way that customers are treated is poor. Professional services sometimes fall into this category, being experienced as arrogant by their clients. They may well know better than their clients, but this does not excuse service that can often be offensive. The medical profession often comes in for criticism in this area, dealing with patients not as human beings but rather as another condition to be treated.

- *Retaining customers in the short term*. It is possible to develop customer loyalty through good customer service. However, if the total service outcome falls below standard, customers will only tolerate this for a relatively short period. If the service experience is excellent, the emotional switching costs are quite high for customers, but eventually they will leave. Some computer companies have used this strategy to retain customers in the period between phasing out an old product and launching a new one.

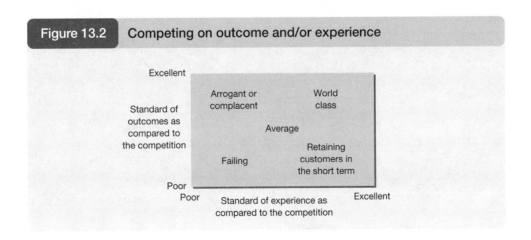

| Figure 13.2 | Competing on outcome and/or experience |

- *Average*. This is the position that many high-volume, business-to-consumer services believe they occupy. In many of these traditional service sectors there are frequently a number of reasonably established competitors, all conducting business in a similar fashion. The consumer financial service sector in the UK was a good example, with several players and little to choose between them. As the competition has become more fierce, many have chosen to try to differentiate themselves through the way that they deal with their customers.

- *World class*. These organisations are universally recognised as being the best in all that they do. There are few of these in existence.

Most large organisations will find that they can position their range of services at different points. Some may be world class, while others are failing. It is important to distinguish between them because each will require a different strategic approach.

13.3.2 Understanding perceived user value

To understand how service or services can be used to create a competitive edge it is essential to understand what is regarded as important by customers. The notion of perceived user value (PUV) can be helpful here (Bowman 1998). PUVs are the criteria regarded by customers as being important, and on which they will base their assessment of the organisation and its services. The PUVs for a supermarket chain might include stock availability, range of products, store location, etc. Figure 13.3 shows a comparison of PUVs for two supermarket chains.

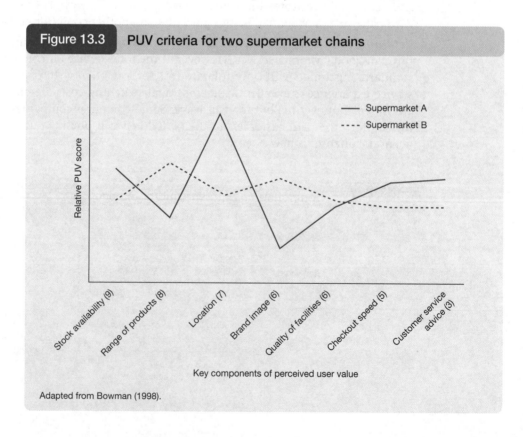

Figure 13.3 | PUV criteria for two supermarket chains

Key components of perceived user value

Adapted from Bowman (1998).

The scores in brackets on Figure 13.3 denote the relative weighting that customers ascribe to each criterion. Therefore stock availability is weighted at 9/10 whereas checkout speed scores 5/10. This analysis allows the operations manager to determine priorities for action (see also section 13.4.3) and also to know in what way operations contribute to the overall competitiveness of the organisation. Operations contribute directly to some aspects of PUV (stock availability, checkout speed and customer service advice) and may contribute indirectly to other aspects of PUV (for example, how the service is delivered may have an impact on brand image and the relationship formed with customers, which may facilitate feedback to revise product range).

By separating out price from the other PUVs we have a useful framework for identifying and assessing current and future strategies (Bowman 1998). This allows the possibility of competing by more than simply being cheaper or differentiated, i.e. competing in both ways (see Figure 13.4).

The analysis from Figure 13.4 shows that Supermarket A is of similar size (depicted by the size of the circle) and strategic positioning (weighted average PUV) to Supermarket B. There is a smaller rival, C, which is perceived to be of higher quality but is very expensive. Likewise, D is the low-cost provider in this marketplace and is only slightly smaller than A and B.

The question to be addressed here is to understand which strategic direction to adopt. If A wishes to maintain the price position but wants to increase PUV, inspection of the analysis from Figure 13.3 will be a good starting-point. Clearly, high stock availability and product range provide opportunities for enhancing PUV. If this strategy is adopted, operations can determine its contribution in terms of improving service standards without increasing operations cost. If the preferred strategy is to increase PUV and decrease price, then operations have a major task if the reduction in price is not simply to be achieved by reducing margins.

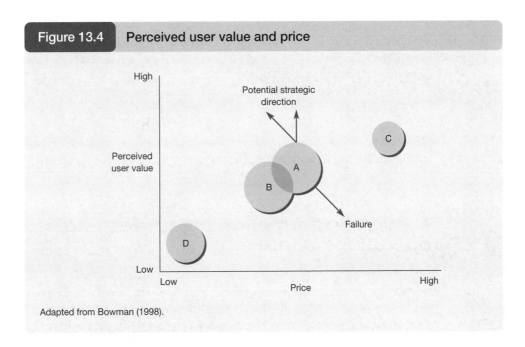

Figure 13.4   Perceived user value and price

Adapted from Bowman (1998).

Telecorp Box 13.1

Telecorp is one of the major global suppliers of telecommunications equipment, with competitors that include Ericsson, Motorola and Nortel. The traditional business of these suppliers has been in the development and production of fixed network equipment – the switches that form the heart of a country's telecommunications structure.

In recent years the traditional business of these telecommunications suppliers has been under threat. Existing stable customer relationships have been broken up. For example, Ericsson, being a Swedish company, has been the preferred supplier to Swedish Telecom, in the same way that Alcatel would relate to France Telecom. In many countries the national telecommunications provider (for example, British Telecom in the UK) has been privatised, with the objective of injecting competitive forces into the industry. Alongside this has been the advent of mobile phone networks. These are often owned by companies that do not have a long history and technical expertise in the telecommunications market, and are operated for profit rather than public service.

These forces have combined to threaten Telecorp's profitability in its traditional business. Manufactured product margins have declined significantly, and in some cases have become non-existent. A possible strategy is to remain as a manufacturer in the 'commodity' area, and to become very lean in its operations, but Telecorp has chosen instead to develop services to be

sold with its manufactured products and systems to help its new, relatively inexperienced, network customers operate more effectively.

While this general approach is agreed and seen as necessary by the senior management group, the interpretation of the vision to develop significant revenues has caused some discussion. There are two main viewpoints. The first view, largely held by those managers brought up in the fixed network environment, is that Telecorp should continue to be seen as an innovator of telecommunications (physical) products and systems, which also helps customers use Telecorp's products more effectively. The opposing viewpoint is that Telecorp should become a service provider, generating solutions for its customers. In this case, Telecorp should act as systems integrator utilising its own or competitors' products in the most appropriate combination. This second view is largely held by managers from the mobile network side, who have often been recruited from other industry sectors.

Questions

1 What are the differences in implications for the service operations manager in implementing the two approaches outlined above?

2 How would you demonstrate the strategic options using the tools described in this section?

This illustration is based on a real organisation, although all names and places have been changed.

The next section develops the strategic positioning analysis from section 13.3, using additional performance objectives and more detailed scales to identify operations priorities.

13.4 Turning performance objectives into operations priorities

While the service concept defines the nature of the service to be provided, the performance objectives define the competitive or strategic priorities for the operations. 'Identifying a service strategy boils down to searching for a match between what needs doing and what the firm can do exceedingly well' (Berry 1995). The operations performance objectives will (or rather should!) include, or incorporate, customer-based PUVs together with the organisation's view as to how it does or should compete as a whole. Performance objectives are also the basis for the development of performance measurement systems and a key way of linking operations performance measures to strategy. Organisations have to do well, and competitive organisations have to compete, on many different criteria. These might include:

- price
- quality
- availability
- reliability
- speed of service
- flexibility
- range of services
- new service development
- uniqueness.

Two dimensions – importance and performance – can be used to help operations managers prioritise these objectives so that they know where it is appropriate to spend time, effort and money.

13.4.1 Importance

The importance of a factor can be assessed in terms of its importance to customers (internal or external). Three categories of importance are order winners, qualifiers and less important factors (see Hill 1993, Slack 1991, Slack *et al*. 2004).

- *Qualifiers* may not win business but play an important part in retaining business, by which we mean customers or sources of funding for example. If performance falls below a certain point compared to other organisations, business may be lost. An internet service provider (ISP), for example, may lose customers if access to its network is slower or more difficult than through its competitors. A university that does not perform well in research league tables may lose out on government funds.

- *Order winners* both maintain and win new business, funds or customers for the organisation. These are special qualifiers that the organisation has chosen as part of its strategy to use as a means of securing an advantage, or a point of differentiation, over other organisations. An ISP may choose price as its order winner, for example. By making its service free to its customers or even providing free phone access to its network, an ISP may gain a significant advantage over its competitors and increase its customer base. A university may attract executive courses by having outstanding facilities, even though its staff may be no better or worse than those in other institutions.

- *Less important factors* are relatively unimportant but should not be ignored because they may become a source of advantage at some future point. In the case of a bank the comfort of the banking hall may be a less important factor, or the speed of the search routines provided may be less important to an internet service provider.

Using the results network from Chapter 11, the order winners are all those factors that contribute to both attraction and retention of business. The qualifiers are those that contribute to retention of business only (see Figure 13.5). Attraction, as before, can be defined as attracting new customers in a competitive environment, attracting new donors for a charity, or attracting new funds for a public-sector organisation, and also attracting good staff. Retention refers to retaining customers, staff and funding.

To help judge the relative importance of individual factors and help identify priorities for improvement, a more discriminating nine-point scale can be used with three points per category (see Table 13.1).

13.4.2 Performance

Performance, the second dimension for assessing performance objectives, is concerned with the performance of each objective against other or competing organisations – whether they are competing in the traditional sense or competing for funds, staff or even kudos! A nine-point scale can again be used to assess relative performance of any of the factors (see Table 13.2).

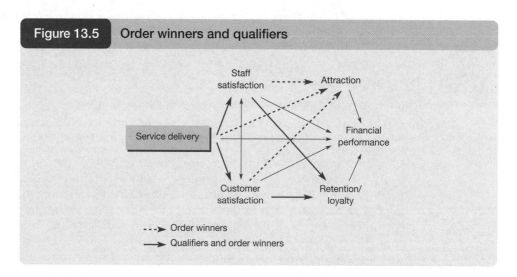

| Figure 13.5 | Order winners and qualifiers |

Table 13.1 Judging importance of individual factors

Order winners (attractors)	Strong	1	Crucially important to attract business
	Medium	2	Important to attract business
	Weak	3	Useful for attracting new business
Qualifiers (retainers)	Strong	1	Vital for retention
	Medium	2	Important for retention
	Weak	3	Useful for retention
Less important	Strong	1	Not usually important
	Medium	2	Rarely considered important
	Weak	3	Not at all important

Adapted from Slack et al. (2004).

Table 13.2 Judging performance of individual factors

Better than others	Strong	1	Considerably better than others
	Medium	2	Clearly better than others
	Weak	3	Somewhat better than others
The same as others	Strong	1	Marginally better than others
	Medium	2	The same as others
	Weak	3	Marginally worse than others
Worse than others	Strong	1	Somewhat worse than others
	Medium	2	Usually worse than others
	Weak	3	Considerably worse than others

Adapted from Slack *et al.* (2004).

13.4.3 The importance–performance matrix

By taking its importance score and the performance score, each performance objective can then be plotted on an importance–performance matrix (Slack 1991, Slack *et al.* 2004). Figure 13.6 shows the matrix, which is divided into four zones:

● *The appropriate zone* is where performance is better than other organisations for the order winners and at least the same as others for qualifiers and less important criteria. Factors in this area may not require action to improve, but the focus of performance measurement systems may have to be to keep the factor in

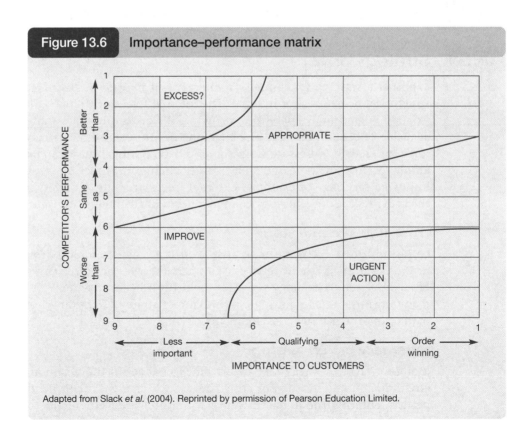

Figure 13.6   Importance–performance matrix

Adapted from Slack *et al.* (2004). Reprinted by permission of Pearson Education Limited.

control. To maintain an edge over other organisations it may be worth considering trying to develop performance in some factors in this zone.

- **The improve zone** identifies factors that need some attention, such as order winners where performance is similar to others and qualifiers where performance is slightly worse. The focus for performance measurement should be an improvement rather than control and strategies should be developed to improve performance (see Chapter 12).

- **The urgent action zone** identifies factors where urgent attention is required to improve performance (see Chapter 12). It is likely to be an immediate priority to move factors in this area up to at least the improve zone and into the appropriate zone in the medium term.

- **The excess? zone** includes factors that may have higher performance than is necessary. Performance that is significantly better than others may be a waste of resources for qualifiers and certainly for the less important factors. On the other hand, if these factors are considered to be emerging qualifiers or winners, such expenditure may well be warranted.

By applying the importance–performance matrix operations managers can translate strategic intentions into clear priorities for the operation, identifying where limited resources may best be spent to support the organisation's strategic intentions.

13.5 Strategy formulation and development

13.5.1 Strategy drivers

Whether a strategy is planned or emergent, it is usually driven by some force, which may be external or internal. The internal forces or strategy drivers might be existing operational capabilities, or new skills or technologies that have become available or been developed. The changing needs of stakeholders may also act as a force for change – pressure from shareholders, political masters, management or employees for an increased share value, change in direction, reduced costs or improved services, for example. External forces or strategy drivers might include the activities of competitors or changing needs of customers (see Figure 13.7).

Operations-led strategy

Opportunities for change may arise from new developments from within the organisation, such as new services, skills, technologies or processes. The availability of e-commerce technology provides opportunities for new delivery channels for many organisations, requiring a rethinking of strategy, including how to manage, market and finance such developments.

Externally driven strategy

Modifications to strategy may be driven by changes in the organisation's external environment, either actual or anticipated. Such changes might include new competitors entering the marketplace; or the strategic developments of competitors

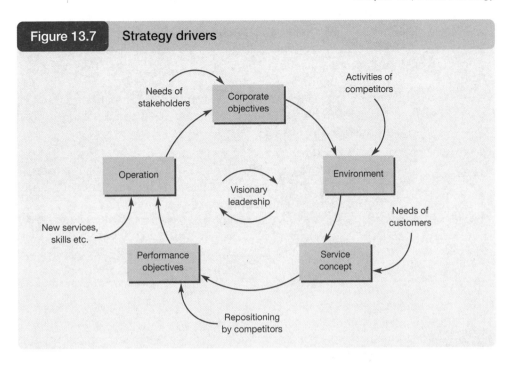

Figure 13.7   Strategy drivers

through different positioning or service developments; or the changing needs of customers who require a different service concept, which may be the result of the activities of the competition; or the loss of customers because their needs are not being met.

Corporate-led strategy

The impetus for change may come from the organisation's executive, driven by a desire or need by its stakeholders for a greater return on assets, or expansion, or retrenchment, or diversification, for example.

Visionary leadership

Any one of the above drivers may be sufficient to begin the cycle of strategy formulation and development, though clearly the more drivers that are in evidence, the more pressure there is on the strategy cycle to move. One condition that we believe has a major impact on the strategy formulation process is visionary leadership. This is usually provided by an individual, usually at corporate level, although it is possibly a senior figure within operations, marketing or finance, who takes responsibility for strategy development and acts as the linchpin in the wheel, pulling all the forces together and helping them move in the right direction.

Visionary leaders understand the current organisation and its service – its processes, people and culture, for example – and are able to create an attractive vision for the future. They are also able to communicate that vision and enthuse others, and thus galvanise the whole organisation to bring about the realisation of that vision (see Figure 13.8).

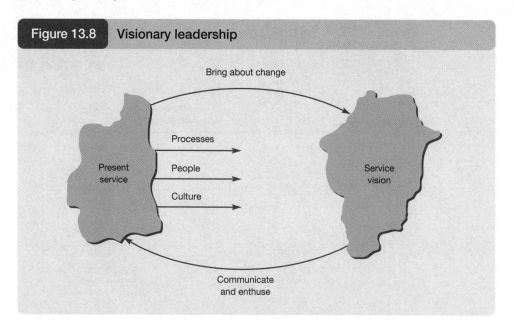

Figure 13.8 | Visionary leadership

13.5.2 Key issues in strategy development

Objectives

The development of clear corporate objectives is based on the strategy drivers – the internal or external pressures or opportunities for change. The objectives may well be expressed in financial or competitive terms over a set period of time, for example return on investment, profit, number of new customers or market share. These objectives need to be clearly stated and will provide the means of measuring and monitoring the success or otherwise of the strategy. The key questions that need to be asked are:

- What are the objectives?
- Are they achievable?
- What investment is required?
- What is the timeframe?
- What methods for review are in place?
- What are the contingencies?

Environment

To ensure that those objectives can be achieved, there needs to be a clear understanding of the market and the environment in which the organisation currently operates, or plans to be operating. This will include an understanding of the size and nature of the competition, the nature and size of the market or potential market, existing competing and complementary products and services, the ways the market is currently segmented, and the likely reaction of the competition. One key outcome of this activity is the identification of a potential target market and an assessment of the perceived needs and expectations of the target customers.

The key questions include:

- What are the characteristics of the market or market segment?
- Is the strategy appropriate for them?
- What are the needs and expectations of customers in this market?
- How well are these needs being served – by this organisation, by other organisations?
- What are the strengths, weaknesses, opportunities and threats?
- What might be the reaction of other providers to a change in strategy?

Service concept

The service concept is a clear statement about the nature of the service:

- The service experience – the customer's direct experience of the service process, including the way the customer is dealt with by the service provider.
- The service outcome – the result for the customer of the service.
- The service operation – the way in which the service will be delivered.
- The value of the service – the benefit that customers perceive to be inherent in the service weighed against the cost of that service.

This identifies not only what customers and providers would have in their mind but also what operations have to provide and marketers market. It also identifies the degree of focus, the extent to which the service attempts to do 'everything for everybody' or focus on meeting particular needs of a particular customer segment. The key questions to be asked are:

- What is the concept?
- Is it aimed at a particular market?
- Is it appropriate for that market?
- Can it be understood by customers and providers?
- How will it be communicated to customers and providers?
- Can it be delivered by the operation?

Performance objectives

Having identified a target market and developed a service concept, the operation needs guidance as to how it should manage its resources and activities. This will ensure that the service it provides will meet the corporate objectives and the needs of the target market and will establish how it will differentiate itself from the competition. A clear understanding of the performance objectives and their relative priorities is required (see the importance–performance model earlier). The key questions include:

- What are the order winners and qualifiers?
- What are the priorities for change?
- What are the measures of performance associated with each objective?
- What are the targets?

- Are they achievable?
- By when have the targets to be achieved?
- What investment is required?

Operation

The design or development of an appropriate operation may be a complex activity requiring a large number of interrelated decisions, connecting processes, employees, customers and infrastructure. New investment may be required or there may be a redeployment of existing resources. The operation plan then needs to be checked against the objectives to ensure that the total strategy is consistent and will achieve the objectives that have been set. Thus the process may have to go through several iterations before a consistent and cohesive strategy is created. The key questions include:

- What changes are required to processes, employees, customer management and infrastructure?
- How will the changes be brought about?
- What resources are required?
- Can the new concept be delivered?
- Will it meet the perceived needs of the target market?
- Can the performance objectives be achieved?

Anglian Water Services Limited | Box 13.2

In the early 1990s Anglian Water Services, in common with the other water companies in the UK, was facing a new challenge. It had been newly privatised and was struggling to understand the new environment in which it was operating.

A new challenge for the water industry was that water users were now to be thought of as customers, not least because in the not-too-distant future the utilities were to become open to competition. Indeed, today, the old demarcations between water, gas and electricity companies have disappeared, with a number of companies providing all three traditional services and offering telecommunications as well.

John Green, then operations director of Anglian Water Services, met with his team of senior managers, including a newly appointed marketing manager, to formulate a customer service strategy. The first requirement was to understand the relevance of customers to the success of the company. The water companies had previously operated more as custodians of water hygiene than as customer-focused organisations. This did not mean that they did not have a service ethic but rather that it was not customer-focused.

The key question to be addressed was 'Did customer service matter?' After all, water users had no choice as to where to go. However, the water companies were subject to close inspection by the industry regulator, OFWAT. This body regularly published statistics, which included customer service performance, comparing the various companies. These statistics were felt to be a significant factor in influencing the stock-market rating of the company, which was essential in competing for investment funds.

Perhaps more important, deregulation was seen not as a threat, but as an opportunity for the company to grow into new areas not directly controlled by OFWAT. The development of a customer service strategy was therefore to be seen as a vehicle for bringing about a culture within the organisation as a whole.

John Green's team set about defining a new service vision. To do this, it carried out an audit of current performance, recognising that there were a number of customer segments with different requirements, including domestic users industrial users and property developers. The points of contact with customers were reviewed and the supporting processes mapped. A number of workshops were held with key staff from all parts of the operation, resulting in a draft customer strategy document to be discussed at board level.

This was the start of many initiatives in the development of service strategy. Early debates as to what perceived quality might mean were an important stage in the process. It was important to consider the possibility that consumers might want water that looked and tasted nice even though it might not be as hygienic in scientific terms. Anglian Water Services has developed this strategy considerably since the initial workshops. A major systems review was carried out, creating a new organisational structure, including the appointment of a director of customer service. Today, Anglian Water has an international business, and a reputation for a commitment to learning.

Questions

1 What were the main drivers for the development of a customer service strategy for Anglian Water Services?

2 How well do you think the strategy development process was carried out? What could have been done differently?

13.6 Sustaining a strategy

Without constant appraisal of the changes to the internal and external environments and consequent adjustments to strategy, organisations may decay. Lovelock (1994) refers to this process as 'institutional rusting'. Strategy therefore involves the process of continually checking the organisation's plans for direction, progress and cohesion in terms of the continually changing environment.

The main operational difficulties faced by organisations in sustaining a strategy are:

- Conflicting objectives, such as the need to provide a customised product using existing processes capable only of delivering a commodity-type service.

- Inappropriate and inflexible operations processes and resources, such as inappropriate equipment and untrained employees.

- Inappropriate investment, including inadequate investment to provide the resources required or develop the existing ones.

- Undetected changes to the service concept as delivered by the operation as opposed to what was originally intended, for example a failure to detect how managers and employees may be reinterpreting the concept in the way with which they are comfortable, as opposed to what is required by customers (concept contamination).

- The addition of multiple (similar) service products to a service process originally designed for one product, resulting in potential compromise of service standards across all products.

13.7 Summary

Service strategy

- Service strategy is the set of plans and policies by which a service organisation aims to meet its objectives.
- A strategy involves the creation of corporate objectives, an understanding of the environment, the development of an appropriate service concept, the identification of appropriate operations performance objectives and the development of an appropriate operation.

Service as competitive advantage

- Organisations may compete on the excellence of their outcomes, the excellence of their experiences, or both.
- Perceived user value provides a means of identifying current and future strategies.

Turning performance objectives into operations priorities

- The importance–performance matrix helps identify operational priorities.

Strategy formulation and development

- Strategy drivers include existing operational capabilities, or new skills or technologies that have become available or been developed, the changing needs of stakeholders, the activities of competitors and changing needs of customers.
- Strategy development is an iterative process, which should result in a consistent and cohesive strategy.

Sustaining a strategy

- It is necessary continually to check the organisation's plans for direction, progress and cohesion in terms of the changing environment.

13.8 Discussion questions

1 Select four organisations in the same sector, such as four food outlets, pubs or libraries, and assess their relative positions in terms of their outcomes and experiences.

2 Identify the PUV criteria for two competing organisations. Score them on each criterion and assess their strategies. What options would they have if they wanted to differentiate themselves from the competition?

13.9   Questions for managers

1 Define and evaluate your service strategy.

2 Do you compete in terms of outcome and/or experience? In what ways could you change?

3 Identify your PUV criteria. How do you score against your key competitors? What are the options for change?

4 Identify all your performance criteria and undertake an importance–performance analysis. Do the priorities identified reflect the organisation's priorities?

5 Evaluate your process for strategy formulation and development.

13.10   Further reading

Mathur S.S. and Kenyon A., *Creating Value: Successful Business Strategies*, 2nd edition, Butterworth Heinemann, Oxford, 2001.

Mintzberg H., Ahlstrand B. and Lampel J., *Strategy Safari*, Prentice Hall, Harlow, 1998.

Normann R. and Ramirez R., 'From value chain to value constellation: designing interactive strategy', *Harvard Business Review*, July–August 1993, pp. 65–77.

Silvestro R. and Silvestro C., 'New service design in the NHS: an evaluation of the strategic alignment of NHS Direct', *International Journal of Operations and Production Management*, vol. 23, no. 4, April 2003, pp. 401–17.

13.11   References

Bailey A. and Johnson G., 'How strategies develop in organisations', in Faulkner D. and Johnson G. (eds), *The Challenge of Strategic Management*, Cranfield Management Series, Kogan Page, London, 1992, pp. 147–78.

Berry L.L., *On Great Service: A Framework for Action*, Free Press, New York, 1995.

Bowman, C., *Strategy in Practice*, Prentice Hall, Harlow, 1998.

Burgelman R.A. and Grove A.S., 'Strategic dissonance', *California Management Review*, Winter 1996, pp. 8–28.

Heskett J.L., *Managing in the Service Economy*, Harvard Business School Press, Boston, Mass., 1986.

Heskett J.L., Sasser W.E. and Hart C.W.L., *Service Breakthroughs: Changing the Rules of the Game*, Free Press, New York, 1990.

Hill T., *Manufacturing Strategy – Text and Cases*, Irwin, Homewood, Ill., 1993

Johnston R., 'Service industries – improving competitive performance', *Service Industries Journal*, vol. 8, no. 2, April 1988, pp. 202–11.

Johnston R., 'Developing competitive strategies in service industries', in Jones P. (ed.), *Management in Service Industries*, Pitman, London, 1989.

Lovelock C.H., *Product Plus*, McGraw Hill, New York, 1994.

Mintzberg, H., *The Strategy Process*, Prentice Hall, London, 1998.

Mintzberg H., Ahlstrand B. and Lampel J., *Strategy Safari*, Prentice Hall, Harlow, 1998.

Normann R. and Ramirez R., 'From value chain to value constellation: designing interactive strategy', *Harvard Business Review*, July–August 1993, pp. 65–77.

Quinn J.B., 'Strategic change: logical incrementalism', *Sloan Management Review*, vol. 1, no. 20, Autumn 1978, pp. 7–21.

Senge P.M., *The Fifth Discipline*, Century Business, London, 1993.

Slack N., *The Manufacturing Advantage*, Mercury, London, 1991.

Slack N., Chambers S. and Johnston R., *Operations Management*, 4th edition, FT Prentice Hall, Harlow 2004.

Smith and Jones, solicitors — Case Exercise

John Smith and David Jones are lawyers and first met when they had been employed in a large firm of solicitors in London. They both felt that London held few attractions for them and that they would prefer their own small country practice. Six years ago they moved to offices just off the main street in a large market town in the west of England and set up in competition with four other firms of solicitors. It was a slow start but both partners were now very busy and had a secretarial staff of five.

John explained that they have two types of client.

There is the personal client who is the local individual with a small legal problem, like a house purchase or a boundary dispute, and there is the commercial client who is a company, a few of which are local but most are based in nearby cities.

The personal client comes through the door when he or she has a problem. There used to be a lot of loyalty to the solicitors that the client or his or her family had used in the past, but this is declining. We don't do any advertising – indeed, it is only allowed in a very limited form. Most of our clients come either because they want a change from the solicitors they have used before or through recommendations from friends. We have worked hard to build up our local personal clients. I like to try to break down the stuffy image of the law and deal at a simple and straightforward level with the client. This personal approach seems to work very well. You see, many ordinary people in the street are very apprehensive about coming to see a solicitor. To them, I suppose, we are a bit like a dentist, only they extract teeth and we extract money! We always make sure that clients are dealt with promptly and

pleasantly by a partner, never by a junior clerk. We see ourselves as a small, local, convenient and friendly firm based on a good, personal and caring image.

When we first came here we obviously had no local work, but we relied upon a few commercial accounts that we brought with us from London. We now work for about ten companies, though no longer for any that are based in London. Some of our commercial work has come about through providing a good service to a personal client. Usually, however, companies have their own favourite firm of solicitors. Sometimes they do give small jobs to other firms just to try them out, so we often get speculative phone calls from potential clients. I reckon sometimes when they ring up they have Yellow Pages in their hands and if you can't help them there and then they will go on to the next firm on the list. Sometimes we get commercial clients through recommendations from other companies or third parties like accountants who have heard that we give a good service. We need to expand our business in this area by giving a good and fast response to our clients.

Now that the firm was well established, John Smith seemed keen not to stand still. He explained:

On local, personal business, solicitors tend to think that if you just sit back, business will just come in and you don't need to make any spectacular effort to keep it. As a result clients are frequently abused. Some solicitors think nothing of telling customers who arrive on the doorstep to go away and come back when they have made an appointment. I think that solicitors have a condescending approach to business. I believe that we have a lot of les-

sons to learn from the modern age and that we can do a lot more thrusting. I am sure there is a lot of scope. I don't believe that everyone is entirely happy with their solicitor.

John felt that the time was right for his firm to expand, and, although these views were less than enthusiastically shared by his partner, John was determined:

It's time the business grew. We are as established as all the other firms in the area, and although we hold on to a share of clients, it never seems to increase, despite a fair growth in the town's population over the last few years. During that time our costs have been increasing. Our overheads on the property and what we have to pay to keep good staff and lease the equipment is considerably greater than what it was even two years ago. It is not easy just to put up our fees to cover these increases. I know you think we pluck figures out of the air, but most of our clients use us several times and they remember how much we charged them last time. As a result our margins have been getting tighter. However, to expand the business we need another solicitor, but it's going to be difficult to attract someone into the office when they see what their share of the spoils might be. Both David and I would also have to take a cut in our slice of the rapidly declining cake. If we are going to expand and bring someone else in, we will need to put a lot of time and effort into generating more work.

I'm also concerned about the role the building societies and banks may play in the future. The Government seems determined to give away our bread-and-butter business. If we lost conveyancing there wouldn't be enough work for even the two of us.

John explained his ideas for getting more business:

With personal work, I think we need to become more visible. We don't make any efforts to sell our services. We are currently thinking about putting a brochure together listing our services, like one of our competitors has done. We could distribute these to potential clients and also to our current clients to maintain our name in their minds and inform them of our other services.

More personal and commercial work can be brought in by making more contacts. It's surprising what work you can get out of meeting people on trains or at croquet matches. All you have to do is mention that you are a solicitor and you find that they have a problem. We have recently had some business cards printed for occasions like this.

You might think that joining Rotary or a golf club would be a good idea, but I have not joined them for two reasons. First because they are full of solicitors touting for trade. And, second, I can't play golf. You see, you can't afford to run the risk of being a 'bad egg': unless you are a 'good' Rotarian or golf player you may tend to lose credibility. I prefer to play croquet and there is only one other solicitor in the club. I'm also not too bad at it! David Jones has some good ideas for getting business clients. He is making contacts with trade organisations and associations like local chambers of commerce. This could provide a lot of good contacts and also give us a feel for local needs.

The problem is that some of the jobs for personal clients are not very profitable. Indeed, margins in this type of work generally are small. But it is an important part of our business: it accounts for about 85 per cent of our income. The rest of our income comes from a handful of commercial clients. This may at first seem small scale but this work does command high margins. The jobs are sometimes relatively simple, like arranging insurances. Our fees are based on a percentage. It only takes one or two large transactions to generate a substantial amount of income.

Because the commercial jobs command higher margins I want to see us make substantial increases in this area. I think that unless we improve our income from commercial work to around 50 per cent of our total turnover in the next two or three years, we will have done badly. I don't think our location is a bad one. We have some big cities quite close by and we have good connections in Bristol and London.

We have a good location with good staff and the latest equipment – photocopiers, fax, PCs, laptops, e-mail, and we even have our own website, thanks to David. I must admit that, although I think there are lots of good possibilities, I am not really sure what more I can do.

Question

1 Develop a new service strategy for Smith and Jones.

chapter fourteen

Service culture

Chapter objectives:

- to understand organisational culture and how to influence it

- to identify types of organisational culture and the implications for service delivery systems

- to describe four dimensions of national cultures

- to describe how organisations might manage cultural change, avoiding the pitfalls.

14.1 Introduction

It is tempting to see organisational culture as some sort of 'magic dust' that may or may not exist but which somehow makes the difference between success and failure. Although this is unrealistic, it is useful to reflect on the reasons why some service organisations have been more successful than their competitors despite having similar technologies, processes and skills.

This chapter explores the nature of organisational culture and its impact on the task of the service operations manager. We outline some ways of describing and diagnosing organisational culture and propose some ways that organisational culture can be influenced to assist the operations manager in the task of providing high levels of service outcome and experience, cost effectively. Many academics believe that understanding and influencing organisational culture is central to delivering a consistent service (see, for example, De Chernatony *et al.* 2003, Browning 1998).

14.2   Understanding organisational culture

There are two broad schools of thought on organisational culture. The first proposes that culture is something tangible, almost to the point where it can be written down in much the same way that an organisation chart can be included in the company's operating manual. In this sense, culture is something that the organisation possesses in much the same way as it might possess a set of resources or products.

The opposing view is that culture is much less tangible, and only really exists when people in the organisation talk to each other and, by their words and behaviours, act out the culture of the organisation. Writers on organisational culture refer to this view as 'culture as personality' (Morgan 1986, Oswick *et al.* 1996). Described in this way, the culture of the organisation is often hidden below the surface of organisational life, requiring a degree of awareness to understand what might be going on.

It is this latter view of culture that informs the major part of this chapter.

14.2.1   Schein's model of organisational culture

Schein (1985) is one of the leading thinkers on organisational culture. His model, shown in Figure 14.1, suggests that organisational culture has a number of levels or layers to it. It is dangerous to assume that what we might observe on the surface is all that there is to the organisation. There is much to organisational life that is 'beneath the surface', often exerting powerful influences on the decision-making process. This is one of the reasons why seemingly irrational decisions are frequently made by senior managers who are influenced by unspoken (and often undiscussable) aspects of the way that the organisation thinks about itself, what it is good at, how it assesses success, and what it values.

Schein proposed the following three levels of organisational culture:

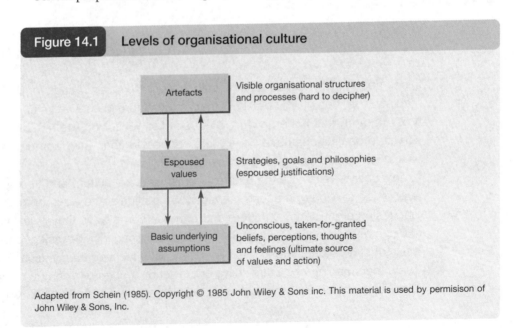

Figure 14.1   Levels of organisational culture

Adapted from Schein (1985). Copyright © 1985 John Wiley & Sons inc. This material is used by permisison of John Wiley & Sons, Inc.

Artefacts

These are the visible aspects of the organisation – its structure and processes, and other physical evidence that can be observed or felt. Although these artefacts may be observed, it is very often not clear what they really mean for the organisation, though they might give some clues.

For the service operation, there may be some understanding to be gained by the celebrations of success of good customer service, or in the position of the champion of service within the organisation (at board level or not). Other visible signs of culture of particular relevance to the service operations manager include the measurement and control systems employed. Control systems that emphasise the importance of customer satisfaction ratings alongside the financial metrics may be evidence of a customer-focused culture.

Even at this level there may be significant differences between operations within the same broad service sector. The hotel that aspires to be a four or five-star operation but which does not invest in replacing tired or broken chairs in the lounge is probably not taking the task seriously. Schein makes the important point that it is very dangerous to draw conclusions from the evidence of the artefacts alone, without knowing the deeper levels of culture that may explain them. However, it is necessary to point out that customers will do just this. Customers will look at the physical evidence and draw their own conclusions.

Most organisations provide instructions to employees as to what to do in the event of fire. The emphasis is normally to leave what you are doing immediately and evacuate the building. A financial services company has a slightly different policy, instructing employees to 'secure company valuables' before leaving. Often, when developing service recovery procedures with operations managers a key concern is that the company's money should not be risked in any way, in any event.

Espoused values

This next level of culture operates at the cognitive level. It describes the stated strategies and beliefs of the organisation. Thus this level may include aspects of the company's mission statement – the general strategy as declared and set down by the leadership team – and statements as to the general values or guiding principles of the organisation. Kwik-Fit's statement that 'Our aim is 100% customer delight' would certainly fall into this category, as would lists of company values that include some of the following:

- we develop teamwork
- we respect the individual
- we are committed to outstanding customer service
- we aim to be the benchmark for the industry
- we operate with integrity
- we encourage initiative.

The issue here is that this aspect of culture still refers to a conscious level of human interaction and thought, and there is frequently a sense that these espoused values and beliefs are what the organisation might like itself to be, rather than what it is in reality. It is relatively common for organisations to prepare statements that might contain phrases such as 'we work together as a team' or 'we value individuals', which do not necessarily reflect the experience of the members of the organisation.

In the same way, the organisation might have stated ambitions in terms of its basic service strategies that are also not borne out in practice. Again, of relevance to service operations managers might be the stated belief of the organisation that delivering 'service excellence' is the key to success. At one level (espoused values) this might be a genuine desire on the part of the organisation's management and employees, while at another, deeper level this may not be as strongly held as one might think at first sight. It is the final level of organisational culture – the basic underlying assumptions – that holds the key to our understanding of why there might be observable differences between what is aspired to and what takes place in practice.

We have found it helpful to encourage organisations to be honest in stating their values and to identify those that genuinely reflect the culture of the organisation and those that might be better described as aspirational or 'work in progress'. So, from the list above, we might identify 'we operate with integrity' as broadly true for the organisation, whereas 'we are committed to outstanding customer service' might be a statement of intent rather than reality at this time. This understanding is invaluable for the operations manager seeking to drive service improvement.

Basic underlying assumptions

The third category of values to be identified are those that the organisation is less happy to publish to the outside world, and frequently prefers to ignore internally. These values are those aspects of the organisation that we are not proud of, but nonetheless are part of our culture. For example, a blame culture or one in which junior employees are not encouraged to challenge management decisions has implications for operational performance and must be recognised.

Basic underlying assumptions refer to those unconsciously held views that are undiscussed and generally unchallenged. Basic assumptions are those beliefs and ways of working that have worked well for the organisation in the past – and are, indeed, its secret of success in the past. These basic assumptions are often expressed in rather more simple, even primitive, terms than many competitive strategies. It is this primitive aspect to the basic assumption that means that it is often deeply held and fiercely defended if anyone (often a newcomer to the organisation) challenges it or suggests it should be changed.

An example of a basic assumption, at an individual level, might be the belief that all workers are lazy. This might lead to some unhelpful behaviour on the part of the management, but also from subordinates as they 'live down' to expectations. Again, applying this idea to a service organisation, it would be extremely difficult to implement long-term customer retention strategies in an organisation that has been extremely successful over a significant period of time by managing short-term revenues.

Almost by definition it is difficult to identify basic assumptions. The individuals in the organisation may only recognise them when deeply held principles are challenged. To make it harder still, the individual may, at a rational level, agree with the challenge, but still resist it unconsciously. An example is provided by medical doctors who agree to a change in surgery procedures so that a patient is seen by the next available doctor. At the rational level they may see the efficiency benefits and agree to the change, but unconsciously they have not changed their basic assumption that the doctor/patient relationship is central to good practice and they will resist the change to the point of ensuring that any pilot scheme is a failure.

We have worked with companies that have a strong track record in producing innovative manufactured products, but realise that they have to develop revenue-earning services to replace declining manufacturing margins, and then find it is much harder to achieve than they thought. Clearly, this can be explained in part by the need to develop new competencies, but a significant issue is the resistance to change brought about by a reluctance to give up the old, tried-and-tested basic assumption that good manufactured product innovation is the way to success. This is often reinforced by the fact that most, if not all, of the senior management come from the 'good old days' and are also reluctant to move away from areas with which they feel competent to deal. This is why significant change is often only brought about by a change of chief executive.

It is important to appreciate that organisational culture is only really understood when the 'unconscious' part of the organisation's personality is revealed. One of the most powerful ways of uncovering the key elements of culture is to provide a framework for members of the organisation to discuss these aspects of their world and to begin to understand the various impacts on their behaviour and, therefore, eventually on the service they may provide to customers. The next section describes the cultural web (Johnson and Scholes 1988 and 1993), which is an instrument that provides a helpful framework for discussion and dialogue.

14.2.2 The cultural web

Figure 14.2 depicts the components of an organisation's cultural web. In this section we first describe the elements of the web and then provide examples of aspects of culture which might help or hinder the generation of a customer-focused organisation or an organisation committed to service excellence.

The paradigm

The word 'paradigm' has unfortunately been somewhat overworked in recent years, but it is particularly important in understanding organisational culture. It basically means the way that we view the world – the sets of values, principles and possibly prejudices that inform our judgements. Another word used for this is 'worldview', which can be likened to the set of spectacles through which we view the world. A simple illustration is a person's reaction to being offered a sum of money. A person whose belief is that the world is a good place might take the money without suspicion, whereas a person whose belief is that the world is a dangerous place would first ask, 'What's the catch?'

The organisation's paradigm may have a number of facets:

- A description of the sector of which the organisation is a part, for example hotels, computer service or financial services.
- The principal customer segments that it seeks to serve: global organisations, small businesses or individual consumers.

Figure 14.2	The cultural web

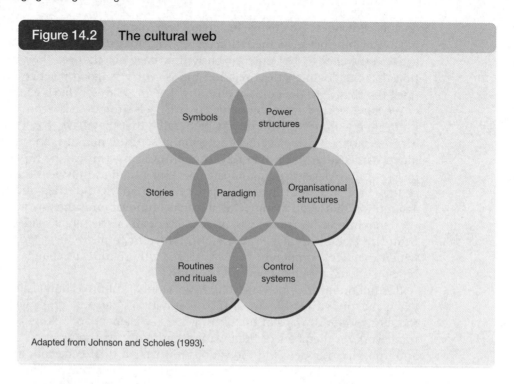

Adapted from Johnson and Scholes (1993).

- In some cases the organisation may express what it does in terms of what the customers are buying rather than what the organisation is providing. For example, the theme park may express its mission as providing magical experiences rather than selling rides; the financial service as providing hope rather than pensions.
- The paradigm may contain some beliefs about what the organisation thinks is good about itself, such as being a risk-taker, innovative, or responsive to customers.
- Finally, it may contain some aspects of the way people think about the organisation that are less positive: it is ruthless, risk averse or arrogant.

There is some commonality between the paradigm as described here and Schein's basic assumptions. Certainly, it may not be obvious to long-serving members of the organisation that the organisation is viewed as somewhat arrogant or ruthless by the world outside. However, if this is the case, the organisation will find it hard to become customer-responsive, having a 'we know best' attitude. A group of managers from a retail service chain carried out a cultural web analysis and were shocked to find that they had not used the words 'service' or 'customer' at any point in their paradigm. They had spoken a great deal about what they thought they were good at, but very little about the need to give the customer what they wanted.

It is important to identify aspects of the paradigm that are helpful for service delivery as well as those which hinder. Organisations that believe that long-term customer satisfaction is more important than short-term profit will generally find a supportive environment for service delivery.

Organisational structures

This aspect of the cultural web deals with the organisation's structure as it works, at least on paper. It is the structure that may be published in the form of organisational charts, showing who reports to whom. Some of the dimensions of organisational culture are:

● Is the structure hierarchical or flat?

● Is it organised geographically or by product area?

● Is it function or process-driven?

● Is it bureaucratic or flexible?

● Is it based on teams or individuals?

The form of the organisation will determine to a large extent how responsive to customers it will be. For customer-facing activities it is helpful if the unit serving the customer is virtually autonomous, and able to satisfy most customer requests from its own resources. This of course may be seen as rather inefficient, and the management may prefer to centralise many activities in order to reduce costs.

Much of the value in recent business process re-engineering (BPR) projects has been a greater emphasis on linking together processes and activities that contribute to customer value rather than functional expertise. This may result in the generation of customer focus rather than operational focus. Examples of this may be found in the creation of teams to handle the entirety of a group of customer transactions. This was the case at Cigma in Greenock in Scotland, a company that handles employee benefits for corporate clients. Cigma reorganised its function-based groups (handling sales, service and credit control, into client-focused teams), and discovered that there were quality and productivity improvements as a result.

Some companies have customer service organisations that are actually set up to protect the company and its workings from the customer. Customer complaints are handled efficiently by this group, but the downside is that fewer people meet and deal with customers or hear what really upsets them. Birmingham Midshires Building Society made a practice of handing complaints to the process owners so that these people could also own the process of customer complaint resolution.

It is clear that organisational design often contains compromise. Ericsson, the telecommunications company, rightly states that it is a global company. Until recent reorganisations, it was true that Ericsson had global presence, but did not act globally in any co-ordinated fashion. The view was that each Ericsson country president should have local autonomy. Although this made Ericsson very flexible and responsive to local needs, it was less appropriate when dealing with multinational customers wanting consistency of approach across the world.

Power structures

This aspect of the organisation's culture is particularly important when it comes to changing the way things are done. Power structures may have nothing to do with the way the organisation chart is drawn. Some individuals appear to have far more power than their status would suggest, either because of the force of their personality or because they exert some power based on expertise.

The importance of power structures as they relate to service delivery might be the negative power sometimes wielded by front-line employees. It would appear to delight some employees to withhold information from customers, because this gives them perverse satisfaction. If this is the case, it is quite possible that these employees feel that they are so powerless and undervalued in the organisation that they will employ this negative power tactic as a means of asserting their importance. Managers must be alert to this, partly because customer satisfaction will suffer as a result, but mainly because it may be that there are issues of leadership and motivation to be addressed.

Leaders use a combination of personal charisma, expertise and positional power to bring about change. In bringing about change it is critical to know where the powerful 'pro-change' people are in order to build alliances to see the change through. It is equally important to identify those who are able to block change. It is often necessary to look beyond the ranks of senior management to find individuals who, by reason of their character or past experience, are extremely influential.

For example, in a water company it became clear that a major factor in the delivery of a customer service strategy was the extent to which a group of relatively junior employees would buy into a new customer-focused approach. Rather like non-commissioned officers in the armed forces, this group had the ability to prevent anything occurring that did not fit with their views. The implementation of the service strategy therefore had to include time for getting understanding and commitment from this group.

Of course, power can also be used very positively to engender customer focus. No one can dispute the influence of Lord Marshall at British Airways or Jack Welch at GE in driving through improvements in customer service.

Control systems

Control systems are the guiding infrastructure of the organisation. What is of interest here is the identification of the control systems that have significant impact on the way things are done. For some organisations, everything must follow well-defined company procedures which, as we have seen in Chapter 7, may deliver consistent results but leave little room for flexibility. Others have very little in the way of formal controls apart from the need to deliver certain long-term goals. The means by which these are achieved are left to the discretion of the individual.

Performance measurement is at the heart of most control systems. Tony Hughes, managing director of Bass Leisure Retail, frequently uses the quote 'What gets measured gets managed, but what gets rewarded gets done'. A good illustration of the effect this produces is provided by the UK's National Health Service (NHS) waiting lists. Waiting-list statistics are used by opposing political parties to demonstrate or attack the effectiveness of current government policies. As a result, waiting lists receive a high degree of attention and there is a view that the statistics are manipulated to ensure that they do not become bad enough to attract attention. There is no great reward attached to removing waiting lists, with the result that the basic question of how to reduce lists often goes unanswered. More significantly, the NHS does not publish regular statistics on waiting *times*, a figure that is of far greater relevance to patients.

More positive examples may be provided by those companies that reward people for customer satisfaction performance above profit, for example Rank Xerox. The company has consistently measured its performance against four key performance criteria: customer satisfaction, employee satisfaction, market share and return on assets (ROA). Until recently, the company has made it clear that the priority has been very much in the order given above, with the firm belief that satisfying customers and employees leads to enhanced market share and therefore ROA.

Kwik-Fit has clearly focused the efforts of branch managers and staff on customer service by managing inventory and other administrative processes centrally. To avoid losing a business focus, each group of branches has its own 'profit and loss' account to understand how the mission of achieving '100% customer delight' links with business success.

A key point here is that organisational control systems often lag behind what is desired to reinforce new behaviours. The manager of a unit responsible for the development of new revenue-earning services for a computer hardware company was frustrated because the regional sales managers were bonused solely on hardware sales. He was on the brink of signing the first major services deal but it was threatened because the hardware content was so small that it would damage the sales manager's bonus. He decided that in order to establish the fact that services were essential for the long-term survival of the company, he would carry the loss-making component on his own budget to maintain the sales manager's support and interest.

Routines and rituals

These are the activities that are not necessarily in the company procedure manual but nevertheless have special significance for the organisation. They might range from the informal system, such as ways of getting round bureaucratic or inflexible procedures, through to celebrations of success, such as pub nights or parties.

The managing director of Credit Card Sentinel sent thank-you cards to people that had done well – a relatively inexpensive exercise that brought about tremendous returns in employee satisfaction. Avis and other companies practise 'visible management', where head office managers spend time each year in the front-line units. Avis finds that this is invaluable for head office staff to understand the issues of the front line, and they frequently discover that renting cars is not as easy as it looks on paper.

Other routines and rituals may be less helpful. The ritual hunt for a scapegoat after each disaster does not contribute greatly to team spirit. Other rituals may become a way of dealing with the difficulties of the job. This is particularly true where staff have to deal with emotionally difficult situations such as in a hospital or at an accident site. Hospitals develop an almost mechanistic approach to their patients to guard against becoming too emotionally involved. This may have an unfortunate impact on patients, who feel they are treated as just another statistic rather than as human beings with feelings.

The analysis of routines is extremely rich as it betrays much of the 'under the surface' life of the organisation. It gives clues about how things really happen as opposed to the sanitised version in the official handbook. When people are able to discuss routines honestly, they may uncover such things as how important decisions are made (corridor conversations and inner cabinets) and how people are promoted (not on merit but on whom they know). Recognising this aspect of organisational life is important in order to influence it to support service delivery.

Symbols

Symbols are the physical evidence of who or what is important in the culture. A couple of decades ago it was relatively easy to see who was important in a large organisation because the managers' status was linked to which floor their office was on, with directors at the top and junior staff at the bottom. Today, with a move towards flatter organisations and a reduction in overt differences between management and staff, the organisational status symbols have become more subtle. Who has a parking space or a fitted carpet in their office (or who has an office at all) become major talking points. In open-plan offices, the size of a person's desk, or who has a special chair, suddenly become all-important. It is as if these symbols take on a life of their own, as anyone who has been involved with a company car scheme will testify. It may seem on the surface that people have accepted quite major shifts in role during organisational change programmes, but their reaction to the loss of a valued symbol may demonstrate that they are far from happy.

Symbols may also be the human role models of the organisation. Certain charismatic leaders may become symbols of change, as, for example, Richard Branson of Virgin, Herb Kelleher at Southwest Airlines, or Tom Farmer of Kwik-Fit.

The relevance for customer focus may lie in how symbols become linked to service. In a security alarm company, sales staff had cars, while service engineers had vans. This might make rational sense, but sent a clear message that service was very much the poor relation. A compromise was reached by providing service engineers with estate cars, which could, of course, be used for private as well as company use.

Stories

The final aspect of the cultural web is the stories that circulate in the organisation. These are sometimes called the 'war stories' and are generally told to new starters early in their stay in an organisation. In some companies, these stories are generally positive ('We're ahead of the competition, this is a good place to work'), while in others they tend to be negative ('Welcome to the mad house, don't take any risks, keep your head down'). In large organisations that have been in existence for several years, and have been through major change, stories relating to the 'good old days' abound.

Part of a process of influencing culture might lie in creating a new set of stories linking heroic acts of customer service to success. The famous stories, such as Federal Express taking initiative to hire a helicopter to get an essential package through, or of Nordstrom refunding a customer for a faulty tyre even though Nordstrom had never sold tyres, do build a culture of customer ownership. On the other hand, stories of staff who have been disciplined for giving relatively small refunds for poor service because they did not follow company red tape are extremely damaging.

Using the cultural web

Table 14.1 shows the cultural web analysis for a financial service company. A typical process for developing this analysis is as follows:

● Develop a common understanding of the key elements of current culture, possibly through the use of facilitated focus groups.

- Examine the current paradigm and decide what aspects would be desirable to change to fit with future strategic direction.
- Identify mismatches between the desired paradigm and current elements of the cultural web.
- Develop action plans to influence or change where possible.

Table 14.1 Cultural web analysis for a financial service company

	Existing cultural web	*Desired cultural web*
Paradigm	Provider of general insurance and pensions Dealing through brokers, not the general public Profitable because of good investment management Generally risk averse A 'nice' company	To be seen as providing freedom from worry for customers To be profitable through acting with integrity, providing innovative financial products to meet the changing needs of customers, and delivering them through excellent service
Organisational structures	Regionally organised with branches and sub-branches Hierarchical, with several management grades Insurance and pensions are separate organisations	Organised in teams around customer delivery processes Providing total solutions for customers in 'one-stop shops' Service delivered direct to consumers
Power structures	Executive management committee Managers who came from Company A prior to the recent merger Actuaries	Executive management committee More influence for those in customer-facing roles
Control systems	Company procedures manual Financial services legislation Risk analysis Sales incentives	Long-term customer retention and profitability Emphasis on developing competence of employees Team incentives
Routines and rituals	Management dinners Senior management visits to branches Promotion on seniority Poor performers 'promoted' to 'special projects'	Recognition of excellent performance in both sales and service Promotion on merit
Symbols	Who has a personal assistant Quality of company car Latest laptop/organiser/IT software	Certificates for achievement
Stories	Amount spent on directors' dining room How good Christmas parties were years ago Senior manager fired for fraud	Celebrations of actions 'beyond the call of duty' Generation of new business through customer referrals

Managers may feel that there is little that they can do to change the organisation's culture. Certainly, to make a major shift in culture is not something that can be accomplished by one individual overnight. However, most managers are part of the power structure, and are able to influence their areas of operation. The value of cultural web analysis as shown in Table 14.1 is that it is possible to identify means of changing aspects of the culture. For example, new reward systems change the emphasis of the control systems relatively quickly. Likewise, it is easy to develop new stories, or to at least ensure that the positive stories are communicated effectively.

14.3 Types of culture

14.3.1 The 'gods' of management

It is important to know the difference between cultures, recognising too that different cultural environments exist within the same organisation. The culture of the boardroom will be rather different from that in the call centre. Likewise, the culture of the accounts department will be very different from that of the sales team. There are a number of factors that influence this diversity, which include individual personalities, the nature of the role undertaken, and the extent to which people have direct customer contact.

Writers on leadership and culture identify various types of culture (see, for example, Kakabadse and Kakabadse 1999, Handy 1991). Handy and Kakabadse both identify power, role and task cultures. Handy, however, uses the term 'club culture' for power culture, and introduces a fourth category, the existential culture.

Handy aligns each of these cultures to a Greek god, giving a useful insight into the various characteristics of these cultures:

- *Zeus – the club culture*. Zeus was the king of the gods, ruling by patronage combined with fear. This culture is found in entrepreneurial organisations and frequently at the very summit of large organisations. It is excellent for speed of decision-making, where key people are chosen because they think and act like the (central) leader. Such organisations can be very effective when they are based on trust, but can be terrible places when an evil Zeus abuses his power.

- *Apollo – the role culture*. This culture is one of rules and order. It is stable and predictable – excellent when the market is not changing rapidly. The individual's role in the organisation is clear, and little initiative is required. The traditional role culture is safe, because nothing changes and someone else (or the system) takes care of things.

- *Athena – the task culture*. Athena is a warrior-goddess, a problem solver. The basis of this culture is expertise, not experience, age or position. Handy states that this culture works well when the product of the organisation is the solution to a problem. This is an expensive culture, because it is staffed by experts and the outcomes are not predictable, often requiring development time and resource. When Athena cultures get large they require Apollonian cultures to manage the routine activities.

- *Dionysus – the existential culture.* Here the emphasis is that the individual is in charge of their own destiny. Handy suggests that in the other three cultures the individual is there to help the organisation achieve its purpose, but that in this culture the organisation exists to help the individual. Professionals may be grouped together in one building because someone can then organise support systems such as telephones and catering, but there is no interdependence between the individuals.

Table 14.2 provides a summary of some of the ways that these different cultures operate.

The shape of organisational life is changing. The large Apollonian cultures are fast disappearing as they need to adapt more rapidly to changing market demands. More organisations are taking on the form of Athena, the task culture, though frequently with Apollo-like support structures, and with a Zeus at the top.

Recently there has been the emergence of 'virtual' organisations or 'hollow' corporations. These are somewhat Athena-like in concept in that the organisation exists for a particular task and then disbands. Film and television programme-makers operate in this fashion, with a producer being commissioned to gather together a team for the one project. Networks of experts, part Athena, part Dionysus, form loose associations constantly changing shape to meet the current need. However, would be wrong to believe that Apollo does not exist any more. There are plenty of Apollo-like organisations in existence still, able to operate consistently and efficiently.

14.3.2 The 'gods' and service delivery

Inspection of Table 14.2 suggests a number of ways that these different cultures might impact service delivery:

- *Zeus.* Zeus cultures are very responsive to customers. They are able to react quickly and harness resources to meet the current need. They are good when a personal relationship between the two chief executives is fundamental to the success of the deal. This relationship, if founded on mutual respect and trust, can be very fruitful in developing long-term business. Service delivery to these valued customers is likely to be of high quality, as Zeus will ensure it. Service delivery to other customers might be less consistent. In terms of the runners, repeaters and strangers, categories described in Chapter 6, Zeus cultures may create repeaters and strangers, while some attention to planning might turn them into runners.

- *Apollo.* These organisations are extremely consistent. Most of the high-volume services, such as retailers, utilities and insurance companies, have much of this culture. The problem is that they may be experienced as rather inflexible by their customers. The attitude of 'that's more than my job's worth' or 'I can't do that' is the downside of the reliability and efficiency that they deliver. This culture thrives on runners, tolerates repeaters and resists strangers.

- *Athena.* This culture is appropriate when the output is a solution for customers, rather than a packaged commodity that an Apollo organisation might deliver. This organisation is therefore flexible, and is good at involving its customers in

Table 14.2 **Summary of different cultures**

	Thinking and learning	Influencing and changing	Motivating and rewarding
Zeus (club culture)	Trial and error Watching other Zeuses Learning by sitting with the 'master' Admission of need to learn is a sign of weakness	Change by replacing people, not development Judged by whom, not what you know Credibility is the key	Money is highly valued Reward is to be given responsibility and resource by Zeus Winning is crucial
Apollo (role culture)	Logical and analytical Acquisition of more knowledge and skills through training courses Appraisals and job rotation	Power from position, role or title Rules and procedures Managers implement directors' decisions	Pensions schemes and career planning Increase in formal authority Status symbols
Athena (task culture)	Problem solving Brainstorming Learning as a team Opportunities for development	Persuasion through expertise Debate and consensus Problem definition Need a new problem to solve	Objectives, not role definitions Variety
Dionysus (existential culture)	Learn by total immersion Give up, having mastered a new skill	Difficult to influence Unpredictable, need to negotiate	Opportunity to make a difference in their terms Freedom

the development process. Specialist software developers and consultants may fall into this category. The problem with these organisations is that, although they are innovative, they get bored with the continual delivery of the same solution. At this stage, an Apollo-like organisation form is more appropriate for consistency and cost. This culture seeks the opportunity to develop new capability for strangers, it tolerates repeaters in order to generate sufficient revenue, and it resists runners.

- *Dionysus*. This culture is a nightmare as far as service delivery is concerned. These individuals will only operate if the task is of interest, and no amount of pleading or bribery will change their mind. Customers are liable to be made to feel that they are somewhat inferior to the service provider, only taken on because they are an 'interesting case'. This culture is only interested in strangers, and will not even consider runners.

Finally, an important point to note is that an understanding of the difference in organisational culture is particularly relevant in a business-to-business relationship. Apollo cultures are likely to be confused and frustrated by Athena cultures and vice versa.

14.4 National cultures

A chapter on culture would be incomplete without at least a mention of the influence of national cultures on service delivery. Hofstede (1980 and 1991) conducted a major cross-cultural study of IBM employees to identify characteristics of national cultures. He identified four dimensions that can be used to rate national culture:

First Direct Box 14.1

Visitors to First Direct's website are bombarded with words that this bank uses to describe itself. These include: foremost, visionary, responsive, futuristic, warm, revolutionary, friendly, safe, invigorated and quixotic.

First Direct, the first 'branchless' telephone bank in the UK, began operations in 1989. Its concept was simple: to provide 24-hour banking for 365 days a year. At the heart of the operation was an information system that allowed the customer to handle any traditional branch transaction in a single telephone call. It would have been tempting to recruit staff for this new operation from First Direct's parent, the then Midland Bank (now HSBC).

The management team took a significant decision to look for people who were fast and efficient, able to work under pressure, but, critically, people with warm personalities. Much of this is due to the vision of its first CEO, Kevin Newman, who is quoted as saying:

I believe that in going forward three things need to be developed. We have to be utterly low cost. We must be able to individualise the manufacturing process and recognise that all our customers are individuals. Third, we must build a strong brand as people need to identify with institutions they can trust.

First Direct identified five core values as central to the way it was to operate, and these were incorporated in the training programme for staff, who were to be known as banking representatives (BRs). The core values were responsiveness, openness, right first time, respect and contribution. These values were reinforced by Newman and his management team, who spent a significant amount of their time talking to BRs. Right from day one, Newman wanted First Direct to have a different culture from traditional banks. Everyone ate in the same cafeteria, and managers were on first-name terms with BRs. The only perk that Newman enjoyed was a company car. There was no 'headquarters' – managers and

directors sat at desks in the same area as the BRs. There was minimal hierarchy, with managers encouraged to concentrate on leadership and guidance rather than interference and instruction.

BRs undertook a seven-week training course before dealing with customers. The first four weeks were dedicated to understanding the bank's products, while the latter three weeks concentrated on telephone role-playing and building techniques. First Direct made limited use of scripting techniques, and BRs were encouraged to build rapport, using language appropriate to the individual customer. BRs worked in teams, with a team leader acting as a coach. The teams were encouraged to develop their own identities, and to create team names. First Direct invested in facilities for the 24-hour workforce. A security firm guards car parks and reception areas, and hot food is available from 7.00 a.m. until 9.00 p.m. Staff are encouraged to attend lifestyle classes covering subjects as diverse as foreign languages and yoga.

Much of the continued success of First Direct has been attributed to its friendly, responsive culture. First Direct's website proclaims that it 'actively promotes a positive working environment'. This has been achieved without the loss of efficiency or consistency. Clearly, this is due in no small part to the culture created by Newman, his management team, and those who followed them.

Questions

1 What do you think are the significant elements in the success of First Direct? What contribution does First Direct's culture make to this success?

2 What actions should First Direct take to maintain the enthusiasm of the initial launch of its branchless banking service?

This illustration is based on personal experience, from information from First Direct's website (www.firstdirect.co.uk), and Insead case study 597-028-1: *First Direct: Branchless Banking.*

- *Power-distance*. A high power-distance rating would suggest that employees are relatively passive, have a liking to be directed, and inhabit a culture that generally expects superiors to wield power. The corollary to this is that superiors frequently exhibit low trust of subordinates. Many Asian cultures have high power-distance ratings. Low power-distance rankings encourage greater mutual trust and an expectation that subordinates will be involved in decision-making. The UK, some of Western Europe and the USA fall into this group.

- *Uncertainty avoidance*. This dimension evaluates the extent to which the culture encourages risk-taking. Cultures with high uncertainty avoidance adopt strategies such as working long hours and enforcing strict obedience to procedures to deal with difficult conditions. Much of the Japanese work ethic exhibits this tendency. Low uncertainty avoidance encourages a more entrepreneurial spirit, with less concern for following rigid procedures.

- *Individualism–collectivism*. The UK, along with the USA and Canada, places high regard on the achievements of individuals, whereas some cultures value loyalty to extended family or tribe more highly. In the latter case, the emphasis is on belonging, duty and group decision making.

- *Masculinity–femininity*. The masculinity-dominant cultures place emphasis on acquisition of money, material possessions and on ambition. Managers are encouraged to press for ever-increasing goals and objectives. Where femininity is dominant, the emphasis is on creating a more collaborative environment.

This work is interesting in that it challenges assumptions that all people are the same. It clearly has implications for the implementation of global operations strategies; for example, teamwork and empowerment may not translate from one culture to another. It is necessary to point out, though, that the assumption that all people from a national culture rank high on power-distance, low on uncertainty avoidance and so on is clearly inaccurate. One hypothesis is that at an organisational level the company culture might be more influential, not least because the company recruitment policies will tend to favour 'people like us'.

A key issue to be addressed is that of flexibility between the organisational values and the elements of national culture (Hallowell *et al.* 2002). If the organisational values are perceived to be fundamental to competitive advantage and they clash with national culture, then the service will fail. For example, if McDonald's had been unwilling to compromise over its products, the company would not have been able to succeed in countries with a strong Islamic culture.

The Four Seasons hotel chain has opened hotels across the globe, each reflecting the local culture, yet each adhering to high standards of excellence. Senior managers speak of being cultural chameleons. Antoine Corinthios, president of Europe, Middle East and Africa, emphasises that there are some global standards such as cleanliness and fast response, but: 'What changes is that people do it with their own style, grace and personality; in some cultures you add the strong local temperament. For example, an Italian concierge has his own style and flair. In Turkey and Egypt you experience very different service' (Hallowell *et al.* 2002). Recognition of this enabled Four Seasons to take over the operation of the legendary George V Hotel in Paris, operating the core standards of the Four Season chain but not insisting on the same service and managerial approach that has been applied in other areas.

14.5 The management of change and service delivery

14.5.1 Strategies for cultural change

There is not sufficient space here to cover all the aspects of the management of change, so we discuss some of the issues that specifically relate to service delivery. Bate (1996) provides a helpful overview of strategies for cultural change. He suggests four basic approaches:

- *Progressive*. This approach is used when there is not time for a consultative approach. Senior managers have to implement change rapidly, frequently upsetting staff in the process. This approach (also termed aggressive) is effective in implementing rapid major change, but is poor in gaining commitment and ownership of the result.

- *Consultative*. This approach is characterised by a great deal of communication and involvement. It is excellent for gaining commitment, but poor at implementing a radical solution.

- *Educative*. Here, the organisation provides material and training to explain why the change is necessary. It is based on the view that if people can (rationally) understand the need for change, they will be happy to support it. Education and training have been shown to be effective (we would say that!), but one problem is that people do not react to change rationally. The other common issue with this approach is that the company 'road-show' is often seen as playing mind-games with the employees. Hence this is also termed the indoctrinative approach.

- *Corrosive*. This is akin to the organisation's grapevine. Senior management 'lets loose' the key messages at key points throughout the organisation. This approach is much favoured by those who must attempt to manage groups of professionals, who often resist any form of direct control.

Most change processes will contain elements of all four approaches. It is important to note that if, in the early process of change, it has been necessary to employ the progressive/aggressive approach, managers must be alert to the danger of disaffected staff displaying unhelpful customer attitudes.

Bate then outlines five parameters to assess the success of the change process:

- *Expressiveness*. This measures the extent to which the change process communicates a new idea. This is what people call 'hearts and minds'. A new mission statement that captures the imagination of the employees will be invaluable here, particularly if this statement is lived up to by senior management.

- *Commonality*. Culture is produced when people speak to each other. This parameter assesses the extent to which everyone speaks the same language and means the same thing. The question here is: 'Is there a sense of solidarity because we know what we are trying to achieve?'

- *Penetration*. To what extent has the change really 'got inside' the organisation? Has it begun to change the way that things are done, particularly at the level of routines and rituals? Has it got to the point where it cannot be ignored?

- *Adaptability*. Is the change process able to deal with the diversity of situations represented in a large, complex organisation? Can those responsible for implementation maintain the essence of the change, making helpful local adaptations? Can it be questioned and rethought in key areas without losing credibility?

- *Durability*. Is it tamper-proof? Will it transcend the departure of the chief executive? Is it clear that this change will not go away?

14.5.2 Pitfalls to avoid

One of the most helpful summaries of the problems of change management is provided by Kotter (1995), who identified the following pitfalls:

- ***Not establishing a sense of urgency***. Kotter quotes a key statistic that 75 per cent of managers must accept the need for major and immediate change if it is to be successful.

- ***Not creating a powerful guiding coalition***. For service organisations it is vital to gaining the commitment of customer-facing staff as well as senior management.

- *Lacking a vision*. Too many organisations implement initiative after initiative without a clear sense of how they fit together. A vision, as with the service concept, should be a unifying factor.

- ***Undercommunicating by a factor of 10***. Employees usually trust their immediate manager or team leader more than the senior management team, which is often remote and seen as pursuing its own agendas. The first-line supervisor or team leader is therefore central to the implementation of a new service vision.

- ***Not removing obstacles to the vision***. It is necessary to ensure that job roles and measurement systems are consistent with the change required, rather than hope that they will catch up. Any significant change will meet overt and covert resistance, which must be faced.

- ***Not planning for short-term wins***. Staff need credible evidence of some success within 12 to 24 months. This needs to be managed.

- ***Declaring victory too soon***. It is tempting to slacken off the pressure at the first signs of success. Unless the changes have taken root in the rituals of the organisation, they have not been not completed.

- ***Not anchoring the change in the organisation's culture***. Managers need to understand the motivators for their staff. Have they changed in line with the new requirements?

The illustration of Amnesty International in Box 14.2 demonstrates the complexity of change in service strategy when those involved have affiliations to more than one group in the organisation. It is insufficient to present a change as 'being the right thing to do', even if this can be supported with rational arguments. In many cases, people's loyalties to local groups may be more powerful than logic.

Amnesty International

Box 14.2

Amnesty International was founded in 1961 by Peter Benenson, a British lawyer, and today it has over 1 million members and supporters spread across over 150 countries. Its objectives are to promote general awareness of human rights and to oppose specific abuses of human rights.

Amnesty has both volunteers and professionals (paid staff). It is organised into two main groups, the International Secretariat in London and over 50 national sections. The International Secretariat is the research headquarters of the organisation, with specialists in many fields sifting and checking information about alleged abuses before initiating action. The national sections contain the 'grass roots' of the volunteer membership, being responsible for activist campaigning, local recruitment, fund raising and so on.

Unfortunately, Amnesty's field of interest is expanding rather than becoming redundant. In many parts of the world there are incidents of human rights abuse. For a number of years Amnesty's work had little co-ordinated international strategy. The approach until the early 1990s was that each of the national sections would be involved to a greater or lesser extent in all aspects of Amnesty's work. This led to a dilution of resources and a somewhat haphazard approach to dealing with abuse of human rights.

The direction of Amnesty is debated in depth every two years at the International Council Meeting (ICM). It was at the ICM in 1991 that the membership of the national sections understood that, in order to meet the increasing challenges, Amnesty would have to act on a basis of international co-ordination rather than simply be an international organisation comprising many national sections.

The impact on the national sections has been that they are no longer left to develop their own plans in isolation. Under an initiative termed 'specialisation' each section must determine its particular strategic focus, taking into consideration its strengths and opportunities. This development of particular strengths for each national section is linked to an international planning process. The International Secretariat in London has the responsibility for determining priority levels for country research and campaigning projects, in consultation with the national sections.

The national sections were initially nervous that they would lose 'universality' and would lose touch with what was going on across the world. In reality, many sections probably never had the ability or desire to address all the potential issues in every place where Amnesty was involved. Most national sections contain a number of local or regional groups. This same process of specialisation has been applied within national sections to these local groups, each taking on a different emphasis of fund raising, public awareness or specific geographical action.

Questions

1 Is it possible to describe the culture of Amnesty International as a whole? What are the essential differences in culture between the national sections and the International Secretariat?

2 In managing this change, what issues should Amnesty International pay attention to at both national and international level?

14.5.3 Capacity for change

Finally, many change initiatives fail because they are under-resourced. This is a concept that should be understood by operations managers. Change fails because managers do not have the capability to manage it. If this is so, the organisation must recruit or buy this ability. Another common problem is that the organisation does not have the capacity to manage the process as well as maintain 'business as usual'. Parker and Lewis (1980) studied managers passing through change and proposed that the experience is similar to the bereavement process, illustrated in Figure 14.3.

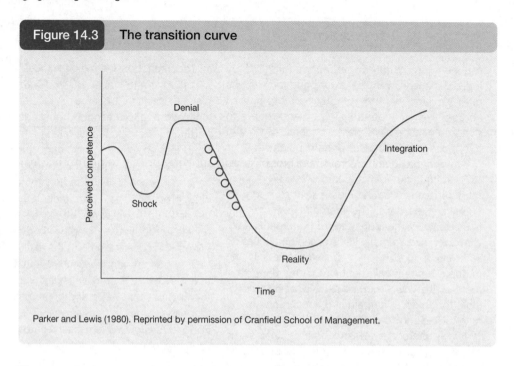

Figure 14.3 The transition curve

Parker and Lewis (1980). Reprinted by permission of Cranfield School of Management.

The transition curve shows the individual's response to a proposed (enforced) change. From a point of relatively high perceived competence, the individual is initially shocked and then fairly quickly moves to the denial state, which can be either pretending that the change will go away, or that they can deal with whatever comes their way. This state leads to a downward spiral into reality as they recognise that the new environment will require the acquisition of new skills and new ways of working. Having reached this low point, the individual needs, often by trial and error, to begin to integrate new approaches into their way of working.

Managers going through a change process need time to understand the impact on themselves, let alone those who work for them. The transition curve is generally estimated to require a period of two years to elapse from beginning to end, though this is only an average figure. The implication for operations managers is that they must dedicate resources to managing staff through any period of significant change if 'business as usual' service is to be maintained to an acceptable standard. At each stage of the transition curve managers must respond appropriately.

Shock

In the early stages, when the employees are in shock, it is important to answer questions as honestly as possible, recognising that since the detail has yet to be worked through it is unlikely that definitive answers can be given. Time must be set aside to be available for questioning, even if in the management's eyes nothing is happening. We worked with two companies who were merging. Because of the requirement to harmonise information systems, there was little action apparent to most employees for several weeks. A senior manager told a group of junior managers, 'We haven't spoken to you about the merger for some weeks, because we felt there was nothing to say'. You can probably imagine the anger experienced by his audience.

Denial

In the denial stage it is important to continue to reinforce the fact that the change will take place – to reiterate the business or market reasons for the change. It is also important to be careful about how the past is described. There is often a temptation to oversell the future in an effort to gain commitment to the proposed change. In so doing there is a danger of 'rubbishing' the past efforts and achievements, forgetting that the very people you are trying to motivate were very proud of what they achieved. It is sometimes useful to have some form of 'rite of passage', recognising the achievements of the past, and allowing people to mourn before moving on.

Reality

There comes a point when it becomes apparent that the change is going to happen. People may be moved to new roles, new organisational structures are put in place, and some people may leave the organisation. Some people may be unsure as to whether they will be able to cope with new roles and will need a fair amount of mentoring initially. They will need encouragement, since they may not perform as well as they would like. Carrying out pilot studies will help build confidence and reduce resistance to change.

Integration

At this point, the change has become part of the organisation. It is easier to go forward rather than go back, but the manager must be careful not to relax too soon. As we saw in section 14.5.2, one of the common pitfalls is declaring victory too soon. Operations managers must now work through the detail of the organisation's culture, such as reward and recognition schemes, promotion criteria and informal routines, to ensure that the desired behaviours are encouraged.

14.6 Summary

Understanding organisational culture

- Culture may be considered to be tangible or intangible, and to exist at three levels: as artefacts, as espoused values and as basic underlying assumptions.
- The cultural web is a useful way of understanding organisational culture and can also be used to help managers understand how they can influence culture.

Types of organisational culture

- Culture can be characterised as gods: Zeus – the club culture, Apollo – the role culture, Athena – the task culture, and Dionysus – the existential culture.
- Each type of culture has a different impact on the service delivery system.

National cultures

- National cultures can be characterised along four dimensions: power-distance, uncertainty avoidance, individualism–collectivism and masculinity–femininity.
- Global businesses must understand potential conflicts between organisational values and cultural norms.

The management of change

- There are four main strategies for change: progressive, consultative, educative and corrosive.
- The pitfalls to avoid include:
  - not establishing a sense of urgency
  - not creating a powerful guiding coalition
  - lacking a vision
  - undercommunicating by a factor of 10
  - not removing obstacles to the vision
  - not planning for short-term wins
  - declaring victory too soon
  - not anchoring the change in the organisation's culture.
  - The transition curve provides insight into the various stages of change, and the manager's role in leading change.

14.7   Discussion questions

1 Give examples of service organisations that fit the 'gods of management' model. What are their strengths and weaknesses in service delivery?

2 What influence can operations managers exert on organisational culture? How important do you think performance measurement is as a component of culture?

14.8   Questions for managers

1 Do you understand what is the principal basic assumption of your organisation? Does it support your service concept, or is the reason for poor performance the fact that your organisational culture is lagging behind your strategy?

2 Can you express the paradigm of your organisation? In what way do you think your interpretation differs from other managers in your organisation?

3 What aspects of your organisation's cultural web can you influence? What action is required to support your organisation's competitive strategy?

4 Which of the 'gods of management' fits your organisation? Is this the type of organisation in which you want to work?

5 What lessons can you learn from Kotter's list of reasons for failure in managing change? How do they relate to your experience of change?

14.9 Further reading

Balogun J. and Hope-Hailey V., with Johnson G. and Scholes K., *Exploring Strategic Change*, Prentice Hall, London, 1999.

Handy C., *Gods of Management*, Random Century, London, 1991.

Sturdy A. and Fleming P., 'Talk as technique – a critique of the words and deeds distinction in the diffusion of customer service cultures in call centres', *Journal of Management Studies*, vol. 40, no. 4, June 2003, pp 753–73.

14.10 References

Bate P., *Strategies for Cultural Change*, Butterworth Heinemann, Oxford, 1996.

Browning V., 'Creating service excellence through human resource management practices', *South African Journal of Business Management*, vol. 29, no. 4, 1998, pp. 135–42.

De Chernatony L., Drury S. and Segal-Horn S., 'Building a services brand; stages, people and orientation', *Service Industries Journal*, vol. 21, no. 3, May 2003, pp. 1–21.

Hallowell R., Bowen D. and Knoop C-I., 'Four Seasons goes to Paris', *Academy of Management Executive*, vol. 16, no. 4, 2002, pp. 7–24.

Handy C., *Gods of Management*, Random Century, London, 1991.

Hofstede G., *Culture's Consequence: International Differences in Work-related Values*, Sage Publications, Beverly Hills, Calif., 1980.

Hofstede G., *Cultures and Organisations*, *Software of the Mind*, McGraw-Hill, New York, 1991.

Johnson G. and Scholes K., *Exploring Corporate Strategy*, 2nd edition, Prentice Hall, London, 1988.

Johnson G. and Scholes K., *Exploring Corporate Strategy*, 3rd edition, Prentice Hall, London, 1993.

Kakabadse A. and Kakabadse N., *Essence of Leadership*, International Thomson, London, 1999.

Kotter J.P., 'Why transformation efforts fail', *Harvard Business Review*, March–April, 1995.

Morgan G., *Images of Organization*, Sage, Newbury Park, Calif., 1986.

Oswick C., Lowe S. and Jones P., 'Organisational culture as personality: lessons from psychology?' in Oswick C. and Grant D. (eds), *Organisation Development*, *Metaphorical Explorations*, Pitman Publishing, London, 1996, pp. 106–20.

Parker C. and Lewis R., 'Moving up: how to handle transitions to senior levels, successfully', occasional paper, Cranfield School of Management, Cranfield, Bedford, 1980.

Schein E.H., *Organizational Culture and Leadership*, Jossey-Bass, San Francisco, 1985.

Security Alarm Systems Ltd   Case Exercise

Security Alarm Systems Ltd (SASL) is a medium-sized company supplying security alarm systems to both organisations and domestic customers. Its main markets are:

- national retail organisations requiring a standard security system across a network of high street branches or outlets in out-of-town retail parks

- manufacturing companies
- other commercial properties, such as office facilities
- luxury domestic premises
- standard domestic premises.

For the first four of these categories, the system can be linked to SASL's central monitoring unit, to facilitate rapid response to alarm activation. In some very sensitive cases, security systems are linked directly to the local police station. These frequently lie in the luxury domestic category – the home of a public personality or an extremely wealthy person.

The industry consists of a few companies providing service nationally. All but one of these restrict their operations to the UK. The exception is the largest company in the market, Intruder Systems, which is a subsidiary of a company based in the USA. There are large numbers of companies that supply and service alarm systems on a local or regional basis. These are often set up and staffed by ex-employees of the national companies.

SASL is organised into four regions: Southern England, Northern England, Midlands and Wales, and Scotland. Each region has a general manager overseeing a number of local depots. A typical depot comprises a depot manager, sales consultants, system installers, service engineers and support staff. There is a small headquarters, which is located in the Northern region and contains the executive team (managing director, sales and marketing director, finance director and technical director), credit control and a team of engineering experts. This central team of system specialists is available as a resource to the sales consultants, particularly assisting them in the design of more complex systems.

Alfred Higgins, an expert in closed-circuit television (CCTV), is annoyed that the company's salesforce does not sell more complex systems, preferring to stick to older technology that they can understand. He says, 'We could charge higher prices for state-of-the-art technology, but many of our sales consultants were originally service engineers and have received very little product training since changing roles'. Higgins also claims that the engineers see a move into sales as an escape from the unsocial hours of service, and a chance to get a company car rather than the service van.

The usual sales procedure is as follows. In response to a customer enquiry, the sales con-

sultant will make a visit or 'survey' to assess the requirements and to present SASL's service portfolio. If the system is a small one, as for example in a typical family home, the sales consultant will provide an initial estimate of price and delivery time during the visit. For larger systems, the sales consultant will develop a more detailed quotation, frequently drawing on the expertise of the central specialist team for details of more complex control systems or CCTV application. SASL does not manufacture any equipment, but is attempting to build stronger links with component suppliers. Better information about component quality would be useful, but is currently held only at depot level.

If the quotation is accepted by the customer, the file is passed to the installation engineers. SASL believes that there are fewer problems with commissioning systems if it retains control over this activity, although other companies, notably Intruder Systems, have outsourced this work. Security systems are normally sold with a maintenance contract, renewable annually. There are various formats for these contracts, ranging from full service and support contracts through to service being charged as costs are incurred. Full service contracts should be most profitable for SASL, although poor organisation means that margins are reduced, and there are significant differences in the depots' abilities to sell these premium contracts.

The local depot structure of the company has provided a good platform for responsiveness, both to sales enquiries and to system problems. This continues to be valuable for domestic customers and for small manufacturing units where the customer deals solely with the local depot. However, this is proving to be less helpful when dealing with national retail chains, where negotiations are normally conducted with a central purchasing department and possibly the customer's own security manager. Joanne Walters, the Birmingham depot manager, says, 'I visit my main customers at least once a year. If there are any problems, I use my discretion as to whether to give a credit note for repairs when we are slightly late in fulfilling preventive maintenance schedules. Customers seem to be quite happy if you apologise and give them some money off.'

Response times to system faults are within the British Standard requirement of four hours, but this is largely achieved at the expense of planned maintenance. This sets up a vicious circle, with system breakdowns occurring more frequently as a result. There are frequently differences in operating procedures between depots, with most local managers having been promoted from the depot's service engineers.

Two of the four regional general managers are long-service SASL employees – both were promoted from service engineer, through depot manager, to regional general manager. The general manager of Scotland (George MacLeod) has recently moved from Intruder Systems, while the general manager of Southern England (Fred Harvey) came to SASL from another competitor, Securiguard, three months after SASL appointed his previous boss, Andrew Porter, as managing director.

SASL has a good reputation for responsiveness to customers, but Porter is worried that quality inconsistency will limit the company's growth. He is also worried that the company's productivity is lagging behind the industry standard. As a result, Porter has decided to strengthen the headquarters team with the appointment of an operations director, whose brief will be to develop consistent processes to be implemented across the network, in order to increase service quality and productivity. Porter's vision for SASL is that it should be positioned as providing security solutions, advising its customers on all their requirements, rather than limiting itself to supplying and servicing equipment. Andrew Porter has asked Fred Harvey to lead a taskforce to investigate the best performing depots with a view to implementing best practice. It is no secret that Porter favours the appointment of George MacLeod as operations director, although the post will be advertised externally.

SASL, under Andrew Porter, is considering withdrawing from provision of security systems to homes, to concentrate instead on its existing commercial base while developing a capability to install and support large security systems. The company has recently completed a major installation in the headquarters of a top financial service company, which required installation engineers to be seconded from all four regions to London to ensure that work was completed on schedule.

Joanna Harris, the sales and marketing director, has developed a marketing plan – a first for SASL. It is based on the assumption that in two years' time over 25 per cent of the business will relate to large projects, requiring a nationwide response. This figure is predicted to grow to nearly 40 per cent in five years. This compares with the current level of less than 10 per cent.

'The challenge for SASL', said Andrew Porter, 'is to reverse a slow decline in our profitability. This will mean significant changes for the organisation as a whole, and particularly for those who have been with SASL for more than ten years, and who remember when it was the acknowledged market leader.'

Questions

1 What problems does Andrew Porter face?

2 How should he deal with them?

15

Operational complexity

Chapter objectives:

- to define complexity

- to explore the operational consequences of complexity.

15.1 Introduction

In this final chapter we will explore what we think is the fundamental problem that underlies all situations and decisions facing operations managers – complexity. The previous chapters have broken service operations management down into handy chunks to enable us to develop each in turn. The reality faced by service operations managers is very different. All of these aspects of operations management – people, processes, culture, improvement, etc. – are invariably and inextricably interwoven so that decisions or actions in one area will have consequences in all others.

This chapter explores the consequences of complexity to try to give a feeling of the nature of operations managers' work. We hope this will provide some insight as to why operations management as a subject, both academic and practical, is both exciting and frustrating.

15.2 What is complexity?

Complexity is both the source of many operational problems and difficulties and at the same time it is the source of inspiration and challenge. Without complexity operations would be an uninteresting, mundane activity that could be assigned as a clerical activity.

The *Concise Oxford Dictionary* tells us that complexity means 'complicated, due to the number of interrelated parts in the system or network'. It also defines a complex as a preoccupation or an obsession with something. Many operations managers we have met have a complex about complexity.

15.2.1 Dimensions of operational complexity

There are several factors that influence the complexity of an operation. The illustration about Oxfam, the international relief organisation, in Box 15.1 is used to describe some of the eight dimensions of operational complexity (see Figure 15.1).

Figure 15.1	Dimensions of operational complexity

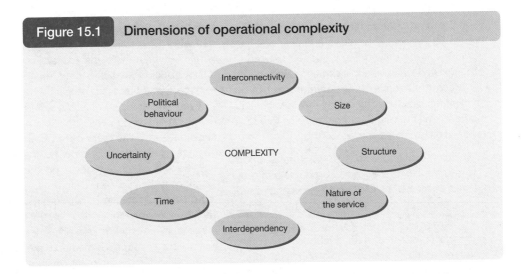

Oxfam   Box 15.1

Oxfam is a major international development, relief and campaigning organisation dedicated to finding lasting solutions to poverty and suffering around the world. Oxfam GB, which is affiliated to Oxfam International (an alliance of 11 organisations), works closely with communities through a network of local partners to help provide safety, dignity and opportunity for many disadvantaged people around the world.

The Oxford Committee for Famine Relief began as one of many relief agencies that sprang up during the Second World War. It continued after the war and extended its remit to provide for the relief of suffering, whatever the cause might be. Oxfam, as it soon became known, set up collection points for donations and opened its first charity shop in 1948. Oxfam's current network of more than 830 charity shops is supported by about 22,000 volunteers and is a key source of income. The shops sell donated items from the British public, as well as Fair Trade goods – food and handicrafts from around the world, giving small-scale producers fair prices, training, advice and funding support. Orders for items can be made by mail or over the internet. Oxfam has also teamed up with Yahoo! to provide free access to the internet in the UK and at the same time raise funds. Together with donations for general use, institutional income and money raised for particular emergencies (restricted funds), Oxfam generated a total income of around £124 million in 1998–9. Oxfam employs around 3,000 staff in total, with about half of these based overseas – mostly local staff from the countries concerned.

Oxfam is perhaps best known for its work in emergency situations, providing humanitarian aid where it is needed. Oxfam has a particular expertise in providing clean water and sanitation facilities. Around 80 per cent of diseases and over one-third of deaths in the developing world are caused by contaminated water, and this can escalate in crises. Yet much of Oxfam's work continues out of the spotlight of disasters. The charity provides continuing help, working with poor communities through a range of programmes concerned with:

- Building livelihoods: e.g. agricultural support, providing seeds and tools so people can grow their own food, building flood-prevention barriers, helping people secure access to markets, credit and land.

- Improving health and education: e.g. providing access to clean water, developing schools.

- Participation in processes: e.g. enabling poor or vulnerable people to gain control over their lives, to have a say and be listened to instead of ignored, bypassed or exploited.

- Gender issues: e.g. working to remove barriers to girls' education.

Oxfam also speaks out on behalf of disadvantaged communities, pressuring governments and decision makers on a range of issues, including trade, Third World debt, education, land issues and workers' rights.

Whether the disasters are natural (such as earthquakes and storms) or political (such as riots and wars), disasters become emergencies when the people involved can no longer cope. In poor countries disasters leave people homeless and vulnerable to famine or disease, and people may become ill or die within days if they do not get aid. In such situations Oxfam, through its network of staff in local offices in 70 countries, is able to advise on the resources and help that are needed and on where they are needed. Indeed, local teams are often able to provide warnings of impending disasters, giving more time to assess need and enable a multi-agency response.

The emergency programmes are mainly run by Oxfam's regional and country offices. The organisation's headquarters in Oxford provides advice, materials and staff, often deploying emergency support personnel (ESP) on short-term assignments when and where their skills are required. Shelters, blankets and clothing can be flown out at short notice from the emergencies warehouse in Bicester. Engineers and sanitation equipment can also be provided, including water tanks, latrines, hygiene kits and containers such as the 'Oxfam bucket', which is light, easy to carry and transport, and has a sealable lid.

Every emergency is different, with differing security situations, aid needs, logistical problems and access issues. The responses of other agencies, such as governments or other relief agencies, will also be different, depending on the nature and location of the disaster. Oxfam relies on its local team, with support from headquarters as necessary, to assess each situation and decide whether the organisation can make a difference. Sometimes it is unable to respond: the security situation may be too difficult or governments respond with all that is needed. Local, regional and head office managers have to weigh up all the factors to decide upon the degree and nature of response.

When an emergency is over, Oxfam often continues to work with the affected communities through its local offices, to help people rebuild their lives and livelihoods.

Questions

1 What, in your view, makes Oxfam's operations so complex?

2 What might be the conflicts between the various stakeholders with which Oxfam has to try to deal with?

Interconnectivity

Complexity is about interconnectivity, created by the many possible interrelationships between different variables. Oxfam has to manage the relationships between its various fund-raising activities: the charity shops and network of volunteers, its head office, and its network of local offices and regional offices. It also has to manage its relationship with the communities that it is trying to serve, and co-ordinate with the activities of other relief agencies and governments. These two very different activities also need to connect, as Oxfam's ability to overcome poverty and suffering depends upon its ability to raise funds.

Size

Complexity is usually relative to size. The greater the size of an operation, i.e. the more elements it has, the greater the number of interconnections. Indeed, as elements increase linearly, the interconnections will grow exponentially. Oxfam is a large organisation with nearly 3,000 staff and about 22,000 volunteers, with offices in 70 countries around the world. This size creates many possible interconnections, which the organisation attempts to manage through its regional structure.

Structure

Some operations will have more complex structures than others. For example, simple structures may have more common routines and straightforward requirements with fewer suppliers. The structure of Oxfam creates a degree of complexity. Oxfam is a global organisation with offices in around 70 countries. Co-ordinating such a structure that is dependent upon volunteers and is focused upon both disasters and ongoing programmes is no simple task.

Nature of the service

The nature of Oxfam's service is also a source of complexity. We may see one of Oxfam's services through, for example, the work of its charity shops, or its clothes and handicrafts. However, its core services are much more complex: the provision of relief when disasters strike, together with attempts to find lasting solutions to poverty through its ongoing programmes. There are few organisations with such intricate, complicated and burdensome services.

Interdependency

Some operations may be large with complex structures, but if there is little interdependency between the parts, then the task will be easier to manage. The many elements of Oxfam's operations are very dependent upon each other: fund raising is needed to provide non-restricted funds, the disasters provide leverage for raising restricted funds, the central emergencies warehouse has to stock the items that may be needed to respond appropriately to unknown disasters. Oxfam has a flexibility in staffing that allows a flexible and focused response to emergencies, yet at the same time its local offices both provide support for its ongoing work and help predict and prepare for disasters. Oxfam is also critically dependent on the goodwill of its volunteers: employees and volunteers give a significant portion of their time and earning potential as a gift. This fact has serious implications for people management; operational decisions must therefore not only address internal efficiency but also respect this 'gift relationship' between the organisation and its workers.

Time

Many tasks undertaken by operations managers are by their nature time sensitive and usually require speedy action or resolution. Although it would be good to be able to hit a 'pause button', this is a luxury not afforded to many operations. Oxfam is often faced with situations where people are dying and will continue to die if help does not get to them within hours. Speed of response, co-ordination with other agencies and preparedness are essential ingredients that help Oxfam to deal with disasters.

Uncertainty

Service is not a physical product and likewise service operations are not machines. The interplay between human actors, both staff and customers, creates a dynamic whose outcomes for the customer as well as time required and costs involved are to some extent uncertain. Oxfam faces great environmental uncertainty – not only is it difficult to predict earthquakes and storms as well as the timing of political events, but it is also impossible to predict the scope and scale of any emergency and the precise needs of communities. Through contingency planning and its staff on the ground, Oxfam can try to manage the impact of these uncertainties. However, when a disaster strikes, nothing can detract from its ability to co-ordinate its efforts into a multi-agency response.

Political behaviour

Here we use the word politics to include a wide range of issues. Most people who have spent any length of time in organisations will recognise that few decisions are made on a purely rational basis, even if that were possible. Organisational psychologists sometimes use the terms 'under the table' and 'undiscussable' to describe some of the dynamics of politics and group behaviour that have a considerable

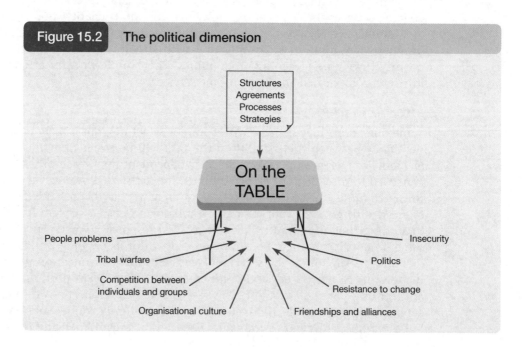

Figure 15.2   The political dimension

impact on how things are done. Figure 15.2 summarises these issues (see, for example, Obholzer *et al.* 1994, Kets de Vries 2001).

The impact of these aspects of organisational life is to increase the complexity of decision making. This is particularly relevant in periods of significant change when individuals and groups may spend vast amounts of energy in ensuring that their particular viewpoint is heard and acted upon. In some ways, we would like to pretend that this dimension of complexity did not exist, but this would be extremely foolish. Politicians today do not always have a good reputation, whether we are referring to those in public life, or those in organisational life. The latter are sometimes seen as being more interested in empire building or game playing – winning for winning's sake rather than doing the best thing for the organisation.

However, to ignore this dimension is folly. Many leadership thinkers (see Kets De Vries 2001) suggest that political behaviour is a key skill for those who wish to influence the organisation's direction. There are few decisions that can be taken where the facts are clear and everyone is in agreement. In these circumstances, it can be far more efficient to build political agreement, recognising that there probably is no one right way, and endless debates delay action.

15.3 Operational consequences of complexity

Complexity to some extent is a fact of life that faces most, if not all, operations managers. While the previous section identified the nature of complexity, the reality is that complexity leads to a number of operational problems. Unfortunately, in many cases there are no remedies – tools or frameworks – that can help us. We would suggest that the operational consequences of complexity can be summarised as follows:

- things don't work as expected
- things fall down holes
- things are misunderstood
- things are missing
- things have to work.

Things don't work as expected

One problem that operations managers face is that any decision they make and any action they take will have a range of consequences. Changing employee shift patterns may have an effect on morale and commitment, which may have an impact on staff satisfaction and retention and costs of recruitment. It may also impinge upon customer satisfaction and then income and profit. Buddhists, although referring to life rather than just operations, call this the law of interconnectivity. They argue that all events and actions are interconnected and interrelated with all other events and actions. Indeed the doctrine of *kamma* is based on the principle of causality – the laws of cause and effect (Plamintr 1994).

In Chapter 11 we developed a structure and suggested methodologies for attempting to understand the links between the many possible operational levers and business outcomes. The reality, however, is that there are just so many interconnected variables with differing relationships, which also change over time, that it is impossible to fully map them or control them all.

Service operations management will always, to some extent, be an art. We have to make judgements, based on a combination of scientific knowledge about the relationships between variables, together with experience and intuition. At best we will improve operational performance, at worst we will prevent entropy – the natural tendency of things to move toward greater disorder or disorganisation (Flood and Carson 1993).

Things fall down holes

Because of the complexity of many operations, things do go wrong and things fall down holes. Even the most efficient bank with the best systems in the world will still occasionally lose a loan application, for example. Even the best public service organisation will occasionally omit to change someone's address, despite having the information. Operations managers cannot therefore be perfectionists – that is not to say that they should not strive to attain perfection, just that it is something that will always be out of reach. Service recovery (Chapter 12) is therefore not an add-on extra but a cornerstone of service operations. The best service operations are those that take recovery seriously and have good systems in place that not only deal with the immediate problem, including the customer, but work to improve the processes.

Things are misunderstood

Service involves people. These are the stakeholders, individuals or groups, who have some form of interest in, or claim over, the organisation. They may be people internal to the organisation, such as managers, staff, officers and board members, or external to the organisation, such as customers, suppliers, political masters, trade unions, local communities and the general public. Most organisations strive to match the varying and sometimes conflicting needs of their stakeholders, although few have the resources to satisfy them all. Stakeholder impact analysis helps managers develop appropriate strategies by identifying stakeholders, identifying their varying needs and concerns, and identifying their relative importance to the organisation (see, for example, Macmillan and Jones 1986, Hill and Jones 1998).

At an operational level we have to deal with the results of these mismatches on a day-to-day basis. They manifest themselves as misunderstandings, misrepresentations and mistakes, brought about by the differing values, mores and expectations of the various stakeholders. They may be nothing more than low-key grumblings at best, or may escalate into disputes resulting in loss of face, loss of office, loss of business, or at worst outright hostility. Managing both personal and business relationships is important for all operations managers (Chapter 3 provides some useful insights).

Things are missing

All managers are blessed with 20–20 hindsight when outcomes are known and certain. Complexity, including a lack of certainty, means that most managers have imperfect knowledge about a situation and its outcomes. Information is usually incomplete, understanding about interconnectivities is limited, and resources are rarely in abundance. As a result, operations managers need to accept the imperfect world, accept that things will always be missing and press on regardless. That is not to say that they should not strive to improve their knowledge, but if they wait until they know everything then they will never make any decisions.

Things have to work

Despite all the above problems, the operation has still got to work. People have to be fed, moved and cared for. If ambulance staff or fire-fighters go on strike, governments have no option but to bring in other agencies, such as the army, to provide some sort of cover. At the other end of the scale a restauranteur whose chef walks out or whose oven breaks down still has to deal with the guests who are booked in for their meals. As a result, operations managers have to be adept at contingency planning. Even 'bodging' is an acceptable way of getting out of a problem in the short term.

15.3.1 Overcoming the problems caused by complexity

At the end of the day, despite the complexity of the task, operations managers have to do their best to make things work smoothly and efficiently, provide good service to their customers and also meet their organisation's business objectives. To try to deal as well as we can with the problems caused by the natural complexity of the operations task, our advice is to:

- obtain as much evidence as you can, but with a view to making timely decisions
- expect things to go wrong and plan for it
- assume that no one understands your thoughts, so take every opportunity to share them
- encourage discussion about your service concept or concepts, their delivery and development
- don't use complexity as an excuse
- understand that you and your colleagues will need to be more flexible in adopting varying approaches to deal with diverse people and processes
- strive for utopia, but accept imperfections
- be innovative.

And, most importantly:

- enjoy.

15.4 Summary

Complexity

- Complexity is the source of many operational problems – and also the source of inspiration and challenge.
- Complexity means complicated, due to the number of interrelated parts in an operation.
- The dimensions of operations complexity are interconnectivity, size, structure, nature of the service, interdependency, time, uncertainty and political behaviour.

Operational consequences of complexity

The operations consequences of complexity are that:

- things don't work as expected
- things fall down holes
- things are misunderstood
- things are missing
- things have to work.

15.5 Discussion questions

1 How do the operational consequences of complexity apply to an activity you have organised, and how did you try to minimise them?

2 Why do you think complexity both fascinates and frustrates many operations managers?

15.6 Questions for managers

1 What are the dimensions of complexity for your operation? How do you try to minimise their effect?

2 What are the consequences for your operation of the complexity you face?

15.7 Further reading

Berry L.L., *Discovering the Soul of Service*, Free Press, New York, 1999.

Kets de Vries M., *The Leadership Mystique*, Financial Times/Prentice Hall, London, 2001.

McElroy M.W., 'Integrating complexity theory, knowledge management and organizational learning', *Journal of Knowledge Management*, vol. 4, no. 3, 2000, pp. 195–203.

O'Connor J. and McDermott I., *The Art of Systems Thinking*, Thorsons, London, 1997.

Stacey R.D., Griffin D. and Shaw P., *Complexity and Management: Fad or Radical Challenge to Systems Thinking*, Routledge, 2000.

Tetenbaum T., 'Shifting paradigms: from Newton to chaos', *Organizational Dynamics*, Spring 1998, pp. 21–32.

15.8 References

Flood R.L. and Carson E.R., *Dealing with Complexity*, 2nd edition, Plenum Press, New York, 1993.

Hill C.W.L. and Jones G.R., *Strategic Management Theory*, 4th edition, Houghton Mifflin, Boston, Mass., 1998.

Kets de Vries M., *The Leadership Mystique*, Financial Times/Prentice Hall, London, 2001.

Macmillan I.C. and Jones P.E., *Strategy Formulation: Power and politics*, West, St Paul, Minn., 1986.

Obholzer A., Roberts V. and Krantz J., *The Unconscious at Work: Individual and Organisational Stress in the Human Services*, Routledge 1994

Plamintr S., *Getting to Know Buddhism*, Buddhhadhamma Foundation, Bangkok, 1994.

Index

Note: Figures and Tables are indicated by *italic page numbers*, and Boxes by **emboldened numbers**